Studying Literature

The Essential Companion

Studying Literature
The Essential Companion

PAUL GORING
Senior Lecturer in English

JEREMY HAWTHORN
Professor of English

DOMHNALL MITCHELL
Professor of English

Norwegian University of Science and Technology

A member of the Hodder Headline Group
LONDON
Co-published in the United States of America by
Oxford University Press Inc., New York

First published in Great Britain in 2001 by
Arnold, a member of the Hodder Headline Group,
338 Euston Road, London NW1 3BH

http://www.arnoldpublishers.com

Co-published in the United States of America by
Oxford University Press Inc.,
198 Madison Avenue, New York, NY10016

The advice and information in this book are believed to be true and
accurate at the date of going to press, but neither the authors nor the
publisher can accept any legal responsibility or liability for any errors
or omissions.

British Library Cataloguing in Publication Data
A catalogue record for this book is available from the British Library

Library of Congress Cataloguing-in-Publication Data
A catalog record for this book is available from the Library of Congress

ISBN 0 340 75945 3 (hb)
ISBN 0 340 75946 1 (pb)

MAR 0 4 2002

1 2 3 4 5 6 7 8 9 10

Production Editor: Anke Ueberberg
Production Controller: Bryan Eccleshall
Cover Design: Terry Griffiths

Typeset in 10pt Times by J&L Composition Ltd, Filey, North Yorkshire
Printed and bound in Great Britain by MPG Books, Bodmin, Cornwall

What do you think about this book? Or any other Arnold title?
Please send your comments to feedback.arnold@hodder.co.uk

Contents

SECTION 2: GUIDE TO THE USE OF ELECTRONIC MEDIA

SECTION 3: THEORIES AND APPROACHES

Introduction

INTRODUCING YOUR COMPANION

'A book which gives one instructions on how to do something; guide.' Thus the *Longman Dictionary of Contemporary English*, providing the fifth of its definitions of the word 'companion'. For our purposes this is undeniably the most appropriate of the six varied definitions of the word given by this dictionary, yet we are tempted to cite definition number two as well: 'a person who willingly or unwillingly shares the work, pleasures, worries, etc., of another: *They were working companions*'.

Our hesitation between these two definitions can be explained by our sense that although we very much hope that the book you are now looking at will be useful in your study of literature, we are not unreservedly satisfied with the suggestion that it will give you 'instructions on how to do something', and are happier with its being described as more of a 'working companion'. The study of literature is not something that can be learned as you might learn how to replace the transmission in a car or to install a new program in a computer. Just as we do not primarily read novels or poems in order to obtain information, nor do we study literature at school or university so as to perfect a mechanical system for analysing or inter-preting literary works. As we repeat many times in the course of this book, the study of literature (like that unacademic reading of literature with which it must never lose life-giving contact) is an interactive or dialogic activity, one which is important as much for the hopeful travelling it provides as for any ultimate arrival. Faced with a broken-down car, only the most fanatical of mechanics would reject the possibility of having a replacement transmission magically installed without labour were this a realistic option, in contrast to the hard work that the real world demands be undertaken. But the student of literature who reads every set text wish-ing that the task were completed is taking the wrong course.

Nevertheless, even travelling hopefully requires good boots, and this is essen-tially what we aim to provide in this book – along with a sense of being able to share your work, pleasures, worries with a printed fellow traveller that will indeed be a *working* companion.

This is a book to which we want you to be able to turn when a particular problem or task has to be confronted. Like all good companions, you will not want to be both-ered by it all the time. But when you are faced with making a presentation in class, when you encounter a critical or theoretical term with which you are unfamiliar, when you need to know a little more about the New Criticism or what is important about the work of William Empson, then this companion will be there to help you.

The entries in Section 3 and many of the theoretical terms in Section 4 of the book have been adapted from Jeremy Hawthorn, *A Glossary of Contemporary Literary Theory* (4th edn, London: Arnold, 2000). Many readers of this book asked for a companion volume which included more general literary and critical terms, along with those additional elements that are contained in Sections 1, 2 and 5. This book is the result of such requests.

USING THE COMPANION

Parts of this book are designed to be treated as a reference work. When first you encounter the distinction between 'story' and 'plot', or you need help understanding what constitutes poetic metre, then there are entries in Section 4 to assist you. Section 3 (Theories and Approaches) and 5 (Theorists) can also be treated as you would treat a reference work. But you might also find it useful early on in your studies to read Section 3 from start to finish so as to gain an overview of the most important movements and positions that have influenced – and even in part constituted – literary studies during the past 100 or so years. If you do, then you will find frequent cross-references to Section 5, in which you can gain more useful information about many of the individuals who created and developed these movements and positions.

The first two sections in the book are designed more for sequential reading, although we hope and expect that you will want to refer back to specific issues and pieces of advice within them when the need arises. These are sections that the new undergraduate student of English is advised to read at the beginning of his or her degree course.

Our book contains a *Table of Contents* that is more detailed than is often the case, and we hope that you will learn to use it to find help in Sections 1 and 2 with particular problems and tasks. The *Table of Contents* will also allow you quickly to locate information about individual schools or approaches in Section 3, as this section is organized thematically rather than alphabetically.

The entries in our final two sections – 4 and 5 – are organized alphabetically, so that finding an entry here should be straightforward.

In addition to a detailed table of contents, this book also makes use of an extensive and comprehensive system of cross-referencing, about which we need to say a few words.

CROSS-REFERENCING

Throughout this book we have used SMALL CAPITALS to indicate a cross-reference. All such cross-references are *to* Section 3, 4 or 5; in other words, no cross-reference will lead you to Sections 1 or 2 (the study guide and the introduction to using the electronic media). But cross-references may be *from* any one of the sections in the book. The contents of Sections 1 and 2 are fully listed in the *Table of Contents* at the front of the book.

How do you know whether to follow a cross-reference to Section 3, 4 or 5? Generally speaking this is easy to work out; Section 3 contains theories and approaches to literature and to criticism, Section 4 is a glossary of literary and theoretical terms, and Section 5 contains information on a number of key theorists.

Let us assume that at some point in the book you meet with the following sentence: 'Although WILLIAM EMPSON is often associated with the NEW CRITICISM, his refusal to rule the use of an author's intention illegitimate in the INTERPRETATION of a work makes this association problematic.' Because *William Empson* is clearly the name of an individual, the fact that his name is given in small capitals should lead you to Section 5 if you want to read more about him, as this is the section that is dedicated to theorists. The *New Criticism* is a particular school or approach, and thus more can be read about it in Section 3. *Interpretation*, being neither school, approach, or individual, should be looked for in Section 4, the glossary of literary and theoretical terms. 'Terms' should be understood broadly: Section 4 contains entries not just on technical terms, but on a range of critical and theoretical issues.

Once you become used to the structure of the book, remembering in which section you need to look in order to follow up cross-references should become second nature. We recognize that there may be a few cases where it is not immediately apparent whether a cross-reference is to an approach or theory (Section 3) or a term (Section 4), but we hope that these will be few and far between. To help in such cases we have provided extra clarification: thus if you mistakenly look for NEW CRITICISM in Section 4, a note will send you on to the right page in Section 3.

In Sections 3, 4 and 5 we have generally restricted the use of small capitals to the first use of a name or a term within a single entry (that is, a single approach in Section 3, a single term in Section 4, or a single theorist in Section 5). In Sections 1 and 2 we have allowed ourselves more flexibility as these sections do not fall into discrete 'units' quite so obviously, and in these sections we have used small capitals to indicate a cross-reference at those points at which we feel it is helpful to the reader.

Remember that cross-references may be to cognate terms, so that INTERPRETING should send the reader to the discussion of *Interpretation* in Section 4. Throughout the book we have used British spelling except when quoting from, say, a source written in American English.

The *Bibliography* at the end of the book lists all works which have been cited in Section 3 and (mainly) 4. It does not list those works included in entries in Section 5, either as the productions of the theorist being discussed or as recommended further reading.

Paul Goring
Jeremy Hawthorn
Domhnall Mitchell

Section 1

Guide to studying literature at university

INTRODUCTION

Who is this guide for?

This guide is intended for students who are studying literature at undergraduate degree level. It is not a guide to the subject of literature itself, but rather aims to give practical advice on the most important techniques and processes involved in the *study* of literature. We offer, for example, advice on how to study a NOVEL but we don't enter into long discussions of the GENRE of the novel or of individual novels. As such, the guide is intended *to complement* the courses you will be taking for your degree and the reading involved in those courses.

We hope that the guide will be useful in two ways. First, for students just embarking upon a degree we aim to provide introductory advice on matters such as how best to prepare for courses, how to get the most from a university library, how to structure your reading effectively, and so on. It may be useful, therefore, for new students to read through the guide as a whole. Second, we hope that the guide will serve as a reference work to be dipped into at various stages throughout the degree course. The advice on essay writing, for example, is intended to help *during the process* of writing with specific guidance on structuring an argument, using evidence, incorporating quotations, the presentation of the essay, using footnotes, and so on. Similarly, the advice on exams may be worth referring to before or during the period of preparation for an exam. The guide is broken down into subsections to make its use as a reference work as straightforward as possible.

Is such a guide really necessary?

If you have got to the stage of being accepted onto a degree programme or of beginning a degree, you may well find it appropriate to ask why a guide to studying literature should be necessary or useful. After all, you have already shown your ability to study literature at an advanced level and have therefore already grappled with many of the issues involved in literary study. This is very true, but it is also true that typically there are significant differences between degree-level literary study and the advanced-level courses which qualify students to begin degrees (i.e., in Britain, A level, Access and International Baccalaureate courses). Many students find that the progression between these levels is not a smooth transition but involves a notable jump. These are some of the principal differences that you are likely to encounter at degree level:

- You are expected to study many more TEXTS, with much less time devoted to each.

- With short teaching times devoted to individual texts – maybe just one lecture or one seminar – the close study of those texts is necessarily a more independent activity.

- Whereas pre-degree study of literature typically focuses upon THEMES, PLOTS, CHARACTERS and poetic or other literary devices, a far wider range of approaches to literature is explored.

- You are introduced to the field of 'literary theory', and to abstract discussions of what is involved in analyzing literature.

Looking over such generalized differences as these, it might be observed first that degree-level study presents many more intellectually exciting challenges than are encountered on lower-level courses. This is not to suggest that pre-degree level courses are unexciting; the point is rather that modern literary studies is a dynamic field of intellectual endeavour and that the new ideas and conceptual frameworks which inform the subject today can make taking a degree in literature an immensely stimulating and rewarding experience – we certainly hope that this will be your experience. From this list of differences, however, it is clear that degree-level study is very demanding for the individual student. Students are expected to read much more, to explore many more methods of INTERPRETATION, and to do so relatively independently with far less close guidance than is usually offered at lower-level courses. The required leap to degree level may not be a quantum one, but it's a leap nevertheless.

'Literary', 'primary', 'secondary': a note on terminology

Although academics often distinguish between TEXT AND WORK, terms such as 'primary texts' or 'primary works' are often used interchangeably to refer to those examples of imaginative literature which will form the central objects of study during your degree. Our own use of the word 'primary' is designed to mark a distinction between 'literary works' and 'secondary texts': all those works which in some way are *about* the literary works – critical studies, studies of authors, works of literary theory, contextual studies, and so on. These texts could also be referred to as 'literature' in its most general sense, but for convenience we avoid that sense in this guide. We additionally distinguish between 'literary criticism' and 'literary theory', but we include both of these categories when we refer generally to 'secondary texts' or 'secondary works'.

GETTING ORGANIZED

■ What preparation is needed at the start of the degree and before courses begin?

■ How should the different teaching formats at university be approached?

■ How to use the library

■ The usefulness of computers to literary study

Studying for a degree is a major undertaking, and it is important at an early stage to find out precisely what your particular degree scheme will entail and what is expected of you in order to complete your course successfully. It is additionally important to become quickly acquainted with the 'tools' that will enable you to conduct your study in as efficient and effective a way as possible. Taking a degree in literature involves the processing of a large amount of information, and part of the technique of becoming a successful student involves developing familiarity and confidence both with information suppliers – libraries, bookshops, the Internet – and with systems that support your subsequent reading, analysis and writing.

The following subsections outline in more detail these *preparatory*, practical aspects of literary study which we feel truly repay the time invested in them. There will, of course, be significant differences between different universities' degree schemes, library systems, computer services, and so on. What is essential for all, however, is to work out on an individual basis how best to navigate your particular degree scheme and how best to employ the resources available to you.

Your degree scheme

What does this degree actually involve? How many courses do I have to take? What possibilities are there for choosing a personalized programme of courses for myself? How many essays do I have to write? How many exams do I have to take and when? Are there any other hoops that I have to jump through before they'll give me a degree?

Successful study depends partly upon careful planning, and it is always helpful to have a strong sense of the long-term requirements of your degree as well as of the short-term demands of individual courses. For example, many degree schemes require or allow students to submit one or more 'project papers' as part of the overall assessment for the course. Usually these projects are undertaken in the later stages of the degree, and there is often scope for students to choose to work on areas of particular personal interest. In such cases, it is useful to have the prospect of the project in mind at an early stage, and to hang on to ideas for the project which may occur along the way. It is also helpful psychologically to know exactly what will be required of you as a student – how many courses you will have to take, the number and length of essays you will have to submit, and so on. Mountaineers maintain that climbing is made easier when the summit is in sight – the same can be said of a degree.

Your department should make available detailed information about the degree and about the individual courses it comprises. Explore this information in depth, and think carefully about what choices you wish to make and about how to develop an effective pattern of work. It is well worth writing down in list form the various courses you need to take and the requirements for each course. Such an exercise can really help in fixing a strong overall picture of the degree and of the plan you need to follow in order to get through the required work. Indeed, we might add a general point here on the usefulness of making lists. Lists often suffer a bad reputation – list-makers run the risk of being dubbed 'anal' – but we three (clearly anal) authors rather like lists. Making a list can be a highly effective way of organizing all sorts of information, and you will find that throughout this guide we both use lists and recommend listing as part of the process of study.

Preparing for courses

As well as preparing for the degree as a whole, it can also be useful to prepare for each course with some care. Before you begin a course, it should be possible to consult a course description and a list of primary and secondary reading. Check through the list of primary reading carefully and work out just how much time you will need to set aside for reading – this is, of course, a particularly important consideration when embarking upon novel courses. You should also check the order in which the texts will be discussed in the course. Good lecturers take the practicalities of reading into consideration when they plan courses, such that longer works do not appear too near the beginning. You will probably need to begin reading some longer works several weeks before the lectures or seminars dealing with those works.

You might also consider such factors as these if you are in the position of choosing which courses to follow. Taking two novel courses simultaneously can be a punishing experience however much you enjoy reading fiction. Inevitably some courses carry a lighter load of reading than others and it may be possible to coordinate when you follow certain courses so as to avoid an impossibly demanding workload.

Before you begin a course, you should also look carefully into its assessment requirements: the number and type of written assignments, exams, seminar presentations, and so on. Again the point is very simple: undertaking the work for a course is made far more straightforward after careful planning. A wall calendar containing the dates when work must be submitted is a very useful aid to effective study.

Getting the most from lectures, seminars and tutorials

The teaching you will receive at university will normally take the various forms of lectures, seminars and tutorials – although you may find that the tutorial is rarely used at your institution. On the whole, the teaching will fill only a small part of your time. In fact, it comes as a shock to many students that actual teaching at university takes up so little time – at many institutions, the total of lectures, seminars and tutorials for a full-time course in literature amounts to no more than six hours per week (no wonder, one might think, the stereotype of the 'idle student' is so common!).

The small number of teaching hours has several implications. One is that you need to be highly self-motivated about your study and to have a fairly disciplined attitude to your own time (unless, of course, you want to fulfil the stereotype). Another implication – the one that concerns us here – is that you should aim to get the absolute most from the teaching that is available. This can be achieved in various ways involving: preparation (again!), fully understanding the functions of the different teaching formats, being an 'active learner', and undertaking productive follow-up work. It is easiest to discuss these issues more closely in relation to the specific teaching formats.

SECTION 1

Lectures

Lectures are used primarily for conveying information and points of view to large groups of people – this is an obvious point, but it is significant with regard to the type of communication involved in a lecture. Of all the forms of teaching at university, the lecture is the most 'one-way': the lecturer may sometimes invite questions and dialogue with the audience, but for the most part the lecturer is there as a source of information and not as a sounding-board for questions.

If the lecture is addressing a specific text from the course, the lecturer will usually assume that the audience is familiar with the text. Since there are not many teaching hours, lecturers do not want to waste time covering straightforward matters such as what happens in the work (unless the lecture is deliberately introductory). So the best preparation you can do before a lecture is simply to *read the work in question* such that you have the mental reference points to which you can then relate the arguments brought up by the lecturer (see 'Reading literary texts', pp. 20–63). It is remarkable how many students do not do this before a lecture, even though it makes listening to the lecture far less worthwhile – and infinitely less interesting. Inevitably there will be occasions during the degree when you don't have time to do the necessary reading or haven't been able to get the relevant book, or whatever. Try to keep these to a minimum, and if sometimes you don't have time to read the whole of a work, you should aim at least to read some passages from it. It is far better to go into the lecture with a 'flavour' of the work than with no sense of it at all. If it is a long work and you know you won't get through it, you might consult the lecturer beforehand and ask if there are certain key passages that will be focused on in the lecture.

It is important to take notes during a lecture, both for following up afterwards and for revising when preparing for exams, but the method of taking notes is a matter of personal preference. Some people go into lectures with an array of coloured pens and then set about producing notes in diagram form; others aim to write down as much of what is said as possible; others note down only keywords or central points. Use whatever method you have found to be successful in your studies so far. Having said that, we might add that it is usually best to be selective in what you note and to use a very spare, skeletal form of words – if you try to note things down in full sentences, you can often find yourself still writing when the lecturer has moved onto a new point. And always make sure that you remember to take with you the work that is the subject of the lecture!

Finally, it can be extremely useful to spend five or so minutes soon *after* the lecture, going through your notes and assessing what the most valuable points from the lecture were. Usually a set of lecture notes will contain key points mixed up with more detailed, incidental points – it can be very productive, while the lecture is fresh in your mind, to go through the notes and highlight the key points or to produce a short summary of the main arguments put forward in the lecture. You might also highlight matters that remain unclear to you, or questions that have arisen from the lecture which you can then pursue either through your own research or in seminars and tutorials.

Seminars

Unlike a lecture, a seminar (sometimes called 'small-group teaching') is primarily a forum for *learning through discussion*. The idea behind this form of teaching is that students do not simply ingest information but rather contribute to a discussion on a particular text or particular issue. In this way, a seminar can be a marvellous opportunity to exchange opinions and to discuss all manner of issues that arise from a literary work – and it is perhaps a particularly effective mode for the study of literature, which has always tended to be a discipline of *dialogue and debate* rather than of *final answers*. A seminar is also an opportunity to engage in the close analysis of individual passages of text (for which large lectures are generally not well suited).

The preparation for a seminar is similar to that required for a lecture: read the relevant text or at least some of it. It's difficult to discuss a text if you've never read it (although we have known students who do just that!). You might also prepare by thinking about or making a few notes on issues pertaining to the text or passages of the text that you find interesting or problematic. You may not always get the opportunity to discuss these, but the chances are that you will be able to raise them at some stage. The lecturer will usually control the general direction of the discussion and will aim to keep it focused, but, in our experience, most lecturers are more than happy to take a back seat when students' discussion acquires a productive energy of its own.

To get the most out of a seminar you need to be prepared to talk and to listen. Actually discussing texts with others will help you develop as a literary critic in two ways. First, it will increase your 'subject-specific' knowledge – that is, it will help you get to know the literary work in question, and it will reveal points of view that may not have occurred to you. In fact, the very act of voicing an opinion can make you more conscious of what you really think about something – it can 'concretize' a previously vague or unformed thought. Second, discussion will enhance your skills in expressing your own point of view – it will help you to put your point of view into words and will give you valuable practice in justifying *why* and *how* you have come to hold that view. We do not want to suggest that seminars are essentially combative battles of words for they are not, but they do very often entail a form of (hopefully productive) debate.

Being prepared to talk also means being prepared to ask questions. Do not be afraid to ask a question because you fear you may have missed something obvious. Often the most informative discussions develop from a very straightforward question. If talking comes very easily to you, you might need to guard against being too dominant in a seminar – remember that some of your fellow students may be less confident than you and that a very dominant member of the group can make contributing to the discussion extremely difficult.

You may want to take a few notes during a seminar, but on the whole taking notes is far less important in a seminar than in a lecture. The seminar leader may present a certain amount of new information, in which case a note or two may be called for, but for the most part you should aim to concentrate upon and engage in discussion. As with lectures, though, it can be useful to spend a few minutes *after* a seminar noting down significant points or avenues you might want to explore further. This takes some self-discipline, as this is typically the time your fellow students are rushing off for a coffee or for lunch, but it is very valuable.

At some point you may well be required to make a presentation in a seminar. This will involve using certain skills that are very specific to the task, but it will also involve some of the same techniques that are used in researching, planning and writing essays. For that reason we offer our advice on how to make a good presentation after the discussion of essay-writing techniques (see pp. 91–3).

Tutorials

Regular one-to-one tutorials, where the student has the opportunity for individual consultation with a tutor, are now very rare at most universities (certainly at most British universities). The tutorial was once a very dominant form of teaching – it remains in extensive use at Oxford and Cambridge – but with greater numbers of students in higher education and with limited teaching resources, it is impossible for many universities to provide tutorials as standard.

If you do have opportunities to attend tutorials, it is important to make the most of them. Tutorials are occasions where close attention can be given to your individual needs and interests, and so you should prepare for the meeting by thinking about what these actually are. If the point of the tutorial is to discuss a particular text, take *specific questions* which have arisen out of your reading of that text. It is probably fair to say that a tutorial will usually be centred around one of your essays, in which case the real objective will be to show you how you might improve your performance *next time* you write an essay. Again, you should ask *specific questions* relating to the development of your writing. If the tutor has recommended, for example, that you 'be more analytical' in a passage of your writing, you might ask exactly what it means to 'be more analytical'.

Using the library

A university library is an essential resource for students of literature, and an ability to use your library effectively is a skill which should be acquired in the earliest stages of the degree. As was remarked above, a degree in literature demands far more *independent* study than most pre-degree level literature courses. Students at degree level are expected to develop their own lines of inquiry within subject areas and to seek out materials individually. Successful study at degree level, therefore, depends to a large extent upon knowing *how to find* information, and despite the massive increase of information available via the Internet (see Section 2, pp. 101–32), knowing how to find information as often as not involves knowing how best to use your library.

So it is worth devoting some time to learning how to use your library with confidence – this is perhaps particularly important if you are working at a distance from your university and are only able to make short, occasional visits to the library. In the long run, you will almost certainly save time if you can familiarize yourself with the various routes which must be followed to find different types of information, such as primary texts, literary criticism and works of literary theory. During the course of your degree, you may well be referring to types of publication that you have never used before – most people, for example, do not encounter academic 'articles' (contained in 'journals' or 'periodicals') before embarking upon a degree – and it is important to get used to referring to all of these various sources that are the regular tools of university work. It is usual for libraries to offer short induction courses or library tours – take full advantage of these if they are available, for they are an excellent starting point. Ultimately, though, some individual investigation and 'hands-on' practice are the best way of learning how to *use* a library.

Productive browsing

Obviously, you will need to spend some time simply working out the layout of the place, and of those sections which will be most useful to you. Libraries can sometimes be off-puttingly labyrinthine and perplexing, but they become less so after a little exploratory browsing and after the classification and cataloguing system has been grasped. Most libraries in Britain (and worldwide) shelve their holdings according to the 'Dewey Decimal Classification' system – a method of categorizing and numbering books which was devised in the 1870s in America by Melvil Dewey. The system is based on a division of knowledge into numbered and lettered classes and subclasses. There are 10 basic classes in the system, numbered as follows:

000 Computers, Information and General Reference
100 Philosophy and Psychology
200 Religion
300 Social Sciences
400 Languages
500 Pure Science
600 Technology (Applied Sciences)
700 The Arts and Recreation
800 Literature
900 History and Geography

The most useful categories to the student of literature are Literature in the 800s (obviously) and General Reference in the 000s, but since studying 'English' is often a deeply interdisciplinary activity (that is, it involves crossing the boundaries which traditionally have divided up areas of knowledge) you may well sometimes find yourself in other sections such as History or Philosophy or even Pure Science. The 800 category incorporates literature in English as well as in other languages and it also includes literary criticism. American literature in English begins at 810, and the subdivision for English literature is the 820s (Old English begins at 820), within which there are further subdivisions according to GENRE:

821 English Poetry
822 English Drama
823 English Fiction (i.e., prose fiction, such as novels and short stories)

These will be the most useful sections in which to browse, and although 'browsing' along a shelf may sound like a rather old-fashioned and unscientific means of inquiry in this age of high-speed information technology, it can nevertheless still be a productive process if you have some idea of what you are seeking. The Dewey Decimal system groups together secondary literature *about* a particular author *after* the primary works *by* that author. So if you are studying an individual author, you can visit that section on the shelves and see what secondary literature is available, rather than just looking at references to those works in the catalogue (discussed below). If you are studying, for example, the novelist Joseph Conrad, you will find his novels shelved together (at 823.92), followed by other writings by Conrad (letters, for example), followed by critical and biographical works about Conrad. The usefulness to you of certain of these critical works will be apparent only when you can actually consult them. For example, you might find in the Conrad criticism section a book called *Conrad Revisited: Essays for the Eighties*, ed. Ross C. Murfin (Alabama: University of Alabama Press, 1985) – the catalogue entry will not reveal much about the actual content of such a book (it's a fairly diverse collection of essays) but a glance at the contents page of the book will soon reveal whether it contains anything of direct use to your area of study. Actually consulting a book will also give you access to its index (assuming it has one), which similarly can provide a quick indication of whether or not the book will be of use to you.

Alongside these subsections containing primary literature in English and secondary criticism about those works, other areas where it can be useful to have a 'browser's familiarity' are the General Literature and General Reference sections. In these sections will be works that you will probably want to refer to again and again during the course of your degree: encyclopaedias; dictionaries; dictionaries of quotations; dictionaries of biography; companions to literature, and so on. It's very useful to know your way around these sections so that when you need to locate a certain factual detail – an author's birth and death dates, for example, or the source of a quotation – you know exactly where to look and are able to find what you want efficiently. We have included, at the end of this 'Using the Library' subsection, a checklist of such works together with some notes on their uses.

It may be that the library to which you have access does not use the Dewey Decimal system. If so, the shelving system will nevertheless probably be much the same as that described above (although some systems separate primary works of literature from secondary criticism on those works). The important thing is to get to know *your* library, whatever system is employed, and to become especially well acquainted with the literature and reference sections. Another area you should aim to get to know is the Periodicals section.

'Periodicals', 'journals', 'articles'

A periodicals section in a library can be a confusing and unwelcoming place. The bulk of a periodicals section is comprised of shelf after shelf of similar-looking volumes; these are often numbered in apparently eccentric sequences – they rarely seem to begin at number one, they have gaps of missing numbers in the middle of the sequence; and on the spines of these volumes can appear titles which are far from alluring. *Studia Neophilologica* vies for attention amidst such treats as *The Lichenologist* and *The Canadian Journal of Corrections*. Reaching a volume down from the shelf can compound the confusion, for on opening it up at the first page, you are often confronted not by 'page 1' but by 'page 248' or something similarly improbable.

Do not be put off by any such superficial obstacles, because periodicals are a wonderfully useful resource and once the means of accessing them has been mastered they can provide an immensely stimulating dimension of degree level study. Periodicals, as the word implies, are titles which are published periodically – that is, they are not 'one-off' publications but ongoing titles to which many authors contribute articles. Most of the works labelled 'periodicals' in university libraries are specialist journals, the function of which is to provide an outlet for new research, and usually they appear between one and six times per year (most specialist literature journals appear between one and four times per year). Academic journals constitute a forum for cutting-edge research and debate, and they serve as a repository for the research carried out over the years. The level of specialism varies greatly: a journal such as *Essays in Criticism* carries articles on a huge range of literary topics, while there are other journals devoted to single themes or authors, such as *The Dickensian*, a Charles Dickens journal.

It can often be more productive (and less time-consuming) to read a single good article in an academic journal than to work through a whole book. So it is well worth getting into the habit of using journals. The periodicals section is not really a place for browsing, although it is usually interesting to look through the latest issues of the literary journals to which your library subscribes. (These are typically displayed separately from the main journal holdings until they are bound together with the other issues from that year.) For the most part, you will probably seek out and read an article after having found or been given a reference to it. Lists of secondary reading provided by your lecturers will contain references to articles, and you might also locate interesting-looking titles from your own searches (discussed under 'How to find relevant criticism', pp. 65–7). With a reference in hand, you will need to locate the relevant volume of the journal using the library catalogue – a tool which, for many other purposes too, it is necessary to master.

The catalogue

Almost all university libraries now have computerized catalogues of their holdings. Computerized catalogues have replaced the traditional card catalogues and they have made searching through library holdings far easier, quicker, and more thorough than ever before. The catalogue can usually be accessed via computer terminals in the library or by logging on to the catalogue at a 'remote' terminal. The catalogue will allow you to perform different types of search, depending upon what you are aiming to achieve – you may simply want to find the location of a book you already know about, or you may wish to see what works the library holds on a particular subject. It is useful to spend some time 'playing' with the catalogue to establish its capabilities and to learn the language of commands it understands. Catalogue searches take different forms, but can be roughly divided into three types:

Author Search This is the quickest route to an entry when you already know the name of the author (of a primary or secondary work); it is also useful if you

SECTION 1

know one work by an author and want to find which other works by that author are available.

Title Search This is the quickest route to an entry when you already know the title. A significant phrase or word from the title will normally be sufficient (e.g., to find *The Life and Opinions of Tristram Shandy, Gentleman,* just search for 'Tristram Shandy' or 'Shandy'). Articles must be located using title searches: search for the title of the journal – not the article – then find the location of the relevant volume (using the volume number or year contained in your reference to the article).

Subject/Keyword Search This is useful for viewing the library holdings in a particular subject area. The computer program will match words exactly, so it's often useful to try several searches with slightly different formulations (e.g., if you were searching for information on Welsh writers, you might try both 'Welsh literature' and 'literature in Wales'). Such searches return a lot of irrelevant entries (e.g., a search for 'Welsh literature' will return *Trainspotting* by Irvine Welsh), so you will need to scan carefully through the list of hits to sort out the useful works. Many systems allow you to use open-ended keywords to broaden the reach of the search: for example, you might search for 'litera*' which would match 'literature', 'literary' and also 'literal'.

The computer terminal through which the library catalogue is accessed may also provide access to other valuable resources, such as **CD-ROM** or **Online** catalogues and databases. For an introduction to using such resources, see Section 2, pp. 101–32.

A checklist of useful reference works
- ▓ *The Oxford Companion to English Literature*, ed. Margaret Drabble, 6th edn (Oxford: Oxford University Press, 1995)
- ▓ *The Bloomsbury Guide to English Literature*, ed. Marion Wynne-Davies, 2nd edn (London: Bloomsbury, 1995)
- ▓ *The Cambridge Guide to Literature in English*, ed. Ian Ousby, 2nd edn (Cambridge: Cambridge University Press, 1994)

Each of the above works provides useful general reference material on literature in accessible and informative entries. For factual details about authors and their works, such guides are an excellent place to start.

- ▓ *Encyclopaedia of Literature and Criticism*, ed. Martin Coyle *et al.* (London: Routledge, 1990)

More a large collection of general essays on literary topics than an encyclopaedia. Its coverage is impressive – different literary PERIODS, GENRES and CULTURES are addressed in an introductory manner, and useful lists of Further Reading are provided. It also includes essays on theoretical and critical issues.

- *The Encyclopaedia Britannica* or *The New Encyclopaedia Britannica* (Chicago: Encyclopaedia Britannica)

A vast, multi-volume store of knowledge from all fields, and very easy to use. It is also available on CD-ROM and via the Internet in a 'free' edition funded by advertisements.

- *The Oxford English Dictionary* ('*OED*'), rev. edn (Oxford: Oxford University Press, 1989)

This 20-volume work is the most complete and detailed dictionary available, providing not only definitions but examples of word usage from different historical periods. It is available in a photographically reduced 2-volume form (complete with its own magnifying glass), and also on CD-ROM. Obviously you will need your own smaller dictionary for day-to-day use. Right from the start of your degree you should get into the habit of *always* looking up the meaning of words you are not familiar with.

- *The Dictionary of National Biography* or *The Concise Dictionary of National Biography: from Earliest Times to 1985*, eds Sir Leslie Stephen and Sir Sidney Lee (63 vols, London: Oxford University Press, 1885–1900), 8 supplements published from 1901 to 1970

An excellent source of authoritative biographical information. The entries are longer and more detailed than those on authors in the literary companions and guides described above. Also available online and on CD-ROM.

- *The Oxford Dictionary of Quotations*, ed. Angela Partington, 4th edn (Oxford: Oxford University Press, 1992) and *The Oxford Dictionary of Literary Quotations*, ed. Peter Kemp (Oxford: Oxford University Press, 1997)

Useful for identifying quotations in literary works where no annotation does it for you, and handy for culling other people's *bon mots*.

It may be that your library does not contain all of the above works – libraries are usually in competition with other sectors of the university for very limited funding, and few libraries are able to order all of the works that students, lecturers, and librarians would like to have available. The important thing, as has already been stressed, is to get to know the resources that are available to you, and to learn how to negotiate the framework of information sources within which you will be working during the course of your degree.

Using computers

First, we suggest that you check the subsection in Section 2 entitled 'Revising and editing electronically' (pp. 125–6). There are three points we would like to add to what is said there.

The first is that it is not essential that you use a PC to write essays or term papers – essays can still be submitted hand-written (although many universities require extended 'project papers' to be typewritten). But if you do have regular access to a PC, we strongly advise you to learn to use it. Many people produce better written work when using a word-processor because the task of making changes and revisions to the text is made so much easier and quicker. (You may, however, find that the task of *planning* and *structuring* an essay is better done with a pencil and a piece of paper.) And the resources of the Web and the Internet (again, see Section 2) are extremely valuable to a student of literature.

Our second point is that becoming too reliant upon computers can be a danger when it comes to sitting exams, because you can get out of the habit of producing an extended piece of prose by hand. A good exam performance partially depends upon this mechanical skill, and so it is important to practise this manner of writing.

Our third point repeats what is said in Section 2, but it deserves repetition: beware of losing your work because of accidents and malfunctions. In other words, *always* make a back-up copy of all of your files on disk, run an anti-virus program regularly and *always* before you open an attached file, and get used to hitting the 'save' button in your word-processing program every time you make an important addition or alteration to what you are writing.

READING LITERARY TEXTS

- What reading techniques facilitate the study of literature?
- Does it matter which edition is used?
- What are the best ways of making notes?
- Which features of a literary text should be noted?
- What specific reading techniques can be brought to the study of prose fiction, drama and poetry?

Reading literature as part of a programme of study is not the same as reading literature purely for enjoyment – although hopefully enjoyment will still play a major role in your reading. To *study* literature means, in part, to become conscious in your reading of *how* the work has created its effects. It is easy to develop impressions about a literary text, but criticism usually involves examining what exactly it is about the text – and sometimes about its reader(s) – that causes those impressions to arise. One might, for example, simply say that 'Jane Eyre is a sympathetic character', but criticism typically requires more: it requires, at some point, an examination of how certain groups of words arranged by Charlotte Brontë have made the character of Jane Eyre appear sympathetic to certain readers. In other words, criticism involves careful explorations of the precise verbal formulations that authors choose to employ in their writing. Clearly there are many different ways of approaching and interpreting literature (see Section 3, pp. 135–97) but it is basically true to say that some sort of careful, self-conscious reading is a fundamental method of all. Developing the skills of a 'critical reader' is clearly vital, therefore, if you are studying for a degree in literature.

As we pointed out earlier, compared with pre-degree level courses a degree in literature can seem very fast-paced, with little teaching time being devoted to each text. The speed at which a degree course whisks students from text to text can mean that it is a major challenge to acquire a critical intimacy with the individual works. On most pre-degree level courses, a great familiarity with a text can be acquired through the meticulously detailed reading and analysis that the pace of the course allows. At degree level it is necessary to develop techniques so as to be able to read relatively quickly while noting and retaining as much relevant material from (and about) the text as possible. In this subsection of the guide, therefore, we offer some general guidelines on how you might refine your reading techniques. Our fundamental aims have been to suggest types of question that you might keep in mind as you read, and to give advice on more mechanical matters such as taking notes.

Reading and studying: general points

Which edition of a text should be used?

Choosing between different editions of a literary work is an important issue that can have major implications for a reading experience and for an interpretation of the work. It is quite usual that our experience of reading literature is partially determined by the work of an editor – intervening between ourselves and what we might be tempted to think of as 'the author's text' will often be numerous editorial changes which have somehow determined the shape of the work. Sometimes these changes are the work of a single editor, or sometimes the modern appearance of a work reflects longer-term transformation. Either way, the editorial manipulation of a text can present certain problems of interpretation, and it is often appropriate to be aware of what has been added, taken away or altered by an editor or indeed by the processes of modern reproduction.

Different editions can present significantly different versions of the text. For example, both of the following passages have been printed as the opening of Charles Dickens' last and unfinished novel *The Mystery of Edwin Drood* (1870):

> An ancient English Cathedral Tower? How can the ancient English Cathedral tower be here!

> An ancient English Cathedral Town? How can the ancient English Cathedral town be here!

The first passage comes from an old but, in its time, highly respectable edition from the London publisher Chapman & Hall; the second comes from the Oxford University Press World's Classics edition of 1982. While the difference may perhaps seem small, it is undoubtedly significant – especially since it appears among the opening sentences, which for Dickens and many other writers typically serve the important purpose of setting the scene of the novel.

Similarly, one finds on the opening page of the still fairly standard Dent edition of Joseph Conrad's *Heart of Darkness* (1902): '. . . in the luminous space the tanned sails of the barges drifting up with the tide seemed to stand still in red clusters of canvas sharply peaked, with gleams of varnished spirits'. Varnished spirits? You might ponder the metaphysical implications of that final image for some time, but you would be reading meaning into an editorial transformation of something much more mundane. Conrad had intended not 'spirits' but 'sprits' – the poles which cross a ship's mast diagonally to hold up a sail – and most modern editions of *Heart of Darkness* print 'sprits'.

In some cases, the choice of the text one reads depends upon factors other than editorial changes. With some works there are several radically different texts which all have authority. Perhaps we should pause here and clarify the terms of that potentially confusing statement: by 'work' we basically mean *a title associated with an author's name*; and by 'text' we mean an actual arrangement of words that is fixed in some material form (see TEXT AND WORK for further discussion of this issue). William Wordsworth's poem 'The Prelude' provides a good example. Wordsworth produced many versions of this poem: there was a brief first draft, composed in 1798 and entitled 'Was it for this?'; then the poem appeared in a 'completed' form in 1799 with the title 'The Prelude'; a new version, again called 'The Prelude', appeared in 1805; and then another version called 'The Prelude' appeared in 1850. There are significant differences between each of the versions, but none has ever really been singled out and designated as *the* ultimate version.

What does all this mean for the undergraduate student of literature? Well, fortunately the decision about which text should be read is usually made for you by your lecturers, who will stipulate a particular *edition* or a particular *version* of a work on a reading list. However, there may sometimes be reasons for you to use an alternative edition: the recommended edition is not available, you already have a copy of the text in a different edition and don't want to buy another, the recommended edition is too expensive, or whatever. If you do use an alternative edition, you should be aware that there may be significant variations between the text you are reading and that to which your lecturer is referring. If you are not recommended to read a specific edition, try to ensure that you are not reading an inferior text – you might consult with your lecturer if you are uncertain about an edition.

We also would like to stress, however, that it is always relevant to keep in mind how the words you are reading came into the world in that particular form. Reading works in modern editions is often far removed from the way in which the works were originally read and the way in which their authors imagined that they would be read. In some cases, the work was never intended for publication at all. For example, many Elizabethan love poems that we now read in mass-produced volumes were originally written not for printing and publishing, but for private circulation in manuscript form. They may have been intended for just a select group of readers well-known to the author, or even intended just for one reader: the object of love addressed in the poem. Such information is not merely incidental – it can help us to understand how the poem produces its meanings. The effect of a private love poem can hinge upon the fact of its intimacy and upon the fact that it is decidedly not a *public* expression. So when you look at such a poem in a modern edition – clearly a *public* document – it is well worth considering that the poem has not always looked like that and the author probably never imagined that it would.

It would be naive to think that as modern readers we can ever 're-capture' the original experience of reading a work, and it would also be wrong to suggest that such 'heritage imaginings' should necessarily be the goal of reading. But by *knowing about* how literary works first appeared and what changes have since been wrought on them, we can often better understand things about how the text functions. Most modern editions contain 'A Note on the Text(s)' where such information can be found, or sometimes it is contained among annotations and notes. In our experience, many students skip over or ignore these passages, but we recommend that they be read with care.

Primary reading should be primary

Aside from reading notes on how the text has arrived in its current form, we recommend that the literary work itself should be the first thing you read when you are studying that work. This may sound obvious, but we want to stress the point because there are many people who prefer to read criticism on a work before they tackle the work itself and we feel that this can be a limiting experience – as limiting as hearing the punch-line before a joke. A secondary work of criticism will usually advance a *partial view* of the literary text. If that view is encountered *before* reading the text it can hold a tremendous influence over the reading experience and it can be difficult to avoid simply interpreting the text such that it reinforces the view. For example, if you read a secondary work which persuasively presents Daniel Defoe's Robinson Crusoe as a representative of early European colonialism, it is likely that such a function will appear as Crusoe's dominant feature and other qualities in the character will be obscured or seemingly diminished.

The same advice applies to reading introductions in the modern editions you will be using: these too will be marked by critical bias, however slight, and it is often preferable to read an introduction *after* reading the text (paradoxical though this may sound). You may notice that some editions of texts – such as many from the publisher Norton – have no introduction, but instead include a section of 'Critical Essays' or of 'Backgrounds and Sources' after the text. This is a very 'honest' approach to the inclusion of secondary material with a text – one that doesn't make any pretence to impartiality.

First reactions – 'knee-jerk', 'gut', 'instinctive', or whatever you want to call them – are valuable and revealing things. They can say a lot both about a text and about you as a reader, and it is well worth leaving yourself open to those reactions before then going about analyzing their causes.

Consulting annotations and notes alongside your reading of a text is another matter. While secondary criticism can limit the reading experience, good annotations enrich reading and can often prevent straightforward misinterpretation. We therefore recommend that you refer to them during the process of reading. Annotations are included in editions of literary works primarily to illuminate potential textual obscurities – problematic language, ALLUSIONS and quotations, cultural and historical references, and any other textual features or points of interest that could easily be overlooked. The usage of many words has changed over time, and annotations can steer readers clear of anachronistic mis-readings. For example, here are two lines from Shakespeare's Sonnet 3:

> Or who is he so fond will be the tomb
> Of his self-love, to stop posterity?

When Shakespeare was writing the accepted meaning of 'fond' was 'foolish' – an annotated text should alert readers to such crucial, but not obvious, information. The couplet certainly makes very odd sense if it is read with the modern meaning of 'fond' in mind.

Taking notes as you read

In ordinary life when we want to preserve something we use aids: photographs, diaries, memo-pads, and so on. And to study literature we have to do the same. We need to take notes. Taking notes might sound like a straightforward process, but it is actually a skilled operation and one which you have to practise in order to be good at it. And it takes time before you can develop your skills to the point at which it does not interfere with your reading. So here are some suggestions.

You can write notes either in the work that you are reading or in a separate notebook. The advantage of the former method is that it does not disturb one's reading too much, and it means that reading is a very 'portable' activity, requiring little more equipment than the literary work and a pencil. The disadvantages are that it spoils the book, it affects one's second reading of the work, there is not always sufficient room on the page for more than the briefest of comments, and *retrieval* of the notes afterwards for purposes of study is time-consuming. One way round these problems is to write very brief notes in pencil as you read, and then to copy these up and expand them in a separate notebook or onto a computer file later. This also allows you to copy out brief extracts from the literary work which strike you as important or which you think you might use as evidence if you intend to write an essay on the work. This method also means that you file for future reference only notes about which you have thought a second time after having finished reading the work. And the pencil marks can be erased leaving any second reading undisturbed (and *undirected*) by earlier notes. If something in the text strikes you as important or significant but you don't want to puzzle over it in case you break your train of thought, then you might mark the passage in question, note the page reference somewhere, and come back to ponder the passage later.

Some people choose to make notes directly onto a computer file. The obvious disadvantage of this is that reading becomes an activity tethered to a desk in the constant company of a humming machine. Or if you use a laptop computer, there is rarely space for both book and machine upon even the most ample of laps. But there are also many advantages to using a computer. If you type your notes onto a computer file, the subsequent process of organizing or transferring notes for use in an essay is made very easy and quick. The notes made during reading will follow the progression of the work, but it can be very useful afterwards to group these into categories – such as notes on a particular character, or theme, or political leaning, or linguistic device, or whatever. The 'cut and paste' facility of a word-processing program is an ideal tool for this type of reorganization.

Whatever method you use for writing up notes – computer or notebook or file – *always* record the page or pages in the literary work to which your notes refer. One of the purposes of notes is to direct you back to the passage that prompted the idea contained in the note, and so it is important to keep a record of where that passage can be found – essential information when you are revising.

Choosing what to note can be a very varied process according to the nature of the literary work you're reading, and so we've chosen to divide points about this into separate subsections according to GENRE. The genre of a work of literature is its type or class, and generic categories can be very wide, such as 'FICTION' or 'drama', or they can be more precisely descriptive, such as 'PICARESQUE NOVEL' or 'COMEDY OF MANNERS'. Here we are using the broad categories of 'prose fiction', 'drama' and 'poetry'. It is common to distinguish among literary works according to these three categories, and it makes sense to do so here because, generally speaking, the groupings represent different *ways of communicating*.

In the following subsections we have again tried to be as *practical* as possible. These sections are not intended as introductions to the genres themselves, but rather explorations of issues that are pertinent when reading and when studying these genres.

Reading prose fiction: novels, novellas and short stories

The language of prose

The modern term 'prose' derives from the Latin *prosa* or *proversa oratio*, meaning 'straightforward discourse' – that is, 'ordinary' written or spoken expression. Implied by the term 'prose' is a distinction from poetry – indeed we wouldn't need a term for straightforward discourse if we knew of no form of 'unstraightforward discourse', which is often seen as the characteristic mode of poetic expression. The writing of poetry, it is sometimes assumed, involves a deliberate manipulation of language, whereas, the argument goes, prose fiction – NOVELS, NOVELLAS and SHORT STORIES – uses language more as a transparent medium for conveying information about the world or about a fictional world.

As a key introductory point, we would like to stress that in general one should definitely *not* treat the language of prose fiction as a transparent window through which simply to regard 'what happens'. As a reader it may be that sometimes you become so involved and caught up in the 'action' of a novel or a short story that you are not arrested by it *as language* as readers typically are when reading a poem. But if you are reading fiction for the purposes of study, you have to learn to resist this process and to 'look at' that which in the past you may have 'looked through'.

With some prose works it is immediately obvious that language is being employed in an unstraightforward manner, and that part of the value of reading the work lies in an engagement with its language. Here is the closing passage of Virginia Woolf's short story 'Kew Gardens' (1919):

> Voices. Yes, voices. Wordless voices, breaking the silence suddenly with such depth of contentment, such passion of desire, or, in the voices of children, such freshness of surprise; breaking the silence? But there was no silence; all the time the motor omnibuses were turning their wheels and changing their gear; like a vast nest of Chinese boxes all of wrought steel turning ceaselessly one within another the city murmured; on the top of which the voices cried aloud and the petals of myriads of flowers flashed their colours into the air.

It scarcely needs pointing out that such writing is far removed from what we think of as straightforward discourse. Certainly this is prose, but it is not every-day prose: its rhythmic qualities, its unconventional syntax and its use of striking IMAGERY clearly mark its difference from the sort of language we might use to discuss the weather or to give someone directions. Woolf's text in fact seems to be so boldly untypical of regular discourse that it *draws attention to itself as language*. As readers we are forced to stop and think about the mode of expression as well as what is being described 'through' that expression. Indeed, part of the interest of the passage can be said to lie in its reformulation *by the means of untypical expression* of how we might think about aspects of the world. By breaking away from the standard, familiar phrases by which we describe the world, the passage invites readers to consider the world anew.

On the basis of that example, the 'prose = straightforward, poetry = unstraightforward' distinction is put under considerable strain. In fact, if one wants to distinguish prose from poetry it might be better to confine the comparison and simply point out poetic qualities that are very rarely found in prose: one might say that prose is a form of language which is typically unrestricted by metrical structures (see METRE) and patterns of RHYME. (Of course, the issue is complicated by the fact that certain poetic forms – FREE VERSE, for example – can also be unrestricted by metrical structures and patterns of rhyme). Such 'definition through negatives' may not be ideal, but it at least allows us to recognize that prose, as it is used in literary works, can be far from straightforward.

Now it could be argued that an example taken from Woolf's 'Kew Gardens' is a special case because it comes from a short story, and that the points one can make about the passage cannot be truly representative for prose fiction as a whole. Indeed, it is partially true that short stories *do* present a slightly special case: they typically employ a prose style that is rich in *implication* and *suggestion*, and such a style often demands more careful close analysis than the prose of a longer work.

But even if the language of short stories does require particularly close attention, this does not mean that attention need not be given to the language of longer prose works such as novels. It is true that novels generally do not repay the type of attention one might lavish upon every word of a SONNET. The novel is sometimes characterized as a loose, baggy genre – one which is capable of absorbing digressions, unconnected subplots, characters that are not fully integrated with the main action, and so on. In other words, novels are often not delicately balanced structures, the interpretation of which will fall apart if you overlook a single comma. But the language of novels does need to be considered with care, even when it seems to be about as 'straightforward' as you can get.

Here is the opening of Jonathan Swift's *Gulliver's Travels* (1726), a work which was written before 'the novel' as such was really settled as a genre but which is now generally seen as an important influence on the development of the genre:

> My Father had a small Estate in *Nottinghamshire*; I was the Third of five Sons. He sent me to *Emanuel-College* in *Cambridge*, at Fourteen Years old, where I resided three Years, and applied myself close to my Studies: But the Charge of maintaining me (although I had a very scanty allowance) being too great for a narrow Fortune; I was bound Apprentice to Mr. *James Bates*, an eminent Surgeon in *London*, with whom I continued four Years; and my Father now and then sending me small Sums of Money, I laid them out in learning Navigation, and other Parts of the Mathematicks, useful to those who intend to travel, as I always believed it would be some time or other my Fortune to do.

It may be that certain technical features of this passage do strike you as unusual, but probably these are largely just the result of eighteenth-century printing conventions and of slightly old-fashioned usages of particular words. The passage is quoted from the Norton edition of *Gulliver's Travels*, which does not print a modernized text, and so retains the now unconventional italics and capital letters that were commonplace in eighteenth-century printed works. Otherwise, though, the passage will probably appear to you as fairly unremarkable in terms of the type of language it employs – indeed, it may even appear linguistically dull. With regard to the passage from 'Kew Gardens', we pointed out Woolf's attention to rhythm, the untypical syntax and the use of imagery – it would be difficult to isolate such 'literary' features in the passage by Swift. The passage is comprised of standard sentences and its descriptiveness appears to be primarily factual. Where Woolf apparently aims to *evoke* a feeling of the city through unconventional images, Swift seems purely intent upon conveying information.

So why are we stressing that attention should be given to the language of prose works even when it can appear as unremarkable as this? Well, first, it is often the case that authors deliberately use 'unremarkable' prose to create particular effects. This is certainly true of Swift. When Swift wrote *Gulliver's Travels* he wanted his readers to believe initially that they were reading a genuine account written by a genuine traveller – the book was partially a hoax. In fact, when the book was first published it was not called *Gulliver's Travels* – this familiar title was attached to the work only subsequently – but it was called *Travels into Several Remote Nations of the World* and the author was supposedly one 'Lemuel Gulliver'. The 'unremarkable' opening passage, then, was all part of Swift's ploy. He sought to trick readers into believing they were reading a genuine work of travel literature before suddenly overturning their expectations. So while the writing seems mundane, it is clearly carefully executed so as to create a desired effect.

But there are further reasons why attention should be paid to the language of prose fiction even if it seems unremarkable. However 'literary' or 'unliterary' the prose, its characteristics will always be crucial to how the novel creates its effects. Notice, for example, the very simple fact that in *Gulliver's Travels* Swift writes in the first person. This is an essential part of how the work functions – not only in the initial passages where deception was Swift's aim, but also later after readers have realized the trick. Imagine how different the effect of the passage would be if it were written in the third person and began: 'Lemuel Gulliver's father had a small estate in Nottinghamshire, and he was the third of five sons. His father sent him to Emanuel-College in Cambridge when he was fourteen years old . . .'. Immediately readers are placed in a strikingly different relationship with the main character: we no longer 'hear his voice' but we observe him from outside through the voice of another narrator. It is to this type of detail that you need to be alert when studying prose fiction – it is just one of numerous factors that are crucial to *how prose works*. (You may find the entry for PERSPECTIVE AND VOICE in Section 4 helpful as a basis for thinking about such issues.)

Making notes on prose fiction: a case study

Let us pursue the issue of what to note in prose fiction by considering in detail the opening passage from Charlotte Brontë's *Jane Eyre* (1847). Following the passage are our suggestions regarding what is important and what might be noted. Before considering our suggestions, we recommend you to read the passage carefully with the following questions in mind:

- What information is being conveyed?
- How is that information being conveyed?

■ What opinions/impressions of the situation and the characters am I acquiring as I read?

■ How is the passage guiding me towards taking up those opinions/impressions?

> There was no possibility of taking a walk that day. We had been wandering, indeed, in the leafless shrubbery an hour in the morning; but since dinner (Mrs Reed, when there was no company, dined early) the cold winter wind had brought with it dark clouds so sombre, and a rain so penetrating, that further outdoor exercise was now out of the question.
>
> I was glad of it; I never liked long walks, especially on chilly afternoons: dreadful to me was the coming home in the raw twilight, with nipped fingers and toes, and a heart saddened by the chidings of Bessie, the nurse, and humbled by the consciousness of my physical inferiority to Eliza, John, and Georgiana Reed.
>
> The said Eliza, John, and Georgiana were now clustered round their mamma in the drawing-room: she lay reclined on a sofa by the fireside, and with her darlings about her (for the time neither quarrelling nor crying) looked perfectly happy. Me, she had dispensed from joining the group, saying, 'She regretted to be under the necessity of keeping me at a distance; but that until she heard from Bessie, and could discover by her own observation that I was endeavouring in good earnest to acquire a more sociable and childlike disposition, a more attractive and sprightly manner – something lighter, franker, more natural, as it were – she really must exclude me from privileges intended only for contented happy little children.'
>
> 'What does Bessie say I have done?' I asked.
>
> 'Jane, I don't like cavillers or questioners; besides, there is something truly forbidding in a child taking up her elders in that manner.'

Here are our thoughts on significant aspects of the passage. They are arranged in the order in which they are prompted by the passage: this is in the nature of notes – notes do not group themselves thematically, but go off in many directions. Arranging notes into categories can be done later when you have finished reading – at which point you'll have a better idea of which categories are relevant.

Paragraph 1: There was no possibility . . . out of the question.

■ The first sentence gives a striking introduction to the novel – it doesn't actually state what the described situation is, but interestingly points to an activity that is prevented from happening (by what we don't yet know). This oblique introduction stimulates curiosity, and at the same time the TONE implies an intimacy between NARRATOR and READER – it is written as though we already know the narrator. Intimacy is also implied with the opening IN MEDIAS RES – we are thrust straight into the action as though we are already familiar with the SETTING and CHARACTERS. Furthermore, the sentence suggests that if things were different, whoever is involved would probably be taking a walk. Already, a certain MOOD is perhaps being suggested – one involving a sense of enclosure or of repressed possibilities.

■ The sentence is very specific regarding *time*. Using the past tense, we are presented with a retrospective view of 'that day'. Perhaps it is a day of great significance that is about to be described.

■ The next sentence reveals more about the NARRATIVE SITUATION. The narrator is one of the characters involved in the action: we are dealing with a first-person narrator, as yet unnamed and apparently one of the community of 'we'. The narrative uses an oblique method of description to set the scene: there is no simple statement that 'It was winter'; rather, the season and weather are more indirectly suggested, first by the 'leafless shrubbery' and then by the description of the wind.

■ Why does the author introduce the book with a scene set in harsh weather? Perhaps the weather is being used to create a particular *atmosphere* – the type of weather, it seems, is not merely incidental, but suggests the use of the PATHETIC FALLACY to reflect aspects of the human drama described in the novel. This seems to be confirmed by the use of a word like 'sombre': this is not simply descriptive of a dark cloud, but conveys the mood of the person describing the cloud. In other words, the *manner* of description is revealing things about the personality and emotional state of the narrator.

■ We also learn about a 'Mrs Reed'. Why does the author inform us about her eating arrangements? Again, it is apparently an indirect way of revealing her character. We are told that sometimes she receives company and she changes her habits when she does so: she is perhaps, then, someone interested in maintaining a particular social status and in creating a particular social image of herself. We may also get a hint about her social status from the 'shrubbery': we cannot tell for sure that this is Mrs Reed's shrubbery but the fact that the characters wander around a *cultivated* area of the outdoors suggests that we are dealing with a family from the middle or upper classes. Not only do they have access to cultivated nature, but they have the time for leisured wandering.

■ If we do draw conclusions such as this from the mention of the shrubbery, we might note that our reading is involving our regarding the novel in relation to an impression of the time and culture in which it was written. We are in part mapping the details given in the novel onto our preconceived notions of nineteenth-century Britain.

Paragraph 2: I was glad . . . Georgiana Reed.

■ The narrator singles her/himself out from the plural 'we'. And this grammatical movement is reflected in what is said of the narrator's position in relation to the other characters. The narrator describes her/his overall dislike of walks with the Reeds, and in doing so suggests her/his feelings of alienation. The narrator suffers the forces of the weather, which leads to (and reflects) the revelation that s/he also suffers among the family and feels apart from and inferior to the others. Perhaps we are starting to feel sympathy for the vulnerable narrator here.

■ We learn more about the class position of the Reeds: they have sufficient wealth to afford a nurse. Their names also signal a class position – 'Georgiana', particularly, has aristocratic associations so we might begin to think that they are aristocratic or aspire to be so. Again, we might note that the author uses an indirect technique for conveying important information. We are not 'told' directly about the situation but have to pick it up from small descriptive hints (compare, perhaps, Swift's Gulliver who, as we saw, simply states his background).

Paragraph 3: The said Eliza . . . little children.

■ The first sentence contains the unconventional construction 'were now'. Strictly speaking, it seems to defy logic and normal grammar with its mixing of a past tense verb and the present tense 'now', but it is effective in giving emphasis to the scene to come. It suggests perhaps that *this* is the important scene that came about 'that day' because 'there was no possibility of taking a walk'.

■ The sense of the narrator's alienation from the family is increased through a description *from the sidelines* of a cosy – almost twee – family group. Particular vocabulary enforces the sense of their cosiness: 'Mrs Reed' has become 'their mamma'; the children are 'her darlings', and these words have a sarcastic or disapproving ring to them. The fireside is a suggestive detail: it indicates warmth – from which the narrator is excluded and which, the previous paragraph has suggested, the narrator craves; it furthermore functions as a symbol of 'the home'. (As the critic David Lodge has pointed out, patterned references to fire and heat play a crucial role in the novel as a whole.)

■ The parenthetical phrase in the first sentence provides a counterforce to the scene of cosy harmony. It undercuts the harmony with a suggestion that the normal behaviour of the Reed children is far from peaceful. Perhaps there is a trace of IRONY here in the narrator's manner of telling – again there is no direct statement concerning the children, but the narrator subtly and ironically introduces their usual 'quarrelling'. The irony of this point resounds further in the latter half of the paragraph when the narrator reports Mrs Reed's many criticisms of the narrator's behaviour: a sense of serious injustice is being suggested.

■ As in the first and second paragraphs, where there was a movement from 'We' to 'I', here there is a movement from the description of the group to a solitary 'Me' and the singularity of this word is given emphasis through its position at the beginning of a sentence and the comma that follows it. Again, the author uses grammar and syntax to enforce what seems to be emerging as a theme: the narrator's sense of exclusion.

▪ To present the words of Mrs Reed, the narrator uses a form that is something in between INDIRECT and DIRECT speech. Quotation marks are used suggesting that these are the actual words spoken by Mrs Reed, but the speech uses the third-person rather than the first-person ('she' rather than 'I'). It is a type of FREE INDIRECT DISCOURSE. Why does the narrator use this form? The presentation of dialogue may be something to keep an eye on as the novel progresses. Perhaps here it is being used to ease the transition to the line following the paragraph which clearly represents direct speech. The move from a retrospective narration to the more 'dramatic' dialogue mode is achieved slickly with Mrs Reed's speech presented in a type of 'halfway' form.

▪ The form of child-rearing promoted by Mrs Reed seems highly constrictive and sentimental. Does she voice these views merely to repress the narrator, while her own children enjoy greater favours? Are her views representative of nineteenth-century British culture? The irony at work in the paragraph suggests that the novel is criticizing these views and Mrs Reed – we might look out for further critique later.

▪ Is there a Mr Reed?

The dialogue: What does Bessie say . . . in that manner.

▪ For the first time, we 'hear' the narrator's voice in the described world. Can we learn anything about the narrator from this question? We might observe that the narrator will not suffer her exclusion without voicing protest. We can tell very little about the TONE of the question: the narrator only supplies 'I asked' and so does not reveal anything about the manner in which the question is asked.

▪ Mrs Reed's response could suggest how the question was asked – she is shocked by 'that manner' in a child. Had Jane (finally we know the narrator's name and sex) perhaps *shouted* the question when faced with such injustice? Clearly we can never truly ascertain any such untold details, but Mrs Reed's response certainly suggests that the question was put in a manner that was far from meek. If this is the case, it has certain implications: it *does* suggest that Jane is a character who will protest at injustice; and it might also hint that Jane, as narrator, does not always reveal all the details that she might. We may want to be alert to further occasions where Jane is not totally open or confessional.

▪ From the novel's title we have probably assumed from the start that the narrator is female, but this is now confirmed. Does this information change our attitude to any of what has gone before?

This list may appear to be an excessively long commentary on a fairly short passage, and we wouldn't for a moment want to suggest that you should write notes on literary works in so expansive a fashion as this. We have deliberately drawn things out here so as to demonstrate the types of things that are of interest to note, and why they are significant in terms of how the fiction is creating its effects. As far as actually making notes is concerned, many of the above points might equate to a single underlined word or a two-word marginal comment.

There is also a lot of material here because the passage is from the beginning of a novel – inevitably a beginning contains a lot of notable details which don't need noting later because they apply throughout the book. In *Jane Eyre* the narrative situation remains fairly constant throughout, so while you might note new details about the manner of narration, you will not need to think about and record its fundamental qualities.

Notice that many of the things we note take the form of questions. When making notes you do not have to stop and think about a point until you have 'worked it out' – indeed, it is desirable to limit interruptions to your reading. Many notes simply mark points of curiosity or details that might be followed up later.

If you were to write about the passage in an essay, it is unlikely that you would need to pursue the range of details we have looked at here – it would be a very rambling essay if you did! But it is always useful to make notes on a wide range of textual features as you read. Then if you come to write an essay on the work, you have a strong body of material which you can use with great selectivity.

Reading long works of prose fiction: a cumulative process

We may read a short story, a novella or a shortish novel in one sitting, while anything up to twenty or more sessions will be required for a long and complex novel such as Tolstoy's *War and Peace*. For those readers who read Victorian novels when they were first published in serial form there was no choice: they *had* to stop and wait at certain stages in their reading. In the eighteenth century, the first readers of Laurence Sterne's *Tristram Shandy* took all of eight years to get through the work, from the first volumes of 1759 to the last of 1767. It is unlikely that reading a novel would take that long nowadays, but it nevertheless remains the case that a novel is something that 'lives with us' over a significant period of time, and this duration has implications for the manner in which we respond to and INTERPRET novels. When we pause in our reading of a novel we tend to go over what we have read, and we might think forward to what we guess might happen or what we would like to happen. Perhaps we might imagine ourselves in situations described in the novel, and ponder how we might act were we in their positions. Some readers can become so involved in the world of a novel that they hold imaginary conversations with characters, and even miss having the characters around them when the reading process is finished.

Put another way: expectation, surprise, disappointment, foreboding, tension, suspense, imagination, fantasy – all form part of our reading a novel. To read a novel is to be involved in a *cumulative process*. Of course, the reading of any literary work takes place progressively over time, but time is a particularly significant factor to take into account when thinking about and studying novels.

One problem which this issue raises for the study of the novel is that there are certain experiences in us, and certain events in the novel, which lodge far more permanently in the mind than do others. Indeed, it is part of the way that a novel works upon us – part of its power as a source of enjoyment – that some aspects of our reading experience should fade more quickly than others. In REALIST fiction, for example, many details are supplied to create a sense of the story's plausibility but ultimately they can often be discarded: when Daniel Defoe informs readers that Robinson Crusoe was 'born in the year 1632' he increases the sense of Robinson as a plausible, tangible character, but the precise date is not of great importance for the narrative that follows and few readers would retain such specific information. But more significant than such minor details, characters and events will strike readers with varying force, and different readers will be struck in different ways. Furthermore, our memory can play tricks upon us once we have finished a novel. If you have read *Wuthering Heights*, but some time ago, then try this test upon yourself: at what stage in the novel does the older Catherine die? Probably, unless you are an unusually retentive and conscientious reader, you are likely to place this event far later in the novel than it actually occurs.

The issue is complicated by the fact that we often read a novel more than once. One of the distinguishing features of good novels (unlike pulp fiction) is that we can get something new out of a second or third reading of the same piece of fiction. On a subsequent reading we are normally less preoccupied with what will happen and so are able to read more carefully and notice many details that slipped our attention on first reading. To go back to the example of the opening passage of *Jane Eyre*, it may be that some of the points we raised would become more conspicuous on a second reading when we know that Jane's story *does* revolve largely around her feelings of exclusion and her quest to find a satisfying home. Rereading the opening we would see that Brontë includes details that *foreshadow* this quest – the term for this technique is PROLEPSIS. The use of prolepsis will certainly have an effect on a first reading, but we may only be subconsciously aware of it. When we reread a passage that employs prolepsis (or when we go back and review our notes), we will become more conscious of how the author has created the effect.

So while we have been promoting the value of reading prose fiction with an attention to the details of the language it employs, the close reading of passages is only part of what constitutes a full critical reading of a novel. In addition to responding to significant detail in the prose of a work of fiction you need also to be able to perceive *larger patterns and movements in the work as a whole*, as well as connections to other works. This is another aspect of reading and studying which is facilitated by making notes.

A checklist of things to note in a novel

This list is intended to serve a double purpose. On the one hand we hope that it will be useful to work from when you are engaged in the analysis of a particular passage from a novel or a short story. In addition, however, we hope that its perusal will serve as a reminder of the sort of points that can be noted in the process of reading or rereading a work of fiction. The golden rule here is: if in doubt, make a note.

Narrative technique All information relating to the manipulation of NARRATIVE in the work: the narrative voice and PERSPECTIVE (is it first-person or third-person? is the NARRATOR involved in the action or distant?); clues about the values or personality of the narrator; things that the narrator *doesn't* know; changes of narrator or narrative perspective; narrative intrusions or comments; TELLING AND SHOWING (are things *explained* by the narrator, or does meaning emerge from dramatized action or dialogue or use of SYMBOLS?); the relationship between STORY AND PLOT (does the narrative follow the time sequence of the action or not?); narrative 'approval' and 'disapproval' (are certain characters or things apparently endorsed or criticized from the narrative point of view?).

TONE Is it familiar or formal, intimate or impersonal? Who (if anyone) is apparently being addressed? Do the vocabulary or syntax suggest a particular style of delivery?

Characterization Information about *how* we learn about the CHARACTERS (are we *told* about them or are their personalities revealed through action, or through repeated 'quirks', or through symbolic associations, and so on?); any indications that characters are changing or developing; significant new information about a character; differences in the way different characters are presented (are some characters ironized while others seem to have narrative endorsement?).

Speech and DIALOGUE Use of DIRECT, INDIRECT or FREE INDIRECT DISCOURSE; do characters speak for themselves or does the narrator intrude, comment or direct? Is the dialogue realistic or conventional? What functions does it perform?

Thoughts/mental processes Do we 'get inside characters' heads'? If so, which heads, and how?

Dramatic involvement Does the narrative encourage readers to become drawn into the events as they happen, or are they rather urged to observe them dispassionately? How is this manipulation of DISTANCE achieved? Are readers urged to become involved with some characters but not others?

Action Any information that advances the PLOT, gives significant new developments in relations between characters or in new events; the ordering of the action
(does the work follow a traditional pattern of 'rising action', 'climax' and 'falling
action' or '*denouement*'?).

DURATION The relation between described time and narrative time. Does the novel
focus in detail on a short period of time, or cover a long expanse of time and
describe extended periods in only a few words? Is the relation between described
and narrative time consistent, or does the narrative sometimes 'shift gear'?

SETTING **and description** What is significant about where the action takes place,
and about the way scenes of action are described? Does the setting add to the
action in any way, or provide a meaningful background for the action? (Think
what the work would be like with a completely different setting.)

Symbol or image Are any details apparently exploited to express meanings
'beyond themselves'? Is there a pattern of IMAGERY (repeated reference to a particular colour, for example)? Are SYMBOLS or images apparently related to others
used elsewhere in the work?

Theme(s) Any topic or point of view that seems, through sustained attention, to
be emerging as a THEME; the development of themes dealt with elsewhere in the
work; introduction of new thematic elements.

Your own response Strong personal preferences/responses the work evokes in you
– or dislikes/disapproval; strong identification with a character – or the opposite;
a sense of tension – a desire to know what happens; particular expectations (especially at the end of chapters/sections, or when a mystery or problem is presented);
any experience of bafflement or surprise; any experience of alienation (when the
novel seems to relate to a cultural or historical situation you are unfamiliar with);
points where you feel you agree or disagree with a narrative opinion (or the opinion of a character).

Reading drama

The stage and the page: reading plays as printed text
Discussions of reading drama from a printed text often dwell upon fundamental
inadequacies of reading when compared with the 'full experience' of seeing a
play performed. A reader of drama, it is often said, is always at one remove from
the real nature of The Play, of which the text in the reader's hands can be, at best,
a mere shadow. Reading drama, it is implied, is the poor, illegitimate relation of
the experience one gains at the theatre.

  We'd like to begin by putting a more positive gloss on the reading of drama –

not least because it will probably be through reading alone that you will encounter most of the plays on your degree course. Reading drama is certainly *different* from seeing a play performed, but there is nevertheless much that can be said in its favour. The nineteenth-century critic Charles Lamb believed as much, and suggested that actors in fact got in the way of a true appreciation of a play. In an essay of 1811, he wrote that after seeing a play 'instead of realising an idea, we have only materialized and brought down a fine vision to the standard of flesh and blood'. Lamb believed that Shakespeare's plays particularly suffered by being staged: 'There is so much in them, which comes not under the province of acting, with which eye, tone, and gesture, have nothing to do.' Lamb's views might be found too extreme or too idealistic, but they usefully stress that *seeing* a play is not the only way in which it might be appreciated. So what are the positive aspects of encountering drama *as text*? We can divide them broadly into three categories:

■ Freedom from the interpretative slant of a performance: one's INTERPRETA-TION is not guided by all the many emphases imposed upon a TEXT by actors, directors, set designers, and so on.

■ Access to *additional* information that may not appear through performance: often the text of a play will contain illuminating prefaces or notes, or there may even be stage directions which cannot truly be brought out in a performance.

■ The possibility to reread and to focus on important or obscure passages. This is particularly useful with older plays containing unfamiliar language. Many people, in fact, struggle to follow plays by Shakespeare in performance unless they already have a good outline of what's going on – with reading you can pause and ponder unclear passages.

Imagining performance

Despite what we have just said, the activity of reading drama is still inseparable from the idea of performance. Reading a play is not like reading a novel or a poem. The sense that a printed play is a 'displaced medium' – that its words are written to be spoken aloud by (usually) several voices – *does* have an influential bearing upon what we do when we read. Reading drama typically involves an imaginative process which partially creates the play as though it were performed with flesh-and-blood CHARACTERS moving around in three-dimensional space. In a way, reading a play involves 'directing' it for the exclusive audience of yourself. You may not actually envisage in detail particular figures, faces and SETTINGS as you read, but reading drama nevertheless entails a significant degree of 'projection' whereby the dialogue and stage directions are transformed into some vision of imagined action. Perhaps you imagine what happens and what is said as though it were performed in a theatre, or you may bypass that layer of artifice and sense the events as though they were really happening – either way the interpretative process involves a view of the text as a skeletal prompt for the mental conception of something altogether more fleshy. Reading drama involves *imagining the unwritten.*

It might be said that reading a novel involves a very similar imaginative process, and it is true that from the words of a novel readers do typically set about creating mental worlds. But a novel usually supplies far more determining information than does a play: a basic difference between reading novels and plays hinges simply upon the *quantity* and *variety* of supplied information. A novel will usually provide numerous details concerning the SETTING, the appearance of CHARACTERS, the manner in which words are spoken, and so on. Furthermore, in novels we usually have a NARRATOR (or several narrators) through whose words the action is mediated.

But when reading a play, we have, as a detective might put it, not much to go on. We read dialogue – usually without much guidance on how it is delivered. We repeatedly read the characters' names to show us the sources of speech. And we read stage directions, which are often sparse and mechanical. In other words, there are many blanks that need to be filled in when you read a play.

General suggestions on reading techniques

As with reading prose fiction, there are skills and techniques which you can develop to facilitate the reading of drama. To begin with some very general points, you might initially adopt reading methods which have a relation to what happens in performance and which can therefore help to capture a sense of the work as a dramatic, vocal event. Specifically, we recommend the following:

■ Read the play without many pauses first time, preferably in one session. Most plays do not take very long to read, so for a play you intend to study closely you can usually afford to read it quite rapidly, and then reread it making notes and looking in depth at important or problematic passages. Reading without a lot of pausing can really help you 'get into' the rhythms of the language and of the dialogue. It can make a sometimes stilted experience flow, and can rapidly give you an impression of the play's main outlines.

■ Read aloud. Again, this is a good method of capturing verbal rhythms and it can expose linguistic features that may pass unnoticed if read silently. Playwrights (*note the spelling*) write plays to be spoken aloud, and they will often revise the text when they actually hear the words spoken in rehearsals. In other words, the language of drama is attuned to ORAL production and by reading aloud we encounter the words in the form for which they were intended. If you are reading a verse play or a play in BLANK VERSE, reading aloud is particularly valuable for recognizing how the verse works and how it contributes to the effects of the play. Reading aloud can also help in penetrating intricate or difficult passages – again this may be particularly relevant where blank verse is concerned. Reading aloud can help you move forward through the *sense* of a passage of blank verse, whereas silent reading can sometimes get ensnared in the line-endings. (Try experimenting with reading a passage of blank verse both silently and aloud to see what we mean.)

■ Read in a group. If you are able to arrange group readings, you will automatically benefit from the two techniques suggested above, and there are other advantages too. You can receive a very good sense of how dialogue functions as an *interactive* form if it is produced by distinct voices, and furthermore the very basic challenge of keeping track of which character is speaking (and who they are speaking to) is largely overcome. Group reading is not a good method for the careful study of a play when you want to pause and take notes, but it is certainly an excellent and sociable way of reading a play for the first time.

In the following subsections, we explore more specific issues pertaining to the text-based study of drama. We suggest further reading strategies and give advice on aspects of drama worth noting as you read. Again, our advice often takes the form of suggesting questions that you might keep in mind as you read. First we would like to consider further the type of imaginative contributions with which readers must augment a script to make satisfactory sense of it – for convenience, we shall discuss interpreting *speech* and *action* separately.

Reading dramatic speech

An arrangement of words can often express several totally different meanings according to which words are emphasized and to the TONE in which the words are delivered. So when we read dramatic speech it is often necessary to give careful thought to where the stresses (see METRE) should or could fall, and more broadly to the manner in which we imagine the lines to be delivered. Consider the simple question: 'Shall you drive to town tomorrow?' According only to emphasis, this question can be given widely divergent meanings:

Shall you drive to town tomorrow? (Or not?)
Shall *you* drive to town tomorrow? (Or will someone else?)
Shall you *drive* to town tomorrow? (Or walk?)
Shall you drive to *town* tomorrow? (Or to somewhere else?)
Shall you drive to town *tomorrow*? (Or today?)

In most cases when we read a line of speech in a play, there are rarely as many possible INTERPRETATIONS as there are in this example. Often the context will narrow down the meaning to just one option, and the emphasis will drop unproblematically into an obvious place. But you will doubtless encounter dramatic speech where the stress pattern is not clear. Here is the first line of an early scene from Shakespeare's *King Lear*, spoken by Lear's daughter Goneril to her servant:

Did my father strike my gentleman for chiding of his Fool?

On which words should emphasis be placed? What different meanings can be made to emerge from the line by altering the way in which it is delivered? Because it is the first line of the scene, we have little contextual information to help us here – we have to conclude that the line is open to varied inflections. If the emphasis falls on 'Did', we imagine Goneril trying to confirm whether something is true: we make assumptions about earlier unseen events – Goneril has heard rumours of her father's behaviour perhaps. If the emphasis falls on 'strike', we find Goneril enquiring into what exactly her father did to her gentleman. Perhaps the second 'my' could be emphasized: this could suggest that Goneril responds to her father's action as a personal affront – he has abused something *belonging* to her. Such an emphasis could suggest aspects of Goneril's character – it could indicate great pride, for example. We could easily continue and draw out more possible ways in which the line might be inflected, but already it should be clear that radically different meanings can be found in a line – or imposed upon a line – simply according to how we choose to emphasize the words.

Variations in emphasis comprise just one aspect of the *manipulability* of dramatic speech. TONE is equally important, if not more so. To remain with the example from *King Lear*, aspects of Goneril's character can be delineated by the type of tone we read into the line: is she angry, or calm and rational, or amused, or impatient, or what? Tone can express an enormous amount and the sort of tone we are to assume is often not signalled precisely or explicitly in the script of a play. We have to supply it as we read. Recognizing tone or deciding what type of tone befits a character's words usually depends upon gathering information cumulatively. You may feel you start to get to know a character the more you read their words and the more you encounter other characters' comments about them. So it is often the case that recognizing or assuming the tone of an utterance is something that 'falls into place' the further you read in a play.

Emphasis and tone are probably the most important variables that you need to remain alert to as you read dramatic speech, but if you really want to push your reading so as to embrace a greater sense of how stagecraft can affect the INTERPRETATION of dialogue, there are further questions that might come under your consideration:

- How might the meaning of the line be modified through gesture or through facial expression?
- How might spatial relations between the characters be used expressively?
- How are other characters responding while speech is delivered?
- What sort of SETTING (including scenery, props, lighting, and so on) frames the utterance, and how might this reflect upon the meaning?

An implication of drama's openness or manipulability is that you need to remain conscious of and record (in the form of notes or marks on the text) the information that you're *adding* to dramatic speech as you read. As with prose fiction you should aim to make notes on many aspects of the play (we further discuss taking notes below), but you should also note significant occasions where you have, as it were, stepped in and made a directorial decision that affects INTERPRETATION. When you encounter cases where the emphasis is AMBIGUOUS, you might underline the words that could receive emphasis and note the possible readings that emerge with different emphases. When it seems that a speech is left open in terms of the TONE in which it is delivered, you might note down the range of options that the text seems to allow or the manner of delivery that you believe to be most appropriate – and you should note *why* you think it appropriate. In short, you should remain alert to and ready to note aspects of the text that seem in any way 'unfinished' as they lie upon the page.

You will notice that we are reluctant to discuss interpreting dramatic speech – and interpreting drama in general – as an activity in which you should necessarily aim to discover a single, 'correct' pattern of meaning. As we remarked earlier, one of the illuminating aspects of reading drama rather than seeing a performance is that you are free from the interpretative slant of a performance, and indeed one of the fascinating things about studying drama is *recognizing* its manipulability. Different productions can illuminate new and interesting facets of a play. Many plays, it is well known, have been moulded by directors to serve particular purposes in particular cultural and political situations: for example, when Shakespeare's *Henry V* was turned into a film by Laurence Olivier during the Second World War, the original text was clearly exploited for the patriotic bolstering of British national identity and spirit during a time of international crisis. Indeed, the history of performances and of the different CULTURAL uses to which plays have been turned is a fascinating area of study in itself. But for the reader of plays, a consequence of this interpretative openness might be that it affects the type of question you ask as you read. When reading drama, it can be interesting to ask not only 'What does this mean?' but 'What could this be made to mean?' and 'What alternative angles could be extracted from these words?'

Reading dramatic action/reading stage directions

Speech, of course, is just one component of drama: *action* is another crucial part of how drama creates its effects. (These comments on action pertain to plays written for theatre or for television; radio plays, which you may read on a degree course, convey action in very different ways.) Some types of play, such as a 'dumb show', in fact contain no speech at all and use only mime and gesture to convey all that is to be expressed: plot, characterization, and so on. In Renaissance and earlier plays, a dumb show was sometimes incorporated before or within a spoken drama: if you read Thomas Kyd's *The Spanish Tragedy* (1587) or Shakespeare's *Hamlet* (1601) you will encounter examples of dumb shows.

You will probably not come across many plays which have no speech, but you will undoubtedly encounter many that have very sparse dialogue and so create much of their effect through action. Perhaps the best-known exponent of sparse dialogue is Samuel Beckett, whose plays typically contain immensely long, word-less passages or passages where just a few words mingle with meticulously-scripted action. The printed text of Beckett's *Krapp's Last Tape* (1958) opens with two pages of stage directions before the first speech begins:

> KRAPP: (*briskly*). Ah! (*He bends over ledger, turns the pages, finds the entry he wants, reads.*) Box . . . thrree . . . spool . . . five. (*He raises his head and stares front. With relish.*) Spool! (*Pause.*) Spooool! (*Happy smile. Pause. He bends over table, starts peering and poking at the boxes.*) Box . . . thrree . . . thrree . . . four . . . two . . . (*with surprise*) nine! good God! . . . seven . . . ah! the little rascal! (*He takes up box, peers at it.*)

The reader of Beckett is actually quite privileged because creating a mental picture of *what* is happening is really quite straightforward. Beckett provides simply so much direction in his script that there are rarely ambiguities in picturing the action. In fact, the challenge when reading Beckett is rather the *interpretation* of what is being expressed by the carefully constructed action.

Most playwrights, however, provide far less direction regarding action than Beckett. And for a reader of drama this can be problematic. Simply keeping track of what is actually going on – which characters are on stage, who is being addressed, when characters are alone, when a dialogue is taking place in private, and so on – can be a challenge, particularly in plays involving many characters and many changes of scene. It is therefore vital to read the stage directions with care and to envisage the implications of those directions. For example, one character's exit may mean that just two characters are left on stage and that the scene is shifting to a more intimate level – at the theatre this would be obvious but reading the scene on the page requires work on the part of the reader. Some people go so far as to write down the characters' names on separate pieces of paper, which they then move on and off an imagined stage as they read of the characters' exits and entrances. Alternatively, you might keep a record in your notes of significant action.

Another reason for reading stage directions with care is that, as we have suggested, they sometimes contain illuminating information, including points to which a member of a theatre audience might not be exposed – or at least points which would be almost impossible to perform. We might consider an example from *Pygmalion* (1912), George Bernard Shaw's play concerning a professor of phonetics, Higgins, and his project to transform a poor flower-seller, Eliza Doolittle, into a 'proper lady'. In one scene, Eliza is sitting almost ignored by Higgins as he discusses the success of his project with a friend. A stage direction reads: '*Eliza's beauty becomes murderous*'. You will probably agree that this is a difficult direction for an actress to follow, and that such a 'subjective' direction is unlikely to be fully communicated in a theatre. When reading the text, however, the direction is clear, and it can actually be seen as contributing to the development of a theme: that

Higgins is suppressing his desire for Eliza. Furthermore, where *Pygmalion* is concerned, the reader is given more than the spectator in other ways too. Shaw wrote both a preface and a prose sequel to *Pygmalion* which are both printed in many editions of the play, and these additional passages contain significant clues as to Shaw's IDEOLOGICAL (and other) purposes in writing the play.

When considering action, you might also think about the nature of the space required for the performance. Is any type of staging essential for the play to work? What type of theatre was the play written for? The development of drama is closely tied to the architectural and technological development of theatres, and so the script of a play can often be better understood when you take into account the framework of performance possibilities within which the playwright was working.

Making notes on drama: a case study

As when we were discussing prose fiction, we would like to look at a passage in detail to demonstrate reading and note-taking strategies that can usefully be applied to the study of drama. The following passage is taken from the beginning of a scene from *The Country Wife*, a comedy by William Wycherley, first performed in London in 1675. The action takes place in London. The previous scene has introduced Mr Pinchwife, a jealous husband recently returned from the country with a new wife. In fear of being cuckolded (look it up!), Pinchwife aims to keep his marriage a secret and he forbids his wife the freedom of the town. This scene introduces Mrs Pinchwife and Pinchwife's sister Alithea. Again, we recommend that before you read our comments you should read the passage carefully keeping in mind the sort of issues and questions we have been discussing thus far.

Mrs Margery Pinchwife, and Alithea: Mr Pinchwife peeping behind at the door.
Mrs Pin. Pray, Sister, where are the best Fields and Woods, to walk in in London?
Alit. A pretty Question; why, Sister! Mulberry Garden and St. James's Park; and for close walks the New Exchange.
Mrs Pin. Pray, Sister, tell me why my Husband looks so grum here in Town? and keeps me up so close, and will not let me go a walking, not let me wear my best Gown yesterday?
Alit. O he's jealous, Sister.
Mrs Pin. Jealous, what's that?
Alit. He's afraid you shou'd love another Man.
Mrs Pin. How shou'd he be afraid of my loving another man, when he will not let me see any but himself.
Alit. Did he not carry you yesterday to a Play?
Mrs Pin. Ay, but we sate amongst ugly People, he wou'd not let me come near the Gentry, who sate under us, so that I cou'd not see 'em: He told me,

none but naughty Women sate there, whom they tous'd and mous'd; but I wou'd have ventur'd for all that.

Alit. But how did you like the Play?

Mrs Pin. Indeed I was aweary of the Play, but I liked hugeously the Actors; they are the goodlyest proper'st Men, Sister.

Alit. O but you must not like the Actors, Sister.

Mrs Pin. Ay, how shou'd I help it, Sister? Pray, Sister, when my Husband comes in, will you ask leave for me to go a walking?

Alit. A walking, hah, ha; Lord, a Country Gentlewomans leasure is the drudgery of a foot-post; and she requires as much airing as her Husbands Horses. *[Aside]*

Enter Mr Pinchwife to them.

But here comes your Husband; I'll ask, though I'm sure he'll not grant it.

Mrs Pin. He says he won't let me go abroad, for fear of catching the Pox.

Alit. Fye, the small Pox you shou'd say.

Mrs Pin. Oh my dear, dear Bud, welcome home; why dost thou look so fropish, who has nanger'd thee?

Mr Pin. You're a Fool. *[Mrs Pin. goes aside, & cryes]*

Alit. Faith so she is, for crying for no fault, poor tender Creature!

Mr Pin. What you wou'd have her as impudent as your self, as errant a Jilflirt, a gadder, a Magpy, and to say all a meer notorious Town-Woman?

Alit. Brother, you are my only Censurer; and the honour of your Family shall sooner suffer in your Wife there, than in me, though I take the innocent liberty of the Town.

■ The first thing to take note of is the opening stage direction which contains important signals concerning how we relate to the whole scene. The fact that Pinchwife is secretly watching the whole conversation – which Margery and Alithea believe to be private – adds a layer of intrigue to all that occurs in the scene. As readers (or members of an audience) we are given a privileged view of the situation – indeed, *we know more about the situation than some of the characters.* The scene is making use of DRAMATIC IRONY. We might want to note at this point that we are apparently dealing with a 'comedy of intrigue', part of the pleasure of which typically involves observing characters interacting in ignorance of information that we possess. Reading the play as a whole, devices that engineer a division between what we know and what characters know will become even more apparent.

■ What does the stage direction actually tell us? It delineates Pinchwife's character: he is jealous and suspicious to the degree that he will spy on his wife. It also suggests that what we hear from the two women will be mostly unguarded truth: they are not feeling the pressure of other people (particularly men perhaps) which might make them temper their words. Margery can talk openly about her husband – and about other men. We might also consider other issues, such as whether the device of the listening husband seems plausible in REALIST terms, or whether it exposes the artifice of the play through obvious CONVENTIONALITY. We should also bear in mind how Pinchwife might be reacting to what he hears as the conversation develops – an actor might be able to make comic mileage from the physical expression of how Pinchwife feels when he hears of his wife's interests in other men.

■ What about the names? 'Pinchwife' appears to have an allegorical quality (see ALLEGORY) – the name expresses the character's main attribute in the play: that he 'pinches' or oppresses his wife. Seeing this name we could again reflect upon the issue of REALISM: the play seems clearly to be employing highly conventional devices. We might note that such names are an economical way of giving characters an accessible and memorable 'handle' – this can be important in plays where it is necessary to keep track of many characters and complex intrigues. 'Margery' and 'Alithea' do not seem allegorical but as the scene develops you may find that they become appropriate for the characters. What associations come to mind when you consider each name?

■ Margery's first line establishes an important theme of the scene and of the play: it reveals that she is unfamiliar with London, but deeply curious to find out about it. Since the play is called *The Country Wife*, we may expect it to deal with city/country issues. What ideas do you associate with the country and the city? What ideas do you think might have been associated with the country and the city when the play was written? It will be worth remaining alert to what points the play makes about this dichotomy.

■ Alithea's reply quickly establishes her as one well-versed in the ways of the city. Perhaps the aptness of the names 'Margery' and 'Alithea' is beginning to come into focus: the former is a fairly ordinary, homely name; the latter has a classical sophistication.

■ In the extract as a whole, are there any differences in the language used by each character that suggest their country/city differences? Note any words or constructions that suggest an idiomatic mode of speech – consider 'hugeously', for example. What TONE do you imagine accompanying these lines? Does Margery, surrounded by the prospect of urban attractions, speak with excitement and enthusiasm? Or could there be yearning and complaint in her tone since she is kept under such tight control away from the attractions?

■ There are very few stage directions in the passage as a whole. Do you need to imagine anything about the physical situation to make sense of the scene?

■ In the dialogue that follows the opening exchange, we might note that Alithea's role is primarily that of a 'sounding board' for revealing the character of

Margery. What do we learn about Margery? One quality that emerges is her ignorance – note her naive question about jealousy and her apparent obliviousness to her husband's motives in restraining her. We might at first suppose that she possesses a 'country innocence' – this would be a traditional, PASTORAL view of the country in opposition to corrupt city values. But since Margery is clearly so keen to immerse herself in city life, we probably want to modify 'innocence' to 'ignorance' (which she is rapidly trying to lose).

■ We can also note that Margery has a keen and discerning appetite for men. Does this justify Pinchwife's motives? Her comments, we can imagine, are adding fuel to Pinchwife's urge to control her, but we may still feel that his behaviour is oppressive and sinister.

■ What is the effect of Margery and Alithea discussing the theatre? It is certainly striking to find contained within a play a discussion of a visit to see a play – it changes the nature of the illusion. On one level, we might say that it makes the play seem more unreal because it voices an acknowledgement of theatrical artifice: the discussion of the play, the audience and the actors cannot help but draw attention – in a self-conscious and witty way – to the fact that *The Country Wife* is also just a play. The scene creates self-reflexive humour as it puts an actor in the position of discussing other actors. On another level, we could say that it makes the play seem more real by breaking through the barrier between the stage and the audience (the 'fourth wall' as it is often called). The world of the performance becomes one where people go to the theatre and gossip about actors – this makes it much like the world of the real audience at that very moment. The discussion of the play also allows for some 'in jokes' to pass between the stage and the audience. You might feel that to understand fully the references to the 'ugly people', the gentry and the 'naughty women' you need to find out about the layout of theatres in Wycherley's time. But even without such knowledge, it is clear that Margery's comments on her place in the audience could be directed to make the real audience think about themselves. The play seems to be making jokes at the audience's expense, as it wittily brands a whole sector of them as ugly.

■ Note also that the extract contains an ASIDE: Alithea's comparison of Margery with a horse. In terms of content, we can say that this illuminates Alithea's urban sophistication and her amusement at country ways. We might also note that it draws attention to Margery's status as Pinchwife's *property* – and it may, therefore, increase our sympathy for Margery. But it is also noteworthy as a FORMAL feature. An aside is another device which tends to break through the 'fourth wall' – there is nothing plausible, in realist terms, about an aside. An aside, like a SOLILOQUY, is a dramatic device which supposedly gives us access to the real thoughts of a character, and for that reason it is worth giving close attention to what is expressed by asides. We could also consider how the aside might be delivered: the actress might speak the line as though to herself, or it could be addressed directly to the audience.

■ In relation to the way in which Pinchwife behaves when he enters, we might consider some of the different overall effects which could be given to the scene (and to the play as a whole). The scene could plausibly be read or performed as fairly light, farcical comedy. Pinchwife could be seen primarily as a comic figure who is laughable because of his fears and because, despite his efforts, the world will always be beyond his control: he shall never prevent his wife from liking other men. But the comedy could be given a far more serious edge. The restrictions Pinchwife imposes upon his wife and the way in which he acts towards her could plausibly be read or played so as to emphasize its horrors. A FEMINIST reading or production of the play might emphasize as much. Consider how Pinchwife might utter his first line in the scene: 'You're a Fool'. We must presume it is with some force because of Margery's reaction, but there are different degrees of force. It might be delivered with the familiar type of blustering comic anger, but suppose the line were delivered with a real sense of malevolence? If you do read the Pinchwife plot in more serious terms, it would probably have an impact upon your reading of much of the scene: Margery might become an almost tragic figure, and her status as property might become even more striking (note that she is *carried* to the play, for example).

You will notice that as we have been suggesting noteworthy details of the passage, we have often had to consider broader issues that pertain to the play as a whole. Reading drama (and other texts) often involves a dialogue between your interpretation of detail and your overall sense of the play – the one informs the other. This is one reason why it can be useful to read a play at least twice.

A checklist of things to note when reading drama

Plot Significant events in the PLOT; moments when the plot seems to be 'changing gear'; major reversals or shifts in the action (see PERIPETEIA); does it follow a pattern of 'exposition', 'complication', 'reversal', 'recognition', 'resolution' (as described in Aristotle's *Poetics* as the typical progression of plot)?; is it self-consciously different from such a format?; does it follow a pattern of TRAGEDY (usually concluding with death or exile), or COMEDY (usually concluding with marriage, a celebration, or a dance)? How is the plot conveyed? Through dramatized action, or through what characters say about off-stage events? Is there a CHORUS who explains development of plot?

Characters/characterization Significant information about CHARACTERS; details of their pasts (what does their past reveal about them now?); motivations for their actions; do they have a 'ruling passion'? (actors sometimes speak of searching for the 'spine' of a character when they are preparing for a part – as a reader it can be useful to have a similar approach). What functions do the characters serve in the plot? Are some characters merely functional, while others are explored in greater depth?

Relations between characters Details of characters' relationships with other characters (keep track of the most important – among only eight characters there are potentially 28 two-way relationships, so considering them all is impossible – of course, the playwright will focus on some relations more than others).

Speech/dialogue Do CHARACTERS make long speeches or are there short exchanges of dialogue? Is speech written as normal prose or in BLANK VERSE? Is the language REALISTIC? How is speech used to convey character? Do characters have their own idiomatic ways of speaking (see IDIOLECT)?

Emphasis and tone How might the lines be delivered? Does the play make clear the tone in which lines should be delivered or is this open to interpretation? What possible forms of delivery are made available by the text?

Asides and soliloquies Does the play employ these devices which puncture the 'fourth wall' of the stage? What is revealed in such speech not directed to one of the other characters?

Action The physical events of the play. Is the action carefully stipulated by the playwright, or is it open to interpretation? *How much* action is there? Does the play depend upon 'spectacle' for any effects, or are its points achieved by verbal means?

Themes and arguments Ideas that are given repeated or extended attention. How does the title relate to the THEMES? Does the title influence your sense of the thematic content? Does the play appear to be advancing a main point or an argument? If so, how is this argument given dramatic form? Does it emerge through PLOT or is it given voice by a character?

Patterns of imagery/symbol/keywords Recurrent motifs. Does the play dwell upon a particular IMAGE? Are particular images or SYMBOLS modified as the play progresses? Are there any words which through emphasis or repetition emerge as especially important? Are keywords tied to individual characters or are they uttered by several?

Tension/suspense Devices that maintain interest. Are there things the play does not reveal so as to maintain curiosity? Does the plot engineer an awkward situation that causes you to wonder how it can be resolved?

Implied type of staging Does the play appear to be written for a particular acting space? How might the type of theatre the play was written for have restricted or shaped the form of the play?

Your own response How do you react to aspects of the play and to individual characters? Do you find yourself sympathizing with certain characters? Does the play use particular devices to bring about your response?

The play's 'manipulability' Aspects of the text of the play that could be inflected differently in performance. How could different aspects of the play be emphasized in performance? What different points could be made through the play by altering the way a character is played?

Reading poetry

Why is formal analysis valuable?

Of the three principal literary GENRES, poetry is often regarded as the most unapproachable and daunting. And if *reading* poetry is seen as difficult, *analyzing* and *studying* poetry are regarded as even greater challenges. Why does poetry suffer from this unfortunate reputation? A key reason is that many readers see difficulty in dealing meaningfully with the technical, formal properties of poetry – all those features which mark the language out as 'poetic' and which distinguish it from prose. Many readers regard poetry as a deliberately (and off-puttingly) oblique mode of expression: a mode which can contain 'hidden' meanings accessible to only an initiated few. And compounding the problem is the fact that the language used to describe the formal qualities of poetry – a language peppered with words like 'trochee' and 'anapest' – is sometimes seen as alien and obscurantist.

Taking these widely perceived obstacles as a starting point, we would like briefly to address and hopefully dispel a little of the daunt that surrounds many readers' experience of poetry. First, we would like to stress that it is absolutely *worthwhile* to grapple with issues of poetic FORM. Examining METRE, RHYME, and other poetic devices is not 'additional' to INTERPRETING a poem's meaning; it is an intrinsic part of the interpretative process. You may sometimes encounter contrary views which suggest that to study the form of poetry – or indeed of any AESTHETICALLY interesting creation – is to miss the point. William Wordsworth argued as much, asserting in his poem 'The Tables Turned' (1798) that:

> Our meddling intellect
> Misshapes the beauteous form of things;
> – We murder to dissect.

Such arguments insist that poetry is above all an art of 'immediate effects', and what readers of poetry should be doing is opening themselves up so as to feel the emotional force of the verse upon them; to begin poking into the workings of poetry is to destroy the direct, almost ORGANIC relation between work and reader. Certainly, poetry is often a highly emotive medium and we would by no means want that potential to be shut off with an insistently 'scientific' approach to reading. When you read a poem for the first time, it is doubtless preferable to be somehow 'open' to its immediate effects. Nevertheless, when a poem does create a powerful emotive effect – or any type of effect – it is almost always the result of careful *craft*. And an understanding and recognition of that craft in operation can, we believe, actually enhance the appreciation of poetry.

Many readers, for example, will find great satisfaction in the opening lines of Samuel Taylor Coleridge's 'Kubla Khan' (1797–98): 'In Xanadu did Kubla Khan A stately pleasure dome decree'. We can appreciate the aesthetic qualities of these lines in rather vague terms – 'there's a pleasing ring to them' – but we do not destroy that appreciation by looking more carefully at how they work. There is much that can be observed about how these two lines create their effects: their metrical arrangement, their use of repeated vowel sounds (ASSONANCE), the careful ALLITERATION, and so on. We do not propose to dwell on these lines here, but you might just read them aloud and note the perfect symmetry of the rhythm. You might also try speaking only the vowel sounds of the first line to see how the second half of the line aurally mirrors the first half. Such contrived, crafted details as these are crucial to the overall effect of the lines.

And in general such details are crucial to how a poem creates its meanings – a process which typically involves an *interaction* between the meanings of words and the effects of their being arranged in metrical patterns. The study of poetry's formal characteristics involves becoming conscious of those devices upon which the meaningful effects of a poem depend. When studying poetry, you can almost always afford to read the work several times: indeed it might be said that a sign of a good poem is that it sustains several readings and presents new things each time. In your first reading, you will usually discover fundamental features of the work, such as: the subject it addresses; perhaps its attitude to the subject; the NARRATIVE SITUATION; and basic features of the FORM (which may suggest that the poem is of a specific GENRE). But when rereading poetry, one of your aims as a student should be to become more alert to those *details* of form of which you may not have become conscious during the first reading.

What is important, is that you should constantly ask yourself *what* these formal details are actually contributing to your experience of the work. Form and meaning are not aspects of a poem that should be considered or discussed in isolation from one another. A common fault in undergraduate writing about poetry is for essays to begin with a mechanical description of a poem's form – 'The poem is written in five stanzas of iambic tetrameters, rhyming ABCABC . . .' – and then to go on with a discussion of the poem's content almost as though it were a piece of prose. Introducing an essay with a general formal description is perfectly acceptable, but it is important to sustain an attention to the formal structure and to other formal devices. Generally speaking, formal features of poetry are only really worth mentioning if they are tied to a tangible effect. To give a very obvious example, let us consider a phrase from Wilfred Owen's 'Anthem for Doomed Youth' (1917), a poem about the appalling casualties of the First World War, which begins:

> What passing-bells for these who die as cattle?
> – Only the monstrous anger of the guns.
> Only the stuttering rifles' rapid rattle
> Can patter out their hasty orisons.

It would generally be considered inadequate merely to point out that the third and fourth lines make use of alliteration, both in the repeated 'r's beginning the concluding words of the third line and in the repeated 'tt's in 'stuttering', 'rattle' and 'patter'. The observation is true but in isolation it doesn't really say much of any significance or interest. Such an observation needs to be pushed further so as to comment usefully on the implications of the device for a reading experience. With this example, it seems fairly clear that Owen is seeking to convey through the *sound* of the words an impression of the sound those words are denoting. Readers of the poem experience aurally a verbal counterpart to the fire of rifles; and we might further observe that this can bring readers experientially closer to the disparity the poem highlights between the typically slow rhythm of a funeral orison and the *staccato* sound of gunfire.

Note that commenting on *how* formal features contribute to a poem does not necessarily require immense interpretative ingenuity or sleight of hand. For example, suppose you were commenting on the metrical pattern and rhyme scheme of a BALLAD – for example, this stanza from Washington Allston's 'Will the Maniac: a ballad' (1813):

> Poor Will was once the gayest swain
> At village dance was seen;
> No freer heart of wicked stain
> E'er tripp'd the moonlight green.

Your principal point might well be that the form is simply very effective for *narrative* poems (ballads are almost always narrative) because the rhythm 'drives the poem forward'; or you might say that the short, regular lines and the stressed rhyme make the poem readily memorable – the form therefore is well attuned to ORAL cultures, in which the ballad, traditionally, has been a prominent GENRE. To give another example, you might say that the rhyming couplet is a form which tends to uphold IDEOLOGIES in which universal truths are validated and propagated. Couplets usually function as short finished units, and poetry written in rhyming couplets tends to progress from one *completed* point to the next *completed* point. On the other hand, rhyme schemes which interlock across units larger than the couplet tend to support discursive explorations of issues –

unlike the couplet, they do not imply a confidence that the essence of a thing can be encapsulated in a short, neat phrase. Formal characteristics, in other words, do not always demand subtle close reading for their *raison d'être* to be explained. Form can be determined by cultural, historical and ideological circumstances, as well as by the particular choices made by an individual writer.

In the subsections that follow, we shall further discuss particular formal features which you might take note of as you read, but first: a brief word about the terminology used in the description of poetic form. Our entries on METRE and RHYME in Section 4 outline the principal terms you are likely to need while studying poetic form for an undergraduate degree – it would be very helpful to read these entries before continuing. Far from obscuring the study of poetry, this specialist terminology streamlines and clarifies critical discussion. And we might add that there are actually not all that many terms which need to be grasped.

How do you identify poetic metre?

Here are some practical suggestions on how to identify the metre of a poem (this is often called 'scanning' a poem, and the study of metre is often called 'prosody' or 'metrics').

- Read through the opening lines of the poem, preferably aloud, and consider carefully where the semantic and grammatical stresses fall.

- Mark the pattern of stressed and unstressed syllables: you could just place a mark on the stressed syllables, or you could use the convention whereby a ˘ is placed over an unstressed syllable, and a ´ is placed over a stressed syllable (as in, Lóndŏn and Nĕw Yórk). It is easiest to mark the stressed syllables first and then go back and mark the unstressed ones.

- Consider whether the poem follows a regular metre – not all poetry does.

- Count the number of feet (see METRE, foot) in each line (it can help to mark the divisions between feet).

- Identify the predominant types of foot and line.

- Having identified the underlying metre of the poem, it is then useful to look out for – or *listen out for* – variations from the regular rhythm as they occur *in the whole* of the poem. (In a few cases you may find that a poem shifts to a different underlying rhythm.) Where you detect changes in rhythm, mark and note the new type of feet.

For example, here is the opening stanza of Thomas Gray's 'Elegy Written in a Country Churchyard' (1742–50):

> The curfew tolls the knell of parting day,
> The lowing herd wind slowly o'er the lea,
> The plowman homeward plods his weary way,
> And leaves the world to darkness and to me.

And here are the lines with marks showing the stressed and unstressed syllables and the divisions between feet:

The cur | few tolls | the knell | of par | ting day, |
The low | ing herd | wind slow | ly o'er | the lea, |
The plow | man home | ward plods | his wea | ry way, |
And leaves | the world | to dark | ness and | to me. |

These lines, then, are each comprised of five iambic feet – in other words, the lines are regular iambic pentameters. You will find that iambic metre is the most common rhythm of English poetry (and it is the rhythm that most closely reflects the cadences of normal spoken English). It is worth noting about our marking of these lines that:

- Divisions between feet do not coincide with divisions between words.

- The marking of stressed and unstressed syllables does not mean that all the stressed and all the unstressed syllables are stressed *equally*.

- There are sometimes grey areas where the poem does not 'fit the foot' as comfortably as it might: for example, some people might argue that 'o'er' cannot be represented as a single stressed syllable. But remember that metrics is an inexact science; and remember also that scansion is not an exercise whereby a poem should be squeezed into a rigid categorizing system – if the poem doesn't quite match the system, it simply shows the limitations of the system.

Let us consider another example – the first line of Edgar Allen Poe's 'The Raven' (1845):

Once upon a midnight dreary, while I pondered, weak and weary,
Once up | on a | midnight | dreary, || while I | pondered, | weak and | weary, |

This line, then, is a trochaic octameter – its eight feet all have a 'falling rhythm' with a stressed syllable followed by an unstressed syllable (notice that we have also marked the main CAESURA in the middle of the line). Trochaic metre, you might note, is very often used to grab the attention of readers: with its stress at the beginning of the foot it doesn't 'ease' you into the line as an iambic metre might be said to do; rather, a trochaic foot begins with the jolt of stress. For this reason, you will find trochees used in many titles which seek to attract attention: 'Monty Python's Flying Circus' is a trochaic tetrameter. You will find that the trochee is often used to break up a predominantly iambic metre, or to create a division where an iambic poem shifts thematically – you will see an example of this in our 'case study' below. As a final note on trochaic metre, it is worth mentioning that the commonest form is the trochaic tetrameter (the example from Poe is basically two tetrameters laid out as one octameter) and that this form is very commonly CATALECTIC (that is, the final foot 'lacks' the final syllable). For example, William Blake's 'The Tyger' (1794) begins with three catalectic trochaic tetrameters:

> Tyger! Tyger! burning bright
> In the forests of the night,
> What immortal hand or eye
> Could frame thy fearful symmetry?

Only the final line of this quatrain is a complete (iambic) tetrameter.

As an example of dactylic metre (with feet consisting of a stressed syllable followed by two unstressed syllables, as in 'fantasy'), consider these lines which begin Alfred Tennyson's 'The Charge of the Light Brigade' (1855):

> Half a league, half a league,
> Half a league onward,
> Half a league, | half a league |
> Half a league | onward, |

Both feet in the first dimeter are dactyls; in the second, a dactyl is followed by a trochee.

As an example of anapestic metre (with feet consisting of two unstressed syllables followed by a stressed syllable, as in 'contradict'), and of a spondee (consisting of two syllables with similar stress), consider the beginning of Algernon Swinburne's 'Hymn to Proserpine' (1866):

> I have lived long enough, having seen one thing, that love hath an end;
> I have lived | long enough, | having seen | one thing, || that love | hath an end; |

This hexameter begins with three anapests (some might say, though, that the third foot consists of three unstressed syllables). There is then a spondee, before the line concludes with an iamb and another anapest. Note the effect of the spondee, which with its even stress has neither a 'rising' nor 'falling' rhythm. The spondee brings about a type of stop, which is very appropriate for preceding the revelation of the 'one thing' that the poet has seen. The spondee functions here almost like a rhythmical colon.

Why do we emphasize the value of noting *changes* in the underlying rhythm? The main reason is that most poets – or at least those who are generally regarded as good poets – often exploit the possibilities of *varying* an underlying rhythm. Indeed, rigidly regular rhythm is normally undesirable in a poem – it can have a lulling, soporific effect. You can become almost hypnotized by the regularity of a de-dum-de-dum-de-dum-de-da rhythm, and your attention is not drawn to the words themselves. Imagine if the lines we quoted earlier from 'The Tyger' were comprised simply of regular trochees – the first line could be something like

'Tyger! Tyger! burning brighter'. We might say that in this manipulated example the rhythm is more regular *and therefore more conspicuous*. And because the rhythm is more conspicuous, the semantic qualities of the words become less striking. In Blake's version, much of the effect of the line depends upon the line being 'brought up short' so as to draw attention to the word 'bright'. The first three trochees set up expectations for a particular rhythm, but then the impact of that final foot comes because it disturbs these expectations.

In conclusion, we should emphasize that it requires hands-on practice to build up confidence with metrical analysis. We should also say that when you have become used to analyzing metre, it will usually not be necessary to go through poems laboriously marking the patterns of stress. You may reach a point where you can sense an underlying rhythm almost instantly, and the main analytical task will then be to note where there are metrical variants and what those variants are doing to the poem. And finally, as a guide to remembering the main types of foot, you may find it useful to know the following lines from Coleridge's 'Metrical Feet' (1806):

> Trochee trips from long to short;
> From long to long in solemn sort
> Slow Spondee stalks; strong foot! yet ill able
> Ever to come up with Dactyl trisyllable.
> Iambics march from short to long;
> With a leap and a bound the swift Anapests throng.

When is it appropriate to note details of rhyme?

A further formal device which is employed in many poems is, of course, RHYME. For a definition of rhyme and descriptions of different types of rhyme, see the entry in Section 4. Here we would like briefly to address how you might approach the matter of rhyme when you encounter its use in a poem you are studying.

The conventional method of describing a poem's rhyme scheme (as in *end-rhyme*) is very straightforward and it will probably already be familiar to you. Letters are used to signify the sounds of the line endings, with the first sound designated as 'A', the second as 'B', and so on. So the lines just quoted from Coleridge's 'Metrical Feet' would be described as having an AABBCC rhyme scheme. Note that unrhymed sounds are still designated with a letter.

As with other formal features, it is rarely worth describing the rhyme scheme of a poem unless you can comment meaningfully on what sort of contribution it actually makes to the poem. But what does rhyme add to a poem? Why do many poets bother with using rhyme when the task of writing could be a lot simpler without it? Undoubtedly, the reasons for this are many and varied, but here are some suggestions, some of which we have touched on before:

▨ Like metre, a use of structured rhyme can add a dimension of musicality to an arrangement of words. It can be used to reinforce an underlying rhythm (as end-rhyme often does), or it can be used to interrupt or disturb a regular scheme. It can, in other words, provide aural satisfactions which run alongside the more intellectual appeals of the poem. It provides a structure or pattern that can reinforce or resist the pattern of overt verbal meaning in the poem.

▨ Rhyme can make poetry memorable. For CULTURES where poetry was (or is) a primarily ORAL form, memorability is clearly crucial to how the poem can be transmitted and preserved. But memorability is not only important for non-literary cultures. Often poets in literary cultures use rhyme to enforce a key point or to convey some type of moral – the memorability of rhyme can help to give such points force and currency within the reading culture. Memorability is a quality of rhyme that is constantly being exploited and not only by poets. Note how often advertisers use rhyme to embed a product's trace in the memories of consumers: few people, for example, would remember that the diurnal consumption of a *Mars Bar* enhances your professional, relaxational and recreational activities, but few can forget that 'A *Mars* a day helps you work, rest and play'.

▨ Related to memorability, rhyme can give pithiness to an observation – for example, in this neat, aphoristic (see APHORISM) couplet from Alexander Pope's 'Essay on Criticism' (1711): 'We think our fathers fools, so wise we grow,/ Our wiser sons, no doubt, will think us so.' As this example demonstrates, the rhyming couplet is the ideal form for pithiness. The rhyming couplets that end Spenserian and Shakespearean SONNETs are often used to give a cogent, pithy, reflective conclusion to the subject explored in the preceding twelve lines.

▨ A pattern of rhyme can impose discipline on a poet – indeed, poets deliberately *choose* to engage in a potentially complex, disciplined activity when they decide to use rhyme (metre, of course, also imposes constraints). Writing poetry is typically not an exercise where following the easiest path is a consideration, and it can be said that one of the pleasures of reading poetry sometimes lies in observing the dexterity with which a poet has overcome a system of self-imposed constraints. Very often this pattern of 'overcoming restraints' at the technical level has parallels in the poem's deeper meanings.

▨ Rhyme can be exploited to emphasize words and to make connections between words. Rhymed words tend to command more attention than unrhymed words – they stand out because they hold a significant position in the pattern of the verse. And it is possible to use this tendency to create juxtapositional effects. For example, in the opening couplet from Blake's 'The Tyger', quoted earlier, the words 'bright' and 'night' operate partly as a pair. Readers are likely to sense a relationship between the words by virtue of their rhyming, and we might say that the vivid contrast between the words' meanings is therefore enhanced.

So when you read a poem that makes use of rhyme, you should ask yourself what the rhyme is actually doing to your reading experience and you should give consideration to why the poet has chosen a particular type of rhyme scheme – answers to these questions may often involve a combination of the type of points we have raised above. If a poem does *not* use rhyme, it may be pertinent to consider *why* not – some poets make a point of not using rhyme, or have reacted against the artificiality of rhyme. John Milton, for example, prefaced his unrhymed epic *Paradise Lost* (1667) with a critique of rhyme as 'the invention of a barbarous age'.

Noting figurative language

Thus far we have focused upon the formal *arrangement* of language in poetry. We haven't commented extensively upon the language of poetry itself, but obviously this is another area which must be addressed when you are studying a poem. More than prose fiction and drama, poetry is known for its unconventional approach to language – poetry is often thought of as a genre in which language is *manipulated*: familiar words and phrases are twisted into new shapes from which new ways of thinking about the world can emerge. Poetry is typically rich in figurative, 'indirect' linguistic constructions – it makes extensive use of METAPHORS, SIMILES, METONYMY, CONCEITS and many other formulations that are something other than bald statements.

We place 'indirect' in quotation marks here because it is clear that the purpose of much poetry is not simply to refer, directly or indirectly, to a thing or an idea in the world outside of the poem. A recurrent tendency in poetry is the exploration and manipulation of language itself (or else why not write in the plainest of prose?) – poetry very often explores the effects that can be achieved when words are combined in unconventional ways. The point of a metaphor, for example, can be to see what things look like precisely through that metaphor. Consider these lines from W.H. Auden's 'As I Walked Out One Evening' (1940): 'The crowds upon the pavement/ Were fields of harvest wheat.' Interpreting a metaphor such as this involves a process of *association*. It is impossible really to paraphrase such an indirect, non-literal formulation – you cannot *substitute* other words for these words. Paraphrasing the lines would inevitably cut off some CONNOTATIONS and introduce a raft of new ones, so it is clear that the metaphor is not an indirect means of expressing a circumscribable 'signified' (see SIGN). Interpretation of the metaphor remains locked inside the metaphor itself but moves outwards along the associations that it prompts in the mind of a reader. Why has Auden chosen to describe the crowds in this manner? What is suggested by likening the crowds to a field of wheat? Why wheat? Why particularly *harvest* wheat? What do we think of the crowds when we view them only through this vivid image? Is the effect fundamentally visual or does it comment further about the state of the crowd or about the state of humanity generally?

These are the types of question that it is important to ask when you encounter such figurative language in poetry. Note that we are not asking 'What do these lines *mean*?' – our questions are more concerned with what the lines and certain individual words *suggest*. Remember always that poets are not short of words to choose from, and it is usual that they choose them with immense care. So close attention should always be given to individual words and to how they function in combination with others. If you come across a striking verbal formulation, you should take note of it and consider what is actually striking about it: underline individual words and note what associations they suggest to you. Note what happens when you encounter conjunctions of words which are not normally used in combination. As we have remarked before, when you are reading you do not need to pause and think about figurative language until you feel you have 'finished' with it – it is quite normal to make notes in the form of questions which you can return to later (and these notes may well often remain in the form of questions).

To give precision to your descriptions of figurative language, you should get into the habit of using the correct technical terms. The terms that you will probably call upon most often are: ALLUSION, CONVENTION, EMBLEM, FIGURE, HYPERBOLE, IMAGE, IRONY, METAPHOR, OXYMORON, PROSOPOPOEIA, SIMILE, SYMBOL, SYNAESTHESIA, SYNECDOCHE.

Making notes on poetry: a case study

As the discussion above shows, studying poetry involves remaining alert to and noting a wide variety of textual features. Let us consider some of these features in interaction with a case study of Ben Jonson's poem 'On My First Son' (1616). It is likely that before reading this poem you would normally encounter in a note or annotation some contextual information: Ben Jonson's first son, called Benjamin, died on his seventh birthday in 1603. The poem can be comprehended without this knowledge, but certain details become more resonant with it.

> Farewell, thou child of my right hand, and joy;
> My sin was too much hope of thee, loved boy:
> Seven years thou'wert lent to me, and I thee pay,
> Exacted by thy fate, on the just day.
> O could I lose all father now! for why
> Will man lament the state he should envy,
> To have so soon 'scaped world's and flesh's rage,
> And, if no other misery, yet age?
> Rest in soft peace, and asked, say, 'Here doth lie
> Ben Jonson his best piece of poetry.'
> For whose sake henceforth all his vows be such
> As what he loves may never like too much.

With a short work such as this, you might read the poem through one or more times and then note observations that apply to the poem as a whole. You can then go on to consider smaller details after you have thought about the overall framework of the poem. General observations would typically focus on the form and principal themes of the poem, such as:

- It is a poem of mourning marking the poet's loss of his son. It is, to use a precise term, an ELEGY.

- The narrative situation is that of a direct address by the poet to his dead son. If you have read other elegies, you may recognize and note that this mode – where the dead are directly addressed by a poetic 'I' – is a common feature of elegies.

- The poem is written in PENTAMETERS – that is, lines comprised of five FEET. The first line is a regular IAMBIC pentameter – that is, its feet are comprised of an unstressed syllable followed by a stressed syllable. But the poem is not regularly iambic throughout. Perhaps the irregular breaks in the rhythm contain points the poet wants to emphasize.

- Glancing at the poem on the page, it looks a bit like a SONNET: more or less square. If the poem were a sonnet, you might expect it to develop an argument according to a predetermined formal structure, but counting the lines it emerges that there are not fourteen but twelve. Nevertheless, the poem still seems to follow a fairly tight structure: grammatical and thematic divisions separate it logically into three groups of four lines (or three 'quartets').

More specifically, you might note details such as the following:
Lines 1–4: Farewell . . . just day.

- The first word immediately establishes the theme of separation and loss. The form of address gives an impression of intimacy: it is not intimacy with the reader; rather the poem invites readers to observe the intimacy the poet has felt with his son. Is it inviting sympathy for the father/poet?

- Referring to the 'right hand' (as in 'right hand man') the poet stresses how much the child has meant to him. It may be that an annotation points out that in Hebrew the child's name 'Benjamin' literally means 'child of the right hand'. If we are told this, we might note the layered meaning at work here, and alert ourselves to look out for further wordplay. Are puns unusual features of the expression of sorrow? Probably they are unusual. Does this verbal sophistication affect how we regard the poet's lament?

- There seems to be ambiguity surrounding the 'joy' – this word is emphasized as the stressed syllable in the foot and as the final word of the line, so we are almost forced to pause on it. Is the poet bidding farewell both to his son and to his joy (as in his general happiness)? Is he stating that the child was his joy? Or was the boy the child of his right hand *and* the child of his joy? This last reading perhaps gives the poem a bawdy edge. There seems to be more wordplay at work.

- In the next three lines, the poet apparently blames himself for something – he interprets the pain he feels as punishment for some 'sin'. Why? Is it an attempt to make sense of his loss?

■ Interestingly, the main focus falls upon his own response to the death rather than on the boy – for a poem supposedly 'On My First Son' the sentiments may seem very self-indulgent! The poem, we might say, does not serve as a memorial to the boy but is more an analysis of personal grief.

■ Financial terminology – 'lent', 'pay', 'Exacted' – is employed to convey the son's short life: the poet presents the son as a type of mortgage that had to be paid off. Again the focus falls upon the poet as debtor. What are the effects of using such terms?

■ Perhaps there is another pun in 'just'. It could refer to the *precise* day when seven years was up (since the boy died on his seventh birthday); or it could refer to a day of justice, when the debt was called in. Perhaps it carries an idea of heavenly justice – a theme picked up in the next quartet. The regular rhythm is distorted here, and it draws attention to 'just'. If the phrase were alternatively 'just the day' – as it could be – the metre would be more regular, the word would not be highlighted, and the ambiguity would not be created. We can note, therefore, how the poem seems deliberately to disrupt the regular iambic form for the purposes of wordplay.

Lines 5–8: O could . . . yet age?

■ There is a sudden shift in TONE. The quartet begins with a bold invocation, which stands out because the metre changes: the line begins with a trochee – the stress falls upon the first 'O' which gives a more 'declamatory' tone to the invocation, and this is increased by the brevity of the phrase, which doesn't complete the pentameter. In this short, highly-charged phrase, the poet seems to wish that he could escape from holding the paternal feelings that cause his grief.

■ The extended question that follows reflects upon this declamation. It suggests a faith in a peaceful afterlife and implies that the boy is in fact fortunate to have left the world so young. The rhyming words that end lines 7 and 8 – 'flesh's rage' and 'age' – highlight where the misery of the world is identified by the poet. It might seem that these are things he suffers himself.

■ Again the focus has been on the poet considering his grief. The lines perhaps express anger about the situation.

Lines 9–12: Rest . . . too much.

■ There is another shift in tone as the final quartet begins – again this is achieved with a new sentence and an opening trochee. From the protestation of the central quartet, there is a movement towards more placid reflection – the poet seems more reconciled to his loss, or at least more resigned to it. The vocabulary is 'mellowed' here, as the traditional phrase 'rest in peace' is augmented with the gentle 'soft'.

■ Still addressing the child, the poet imagines his son being asked about his own grave. The response he urges upon his son again focuses attention on the poet, and it focuses attention on him *as a poet* – the poet views his son as his finest artistic creation.

■ We might wonder about the child's mother – she might seem strikingly absent in this image of the child's creation. Again perhaps the poem seems self-indulgent – indeed the child himself is only described as a product of the poet.

■ The final couplet expresses further reconciliation and a resolution on the part of the poet to approach future affections with a wariness of the suffering they might cause. The final line is another regular iambic pentameter – the regular rhythm enforces the aphoristic, 'pithy' quality of the moral ending.

A checklist of things to note when reading poetry

Title What expectations does the title set up? What does it suggest about the subject and GENRE of the poem? Is the poem comprehensible without the title? Does it focus your reading in some way?

Visual appearance What visual form does the poem take on the page? Is it divided into STANZAS? Does its appearance immediately suggest its GENRE? Has the poet exploited any typographical devices for meaningful purposes?

The 'speaker' Who is 'speaking'? Is the personality of the speaker revealed, or does it remain obscure? What are the circumstances of the NARRATIVE SITUATION? Does the narrative situation have a specific time or place? Does the poem use the first-person pronoun 'I'? Do you associate the speaker with the actual poet or do you see the speaker as a fictional PERSONA?

The implied narratee To whom is the poem addressed? Is a particular individual addressed? Is it addressed to you as a reader or to another figure? Can you deduce an intended readership? Is the poem only *supposedly* addressed to a particular NARRATEE – an absent lover, for example, or a dead person? Is it clearly not addressed to an individual but has a more *public* implied audience?

Subjects/themes What is the predominant subject/THEME of the poem? This is a question to ask on first reading and to keep asking as you refine first impressions with more detailed analysis. What attitudes does the poem/poet take to its subject? How does it order its treatment of the subject: is there a clear progression in the way the subject is addressed, or a progression in the attitude of the poem/poet to the subject?

Public/private Relating the narrative situation and the thematic content: does the poem deal with private, intimate themes, or are the issues it treats clearly public?

Details of the poem's composition and publication are of interest here: was the poem written for private reading or for mass distribution?

Metre What type of METRE is used in the poem? Are the lines all the same length? How many FEET are there in each line? What sort of foot is used? Is the metre regular, or is there a predominant metre which is sometimes disrupted? Is there no metrical regularity at all? Do grammatical divisions (signalled by commas, full stops and so on) coincide with metrical breaks? Is the poem divided into STANZAS, or do the lines follow on continuously from one another? What effects are created by the chosen metrical form? Does it suggest a particular TONE, or is it used so as to shift the tone? Are certain words made to stand out through their metrical position? If so, why are these words important?

Rhyme Does the poem use RHYME? If so, what is the rhyme scheme and is this scheme regularly adhered to? Do rhyming words fall mostly at the ends of lines or are there rhyming words within lines? Does the poem use ASSONANCE? What are the effects of the rhyme scheme? Does it help to enforce a particular rhythm? Are certain words emphasized through rhyme? Are significant associations drawn between rhyming words?

Other 'sound effects' Does the poem use aural devices other than rhyme: ALLITERATION, for example, or ONOMATOPOEIA? To what effect? Reading aloud can help to expose such devices.

Genre Looking at the metre and the rhyme scheme, does the poem match the criteria of a formally defined GENRE? If so, why might the poet have chosen this form? What expectations do you have of the form? Is the form appropriate to the theme? Is it used seriously? Does the poem contain any self-conscious or IRONIC reflection on the chosen form? Does the poem fall within another generic category that is not defined according to form (the elegy, for example)? Does the poem fit into more than one generic category (for example, an elegiac sonnet)?

Figurative language Does the poem employ figurative devices such as METAPHOR, SIMILE, METONYMY, and so on? Does the poem have a dominant CONCEIT or an extended metaphor that it explores in depth? If so, in what way is the metaphor appropriate (or otherwise) to the subject?

Cultural and historical context Does the poem's meaning depend upon knowing details of the situation in which it was written? Does it allude to certain historical people, things or events? Was the genre of the poem particularly favoured (or otherwise) when the poem was written?

LITERARY CRITICISM

- ▪ What is literary criticism?
- ▪ How is criticism distinct from theory?
- ▪ How do you find relevant criticism?
- ▪ What are the most effective ways of using criticism?

As well as reading primary literary texts, studying for a degree in literature entails reading and assessing works of 'literary criticism'. This is one of the major differences between degree level literary studies and lower level studies, which typically demand only limited attention to the secondary literature that has been written *about* works of imaginative literature. As a student of literature, you will, of course, be involved in the production of 'literary criticism' yourself, and, as the previous subsection has outlined, this necessitates a close engagement with the literary text on your part. But it often also involves a further interaction between you and previous critics who have thought and written about that text. As such, it is useful to think of literary criticism as in part a collective enterprise. No literary critic is a lone pioneer, forging ahead independent of others; rather, literary critics, including degree students, work within a *field of study* involving the contributions of many.

This might make literary study appear very daunting: for one thing, there is simply *so much* that has been written about literature, and there seem to be umpteen books and articles on even relatively unknown authors. And within that mass of secondary literature, it is not always clear what will actually be useful and *how* one can best make use of it. Our aim in this subsection, therefore, is to suggest ways of navigating and making productive use of literary criticism, giving practical directions on how to find relevant works and on how to get the most from them. But first it is worth pausing to consider what exactly we mean by 'literary criticism' and how this term is distinct from 'literary theory'. You may find it useful to read the following in conjunction with the opening pages of Section 3, in which among other things the relationship between theory and critical method is discussed.

What is literary criticism?

'Literary criticism' is a very broad term which can really refer to any discourse on the subject of literature. It is perhaps most widely used to refer to the evaluative activity of literary critics or reviewers who pass judgement on works of literature in newspapers and magazines. It is this meaning of 'literary criticism' which predominates outside of academic study, and it is one which is tied closely to its etymology. 'Criticism' derives from the Greek word *krinein*, meaning 'to judge', and so the idea of *evaluation* has always been inherent in the term. The noun *kritikos*, meaning a 'judge of literature', has a very long history and was in use as early as the 4th century BC.

The term 'literary criticism', however, tends to be used rather differently within modern academic circles and while its usage here retains an idea of 'judgement', it is often judgement in the sense of 'analysis' rather than 'evaluation'. For example, a descriptive work of literary history – perhaps an account of how the genre of the novel emerged – could still be termed 'criticism' even if it did not seek to assess in any *qualitative* sense the literary works under investigation. So 'literary criticism', in this sense, is another way of saying 'literary analysis' – and in this sense it, of course, remains a very wide term encompassing an array of different types of analysis. Criticism, in this academic sense, can of course involve qualitative evaluation, but it is important to recognize that it need not necessarily do so.

It is probably obvious, then, that the academic use of 'criticism' does not carry the ideas of 'negative assessment' or 'condemnation' which are associated with the term in general discourse. Many non-academics might assume that a book called *Wordsworth: A Critical Study* was a lengthy discussion of all that's wrong with Wordsworth, but this is unlikely to be the case.

'Criticism' and 'Theory'

'Literary theory' can also be seen as an aspect of 'literary criticism', but we believe that it is useful to distinguish these two terms – and not only so as to clarify the types of works we refer to as 'criticism' later. 'Theory' and 'criticism' are usually treated as separate categories in literary degree courses; there are often separate courses on 'Literary Theory' and 'The History of Criticism' (although the latter is becoming less common). And furthermore, tangible differences can be identified between the two categories.

It is perhaps best to distinguish 'criticism' from 'theory' by saying that they have different *objects* of investigation. The object of investigation in 'literary criticism' is typically a particular literary work or a group of literary works. The object of investigation in 'literary theory' can vary (see the discussion on p. 137 at the start of Section 3), but to generalize we can say that it involves *the way in which we might think about* a literary work or group of literary works. To use an analogy from industrial production, we might say that 'theory' is the tertiary enterprise generating the tools which are used in the business of 'criticism'. The tools, in this case, are *conceptual* – they are the patterns of thought that underlie the *approach* of the criticism.

This distinction is one that perhaps 'purifies' the categories, and any extended reading of works of theory and criticism will show that there are many overlaps between the two. A theory cannot emerge from a vacuum and new directions in theoretical understanding can be sparked off through critical analysis, and will then be tested and further explored through critical analysis. And primarily critical works may well involve long passages of theoretical discussion and refinement. Overlaps aside, as a working definition of 'literary criticism' we can say that it refers to studies which aim to analyze particular literary works or groups of works.

Note that this is not to say that 'literary criticism' and 'practical criticism' (see the entries for I.A. RICHARDS and NEW CRITICISM) are the same thing. Whereas 'practical criticism' refers to analysis based upon the close reading of a text with minimal attention to biographical, historical, or other 'extrinsic' details concerning the text, 'literary criticism' is used in a broader sense and can describe an array of approaches which do draw on extrinsic information.

How to find relevant criticism

Literary criticism, as we have suggested, can perform many different functions. This becomes immediately apparent from even the most cursory reading of works of criticism – critics have asked and continue to ask many different types of question when writing about literary works, and these various questions typically bring forth very different types of answer. We discuss the diversity of approaches to literature in Section 3, but it is also worth stressing here that there is no *one* way of 'doing' literary criticism, no standard set of aims or methods according to which criticism is conducted. In fact, part of the excitement of studying literature lies in the exploration of different critical approaches and of the alternative ways of thinking about a literary work that they can generate.

This diversity in literary criticism has implications of a practical nature when you wish to supplement your own impressions of a literary work with the views of another critic. Often specific works of criticism may be part of the required reading for your courses, but there will also be occasions when you need to explore a field of criticism for yourself. And when confronted by a number of critical works – so many that reading or even skimming them all will simply not be possible – you may well find yourself wondering which works it will be most valuable to read. In relation to this problem, we should say first of all that: (i) it is valuable to read widely and to become acquainted with a broad range of approaches to literature; (ii) you may well come to favour a particular approach to literature, but you will benefit in your degree if you have thoroughly explored how other approaches are applied; and (iii) in preparing for essays or exams, it can be as useful to gather material you can *disagree* with as material that simply upholds your view of a text. That said, you still have to be selective. So how should you find your way around the diverse field of literary criticism? How should you identify the work(s) which will be most valuable to your study of a text?

Essentially, finding relevant criticism involves becoming skilled in using bibliographies of different kinds – printed and electronic – so that you are able to isolate references to the books and articles that will be most valuable. When you are using a bibliography of any kind, it is useful first to ask yourself what it is you want or need to find out about a text – browsing a bibliography can be productive but it is usually better to have a sense of the broad areas you should browse in. Your questions might arise from a curiosity that has arisen during your reading of the text, or most probably they will be related to a particular assignment –

an essay topic, a presentation, or preparation for an exam. You might, for example, want or need to explore:

- alternative INTERPRETATIONS of the TEXT (remember that TV or film adaptations can also be considered as interpretations – but don't assume that watching them is a substitute for reading the text)
- details of the AUTHOR's life, or personality, or other writings
- the GENRE of the work
- the CULTURAL circumstances or the PERIOD in which the text was written
- how the work relates to other works, literary and non-literary
- issues regarding READERSHIP when the work was written, or the work's subsequent readership

Knowing roughly what you want to explore will enable you to refer to the appropriate part of a printed bibliography, or it will help you in selecting 'search terms' when you use an electronic resource. In short, it will help you recognize titles of works that may be worth reading – titles or subtitles of critical works tend to be helpfully descriptive. Here are the main types of bibliography that you will encounter during your degree course, with notes on how best to use them:

Lists of secondary reading provided by your lecturers Probably these will be the most useful bibliographies you encounter during an undergraduate degree. Such lists will usually be tailored to the particular identity of the course; they will contain the most up-to-date works; and, perhaps most important of all, the lecturer is likely to have selected works that are available in your library.

Lists of further reading in editions of texts These are usually very selective and therefore very accessible; typically they list those works that have proved particularly important or influential, and they cover a wide range of areas: textual interpretation, history of the work's RECEPTION, biography, and so on. Check *when* the list was compiled or was last revised – an old list may give an outdated picture of the critical field.

A library catalogue search (see 'Using the Library', pp. 14–19) This is a good method of quickly compiling a rough, general bibliography where you can be fairly sure that all the items found will be available to you. Note that such a search will *not* locate titles of articles.

Annual printed bibliographies covering literary studies in general Specifically: *MLA International Bibliography of Books and Articles on the Modern Languages and Literature* (New York: Modern Language Association, 1922–); *Annual Bibliography of English Language and Literature* (Cambridge: Bowes and Bowes, 1921–), published by the Modern Humanities Research Association and known as ABELL; *The Year's Work in English Studies* (London: English Association, 1919–). These were once indispensable bibliographies: they have excellent coverage and their systematic arrangement makes the individual volumes easily accessible. A drawback is that you can only search one year at a time. They have now been largely superseded by electronic databases.

Online and CD-ROM databases These are by far the most readily searchable and thorough databases available. See Section 2 for a detailed description of how to use these resources.

Bibliographies contained in critical works (and references contained in footnotes) Critical works themselves may lead you on to a new stage of reading if you follow up the references supplied by a critic. Even if you don't have time to pursue further works, it is still helpful to consider what a critic has referred to while researching and writing.

Using criticism

Whatever route you have used to locate a work of criticism – following your own research or a recommendation – there are certain methods that you can use to make your reading as productive as possible. Here are some suggestions:

- Think of reading criticism as a two-level activity: on one level you are discovering things about a particular text or author or about some other aspect of literature; on another level you are observing a critic at work, and are seeing in practice the application of particular critical methodologies. In the wider scheme of the degree, the latter is just as important as the specific knowledge gained from the former.

- Relating to the above, try to pinpoint where the critic 'is coming from'. Literary critics are not always explicit about their priorities and their methods, but as a reader of criticism you should try to isolate what these are. As you read, ask yourself questions such as: what are the underlying aims of this critic? What types of question is s/he really asking about the literature under investigation? What assumptions does s/he make about literature or about textual production? What interpretative methods does s/he employ? Are certain aspects of the literary text being prioritized over others?

- Note how the critic locates their own work within the field of study. How does s/he treat other critics who have written on the topic before? Does the engagement with other critics serve to delineate the approach of the study?

- Always make careful notes on what you read. With critical works, you will mostly be reading borrowed copies so making notes on the text itself is generally not desirable (for you or for the next reader!). We recommend taking notes straight into a computer file, but, of course, using a paper notebook or file is perfectly adequate.

■ You may want to quote from the critic in an essay or project, in which case make sure that you copy the quotation down *exactly*. It is irritating and time-consuming to go back and check a quotation for a second time, especially when the work may well be being used by another reader. And ensure that you signal in your notes that it *is* a quotation – otherwise you could possibly go back to your notes and mistake a quotation for your own paraphrasing.

■ Make notes not only on local points raised by the critic, but on the overall argument that the critic puts forward. In fact, it can be useful to write a brief summary of the argument when you have finished reading the work: this can help to fix the argument in your mind; it is useful for the purposes of revision; and in exams it is generally better to know the main outlines of an argument or approach than specific, easily forgotten details.

■ Be attentive to your own impressions of the text under discussion as you read the critical work. Is the critic reshaping your view of the text? Does the approach offer a perspective on the text that you hadn't previously considered? Do you find yourself resisting ideas about the text put forward by the critic?

■ Do not just record points that you find illuminating or points that reinforce what you already think. Noting views contrary to your own can be just as valuable, especially when it comes to formulating an argument for an essay.

■ Always keep page references with your notes and with any quotations you have copied down. You will need these when you come to use the critical material in essays and projects.

■ Always keep a full record of the work including details of: the author, the title, the place and date of publication, the publisher, the journal name (if it's an article), relevant page numbers (if it's a chapter in a book or an article), the editor of the collection (if it's a chapter in a book).

■ When reading books, be selective and isolate the passages that will be most relevant to your specific area of study. Reading the preface or introduction is advised because that should outline the general framework of the work and will help orientate your reading of subsequent passages. Make full use of the index and contents pages to locate the most relevant passages.

WRITING ESSAYS

■ What are the best techniques for writing a good essay?

■ What types of preparation will benefit essay writing?

■ How can 'literary theory' be incorporated in an essay on a literary text?

■ The writing process: from notes to finished essay

■ Guidelines on the presentation of essays

■   What is plagiarism and how can it be avoided?

■   Guidelines on making a presentation

When it comes to writing essays there is no substitute for practice. The more you write and have your writing commented upon, the more clearly and easily will you come to write. Since practice is so essential to writing well, it is difficult to offer much specific advice on actual techniques: we are suspicious of student guides that treat essay writing rather like learning how to use a computer program – some examples almost give a standard essay with blanks for the student to fill in with the appropriate words taken from the topic. What follows in this subsection, therefore, aims to give advice about the conventions which *can* be learnt, but for the most part our remarks are tentative suggestions intended to help you think about how you prefer to write. We have attempted to give some general advice about academic writing and to explore some of the specific problems involved in responding to questions about literature. But different lecturers, different colleges, and different cultures have different expectations concerning the writing of essays. Listen to the advice of your lecturers, take note of their comments on your work, and ask them about their comments or request further advice if you are in any doubt. Above all, practise. It is generally better to write ten two-page essays in a term or semester than one twenty-page essay (and it's much less boring). That way you learn to think about how to respond to questions and how to structure answers.

Analyzing the question

In most cases when you write an essay, you will be responding to a specific question or topic which has been set by a lecturer. Your essay will be judged partly on the basis of how well it relates to the set question, and so a crucial part of the process of writing a good essay lies in analyzing the question. It is well worth investing time and careful thought in this stage of preparation – by developing a good sense of the areas to be considered in your essay, the subsequent selection of material and the actual writing will flow much more smoothly. Analyzing the question involves:

■   Ensuring that you have fully understood what the question is asking

■   Checking any technical terms you are unsure about

■   Noting what *must* be included in the essay if it is to be a full response to the question

■   Considering the different directions the essay could take within the scope of the question, and considering which direction your essay will take

Let us look at an example to explore how this analysis might work in practice. Here is a question which, like many you will encounter, seems at first glance to be very specific and to indicate fairly clearly what the essay should contain:

Discuss the idea that Adrienne Rich's poem 'Diving into the Wreck' is simultaneously a personal and political allegory. Briefly comment on the implications of the poet's choice of free verse, define the genre of the poem, and then go on to give a thorough analysis of the poem's themes and imagery.

Even if the task seems to be stated in fairly explicit detail, it is still worth pausing to think about what is actually required and what lines of investigation might be pursued. Looking closely at this question (strictly speaking, of course, it isn't actually a question) you might note the following points – some of these take the form of questions which would need to be addressed as you further plan and write the essay:

- The central issue being raised here is apparently the poem's double layer of ALLEGORY. Perhaps this topic can provide a 'backbone' for the essay – it can be the main thread to which local details in the poem and other points of information can be related. The question doesn't make it absolutely clear, but probably the 'thorough analysis' of 'THEMES and IMAGERY' can be interpreted to mean 'an analysis of themes and imagery *with a view to demonstrating how the poem uses allegory*'. Otherwise the essay may end up being very fragmented. An idea of how the essay could be structured is emerging.

- Again relating to structure, the writer of the question wants the response to include *brief* comments on the FORM of the poem, and these are to precede the 'thorough analysis'. Such instructions should be followed – if they are not, the essay could lose marks simply on the grounds of not answering the question, however good it is otherwise.

- The phrase 'thorough analysis' suggests that much of the essay should be devoted to close reading of the TEXT; it is probably expected that the essay should contain extensive, analytical close reference to the text.

- The question contains some technical terms – if you are not absolutely confident with the terms used in a question, you should look them up (in our Section 4, for example).

- Is it, in fact, correct to identify the poem as 'a personal and political allegory'? The invitation is to 'discuss' – the idea may be rejected or accepted. In preparing for the essay, it will be important to read and reread the poem with that idea in mind and to *test* it against the evidence of the text. It will be best to develop an opinion on the matter *before* you begin to outline a plan for your essay (but you may well *refine* your view through the actual process of writing). If you decide that this idea does adequately describe the poem, your essay might progress as an account of this 'double allegory' through the whole poem. If you reject the idea, your essay might show where the flaws lie and you might suggest a preferable way of characterizing the poem. Perhaps you might find that the idea is *partially* convincing but there are areas of the poem where it does not seem so pertinent. If this is the case, how could you structure the essay? Should the essay follow the progression of the poem? Or would it be better to arrange the essay thematically, with the points highlighting the weakness of the idea grouped together? Either approach could be used, but perhaps the latter would produce a neater, more cohesive argument.

■ Although the essay invites close attention to the text, the suggestion that the poem can be read as a *personal* and *political* allegory also invites a broader focus. It may be appropriate to investigate details of the author's life, so as to see whether the poem does indeed allegorize personal experience. Or perhaps you might consider interpreting 'personal' in terms of 'relating to individuals' rather than relating specifically to the actual author. The political aspect will also need to be clarified and set in context. Of what nature is the poem's political content? This will need to be stated clearly in the analysis.

■ Remember that many FEMINISTS have suggested that 'the personal is political'. It would not be against the spirit of Rich's poem to argue that although the question attempts to combine the personal and the political, it perhaps still treats them as generally separate spheres, and to comment on this.

These points should demonstrate that when you respond to even a fairly detailed question, there is still a good deal of room for manœuvre in how you plan and write the essay. Other questions will not contain so much direction. At some point, you will almost certainly encounter this classic type of assignment: a quotation followed by 'Discuss'. For example,

> 'The most remarkable effect of Laurence Sterne's *A Sentimental Journey* (1768) is that the first-person narration constantly leaves readers with impressions of things that have not been said.' Discuss.

Analyzing such an assignment involves applying many of the same techniques of 'dissection' that we have outlined already. It demands scrupulous attention to the details of the quotation, and it demands that you test the validity of the quotation against your own impression of the text. Again you have the option either to support the quoted statement or to disagree with it – this point is worth stressing because you may encounter deliberately provocative quotations where it seems you are almost expected to disagree. Perhaps, though, the most important thing to emphasize here is that, in such contexts, the word 'discuss' tends to carry with it all sorts of undeclared assumptions. What do academics mean when they use 'discuss' like this? Generally speaking, you can assume that 'discuss' means some or all of the following:

■ 'Discuss the validity of this statement with close reference to the mentioned text.'

■ 'Elaborate upon and explain the particular issues or textual features mentioned in the quotation.'

- ■ 'Express whether or not you believe the statement to be true and support your claims by using evidence from the text.'
- ■ 'If you wish, digress into broader areas so long as the points you make are relevant to the central issue.'

In other words, essay questions often employ a type of shorthand and it is important to become accustomed to this shorthand in order to determine what is really expected in an essay. You may well encounter other shorthand formulations, such as: 'Give an account of . . .'; 'Consider . . .'; 'State your opinion on . . .' – these typically carry similar invitations to *expand* upon the issue as are implicit in 'Discuss'. If an assignment begins with 'Give a critical analysis of . . .', you are really being asked to conduct a detailed investigation of the text and of how it creates its meanings; the phrase is not inviting you to *evaluate* the literary work; although analysis very often carries with it evaluative implications, these are secondary so far as the question asked is concerned.

What about that other classic phrase of essay questions: 'Compare and contrast . . .'? Generally speaking, whenever you are invited to 'compare and contrast' things – literary WORKS, GENRES, CHARACTERS in the same work, and so on – your essay should go beyond simply listing a range of similarities and differences. You might take the phrase to mean 'Compare and contrast *with a view to highlighting significant features of the things under your scrutiny*'. The phrase really derives from the belief that productive analysis can proceed by means of comparison – the belief that the nature of a thing can sometimes be best identified by exploring its differences from and similarities to other things.

There may be occasions where you are not given a specific assignment or question, or where the question is very open. If this is the case, set yourself a clear theme for the essay and make sure you have a strong sense of the direction in which it will lead (you might discuss your ideas with your lecturer before you embark upon the actual writing). If you set off with a vague set of goals, you're likely to produce a vague, rambling essay. With a very general question, a good approach is to discuss the issue generally first and then to narrow matters down and to examine in detail some specific examples. If you are addressing a specific question which allows you to select the literary texts in which you will explore the issue, try to justify why you have chosen a particular text – provide a thoughtful rationale.

Formulating and structuring an argument

In exploring how to analyze questions, we have already begun to consider how to formulate and structure your answer as an argument. Indeed, several of the points that emerged from our dissection of the sample question were considerations of the material you might use in an essay and of how the essay might be structured. It is almost always beneficial to further develop such preliminary thoughts before you actually begin to write the essay. Typically the next stage of preparation involves two processes:

- gathering material for the essay from both primary texts and secondary texts
- planning how best to organize that material – in other words, refining the structure of the argument

What does gathering material involve? Most importantly it involves your going back to the literary text(s) or reviewing your notes on the literary text(s) so as to select and examine the passages that are most relevant to the topic. In a sense it involves a *directed rereading* or *directed reassessment*, in which you look again at the text with the issues under investigation as your primary focus. When we discussed reading techniques earlier, we suggested that you should be attentive to a wide range of textual features; reading with a view to writing an essay typically demands a more focused approach to the text. As you go through the text or your notes, you should note down relevant passages and transcribe quotations that substantiate the points you think you will make in your essay – you will save time if you type this material straight into a word-processing file. Keep an open mind as you revisit the text: think of it as a process in which you are still weighing up the evidence and considering the argument you will put forward in the essay. The *process* of writing an essay is not simply the expression of a point of view; it is very often, in fact, the *discovery* of that point of view. Note that it is best to gather more material than you will finally need – you can continue to be selective as you actually write the essay.

As well as gathering material from the primary text(s), it will usually be advantageous to locate relevant material from secondary works of criticism. If you have already considered some critical views of the text, this will again be a process of revisiting notes. Alternatively, you may need to conduct some new research into the specific subject area of the essay – for advice on this, see the earlier discussions of 'How to find relevant criticism' and 'Using criticism' (pp. 65–8).

Organizing the textual material you locate and organizing the way in which you address that material are crucial to writing a good essay. An essay question requires an answer, not just a response. It is expected that when writing an essay you will take up a position to what has been asked and advance in a logical fashion *an argument* (sometimes alternatively called a 'thesis', 'claim', 'position' or 'point of view' – see THEME AND THEMATICS). So you should think carefully about what points you intend to make and consider how you can make logical, persuasive connections between these points. A technique preferred by some writers is to note down a fairly random list of points, and then think about the most effective order in which they can be connected. You might try to categorize your points into logical groupings, which could be addressed under sub-headings in your essay. You should always aim to isolate what your main argument is – as we suggested earlier, essays benefit from having some sort of backbone. As a reader you will no doubt have noticed that it is more satisfying to read a text which has a clear direction than one that rambles in a random fashion.

On the whole, we advise against adopting an essay structure that mechanically follows the progression of the text. This can sometimes work when short texts are being discussed, but it is usually not the most effective way of arguing a case. An argument should have its own logic – different from the logic of the literary work – so it is normal that its structure will not echo the development of the work it discusses. Relatedly, if the work you are writing about is NARRATIVE (i.e., it tells a story), *do not retell or summarize the story*. There may be occasions where you need to use brief moments of summary – if, for example, you want to make clear at what point a particular phrase or passage appears – but as a general rule do not summarize. Perhaps we should concede here that it is possible that one day you might encounter an essay topic or exam question which starts, 'Tell the story of *Wuthering Heights* and then proceed to comment on . . .'. This apart, 99.9 per cent of essay topics and questions do not require you to open with an obligatory three-page précis of what happens in the work in question. You have to assume that the person marking the essay has read the work and knows what happens: s/he does not need or want to be reminded of this. Telling the story is a remarkably common flaw in responses to questions about prose fiction and drama. Remember that you are a literary critic, and that your task is to comment on the work, not to reproduce it in abridged form.

Finally, do not be afraid to take risks with your argument. So long as an argument is backed up with convincing evidence, many lecturers and examiners would prefer to read an essay with some flashes of originality (even if they disagree!) than to plod through a predictable, 'safe' essay. If you feel unsure about 'risky' passages, you might still include them but with some rhetorical 'hedging' ('It may even be the case that . . .', 'One could almost assert that . . .').

Applying literary theory in essays

It is now quite usual for an undergraduate degree in literature to include the study of literary theory – your degree scheme may well, in fact, contain a separate course devoted purely to literary theory. Literary theory, we might say, is now more or less a standard component of a degree in literature, and students today generally become far better informed of the theoretical underpinnings of literary analysis than students of 20 or even only 10 years ago. But despite this *knowledge* of theory, many students still find the *application of theory within their own writing* a highly problematic issue – this has become apparent to us both through reading students' essays and through discussing with students the aspects of writing that are found particularly challenging. Applying theory is regarded almost like glass-blowing – as a difficult and hazardous business which many find interesting to watch from a distance, but then few expect to produce a good result if they have a go at it themselves.

Such an impression of literary theory is sometimes actually upheld by advisors on literary study. For example, we came across the following warning contained in a respectable American web site giving guidance on writing essays: 'If you have never analyzed a literary text using a specialized approach before, you should probably consult your instructor.' Such a warning might almost have been issued by the Surgeon General, and it would come as no surprise to read next that 'a specialized approach will work only as part of a calorie-controlled diet'. Taking 'a specialized approach' certainly sounds like a big event here, and it is presented as a major undertaking which students may never have faced before.

We would like to suggest, however, that taking a specialized approach – or, to put it another way, performing analysis within a particular theoretical framework – need not be a massive leap forward from the textual analysis you have undertaken previous to studying for a degree. And we would also like to suggest that if you have analyzed literature at all, it is highly likely that you have already taken some sort of specialized, 'theoretical' approach, even if you were not consciously aware of its nature (for further discussion of this issue, see the beginning of Section 3, pp. 135–7).

The moment you start thinking about a text, you are in some way using a theory of interpretation or you are regarding the text from a 'theorizable' view of literature's place in the world. If, for example, you read the poetry of Sylvia Plath and find in its IMAGERY signs of the AUTHOR's depression, your interpretation is founded upon certain assumptions concerning the relationship between text and author, and you are implicitly subscribing to a theory that sees literature as a space in which authors may indirectly express aspects of their psychological make-up. Perhaps without knowing it, you have been engaging in a type of 'psychoanalytic reading'. In other words, theories of literature are essential to any discourse on the subject, although the particular identity of the theory is very often not made explicit. So when we call this subsection 'Applying literary theory in essays', we do not wish to suggest that 'theory' is some sort of garnish or fashionable accessory – something that can be sprinkled over or bolted on to an essay. Rather, 'theory' is something that is already present in the form of assumptions and methods.

Having said that, degree level study will doubtless introduce you to new theories and new ways of reading that you may not have considered before – this is part of the challenge of studying literature and part of what makes it intellectually exciting. In addition, there is considerable work to be done to sharpen one's awareness of different theories and to strip away some of the veiling familiarity that makes our assumptions seem simply 'natural' or 'commonsensical'. And on top of that, an ability to use theory effectively within essays is something that comes through gaining knowledge of the field(s) and through extensive practice.

The advice that follows should be read in conjunction with Section 3 (pp. 139–97). Our intention here is not to explain different theories, but to offer some thoughts on *how* theory might be used in your own literary criticism. Our suggestions are arranged so as to reflect three stages in the writing process: (i) choosing which theoretical framework(s) will benefit the essay; (ii) investigating the theoretical field so as to ascertain what will be useful for the essay; and (iii) incorporating statements about the theoretical orientation of an approach within an essay.

Which theory?

How can you tell which theories may be useful to your analysis of a text (or which theories already underpin your intended approach to performing analysis)? First, we should say that an ability to recognize this will increase primarily as you develop your knowledge of and confidence with different theories and approaches. More specifically, though, you might consider the following points:

- A theoretical approach is often inherent in the nature of an assignment. For this reason, consideration of which theoretical field(s) will be most pertinent is often another part of analyzing the question. Suppose, for example, you were confronted with the following exercise:

  'In his short story 'The Dead' (1914), James Joyce employs a subtle narrative technique whereby the 'story' and the 'plot' are unsynchronized. Giving some definition of 'story' and 'plot', write an account of Joyce's technique and of the effects it has upon the reading experience.'

  This question is very pointed with regard to the textual features that you should focus upon – it is quite explicitly inviting you to discuss NARRATIVE technique. And with the instruction to define certain terms, the question invites you to look not only at Joyce's short story but more generally into the discourse used to describe narrative technique. In other words, the question is offering you several leads into the theoretical field of NARRATOLOGY. As you become familiar with different theories and approaches, you will probably begin to recognize such connections between questions and theoretical fields quite easily. Alternatively you might make the connection by following up the terms used in a question – looking up STORY AND PLOT (in Section 4 of the present book) would bring you in touch with discussions of narratology (and the narratological aspects of RUSSIAN FORMALISM).

- Note that an essay might incorporate more than one perspective and that these might be derived from distinct theoretical groups. Different approaches typically illuminate or emphasize different literary issues, and so you may well find yourself applying several interpretative approaches in order to address a question. To return to the example concerning Joyce's 'The Dead', some writers may feel that the phrase 'the reading experience' demands some discussion – the question is actually about narrative technique *and* reading. Perhaps certain ideas from the field of READER-RESPONSE criticism will also be useful in the essay. A general point to be made here is that no single theory provides an ultimate key for unlocking a 'full' reading of a text.

■ If the assignment is very open – of the 'Write a critical analysis of *Great Expectations*' type – your options regarding a theoretical orientation are clearly wider. Such assignments imply little about *how* you should conduct your analysis. If you want your essay to be theoretically explicit, you might approach the openness of the question in one of two ways: (i) you might think about what issues you want to raise in your critical analysis, and at the same time make an effort to remain conscious of the *type* of analysis you are pursuing and of the theoretical assumptions it depends upon; or (ii) you might isolate a theoretical approach that interests you and consider what interpretations of the text arise if you apply the interpretative methodologies advanced by the theory.

As a final general point, we should emphasize that 'choosing a theory' should really be seen as 'choosing an intellectual field which might prompt some useful ideas for the analysis of a particular text'. A 'literary theory' is not a sausage machine or a mathematical formula: you can't feed something in at one end, and then let the theory do its stuff while you stand back and admire what comes out. It is probably more correct to describe a 'literary theory' as a set of contestable suggestions regarding what readers and critics might opt to do when they read literary works. And as such, when you 'choose a theory', you should think of the exercise as a search for fruitful ideas regarding reading and interpretation rather than a search for a map which can lead to 'the answer'. And remember that there may be occasions when it is useful to home in on a theory with which you have little or no sympathy – using analysis of a text to show, for example, that the text has complexities to which the analytical categories of the theory in question are blind or unresponsive.

Investigating the theoretical field

If you take a course in literary theory as part of your degree, you will in most cases have a good impression of the field before you think about working with the theory in an essay. But it is likely that you will need to conduct further investigations – or more *refined* investigations – into the field before embarking upon your essay. Here are some suggestions on how to go about this process:

■ Remind yourself of the main characteristics of the theory, but aim to isolate those factors which are truly relevant for your essay. These may be particular theoretical *aims* or they may be particular interpretative *tools* or sets of terminology that have been generated by a theory. Begin your investigations with secondary discussions of theories (we hope that the material in this book will be useful here) but do not *only* read secondary material. If you can isolate a primary theoretical text which is relevant to the issue, read it carefully and make notes on it. Relatedly, take note of any key theor*ists* who are associated with the theoretical concepts you want to apply in your essay. You may have occasion to mention a particular theorist in your essay if s/he has been particularly crucial in the generation of a concept.

■ Do not lose yourself in the theoretical field. If you are reading about theory so as to support your analysis of a particular literary text, remember that the literary text is your primary object of investigation. Points about the theoretical orientation of your essay may only amount to a few words in the finished essay – consider this when you plan the time you will devote to preparing for and writing an essay.

Incorporating statements regarding theory in essays

What should you actually write about a theory in an essay? How much should you write about the theoretical orientation of your essay? Should theoretical issues be addressed in a general introductory statement, or should they be mentioned along the way? There are no final or straightforward answers to such questions – every essay will have its own logic and may benefit from a different type of theoretical content – but the following general points can be made:

■ When you make a point about theory, always ensure that it is *relevant* to your argument. You should generally avoid entering into digressive discussions of the theory itself unless it is important for your overall argument to do so.

■ It is often helpful in an introduction to describe the *type* of analysis you will be pursuing. Outlining the theoretical orientation of an essay can be seen as part of the general purpose of an introduction – that of showing your reader the direction(s) in which the argument will be leading. This can usually be achieved in just one or two carefully crafted sentences.

■ Relatedly, the purpose of statements regarding theory is in many cases simply to make explicit the orientation of the analysis. This can often be achieved in a single sentence or even just a subordinate clause: 'Looking at the passage from a psychoanalytical point of view . . .'; 'A post-colonial perspective can illuminate . . .'. However, to be even more explicit, it may be useful to state more fully what exactly is implied by the chosen point of view.

■ If you are applying a specialist term that has come into use via a particular field of theory, it can often be helpful to show your awareness of the term's origins. This is especially important where the term has a specialist meaning and a more everyday meaning – such as 'story' and 'plot' – because it will clarify the sense in which you are using the term.

■ Avoid bluffing. As we have said, theory is not a garnish – merely scattering some jazzy theoretical words and phrases over your essay will not improve it.

Finally, we repeat that you should not be afraid to discuss the limitations of a theory or problems that you encounter when you apply a theory. Mentioning limitations can be a good way of demonstrating your confidence with a theory. And exploring the way in which a theory's interpretative approach conflicts with other approaches or falls short of offering a satisfactory reading can give a very productive tension to a discussion.

Writing

We have been stressing the *preparatory* processes of essay writing not only because it is through these processes that you gather and structure the material for a good essay, but also because the actual writing of an essay is very much easier after thorough preparation. For one thing, you will, in a sense, already be well advanced in the writing process. If you have collected and arranged notes on the text, quotations from the text, notes on secondary criticism, quotations from critics and so on, you will already have assembled the skeletal framework of the essay. You will not have the problem of staring at a blank page or screen. Relatedly, and more importantly, you will also have worked out roughly what you are going to say – and writing, we cannot emphasize enough, is always easier if you know what you are going to say, not in every detail, but in terms of the broad movement of your argument.

But how can you transform a skeletal set of notes and quotations into a finished, polished essay? Our suggestions regarding this process follow below. But, although you will find some useful ideas here, we urge you to read our points with a critical eye – as we have said, writers work in different ways and so it is impossible to provide a blueprint for an ideal writing method. The important thing is to practise and to get to know the techniques that work best for you.

Writing a first draft

A good essay is usually the result of several drafts – or it is, at least, the result of writing and subsequent revision. For this reason it is usually best to write a first draft fairly quickly. At the early stage of writing, it is generally counterproductive to agonize over getting a particular phrase exactly right; it is better just to get something written which can then be polished later. Otherwise you can spend a lot of time on writing passages that you may ultimately reject altogether. Writing quickly, however, does not mean writing carelessly. You should aim to be precise in what you say: choose your vocabulary with care, and construct your sentences so that they express accurately and clearly what you wish to convey.

When you write a first draft, you should not feel that you have to begin at the beginning and write in a straight line towards a planned conclusion. Indeed, it is often better to write an introduction *after* you have drafted the main body of the essay, because the structure of the essay may change during the writing process. You may feel that there is a key point or a key passage that you really want to write about – if so, this is a good place to start. You can fill in the other parts that will surround that issue later.

Even though we have emphasized the value of planning an argument before you begin to write, you should be prepared to make adjustments to the argument – in terms of both content and structure – if you recognize ways in which it might be improved. Often the actual process of writing about a particular passage of text can throw up previously unnoticed ideas or problems – you should try to incorporate such ideas or redress the argument if they suggest alternative possibilities. And it is largely for this reason that it is often best to write introductions (and conclusions) when you have drafted the main body of your essay. The business of making changes to an essay is obviously an area where word-processing facilities are immensely valuable. Swapping paragraphs around, adding words or sentences, introducing new quotations – all these can be performed in seconds, such that you can devote your time to thinking and writing and not to repetitive copying. And an essay is not a political speech: conceding points to the 'opposition' generally strengthens rather than weakens an essay.

As you write, try to include regular textual 'signposts' to remind your reader where the essay is going. If you are moving on from one stage of your argument to another, you should signal this move clearly and state why the essay is progressing in this way. If you are unable to think of a reason why you are making a point, it may be that the point is not valuable to your essay. As a general rule, remaining self-conscious about the *reasons* for including particular points is a good way of keeping your argument cohesive, of remaining relevant, and of avoiding waffle. And expressing the reasons for those points is a good way of keeping your reader 'on track'.

Writing introductions

There are many ways of introducing an essay: with a straightforward statement of the coming argument; with the description of a particular problem that will be explored in the essay; with a passage of a literary text together with a commentary which highlights a particular problem; with an illustrative anecdote; with a quotation from a critic which you may disagree with or support – these are just some of the numerous ways in which you might begin an essay. None of these methods is necessarily better than another, so we will not recommend any single approach to introducing an essay. But we will make some general observations about what should be included and what, on the whole, should be avoided.

■ Try to be interesting. This may sound very obvious, but it's worth stressing that your first few sentences can be crucial in determining how fully you engage your reader's interest and attention. Consider how others have introduced texts (of whatever kind) and think about what techniques you have found interesting as a reader.

■ However you begin the essay, the point should be relevant to the argument.

■ Relating to relevance, it is usually better to avoid opening with a very general comment about a literary work or its author, such as 'Samuel Beckett was born in Dublin in 1906 . . .'. You might well mention such details later in the introduction, but they are unlikely to be central to the argument and so they generally should not be given pride of place at the beginning of an essay.

- If you begin with a anecdote or a passage of text, remember that *at some point* in the introduction it is useful to include an explicit statement of your thesis. Such openings can be stylish and interesting, but you must remember that an introduction should actually *introduce* what is to come.

- You do not need to give away your conclusions in the introduction – in fact, it is often better to keep these in reserve so that you have something to add in your actual conclusion. An undergraduate essay is not a suspenseful thriller, but it can still be good to keep information in reserve: this is a way of making readers want to read further.

Writing conclusions

A conclusion may contain some recapping of the argument, but a good conclusion will usually go beyond a restatement of what has already been said. You might save a clinching point in the argument for the conclusion, or you might suggest a further direction in which the analysis could productively lead. Another effective way of concluding an essay is to 'take a step back' and reflect upon what the analysis has actually achieved or upon what types of interpretation the approach has brought forth (including, if relevant, reflection upon what the approach does *not* illuminate).

As a general rule, avoid the temptation to conclude with a grandiose judgement of the text's value. Many writers end essays with something along the lines of: '. . . and it is for this reason that Skelton's poetry has for so long retained its incredible, affective power . . .'. Usually such conclusions contribute very little and their connection with the main body of the essay is often spurious. With conclusions, then, the rule remains: *be relevant*.

Using and presenting evidence

A good argument will need to be supported by *evidence* – this is why we emphasized earlier the importance of gathering quotations from primary and secondary texts. And knowing how to present and how to engage with the evidence you adduce is one of the most valuable skills in essay writing. Unless the question specifically focuses upon extra-textual matters, the most important evidence that you can bring forward is likely to be *textual* – in other words, material from the literary work itself. Textual evidence is important because it reveals to the reader that your argument has a foundation in the realities of the literary work under scrutiny – it shows whether your argument holds water when tested against the text close up.

Inevitably, some points will require more textual evidence than others. If you are describing the effects of a particular use of IMAGERY, for example, it is likely that you will need to *show* particular instances of the imagery at work. If, however, your point concerns the general structure or progression of a work, a brief and accurate description of that structure may be more effective than actual quotation. Most essays will involve some passages of this 'broad brushwork' as well as more detailed reference to the text.

When quoting, avoid including more of the source than is absolutely necessary. You should quote only enough to make your point. It may be that your point is proved by a key phrase, in which case that is all that should be included. If you don't wish to quote a complete sentence, try to incorporate the phrase logically and smoothly within your own sentence. For example:

> When the speaker of Shakespeare's Sonnet 18 wonders whether to compare his beloved 'to a summer's day', he begins an intense interrogation of the relationship between art and nature.

If the significant points in the quotation are separated by words you do not wish to include, edit the quotation down and indicate where you have cut material with: . . . or [. . .] . You can also add words in square brackets so as to maintain the grammatical sense.

When using evidence, make sure it is clear *why* it is there. Introduce the quotation such that its purpose is clear, and comment upon what it is revealing or upon how it is supporting your argument. Often the most effective way of using a quotation is to comment generally on the passage when introducing it and then to engage with it in more detail afterwards. For example:

> The first line of Shakespeare's Sonnet 18 can create an initial impression that the poem will be highly conventional: 'Shall I compare thee to a summer's day?' As an iambic pentameter with an opening trochaic substitution, the line follows the standard sonnet metre, and in terms of content, it seems to be introducing a stock comparison between nature and a loved one. But, in fact, the line is questioning the value of the stock comparison, and this examination of poetic convention continues as the poem progresses.

In short, every time that you quote from a text you should explain what it is in the quotation that is important – you should point to *particular* words, *particular* phrases, *particular* techniques.

Apart from textual evidence, there are various forms of extra-textual evidence that can be incorporated in an essay: comments and opinions from critics, statements from or about the work's author, illuminating parallels with other works either by the same author or by others, information about relevant social, historical or cultural events or circumstances, significant details of the work's publication or distribution. With all of these form of evidence, two issues should be borne in mind: (i) *influence*, and (ii) *relevance*. (And the theoretical implications of issues of 'influence' and 'relevance' should also be borne in mind.) You may reproduce a lot of accurate facts, but did they have any influence on the writing (or do they have any influence on the reading) of the work? Are they relevant to the question asked? In incorporating extra-textual evidence into the essay, you can generally apply the same guidelines that pertain to the presentation of textual evidence. Do not quote more than is necessary and ensure that you signal what the evidence is adding to your argument.

Remember that there is a difference between evidence or proof, and support. A statement by a critic who agrees with your position represents support rather than definitive proof that you are correct. Students often misuse verbs such as 'demonstrate' and 'prove'. It is not just unwise to write, 'As Derrida has proved, there is nothing outside the text', it is wrong – even if you agree with Derrida – because this is something that he has *claimed*, or *argued*, but not definitively established.

Writer's block

At some point, most writers will suffer the condition known as 'writer's block'. It is a deeply frustrating experience: you sit at your desk staring at the screen or the paper, and no matter how much you want to write, the words will simply not flow. Sometimes your mind is blank and you don't know what to write, while at other times you have ideas about what you want to say but it seems to be impossible to form them into words and sentences.

Writer's block can be caused by many very different factors: the stress of a heavy workload or other types of stress; too infrequent sessions of writing; a lack of information about the subject under investigation; unrealistic perfectionism; a sense that someone else has already written what you want to write. Certain Californian psychotherapists have suggested that writer's block is as often as not caused by feelings of personal inadequacy and that the way to combat it is to make a list of all those things about yourself that you find particularly splendid. Here are some other suggestions:

- Stop trying to write and do something completely different – preferably something non-intellectual, involving physical exercise or at least movement – for an hour or two.

- Write something else: a letter or an email – something that does not require careful composition or a polished finish.

- Move onto a different part of the essay and try writing. You can return to the passage that was proving problematic later or leave it until last, or you may even find that the essay is fine without it.

- Choose a passage from a relevant literary text and write about it in detail or just make detailed notes on it – having some concrete text to write about is often a good way of getting going again.

- Try writing as badly as you can – believe it or not, this is very effective for some writers. You may end up discarding or completely rewriting what you've written, but it can help the writing to flow again.

SECTION

Revising a first draft

A first draft can always be improved, and even if you ultimately make only a small number of changes and corrections, it is always worth going to the trouble of rereading and revising your first effort. Indeed, if you have time you might well revise the essay more than once – you will almost certainly notice new ways in which it can be improved each time.

As a general point, you may find that seeing where changes could or should be made is easier after you have put the essay aside for a short time. Leaving the essay for a couple of days, or even for just a few hours, will help you to gain a degree of critical distance from your text – problems will then usually stand out more than if you were to read it straight after having finished writing. As another general point, we always find it much easier to spot flaws or areas for improvement when reading a hard copy of a text (i.e., a paper copy). Regrettably, this method wastes paper but we generally think the sacrifice to be worthwhile since small details of a text can often be overlooked when you read a text 'on-screen'. The following list indicates specific features of the text which you should attend to as you revise:

- Is your argument conveyed clearly and persuasively? You may need to insert more directive phrases showing where the discussion is going.

- Is the argument backed up with sufficient evidence? And is the evidence presented so that the reasons for its inclusion are absolutely clear? Perhaps there will be places where you can edit quotations, so that you do not include unnecessary material.

- Do not be reluctant to reject material. Delete passages if they are irrelevant or if they reiterate what has already been clearly stated.

- In addition to deleting passages, look carefully at your text at a closer level and delete any words that are unnecessary. Verbosity is not a strength in essay writing.

- Check that every sentence makes grammatical sense. And look out for clumsy writing – that is, writing that may be grammatically correct but is nevertheless not the clearest means of expressing what you mean. Check that you haven't used sentences that go on for too long – if you have, break them down into shorter sentences.

- Consider your vocabulary with care. Are you really using the most appropriate and accurate terms for describing your subject? If you think any words may be rather loose, think about how you might replace them or how you might rephrase the point to make it clearer.

- Check your spelling. You should do this as you read a hard copy, and also on-screen if your word-processing program includes a spell-checker. But . . .

- Do not rely too heavily upon a spell-checker. A spell-checker will fail to pick up certain errors, especially in cases where a wrongly spelt word is another word correctly spelt. 'Do knot rely two heavily up on a spell-chequer' would pass the scrutiny of many spell-checkers.

On the whole, we are sceptical about the value of those automatic grammar programs that are included with many word-processing packages. In our experience, their model for good writing is limited and the advice they offer can be more constraining than helpful. Such programs certainly don't approve of our writing styles and nor, incidentally, do they approve of the styles of most authors studied on a literature degree. You'll find that they like Ernest Hemingway's short sentences and his fondness for the active voice. But test a passage from a Henry James novel, and it seems remarkable that he ever got published. Grammar programs can provide an entertaining half hour, but they are generally not useful writing tools.

The tradition in North American and European universities is that an essay should be your own work. However, our own opinion is that there is nothing wrong in two friends exchanging essays and commenting on them. When we read something we have written we frequently miss problems with expression because we know what we mean, but reading what someone else has written is a different matter. It is probably safest to check that your lecturers have no objection to such a procedure, and certainly any changes to what you have written should be written by you and you alone. But an element of constructive mutual criticism – of DIALOGUE – is, in our opinion, natural to academic work.

Guidelines on presentation/style

It is important that essays and projects are presented in a clear and readable form. There are at least three reasons for this: (i) it demonstrates a serious, careful, professional approach to the task, (ii) it is crucial to the clarity of the content (for example, 'Jane Eyre' and '*Jane Eyre*' mean different things but this may be signalled only through presentation), and (iii) it will endear you – or at least your work – to whoever is grading the essay. When lecturers and examiners come to assess and comment on your work, it is probable that your essay will be one of many such works demanding attention, and unsurprisingly the task of ploughing through a mound of essays is not always seen by lecturers as the most pleasurable aspect of their jobs. So it is important for you as a writer to try to 'get on the right side' of the marker. Of course, what the marker will ultimately be looking for is good content, but you should aim to make that content as readily accessible as possible.

You will ease the task of your lecturer or examiner if you provide two basic elements in your essay: (i) complete legibility, and (ii) space for writing comments. 'Good presentation', therefore, is not the result of hours of fiddling around with the graphics facilities on your computer (indeed, when essays are ornamented with an array of decorative fonts, wingdings and curlicues, it can seem as though too much effort has gone into the appearance and not enough into the actual writing). 'Good presentation' basically implies clarity, and it can be achieved by following some simple guidelines.

There is no single set of conventions that is accepted worldwide as *the way* to present an essay. Your own university or university department may have its own recommendations regarding essay style and presentation – if so, follow these with care. Alternatively, the university may recommend that you follow one of several systems that are used around the world and are laid out in such publications as: the *MHRA Style Book* (from the Modern Humanities Research Association), *The Chicago Manual of Style*, and the *MLA Style Manual* (from the Modern Language Association). Most universities do not rigidly *demand* that a particular system be followed for undergraduate work; the main expectation will be for *clarity* and *consistency*.

The following guidelines are intended to convey the very basic requirements of good presentation. The suggestions are fundamentally in line with the *MHRA* system. The suggestions mostly assume that you have access to a word-processor, but if you are handwriting your essays the advice is still relevant.

- Print or write on one side of the paper only.
- Leave generous margins on both sides of your text.
- Use line spacing of at least 1.5 lines (or write on every other line).
- Use a clear 12 point font.
- Number the pages.
- Use single quotation marks. A quotation *within* a quotation should be indicated with double quotation marks. (Note that this is the British standard; the American standard is the reverse.)
- Long quotations (as a general rule, those that stretch more than two lines/those over 30 words) should be left-indented and single spaced. Quotation marks are *not* required for indented quotations.
- Verse quotations stretching over two or more line-breaks should be laid out as verse (as they appear in the original). With a shorter verse quotation you can indicate a line-break with: /. For example, 'Pike, three inches long, perfect / Pike in all parts'.
- Italicize titles of books (or underline them).
- Place titles of poems, chapters in books, articles in journals in single quotation marks.
- Provide references to work that you cite (i.e., works that you mention or quote from), for advice on which, see below.

References

For an undergraduate level essay, you may not actually be *required* to provide references to the evidence you cite in an essay, but it is as well to get into the habit of giving proper references. Footnotes (or endnotes) and a bibliography will almost certainly be required for an extended 'project paper'. The purpose of a reference is to show exactly *where* your evidence has come from: which edition of a text, the relevant page, which critical work, and so on. Your reader might, for example, want to go back to the text to see a quoted passage in its fuller context (or to check that it is quoted accurately), or maybe the reader will be interested to see the dates of quoted critical works – references make any such 'follow-up' much easier. Good footnotes can also have a rhetorical effect, giving assurance that the essay is grounded in a sound use of source material.

With a word-processor, creating footnotes is very straightforward indeed: place the cursor where you wish the footnote to appear, then click on 'Footnote' (probably on the pull-down 'Insert' menu). Then simply type the reference into the footnote. All the numbering is done automatically, and even if you shift your text around, the program will re-order and re-number the notes.

The actual form of the most common types of reference is described below. In addition to consulting this *very basic* list, you might keep half an eye upon how critics use footnotes when you're reading secondary literature – it can be easier to grasp the form and function of footnotes 'in action' than out of context. Note that you only need to provide a full reference once: references to an already-cited work can be abbreviated; and if you are referring many times to a work – your primary text, for instance – it is often best for subsequent page references to be given in parentheses directly after the quoted passage in your text.

References to books Include in this order: the author; the title (in italics); the editor(s) (if applicable); the translator (if applicable); place of publication; publisher; date of publication; page reference (if you are referring to a specific page). A standard way of presenting and punctuating these details can be seen in these examples:

Martin Amis, *London Fields* (Harmondsworth: Penguin, 1989), p. 87.

Arthur Clayborough, *The Grotesque in English Literature* (Oxford: Clarendon Press, 1965), p. 3.

Jürgen Habermas, *The Structural Transformation of the Public Sphere: An Inquiry into a Category of Bourgeois Society*, trans. Thomas Burger (Cambridge: Polity Press, 1989).

Abbreviated forms of these titles might be: Amis, *London Fields*; Clayborough, *The Grotesque*; Habermas, *Structural Transformation*. Often you will be referring to editions other than the first edition – it is good practice to state either in the main text or in a footnote the date of the first publication. In the main text you can include the date parenthetically after the first mention of the title, for example: 'Samuel Richardson's first novel, *Pamela; Or, Virtue Rewarded* (1740), was a sensation among the reading public . . . '. In a footnote, the original date can be included within a reference to a modern edition thus:

Samuel Richardson, *Pamela; Or, Virtue Rewarded* (1740), ed. Peter Sabor (Harmondsworth: Penguin, 1980).

References to works (primary or secondary) in edited anthologies Include in this order: the author; the title of the individual work (in quotation marks); the title of the anthology (in italics); the editor(s); place of publication; publisher; date of publication; first and last page numbers of the individual work; specific page number (if you're referring to a single passage). For example:

Jane Spencer, 'Women writers and the eighteenth-century novel', in *The Cambridge Companion to the Eighteenth-Century Novel*, ed. John Richetti (Cambridge: Cambridge University Press, 1996), pp. 212–35 (223).

Seamus Heaney, 'Punishment' (1975). In *The Norton Anthology of Poetry* (4th ed), ed. Margaret Ferguson, Mary Jo Salter and Jon Stallworthy (New York and London: Norton, 1996), pp. 1790–91.

References to articles in periodicals Include in this order: the author; the title of the article (in quotation marks); the title of the journal (in italics); volume number and year; first and last page numbers of the article; specific page number (if you're referring to a single passage). For example:

Susan Staves, 'Don Quixote in Eighteenth-Century England', *Comparative Literature*, 24 (1972), pp. 193–215 (202).

Annette Kolodny, 'A Map for Rereading: Or, Gender Interpretation of Literary Texts', *New Literary History*, 11 (1980), pp. 451–67.

Electronic references If you cite or use material that you have taken from a web site or from another electronic source, you should also give a reference for such use. We have included advice on referencing electronic material in Section 2, p. 126–31. This is because conventions for referencing electronic material are less firmly established than they are for printed sources, and so we have given rather more extensive information on this topic, information which finds a more natural place where we discuss using the electronic media.

Bibliographies

When listing cited works in a bibliography, the standard format is very similar to that used for references in footnotes. The main difference is that you should begin a reference to a work with the author's last name; the works are then ordered alphabetically according to the authors' names. It is common, but not obligatory, to separate works into primary and secondary lists: here it is not necessarily the case that 'primary' equals 'literary' and 'secondary' equals 'critical and theoretical'; 'primary' usually refers to the central, core texts, so 'literary' texts may sometimes be included under 'secondary'.

Plagiarism and how to avoid it

We will end this discussion of essay writing with a word of caution about plagiarism. To plagiarize, as the *Oxford English Dictionary* puts it, is 'to take and use as one's own the thoughts, writings, or inventions of another'. Plagiarism, then, is the reproduction of something without acknowledgement of the sources that are being reproduced and without acknowledgement *that* they are being reproduced. It involves creating a pretence that the source is actually oneself. Had we simply written above that plagiarism is to take and use as one's own the thoughts, writings, or inventions of another, with no mention that this very phrase came from the *Oxford English Dictionary*, we would ourselves have been guilty of what we are describing.

Plagiarism is undeniably a very serious issue where the writing of essays is concerned – so serious that in some cases where students have been found to have plagiarized they have not been permitted to complete their degree. So it is clearly something to avoid. There are different ways in which you can plagiarize in an essay. The most serious form of plagiarism is the simple reproduction of a complete essay that has been written by someone else – and it is well known that there are several successful Internet businesses offering students the easy opportunity to do this. Obviously you can steer clear of such practices without us pursing our lips and wagging discouraging fingers at you. The next level of plagiarism would be the straightforward reproduction of passages of another writer's work within an otherwise original essay. Here again, we hope that the fact that this constitutes plagiarism is sufficiently obvious that no warning note need be sounded. But it is just about possible to plagiarize by accident or through misunderstanding, and in this regard we may be able to provide some worthwhile advice.

Accidental plagiarism can arise basically through the improper presentation of secondary material. There are certain *only slightly wrong* ways of presenting secondary material, which constitute or border upon plagiarism. Suppose you wish to incorporate within your essay certain points put forward in the following extract from John Brewer's book, *The Pleasures of the Imagination: English Culture in the Eighteenth Century* (New York: Farrar, Straus and Giroux, 1997):

> The reopening of the theatres in 1660 did not mark a return to the flourishing days of English Drama in the Elizabethan and Jacobean era. Charles II loved the theatre dearly (just as he dearly loved some of its performers), but he wanted it regulated and loyal, not encouraging of opposition or dissent.

Basically there are two *acceptable* ways of drawing upon this quotation in an essay. First, you could *quote* the passage or parts of the passage: this involves placing all the quoted words within quotation marks, and giving a clear, unambiguous indication of where the quotation has come from. So your essay might include something like this:

As John Brewer has argued, when the theatres reopened there was no 'return to the flourishing days of English Drama in the Elizabethan and Jacobean era'.

And you would add a footnote or reference giving the source. The second acceptable method of drawing on the passage would be to *process the ideas it contains*, present them in a paraphrased form, and to acknowledge where you have taken the ideas from. So your essay might read:

As John Brewer has argued, when the theatres reopened in 1660, Charles II was concerned that they should be tightly controlled – the king wanted the theatre to support his monarchy and not to function as an outlet for radical, oppositional expression.

Again, you would add a footnote or reference to show details of the source.

So how can you get it wrong? The most obvious wrong way would be the simple reproduction of Brewer's words, with no mention of Brewer and no suggestion that the words are anything other than your own composition. Such a use of a source is straightforward plagiarism. But other improper ways of presenting the material are not so obviously wrong. The following use of Brewer might well be considered to verge on plagiarism:

As John Brewer has argued, the reopening of the theatres in 1660 did not mark a return to the flourishing days of English Drama in the Elizabethan and Jacobean era.

This is actually a quotation but it is not presented as a quotation – the presentation acknowledges that the ideas have come from Brewer but it suggests that the form of words has not. Equally, if the passage were reproduced but with only *very slight* paraphrasing, it may not be considered to be plagiarism *per se*, but it would usually be regarded as 'bad practice'. So it would not be advisable to include in an essay:

As John Brewer has argued, the 1660 reopening of the theatres did not bring about a return to the prospering days of English Drama in the Jacobean and Elizabethan era.

The fundamental issue here is that the passage demonstrates an ability to use a thesaurus, but it shows no sense that the writer has thought about and processed the points made by Brewer. In fact, as a good rule of thumb, if you have mentally *processed* all the secondary material you are drawing upon in an essay (but which you are not quoting) there will not normally be a risk of accidental plagiarism.

We do not wish to inspire any paranoia about the way in which you use sources. You do not need to smother your essays with dozens of references to other critics. In fact, it is worth mentioning that an essay will usually contain much information that does not need to be accompanied with a reference to a source. Established facts can normally stand alone. If, for example, you wrote in an essay that 'the theatres reopened in London in 1660' or 'William Wordsworth died in 1850', you would not need to cite a source. These are established facts that can be found in any number of reference works, and as such are public 'intellectual property'. References to sources are generally only needed where you are drawing upon an *argument* or an *idea* that is clearly related to a particular work. If you are in *any* doubt about what constitutes plagiarism you should seek advice from your lecturers – most lecturers would far rather give an explanation of plagiarism than discover it in an essay.

Making a presentation

We have reserved until now our discussion of the skills needed for making a presentation because many of the techniques are closely related to those required for writing a good essay. Indeed, you might think of a presentation as a type of oral essay. Of course, the nature of a presentation depends upon the assignment you have been invited to pursue, but it is usually the case that, like an essay, a presentation will require the development of an argument, the application of supporting evidence, an introduction that lays out clear directions for what is to come, and a coherent conclusion. And like an essay, a presentation should be interesting – indeed, you may feel that, with an audience before you, the need to be interesting is especially pressing.

Presentations are a fairly recent component of degree work (it may be that your degree scheme does not include them) and there is no accepted set of expectations about their form and their importance. But looking into this increasingly common aspect of study, we have found that they typically involve speaking for between 10 and 30 minutes on a pre-arranged topic to an audience comprised of a seminar group and a lecturer. In some cases they are non-assessed, in others they are graded and the grade can contribute to the overall assessment of the degree. So how should you go about preparing for and delivering a presentation? Many students feel extremely nervous about giving presentations – being properly prepared is one way of overcoming those nerves.

The main preparation is, as we have suggested, much like the preparation for an essay. It involves: careful analysis of the question or assignment; gathering evidence from primary and secondary sources; arranging that evidence into a progressive, logical structure; and building a cohesive argument around the evidence. But there are also decisions to be made about *how* you will convey your points to your audience – you will need to consider questions and issues such as:

■ Should you write a text in full, or just make notes, or just speak from memory? Certainly it can be a useful part of the preparatory process to write a fairly finished version of the text – you needn't do all the polishing you would for an essay, but you might nevertheless write a fairly advanced 'sketch'. The discipline of writing will help you develop the ideas you wish to put forward. And if you are unaccustomed to public speaking, you may want to have the security of a fairly complete text to speak from. Remain aware, however, that actually reading from a text can sometimes be a very boring, unengaging method of presentation. If you do read, you should aim not only to give voice to the words but to think through the words as you present them. Remember you are actually *talking to people* (doubtless you will have heard experienced speakers who seem to forget this). Speaking from memory is generally not advisable: you avoid being a 'dull reader' but a carefully prepared argument can easily become garbled if it is badly recalled. Speaking from notes is a good compromise between the two: you have the security of your presentation's outline before you, but you are forced to formulate the words as you present them, and this generally is the most interesting and engaging means of delivering ideas to other people. You should aim to meet the eyes of your listeners as often as possible – and this can be hard if you are just reading a text.

■ How do you keep within a time limit? First, we should say that it is very important to fill but not exceed your time limit. Some presentations peter out after a couple of minutes, while others can seem to drag on for ever – neither error makes for a satisfactory presentation. At an early stage in your preparation, you should time yourself reading a passage aloud and then calculate roughly how many words you need so as to fill the time (this is another advantage of writing a text fairly fully). And when you have finished writing, you should practise reading the whole presentation aloud – make cuts or additions accordingly. However much you practise, you may well find on the day that you have too much material. So it is useful to have ideas of passages that can be cut without disrupting the whole presentation. It is especially useful to have a 'reserve' passage *before* the conclusion, which can be included if you have time, but cut if you don't. Avoid cutting your conclusion when you deliver the presentation.

■ Should you use illustrations? If the equipment for showing illustrations is available, yes. It is almost always beneficial to add some visual interest to a presentation, even if it is sometimes not crucial to the argument itself.

■ Should you use handouts? Again, yes. A handout might contain a list of your key points – this can make a talk easier to follow. Or you might include on a handout the key passages from primary or secondary sources which you will consider. If you are discussing the details of a particular passage, it is *much* easier for your audience if they are able to look at the passage as you talk about it.

Finally, as with writing essays, *practice* is probably the most valuable way to become skilled in giving presentations. Whereas with writing you can practise as much as you wish or have time for, it is not always easy to find opportunities to practise giving presentations – in other words, it is not always easy to find a willing audience. For this reason, it can be useful to work in a group and to rehearse a presentation in front of a friendly audience before having to present it formally. This can also allow you to see how other people give presentations, and to discuss with others how you (and they) could improve presentational techniques. Here as elsewhere, we believe that all study benefits from collaborative dialogue with fellow students, and that this is not to be seen as next-door to cheating. Such collaboration and dialogue are especially valuable in the study of literature.

EXAMS

■ Preparing and revising for an exam

■ How to perform well in the exam room

If you have reached the stage of studying for a degree, then no doubt you will already have developed your own techniques for preparing for and taking exams. You may nevertheless find it helpful to consider the following specific advice on how to revise the subject of literature and how to write essays on literature under the pressure of exam conditions.

Preparation and revision

One of the first preparatory things you should do when the prospect of exams looms is ensure that you are fully aware of the format of each of the exams you must take: the duration, the number of questions you will be expected to answer, and the amount of weight each question carries in the final assessment. Knowledge of these details will help significantly in your preparation, and it will prevent any unsettling surprises when you come to take the exam. Also, ensure that you know what you're allowed to take into the exam with you – most importantly, check whether it is permitted to take the primary texts and check which editions are allowed and whether they can contain marks or comments of your own.

With these details in mind, you should *plan* how you intend to revise – revision can easily becomes a shapeless, wandering activity, but it will benefit your exam performance if you actually structure your preparatory work. Specifically, we suggest the following:

■ Work out a realistic revision schedule: you should aim to work intensely, but not to the point of collapse. The schedule should divide your time according to the number, scale and importance in the exam(s) of the topics to be covered. *Always* begin with your areas of weakness – even if it is tempting to leave these to the end!

■ Work in short sessions and reward yourself with guiltless breaks. A normal attention span for revision is apparently about 20 minutes: it is better to work intensely for this time and then have a break than to devote a whole, uninterrupted day to half-hearted efforts.

- Concentrate on the subject areas with which you feel least confident, and don't avoid any areas because of dislike or uninterest.

- When re-reading literary texts or notes, make more notes. The act of writing helps to anchor thoughts, and the new notes can serve as study aids for last-minute revision.

Revising literary texts

You might take an exam requiring knowledge of several texts over a year after you have read some of them. With the rise of 'modular' degrees, the gap between studying a work and being examined on it is now usually shorter than this, but refreshing your memory of the primary texts is still a necessary exercise. With short texts, you should aim to reread them in full and in detail. With long texts – novels and longer poems and plays – full rereading is impossible, but it is useful to reread certain passages in detail.

If you have taken detailed notes from your reading, the process of revision will have been made much easier for you. But do not study your notes in isolation: always consider them in conjunction with the literary work concerned. (It makes no sense to memorize a set of notes if you have forgotten the salient details from the work itself!) With longer works, if some of your notes are marked on the text itself, it can be helpful to turn through the pages to review the passages you high-lighted and commented on, but on the whole skimming a complete text is less effective than concentrating upon reading selected passages with care. These passages should always include the opening and closing pages of the work – beginnings and endings are almost always revealing and important. In revising novels, rereading the beginning will remind you particularly of details regarding the narrative technique – these are often forgotten more readily than thematic content or the plot. (You might try this exercise: think of a novel you read over a year ago but have not looked at since, and then try to describe the narrative technique.) Apart from opening and closing pages, you should pick some key passages – either those that seemed important to you, or those which critics have found of great interest. And pick a couple of passages at random, preferably ones that seem unfamiliar on leafing through the work. Analyze these in detail.

Quotations: To memorize or not to memorize?

If you are not allowed to refer to the texts in the exam, we suggest that it is *not* worth spending hours learning long selected passages by heart. Not only is this extremely time-consuming, but there is also a tendency for those who have shed blood learning quotations to insist on demonstrating the fact in the examination room, and the quotations that have been learned may well not be relevant to the question asked. Having said that, it can be useful to learn (or at least getting to know very well) some short key phrases. Arguably this is most important where poetry is concerned – where the point of the work is dependent upon an exact use of words – and fortunately it is usually easier to learn a passage of poetry than a passage of prose. A good way of learning poetry is to make a tape recording of the poem which you can then play back repeatedly – this method has the advantage that you can listen to the tape and do something else at the same time.

If you are unable to quote at length in an exam, you can still be detailed in your reference to the text. Refer to particular scenes, isolate the operative events and actions, describe important utterances (you do not have to quote these), draw attention to relevant aspects of narrative technique, and comment on such things as symbolism and imagery if they play a significant role.

Note that when examiners grade exams, they usually take into account whether access to the texts is available: few examiners will expect students to quote extensively from memory; equally, if access is allowed, many examiners may expect some close attention to details of the text.

Revising secondary material

Your main object of attention when revising should be the primary texts, but it may also be useful to refresh your memory of *significant* critical debates that surround those texts. You do not necessarily have to tie these points in with the names of the critics involved in the debates – although if you can attach a name to a point of view, it certainly won't hurt. And you do not need to remember extended quotations from critics – unless perhaps a *key phrase* has been used repeatedly in discussions of a work. The main thing is to remember the broad directions of the *arguments* involved in the text's critical reception, or the *arguments* that have affected the way in which you view the text. Unless the exam is specifically on literary theory itself, you can take a similar approach to revising the theoretical concepts that are important to your sense of a text.

Practising before an exam

As well as revising, it is important to practise writing exam answers under conditions similar to those you will face on the day. As we remarked earlier, this is particularly important if you normally write using a computer. Many screen-based writers get quite out of the habit of writing by hand, and it can be genuinely problematic for them to write non-stop for three hours or more – and not only because of manual pain. There are different composition methods for writing by hand and writing on-screen. Writing by hand is generally a more linear process: you can't move text around as you can with a word-processor, so it is important to come up with a plan before you begin to write and then to stick closely to that plan. It is possible to add passages when you write an exam – include them at the end of your answer and indicate their position in the text with an asterisk or note. But, on the whole, it is better to avoid this if you can: you will not endear your work to the examiner if s/he has to keep jumping around in the answer simply to read what should be a linear argument.

To practise writing exam answers it is useful to acquire old exam papers – most universities retain past exams and they are available to students for the purpose of practice. Alternatively you might ask your lecturer for some practice questions (particularly if the exam is for a new course and past papers are not available), or you might set yourself some questions. Whatever way you assemble a 'mock exam', it is best if you can place yourself in 'pseudo-exam conditions' when you address it – in other words, set aside the requisite time and try to avoid disturbances or interruptions. And when you write your practice answers, be strict about sticking to the time – there will be no leeway in the real exam. As for evaluating your performance, you should look carefully through your work yourself, but you might also consider taking mock exams in a group and then evaluating the work collaboratively. When you assess your performance, try to identify where your work is weakest and try to address these areas as you revise and practise writing further.

Taking exams

A good exam performance depends not only upon your knowing the subject well. It also depends upon an ability to work well under pressure and to make the most effective use of limited time. In most exams there will be more than one part: you may be required to write several essays, or there may be a 'definitions' section as well as an essay section. Whatever form the exam takes, you should divide your time according to how much credit is given to each part. Calculate accurately how much time you have for each answer, making sure you allow about five minutes for reading through the paper – we recommend that you should be fairly precise and inflexible about this. Exams are almost always graded strictly. If a particular section counts for only 10 per cent of the final grade, you will not be able to earn more than 10 per cent for your response, however good it is. The most capacious swathe of shining erudition will simply not earn more marks than are available. So it is not worth sacrificing some sections so as to devote an unnecessarily long time to those that you feel you can treat most competently. Furthermore, you should aim always to write at least *something* for every part of the exam – a blank space will earn no marks, whereas an attempt to address the question will usually earn at least some marks. Where minimums are concerned, the quantity you write can be an influential factor, so you might aim to write at least three pages for each essay. In terms of gaining marks, it can be said that a law of diminishing returns applies to the length of an essay: it is much better to write a third or a fourth page for one essay (and raise your mark for it from 45 per cent to 55 per cent), than to add a tenth or eleventh page to another (and raise your mark for it from 67 per cent to 70 per cent).

Writing essays under pressure

As well as making the best use of the exam time as a whole, you need to maximize the time available to you for each section. Here are some suggestions on how to write an essay in limited time:

- Allow a short time for interpreting and planning your answer. Looking around an exam room, some people seem to begin writing just seconds after turning the exam paper over, but this generally is not advisable. It is worth spending a few intense minutes 'brainstorming': analyzing the question and writing down, in brief, any ideas you have about how you will respond. At first, don't worry about the order of what you note – just write down the relevant ideas as they come to you. Then try to impose some structure on your notes and work out the order in which you will address the points in the essay – you might number the notes, rather than write them out again. Such planning is not a waste of time, even if it may seem as though the time could be used actually writing the answer. Examiners prefer concise, well-structured and clearly-argued answers to long, rambling ones without a clear direction.

- Do not waste time writing out the question: the number of the question will be sufficient. Here is a comment made by the admittedly unsympathetic character Morris Zapp in David Lodge's novel *Small World* (1984): 'You can always tell a weak examinee. . . . First they waste time copying out the question. Then they take out their little rulers and rule *lines* under it.'

- Write an introduction, but make it short. A good exam answer should explain the attitude you are taking to the question and how you are going to answer it. The introduction need only be half a page long.

- Following the introduction, you should provide, in as ordered a way as possible, evidence to substantiate the position you have taken up. At each stage in the answer, the reader should be aware of what you are trying to argue and how this fits in to your general thesis or response to the question. Anyone who has marked exams knows that a sure sign that there is something wrong is when you have to flip back to page 1 to check exactly which question the script is supposed to be answering.

- Do not waste time on conclusions that simply reiterate all the points made during the course of the answer. If you have something to add in a conclusion, then you should use it. But recapitulation is usually not worthwhile in an exam, unless it is very brief and necessary in some way.

- Try to allow yourself five minutes to read through your answer to correct obvious errors – there will almost always be some. Examiners know that exam answers are written under pressure and so they do not expect the most polished prose, but it is advisable to present a text which is as accurate as is possible given the limited time.

It is quite common that the pressure of an exam causes people to forget certain apparently obvious details: names of characters, titles of works, literary terms, even the names of authors. If you experience such a blank in an exam, don't panic and don't abandon any plans to write about that topic. Just leave a blank and go on writing. If the word doesn't come to you by the end of the exam, then asterisk the gap and write a footnote explaining that you have forgotten the word and indicating what it is that you are discussing by other means ('Heathcliff's son', or even at a pinch 'the French anthropologist whose name is the same as a well-known brand of jeans').

A final point. The following is taken again from David Lodge's novel *Small World*. It gives the reader a (fictional) examinee's written response to the question, 'By what means did Milton try to "justify the ways of God to man" in "Paradise Lost"?'.

> 'Paradise Lost' is an epic poem in blank verse, which is another way of justifying the ways of God to man because if it rhymed it would seem too pat. My tutor Professor Swallow seduced me in his office last February, if I don't pass this exam I will tell everybody. John Milton was the greatest English poet after Shakespeare. He knew many languages and nearly wrote 'Paradise Lost' in Latin in which case nobody would be able to read it today. He locked the door and made me lie on the floor so nobody could see us through the window. I banged my head on the wastepaper bin. He also considered writing his epic poem about King Arthur and the knights of the Round Table, which is a pity he didn't as it would have made a more exciting story.

While we do not recommend this as a model for an examination answer (blackmail is illegal!), we draw your attention to the fact that part of the comic effect of this extract comes from the shock effect of juxtaposing a rather boring and weak response to the question with striking personal revelations. Examination answers should not be chatty or full of irrelevant personal detail. But the examination grader who is working through many, many scripts will welcome the occasional element of personal response and original opinion – *so long as it can be made relevant to the question asked*. If you can arouse the interest of the person marking your examination answer, and display something personal in your engagement with the question, then you stand a good chance of winning the sympathy of the person who has to mark your script – and that is no bad thing.

Section 2

Guide to the use of electronic media

SOME INTRODUCTORY COMMENTS

The revolution brought about by the development of computers has impacted upon the academic study of literature (and other things) in many different ways. In some cases it is a matter of the development of a new and quicker way of doing the same thing: an electronic library catalogue instead of a card-file one, cutting and pasting on-screen instead of with scissors and paste and bits of paper. And even where it is a matter of 'the same – only faster', the increase in speed is so enormous that we are effectively talking of a quite new sort of resource. But in other cases entirely new possibilities of searching for and retrieving information – and of discussing its significance with other people – have been enabled by the development of computers and their ancillary systems. An undergraduate with a PC and an Internet connection can now do in two minutes what, 20 years ago, an experienced scholar with knowledge of how to search in the depths of a dusty library could take days or even weeks to accomplish.

In short, the computer has become an essential tool in the research and study process at all levels. What follows is a set of guidelines for using this tool in an academic environment. We presuppose a degree of familiarity with certain elementary procedures, though our own experience tells us that even people with a satisfactory working knowledge of computers will not always remember the meanings of every common term. For that reason, we supply definitions of abbreviated terms as and when they appear, but our primary aim is to discuss the kinds of data available electronically, how and where to find relevant information, and what to do with it afterwards. And we further take it for granted that you are already familiar to some extent with a few of the basics: how to use *Word for Windows* or *WordPerfect*, for instance, or how to start up *Netscape Navigator* or *Communicator* and *Microsoft Internet Explorer*, the most common 'browsers', or software programs, which convert HTML-encoded files into images, sounds, and text (HTML stands for Hypertext Markup Language, or the system of codes by which Web pages are set up, designed and distributed). (We remind British

Note: in this section we have followed the convention of using angled brackets – < > – to enclose electronic addresses (e.g. e-mail addresses, www pages, etc.). If you want to use any of these addresses, type everything inside the angled brackets, but not the brackets themselves.

readers that we use the American spelling 'program' where the electronic media are concerned.)

Electronically available materials are useful for any number of reasons. Take the Internet:

■ Information that can expand and strengthen your research is quickly accessible, in the shape of primary TEXTS (copies of NOVELS, plays and poems) and secondary sources (bibliographies, critical articles, concordances, dictionaries, encyclopaedias)

■ The Internet widens what the American critic STANLEY FISH called the INTERPRETIVE COMMUNITY: researchers with e-mail can discuss and share information with others, including experts in the field, either directly (one-to-one) or through listservs and news groups (defined in the next subsection)

■ The information on the Internet is often more current than traditional forms of scholarship, which can typically take anything from a year (in the case of journal articles) or several years (in the case of books) to be published. E-mail discussion groups can in theory supply more up-to-date developments in a field

But there are disadvantages:

■ There is such an abundance of information that it takes a long time to read and sort through for relevance (traditional print sources are no less limited, but in a library the materials have already gone through a process of selection and categorization that make it easier for us to find what we need)

■ The information is so varied that it is difficult to keep focused on what you are looking for, so that you begin to follow other threads and topics instead

■ The information is often suspect or biased, badly informed or irrelevant

In what follows, we have adopted a roughly chronological approach to the process of READING and writing electronically, which is meant to follow and supplement aspects of the more comprehensive study guide in Section 1. We look at different levels or phases of reading, and the kinds of contributions electronic media can make to these, before examining the impact of new technologies upon the process of writing itself. What we hope to develop is the ability to evaluate, filter and manage information critically. But first, we want to begin by defining what some of the major electronic media consist of.

ELECTRONIC MEDIA: OPENING DEFINITIONS

The technology of literary publication and distribution is in a constant and rapid state of change. But basically, there are two main categories of electronic media: physical materials such as CD-ROMs (Computer Diskette Read-Only Memory) and other diskettes; and online sources, such as academic and commercial databases, e-mail discussion groups, listservs and newsgroups (more on these later). Books on CD-ROM – especially reference books, dictionaries, encyclopaedias, and archival materials (electronic versions of manuscripts, or back-issues of newspapers) – are by no means uncommon, and certainly useful, but they are expensive and usually only affordable by libraries. (You can check your University Library's home page to see if they have any primary or secondary materials on CD-ROM.) Nevertheless, the fact that CD-ROMs are expensive to produce and purchase means that they are often of good quality: such editions of literary works, for example, are usually reliable because they have been generated by academics and publishing houses with reputations that they want to protect and advance. Generally speaking, if you can get access to materials on CD-ROM, you will find that their reliability is less an issue of concern than with free online editions and criticism generated by private individuals.

In addition to printed and CD-ROM copies, books are now available in other electronic forms, either on the Web or (increasingly) as e-books. E-books may be downloaded directly from a commercial site to your computer as PDF files (which look very much like the pages of a book) or as HTML (which looks like plain running text). Some books may be borrowed, for a fee, by those who have the technology needed to view them: they are then available for a limited time-period only. But already, some libraries are beginning to circulate handheld devices (such as the Palm Pilot), which are easily carried in the pocket and which display the book on a screen. At the time of writing, traditional printed books are still the primary resource. They remain cheaper than e-books and, on the whole, are easier to get hold of. Printed texts are also less taxing on the eyes than computer screens – at least at this point in the history of the two technologies of the book.

It is now the case that publishers with solid reputations who once specialized in CD-ROM ventures are increasingly migrating to the World Wide Web, and most of the information we will be looking at in the pages that follow is provided through the Web. The Web is one way in which the computers linked to the Internet can connect and make information available to each other through a system known as HTTP (HyperText Transfer Protocol: a protocol is the procedure by which information is formatted for viewing in Netscape or Microsoft Explorer). E-mail systems (such as Eudora) are also part of the Internet, but they communicate through a system known as Simple Mail Transfer Protocol (SMTP, which facilitates the sending and receiving of messages and the exchange of computer files as attached documents).

Listservs are closed groups of e-mail users, who are interested in specific topics (such as science fiction, or the novels of Joseph Conrad); one normally has to subscribe to join a group, and the discussions are checked first by a moderator before being released to the other members. IRCs or MUDs and MOOs use different protocols to allow users to communicate 'synchronously', or live in 'real time'. (A MUD Multi-User Dimension, originally developed for the *Dungeons and Dragons* game, facilitates synchronous conferencing and distance education applications. A MOO is a MUD, Object-Oriented.) Newsgroups tend to be less formal, and are asynchronous: these are electronic bulletin boards that allow people to participate as and when they want. Newsgroups are typically informal, but can be useful if they are set up to discuss specific critical, literary and theoretical issues, or in connection with particular conferences, allowing delegates to initiate discussion before the conference begins, and to continue after it has finished. These services use a system called News Protocol.

In addition, there are older ways of facilitating the storage and exchange of documents and programs: these include Telnet (or remote login, which allows your computer to log onto another and to use it as if you were physically present); FTP (File Transfer Protocol, an application which permits your computer to access files from a remote computer and view or save them on your computer); and Gopher (an early way of retrieving Internet documents which has largely been replaced by the Web). Gopher and Telnet have their own directories – Veronica, for example, or the directory for gopher databases in the United States, which at the time of writing is listed at the site:

<gopher://gopher.tc.umn.edu/11/Other%20Gopher%20and%20Information
    %20Servers/North%20America/USA%09%09%2B>

– but most of their information is available through the Web.

FINDING PRIMARY ELECTRONIC INFORMATION

Books purchased in electronic form in order either to be added to a library's holdings, or downloaded to any of the new e-book reading devices, are a relatively recent development within contemporary publishing. But electronic copies of much older (and thus non-copyright) works have been available free via the Internet for some time. A variety of sites allow you to view or download such literary texts – the plays of William Shakespeare, the prose of Aphra Behn, or the poetry of Christina Rossetti, to pick some random examples.

Finding these involves nothing more difficult than having access to a computer linked to the Internet, and a good search engine. (A search engine is a program which allows you to look for information files using relevant search terms.) The most common search engines include Alta Vista, Excite, FastSearch, HotBot, InfoSeek, Lycos, Magellan, Webcrawler and Yahoo (others include About, All4One, AskJeeves, DirectHit, Dogpile, Google, Mamma, NorthernLight, OneKey, ProFusion, Raging Search and Starting Point). Browsers such as Netscape and Microsoft Internet Explorer have their own search engines, which you can also use. Some search engines, such as the ones we have listed, limit themselves to specific sites or types of files; others, like MetaCrawler, will search many sites simultaneously for sources of information (at the time of writing, it will combine search engines from Excite, InfoSeek, LookSmart, Lycos, WebCrawler, About, DirectHit, Google, and Internet Keyword). A meta-engine such as this one does not have its own database: instead, it searches the databases of others.

These are the kinds of search that you can carry out:

■ Simple or General Searches. You type in a topic or keyword. This is the fastest and most straightforward approach to take, but it can yield hundreds of results, many of them unrelated to your topic.

■ Specific or Advanced Searches. Boolean operators (more on these below) and/or other ways to make a search more specific. The results tend to be fewer, and more relevant.

■ MetaSearches. A metasearch engine will look in several databases. Though it is often very fast, such an engine may be limited to only a certain number of returns per database: in addition, it may be programmed to search in slightly different, but significant, ways from certain databases, causing compatibility problems.

■ Successive Searching. With InfoSeek, for example, you can perform one search, and then perform another more specific search within your results. This helps you to narrow your search, and get more relevant results.

■ Category Browsing. Search engines such as Yahoo and Looksmart have categories which you can use to begin your search. These are good if you are slightly uncertain about what you are looking for, and want to start generally and be guided to relevant materials. The drawback is that you are constrained by the choices and definitions of the site-organizers.

The point to make here is that if you don't find anything relevant on one search engine, try another engine or another kind of search. Generally speaking, there is an overlap of approximately 60 per cent between searches on different engines, but the 40 per cent that is different can make a crucial difference. As an exercise, you might want to submit a query to different search engines and then compare 'hits' or 'matches' (the results): the one that produces the most relevant information may be the one you should use first (but not exclusively) in future searches. And make sure that you 'bookmark' (in Netscape) or 'add to favorites' (in Microsoft Explorer) in order to create shortcut links that will enable you to return quickly to these sites at any time in the future. (In Netscape, you click 'Bookmarks' on the Menu Bar at the top of your screen, and then click on 'Add Bookmark'. In Microsoft Explorer, click on 'Favorites' and then 'Add to Favorites': you will then be asked to confirm this.) Such procedures allow you to set and save up a list of worthwhile sites and their URLs: you can also organize these into different folders according to topics (newspapers, sports, journals), making them easier to manage and quicker to access.

Later, we will look more closely at how to cite information to which you refer, but for now you should be aware that if you find something, you should make a note of its URL (the uniform resource locator which functions as a path or address to the file: typically, it will begin with <http://www> and the date when you accessed it. This is because information is altered, deleted, or updated so often on the Internet that when you look at a file, you are really looking at a particular edition of the file, which may change.

There are of course problems with searching the Internet. Take these examples of texts which we found online: in looking for *The Waste Land*, not only did we get T.S. ELIOT's poem of that name, but also information about the most recent developments in toilet flushing technology. And for H.D. (Hilda Doolittle), we scored a number of hits that included a firm which manufactured automobile lubricants, in addition to the Home Page of Harley Davison, the motorcycle company.

The standard way of avoiding this problem is to use what are called boolean operators, which help you to refine and limit the results that you get. To return to T.S. Eliot once again: by writing <waste land> in the search box, and clicking on Find or Search, we effectively ask it to look for all documents that include the word <waste> *and/or* the word <land>. (Capitals are another matter: unless otherwise stated or directed most search engines are not case-sensitive, which is to say that they do not distinguish between capital and small letters.) Or to put it another way, if we had searched for John Milton, the engine would have recorded every instance where the word John had been included in a document, as well as every occurrence of Milton (Milton Keynes, for example), in addition to instances with both.

More often than not, you will get some useful results relating to the author of that name, or to the poem entitled *The Waste Land*. But by writing <waste And land>, we will get sites that include *both* terms, rather than one or the other. When we did this, for instance, it didn't prevent us from being given information about the latest advances in sewage management, but it did mean that T.S. Eliot's poem appeared first in the list of results, rather than (as previously) fifth. In short, the use of a boolean operator makes your search more advanced and efficient, meaning that you are more likely to get relevant results. Alternatively, by writing <'Waste Land'> in quotation marks, you will instruct the search engine to look for those words as a phrase, and not as separate elements.

Here is a list of some common terms that can help you to focus a search:

- By writing <Eliot NOT George> you will ensure that you will get returns that do not include George Eliot, the nineteenth-century female novelist.

- Another way of doing this is to use the minus sign ('−') to exclude irrelevant materials. For example, <eliot−george>.

- By writing <*Great Expectations* OR *Middlemarch*>, you indicate that you want files that have either term, but not necessarily both.

In fact, when we used the search engines mentioned above, Excite, Hotbot and Webcrawler responded to the boolean operators, excluding answers with

<george> in them (though not other names in every instance). The others – Altavista, Fast, InfoSeek, Lycos, Yahoo and Metacrawler all responded in the opposite way, by providing us with sites that included eliot and george. However, most of these sites use a very simple search engine initially: Altavista, to take only one example, allows you to adopt a more advanced search which accepts boolean terms. And InfoSeek allows you to search within your own search results, so that (for instance) you can begin with 'eliot', then scroll down the page of results, find the search window at the bottom, enter 'george' and ask it to search within the results you already have. You can continue this process so that you eventually produce a very narrow query that may yield more precise results.

We will review our discussion of boolean operators, and provide further tips on search techniques, later when we come to consider criticism and other secondary materials on the Internet.

ISSUES OF RELIABILITY

The very things that make the Internet a wonderful resource – the relative cheapness and ease of producing materials, the lack of formality or bureaucratic procedure, the convenience of access – do not always provide the ideal circumstances for more scholarly productions. A famous cartoon which appeared in the *New Yorker* showed two dogs sitting in front of a computer screen; one says to the other, 'On the Internet, nobody knows you're a dog'. Like many jokes, this one is not entirely accurate, but it does gesture in the direction of a fair comment: whereas traditional, typeset, editions frequently involve years of careful research by individuals or teams selected because of their work in an appropriate field or discipline, and whereas such books go through a lengthy process of proof-reading and editing, a text on the Web may involve little more than a scanner or good word-processing software.

One of the major issues associated with electronic texts, then, is that of reliability or authority. (This is essentially a development of a problem that has existed for some time, and which we cover in Section 1, pp. 21–3: the question of which edition to choose.) Keep in mind that the printed books in your university library are usually recommended by lecturers and researchers who vouch for their quality or centrality in some way. Where electronic texts are concerned, there are few economic restrictions: enormous amounts of information can be presented with little expertise or cost. And there is frequently no review process – no team of editors ensuring that what is published has a basic standard or objectivity.

In most cases, too, your tutor or lecturer will recommend that you use a certain standard edition as the basis for discussion – either in the class, or for a written assignment. More often than not, these printed editions carry with them a certain degree of legitimacy that comes from tradition: we know almost without looking that the Oxford edition of Wordsworth's poems, for instance, has been collated and edited by leading scholars. This does not mean that such books are flawless, but it does make them generally reliable. However, this is frequently not the case with Web editions. For example: there are many, many sites containing Emily Dickinson's poems and letters on the Internet. Often, these are based on four editions that were published during the 1890s, after Dickinson's death. As critics have pointed out, however, these editions misrepresent Dickinson's originals in many, and often serious, ways: by altering her punctuation, for example, 'correcting' her syntax, inserting different words in order to produce fuller, and more conventional, RHYMES. The poems are organized according to themes which Dickinson herself never formulated or approved, and they are assigned titles (again in contrast to her practice). Such editions have an historical value – they show us the kinds of poetic norms Dickinson's early editors worked with – but when published electronically there are very rarely footnotes explaining their source or suspect status.

In short, there are problems associated with the kinds of materials that are available free of charge in electronic format, and you should be aware of these before you begin looking:

■ Many of the results will be advertisements for books by or about the author you are interested in. In other words, they will contain little or no relevant information.

■ Home pages often contain favourite poems, and your results will inevitably include a fair proportion of these, with no guarantee that they are accurately transcribed or taken from reliable sources.

■ Some of the texts will be wrongly dated: any dates should be routinely corroborated by looking at information in print.

■ With poems, it is very easy to mis-transcribe punctuation, STANZA breaks, and indenting.

Assessing authority and reliability

Later, we will provide you with a comprehensive list of basic questions you can ask which can help you to gauge the accuracy and quality of *secondary* information you are reading. But there are useful points to keep in mind when trying to assess the authority of both primary and secondary texts – the way the page looks, for instance, its language, title and overall structure. An absence of typing errors is a sign that may inspire some confidence. But one of the first and best ways of evaluating the seriousness or authenticity of a text is through its URL. The Universal Resource Locator is the address of the file, and learning to recognize what some of its elements refer to can be useful. Here are four examples:

<http://disney.go.com/>

<http://www.amherst.edu/>

<http://www.pbs.org/>

<http://www.homeoffice.gov.uk/

The first part of the address (before the colon) indicates the type of communications system or protocol being used (in this case, it is http, the most common, but it could just as well have been ftp or gopher). What follows the double forward slash (//) is the address of the server, or the name of the institution or site providing the service. (After the single slash, there will be an optional port number, where the server is situated, and some file and resource details, which are not immediately interesting to us.) It is the kind of institution indicated by the main part of the address – the kind of host – that we need to understand, and this is provided by the domain indicator at the end.

The first address (disney.go.com) probably doesn't require much explanation, but the end of the address features the typical domain identification of a business (the .com indicates that it is a commercial site, in other words). The second address corresponds to the home page of Amherst College, one of America's leading institutions of higher education (.edu is equivalent to an educational site). The third is the address of public broadcasting services in the United States, which relies heavily on public funding in order to provide quality programmes (.org stands for organization, but is not necessarily commercial). The final domain indicates a government site, this time in the United Kingdom (most national or geographic domain indicators are fairly easy to interpret once you get used to them: .no for Norway, .jp for Japan, for example).

The point to make is that a text which is located under a university or educational address will often have the implicit approval or imprimatur of someone or some group affiliated professionally with that institution, and is therefore an early indicator not only of good quality or seriousness but also relevance or pertinence (though it is not an absolute guarantee). It is not so much, or not even, that a commercial site will be poor: it is more that different organizations have different aims and audiences, and knowing how to read a URL can help you to guess what those might be and whether they are likely to be appropriate to your immediate needs. (A commercial site will contain advertising, for instance: this may mean that the information it offers takes longer to access, and it may even have an impact on content.) Additional indicators of validity include the presence or otherwise of the name of the person responsible for the information: it is relatively easy to find out if he, she or they is/are qualified to produce it – and indeed whether they provide a contact address as a token of their willingness to answer for the materials, and to respond to questions about them.

Knowing how to read a URL is useful in other ways too. For example: if we perform a search for Christina Rossetti, what we might find (and this is an invented address, please don't try it!) is a URL that says <http://www.university college.edu/preraphaelites/crossetti>. The address tells us the type of service (http), the name of the institution providing the resource (universitycollege), the type of institution (educational), and the location of the file in the directory structure of the server. We click on the link, and find a page that is so good that we would like to get more information about the site. But there are no links to the home page, and we cannot use the 'back' button on the browser (which normally returns us to the step we took before accessing the present page). By deleting </crossetti>, however, we enter a new URL, which should (in theory, but not always in practice) take us to the Pre-Raphaelites page. Alternatively, we can remove all of '/preraphaelites/crossetti', and find University College's Home Page, which will have its own search box, which we can then instruct to look for materials on the Pre-Raphaelites.

But what happens when we find literary texts: in what ways are they useful to the process of research? One of the first issues to address here is that of downloading texts, or excerpts of texts.

DOWNLOADING LITERARY TEXTS

As we shall see shortly, having an electronic copy of a text on your computer has its advantages: you can cut and paste large quotations, for example, or search a text for a key word. (Netscape and Microsoft Explorer both allow you to search files for words and phrases, and some electronic texts are formatted with built-in search engines, which are often useful.) The disadvantages are that HTML texts do not always have page numbers, so that you may copy something but still have to look through the original in order to find a reference.

Another, more practical, problem is that (in the case of novels and plays, for instance) texts can take up a lot of memory (though this can be solved if you have the right software, or if you save to disk) and/or may contain macros (hidden codes) that can cause you problems later on. All of this presumes that you own your own computer, of course: downloading on a university-based machine is not recommended (unless you save to disk, or you have your allotted area of storage space on a university server). And even if cutting and pasting from an electronic copy seems faster than copying manually from a printed book, you will often find problems of formatting compatibility: a poem may be recorded with indents, for example, which do not transfer properly into Word or WordPerfect; a passage of prose transferred into a Word document will suddenly have lots of blank spaces which you then have to delete. In other words, you *may* find it just as straightforward to type the quotation yourself as to copy it.

In addition, downloading from a remote site may require that you have the right software: if you don't, your efforts will be frustrated, and your computer may freeze during the attempted transfer. Always keep such an eventuality in mind: save whatever you are working on before you begin to download (or you may lose parts or all of what you have written). For instance, check to see if you have a program for decompressing files (such as WinZip). Many FTP sites make files smaller for the purposes of saving storage space: rather like packets of soup, you need to add something in order to make them normal sized again (though some files, ending in <.exe> are usually self-extracting). Archived or compressed files often end with a <.zip> or <.tar> suffix: <.hqx> is coded for Macintosh users. Software enables you to decompress, or unzip, these files – and your browser will usually tell you if you need a new application and ask your permission to download it. If your university hasn't already installed this kind of software in your machine, you can get it free from various 'shareware' sites, but you need first to make sure that the downloading is not against university policy. Once you reach a shareware site (for example, at <www.winzip.com> or <www.shareware.com>), follow the instructions or get a technician to help you.

Keep in mind too that electronic editions are often transcribed, and that human errors can and do occur during transcription (the text is not always proofread). If you do cut and paste you should make it a routine to cross-check your quotation against a print edition to ensure that there are no discrepancies. You might think that a scanned copy would be better, but again we come up with the problems of reliability we mentioned earlier (a copy is only as good or as bad as the original). Finally, be sure to check if the file you are reading is incomplete – either a selected edition (for example), or one still 'under construction', and therefore incomplete, or an amended one (where some passages have been removed for some reason). Finally: having carefully reviewed your reasons for downloading, before beginning you should check that (i) you have enough memory available, (ii) that you have a current anti-virus program, (iii) that there is some kind of documentation to accompany the text you are interested in (in terms of both information about the person doing the producing, and the textual source of the production).

READING IN THE ELECTRONIC AGE

How have these new developments in electronic technology affected habits of reading? At a very basic level, the answer is very little: the first reading of any literary text is still, as Vladimir Nabokov argued, a fairly basic activity. The eyes still have to move from left to right (in English, at any rate), line after line, and from one page to another, as an impression of the world of the text is pieced together. Although books are now available in electronic format, as we wrote above, most of these require traditional methods of reading. The texts which do demand different skills are those which proceed in a nonlinear fashion, like HYPERTEXTS, where one proceeds very much as one wants to, clicking on different links and producing a narrative (or anti-narrative) of one's own. Even here, however, there are restrictions: the paths chosen may differ from reader to reader, but they are rarely random, having been programmed beforehand.

What has changed are the procedures of reading *actively*: Nabokov recommended his students to read with a pencil handy, marking dates and the names of people and places, making marginal comments that may seem banal and obvious at the time (the colour of eyes, aspects of clothing, a manner of speaking, the first meeting between characters) but which may come to help you develop and organize your reading later. And he thought that it was especially important to have a dictionary, and to look up (i) words that you can't easily define (you may know their meaning, but find it hard to formulate this fully) and (ii) the variety of meanings that a word may have (particularly if you feel that the word is important). For Nabokov, the imagination was less important, or at least less primary, than having a dictionary during this phase of reading. This is still sound advice, and computers can make a contribution to this process. Many dictionaries – such as Webster's – are available online, and there are even copies of historical editions that can be purchased as CD-ROMs. In fact, recent studies have suggested that Emily Dickinson, often ranked as America's foremost lyric poet, used her dictionary when composing poems, looking up different definitions and meanings in order to extend her ideas in new directions – and having an electronic copy of the dictionary she read obviously then becomes useful and relevant.

SEARCHING AND ANALYZING ELECTRONIC TEXTS

In Herman Melville's *Moby Dick*, there is a chapter entitled 'The Whiteness of the Whale'. Reading through the print copy of the book, it would take days to put together a list of every time the colour white appears (or, by extension, every time Melville refers to any colour at all) – unless your university library has a concordance to Melville's work. (A concordance provides an alphabetical list of all, or some, of the words in a particular text, along with page and line references to a given edition.) An electronic copy enables you to search and find these occurrences in seconds. This then allows you to locate and analyze the passages where the colour appears, and to consider whether or not there is a pattern which is worth commenting on (a connection between whiteness and divinity, for instance, or whiteness and indecipherability). By extension, in Sarah Orne Jewett's 'The White Heron' (which is sometimes available on the Internet – it comes and goes!), you could perform a similar search for a particular colour, or for colours in general. You can even begin to make comparisons between Melville and Jewett, or between patterns of IMAGERY or THEMATIC preoccupations in writers on your course.

As we have already said, there are many electronic editions of literary works available on the Internet – though these tend to be older works, out of copyright. You can search for specific authors or texts (of poems, prose or dramatic works): retrieving an electronic text can be useful because it can then be searched for a particular phrase or word or image.

Other ways in which searches can be useful include the ease with which a half-remembered quote can be found and checked, and if a critic quotes a snippet from a literary work, you can locate it and view it in a wider textual context. If you are curious about an author's use of a word, you can search a corpus of texts from a particular period to find out who else uses it, and in what ways (you can of course also do this for a single author).

Electronic media can assist the research process in other ways. For example, although we recommend that you disable spelling and grammar software during free-association work (discussed shortly), it can be very interesting to download a passage of writing and then see what happens when you allow them to be checked for irregularities. Part of the lesson is learning that such software is very limited: it applies standards that are often very rigid and conservative. But the other point is that you can begin to see the ways in which a writer may or may not conform to such usage, and you may want to ask questions about this: are long sentences or unusual syntactic sequences a common part of the author's style, for example, or does he or she use these only now and then? Are grammatical and spelling anomalies rhetorical (deliberate) or historical (to do with changing usage)? Are there materials here for an essay, or can they be part of a larger critical argument?

BROWSING THE WEB

As we have seen from Section 1, the best inquiries into works of literature begin with a personal response – partly because it is often easier to derive initiative and momentum from an idea you have had yourself, rather than a topic imposed upon you. At its initial stages, research is an extension of this first response, and electronic media can help this process. In what follows, we will look at the ways in which the different media can help. We begin first with online resources: search engines and procedures, e-mail discussion groups (listservs), before looking at bibliographies, dictionaries, encyclopaedias and journals, both as online services and as CD-ROMs.

The essential paradox of the Internet is this: information is easy and quick to access – but it is not necessarily relevant or helpful. The problem is that you can spend a lot of time getting very basic information: when a writer was born and died, what he or she wrote, and perhaps a few standard excerpts from their works. Frequently, the pages are put there by fans – people who are interested in a particular writer, but who do not always have original or useful things to say about her or him. There is nothing wrong with this: it's a legitimate way of expressing an allegiance or affection. But more often than not, what you will get is a brief biography taken from a printed text, a list of books, some photographs and perhaps a few short summaries.

By and large, biographies on the Internet are not going to be very useful to you. There are almost certainly better ones in the library. (It is extraordinary, for instance, how often even basic things like dates of birth, or publication dates, differ from one site to another.) And a page of favourite quotations is not going to be very pertinent either – unless you haven't seen them before and feel that they can be applied during your essay.

So how can browsing the Web actually benefit the study of literature? Let us consider how your initial ideas about a text can be explored and developed through Web searches.

■ You can begin by using a search engine to look up a word or technique or topic which you think may possibly be relevant. Often, there will be tens of thousands of results, and it is the first 20 to 30 which will either be most relevant or which will show that the search topic is either too wide or unsatisfactorily covered by the Web.

■ You proceed by refining your topic, by (for instance) using boolean operators, or by clicking progressively on categories until you have found a specific area. A typical topic path might involve clicking on subject areas such as 'arts and humanities', 'literature', 'genres', 'poetry', 'British poetry', 'period', 'nineteenth century', 'Tennyson', which will then narrow your search down to a small number of files on Alfred, Lord Tennyson. Yahoo works in this way: unlike the other tools, it does not search databases, but employs people to describe, review, and rank them. It then organizes these sites according to different categories. This is very valuable: it is the equivalent of an annotated bibliography. But the flip side is that it is partial: someone, somewhere, makes decisions about what is and isn't relevant. A robot search engine (Altavista, Excite, InfoSeek, Lycos, HotBot, Webcrawler) intervenes less: it more or less retrieves all of the data, and lets you decide what you need or want. InfoSeek is especially useful in this respect, for it prompts you to begin a search within your search results, thus enabling you to create a more precise grid for looking.

■ You evaluate your information: immediately after the section that follows, we offer some tips on how to do this. But you should note that some engines already evaluate or attempt to manage the information on your behalf: Yahoo, in the ways we have just mentioned, for example. But if you search for Hamlet on Altavista, it will offer you related searches on 'Shakespeare's Hamlet', 'Hamlet essays', 'Hamlet synopsis', and 'Hamlet quotes'. (InfoSeek does something similar, offering you a variety of paths in addition to results.)

Earlier in this section, we mentioned the usefulness of boolean operators in refining searches for primary texts. In looking for critical materials, knowing how to narrow your search down so that you do not produce irrelevant and distracting information is useful. Here are some standard boolean operators that you may find helpful:

■ <romantic AND poetry> This confines your search to files that contain both terms, not either.

■ <romantic ADJ poetry> The search will look for romantic poetry as a phrase (with the words *adjacent*, or next to each other). Whereas <romantic AND poetry> in theory may produce results where the word *romantic* is on page 4 and *poetry* on page 5 (though most engines automatically give precedence to results where both words are adjacent), this method ensures that they are kept together. One can extend this: for example, <nineteenth ADJ century ADJ romantic ADJ poetry> will look for the phrase 'nineteenth century romantic poetry'.

■ <'romantic poetry'> Using quotation marks is a short-cut way of searching for the two words as a phrase. This is a literal search.

■ <+romantic+poetry> Placing a plus sign like this before the terms you are interested in will ensure that each term will be searched for. It is a shortcut for romantic AND poetry.

■ <romantic NOT prose> This will limit your search to documents with the word 'romantic', but not ones which include 'prose'. Alternatively, you can be more specific: <romantic AND poetry NOT prose>.

■ <+romantic−prose> The minus sign will eliminate certain terms from your search results. It is a shortcut for <romantic NOT prose>. Again, you may be more specific: <+romantic+poetry−prose>.

■ Using brackets allows you to combine items in more complicated ways. For example: <['romantic poetry' AND 'romantic criticism'] NOT prose>. This is called 'nesting' search terms. Many search engines will accept either square brackets [] or round ones ().

■ <romantic OR poetry> This will perform a search for romantic and/or poetry. In other words, you may get answers that include one but not the other. If you are writing an essay on Wordsworth and Coleridge, this kind of approach is useful because files may not always contain both.

■ <romantic AND (poetry OR prose)> This is another way of looking for romantic and poetry or romantic and prose.

■ <(prose OR poetry) AND romantic> The search will look for romantic and poetry or romantic and prose.

■ <(british or american) AND (romantic ADJ poetry)> The phrase 'romantic poetry' that further includes either 'british' or 'american'.

■ <roman*> Asterisks (or wild cards) allow for greater flexibility in your search. A search like this one will return pages containing 'roman', 'romanesque', 'romance', 'romantic', 'romanticism', and so on. They are useful if you do not want to distinguish (for example) between singular and plural terms (theor* instead of theory, theories and theorists). As their names suggest, fuzzy or wild card searches can be very much hit-and-miss affairs.

Another handy trick to keep in mind is the Link command, which works on Altavista and InfoSeek. It enables you to find sites that have links to one about which you are interested in finding out more. For example: you have to deliver a class paper on *Hamlet*. You find a Web site with the text <http://www.hamlet.org/>, and then copy and paste this URL into the search box for Altavista or

InfoSeek (you can try it for other engines as well). Preface the address with link: (that is, in this case, write <link:http://www.hamlet.org/>), and click on the find or search button. The engine will now find all the sites it knows that have links to the 'Hamlet' file: for example, <http://www.bowernorth.com/greenroom/links/linksshakes.htm>, a site with many links to Shakespeare files. In other words, the link option allows you to discover sites that critically analyze, discuss or review the materials in which you are interested.

EVALUATING SECONDARY SOURCES

Previously in this section, we wrote about how URLs can speed up the browsing process by giving you valuable initial information about the nature of a site. Knowing that an address is commercial rather than educational, for instance, can help you a lot, depending on what you are looking for – Mickey Mouse or Marianne Moore.

The title of the file (which can be the name of an author, or a time-period such as the eighteenth century), can tell you a lot. For example:

■ <http://andromeda.rutgers.edu/%7Ejlynch/Johnson/>: For someone looking for materials on Samuel Johnson, this is likely to be a good site because (i) it comes from a university site and (ii) includes Johnson in the title (which is to say that Johnson is not likely to be mentioned only once in 60 pages, since he appears to be the subject).

■ <http://www.weems – plath.com/>: The first return on a search query for Sylvia Plath, this one seems unpromising (in fact, it has nothing to do with the poet at all).

■ <http://www.geocities.com/~emily777/PlathLinks.html>: The .com ending shows that this is a commercial organization, which is not promising (often it means that what you get is a fan page, with poems, photographs, and some e-mails). But the PlathLinks suggested something more substantial, at least to us, and indeed the site is quite a good one: well organized, and with links to good essays and papers on Plath.

These are matters of pertinence, perhaps, more than reliability. But when you get access to a site, how do you know it is serious and worth using? Early indicators, we have said, include such things as the overall structure and appearance of the site, and its use of language (informal, formal): these show its goals and projected audience. In addition, it is always worthwhile trying to find out more about the author(s) behind the site: what are her or his professional affiliation and/or qualifications? For example:

■ <http://www.csustan.edu/english/reuben/pal/TABLE.HTML>: the title of the page is Perspectives in American Literature – A Research and Reference Guide. It is aimed at academics, then, and seems scholarly.

■ It bears the name of the California State University at Stanislaus – so it has a degree of approval from them. It also suggests that this is a public service, rather than something commercial (some Web sites on literature charge for the information they give you).

- It has the name of the person responsible for the site: Paul P. Reuben.
- By deleting the last part of the URL, we can get to the home page of CSU and follow links from there to a campus directory, which lists the departments and staff, and confirm that Reuben is a Professor of English at CSU.
- Reuben includes his e-mail address: he is willing to be contacted, and to receive advice about his page. More importantly, we can verify the page as legitimate.
- The site has been in existence since 1995. It is superbly organized, according to author, genre and time-period. Each chapter contains an introductory essay, selected bibliographies, and information on authors. It has its own search-engine. All of this means that the author is serious about what he is doing, has put a lot of effort into his project, and that the information he makes available is sufficiently useful for it to stand the test of time.

PAL has also received various awards and citations. Now, awards in themselves are not a useful guide to seriousness or relevance: commercial organizations often give awards to sites in which they have some vested interest. But some of the citations Reuben includes (a reference in the College and Libraries news bulletin, for instance) are credible. More importantly, teachers in the field of American literature are willing to be quoted as saying that this is a useful research resource, and these quotations are a kind of peer review: that is, PAL has been evaluated by informed sources and found to be reliable.

Not all sites are this easy to judge. And in singling PAL out, we are less interested in promoting its merits than in pointing out that there are a number of ways by which information can be checked. One of them is to find out more about the competence of the individual(s) responsible: Reuben makes this easy, but if he had not included supporting citations, we would have instigated a search to find out more. For example, we might have checked Amazon or Barnes & Noble online to see if Reuben had any print publications, and if so, what reviewers had to say about these. Or we could have looked in the index of other books about American literature to see if he was mentioned. In other words, we would try to find out how qualified Paul P. Reubens (or anyone else for that matter) was:

- What are the author's credentials (level of education, pedagogical experience, publications, responsibility for courses) in this field? Does the site reflect this experience (that is, is the expert in the eighteenth century writing on something he may know little about, such as the literature of the American South?).
- Is there a university or otherwise relevant affiliation?
- What are the basic goals or values of the organization or institution promoting the site? Do you share these values, and are they likely to distort or enhance the materials you read?

■ What do other scholars say about your source? Has your lecturer recommended her or him? Check other critical materials and bibliographies.

■ Is there evidence of bias or objectivity? For instance, Reuben's introduction to American literature includes women writers, African-Americans and Native Americans. He does not attempt to exclude on the basis of gender or ethnicity.

■ Internally, that is in files that take narrower subjects (a poet, rather than a survey of all American literature), you should check that there is a bibliography and/or footnotes, so that you can cross-check sources to review the fairness and accuracy of the opinions being expressed.

■ How current is the information? If it is written in 1991, for instance, will it make the same kind of impact on your research as a more recent book or journal article? Be cynical: will this make a difference?

■ By extension, how recent is the last revision? Most web sites will have a statement at the bottom of the opening page saying something like 'Last Revised October 1997'. Such a date may suggest that the author has lost interest: more importantly, it will also mean that the article may not be entirely current.

■ How relevant is the site in terms of your needs? Again, PAL is a very useful starting point – both in terms of authors, genres or time periods. And it has several links to other sites. But you may be looking for something more specialist: evidence of homosexual attraction in *The Adventures of Huckleberry Finn*, for instance, or the use of dialects in Kate Chopin. You need to weigh up the value of the site in relation to your immediate needs.

■ How useful is the information you get in comparison with the range of information resources available in a traditional library collection?

SECONDARY SOURCES

Bibliographies

Using CD-ROMs in combination with the Web can be a quick and efficient way of building up a list of articles, books and essays on almost any subject matter. Again, it is a good idea to start with own your library, since it will include links to important electronic databases and publications (such as the MLA Bibliography, and Literature Online, discussed below). In addition, many libraries now provide access to details about off-site as well as on-site materials through their computer-based information retrieval systems. And there have been other improvements: a recent development in cataloguing is the inclusion of details from the table of contents or from a book's index, thus increasing our ability to judge the relevance of secondary materials at an early stage. Some systems, rather than just listing the abstract of a journal article, include full text files of the entire article (there will be more on this under the section dealing with periodicals). Already, you can see how electronic media have made a physical impact on research: they have made redundant the intermediate step characteristic of previous systems in which users first performed a search and then had to get the articles themselves in print or microfilm.

One CD-ROM that we strongly recommend is the MLA (Modern Language Association) International Bibliography of Books and Articles on the Modern Languages and Literatures, to which most libraries subscribe. The print editions (which consist of two large volumes) contain a list of articles, books and doctoral dissertations (from DAI, Dissertation Abstracts International) published each year in the disciplines of folklore, modern languages and literatures, and linguistics. The CD-ROM and Internet editions (the latter is updated 10 times annually) feature all the information contained in print entries going back to 1963. The Bibliography can be searched by author, classification headings, nationalities, subject-index terms, time-periods, or a combination of these elements. The subject-index, for example, is arranged alphabetically and features the names of authors ('Dickinson, Emily'), critics ('Bercovitch, Sacvan') as well as topics ('Symbolism' and 'Black English', for example). The advantage of these search tools is that they allow you to construct detailed and current bibliographies on a particular subject or text, and quickly to assess what is available to you (in your library, through inter-library loan, or in electronic format).

As we also wrote previously, however, publishing houses that used to specialize in CD-ROM collections are increasingly migrating to the Web. One example of such a database is Lion-Chadwyck's 'Literature Online', which used to be an extremely expensive CD-ROM, but which now exists only as a Web publication with an annual subscription. It is a massive collection of over 290,000 works of poetry, drama and prose with complementary reference resources. Depending on the kind of subscription your university has chosen, the primary texts include English poetry from 600 to the present, American and African-American poetry from 1603 to the present, English fiction from the sixteenth to the nineteenth century, English drama from 1280 to 1915, and American drama from 1762 to 1832. Secondary Sources include LIFT, a literary journal index with full text of many articles, Webster's Dictionary, the Annual Bibliography of English Language and Literature, the King James Bible, links to other Web resources, bibliographies for over 400 authors, and biographies for over 1,000 authors.

The Annual Bibliography of English Language and Literature (ABELL) in itself is an important standard reference resource, and has existed in print form for over 70 years. Compiled by a team of advisors, contributors and editors under the direction of the Modern Humanities Research Association (MHRA), the bibliography features world-wide publications such as book reviews, collections of essays, critical editions of literary works, doctoral dissertations, monographs and periodical articles.

Periodicals

As we have said again and again, not everything on the Web is reliable. Of course, not everything in print is necessarily reliable either. But there are certain procedures that are designed to ensure that the information published (for example) in journals is informed and interesting, well documented or supported with evidence of extensive reading, and well written. Open any of the best journals (*PMLA*, *American Literature*, etc.), and you will see in the first pages a list of the board of editors and a further list of readers (usually experts in particular fields): to be accepted for publication, most articles have to go through both levels first. This may not guarantee the truth or accuracy of the contents, but it will suffice as an assurance of good faith – of a combination of quality and seriousness.

To take one example: *Modern Fiction Studies* has an editor, an editorial staff and two editorial boards, the Purdue Advisory Board and the Editorial Advisory Board. Board members act as referees for submitted essays that have passed through an initial screening process. The Purdue Advisory Board consists of 15 faculty members from the English Department at Purdue who have some expertise and interest in the disciplines covered by the journal. The Editorial Advisory Board is made up of 42 distinguished critics and scholars from colleges and universities in the United States and abroad who work in the fields of modern and contemporary narrative, theory, and cultural studies. This is not to say that every article will be read by each and every one of the members comprising the two advisory bodies, but it does guarantee a process of filtering by serious scholars able to judge the competence and relevance of what they are reading. A Home Page on Walt Whitman or Stevie Smith does not require those levels of review – and nor should it. But the point is that there are few sites on the Web which go through the same process of critically evaluating the information which they distribute.

Electronic editions of academic and critical journals are an exception. And many journals and periodicals are now available in online electronic editions, with searchable archives: the *Times Literary Supplement*, for example, as well as *New York Review of Books*, in addition to the arts pages of the *Times*, *Telegraph*, and *Independent* (to name a few). As a student, you should be able to take advantage of the fact that many university libraries subscribe to some of these electronic editions. Project MUSE, for example, from Johns Hopkins University Press, allows institutional full-text subscription access to over 100 scholarly journals in the arts and humanities, social sciences and mathematics. Keep in mind that if a journal is physically available in your library, then it has gone through a process of peer evaluation, which is to say that it is judged worthwhile by people with some competence in the field. It is often a good idea to make a list of these journals, and then find out which ones are available electronically. But remember that not all editions will be equally relevant to every research requirement: some specialize in specific authors (*The Shandean*, *The Keats– Shelley Review*) which will make them useful for certain assignments, but not others. And even in journals that take (say) Anglo-Irish literature for their subject, not every issue will be helpful. Again, however, electronic media make the job of finding this information physically less demanding: most journals have search-forms that will help you find what you are looking for.

Web sites

There are some sites such as the *Voice of the Shuttle* (VoS) which attempt to structure as much information as possible into manageable categories: this one has over 70 pages of links to humanities and humanities-related resources on the Internet. Its goal has been to provide an organized and annotated guide to online resources that reflects the kinds of disciplinary boundaries in the humanities, and also reflects new interdisciplinary constellations involving interaction with the sciences and social sciences. VoS catalogues both primary, secondary and theoretical resources, and is aimed at people seeking an academically respectable approach to the humanities.

There are two things to say about this site. First, it is unusually permanent: it has existed continuously since March 1995 (when it became open to global Web access, and not just to students and staff of the humanities at the University of California at Santa Barbara). Most Web sites come and go fairly quickly. Second, *Voice of the Shuttle* remained at the same address on the Humanitas server from its origin until October, 1999: normally, such addresses also change regularly. Nevertheless, when we attempted to follow a link from *Modern Fiction Studies* to VoS, it had changed from <http://humanitas.ucsb.edu/humanitas_home. html> to <http://vos.ucsb.edu/>. This did not prevent us from successfully accessing the site, but it does show that the information on the Web is in constant evolution. If you find that an old address doesn't work and that there is no automatic link to the new one, type in the name of the site (in this case, Voice of the Shuttle) into your search engine and you will probably be able to track down its new whereabouts.

Keep in mind our advice about evaluating Web sites: review the competence or the person responsible for uploading the materials, and try quickly to assess their relevance and currency.

Listservs (e-mail discussions groups)

E-mail (electronic mail) is a program that allows individuals with computers connected to the Internet to post, receive, store, and manage correspondence electronically. Most systems (such as Eudora – named after the American writer Eudora Welty) allow you to view messages without opening them, to print and save them, copy and paste from one program to another (from Eudora to WordPerfect, or from WordPerfect to Eudora), and to edit or quote them in replying. We can also attach files in Word for Windows and WordPerfect, and include links to e-mail addresses and Web pages that will open automatically when the user clicks on them. The e-mail systems used by the authors of this book have sound features that alert us to incoming messages: a degree of privacy is also possible because each of us has his own password, and we can create additional passwords so that specific messages cannot be read.

Technically speaking, a 'listserv' is a type of software which permits e-mail messages sent to a designated address to be distributed automatically to a group of people who subscribe to a list. However, 'listserv' is now used more or less interchangeably with the 'mailing list' (or just 'list') itself, rather than the program that enables it to happen. The obvious advantage of a specialist discussion group is that you can get interested participants to respond to your ideas, and to make suggestions. Such a group will often include members who are experts in their field. But like everything else on the Internet, the quality and reliability vary (not just from group to group, but from one topic of discussion to another). To take Emily Dickinson, again, there are two major listservs for her: the first of these is called DICKNSON. (In order to join, you send a message to <listserv@listserv.uta.edu>, and write <subscribe dicknson> (leave out the second 'i' of her name). This is a 'moderated list', which means that all messages go to the editor first, where they are screened before being posted to everyone on the list. The moderator (rightly) wants to filter out *spam* (useless messages), *junk* (commercial messages), or *flames* (personal attacks on other readers). Another list is EMWEB at Brigham Young University (to subscribe, you send an e-mail to <majordomo@lal.cs.byu.edu>, with the message <subscribe emweb>). Its editors inform us that the list was created for discussion of the lexical play of words in Dickinson's poems, as a resource for the *Emily Dickinson Lexicon* to be published by the Greenwood Publishing Group.

Both of these are serious, scholarly fora for the discussion of Dickinson's poems. (Note that both have the abbreviation <edu> – indicating an educational organization, an early indicator of quality.) Both are good places to join if you are writing about Emily Dickinson: not only can you discuss ideas (we give you some pointers about how to go about doing this below), but you can also access archive discussions, and find out what people have been saying in the recent past about poems and issues related to Dickinson. Be aware, however: even though many of the people who take part in these discussions are experienced and respected scholars or critics, the information that they supply does not always come with the standard scholarly apparatus that enables us to check what they say for accuracy. There are very few footnotes or references that support the argument, in other words. Nor should it necessarily be otherwise: e-mail messages are meant to be informal. But the point is that e-mail messages often display poor critical practice. They can feature apparently authoritative and unqualified statements which are stated as fact but which may be highly contentious. In short, maintain your critical guard when reading e-mails.

As we said, e-mail discussions are useful because you ask questions and get quick, sometimes immediate, directions from experts in the field (many of whom subscribe to both groups). But both have their fair share of dross, and the fact that a message goes through a moderator does not guarantee its quality. In the past, for instance, there have been very lively discussions about the hair-colour of Dickinson's dog, Carlo. Knowing that Dickinson had a dog and that she named it (probably) after a dog in *Jane Eyre* is potentially useful information: it shows that she read and enjoyed nineteenth-century English women writers, and brings up the possibility of a comparative study. What difference the hair of the dog makes, we are not so sure about. Other, regular, discussions include the identity and gender of Dickinson's secret lover, or whether she had one, and there have been outraged postings about Dickinson's brother's mistress (some scholars refuse to engage in discussions that mention her name, for instance). Again, knowing that Austin (Dickinson's brother) had a mistress (Mabel Loomis Todd), and that she edited many of Dickinson's poems after Emily's death, while Susan (Austin's wife, and a close friend of Emily's) also worked separately on another posthumous edition, is instructive, and explains in part why Dickinson's manuscripts are housed in two different institutions (Amherst College and Harvard University). It further gives an interesting human twist to matters of publishing history. The morality of the affair would not seem especially relevant, however.

In short, e-mail discussion groups are fairly open and informal, and this means that they are reasonably unintimidating, that they welcome contributions from new members – but perhaps also that people feel free to discuss anything and everything, which is entertaining but not necessarily educational.

There are certain procedures that it makes sense to follow if you join such a group. For instance, include a brief paragraph or a couple of lines about yourself, and which course or writer you are studying. If you want help with an assignment, make this clear right away (academics are nervous about giving information that may be used uncited in other contexts). You should probably not submit an independent query until after you have checked the traditional print resources in the library, and consulted bibliographies and other materials online. In other words, don't antagonize others by asking immediately what books there are about (for example) Dickinson: the classic response will be that someone will tell you to try finding a library. Often, the best approach is simply to cite a problem (either a question or an interpretive dilemma of some kind) and then offer your angle on this – at least, a few ideas of your own. Alternatively, you might want to answer a statement made by someone else in the group: in such a case, make sure you quote from the message to which you are replying, or otherwise contextualize your remarks ('In a message dated 25 November 2001, John Doe suggested that . . .'). You will find that contributors will respond much more positively and quickly if you voice an opinion. Always indicate your sources clearly if you use anything from an e-mail: you may not get credit for the idea (unless you had it to begin with, and are simply quoting for support), but you will certainly get recognition for your initiative. As long as the mailing list you belong to is relevant (in terms of nationality, time period, subject, genre or author), you should include it in the bibliography, even if you don't find anything immediately pertinent: e-mails are legitimate secondary sources, after all.

In addition, take the time to choose what listserv, if any, you want to belong to. Mailing lists tend to have narrow areas of focus: you are not likely to get much joy about Dickinson if you join Ishmail (the Herman Melville discussion group). In order to find a listserv, you will first have to initiate a search on the World Wide Web. There are also search engines that specialize in Internet discussion and information lists: one of the most enduring is <http://tile.net/lists/>, which has catalogues of such groups, but also a search box where you can enter a topic (post-modernism, American studies) and hopefully find something appropriate.

Finally, you will note from the addresses we supplied above that one begins with <listserv> and another <majordomo>. These are two out of the main three (the other one being <listproc>) types of mailing list programs. Each has its own procedure for subscription.

- With a group like American Literature (or AMLIT), the convention is to mail <listproc@lists.missouri.edu>, leave the subject line open, and write <subscribe AMLIT-L jane doe> in the body of the text (that is, in the blank space where you normally write messages).

- For the Native American discussion group, send a message to <majordomo@ listserv.prodigy.com>, leave the subject line open and, and write <subscribe native-american>.

- For the African-American Women's literature list, write to <listserv@ cmuvm.csv.cmich.edu>, leave the subject line open and write <subscribe AAWOMLIT jane doe>.

- To unsubscribe, follow the same procedure and write <unsubscribe> instead of <subscribe>.

These addresses are accurate at the time of writing, but we list them simply to show that different groups and programs have different procedures for membership.

Newsgroups

A newsgroup is like an e-mail discussion group: people subscribe because they share an interest in a specific topic, and want to exchange information with others. Such discussions can be a useful way of initiating or expanding research projects. Like discussion groups, they are not in 'real-time' (where you write and someone answers immediately) but they use different software and they tend to be more topical than listservs. For this reason you are more likely to find recent, minority-interest, authors analyzed on newsgroups than on e-mail discussion groups. And you do not have to become a member to take part. The easiest way to locate something related to your topic of interest is to go to a specialist search engine like TileNet (<http://www.tile.net>) or Liszt's Usenet Newsgroups Directory (<http://www.liszt.com/>). The latter catalogues some 30,000 Usenet

Newsgroups, 80,000 Mailing Lists, and 25,000 IRC (Internet Relay Chat) Channels. Both organize discussion groups according to categories (humanities) and topic (literature), but also have their own search engine. At DejaNews, (<http://www.deja.com/usenet>), you can browse the most recent discussions and decide if the level and topic are sufficiently relevant for you to join. Alternatively, you can use the built-in newsreading interfaces carried by Netscape Navigator and Communicator, or Microsoft Internet Explorer, on the condition that your ISP (Internet Service Provider) gives access to that group.

Much of the advice we offered for e-mail discussion groups applies to newsgroups. If you post a message, don't ask for information that you can find in a library catalogue or bibliography. Try instead to formulate a topic or a problem, and then offer your own take on this. You can finish the letter by adding that you are working on a class paper, and that you would be grateful for assistance.

But one of the big differences between listservs and newsgroups is that the former 'owns' a space, so that it can archive materials, while most newsgroups have a limited amount of storage space. Thus, if you read something useful, try saving it to disk and documenting your source, for new postings generally replace older ones fairly quickly.

REVISING AND EDITING ELECTRONICALLY

Writing an essay, delivering a paper, preparing a class presentation – these are all aspects of the research process that are covered more fully in Section 1. But a note of warning concerning using a PC to help you do these things belongs in the present section.

It is so easy to edit on a computer screen that there is a temptation to write straight on to screen without planning at all. After all, 'I can always tidy it up later'. We are not against brainstorming sessions where you just list all the ideas you have as they come to you, either on screen or on a piece of paper – in fact we think that they are an excellent way to start. But before you actually start to write an essay, a presentation or a term paper we very strongly advise you to try to *plan out the structure of your argument*. Otherwise you risk getting a rambling and confusing mish-mash of ideas that will infuriate your teacher.

If you do brainstorm onscreen, it is a good idea to disable the automatic spell-check and grammar-check on your machine (these functions highlight words which are misspelled, and sometimes phrases that are ungrammatical or over-long: in WordPerfect you will find them under Tools and then Proof-read). The spell-check can be very distracting. Try not to correct or even evaluate what you have written in any form as you proceed: you should simply try to get your ideas down for as long as it takes, typing for 5 to 10 minutes at a stretch if necessary. Use the Enter key to distinguish between sequences of thought or ideas, rather than attempting to create a link between them. Resist at all costs the instinct to correct what you have written until you have got all your major ideas written down.

When the time does come for revising what you have written, it is a good idea to take into account the following:

■ Consider whether or not you want to use the same file during revision, or if you want to create different drafts (WoolfEssayOne, WoolfEssayTwo). The latter approach can be useful if you decide to cut things at some stage: you can always return later, and cut-and-paste from EssayOne to EssayTwo if you change your mind. Alternatively, create a section at the end of your document where you can paste excisions, and then review their pertinence later.

■ Highlight, or mark in bold or capitals or with extended question marks, passages of writing that may need reworking or tidying.

■ Highlight in bold or capitals sources that remain to be documented, or places that require a footnote.

■ Make sure that you do a spell check before submitting.

■ Decide what you think of the grammar-check facility in your word-processing software (we have our doubts – see Section 1 – but you may find it a useful tool).

■ Keep in mind that you can cut and paste to enhance coherence.

■ If you are making an oral presentation, think about font sizes and types. In other words, make sure that what you write is physically easy to read (use a large font), and vary the application of bold, italics and underlining in places where you want to emphasize an argument or allow for some improvisation (it creates a varied and interesting paper if you can leave the written script now and then and extemporize, however briefly).

■ Again, in the event of an oral presentation, consider printing handouts with quotations written down and sources cited: alternatively, or additionally, use a transparency that includes the main points of your argument, arranged in the same order as your paper.

■ Always print out a copy for proof-reading. Keep in mind that your spell-checker may miss some typing errors (from for form, for instance). Reading a print copy lets you see how well the essay reads (and if you are giving a presentation, make sure you read it aloud beforehand to see if the sentences are the right length: too long, and you will be out of breath).

DOCUMENTING ELECTRONIC MEDIA

As we have said repeatedly, there are two main categories of electronic media: physical materials such as CD-ROMs and diskettes, and online sources, such as academic and commercial databases, e-mail discussion groups and network sites. Most commercial CD-ROMs are updated regularly, normally at least once a year, while web sites are revised more often: the MLA Bibliography, for instance, changes 10 times a year. Since the physical media are changed annually, it is generally sufficient to supply a year when you quote from, or refer to, them in your footnotes. But since the online entities change much less predictably, often many times in a single year, it is important that you give the exact date when (or period during which) you accessed them in addition to their year of publication. And since online materials have specially formatted addresses (URLs), indicating which protocol (or means of transferring data), server network, domain, directory, file path and code the file is written in, then as much of this information has to be included as possible in order for other readers to be able to access and/or to verify your source (some of it may not be available, in which case you should report this).

You should treat the information given below as a supplement to the information on referencing sources given in Section 1, p. 87. Remember, however, that conventions for referencing electronic sources are less fixed than are those for referencing printed sources, so that you should check in the standard guidelines (see below) for the most up-to-date conventions.

The four most common ways of documenting electronic sources are: those which follow the guidelines of the MLA; the Chicago Manual of Style (which is slightly more complicated because it has two sets of guidelines); the *MHRA Style Book* (from the Modern Humanities Research Association); and the APA (American Psychological Association). You can find instructions and practical examples for each on the Web – for example, at the MLA's homepage <http://www.mla.org/>: click on the MLA Style link, and if the address is no longer current, perform a search for the Modern Language Association, the MLA Style, or citations of electronic sources. Other useful sites are Janice Walker's 'The English Pages Citation Guide' (at <http://www.awl.com/englishpages/ citation_walker.htm>) and James D. Lester's 'Citing Cyberspace: A Quick-Reference Guide to Citing Electronic Sources in MLA and APA Styles' (at <http://www.awl.com/englishpages/cyber.htm>). Again, keep in mind that online information is continually updated, not always with notification to users. If you find that the addresses here are no longer current, then type in key words from the titles we have given (or do the category searches we have suggested) and you will find the same information, or something similar to it. In addition, your college or university library will certainly have several copies of the *MHRA Style Book* or *The MLA Handbook for Writers of Research Papers* (try to get the most recent edition). The important thing, once you have decided on a style, is to follow it consistently, and to provide as much information as possible (electronic sources do not always provide author names, for instance, or the date when the information was put online: then you have to supply the date of the last revision, when applicable).

A common problem with documents on the Web is that they generally lack fixed page numbers: if you document such a source, you should leave out numbers from your parenthetical references. Avoid trying to get around this by supplying the page numbers of a printout, because the pagination will differ depending on the font size, paper size (US standard paper size is different from

European A4), print settings and word-processing program. However, if your source includes fixed page numbers, paragraph numbering or section numbering, cite the relevant details using the appropriate abbreviation before the numbers.

The basic convention for citing electronic documents is that the author's name (if known) is given first, in inverted form (last name first); if there is more than one author, you invert only the first author's name, and then list the others in alphabetical order; the full title of the work in quotation marks; the title of the complete work, if applicable, in italics; the document date, if known and if different from the date accessed; the full http address; and the date of visit. And use either underlining or italics (they are equivalent), but be consistent.

Here are some examples of information we think you might find on the Internet. We supply an abstract statement of documentation principles, followed by one or two examples. The MLA guidelines from the (fifth edition) of *The MLA Handbook for Writers of Research Papers* have been consulted in drawing up these guidelines, but we have adapted them to conform to standard British conventions such as those given in the MHRA Guide, and so that they conform with the conventions followed in Section 1, pp. 87–8. Note in particular that in accordance with the MLA convention commas and full stops should be placed *inside* quotation marks in these examples, but in accordance with standard British practice we have placed them *outside*.

Abstract Give the name of the author, surname first; the title of the article in quotation marks; the title of the original place of publication, underlined or in italics, with place of publication, publisher, volume, issue number and (in parentheses) year (where applicable); followed by pagination (or n.p. for no pagination available); the date of access; the protocol and address in angled brackets.

> Cole, Phyllis, 'The Nineteenth-Century Women's Rights Movement and the Canonization of Margaret Fuller', *Emerson Society Quarterly* 44: 1 and 2 (1998), n.p. Abstract, 29 Sep. 2000.
> <http://www.wsu.edu:8080/~english/ESQCole.html>.

Archive Give the title of the archive, underlined or in italics; the name of the editor(s); the place of the server or host and the year of first access or of latest revision (if available); the date of access, and the protocol and address enclosed in angled brackets.

> *Dickinson Electronic Archives*, ed. Martha Nell Smith and Ellen Louise Hart, University of Virginia (1992), 28 Sep. 2000.
> <http:jefferson.village.virginia.edu/dickinson>.

Article from a scholarly journal online Give the author's name, surname first; the title of the article in quotation marks; the title of the journal, underlined or in italics, with volume, issue number and (in parentheses) year; followed by pagination (or n.p. for no pagination available); the date of access; the protocol and address in angled brackets.

> Franklin, R.W., 'Emily Dickinson to Abiah Root: Ten Reconstructed Letters', *The Emily Dickinson Journal* IV.1 (1995), 1–43, 29 Sep. 2000. <http://www.colorado.edu/EDIS/journal/articles/IV.1.Franklin.html>.

CD-ROM editions List the name of the author or authors, if known; the title of the publication underlined or in italics, together with any version or edition numbers; the medium of publication (CD-ROM); the name of the distributor, with the year. Note that the date of access is not included for electronic publications on fixed media such as CD-ROMs.

> Kiernan, Kevin S., *The Electronic Beowulf*, CD-ROM (The British Library and The University of Michigan Press: 2000).

Database online List the name of the author or authors (if known and applicable); the title of the publication underlined or in italics, together with any version or edition numbers; the name of the distributor; the date of access; the protocol and address in angled brackets.

> *Guide to African-American Documentary Resources in North Carolina.*, ed. Timothy D. Pyatt (University of Virginia Press: 1996), 30 Sep. 2000. <http://www.upress.virginia.edu/epub/pyatt/index.html>.

Dictionary online List the title of the publication underlined or in italics, together with any version or edition numbers; the name of the distributor, with the year; the date of access, and the protocol and address in angled brackets.

> *Merriam-Webster's Collegiate Dictionary, Tenth edition*, Merriam-Webster Inc., 2000, 30 Sep. 2000. <http://www.m-w.com/cgi-bin/dictionary>.

Editions online List the name of the author, inverted; the title of the publication underlined or in italics; the year of first publication; the name of the electronic server, with the year; the date of access, and the protocol and address in angled brackets.

> Caird, Mona, *The Daughters of Danaus*, (1894) (Bloomington: Indiana University, 1998), 30 Sep. 2000. <http://www.indiana.edu/~letrs/vwwp/caird/daughters.html>.

E-mail messages Give the name of the author, surname first; the subject line of the message in quotation marks; the date of the message if it is different from the date accessed; the address (omit for personal e-mail, and replace with 'E-mail to [name of recipient or] the author'); and the date of access.

> Miller, Cristanne, 'RE: FW: yes, this is it', e-mail to the author, 28 Sep. 2000.

Encyclopaedia online List the title of the complete publication underlined or in italics; any version or edition numbers with year of publication (if applicable); the name of the publisher; the date of access; and the protocol and address, in angled brackets.

> *Encyclopaedia Britannica Online*, Britannica.com, Inc., 1999–2000, 30 Sep. 2000. <http://www.britannica.com>.

Encyclopaedia entry online List the author's name, if available; the title of the article in quotation marks, if applicable; the title of the complete publication in italics, with any version or edition numbers; the place of publication (if available), the name of the publisher and the year of publication; the date of access; and the protocol and address in angled brackets.

> 'Bishop, Elizabeth', *Encyclopaedia Britannica Online*, Britannica.com, Inc., 1991–2000, 30 Sep. 2000.
> <http://www.britannica.com/bcom/eb/article/
> 9/0,5716,15609+1+15410,00.html?kw=bishop%20elizabeth>.

FTP (File Transfer Protocol) files List the author's name (if known); the full title of the paper in quotation marks; the document date if known and if different from the date accessed; the date of access (if applicable); the protocol and address in angled brackets.

> Bruckman, Amy, 'Approaches to Managing Deviant Behavior in Virtual Communities', Apr. 1994, 30 Sep. 2000.
> <ftp://ftp.media.mit.edu/pub/asb/papers/deviance-chi94.txt>.

Gopher files (and telnet) List the author's name (if available); the title of the paper in quotation marks; any print publication information, including the date of publication if known and if different from the date accessed; the date of access (if applicable); the protocol and address, in angled brackets.

> 'A Guide to the Alice M. Jordan Collection in the Boston Public Library', Boston Public Library, 1998, 30 Sep. 2000.
> <gopher://bpl.org/00gopher_root:%5Bspec_coll%5Dabout_jordan.doc>.

Listserv, and Newsgroup citations Give the author's surname and first name (or alias, if known); the subject line from the posting in quotation marks; the date of the message if different from the date accessed; the name of the listserv or newsgroup, underlined or in italics; the date of access (if applicable); the address of the listserv or newslist in angled brackets.

> Scott, Megan, 'Re: Visiting Emily (fwd)', *Dicknson*, 29 Sep. 2000.
> <DICKNSON@LISTSERV.UTA.EDU>.

Online article or chapter List the author's name, if available; the title of the article in quotation marks, if applicable; the title of the complete publication, underlined or in italics, with any version or edition numbers; the date of access; and the protocol and address in angled brackets.

Reuben, Paul P., 'Chapter 9: Harlem Renaissance – Zora Neale Hurston', *PAL: Perspectives in American Literature – A Research and Reference Guide*, 30 Sep. 2000. <http://www.csustan.edu/english/reuben/pal/chap9/hurston.html>.

Review List the author's name, if available; the title of the article in quotation marks; the title of the complete publication, underlined or in italics, with volume and issue numbers, and (in parentheses) the year; the pagination (if available); the date of access; and the protocol and address in angled brackets.

Iyer, Pico, 'Foreign Affair: Review of *When We Were Orphans* by Kazuo Ishiguro', *New York Review of Books* XLVII: 15 (2000), n.p., 29 Sep. 2000. <http://www.nybooks.com/nyrev/WWWfeatdisplay.cgi?20001005004R>.

Serialized article List the author's name, if available; the title of the article in quotation marks; the title of the complete publication, underlined or in italics, with volume and issue numbers, and (in parentheses) the year; pagination; the dates of other articles in the series (if applicable and available); pagination; the date of access; and the protocol and address in angled brackets.

Scarry, Elaine, 'The Fall of EgyptAir 990', *New York Review of Books* XLVII: 15 (2000), n.p. Second part of the article, 'Swissair 111, TWA 800, and Electromagnetic Interference', begun 21 Sep. 2000. 29 Sep. 2000. <http://www.nybooks.com/nyrev/WWWfeatdisplay.cgi?20001005049F>.

Synchronous Communications (MOOs, MUDs, IRC, etc.) Give the name or alias of the speaker(s); the title of the event (if applicable) or type of communication (i.e., 'personal interview'), the name of the forum; the date of access; and the MOO (or MUD, etc.) address of the site, in angled brackets.

Patuto, Jeremy, Simon Fennel, and James Goss, 'The Mytilene Debate', 9 May 1996. MiamiMOO. 28 Mar.1998. <http://moo.cas.muohio.edu/cgi-bin/moo?look+4085>.

SAFETY MEASURES

Finally, we would like to take this opportunity to remind readers of the importance of learning and maintaining good computer routines. Otherwise, you could find yourself in the same situation as the author of a pitiable note fixed to the front door of a college library in Massachusetts: on it, he had given his name and asked that the individual who stole his laptop please return the diskette that was inside in it to his address, since it contained the only copy he had of the PhD thesis he was in the process of preparing for submission. You should get into the habit of making regular back-ups of whatever it is you happen to be working on. (In WordPerfect and Word for Windows, you can programme your machine to save every three or four minutes, so that if there is an electrical surge, a power cut or any other problem, you will have lost comparatively little work.) At the end of the day, make sure that you copy to both the hard disk and to a diskette: if you don't own your own machine, make two back-up copies to separate diskettes, and keep these in different places. You should not keep diskettes with a laptop, for instance: if the laptop is stolen, the diskette will be lost too. (In the case of this book, each of the authors had copies on a computer hard-drive, a site on the university server, a laptop, and a diskette.) Remember the adage: there are two sorts of hard-disk; those that have failed, and those that will fail some day.

If you download materials often, or if you are collaborating on a project where several people exchange diskettes or attached files (through e-mail), you should also run an anti-virus program regularly – and make sure that it is regularly updated. A good rule is to run your anti-virus program every time you receive attached files by e-mail, and *before* you open such files. (Most anti-virus programs can be asked to target just the folder that contains attached files.)

Section 3

Theories and approaches

WHY THEORY?

Thirty years ago, few if any Literary Studies degrees contained any courses with the word 'theory' in their titles. A student taking an English degree in Britain might well face courses entitled 'Practical Criticism', or 'The History of Criticism' at some stage during his or her studies, but these would contain relatively little of what now fills courses in (literary) theory. Practical criticism courses would train students in the close READING and ANALYSIS of literary WORKS or extracts, while the History of Criticism would generally survey the most important literary critics from the early modern period onwards: Sidney, Dryden, Johnson, Wordsworth, Arnold – ending with a short look at a number of twentieth-century critics: I.A. RICHARDS, T.S. ELIOT, and perhaps F.R. LEAVIS, and in some cases a backward look to Aristotle.

But in the course of the final three or so decades of the twentieth century most Literary Studies degrees – and English degrees in particular – have come to involve much more concern with what is now generally termed literary theory. What is new about the body of knowledge studied in such courses is that: (i) much of it is far more abstract and philosophical than the material that would have been studied in 'History of Criticism' courses, often including elements that in a previous generation would have been included, if at all, as part of the study of Aesthetics in a Philosophy degree; (ii) much of it involves theorists belonging to traditions unconnected with Anglo-American Literary Studies (note how many of the theorists in Section 4 wrote in languages other than English); (iii) many of the theories considered have a global scope and, at least in their initial phases of development, had little or nothing to do with literature (MARXIST theory, PSYCHO-ANALYTIC theory, QUEER THEORY, for example).

This change in the nature and scope of Literary Studies degrees has its positive and negative elements. On the one hand, Literary Studies has become less parochial and self-enclosed, and is now open to traditions of debate and enquiry that previously were deemed to be foreign to it. It has become a more self-conscious discipline, more concerned to question what it does, and to recognize that there are many different ways of studying literature, not all of which are compatible with one another. On the other hand, there is certainly a danger that 'theory' can become even more self-enclosed and self-justifying than Literary

Studies was 30 years ago, living a life of its own that influences, and is influenced by, the actual reading and criticizing of literary works, only on rare occasions.

Like it or not, literary theory will form a significant part of the syllabus that students on English and other degree courses involved with the study of literature will face in the foreseeable future. For us there are two main reasons why Literary Studies degrees are the better for containing courses on literary theory. These have been formulated before, but it is worth restating them.

Molière's Monsieur Jourdain

In Molière's play *Le bourgeois gentilhomme*, Monsieur Jourdain – the 'bourgeois gentleman' of the title – discovers in conversation with the *Maître de philosophie* that, without knowing it, he has been speaking prose for 40 years. In like manner, one of the things that students who follow courses in literary theory typically discover is that they have been confronting, and resolving, literary-theoretical problems for many years without necessarily being aware of the fact. Every time you write an essay, you make decisions about issues which have exercised the minds of theorists, and about which they have probably clashed swords. Your decisions will emerge from a set of assumptions which together constitute a theoretical position. In our opinion, it is better to be conscious of the nature of those assumptions and that position. This is because once one is so conscious, one can modify one's theoretical position in the light of one's critical practice, and vice versa. Unconscious assumptions are often hard to modify.

Reinventing the wheel

That body of knowledge that we know as 'literary theory' contains the fruits of generations (even millennia) of engagement with certain recurrent problems which the reading and interpretation of literary works throws up. It makes no better sense for students of literature to start from scratch by discovering these problems and engaging with them alone than it does for each new generation of students of physics to reinvent Einstein's theory of relativity. This is not to say that a student of literature must accept a set of rules laid down by a number of theorists, but merely that he or she ought to be aware of the issues that have been argued about in the history of the discipline.

We believe that what the study of literary theory does is to make students *aware* of the theoretical issues which they will face and resolve one way or another whether or not they study theory. In our view it is preferable to make informed decisions that rely *both* on more practical skills developed through the reading and study of literary works and *also* on the theoretical and more abstract understanding that the study of literary theory provides. Indeed, there should be a creative interaction between such practical skills and experience on the one hand, and that more abstract understanding of theoretical issues that comes with the study of literary theory, on the other. Your skills as a reader and critic will, we believe, be enhanced by a sound knowledge of literary theory.

Most of this section of the book will consist of introductory accounts of different theories and critical schools, gathered into what we hope are convenient groupings. But students need to be aware that these different theories typically carry with them different aims, assumptions, objects of study, methods, and forms of evidence. We are, accordingly, prefacing our actual presentation of the theories themselves with some introductory comments relating to the different types of theory you will encounter in the following pages. Theories differ not just because they disagree on how to achieve a common goal, but also because they may have quite different goals. We would like to start this section by asking you to think a little about the varied types of goal that a theory may set itself.

THE THEORETICAL 'OBJECT'

'Object' is in inverted commas because some of the possible objects of study with which theorists are concerned are better described as processes or relationships. What we mean by the word is, however, that body of material at which the theories in question are directed. At one time – for the two or three decades after the Second World War when the ideas of the NEW CRITICS were dominant – it would have been assumed that the 'body of material' in question consisted of a set of literary works. But many critics and theorists have disagreed with the New Critics, and have argued that to study a literary work we need to study more than 'the work itself'.

Let us list – very schematically – some of the main elements in this 'more'.

- The writer (including his/her social and personal background, upbringing, beliefs, etc.)
- The process of composition (conscious aims, generic constraints, 'inspiration')
- The literary apparatus (publishing houses, censorship, possible READERS/ audience)
- The single literary TEXT or WORK
- A writer's total literary production
- A GENRE
- A particular response to a work
- How readers in general have responded to a work – with changes over time
- An INTERPRETATION of a work – or historical changes in how a work is interpreted
- The IDEOLOGY underlying a work
- The existence, and the quality, of the literary CANON or canons
- The function played by literature in a particular society
- The writer's GENDER; how gender is used in a work; gender variations in the way the work is read
- Political and power relationships in the world of the writer or reader

This is only a partial list, but even as it stands we can recognize that different theories will entail a greater or lesser concern with some of the different items listed. Not surprisingly, READER-RESPONSE critics will be interested either in a particular response to a work, or to the responses of readers in general. FEMINIST critics are likely to focus in on the issue of GENDER. POSTCOLONIALIST critics will inevitably be concerned with the effect of unequal power relationships on the way in which a writer experiences the world or a reader experiences a text. One important implication of such diversity is that alternative theories may or may not be mutually exclusive. However, perhaps the main point to be made is that if we take the totality of elements and relationships that are involved in the writing and READING of literary WORKS, few theories devote an equal amount of attention to all of them.

What you should also be aware of, is that not all theories have as their primary concern the issue of how to read, interpret or ANALYZE individual literary works, so that for example it makes rather better sense to talk of a NARRATOLOGICAL analysis of a novel than it does to talk of a reader-response analysis of a novel. This is because reader-response critics are by definition interested not so much in *analyses of texts or works* in themselves, but in the study of *responses to texts or works*. This is not to say that there is no overlap between these two activities: if you isolate significant aspects of a writer's use of – say – FREE INDIRECT DISCOURSE, then you may learn something about how readers are likely to respond to the text in which this technique is used. But the overlapping is only partial.

TYPES OF THEORY

Let us make use some simple distinctions to illustrate the different sorts of aims that theorists may have.

Descriptive or prescriptive?

First, a theory can either be *descriptive* or *prescriptive*. In other words, it may either attempt to describe how things *are* (how a literary work is read, how generic constraints function, how particular techniques work), or how they *should be* (this way of reading or interpreting rather than that, this way of presenting women rather than that, this underlying set of ideological assumptions rather than that). To give examples, we can say that STRUCTURALISM and the theories that it informs (such as SEMIOTICS and narratology) tend to be descriptive rather than prescriptive, whereas theories such as MARXISM and feminism have a strong prescriptive impetus. Both Marxism and feminism typically involve the making of moral judgements, while structuralists and semioticians are interested not in how things can be changed for the better, but in how best to describe things as they are. No structuralist has ever claimed that structuralist theory can build a better world, merely that it can enable us to describe and analyze this world more accurately.

This is not to argue that narratologists never make value judgements and feminists are incapable of disinterested description. But it is to argue that such activities are subsidiary and secondary in each case, and that these two theoretical positions represent fundamentally different sets of assumptions. In brief: narratology and feminist theory not only have dissimilar aims, they are essentially different *sorts* of theory.

Literature-specific?

A second way of distinguishing between different sorts of theory is by asking whether or not a theory is literature-specific. Thus we can say that the NEW CRITICISM was developed by literary critics and was originally intended to be applied only to works of literature, although New Critical assumptions and methods did subsequently inform other practices. With Marxist theory we are clearly dealing with a theory that develops largely (although not completely) independently from theorizing about literature, one which develops certain all-embracing ideas about society, CULTURE and history which are then *applied to* literature through adaptations and refinements. Narratologists are interested not just in literary works, but in both ORAL and written NARRATIVES, and both fictional and non-fictional ones.

A neat way of labelling this distinction is to distinguish between 'top-down' and 'bottom-up' theories. Top-down theories generally have a wide and comprehensive scope, the detailed implications of which are then applied to particular instances, whereas bottom-up theories are constructed on the basis of the resolving of problems at a lower or practical level. Not surprisingly, literature-specific theories such as the New Criticism tend to be bottom-up, whereas more all-embracing theories such as Marxism or feminism tend to be top-down. (Which is not to say that grappling with practical problems has not contributed to the earlier development of both Marxism and feminism: a single theory may start as bottom-up and then be developed as top-down.)

As a general tendency we can say that during the second half of the twentieth century, Literary Studies moved to endorse more and more top-down theories and to exhibit more reservations about exclusively bottom-up ones. Why this should be is not easy to establish. In part it may be because newer disciplines tend to be more protective regarding their autonomy and thus more inward-looking than older ones, but it is doubtless also connected to more complex factors concerning the way in which the humanities have developed in the higher-education systems of developed countries.

Butcher or biologist?

Here is another way of thinking about some of these issues. Old-fashioned butchers' shops very often used to have on their walls schematic sideways-profile pictures of bulls, divided up into the common joints or cuts in which meat was conventionally sold. If you compare such a diagram with an illustration of a bull taken from a biology textbook, you will notice that the units into which the animal is divided are quite different. This is because while the biologist is attempting to understand the bull's structure as it works for the bull, the butcher is attempting to compartmentalize the bull in a way that reflects the interests not of the bull but of the human meat-eater. We can suggest that while the biologist looks for *intrinsic* elements in the animal, the butcher imposes *extrinsic* categories on it – something we realize when we travel to a different country and discover that animals are divided in a quite different manner for sale to the non-vegetarian public.

In one sense, we can say that different literary theories incline either to the logic of the biologist or the butcher. A strong critical tradition that stretches back centuries and that is represented theoretically by the Anglo-American New Critics involved the search for elements believed to be not only *in* the literary work, but fundamental to its value. When the New Critics isolated tensions, paradoxes, the productive interplay between FORM and content, they did not think of themselves as imposing their ideas on the work, but as discovering what was actually there, and what enabled the work to function for readers. But other theorists, without necessarily admitting that they are engaged in the task of butchering the literary work, certainly concede that the categories with which they work are not so much discovered in the work, but are, rather, taken to the work so as to enable certain insights – responses, INTERPRETATIONS – that would not exist without them.

Having made this distinction, we need to urge caution. When dealing with literary works the distinction between the intrinsic and the extrinsic has the appeal of neatness, but since the days of the New Critics many commentators have pointed out that although it enables useful working distinctions it crudifies the complexities of the writing and reading processes. We need to recognize that the reading of literary works is an *interactive* process. What happens when we respond to a work is not just the result of the transference of something 'in' the work 'into' us. Even in the case of the New Critics, the expectations they brought to literary works had an effect upon what they found 'in' them.

And even with our butcher and biologist, the difference is not absolute. The butcher has to pay some attention to the structure of the animal when cutting it up; the biologist follows certain preconceptions and needs when deciding how to distinguish the working parts of the bull. Even so: when dealing with a new theory, or with the work of a given critic, it often helps to ask oneself: 'butcher or biologist?'. Not that one is better than another, merely that these very crude distinctions represent different sorts of theoretical or critical practice.

School or theory?

A third distinction to bear in mind is that between 'theoretical school' and 'theory'. A theoretical school (RUSSIAN FORMALISM, for instance) requires the development of a coherent set of ideas by a group of individuals who work together, commenting upon one another's ideas and generally presenting something of a united front in public declarations or polemics. The Russian Formalists, like the members of the PRAGUE SCHOOL, enjoyed this sort of mutually supportive contact. One of the implications of such a collaborative endeavour is that once this collectivity is lost, the name can no longer be applied to further individuals even if they agree with everything that was publically asserted by the school. Whatever you now believe and argue in favour of, it would be hard for you to become a Russian Formalist. A theory, in contrast, may enjoy an existence that extends beyond the life-span of any individual or group of individuals. You can claim to be a Marxist critic even if you advance ideas and theoretical formulations that Marx never assented to, so long as you can convincingly argue that your own position represents a logical development of ideas and theoretical formulations that were acceded to by Marx.

Chosen or thrust-upon?

Like greatness, the titles of some theoretical schools are achieved: they are mutually agreed upon by their members. In the case of other such schools, titles have been thrust upon their unwilling recipients. Some of the theories with which we are concerned are ones which have been identified and claimed by those associated with them. The Russian Formalists were content to be known as formalists and thought of themselves as a group (although this may partly have been as a result of having been attacked both as formalists and as a group). But sometimes a theoretical position is imposed retrospectively. Not all of those who are now named as New Critics thought of themselves as New Critics (in fact as the entry for this particular position is concerned will show, hardly any of those now known as New Critics seem to have welcomed the term, and its attribution to some individuals – WILLIAM EMPSON, for example – seems highly questionable).

Another way of putting this point is to suggest that certain theoretical principles may be the result of a conscious and deliberate choice on the part of those concerned, whereas in other cases what we may find is that a critic's work is motivated and directed by principles which are underlying rather than overt, principles of which he or she may be at least partly unaware. Even within, say, FEMINIST criticism, we may be able to distinguish between a critic who is possessed of an instinctive sympathy for the women and an unformulated but keen ability to recognize and to react against the oppression of women, and a critic who calls him- or herself a feminist and is able to define what he or she means by this. It is especially the case in our field of study as against many others that the acute reader or critic may respond to an aspect of a literary work before the theoretical formulation that allows the aspect in question to be categorized has been arrived at. A good close reader of texts may well be able to recognize the significance of a switch into FREE INDIRECT DISCOURSE before she or he has learned how to define that particular narrative technique.

THEORY AND METHOD

Theories typically carry with them implications regarding what we can term critical method. By common consent one of the best examples of this is the way in which the critical assumptions of the New Critics (in a good poem tensions and paradoxes, form and content combine in productive ways to produce a unified whole) involve the endorsement of certain methods (interpretation based on close reading and analysis) along with the rejection of others (speculation about authorial INTENTION, the relating of textual detail to socio-economic factors in the writer's society). By implication, too, the New Critical commitments had strong implications not just for the critic but for the writer, too (to be acceptable, a literary work needed to be a unified whole, with formal–technical elements contributing to overall effect). At an obvious level, to be a reader-response critic is to be committed to (what in general the New Critics were at least formally opposed to) the analysis of actual responses by individual readers to literary works.

Similarly, it would be illogical to criticize someone who was attempting to apply VLADIMIR PROPP's ideas about functions to a NOVEL by Charles Dickens, for failing to reveal those techniques of characterization that allowed for the creation of a set of unique CHARACTERS. And this because Propp's method of analysis requires that the apparently unique should be subsumed into a finite set of pre-existing categories. (At the same time, it would be neither illogical nor inadmissible to argue that because Dickens's novels have traditionally been valued for their presentation of large numbers of unique and idiosyncratic characters, a Proppian analysis would most likely fail to explain everything about Dickens's fiction that readers have valued.)

Other theoretical positions and allegiances have less clear methodological implications. A feminist critic may find that the tools of the New Critics (analytical close reading leading to interpretation of single works) are extremely useful in exploring, say, the difference between two poems on a shared THEME by a male and a female poet. But feminist critics have also take elements from Marxist and STRUCTURALIST theories in building up an armoury of critical methods.

Some theoretical positions require certain methods and prohibit others; some methods of reading, analyzing or interpreting literary works are open to use by critics of very different persuasions. Generally speaking, what is known as *scholarly method* represents a set of commonly accepted standards and conventions which govern academic writing, although even here the adoption of a given theoretical position may well have implications for one's attitude to certain of these standards and conventions. Thus if you write a term paper or a doctoral thesis, you will be expected to present in it references to cited texts in a consistent manner that follows one of the standard scholarly guides, and you will be expected to quote accurately – whether you are a POST-STRUCTURALIST or a reader-response critic!

And, finally, you should remember that some of these issues have other implications for the writing of essays and examination answers. The evidence that you
bring to bear in an essay may be in part determined by the theoretical position
that you adopt. To take one crude example: if a writer comments on his or her
own understanding of a poem ('When I wrote this I was trying to respond to the
Vietnam War, and this really is what the poem is about'), then the force of such
evidence will be diminished if you are arguing from a PSYCHOANALYTIC
perspective that the author is no more able to understand what a poem is about
than a dreamer is able to understand the import of his or her own dreams.

A NOTE ON OUR GROUPINGS

We have warned you that the way in which we have grouped together our schools
and theorists is crude and involves an element of arbitrariness. What we have
tried to do is to gather together those schools and theories which are related to
one another either through direct influence, or because their ideas and principles
have something in common. Within each grouping we have attempted to deal
with individual schools or theories in roughly chronological order.

One of the dangers of such groupings is that they stress certain connections at
the expense of others. Thus reader-response theory is listed as a variety of
HERMENEUTICS because those German theorists who contributed to the development of reader-response theories were heavily influenced by the German
hermeneutical tradition. But many reader-response critics are also significantly
indebted to psychological and psychoanalytical theories. A more significant
problem emerges as a result of separating 'Formalisms' from 'Structuralism and
its Progeny', as this tends to obscure the common debt owed by both the Russian
and Czech formalists, and the structuralists, to the seminal work of FERDINAND
DE SAUSSURE. We feel, however, that it is more useful to direct attention to the
common elements in, first, the main groupings of formalists, and second, those
we have described as structuralists and their progeny. But it is very important that
you bear in mind that connections between groupings may in some cases be as
strong as those between theories or schools within a particular grouping.

Moreover, some of our groupings are tighter than others. Our final group,
which we have (perhaps weakly) entitled 'Isms', gathers together theories that
have a globalizing imperative, a political agenda, and often a polemical style. But
across these common elements there are very significant differences. And of
course a number of 'isms' – Russian Formalism, New Criticism, structuralism,
and post-structuralism, are not included in this grouping.

FORMALISMS

The term 'formalist' is now frequently used very loosely to denote a view of literature which (i) excludes or downplays consideration of social, historical, and
political or IDEOLOGICAL issues, and (ii) looks at either the individual literary
WORK, or a larger grouping of literary works such as a GENRE, or literature in

general, as a closed or relatively closed system. The term also implies a concern with formal–technical issues at the expense of matters of meaning or THEME.

Three different groupings of theorists are associated with formalism, and in spite of the similarities between them, they differ in important ways.

Russian Formalism

It is largely thanks to this particular group of theorists that the term 'formalist' has entered Literary Studies. The term's CONNOTATIONS are now relatively neutral, but 'formalist' was used in a pejorative sense by the group's contemporaries, especially by those attacking the group from a MARXIST perspective, who claimed that the group's members concentrated on questions of form and technique at the expense of meaning and of matters of social and historical context – serious accusations in post-revolutionary Russia. Two related groups of theorists – the Moscow Linguistic Circle and the *Opojaz* group (Society for the Study of Poetic Language) – are today generally taken to represent what is now seen as the single movement known as Russian Formalism. The most important Russian Formalists are VIKTOR SHKLOVSKY, Boris Eichenbaum, Boris Tomashevsky, Yuri Tynyanov, and ROMAN JAKOBSON – who was subsequently involved with the PRAGUE CIRCLE of theorists and eventually moved to the United States. (Different systems of transliterating Russian letters result in there being a number of different spellings of these names.) VLADIMIR PROPP, author of *Morphology of the Folktale*, is not now generally classed as a member of the group, although he has been so classified at various times in the past. Roman Jakobson's work subsequent to his leaving the Soviet Union is, again, not normally classified as 'Russian Formalist' today.

Russian Formalism developed during the years of the First World War and was, as Victor Erlich has put it, a 'child of the revolutionary period . . . part and parcel of its peculiar intellectual atmosphere' (quoted by Bowlt: 1972, 1). The child was, however, eventually disowned by its parent (or putative parent): Russian Formalism came under increasing pressure in the Soviet Union as a more monolithic and repressive attitude to literary theory developed there, and by 1930 it had been forced into exile.

The first sentence of Eichenbaum's essay 'The Theory of the "Formal Method"' gives a fair indication of its characteristic trajectory: 'The school of thought on the theory and history of literature known as the Formal method derived [Eichenbaum is writing in 1925] from efforts to secure autonomy and concreteness for the discipline of literary studies' (Èjxenbaum: 1971, 3). Words such as 'autonomy' and 'concreteness' inevitably call to mind the NEW CRITICS (see below), but the autonomy in which the Russian Formalists are interested is less that of the individual work and more that of Literary Studies in general and of LITERARINESS; its CONCRETENESS is less what, following F.R. LEAVIS, we think of as the literary work's local effects and enactments of 'life', and more a matter of the isolation of technical devices and linguistic specificities. But it certainly shares with the New Critics a suspicion of any literary criticism which relies upon biographical details about the AUTHOR or socio-cultural information about his or her age. To this extent it shares with the New Critics a desire to establish Literary Studies as a discipline independent from History, Philosophy, Biography, Psychology, and so on. But in its insistence upon the need for an independent *theory* of literature it stands at some distance from the New Critics and their view of what Literary Studies should be. According to Eichenbaum, opposition to the Symbolists also bequeathed to the group 'the new spirit of scientific positivism that characterizes the Formalists: the rejection of philosophical premises, psychological or aesthetic interpretations, and so forth' (Èjxenbaum: 1971, 7). The word 'positivism' may jar on the ears of a modern reader, but what the use of this word seems to signal for the Russian Formalists is a close attention to textual detail. As Eichenbaum puts it, 'It was time to turn to the facts and, eschewing general systems and problems, to start from the center – from where the facts of art confront us. Art had to be approached at close range, and science had to be made concrete' (Èjxenbaum: 1971, 7).

As indicated, however, this is not a concreteness to be found in the individual work: Eichenbaum quotes Jakobson to the effect that the object of study in literary science is not literature but 'literariness', and the Formalists exhibit a good deal less respect for the value and autonomy of the individual work than do the New Critics: indeed, they could often be described as looters, stripping literary works of useful examples to help in the construction of more general theories.

Three important Russian Formalistic bequests to Literary Studies need to be mentioned here: first, the now unfashionable belief in a distinction between poetic language and ordinary language. Second, the importance of DEFAMILIARIZATION, a concept which enjoys considerable currency today. And third, the distinction between *fabula* and *sjužet* (see the entry for STORY AND PLOT), which plays a pivotal role in modern NARRATOLOGY.

One of the most potent critiques of the Formalists was actually first published in the Soviet Union in 1928: P.N. Medvedev's *The Formal Method in Literary Scholarship*, which some have claimed was actually written by MIKHAIL BAKHTIN (Medvedev was a member of Bakhtin's circle). Medvedev's book recognizes the positive elements in the work of the Formalists (his attack should not be equated with the Stalinist suppression of them), but he criticizes their rigid distinction between internal and external factors, and their inability to recognize that an external factor acting on literature can become 'an intrinsic factor of literature itself, a factor of its immanent development' (1978, 67). Medvedev is shrewd in his criticism of some Marxist attacks on the Formalists: for him what was important was not that the Formalists denied that external factors could influence literature, but that they denied that such factors could affect it intrinsically. Medvedev is also effective in his critique of the Formalists' commitment to the existence of a separate poetic language; as he puts it, '[t]he indices of the poetic do not belong to language and its elements, but only to poetic constructions'

(1978, 86). However, as one would expect from a member of Bakhtin's circle, Medvedev's strongest criticism is reserved for the ahistoricism of Formalism (1978, 97), and for its failure to recognize that '[e]ven the inner utterance (interior speech) is social; it is oriented toward a possible audience, toward a possible answer, and it is only in the form of such an orientation that it is able to take shape and form' (1978, 126). Finally, he notes that though the Formalists attempted to escape from a psychological subjectivism in their approach to literature, their basic theories (including the need to 'deautomatize' perception) 'presuppose a perceiving, subjective consciousness' (1978, 149).

Prague School

Alternatively *Prague (Linguistic) Circle*. A group of theorists writing in Prague from the late 1920s through to the German invasion of Czechoslovakia and a little beyond, some of whom were émigrés from the Soviet Union (the best-known amongst whom was RUSSIAN FORMALIST exile ROMAN JAKOBSON, who moved to Prague in 1920 and was a founder member of the group at its inception in 1926). The best-known members of the group, apart from Jakobson, were RENÉ WELLEK, Felix Vodička and Jan Mukařovský.

According to many commentators the Prague School writers constitute a clear bridge between RUSSIAN FORMALISM and modern STRUCTURALISM – a claim which can be confusing to the uninitiated as English translations of Prague School writings often have their authors describing their own position as structuralist. The structuralism of the 1960s and later is, however, somewhat (but not completely) different from the structuralism of the Prague School. What the two have in common is a significant debt to the writings of FERDINAND DE SAUSSURE, and an attempt to extend the application of Saussure's theories beyond language. The subtitle of *A Prague School Reader*, Paul L. Garvin's useful collection of some of the more important non-linguistic Prague School texts, 'On Esthetics, Literary Structure, and Style', helpfully indicates the extent to which their work moved beyond Linguistics as such (see Garvin: 1964). The starting point may be Saussure and language, but the work of the Russian Formalists, upon which the Prague writers built, is at least as important a source as is the work of Saussure. Much of the work of the group had a specifically linguistic focus – working with phonetics, phonology and semantics and attempting to define such concepts as 'phoneme', 'distinctive/redundant feature', and so on, but from this base the members of the group moved into a number of cognate areas, including those of literature and aesthetics. But none of this work was untouched by formalism and formalist ideas: Mary Louise Pratt argues that although the School's members made a point of calling their linguistics 'functional', in common with Saussure they were concerned almost uniquely 'with the function of elements within the linguistic system rather than with the functions the language serves within the speech community' (1977, 7), although she notes that in the pre-Second World War period the poeticians of the group *were* concerned with this latter issue – as can, incidentally, be seen from the essays in Garvin's *Reader*. This, she adds, meant that from the publication of the important Prague School Theses of 1929, an opposition between poetic and non-poetic language is built into the group's pronouncements on the social function of language. The position is clearly expressed in Jan Mukařovský's essay 'Standard Language and Poetic Language' (reprinted in Garvin: 1964).

We can trace this distinction right through to Roman Jakobson's much later, and no less influential, argument about the different 'functions of language'. The poetic function, as defined by Jakobson, involves 'a focussing on the mèssage itself for its own sake'. This is a definition which, although it maintains the Prague School's commitment to a distinction between poetic and ordinary language, effectively denies literature any significant social role and can be seen as a step away from some of the pre-Second World War positions of the group's members concerning literature. It is not surprising, following this, to find Mukařovský arguing a standard formalist case in 'Standard Language and Poetic Language': 'the question of truthfulness does not apply in regard to the subject matter of a work of poetry, nor does it even make sense' (1964, 22–3).

With the movement of René Wellek to the United States another important link – between the Prague School and Anglo-American NEW CRITICISIM (see below) – can also be traced. *Theory of Literature* by René Wellek and Austin Warren first appears in the United States in 1949, at the beginning of the period of the New Criticism's greatest influence (perhaps a more accurate word would be HEGEMONY) in that country. Garvin's *Reader* prints as frontispiece a statement of Josef Hrabák's which was first published in 1941 in *Slovo a slovesnost*, the journal of the Linguistic Circle of Prague, and which can serve to indicate the common ground between these different critical schools and movements:

> Structuralism is neither a theory nor a method; it is an epistemological point of view. It starts off from the observation that every concept in a given system is determined by all other concepts of that system and has no significance by itself alone; it does not become unequivocal until it is integrated into the system, the structure, of which it forms part and in which it has a definite fixed place. . . . For the structuralist, there is an interrelation between the data (facts) and the philosophic assumptions, not a unilateral dependence. . . . In one word, the entire structure is more than a mechanical summary of the properties of its components since it gives rise to new qualities.
>
> (Garvin: 1964, vi)

Here we see the Saussurean emphasis on relation (or difference) instead of self-identity, but within the individual system rather than in language in general. And for the Prague School, so far as literature is concerned the individual system tends to be the individual literary WORK rather than 'LITERARINESS' in general although, as the above quotation demonstrates, there is a generalizing impulse in

Prague School theory which helps to prevent it from being imprisoned in pre-existing categories such as 'the work'.

At any rate, a view of the literary work as a structure which had to be seen as a whole generated by the dynamic relationships between its component parts (a view which probably also owes a lot to Gestalt psychology), encouraged ANALYSIS of these dynamic relationships. Thus Prague School theories can be said to have contributed to the already existing emphasis upon close reading made much later by the New Critics. And it is fascinating to read Felix Vodička's 1942 essay 'The History of the Echo of Literary Works' in conjunction with W.K. Wimsatt's and Monroe Beardsley's highly influential 'The Intentional Fallacy' and 'The Affective Fallacy' (1946 and 1949). Two brief quotations from Vodička's essay must suffice to make this point:

> The literary work, upon being published or spread, becomes the property of the public, which approaches it with the artistic feeling of the time.
>
> . . .
>
> Subjective elements of valuation, stemming from the momentary state of mind of the reader or his personal likes and dislikes, must in the historical criticism of sources be separated from the attitude of the times, because the object of our cognition are those features which have the character of historic generality.
>
> (1964, 71)

It is probably fair to say that, in common with the Russian Formalists, the Prague School theorists responded to critical pressure from orthodox MARXIST critics by stressing the internal relationships in the literary work at the expense of its external relationships with AUTHOR, READER, or socio-historical reality, although at the same time a writer such as Mukařovský was able to incorporate views of the literary work's internal dialectic in a way which suggested some absorption of Marxist ideas.

So far as literary theory and criticism are concerned, the development of the Russian Formalist concept of DEFAMILIARIZATION into the similar concept of FOREGROUNDING represents perhaps the most influential of Prague School theoretical contributions, especially within the fields of NARRATOLOGY and STYLISTICS. The Prague School belief in the existence of a separate 'poetic language' which can be distinguished from 'ordinary language', ties in with the concept of 'foregrounding': according to Mukařovský, the function of poetic language 'is that of the maximum of foregrounding of the utterance' (Mukařovský: 1964, 19). There are also strong points of resemblance between the Prague School concept of foregrounding and certain aspects of BERTOLT BRECHT's theories concerning the ALIENATION EFFECT.

New Criticism

In an article entitled 'In Search of the New Criticism', Cleanth Brooks – whose name is almost always mentioned in the list of those who are presumed to have been New Critics – states that 'the New Criticism is not easy to describe or locate' (1983, 41). Brooks points out that the name comes from a book by the poet and man of letters John Crowe Ransom entitled *The New Criticism*, published in 1941. Brooks continues:

> In it [Ransom] discussed the critical aims and methods of Yvor Winters as the 'logical' critic, T.S. Eliot as the 'historical' critic, and Ivor A. Richards as the 'psychological' critic. He mentions more briefly R.P. Blackmur, William Empson, and a few others. Though Ransom treated all with respect, he put on record his reservations and disagreements. He neither defined an entity called the New Criticism nor did he attempt to promote it. In fact, his last chapter is entitled: 'Wanted: An Ontological Critic.'
>
> (1983, 41)

Brooks suggests that the belief that there was a group of critics called 'The New Critics' stems from people who either had not read Ransom's book or had mis-read it, and who assumed that Ransom was the primal New Critic and that his former students and friends were the others.

Other accounts of the emergence and development of the group (or the belief that there was such a group) take a different starting point. Jonathan Culler suggests that it originates in debates about the nature of poetry in T.S. ELIOT's *The Sacred Wood* (1920), and was continued by a group of poets meeting at Vanderbilt University under the tutelage of John Crowe Ransom who published – from 1922 to 1925 – a review called *The Fugitive*. Culler sees a collection of political essays published by this group under the title of *I'll Take My Stand* (1930) as an important ancestor of the New Criticism. The essays defended the Southern way of life against those who, following the Scopes 'monkey' trial (at which a teacher was tried for teaching Darwinism), denigrated it: 'Contrasting the agrarian with the industrial, the traditional and the organic with the alienated and the mechanistic, the contributors celebrated the life of yeoman farmers in small communities and argued for a spiritual superiority of subsistence farming over cash crop farming and industrial manufacture' (1988, 9). According to Culler, as a result of a lack of success on the political front the writers concerned (known as the Agrarians) abandoned the cause of the autonomous, self-sufficient farm for that of the self-sufficient poem. Whether or not we accept this account, the political element introduced by Culler is an important one, and explains why a number of commentators (normally but not always American ones) have included the English critic F.R. LEAVIS in their list of New Critics. There are cer-tainly passages in which Leavis sings the praises of the 'organic community' which are very reminiscent of the political arguments of the Agrarians – especially when taken in conjunction with Leavis's own brand of insular conservatism.

Another important father figure for the New Criticism is undoubtedly I.A. RICHARDS, although he is infrequently named as a New Critic himself – perhaps because by the time the term came into common use Richards was pursuing interests very different from those associated with New Criticism. If the Agrarians are important IDEOLOGICAL forebears of the New Criticism, Richards's main importance lies more on the practical level, in the *method* of close reading or practical criticism that he bequeathed to the New Critics.

Brooks points out that Ransom's *The New Criticism* also mentions the English critic WILLIAM EMPSON, who often figures on lists of prominent New Critics. Empson's *Seven Types of Ambiguity* (1930) was extremely influential by virtue of what many saw as a continuation of the lessons of *Practical Criticism* (and Richards was Empson's tutor at Cambridge). *Seven Types of Ambiguity* was full of close and detailed *analytical* readings of poetry which – unlike the biographical criticism of a previous age or the MARXIST criticism of a slightly later one – kept the reader's attention firmly and consistently upon matters of textual detail. Empson was certainly a very important influence on those American critics who became known in the 1940s and 1950s as the leading New Critics: an essay written by Cleanth Brooks for the journal *Accent* and entitled simply 'Empson's Criticism' singles out what Brooks sees as the most important elements in Empson's criticism: 'the significance of Empson's criticism is this: his criticism is an attempt to deal with what the poem "means" in terms of its structure *as a poem*' (1946, 498). This, Brooks goes on to argue, is radically different from what 'the critic in the past' had attempted to do: either to find the goodness of the poem in terms of its prose argument and its 'truth' – thus making poetry compete with philosophy or science – or else trying to find the poetry in the charm of the decorative elements. For Brooks, Empson's great virtue as critic is that he moves beyond such positions, showing how poem after poem ' "works" as a complex of meanings', with metaphor playing a functional (not decorative) role, metrics also performing a function, corroborating the play of meaning throughout the poem, and connotations no longer seen as hints of decorative, mysterious beauty, 'but active forces in the development of the manifold of meanings that is the poem' (1946, 498).

If we go back to 1938, when Brooks and Robert Penn Warren had published a book entitled *Understanding Poetry* (revised edition, 1958), we can see that both Empson and Richards must have had a profound influence upon the writing of this book, a book that was perhaps *the* most influential in establishing a new set of critical principles and practices. According to Brooks's 1983 essay, he and Warren faced a similar problem to that faced by Richards: their students were 'bright enough young men and women', but 'very few of them had the slightest conception of how to read a short story, let alone a poem' (1983, 42). *Understanding Poetry* contained a 'Letter to the teacher' which noted that there were three substitutes for the poem as object of study: paraphrase of logical and narrative content; study of biographical and historical materials; inspirational and didactic interpretation. These three substitutes were to be avoided, although paraphrase was allowable as a necessary preliminary step in reading a poem.

'The teacher', then, (who was typically hard-pressed and faced with the problem of how to interest his or her pupils) was handed the perfect pedagogical recipe: concentrate upon the poem as poem; study the words on the page; use the poem as your teaching material – it can be read in class, and analyzed and discussed there and then, with no need for extra study or information.

By the end of the Second World War the stage was thus set for the confirmation on the theoretical plane of what was seen by critics such as Brooks to be a new set of working practices for critics. Key documents here are the two essays 'The Intentional Fallacy' and 'The Affective Fallacy', written by critic W.K. Wimsatt and aesthetician Monroe Beardsley, and published respectively in 1946 and 1949. These elevated the pedagogical techniques of Richards, and of Brooks and Warren, and what was perceived to be the working practice of a critic like Empson, to the level of a set of theoretical injunctions. The poem had to be treated as poem and not as anything else; it had to be read and analyzed 'in itself'; criticism that contained references to the author's INTENTION or the poem's 'affects' in the reader was deemed illegitimate.

In the 1940s and the 1950s the new doctrine spread like wildfire in schools and establishments of higher education in Britain and the USA, and there are many educated in the 1950s and 1960s who can remember red lines through paragraphs in essays which dared to bring in biographical or socio-historical information, or to make use of words such as 'INTENTION'. The rise to HEGEMONY of what were seen to be New Critical principles was certainly helped by the fact that this was the period of the Cold War and one of the consistent targets of the then practitioners of New Criticism was that of MARXIST criticism.

What is interesting, however, is that the remarkable degree of consensus concerning the New Critical principles in the 1950s and 1960s, at all levels of the educational systems of Britain, the United States, and many Western European countries, does not actually match with the actual beliefs, theories, and even practice of many of the revered father figures. Richards's psychologism, Empson's lifelong commitment to the use of biographical information and speculation in poetic analysis (only noticed by many when books such as *Milton's God* and, especially, *Using Biography* appeared, and when Empson started to criticize the intentional fallacy loudly and sarcastically) – even Brooks's use of paraphrase as a critical tool at much the same time as he rejected it on the theoretical plane – none of these seemed to have disturbed the still waters of New Critical consensus too much for at least a couple of decades. And this suggests that the New Criticism took its nourishment as much sideways (from contemporary non-literary IDEOLOGY) as it did from the past and the father figures. The consensus, in other words, seems to have been established between the followers of the father figures more than between the father figures themselves.

SECTION 3

Thus the New Criticism presents us with the paradoxical picture of a remarkable hegemonic consensus overlaying what (as Brooks quite rightly points out in his 1983 essay) was a much more pluralistic set of critical practices. Was, and is. In 1981, Jonathan Culler wrote that: 'Whatever critical affiliations we may proclaim, we are all New Critics, in that it requires a strenuous effort to escape notions of the autonomy of the literary work, the importance of demonstrating its unity, and the requirement of "close reading"' (1981, 3). It is in particular the analytical *methods* of the New Criticism which are perhaps its most valuable gift to its successors: even a Marxist literary critic today will ignore the need for close attention to textual detail at his or her peril, and it seems impossible for us to return to the sort of criticism whose inadequacies brought the New Criticism into being.

THE HERMENEUTIC TRADITION

Contemporary use of the term 'hermeneutics' generally implies some reference to the German hermeneutic tradition, a tradition which has become better known in Britain and America during the past three decades through the work of E.D. HIRSCH and WOLFGANG ISER. Anglo-American critics and theorists do sometimes use the term as a loose synonym for INTERPRETATION, or 'theory of interpretation', however. We use the word 'tradition' here, because the different groupings examined in this section are related not just by similarities, but by traceable lines of influence.

Hermeneutics

The undisputed founding fathers of the German hermeneutic tradition are Friedrich Schleiermacher (1768–1834) and Wilhelm Dilthey (1833–1911), although both built on the work of German Protestant theologians of the seventeenth century whose development of methods of Biblical INTERPRETATION had a clearly theological imperative. It is to Schleiermacher that we owe the concept of the hermeneutical circle (see below), although it was Dilthey who gave it its name.

The philosopher and historian Wilhelm Dilthey, according to a useful discussion by Ian Maclean,

sought to make hermeneutics the equivalent in relation to the human sciences (*Geisteswissenschaften*) of the scientific method of the natural sciences (*Naturwissenschaften*). For him, explanation was the appropriate mode of intelligibility for the natural sciences, whereas understanding was that of the human sciences. Understanding has to do with the experience of other subjects and minds than our own; it relies on the meaningfulness of all forms of expression in which experience is couched (but especially written expression); this meaningfulness is bestowed on expression by interpretation.

(1986, 124–5)

Three other very important names in the German hermeneutic tradition are those of Edmund Husserl (1859–1938), Martin Heidegger (1889–1976), and Hans-Georg Gadamer (1900–). Husserl's development of PHENOMENOLOGY (see below) had a number of very important implications for theories of interpretation, especially in terms of the active and 'completing' role that the act of consciousness has in CONCRETIZING its incompletely perceived objects of perception. Heidegger's main contribution to hermeneutical theory is, arguably, his anti-individualistic and historicist view of the process of interpretation.

The word hermeneutics is etymologically related to the name of the messenger-god Hermes, who, as Richard E. Palmer points out in his book *Hermeneutics*, is, significantly, 'associated with the function of transmuting what is beyond human understanding into a form that human intelligence can grasp' (1969, 13). Palmer points out that hermeneutics has traditionally had two main focuses of concern: 'the question of what is involved in the event of understanding a text, and the question of what understanding itself is, in its most foundational and "existential" sense' (1969, 10). Hermeneutics thus has often had a dual identity, being treated on the one hand as a philosophical study with the aim of understanding (rather than changing) the practice of interpretation, and on the other hand as the search for a set of correct principles and methods that will enable correspondingly correct interpretations to be arrived at.

At different times this dual identity has led to disagreements concerning the 'true' role and function of hermeneutics. It is arguable that this tension can be traced back to the development of hermeneutics within Biblical scholarship and EXEGESIS. Richard Palmer certainly argues for the existence of *two* hermeneutic traditions:

> There is the tradition of Schleiermacher and Dilthey, whose adherents look to hermeneutics as a general body of methodological principles which underlie interpretation. And there are the followers of Heidegger, who see hermeneutics as a philosophical exploration of the character and requisite conditions for all understanding.
>
> . . .
>
> Gadamer, following Heidegger, orients his thinking to the more philosophical question of what understanding itself is; he argues with equal conviction that understanding is an historical act and as such is always connected to the present.
>
> (1969, 46)

Perhaps the aspect of the hermeneutic tradition which is best known in Anglo-American circles is that rendered by the term 'the hermeneutic circle'. The term is used to express the seeming paradox that the whole can be understood only through an understanding of its parts, while these same parts can be understood only through an understanding of the whole to which they belong. Allan Rodway suggested back in 1970 that the way we escape from such situations is by 'edging out', 'tacking from evidence to hypothesis to further evidence to renewed hypothesis' (1970, 94) – although it is arguable that such a solution to the problem of the hermeneutic circle is already implicit in the work of both Dilthey and Schleiermacher.

E.D. HIRSCH is the theorist who has done most to bring the work of the German hermeneuticists to the attention of Anglo-American readers. Indeed, in his essay 'Objective Interpretation' (first published in 1960 and reprinted in *Validity in Interpretation* [1967]), Hirsch states that 'my whole argument may be regarded as an attempt to ground some of Dilthey's hermeneutic principles in Husserl's epistemology and Saussure's linguistics' (1967, 242, n. 30). In his subsequent book, *The Aims of Interpretation* (1976), Hirsch describes his relationship to the German hermeneutic tradition in more detail. Like Richard Palmer, he sees two main 'lines' within this tradition, although these he defines in a rather different manner from Palmer:

> In this book I write as a representative of general hermeneutics. In the history of the subject, the important distinction between local and general hermeneutic theories has served to define the tradition of Schleiermacher over against more narrowly conceived hermeneutical traditions. Within this line of general hermeneutics stemming from Schleiermacher can be found Boeckh, Dilthey, Heidegger, and Gadamer in a direct, unbroken lineage. (Just as Heidegger was a student of Dilthey's, so was Gadamer a student of Heidegger's.) But the tradition is by no means a uniform one. The relativism of Heidegger and Gadamer runs counter to the objectivism of Boeckh and Dilthey, so that my own objectivist views can be considered a throwback to the 'genuine' or 'authentic' tradition of Schleiermacher. But whether one takes an objectivist or relativist position, certain arguments favoring general hermeneutics over local hermeneutics seem to me very strong.
>
> (1976, 17)

It is for Gadamer that Hirsch reserves his strongest criticisms, focusing on his *Truth and Method* in an essay entitled 'Gadamer's Theory of Interpretation', first published in 1965 and reprinted as an appendix to *Validity in Interpretation*. *Truth and Method* was first published as *Wahrheit und Methode* in Tübingen in 1960; the English translation (1975, revised 1989) is of the second edition, published in Tübingen in 1972.

Hirsch sees Gadamer's book as a 'polemic against that nineteenth-century preoccupation with objective truth and correct method' that is represented by August Boeckh's *Encyclopädie und Methodologie der philologischen Wissenschaften* (1877), to the title of which Gadamer's own work's title responds (Hirsch: 1967, 245). According to Hirsch, Gadamer's 'primary concern is to attack the premise that textual meaning is the same as the author's meaning' (1967, 247). Hirsch is also extremely critical of Gadamer's argument that the author's perspective and the interpreter's perspective must be merged by means of a fusion of horizons (*Horizontverschmelzung*), asking, 'How can an interpreter fuse two perspectives – his own and that of the text – unless he has somehow appropriated the original perspective and amalgamated it with his own?' (1967, 254).

Hirsch's own distinction between MEANING AND SIGNIFICANCE has been seen by more than one commentator as an attempt to break the then current orthodoxies of NEW CRITICAL anti-contextualism by going back to the origins of the German hermeneutic tradition – and, in particular, to the work of Friedrich Schleiermacher. Schleiermacher believed that the process of understanding reversed the process of composition, for instead of starting with the AUTHOR's mental life and proceeding to textual embodiment or projection it started with the text and worked its way back to its originating mental life. It is easy to see how Hirsch's insistence on equating *meaning* with authorial INTENTION builds on such a view.

At a time when the DEATH OF THE AUTHOR was being confidently announced one can readily understand that this particular position did not meet with general acceptance. T.K. Seung has offered a representative objection to Hirsch's position: 'If authorial intention were available for direct inspection and observation by readers, it could readily be used for settling the claims of competing interpretations. Unfortunately, authorial intention can be reached only through textual interpretations' (1982, 13). We are back to another vicious circle. In this case, however, the argument that authorial intention can be reached only through textual interpretation seems unnecessarily limiting, and arguably lands us back in a sort of New Critical formalism (which is not to suggest that Hirsch's own views are unproblematic: see the entry for MEANING AND SIGNIFICANCE and the discussion of his work in Section 5).

If the historicist emphases of the German hermeneutic tradition militated against its catching the interest of many Anglo-American theorists during the heyday of STRUCTURALISM and DECONSTRUCTION, two new developments are helping to change this situation. The first is the rise of the NEW HISTORICISM, which has helped to make the historicist emphases of the hermeneutic tradition much less unfashionable, and the second is the fact that a growing interest in the work of MIKHAIL BAKHTIN and his emphasis on the DIALOGIC may, similarly, make some of the arguments of Hans-Georg Gadamer sound a little more relevant to Anglo-Saxon ears.

In 1984 Iain Wright argued persuasively for a far more positive consideration of Gadamer's work than had E.D. Hirsch. Wright claims that Gadamer has been unjustly neglected in Anglo-Saxon circles – a neglect which Wright explains in part by the fact that his major work, *Truth and Method*, is available in English only in a translation which is 'woefully inadequate' (since Wright wrote it has been revised [1989]).

Even so, Wright argues, Gadamer offers modern theory of interpretation a middle way between 'doctrinaire objectivism versus doctrinaire subjectivism, pure intentionalism versus pure anti-intentionalism, slavish "homage to the truth of the past" versus "intelligibility for our time", ultra-Rousseauism versus ultra-Nietzscheanism, the rights of the text versus the rights of the reader' (1984, 93). It is here, according to Wright, that the idea of dialogue comes in. For Gadamer insists on the tension between past and present, and the need to resolve this through dialogue: 'A false dialogue is one-sided. A true one (and Gadamer's ideal touchstone is the Platonic dialogue) involves a mutual learning-process in which each interlocutor retains his or her identity but is prepared to learn from the other' (1984, 95). It seems likely that a fruitful interplay between the (very fashionable) ideas of Bakhtin and the (far less fashionable) ideas of Hans-Georg Gadamer is now possible within Anglo-American theoretical circles.

Other theorists who have been particularly influenced by the German Hermeneutic tradition are Roman Ingarden, PAUL RICOEUR, the members of the Geneva School of Criticism (see below, in the discussion of phenomenology) and those of the German RECEPTION THEORY school (see below).

Phenomenology

Phenomenology originates in the writing of the German Edmund Husserl (1859–1938), whose philosophy takes as its starting point the world as experienced in our consciousness. It thus rejects the possibility of considering the world independently of human consciousness, but seeks rather to get back to CONCRETE reality through our experience of it. For Husserl, consciousness is always *consciousness of something*: it is directed outwards rather than inwards – even if it is directed on to something imagined. It is thus too simple to describe phenomenology as idealist, for although it posits the impossibility of our gaining a knowledge of the world which is untouched by our perception of that world, it does suggest that through an *eidetic* method we can build up a successively more and more accurate understanding of the objects of our consciousness by filtering off accidental and personal elements in our perception of them. In order so to analyze our consciousness we must suspend all preconceptions about the objects with which it is concerned. TERRY EAGLETON comments that although

> Husserl rejected empiricism, psychologism and the positivism of the natural sciences, he also considered himself to be breaking with the classical idealism of a thinker like Kant. Kant had been unable to solve the problem of how the mind can really know objects outside it at all; phenomenology, in claiming that what is given in pure perception is the very essence of things, hoped to surmount this scepticism.
>
> (1983, 56–7)

It is not hard to understand the interest that such ideas aroused amongst students of art and literature, for whom the pseudo-objectivity of positivism seemed no more applicable to the study and appreciation of art-works than did variants of Kantianism which too soon could end up in solipsism and an abandonment to unfettered personal 'taste'. A range of literary theorists and aestheticians found in Husserl's ideas something upon which they felt they could build. One of the earliest was the Polish aesthetician Roman Ingarden, who argued that a READING of a WORK of literature CONCRETIZES it (much as the PERFORMANCE of a play concretizes the written TEXT).

The Geneva School of criticism owes its largest debt to Husserl and phenomenological ideas. Its members were mostly associated with the University of Geneva, and have on occasions been referred to collectively as the 'Critics of Consciousness'. J. Hillis Miller, who was for a time closely identified with the school, has written a useful survey-account of the school which is reprinted in his book *Theory Then and Now* (1991). According to Miller, for the Geneva critics literature is a form of consciousness (1991, 14), while criticism is

> fundamentally the expression of a 'reciprocal transparency' of two minds, that of the critic and that of the author, but they differ in their conceptions of the nature of consciousness. From the religious idea of human existence in [Marcel] Raymond and [Albert] Béguin, to the notion in [Georges] Poulet's criticism that what counts most is 'the proof, the living proof, of the experience of inner spirituality as a positive reality,' [Jean] Rousset's belief that the artist's self-consciousness only comes into existence in the intimate structure of his work, the unquestioning acceptance of an overlapping of consciousness and the physical world in [Jean-Pierre] Richards's criticism, and the fluctuation between incarnation and detachment in the work of [Jean] Starobinski, these six critics base their interpretations of literature on a whole spectrum of dissimilar convictions about the human mind.
>
> (1991, 29)

This is criticism that is a long way away from the death of the author; the idea of writing as self-expression or self-projection is central to the work of Jean Rousset, and according to Miller, Georges Poulet believes that

> [c]riticism must therefore begin in an act of renunciation in which the critic empties his mind of its personal qualities so that it may coincide completely with the consciousness expressed in the words of the author. His essay will be the record of this coincidence. The 'intimacy' necessary for criticism, says Georges Poulet, 'is not possible unless the thought of the critic *becomes* the thought of the author criticized, unless it succeeds in re-feeling, in re-thinking, in re-imagining the author's thought from the inside . . .'.
>
> (1991, 15)

SECTION 3

READER-RESPONSE CRITICISM (see below) owes an important debt to phenomenology and the Geneva School, particularly in the person of the German critic WOLFGANG ISER. Iser's essay 'The Reading Process: a Phenomenological Approach' (reprinted in Iser: 1974) is a good example of the creative development of a number of aspects of phenomenology – and, too, of the way in which phenomenology leads naturally to some of the preoccupations of reader-response critics. Take, for example, the first sentence of the essay: 'The phenomenological theory of art lays full stress on the idea that, in considering a literary work, one must take into account not only the actual text but also, and in equal measure, the actions involved in responding to that text' (1974, 274). Iser then moves on to discuss Ingarden's theory of artistic concretization, and concludes that the literary work has two poles: the artistic pole (the text created by the AUTHOR), and the AESTHETIC pole (the realization accomplished by the READER) (1974, 274). The argument is an interesting one, although the proposed nomenclature is perhaps odd, suggesting as it does that there is nothing aesthetic about the author's created text and nothing artistic about the reader's realization.

Iser stresses in particular the work's *virtuality*: like the text of a play which can be produced in innumerable ways, a literary work can lead to innumerable reading experiences. He also makes use of Husserl's argument that consciousness is *intentional*, that it is directed and goal-seeking rather than random and all-absorbing. So far as the reading of literature is concerned, this allows Iser to place a high premium not just upon the reader's 'pre-intentions' – what he or she goes to the text with – but also upon the INTENTIONS awakened by the reading process itself (and, indirectly, by the text). One of the best-known of Iser's arguments involves the literary work's 'gaps'. According to him, no literary work is, as it were, complete: all have gaps which have to be filled in by the reader, and all readers and readings will fill these in differently (1974, 280; Iser makes similar points in a number of other essays). Iser's gaps bear a close relationship to Roman Ingarden's 'spots of indeterminacy': see the entry for CONCRETIZATION.

It will be seen that such a position offers something of a compromise position: it shows how readers' responses can be taken account of without giving the individual reader absolute freedom to do with the text as he or she wishes: the reader has licence to fill in only the gaps.

Reception theory

A term generally used both in a relatively narrow sense to describe a particular group of (mainly German) theorists concerned with the way in which literary WORKS are 'received' by their READERS over time, and also sometimes used in a looser sense to describe any attempt to theorize the ways in which art-works are received, individually and collectively, by their 'consumers'. The names most frequently mentioned as core members of the particular group of theorists are Hans Robert Jauss, WOLFGANG ISER, Karlheinz Stierle and Harald Weinrich.

The translators of an article by Karlheinz Stierle entitled 'The Reading of

Fictional Texts' suggest that the German term *Rezeption* as used by those known as 'reception theorists', 'refers to the activity of reading, the construction of meaning, and the reader's response to what he is reading' (Stierle: 1980, 83 n.1). In analyzing the activity of reading, reception theorists make considerable use of a concept defined by Hans Robert Jauss – along with Wolfgang Iser the most important founder-member of the group. In an early and influential essay entitled 'Literary History as a Challenge to Literary Theory', Jauss singles out three ways in which a writer can anticipate a reader's response, and these appear to represent his view of the component parts of the reader's *horizon of expectations*:

> first, by the familiar standards or the inherent poetry of the genre; second, by the implicit relationships to familiar works of the literary-historical context; and third, by the contrast between history and reality . . . . The third factor includes the possibility that the reader of a new work has to perceive it not only within the narrow horizon of his literary expectations but also within the wider horizon of his experience of life.
>
> (1974, 18)

All of these elements may fuse into a single if complex tradition which a TEXT accumulates as it becomes well known, a tradition with which its reader has to contend or grapple as he or she reads and responds to it. A well-known text, in other words, raises more specific expectations for the reader than one that has accrued no such tradition. (The implication of the last-quoted sentence above is that the reader of an *old* work does *not* have to perceive it within the wider horizon of his or her experience of life, and this implication perhaps reveals a certain limitation in the theory.)

An important part of the theory as it has developed and matured involves a view of literary texts as partially open, and of the responses engendered by them to be (again partly) the creation of their readers. Thus in a much-quoted example, Wolfgang Iser sees the sense a reader actively *makes* of a literary text to be contained within certain limits imposed by the text itself.

> In the same way, two people gazing at the night sky may both be looking at the same collection of stars, but one will see the image of a plough, and the other will make out a dipper. The 'stars' in a literary text are fixed; the lines that join them are variable.
>
> (1974, 282)

This argued element of textual containment has, incidentally, led the American critic STANLEY FISH to distinguish his own concept of the INTERPRET[AT]IVE COMMUNITY from the reception theorists' horizon of expectations: for Fish the text is itself constituted by the pre-existing CONVENTIONS of the interpret[at]ive community.

Reader-response criticism

According to the American critic STANLEY FISH, in a book published in 1980: 'Twenty years ago one of the things that literary critics didn't do was talk about the reader, at least in a way that made his experience the focus of the critical act' (1980, 344). Since the time about which Fish was writing, however, more and more attention has been devoted to the identity, role and function of readers of literature, and this has led to the coining of a range of new terms. Much of this attention has stemmed from a number of different critical theories and approaches which are often collectively described as *reader-response criticism*, but some of it can best be seen in relation to the loosening of NEW CRITICAL dogmas. Once appeal to the INTENTIONAL and AFFECTIVE fallacies lost its force, curiosity about the reader faced no interdiction. A sure indication of this sense of new-found freedom is the gradual movement away from talk of 'the reader' towards reference to 'readers' – a movement accompanied by the willingness of critics to say 'I' rather than 'we', which in its turn has to be related to a growing awareness of the dangers of ethnocentricity and parallel GENDER and CLASS biases. For this reason it may be a little misleading to think of reader-response criticism as a school: the term gathers together a range of attempts to theorize about readers and to study them and the reading process, and TERRY EAGLETON's joke description 'The Reader's Liberation Front' catches some of the diversity in the reality described. Indeed, not all criticism categorized as reader-response criticism is actually concerned with readers' response(s); much of it is concerned with other issues: readers' COMPETENCE, the reading process *in toto*, the TEXT's formation of the reader, and so on.

Perhaps not surprisingly, much of the criticism described as reader-response criticism is concerned with the novel. We are much more conscious of reading as a process when reading a novel than when reading a poem – especially a LYRIC poem which can be held as a finished unit more easily in the memory. Wayne Booth's 1961 book *Rhetoric of Fiction* popularized the notion of the 'implied author', and by extension the term 'implied reader' was coined to describe the reader which the text (or the author through the text) suggests that it expects. Booth himself talks of the *postulated* or *mock* reader; another very similar term – *extrafictional* or *authorial voice* – is suggested by Susan Sniader Lanser:

> The authorial voice is an *extrafictional* entity whose presence accounts, for example, for organizing, titling, and introducing the fictional work. This extrafictional voice, the most direct textual counterpart for the historical author, carries all the *diegetic authority* of its (publicly authorized) creator and has the ontological status of historical truth.
>
> (1981, 122; quoted by Aczel: 1998, 474)

It should be noted that this term, like all other terms with the form 'the X reader', although singular, actually has the purpose of describing a group or category of readers. JACQUES DERRIDA has argued that all reading is transformational, and in the same comment warned against reading (in this case the classic texts of MARXISM) 'according to a hermeneutical or exegetical method which would seek out a finished signified beneath a textual surface' (1981, 63). Although Derrida is not normally thought of as a reader-response critic, the same insistence upon those transformational and creative aspects of reading which we associate with this group of critics can be found in his work.

Closely related to the implied reader is the *inscribed reader*, that is, the reader whose characteristics are actually there to be discovered in the text itself, waiting for the actual reader to slip on like a suit of clothes. UMBERTO ECO has introduced the similar concept of the *model reader*; he argues that '[t]o make his text communicative, the author has to assume that the ensemble of codes he relies upon is the same as that shared by his possible reader (hereafter Model Reader) supposedly able to deal interpretatively with the expressions in the same way as the author deals generatively with them' (1981, 7). This may be taken to imply that the model reader is external to the text, but later in the same chapter of his book Eco makes it clear that for him the concept is more intra-textual in nature and that the model reader is thus also to be understood to be inscribed in the text: 'the Model Reader is a textually established set of felicity conditions . . . to be met in order to have a macro-speech act (such as a text is) fully actualized' (1981, 11; for *felicity conditions* see SPEECH ACT THEORY, p. 174).

Rather different is the *intended reader*, because here the evidence may be either intra- or extra-textual: an author's comment in a letter that a WORK of literature was written to be read by a particular person or group of people can be used as evidence substantiating a case for a particular intended reader, but clearly not for a particular inscribed reader. Again related but slightly different are the *average* and the *optimal* or *ideal reader* (sometimes translated as *super-reader*). Super-reader comes from Michael Riffaterre (he later replaces it with *archi-lecteur* or composite reader), and describes (paradoxically) as much readings as readers, in other words, the responses engendered in different readers by particular textual elements. Riffaterre has also coined the term *retroactive reading* to describe a second-stage, HERMENEUTIC reading which comes subsequent to an initial, *heuristic reading* or reading-for-the-meaning process (1978, 5; see the entry for MEANING AND SIGNIFICANCE).

Different again is *symptomatic reading*: if we define a SYMPTOM as a non-intentional SIGN then it follows that a symptomatic reading treats a WORK much as a doctor examines a patient for symptoms. The doctor (in the exemplary situation) does not ask the patient what is wrong with him or her, but looks for clues which the patient is unable to recognize or interpret. A symptomatic reading, then, seeks to use such clues in a work as a way into the secrets of the AUTHOR, or of his or her society or CULTURE, or whatever.

JEROME J. MCGANN has coined the term *radial reading* for the sort of reading that 'puts one in a position to respond actively to the text's own (often secret) discursive acts'. As an example he refers to the two volumes which form the first edition of Ezra Pound's first 27 cantos, each of which

> 'makes a clear historical allusion not only to William Morris and the bibliographical face of the late nineteenth-century aesthetic movement, but also to the longer tradition which those late nineteenth-century works were invoking: the tradition of the decorated manuscript and its Renaissance bibliographical inheritors' (1991, 122).

The *optimal/ideal reader* is a term used to refer to that collection of abilities, attitudes, experience, and knowledge which will allow a reader to extract the maximum value from a reading of a particular text. (For some commentators, the maximum *legitimate* value.) It should be noted that whereas for some critics the optimal/ideal reader is a universal figure, for most he or she is particular to given texts: the ideal reader for *Humphry Clinker* may not be the ideal reader for 'My Last Duchess'. Closely related again is the *informed reader*, a term given currency by STANLEY FISH. According to Fish:

> [t]he informed reader is someone who (1) is a competent speaker of the language out of which the text is built up; (2) is in full possession of 'the semantic knowledge that a mature . . . listener brings to his task of comprehension,' including the knowledge (that is, the experience, both as a producer and comprehender) of lexical sets, collocation probabilities, idioms, professional and other dialects, and so on; and (3) has *literary* competence. That is, he is sufficiently experienced as a reader to have internalized the properties of local discourses, including everything from the most local of devices (figures of speech, and so on) to whole genres.
>
> (1980, 48)

For *contrapuntal reading*, see the entry for EDWARD SAID in Section 5.

In spite of the fact that all of these terms have sprouted on the grave (or the sick-bed) of the New Criticism, it can be argued that all of them except the intended reader retain a certain text-centredness. Rather different is the *empirical reader*, used to describe those actual human beings who read a given literary work in varied ways and get varied things out of their readings. This concept arises perhaps more from the sociology of literature than from literary criticism as such, but study of the empirical reader and of empirical readings can have important implications for literary criticism. In particular, confirmation that one literary work can generate a range of different reading experiences, over time, between cultures or groups (or within them), and even for the same individual, leads necessarily to the question of the status and authority of these different reading experiences. If there is an optimal reader, is there also an optimal reading, or is it a characteristic of major literature that it can generate a succession of new reading experiences as the individual reader or his or her culture changes? It has to be said that study of empirical readings is at a very early stage; Norman N. Holland's *5 Readers Reading* (1975) contains interesting material, but it could more accurately have been entitled *5 Readers Remembering What They Read*. Lynne Pearce's *Feminism and the Politics of Reading* (1997) combines empirical study of her own and other reading processes with a view of the reader–work relationship as a form of ROMANCE, a romance which proceeds through a set of standard phases which Pearce borrows from ROLAND BARTHES's *The Pleasure of the Text* (1976).

STRUCTURALISM AND ITS PROGENY

It is helpful to distinguish modern structuralism, which is essentially a post-Second World War development, from the structuralism of the Prague School theorists (for which see the entry for PRAGUE SCHOOL earlier in this section). Although these have something in common – notably a central and substantial debt to the work of FERDINAND DE SAUSSURE – the close relations between the Prague School and RUSSIAN FORMALISM mean that it makes good sense to consider both in the same subsection.

The present entry will therefore concentrate upon what we can term modern structuralism, with a more restricted consideration of its roots in the early part of the twentieth century. In its initial phase in the 1950s and 1960s modern structuralism is a largely French phenomenon whose most important figures are probably the anthropologist Claude Lévi-Strauss (whose work has ensured that MYTHIC and archetypal literary criticism has significant connections with structuralism), and the literary and CULTURAL critic ROLAND BARTHES. Following them, however, many other individuals produced work which has been labelled structuralist. These include a group of MARXIST theorists of differing persuasions within Marxism such as Louis Althusser and LUCIEN GOLDMANN (often referred to as a 'genetic structuralist'); NARRATOLOGISTS such as GÉRARD GENETTTE, and MICHEL FOUCAULT who, for want of a better classification, we can call a historian. We can add that in his insistence that the UNCONSCIOUS is structured like a language, JACQUES LACAN also advances a classic structuralist position (see the entry for linguistic paradigm).

Common to all of these is (i) an interest in structures or systems which can be studied SYNCHRONICALLY rather than in terms of their emergence and development through traceable processes of historical causation; and (ii) a related debt to the theories of Saussure – often involving a commitment to the implications of the linguistic paradigm. Put crudely, structuralism is (at least in its early or 'pure' form) interested rather in that which makes MEANING possible than in meaning itself.

Structuralism

A classic early example of a structuralist involvement with *literature* (or at least with NARRATIVE) is to be found in VLADIMIR PROPP's *Morphology of the Folktale*, first published in Russian in 1928. Typical features of Propp's study are its concern to generalize features (or 'functions') across TEXTS, and thus to concentrate upon a system capable of generating meanings which goes beyond the confines of the individual WORK, and a concomitant lack of interest in the INTERPRETATION of individual works or, even, in their individual specificity. (ROLAND BARTHES's proposed CODES of reading can be seen to be the direct descendants of Propp's functions.) From this perspective it is as if the work is written not by its AUTHOR (collective or individual), but by the 'grammar' or system of transformations that pre-exists its creation (see the entry for LINGUISTIC PARADIGM). A fundamental distinctive feature of structuralism can perhaps be indicated by comparing this to the way in which Claude Lévi-Strauss can treat the system of gift-giving in a culture, or Roland Barthes can treat 'Steak and Chips' or 'Striptease' in his *Mythologies*. What all of these studies have in common is a concern with the pre-existing system which allows individual UTTERANCES to be generated. Indeed, use of the linguistic paradigm means that for the structuralist a particular meal, or giving of a gift, can be treated as a sort of utterance, an example of PAROLE behind which lies a complete LANGUE. When we give a visitor a meal of steak and chips, the meaning which this has for him or her is determined not just by (or not perhaps even primarily by) the actual taste and appearance of the meal, but the grammatical function which 'steak and chips' is allowed to play in the *langue* of meals. How and why this *langue* has developed into the system that exists is a matter of less (or no) interest to structuralism.

Clearly, this downplays the importance of 'the meal itself' and of the individual cook's skill, and thus it is not surprising that when structuralism is applied to literary works, it downgrades or rejects the view that either the 'work itself' or the author determines how the work is to be read. As GÉRARD GENETTE puts it,

[t]he project [of structuralism], as described in Barthes's *Critique et verité* and Todorov's 'Poétique' (in *Qu'est-ce que le structuralism?*), was to develop a poetics which would stand to literature as linguistics stands to language and which therefore would not seek to explain what individual works mean but would attempt to make explicit the system of figures and conventions that enable works to have the forms and meanings they do.

(1980, 8)

Many structuralists have used Saussurean linguistics as a basis to argue that such structures, like language, are self-enclosed and are neither affected (or caused) by extra-structural pressures (the 'real world'), nor can they change or even refer to an extra-structural reality. We can see this emphasis as representative of the formalist wing of structuralism. In fact, Saussure provides a dubious basis for such an assertion, which is as questionable as the argument that Saussure rejects the historical approach in favour of the synchronic one (in actual fact he argues that both are necessary). Be this as it may, structuralist literary theory and criticism often tend to be characterized by a commitment to such closed systems, although in the work of, for example, Roland Barthes, structuralist analyzes can also be directed outwards towards social, IDEOLOGICAL and political realities.

Although structuralism has been (and remains) a controversial movement, it has undoubted successes to its credit across a range of disciplines and subject matters. Within literary criticism its most unqualified successes have probably been within the field of NARRATOLOGY. Gérard Genette – one of its leading practitioners within this field – has argued that structuralism is more than just a method and needs to be seen as a general tendency of thought or an ideology (1982, 11). Interestingly, Genette sees the concern of structuralism with form at the expense of content as a *corrective* one, as can be seen from his (much-quoted) comment that 'Literature had long enough been regarded as a message without a code for it to become necessary to regard it for a time as a code without a message' (1982, 7). He explains the need for such a corrective shift of focus by characterizing structuralism as a reaction to 'positivism, "historicizing history" and the "biographical illusion"', and sees structuralism as

> a movement represented in various ways by the critical writings of a Proust, an Eliot, a Valéry, Russian Formalism, French 'thematic criticism' or Anglo-American 'New Criticism.' In a way, the notion of structural analysis can be regarded as a simple equivalent of what Americans call 'close reading' and which would be called in Europe, following Spitzer, the 'immanent study' of works.
>
> (1982, 11–12)

This broadens structuralism very considerably, as does Genette's claim that 'any analysis that confines itself to a work without considering its sources or motives would, therefore, be implicitly structuralist' (1982, 12).

Semiology/semiotics

Semiotics overlaps significantly with structuralism, but enjoys sufficient independence to merit separate treatment. The term *semiotic* was coined at the close of the nineteenth century by the American philosopher Charles Sanders Peirce to describe a new field of study of which he was the founder, and *semiotics* traces its descent from this point. *Semiology* was coined by the Swiss linguistician FERDINAND DE SAUSSURE, and in his posthumously edited and published *Course in General Linguistics* he defended the coinage as necessary for the naming of that new science which would form part of social psychology and would study 'the life of signs within society' (1974, 16).

Today 'semiology' and 'semiotics' are generally used interchangeably, although attempts have been made to give each a distinct meaning; at one time *semiology* seemed generally preferred in Britain (perhaps because French theorists preferred the term *sémiologie*) while *semiotics* was more common in the United States. The latter term now appears to be rather more common in both countries, and will thus be adopted in what follows. (Both terms are based upon adaptations of the Greek word *sēmeion*, meaning 'sign', and the spelling 'semeiology' is sometimes encountered in older texts.)

Saussure's comments are general and predictive, whereas Peirce's are more detailed and comprehensive in scope, and attempt to present a more integrated and formalized system. (It is Peirce we have to thank for the distinction between ICON INDEX and SYMBOL: see the entry for SIGN.) W.T. Scott has suggested that it was precisely the 'abstractness, density and range' of Peirce's proposal that militated against its being developed, either by scholars who were neither philosophers nor logicians, or by others with an interest in abstract universals of mind and meaning. In contrast, Scott continues, 'the sketchiness and concreteness of de Saussure's work makes it more approachable', and its association with Linguistics helped to attach semiology to what has been perhaps the most theoretically prestigious of the human sciences during recent decades (1990, 71). Central to this association has been the use by semioticians of the LINGUISTIC PARADIGM.

What is certain is that, between the 1960s and the 1980s, attempts to establish such a unified science of signs to be known as *semiotics* flourished, and that this threw up an extended terminology and set of concepts that have been pressed into use in a very wide range of fields of study – including that of literary criticism. Although Saussure himself was certainly no narrow formalist, semiotics has often been characterized by a formal-technical approach to the study of signs which, although it may have a place for terms such as *context*, has not emphasized social and CULTURAL determinants. On occasions many of Saussure's terms – SIGNIFIER and SIGNIFIED, LANGUE and PAROLE – have been recruited into the service of more or less acultural and asocial variants of semiotics, often under the aegis of STRUCTURALISM.

In contrast, other versions of semiotics have seen themselves, following Saussure's own suggestion, as a part of the Social Sciences rather than as an abstract, formal and technical discipline, and have seen their work to be closely related to CULTURAL STUDIES. It is significant, for example, that the English translation of UMBERTO ECO's 1972 essay 'Towards a Semiotic Inquiry into the Television Message' was first published in *Working Papers in Cultural Studies* in Britain, and that although this essay states an initial concern to consider television outputs as 'a system of signs', it also commits itself to a belief in the importance of empirical investigations into how viewers actually 'read' and understand what they see – what they actually 'get' (1972, 104).

For Jonathan Culler, semiotics is not primarily concerned to produce INTERPRETATIONS, but rather to show how interpretations, or meanings, are generated.

Semiotics, which defines itself as the science of signs, posits a zoological pursuit: the semiotician wants to discover what are the species of signs, how they differ from one another, how they function in their native habitat, how they interact with other species. Confronted with a plethora of texts that communicate various meanings to their readers, the analyst does not pursue a meaning; he seeks to identify signs and describe their functioning.

(1981, vii–viii)

The debt owed by semiotics to structuralism – indeed, the overlap between the two – should be apparent here.

Semiotics is less fashionable today than it was in the 1970s and 1980s, and work which would have been described as belonging to semiotics then generally receives a rather looser categorization today. Those who do describe themselves as semioticians today are very likely to attach a much greater IDEOLOGICAL significance to the sign than was the case in the 1970s and 1980s. One source of this shift of emphasis is probably the work of MIKHAIL BAKHTIN and his circle, work which reached the English-speaking world only in the 1970s and 1980s, even though much of it was written and/or published in the 1920s and 1930s. V.N. Vološinov's *Marxism and the Philosophy of Language*, for instance, which was first published in Russian in 1929, appeared in English only in 1973. The first chapter of Vološinov's book is entitled 'The Study of Ideologies and Philosophy of Language', and it devotes particular attention to the nature of the *sign*: 'The domain of ideology coincides with the domain of signs. They equate with one another. Wherever a sign is present, ideology is present, too. *Everything ideological possesses semiotic value*' (1986, 10).

As suggested above, a use of the linguistic paradigm has often been crucial to semiotic analyzes: widely different systems such as complete CULTURES (Lévi-Strauss), striptease (Roland Barthes), or the UNCONSCIOUS (JACQUES LACAN) are examined as sign-systems operating like a language, and what a component of the system *is* is subordinated to, or explained in terms of, what semiotic function it performs. Not surprisingly, this can take semiotic ANALYSIS close to aspects of traditional literary analysis. Thus Robert Scholes's 'semiotic analysis' of 'Eveline', one of the stories in James Joyce's collection *Dubliners* (Scholes: 1982, 87–104) relies heavily on the codes of reading defined by Roland Barthes in his *S/Z* (see the entry for CODE).

Perhaps because modern literary criticism was long dominated by the need to generate INTERPRETATIONS, semioticians have been less interested in literature than one might have expected, although Jonathan Culler has argued that literature is the most interesting form of semiosis, as it is cut off from the immediate pragmatic purposes which simplify other sign situations, something which allows the 'potential complexities of signifying processes [to] work freely in literature'. Moreover, Culler claims, literature presents us with a difficulty in saying exactly what is communicated at the same time as we are aware that 'signification is indubitably taking place' (1981, 35).

Literary semiotics, like semiotics in general, comes in what we can term 'formalist' and 'cultural' editions. Robert Scholes points out that Yuri Lotman's *Analysis of the Poetic Text* (1976) and Michael Riffaterre's *Semiotics of Poetry* (1978), both 'approach poems through conventions and codes but share with the New Critics a sense of the poetic text as largely self-referential rather than oriented to a worldly context', whereas Barbara Herrnstein Smith's *Poetic Closure* (1968), although it also concentrates upon codes and CONVENTIONS as a way into the INTERPRETATION of texts, reveals a 'willingness to speak of a poem's "sense of truth"' that links her to other critics concerned with the emotional and intellectual impact of a text on READERS (1982, 12). An interest in the reader, then, is typical of what one can define as non-formalist literary semiotics. An interest in the AUTHOR is much less common among critics of this persuasion, many of them writing when a belief in the death of the author was strongest.

Robert Scholes argues, thought-provokingly, that semiotics has become not so much the study of signs as the study of CODES, 'the systems that enable human beings to perceive certain events or entities *as* signs, bearing meaning' (1982, ix).

The work of JULIA KRISTEVA presents some complications with regard to the terms *semiotics* and *semiotic*. Kristeva has written an essay entitled 'Semiotics: A Critical Science and/or a Critique of Science' (first published in French in 1968, reprinted in Moi: 1986a), in which she defines semiotics as 'the production of models' (Moi: 1986a, 77) and she notes that 'literature' does not exist for semiotics as it

> is *a particular semiotic practice* which has the advantage of making more accessible than others the problematics of the production of meaning posed by a new semiotics, and consequently it is of interest only to the extent that it ('literature') is envisaged as irreducible to the level of an object for normative linguistics (which deals with the codified and denotative word [*parole*]).
>
> (Moi: 1986a, 86)

But at the same time, in her *Revolution in Poetic Language* (first published in French in 1974), Kristeva distinguishes between 'the semiotic' and 'the symbolic' in a context that is PSYCHOANALYTIC and Lacanian. According to Kristeva she understands the term 'semiotic' in its Greek sense, meaning 'distinctive mark, trace, index, precursory sign, proof, engraved or written sign, imprint, trace, figuration' (Moi: 1986a, 93). The semiotic is connected by Kristeva to 'a precise modality in the signifying process' – 'the one Freudian psychoanalysis points to in postulating not only the *facilitation* and the structuring *disposition* of drives, but also the so-called *primary processes* which displace and condense both energies and their inscription' (Moi: 1986a, 93). The argument is complex, but it seems that for her the semiotic has a subversive role *vis-à-vis* the symbolic, which is connected to the Law of the Father and PATRI-ARCHAL power. According to Kristeva, the semiotic 'dismantles' the symbolic in poetry (Moi: 1986a, 115). For further discussion of the work of Kristeva, see the entry on her in Section 5.

Narratology

According to Richard Macksey (1997, xiii), Narratology was so-named by TZVETAN TODOROV in 1969. Onega and Landa claim that as the title was popu-larized in the 1970s by a number of STRUCTURALIST writers, 'the definition of narratology has usually been restricted to structural, or more specifically struc-turalist, analysis of narrative'. And indeed, Gerald Prince suggests that 'narra-tology' can refer to the structuralist-inspired theory which studies the functioning of NARRATIVE in a medium-independent manner, and he attempts to define both narrative COMPETENCE as well as what narratives have in common and what enables them to differ from one another (1988, 65).

Onega and Landa add, however, that narratology 'now appears to be reverting to its etymological sense, a multi-disciplinary study of narrative which negotiates and incorporates the insights of many other critical discourses that involve nar-rative forms of representation', and that today narratology 'studies the narrative aspects of many literary and non-literary genres and discourses which need not be defined as strictly narrative, such as lyrical poems, film, drama, history, adver-tisements' (1996, 1).

The leading proponent of structuralist narratology is undoubtedly GÉRARD GENETTE, and it is particularly with respect to his extended use of the LINGUISTIC PARADIGM that his narratology displays its structuralist allegiance, with terms taken from the system of linguistic grammar being used to denote elements of a proposed 'grammar of narrative'. There is arguably a direct line of descent trace-able from VLADIMIR PROPP's 'functions' through to those grammatical terms used by Genette to indicate the presence of a narrative grammar.

Post-structuralism

This is a descriptive title that is sometimes used almost interchangeably with DECONSTRUCTION while at other times being seen as a more general, umbrella term which describes a movement of which one important element is decon-struction. Satya P. Mohanty's statement 'I use "poststructuralist" to refer to the dominant strand of postmodernist theory, whose focus is on language and signi-fying systems but whose claims are basically epistemological' (1997, 28 n. 4) is representative of a widespread attitude. The two terms are discussed separately in this section, but the imposing presence of JACQUES DERRIDA in both discus-sions should signal their considerable overlap.

Richard Harland suggests that the post-structuralists fall into three main groups: the *Tel Quel* (a French journal) group of JACQUES DERRIDA,

JULIA KRISTEVA and the later ROLAND BARTHES; Gilles Deleuze and Félix Guattari (authors of the influential *Anti-Oedipus: Capitalism and Schizophrenia*, [published in French in 1972]) and the later MICHEL FOUCAULT; and (on his own) Jean Baudrillard (Harland: 1987, 2). Whether JACQUES LACAN is a structuralist or a post-structuralist (or both) is a matter for continuing debate.

The degree of uncertainty that surrounds the use of this term can, however, be suggested by noting that Alex Callinicos proposes a rather different division of post-structuralism into two main strands of thought. The first of these is what Richard Rorty has dubbed TEXTUALISM, while the second is one in which the master category is Michel Foucault's 'power/knowledge'. This 'worldly post-structuralism', as Callinicos calls it, using a term of EDWARD SAID's, involves an 'articulation of "the said and the unsaid", of the discursive and the non-discursive' (Callinicos: 1989, 68). Callinicos argues that whereas the textualists see us as imprisoned in TEXTS, unable to escape the discursive (or unable to see any reality unmediated by DISCOURSES), 'worldly post-structuralism' leaves open the possibility of contact with a reality unmediated by or through discourses. If one accepts this division, then it has to be said that at least part of Foucault's work seems to belong with the textualists. It also has to be said that post-structuralism in its textualist version has had a far more significant impact upon Literary Studies than has the worldly variant, although many of Foucault's ideas have been taken up for criticism and development by FEMINIST critics. The parallel with the distinction proposed earlier in this section between 'formalist' and 'cultural' variants of structuralism should be apparent.

'Textualist' post-structuralism represents both a development and a decon-struction of STRUCTURALISM – a demonstration of its argued inner contradictions. A classic example of this is to be found in an early (1968) interview of Derrida by Julia Kristeva, published in *Positions*. Derrida here takes issue with what he claims is SAUSSURE's maintenance of a rigorous distinction between 'the *signans* and the *signatum*, [and] the equation of the *signatum* and the concept', which, he argues, 'inherently leaves open the possibility of thinking a *concept signified in and of itself*, a concept simply present for thought, independent of a relationship to lan-guage, that is of a relationship to a system of signifiers . . .' (1981, 19).

Within Saussure's revolutionary view of language as a system of DIFFERENCES with no positive forms, that is, Derrida argues that one can discover (by decon-structing Saussure's argument) a relic of the old ideas, an extra-systemic entity, a 'transcendental signified'. Poststructuralism is thus an attempt to push the logic of structuralism's Saussurean base through to its logical conclusion.

Derrida's own position is best followed through certain key terms such as *deconstruction*, LOGOCENTRISM, DIFFÉRANCE, *transcendental signified*, meta-physics of PRESENCE, and so on – which to avoid repetition will not be reconsid-ered here. Suffice to say that central to his endeavour (as he himself admits) has been a commitment to the rooting out of a belief in absolute and extra-systemic determinants of meaning, and in this respect he occupies the same relation towards philosophy as Einstein does towards classical physics. Thus central to the post-structuralist impact on literary theory and criticism has been its argument that the play of SIGNIFIERS cannot be stopped or made subject to the sway of any extra-textual authority: there is, as Derrida infamously puts it, nothing outside the text (1976, 158). Post-structuralism is therefore implicated in the DEATH OF THE AUTHOR, and in consistently opposing any textual INTERPRETATION laying claim either to finality or undeconstructable authority. It has also contributed to a suspicion of any argument or position which grants the individual human SUBJECT powers of self-determination or of historical causation: Louis Althusser's long-lasting attack on HUMANISM prefigures many later post-structuralist attempts to see the subject as site rather than CENTRE.

Deconstruction

Deconstruction is perhaps best described as a movement rather than a school; its name originates in the writings of the French philosopher JACQUES DERRIDA, and rests upon the implication, as Jonathan Culler puts it, that the hierarchical oppositions of Western metaphysics are themselves constructions or IDEOLOGICAL impositions (1988, 20). Deconstruction thus aims to undermine Western metaphysics by undoing or deconstructing these hierarchical oppositions and by showing their LOGOCENTRIC reliance upon a CENTRE or PRESENCE, which reflects the idealist desire to control the play of signifiers by making them subject to some extra-systemic transcendental signified. As will be seen, Derrida is a great coiner of neologisms, and to avoid the necessity for repetition the reader is advised to look up these separate terms – along with DIFFÉRANCE, DISSEMINATION, and 'phonocentrism'. Deconstruction is generally taken to represent an important – even dominant – element in POST-STRUCTURALISM, and can be categorized as one of the progeny of structuralism only by remembering that children typically define themselves by quarrelling with their parents.

In spite of the fact that Derrida in particular and deconstructionists in general are hostile to or dismissive about accounts of intellectual heritage and lines of descent, Derrida has not been without his formative influences. According to Martin Jay it is difficult to ignore hearing in Derrida's work the echo of other arguments, some of which he lists:

Bergson's protest against the spatialization of time, Nietzsche's critique of Apollonian art, Bataille's strictures against heliocentric notions of form, Starobinski's exposure of the dialectic of transparency and obstacle in Rousseau, Heidegger's attack on enframing in the age of the worldview, Merleau-Ponty's interest in the chiasm of the visible and invisible, and Barthes's rejection of the traditional French fetish of linguistic clarity all provided threads for the intertextual web that can be called deconstruction. So too did Emmanuel Levinas's elevation of Hebraic iconoclastic notions of ethics over idolatrous Hellenic ontology and Edmond Jabès's stress on

> the word over the image. . . . Here the effects of Derrida's own Jewish background must be acknowledged. And finally, the impact of the twentieth-century revolution in communications media, which was so important for thinkers from Heidegger to Baudrillard, may also be detected in Derrida's work.
>
> (1993, 498–9)

There is no absolute agreement concerning the implications that Derrida's more general positions hold for literary criticism and theory. At one extreme their implications can appear modest: Jonathan Culler quotes Barbara Johnson to the effect that deconstruction is 'a careful teasing out of warring forces of signification within the text' (Culler: 1981, ix) – a statement with which the NEW CRITICS would surely have been in full accord. In an interview with Imre Salusinszky, Johnson has further commented that:

> if it is indeed the case that people approach literature with the desire to learn something about the world, and if it is indeed the case that the literary medium is not transparent, then a study of its non-transparency is crucial in order to deal with the desire one has to know something about the world by reading literature.
>
> (Salusinszky: 1987, 166)

This, one may be forgiven for noting, is so buttressed with qualifications that it would be hard to disagree with – although it does hedge its bets on whether it really is possible to learn something about the world through literature or whether this is a delusion experienced by 'people' who can be relieved of their inappropriate 'desire' through a study of the literary medium's non-transparency.

Johnson does, however, go on to distance herself and deconstruction from the 'self-involved textual practice of "close reading"' of the New Critics mentioned by her interviewer, suggesting that deconstruction necessarily involves a political attitude, one which examines authority in language, and she notes that Karl Marx was as close to deconstruction as are a lot of deconstructors – particularly by virtue of his bringing to the surface the hidden inscriptions of the economic system, uncovering hidden presuppositions, and showing contradictions (Salusinszky: 1987, 167).

It would certainly seem that deconstruction involves one inescapable implication for the process of INTERPRETATION – literary or otherwise. This is that the interpretation of a TEXT can never arrive at a final and complete 'meaning' for a text. As Derrida himself remarks about a READING of the Marxist 'classics': 'These texts are not to be read according to a hermeneutical or exegetical method which would seek out a finished signified beneath a textual surface. Reading is transformational' (1981, 63). Not just reading in general, but (clearly implied) each act of reading. Thus for Derrida the meaning of a text is always unfolding just ahead of the interpreter, unrolling in front of him or her like a never-ending carpet whose final edge never reveals itself. Introducing a volume of essays entitled *Post-structuralist Readings of English Poetry*, the volume's editors, Richard Machin and Christopher Norris note that post-structuralist readings tend to 'feature the text as active object' (1987, 3): the AUTHOR is no longer seen as the source of meaning, and deconstruction is guilty of being an accessory after the fact with regard to the death of the author. Later on in their Introduction they seek to establish that whereas each reading in the collection 'develops an insistent coherence of its own that drives towards conclusive and irrefutable conclusions', the possibility is none the less held open of 'a multitude of competing meanings, each of which denies the primacy of the others' (1987, 7). The possibility of such a paradoxical blending of linear rigour and pluralistic co-existence has not always convinced the sceptical, however, and one of the most recurrent criticisms of the readings or interpretations generated by deconstruction is that they are not subject to falsification. Another objection is that these readings and interpretations have a tendency to end up all looking the same, all demonstrating the ceaseless play of the SIGNIFIER and nothing much else, just as crude psychoanalytic readings of the 1930s and 1940s tended all to end up demonstrating certain recurrent items of Freudian faith. And indeed the more a criticism holds that interpretations are not subject to the control of textual meaning (however defined), the more it has to cope with the problem that the choice of text necessarily becomes a matter of less and less moment. How can one talk about rigorously grappling with a text if there is said to be nothing fixed 'in' the text?

Pragmatics and the reaction against structuralism

A cluster of theoretical positions can perhaps be seen as the return of structuralism's 'repressed'. Two important early theorists of SEMIOTICS, Charles Morris and Charles Peirce, proposed a tripartite distinction between *syntactics* (SIGNS and their relations to other signs), *semantics* (signs and their relations to the 'outside world'), and *pragmatics* (signs and their relations to users). While this distinction enabled theorists such as FERDINAND DE SAUSSURE to isolate different systems of formal rules (syntactic and semantic) from language in its actual, day-to-day use (its pragmatic existence), it also of course allowed others to pinpoint exactly what it was that structuralism left out of its reckoning. Saussure and his disciples argued that language at the pragmatic level was subject to too many random and unquantifiable pressures to constitute a proper object of study, but a loosely associated group of recent theorists have disagreed, and in recent years more and more disquiet has been expressed at the banishing of the realm of the pragmatic from the concern of the theorist of language, and pragmatics, which has its primary origin within the discipline of Linguistics, involves a reaction against the ideas and practices of both Saussure and the American theorist of language Noam Chomsky. Thus Stephen C. Levinson, in his *Pragmatics*, suggests that the growth of interest in pragmatics

SECTION 3

owes much to a reaction against Chomsky's treatment of language as an abstract device or mental ability which is dissociable from the uses, users, and functions of language (1983, 35). He adds, however, that this is not the whole story:

> Another powerful and general motivation for the interest in pragmatics is the growing realization that there is a very substantial gap between current linguistic theories of language and accounts of linguistic communication. . . . For it is becoming increasingly clear that a semantic theory alone can give us only a proportion, and perhaps only a small if essential proportion, of a general account of language understanding.
>
> (1983, 38)

This development in Linguistics has its parallels in other disciplines, including Literary Criticism. A collection of essays edited by Roger Sell and entitled *Literary Pragmatics* contains a number of attempts to transpose some of the more general principles of pragmatics to a literary context. Central to such a project is a commitment to moving away from the study of literary WORKS as closed or purely formal structures of TEXT to a recognition of them as mediating elements in chains of communication.

> Literary pragmatics takes for granted that no account of communication in general will be complete without an account of literature and its contextualization, and that no account of literature will be complete without an account of its use of the communicative resources generally available. In effect, it reinstates the ancient linkage between rhetoric and poetics . . . .
>
> (1991, xiv)

Perhaps paradoxically, such emphases can take us back to formal systems. It is well known that ancient rhetoric tended to generate these: in its modern variants, attempts to isolate the sets of rules and CONVENTIONS that bind writers to READERS, and which can be seen as the forces which choreograph actual readings of works of literature, can lead straight into SYSTEMS as formal and formalized as grammars. Literary pragmatics typically tries to bring together CENTRIFUGAL AND CENTRIPETAL movements: moving into the text and isolating pragmatic techniques (implicature, presupposition, persuasion), and relating these to forces outside the text in the worlds of writer and reader, such as power relations, CULTURAL traditions, systems of publishing and distribution, censorship, and so on, with a stress throughout on *particular* pragmatic conjunctions and interactions.

Speech act theory

Speech act theory can best be categorized as a way of studying what happens when people talk to one another which focuses on aspects other than that of the semantic content of what is actually said. To this extent speech act theory can be seen as a strain or element in pragmatics, one which originates not in the discipline of Linguistics but in Philosophy. Speech act theory originated with the philosopher John Austin's book *How to Do Things with Words* (1962), in which Austin argues against the philosophical assumptions that verbal statements can be analyzed in isolation and in terms only of their truth or falsity.

A number of other philosophers – most notably John Searle but also H.P. Grice and P.F. Strawson – have developed and extended Austin's arguments. They have drawn attention to the manner in which the public UTTERING of statements is governed by rules and CONVENTIONS which have to be understood and abided by on the part of utterers and listeners if effective communication is to take place, and also to the fact that statements not only *say* things, but they typically also *do* things. In Searle (1969) we find a useful distinction between a number of different sorts of verbal act.

1. Uttering words (morphemes, sentences) = performing *utterance acts*

2. Referring and predicating = performing *propositional acts*

3. Stating, questioning, commanding, promising, etc. = performing *illocutionary acts*

Austin distinguishes between *constatives* – utterances which can either be true or false because they claim to report that certain things are the case in certain worlds – and *performatives*, which are utterances used to do something rather than to say that something is the case (e.g. 'I promise to marry you') and of which it makes no sense to claim that they are either true or false. One should add that a constative can also have a performative aspect – by pragmatic implication, for example.

Utterance acts are also referred to as *locutionary acts* if they involve the production of a recognizably grammatical utterance within a language community. *Illocutionary acts* include such things as asserting, warning, promising and so on, and Austin claimed that over a thousand different possible such acts can be performed in English. Searle has suggested that illocutionary acts can be classified into five basic categories: *representatives*, which undertake to represent a state of affairs; *directives*, which have the aim of getting the person addressed to do something; *commissives*, which commit the speaker to doing something; *expressives*, which provide information about the speaker's psychological state, and *declarations*, which bring about the state of affairs they themselves refer to (e.g. 'I now declare you man and wife') (1976, 10–14; compare ROMAN JAKOBSON's 'functions of human communication' on p. 357).

Searle has also pointed out that a person who performs an illocutionary act may also be performing what he has dubbed a *perlocutionary act*, in other words, achieving certain intended results in his or her listener. He gives as examples, *get him to do something, convince him (enlighten, edify, inspire him, get him to realize)* (1969, 25).

The conventions underlying successful conversation are known as *appropriateness conditions* or *felicity conditions* by speech act philosophers, and together are taken to constitute the *co-operative principle* (a term suggested by H.P. Grice) that governs conversation in ideal situations. They include (i) *maxim of quantity*: (make your contribution no more or less informative than is required); (ii) *maxim of quality*: (make your contribution one that is true, and that does not include either false or inadequately substantiated material); (iii) *maxim of relation*: (be relevant); (iv) *maxim of manner*: (be perspicuous, avoiding obscurity, ambiguity, unnecessary prolixity). (Based on Pratt: 1977, 130; following Grice.)

A theory of utterances which reduced the importance of truth REFERENCE and emphasized instead the compact formed between utterer and listener by the mutual adoption of a set of conventions, made literary critics sit up and take notice, for it seemed of far greater potential use in literary criticism than more traditional philosophical approaches to verbal statements had been. An obvious application of such a theory was to the conversations between CHARACTERS in plays and literary NARRATIVES, but there were more interesting and sophisticated ones. In his essay 'The Death of the Author' ROLAND BARTHES suggested that the word *writing* (see ÉCRITURE) no longer designated 'an operation of recording, notation, representation, "depiction",' but rather 'a performative . . . in which the enunciation has no other content . . . than the act by which it is uttered' (1977, 145–6; see also the entry for AUTHOR). Barthes's use of a term from speech-act theory here shows how difficult his (typically shifting) theoretical position is to ascertain: his earlier structuralism seems here abandoned as he appropriates a term from a tradition highly critical of structuralism.

In a very different way the theory of implicature seemed especially promising for literary-critical application. When a writer wrote something that seemed to be irrelevant to what the READER had been led to be interested in, was this not because the writer could rely upon the reader's *searching* for relevance in the TEXT? Do not readers assume that everything that is there in a literary text is there for some purpose, has in other words some implicature? The problem with this use of speech act theory would seem to be that all it did was to give a new name to something about which literary critics and readers had known for a very long time anyway. Moreover, were not author and reader, and their intercourse, comparable to the participants in a conversation governed by the co-operative principle? Was it not the case that just as a conversation which did not abide by the different Gricean maxims would necessarily be ill-fated and unproductive, so too that any reading of a literary work which did not respect the conventions of literary communication would become pointless and unproductive?

There are a number of possible objections to such an argument. The first is actually a criticism of speech act theory itself, that speech act theory tends to stress co-operation at the expense of struggle and disagreement. Most conversations are not conducted between equals whose interests are identical; they are conducted between individuals who have divergent interests and who either possess, or are subject to the exercise of, social power and authority. Most participants in conversations thus, the argument continues, typically break many of the maxims quoted above to further their own interests, and they expect their fellow conversationalists to do the same. Much the same is true of literary reading: the author and the reader have different interests and are as much trying to outwit as to co-operate with one another. In her poem 'Murder in the Dark' Margaret Atwood (1983) compares the literary process to the party game referred to in her title, with the writer as murderer and the reader as detective!

The second objection to a literary-critical appropriation of speech act theory is that literary works are not orientated to the achievement of specific goals in quite the way that the typical conversation is. Literary works are objects for appreciation, INTERPRETATION, and (sometimes) performance. They thus have the potentiality to generate new experiences, new SIGNIFICANCE, in a manner quite different from that of a conversation. Literary works have, too, an AESTHETIC dimension which conversations lack. This explains why it is that literary works seem actually to be prized to the extent that they break some of the Gricean maxims – that involving AMBIGUITY, for example.

PSYCHOLOGICAL AND PSYCHOANALYTIC THEORIES

Some of the earliest recorded commentators on art and (in a broad sense) literature remarked upon the mysteriousness of the processes which went on in the artist's mind. It is thus not surprising that as attempts to illuminate the mysteries of the human mind became organized in academic disciplines and medical practices from the middle of the nineteenth century onwards, those interested in literature should attempt to apply them to the study of literary works. The application of psychological and psychoanalytic theory to such study has not, however, restricted itself to the mental processes of the artist or writer.

So far as the application of Freudian theories to the study of literature is concerned, readers are referred to the entries for CONDENSATION AND DISPLACEMENT, INCORPORATION, MIRROR STAGE, PROJECTION CHARACTERS, REVISIONISM, UNCONSCIOUS and the comments on 'the uncanny' in the entries for the FANTASTIC and MAGIC REALISM. In like manner, in addition to the entry for JACQUES LACAN in Section 5, the entries for OTHER, DESIRE, JOUISSANCE, and MIRROR STAGE provide information about the application of Lacanian theories within Literary Studies.

As will be apparent in the accounts given below, psychoanalytic theories have often been raided and put to use by an array of other theorists, ranging from the MARXIST philosopher Louis Althusser to whole schools of FEMINIST theorists. Many of these appropriations have been concerned with investigations into the construction (or DECONSTRUCTION) of the SUBJECT AND SUBJECTIVITY – a central concern for many recent theorists. As the entry for UNCONSCIOUS also indicates, both Freudian and Lacanian theories concerning the Unconscious have reached into some perhaps unexpected branches of literary theory in recent years – witness the Marxist FREDRIC JAMESON's 'political unconscious'.

Psychoanalytic criticism

Perhaps the most striking difference between the literary criticism influenced by or based upon psychoanalytic theories of the pre-Second World War period, and that based upon psychoanalytic theories of the past few decades, is that the latter is unlikely to be built purely upon such psychoanalytic theories. Freudian literary criticism of the 1920s and 1930s, for example, generally presented a rather exclusivist appearance: distinguishing itself from other literary criticism and relying very little upon theorists other than Sigmund Freud or his followers. In contrast, the modern literary critic or theorist who relies heavily upon the writings of, say, JACQUES LACAN, is likely also to exhibit a more general interest in DECONSTRUCTIONIST and POST-STRUCTURALIST theory, and probably FEMINIST theory too.

An extremely useful and accessible introduction to and overview of psychoanalysis and psychoanalytic criticism can be found in E. Ann Kaplan's Editor's Introduction to her 1990 book *Psychoanalysis and Cinema*, entitled 'From Plato's Cave to Freud's Screen'. Kaplan differentiates the following six different aspects of psychoanalysis:

1. Psychoanalysis as a 'talking' cure (Kaplan divides this into two parts: the analytic scene, and 'the theory of human development ... found in Freud's basic concepts');

2. Psychoanalysis used to *explain* literary relationships, actions, motives, and the very existence itself of the text;

3. Psychoanalysis as *structurally* an aesthetic discourse (Kaplan refers here to narrative theory, and notes that '[t]he analyst and the analysand are seen to construct "fictions" in the course of their interaction that are not dissimilar from literary use of language');

4. Psychoanalysis *in* a narrative discourse – used as the subject of literary or film texts;

5. Psychoanalysis as an historical, ideological, and cultural discourse;

6. Psychoanalysis as a specific process or set of processes, that the literary or film critic uses as a *discourse* to illuminate textual processes and reader/spectator positions *vis-à-vis* a text.

(Abridged/adapted from Kaplan: 1990, 12–13)

Kaplan's account of the emergence of psychoanalytic literary methods in Germany in the 1930s, and of their development in the United States in the 1940s and subsequently is an ideal starting point for anyone wishing to pursue this topic.

Jacques Lacan is the psychoanalytical theorist who has been most influential on literary theory and criticism in recent years, particularly with regard to his development of the theories of both Freud and FERDINAND DE SAUSSURE. Lacan's assertion that the Unconscious is structured like a language involves an extension of the LINGUISTIC PARADIGM into the realms of psychoanalysis, and has been seen to have important implications for our understanding of the concept of the SUBJECT and of language itself. In terms of studies of particular literary TEXTS it is harder to point to a great influence on Lacan's part. His study of Edgar Allan Poe's short story *The Purloined Letter* is less a piece of literary criticism and more the use of a literary text to exemplify certain psychoanalytic issues, and although it has inspired a number of subsequent studies it is doubtful to what extent the student of Poe will find too much of local interest in these.

Since the 1980s psychoanalytical theory has typically entered Literary Studies in company with FEMINISM. Stevi Jackson and Sue Scott point out that the centrality of the concept of repression to psychoanalysis has encouraged both MARXIST and socialist feminists to use psychoanalysis in their exploration of female sexuality (1996, 7), and many feminist literary-critical appropriations of psychoanalysis have been concerned with issues of GENDER formation, repression, and sexuality. For Jackson and Scott, the attraction of a perspective on Freud mediated through Lacan, 'is its emphasis on the cultural and linguistic structures in which we are positioned in becoming sexed subjects, and its representation of feminine sexual identity as a precarious accomplishment'.

Laura Mulvey has explained the considerable influence of Lacan's writings within Film Studies and feminism as follows.

> His influence broadened and advanced ways of conceptualising sexual difference, emphasising the fictional, constructed nature of masculinity and femininity, the results of social and symbolic, not biological, imperatives. From a political point of view, this position has an immediate attraction for feminists: once anatomy is no longer destiny, women's oppression and exploitation can become contingent rather than necessary. The Lacanian account of the Oedipus complex pivots on the relation of the Father to law, culture and symbolisation, so motherhood under patriarchy gains an important psycho-analytic dimension.
>
> (1989, 165)

She adds, however, a note of warning.

> But, in the last resort, the theory and the politics remain in tension. The Lacanian representation of sexual difference (defined by the presence or absence of the Phallus) leaves woman in a negative relation, defined as 'not-man' and trapped within a theory that brilliantly describes the power relationships of patriarchy but acknowledges no need for escape.
>
> (1989, 165)

The sceptical note is also struck by Stevi Jackson and Sue Scott, who note that many feminists 'remain sceptical of the entire psychoanalytic enterprise', since the 'universalistic theory of subjectivity' which it offers is 'very difficult to reconcile with historical understandings of sexuality as changing over time' (1996, 10).

Another very useful critical overview of psychoanalytic literary criticism is to be found in Peter Brooks's essay 'The Idea of a Psychoanalytic Criticism', which is one of the essays (originally lectures) in his 1994 book *Psychoanalysis and Storytelling*. In this essay Brooks admits that an initial and basic problem is that 'psychoanalysis in literary study has over and over again mistaken the object of analysis' (1994, 20), concentrating upon either the AUTHOR, the READER, or the FICTIVE persons of the text as objects of ANALYSIS. Brooks proposes an alternative:

> I believe that the persistence, against all the odds, of psychoanalytic perspectives in literary study must ultimately derive from our conviction that the materials on which they exercise their powers of analysis are in some basic sense the same: that the structure of literature *is* in some sense the structure of mind – not a specific mind, but what the translators of the *Standard Edition* of Freud's Works call 'the mental apparatus' . . . a term which designates the economic and dynamic organization of the psyche, to a process of structuration. . . . We continue to dream of a convergence of psychoanalysis and literary criticism because we sense that there ought to be, that there must be, some correspondence between literary form and psychic process, that aesthetic structure and form, including literary tropes, must somehow coincide with the psychic structures and operations they both evoke and appeal to.
>
> (1994, 24–5)

This is clearly the statement of a man who feels himself swimming against the current: 'against all the odds', 'in some sense', 'dream', 'sense', 'that there ought to be, that there must be', 'some correspondence', 'somehow coincide' – Brooks's argument is hardly brimming with confidence, and itself invites the sort of analysis that is popularly thought of as psychoanalytic.

Brooks himself rehearses two of the major criticisms of psychoanalytic criticism, first 'that psychoanalysis imperialistically claims to explain literature' and second the 'more subtle (and contemporary) charge that psychoanalysis may be nothing *but* literature, and the relations of the two nothing more than a play of intertextuality, or even a tautology' (1994, 36). Psychoanalytical criticism, in other words, after being attacked early on for being outside the text and unresponsive to its subtleties and uniqueness, now has to adapt to a world of poststructuralist doubt in which many believe that there is no longer anything at all outside the text.

In another essay collected in the same volume, 'Changes in the Margin:

Construction, Transference, and Narrative', Brooks takes a rather different tack, focusing not on parallels between literature and mind, but on parallels between telling stories to an analyst and telling stories to a literary reader. He notes that 'there appears to be increasing agreement, even among psychoanalysts themselves, that psychoanalysis is a narrative discipline'. The psychoanalyst is concerned with the stories told by 'his' patients, which typically suffer from a 'faulty syntax', full of gaps, contradictions in chronology, and screen memories concealing repressed material (1994, 47). The analyst must therefore reconstruct this narrative DISCOURSE, along with the analysand (1994, 54), and in doing so with the help of concepts such as transference and construction, Brooks suggests, in perhaps his boldest move in the essay, that psychoanalysis may

> 'suggest a properly dynamic model of narrative understanding that allows us to recapture, beyond a formalist "narratology", a certain referential function for narrative, where reference is understood not as a naming of the world, and not as the sociolect of the text, but as the *movement of reference* that takes place in the transference of narrative from teller to listener, and back again' (1994, 72).

Archetypal criticism

A type of criticism that attracted renewed attention in the 1970s and 1980s, largely as a result of a FEMINIST interest in the implications that a new form of archetypal criticism might hold for an understanding of women's experience of PATRIARCHY.

The reason (or excuse) for seeing archetypal criticism in relation to psychological and psychoanalytic theories is that one of its founding fathers was the Swiss psychologist and psychoanalyst Carl Gustav Jung, whose concept of the 'collective unconscious' was extremely influential with regard to the development of mythic and archetypal criticism. Jung developed a theory of archetypes which combined with that of the collective unconscious, and attempts were made by him and by others to use these associated theories to explain similarities in myths and archetypes found in widely varying cultures at different times. The other founding father of archetypal criticism was Sir James Frazer. Frazer's *The Golden Bough* appeared in 12 volumes from 1890 to 1915, and represents an exhaustive study of the interconnections of art, religion and MYTH through long processes of historical transmission and transformation. In addition to having a significant influence upon the study of ancient art and CULTURE, the work left its mark on *contemporary* literature: in his prefatory comments to the notes to *The Waste Land* (1922), T.S. ELIOT acknowledges his deep indebtedness to Jessie Weston's *From Ritual to Romance* (1920) and adds the following comment:

> To another work of anthropology I am indebted in general, one which has influenced our generation profoundly; I mean *The Golden Bough*; I have

> used especially the two volumes *Adonis, Attis, Osiris*. Anyone who is acquainted with these works will immediately recognise in the poem certain references to vegetation ceremonies.

The widespread influence of Eliot's poem in the twentieth century is certainly one important factor in the spread of interest in archetypes (from the Greek words *archi*, a beginning or first instance, and *typos*, a stamp or impression), that is, in particular SYMBOLIC patterns and motif-complexes which span cultural and historical boundaries. (Archetypal critics tend to divide into two camps when it comes to explaining this spanning process: we can call these, crudely, the 'spontaneous generationists' and the 'complex processes of transmissionists'.) But other MODERNIST writers of the same period exhibited great interest in the archetypal content of myths: we can cite Yeats, Joyce and Lawrence as obvious examples.

Outside of the work of creative artists we come near to archetypes in the work of Sigmund Freud, and certain Freudian uses of, for example, the Oedipus complex come close enough to universalized cross-cultural patterns of meaning to invite the term 'archetypal'. But the theory of archetypes is given more direct theoretical justification in Jung's theory of the collective UNCONSCIOUS, the survival of primitive forms of thought in the psyches of the members of developed cultures.

The primary accessible source for these archetypes is myth, and in its first flowering archetypal criticism is very closely related to the study of ancient myth: so much so that it is sometimes known as mythic or mythopoeic criticism.

It is with Maud Bodkin's *Archetypal Patterns in Poetry* (1934) that archetypal literary criticism comes of age, and this study initiated a flood of myth-seeking analyzes of literature, especially in the United States.

By the 1950s, however, archetypal criticism was under pressure. It was treated as a variant of extrinsic criticism by the NEW CRITICS, while simultaneously incurring the disfavour of MARXIST and sociological critics for its alleged failure to confront the socially or culturally specific nature of myth – although the critical theories of NORTHROP FRYE helped to keep an archetypal light burning during the decades after the Second World War, and Leslie Fiedler's *Love and Death in the American Novel* (1960, revised edition 1966) demonstrated that it was possible for a literary criticism to trace archetypal patterns in modern literature in a manner that was both creative and culture-specific.

With the resurgence of FEMINIST criticism, however, a new approach to the study of archetypes emerged. If the oppression of women was universal, then this would explain why myths reflecting this repression appeared at all times and all places – without the need for any mystical or even biological explanation. Annis Pratt's *Archetypal Patterns in Women's Fiction* (1982) is representative of the feminist appropriation of archetypal criticism. Pratt argues that Jung defined archetypes as primordial forms springing from the preverbal realm of the unconscious, and that he did not intend his archetypal categories to be taken as fixed absolutes but more as 'images, symbols, and narrative patterns that differ from stereotypes in being complex variables, subject to variations in perception' (1982, 4). Her book focuses upon such examples as the 'rape-trauma archetype' which can be traced from the Apollo–Daphne myth to much women's FICTION, the 'green-world archetype' which, in many female BILDUNGSROMANE, represents a special world of nature in which the pain and suffering experienced by the heroine will be unknown, and the 'growing-up grotesque archetype'. She concludes that it is possible to trace a relationship between the rise of women's fiction and three interrelated repositories of archetypal materials: 'the *Demeter/Kore* and *Ishtar/Tammuz* rebirth narratives, the *grail legends* of the later Middle Ages, and the cluster of archetypal and ritual materials constituting the *Craft of the Wise*, or *witchcraft*' (1982, 167). She concludes that the archetypal patterns to be found in women's fiction constitute signals from a buried feminine tradition that conflict with cultural norms, and this view of archetypes as potentially *oppositional* sums up much of the attraction that investigation into archetypes holds for feminist literary critics today.

'ISMS'

As we have admitted in the introduction to this section, there is a sense in which the defining logic of this fifth sub-section is the weakest of the section. But the theories considered below do have a stronger common element than that of not fitting into the previous four. Although there are very significant and fundamental differences between – say – QUEER THEORY and MARXIST theory, along with the other theories and schools considered in this subsection these two groupings share what in our introduction we have summarized as 'a globalizing imperative, a political agenda, and often a polemical style'. It is also the case that all of the theories and schools looked at in this subsection can be described as 'top-down' rather than 'bottom-up'. In other words, all of them have their roots wholly or partly outside the study of literature. This is not to say that in the application of more global or universalizing theories to literature, the specificity of literature is necessarily ignored. Nor is it to assert that the development of the larger theory took place in a totally literature-free environment; as we point out below, literature and its study have played an important role with regard to the development of 'second-wave feminism'. But when all of these provisos and qualifications have been expressed, it remains the case that the systems of ideas behind the schools and categories dealt with below have encountered the specialist study of literature late rather than early in their development.

This means that the schools and theories dealt with below are likely to have the advantage of a broader view, a sense of the way in which the writing and reading of literature fit into CULTURE and society at large. It also means that all of them also own some sort of commitment to a historical perspective, in contrast to the SYNCHRONIC approach associated with STRUCTURALISM and with certain varieties of FORMALISM. On the other hand, a general characteristic of more global or top-down theories is that they bring less specialist tools with them. The concepts, categories and methods of Marxism have not been developed with literature in mind – unlike, say, the concepts, categories and methods of the NEW CRITICS. Top-down theories are typically accused of clumsiness in their dealings with literary WORKS, a clumsiness which it is often alleged stems from attempts to stretch literature on to the Procrustean bed of a more general set of ideas. As a result, it is often the case that while the proponents of such theories attempt to adapt their inherited 'concepts, categories and methods' to the needs of literary study, they often raid more literature-specific theories and approaches for tools. Thus in spite of the fundamental differences between the New Critics and Marxist literary critics, it is often the case that the latter make use of some of the tools and methods of the former.

It is also worth noting that the development of a separate area of study known as Cultural Studies in both Britain and the United States owes much to the groupings listed below, and to their encounter not just with Literary Studies but also to Media and Film Studies.

Especially in Britain, Cultural Studies owes much to the academic discipline of English: the highly influential Birmingham Centre for Contemporary Cultural Studies was for many years located within the Department of English at Birmingham University. A 1970 essay by Richard Hoggart entitled 'Contemporary Cultural Studies: An Approach to the Study of Literature and Society' – which echoes debates between F.R. LEAVIS and the Marxist critics of the 1930s – is prefaced by a bibliographical note which references a number of important issues and figures from English Studies. These include what Hoggart calls the English 'culture and society' debate, including of course RAYMOND WILLIAMS's *Culture and Society* (1958), but also L.C. Knights's *Drama and Society in the Age of Jonson* (1937), Lionel Trilling's *Beyond Culture* (1966), GEORG LUKÁCS's *The Historical Novel* (English translation, 1962), and other work on 'the sociology of literature'. The bibliography then moves to list material concerned with the analysis of popular literature, starting with Q.D. Leavis's *Fiction and the Reading Public* (1932) and ending with *The Popular Arts* by Stuart Hall and Paddy Whannel (1964). There are then works on mass communication, and works related to the social sciences, including psychology. Works on STRUCTURALISM and SEMIOTICS follow, along with texts concerned with 'mass culture' and with the sociology of knowledge.

The approaches listed below, then, have contributed importantly not just to Literary Studies, but also (often via an engagement with Literary Studies) to wider developments such as Cultural Studies.

Marxist theory and criticism

Marxism is a materialist philosophy, one which insists upon the primacy of material living conditions rather than ideas or beliefs in the life of human beings. It sees history as, in Marx's words, 'the history of class struggle' – the history of struggle for control of the material conditions upon which life rests. It is on the basis of these material conditions, and in response to the struggle for them, that ideas, philosophies, mental pictures of the world, develop – as secondary phenomena. These secondary phenomena may provide human beings with an accurate picture of reality, including themselves and their situation, but they may not. IDEOLOGIES are all related to CLASS positions and thus, in turn, to material conditions and the struggle for their control, but this is not to say that they provide a reliable picture of these. Traditional Marxists have laid great stress upon the distinction between BASE (or basis) and SUPERSTRUCTURE, seeing the social base as essentially economic in nature, and the superstructure as constituting the world of mental activities – ideas, beliefs, philosophies, and (in the opinion of some but not all Marxists) art and literature.

Marxism is an anti-ESSENTIALIST philosophy; for Marxists, all is in movement, and – because there is no separate or pure realm of ideas, or values, or spiritual phenomena – all is interconnected, however complex and mediated the interconnections turn out to be. The complexity of these interconnections takes, according to Marx, a characteristic form: a dialectical rather than a mechanical and purely hierarchical one. And this opens up the possibility for human beings to gain at least partial control over their life-circumstances: Marxism has traditionally been an active and interventionist philosophy, not a spectatorial or passive one, although this may be changing with a growing suspicion of the dangers of too partisan an attitude to theory.

Marxist ideas about literature have a long history. Marx himself was extremely well read in classical and contemporary literature, and literary allusions and references abound in his work. A number of early Marxists sought to apply Marx's ideas to literature: both in terms of the INTERPRETATION and evaluation of existing literary WORKS, and also in terms of advice to writers and those with (or seeking) political power about what sort of literature should be encouraged. The active and interventionist nature of Marxism has recurrently led to attempts to *use* literature for social or political ends: some of these have gained a bad press in the reviews of history, as in the case of Soviet Socialist Realism; others have received a more positive response, as in the case of BERTOLT BRECHT's attempt to use his political theatre in the interests of social revolution. It should be noted that Marxism did not introduce the political use of art and literature to the world; there is a long tradition of such attempts – one which it is fair to say the modern academic study of literature consistently underplays and undervalues.

Early Marxist writings on literature and art tended to be of a generalizing nature, seeking to explain why large bodies of writing took the form that they did by relating them to the social and economic conditions of their emergence. Thus G.V. Plekhanov's essay *Art and Social Life* (first published in 1912) has a long opening section on 'French Drama and Painting of the Eighteenth Century' which attempts to relate the class STRUCTURE of eighteenth-century France with the more general characteristics of the drama and painting of the period. To a large extent this sort of impulse has remained central to Marxist literary criticism, although it can take a crude 'vulgar Marxist' form in which art is seen directly and unproblematically to mirror or reflect a society's class structure or economic base, or it can take a more sophisticated form in which increased attention is paid to complex processes of mediation between a society and its art and literature. A good example of the latter would be the work of LUCIEN GOLDMANN.

Marxist literary criticism has had two periods of significant influence: in the 1930s, and in the 1960s. In both periods this influence has been related to a more general interest in and commitment to Marxist ideas. Undoubtedly the most influential and important Marxist literary critic of the 1930s (and after) was the Hungarian GEORG LUKÁCS, associated in particular with a strong defence of the REALISM to which he believed his Marxism committed him, alongside a concomitant hostility on the artistic and the political level to all forms of MODERNISM.

Since 1960 Marxist literary criticism has reflected the diversities of Marxism in the modern world, and in certain usages today a point is made of dropping the capital 'M' so as to indicate less dependence upon the particular historical individual whose name is borrowed for the term. As a generalization we can say that the less contentious it has become to see literary works in the context of their emergence and subsequent life, the more Marxist ideas have penetrated literary criticism in general. Committed modern Marxist critics are more likely than their predecessors to be engaged in the study of mediating processes: ideology, the 'political unconscious' of the American Marxist FREDRIC JAMESON, the 'literary modes of production' of the British Marxist TERRY EAGLETON, and the STRUCTURE OF FEELING of the Welsh cultural theorist and novelist RAYMOND WILLIAMS (who became progressively more critical of orthodox Marxism). They are also less likely to be happy with a straightforward relegation of literature to the realm of the superstructure. The influential French Marxist Pierre Macherey's *A Theory of Literary Production* (first published in French in 1966), for instance, by seeing the writing of literature as a form of production necessarily sees it as more than the simple reflection of economic facts that vulgar Marxism attributed to literature.

Since the 1970s one is likely to find literary critics or theorists describing themselves as 'Marxist-FEMINISTS', or 'structuralist-Marxists', or seeking to combine or relate Marxism and POST-STRUCTURALISM. What we can call monolithic Marxism seems very much a thing of the past, and after the collapse of communism in Eastern Europe it seems unlikely to make a particularly strong comeback.

Frankfurt School

The term is generally applied nowadays to those individuals and works associated with the Frankfurt School of Critical Theory. The School grew out of the Frankfurt Institute of Social Research, which was founded in 1923, and especially out of Max Horkheimer's directorship of the Institute. Horkheimer's own work, and that of others such as Herbert Marcuse, Theodor Adorno, and Erich Fromm, established itself as an important development (or revision, depending upon one's perspective) of MARXISM, and is generally seen as a founding element in what is now referred to as Continental Marxism. The School was pro-MODERNIST and anti-Stalinist (especially in its view that the industrial working class of advanced countries was no longer a revolutionary force), and was sympathetic to an open attitude towards PSYCHOANALYSIS. In spite of its name the School was not always located in Frankfurt; its members regrouped in the United States during the Nazi period, but returned to Frankfurt in 1950.

During the 1960s and 1970s the ideas of the Frankfurt School seemed to offer a non-Stalinist application and development of Marxism to issues of culture and IDEOLOGY, and in 1977 FREDRIC JAMESON was able to write that the Frankfurt School had transmitted 'fundamental themes and concerns' from debates around Marxism in the 1930s to 'the student and anti-war movements of the 1960s' (Bloch *et al.*: 1977, 197).

The standard study of the Frankfurt School is Martin Jay's *The Dialectical Imagination: A History of the Frankfurt School and the Institute of Social Research 1923–50* (1973). For students of literature, Adorno's contributions to the debates collected in the volume *Aesthetics and Politics* (Bloch *et al.*: 1977) – including letters to WALTER BENJAMIN and a critique of the work of GEORG LUKÁCS – are of abiding interest.

New Historicism and cultural materialism

Victor Shea has pointed out that Wesley Morris used the term 'New Historicism' in 1972 'to designate a mode of literary criticism derived from German historicists such as Leopold von Ranke and Wilhelm Dilthey, and American historians such as Vernon L. Parrington and Van Wyck Brooks' (1993, 124). Kiernan Ryan has suggested that the term is foreshadowed even earlier, in the title of Roy Harvey Pearce's 1969 book, *Historicism Once More*, but he concedes that

> it is Stephen Greenblatt who gets the credit for slipping the term into circulation in its current sense in his Introduction to 'The Forms of Power and the Power of Forms in the Renaissance', a special issue of *Genre* (15 1–2 [1982]) devoted to what was already billed as a fresh departure in critical practice.
>
> (Ryan: 1996, xiii)

Nowadays the term is restricted to this later usage stemming from STEPHEN J. GREENBLATT, and describing groupings of critics and theorists who have rejected the SYNCHRONIC approaches to culture and literature associated with STRUC-

TURALISM and who have attempted to provide more adequate answers to various problems associated with the tensions between aesthetic, cultural, and historical approaches to the study of a range of different sorts of TEXT.

Most of those known as New Historicists (some of whom have gone on record with their preference for the term 'cultural poetics') are from North America, while cultural materialism is by and large a British phenomenon. On occasions, however, New Historicism is used as an umbrella term to include members of both groupings.

The writings of MICHEL FOUCAULT and RAYMOND WILLIAMS constitute a major influence on the New Historicists, who have succeeded in defining (or suggesting) new objects of historical study, with a particular emphasis upon the way in which causal influences are mediated through discursive practices (see the entry for DISCOURSE).

Stephen J. Greenblatt is a key figure in the rise of the New Historicism, and in his collection of essays *Learning to Curse* (1990) he admits that for him the term describes not so much a set of beliefs as 'a trajectory that led from American literary formalism through the political and theoretical ferment of the 1970s to a fascination with what one of the best new historicist critics [Louis A. Montrose] calls "the historicity of texts and the textuality of history"' (1990, 3). Elsewhere he describes the New Historicism as a practice rather than a doctrine (1990, 146). Greenblatt sees the New Historicism's creation of 'an intensified willingness to read all of the textual traces of the past with the attention traditionally conferred only on literary texts' (1990, 14) to be central to its value. Thus in a study of a design by Dürer for a monument to commemorate the defeat of peasants involved in protest and rebellion, Greenblatt notes that INTENTION, GENRE and historical situation all have to be taken into account, as all are social and IDEOLOGICAL and must be involved in any 'reading' of the design (1990, 112). He continues:

> The production and consumption of such works are not unitary to begin with; they always involve a multiplicity of interests, however well organized, for the crucial reason that art is social and hence presumes more than one consciousness. And in response to the art of the past, we inevitably register, whether we wish to or not, the shifts in value and interest that are produced in the struggles of social and political life.
>
> (1990, 112)

The New Historicist, in other words, has as much to say about the READING of texts as about their composition.

For those who like negative definitions, Greenblatt cites three definitions of the word 'historicism' from *The American Heritage Dictionary*, all of which he sees as counter to the practice of New Historicists:

1. The belief that processes are at work in history that man can do little to alter;
2. The theory that the historian must avoid all value judgments in his study of past periods or former cultures;
3. Veneration of the past or of tradition.

(Quoted in Greenblatt: 1990, 164)

Although Greenblatt and other New Historicists pay tribute to the work of various POST-STRUCTURALISTS, the anti-formalist element in their work clearly distances them from important aspects of post-structuralism.

Graham Holderness has produced a useful checklist of what he considers to be the differences between the (mainly British) cultural materialism and the (mainly North American) New Historicism. According to him, cultural materialism

is much more concerned to engage with contemporary cultural practice, whereas New Historicism confines its focus of attention to the past; cultural materialism can be overtly, even stridently, polemical about its political implications, where New Historicism tends to efface them. Cultural materialism partly derives its theory and method from the kind of cultural criticism exemplified by Raymond Williams, and through that inheritance stretches its roots into the British tradition of Marxist cultural analysis, and thence into the wider movement for socialist education and emancipation; New Historicism has no sense of a corresponding political legacy, and takes its intellectual bearings directly from 'post-structuralist' theoretical and philosophical models. . . . Cultural materialism accepts as appropriate objects of enquiry a very wide range of 'textual' materials [. . . whereas] New Historicism concerns itself principally with a narrower definition of the 'textual': with what has been written . . . .

(1991, 157)

Faith Nostbakken has pointed out that the term 'cultural materialism' emerges independently in two different academic contexts. As she explains, 'Marvin Harris applied the name "cultural materialism" to a scientific method of studying the interaction between social life and material conditions (*The Rise of Anthropological Theory* 1968)' (1993, 21). In Literary Studies, however, the term has a rather different ancestry from this, as it owes not just its theory and method to RAYMOND WILLIAMS, but also its name. In his essay 'Notes on Marxism in Britain since 1945', Williams gives an interesting account of the intellectual journey which culminated in cultural materialism for him.

It took me thirty years, in a very complex process, to move from that received Marxist theory [= cultural theory from Engels and through

Plekhanov, Fox, Caudwell, West, and also Zdhanov] (which in its most general form I began by accepting) through various transitional forms of theory and inquiry, to the position I now hold, which I define as 'cultural materialism'. The emphases of the transition – on the production (rather than only the reproduction) of meanings and values by specific social formations, on the centrality of language and communication as formative social forces, and on the complex interaction both of institutions and forms and of social relationships and formal conventions – may be defined, if anyone wishes, as 'culturism', and even the old (positivist) idealism/materialism dichotomy may be applied if it helps anyone. What I would now claim to have reached, but not necessarily by this route, is a theory of culture as a (social and material) productive process and of specific practices, of 'arts', as social uses of material means of production (from language as material 'practical consciousness' to the specific technologies of writing and forms of writing, through to mechanical and electronic communication systems).

(1980, 243)

If the model presented here is one of the relatively gentle evolution of cultural materialism from MARXISM, elsewhere Williams suggests that more of a sharp break took place.

What is actually latent in historical materialism is not, in Lukács's categorical sense, a theory of art, but a way of understanding the diverse social and material production (necessarily often by individuals within actual relationships) of works to which the connected but also changing categories of art have been historically applied. I call this position cultural materialism, and I see it as a diametrically opposite answer to the questions which Lukács and other Marxists have posed.

(1989, 273)

John Higgins has commented that in Williams's work cultural materialism looks two ways: 'As *cultural* materialism, it is the name Williams gave to his distinctive version of Marxist theory, but, as cultural *materialism*, it refers to his response to the theory and practice of literary analysis at work in the existing institutions of English studies' (1999, 125). Put another way: the word *culture* represents a challenge to traditional Marxists, whereas the word *materialism* represents a challenge to the apolitical tradition of English literary criticism.

What Williams does not mention overtly, though, is the now-typical cultural materialist insistence upon situating cultural artifacts and art-works in the varied and successive contexts of their 'consumption' or interactive enjoyment. Thus according to Alan Sinfield, the 'rough programme' of cultural materialism involves the placing of a text in its (plural) context*s*:

> a strategy [which] repudiates the supposed transcendence of literature, seeking rather to understand it as a cultural intervention produced initially within a specific set of practices and tending to render persuasive a view of reality; and seeing it also as re-produced subsequently in other historical conditions in the service of various views of reality, through other practices, including those of modern literary study.
>
> (1992, 22)

In his book *Shakespeare Recycled*, Graham Holderness suggests that the New Historicists have preferred to 'reproduce a model of historical culture in which dissent is always already suppressed, subversion always previously contained, and opposition always strategically anticipated, controlled and defeated' (1992, 34). By implication, therefore, the cultural materialists see a culture far more as a battlefield: riven with struggles, tensions, and contradictions on a number of different planes. Alan Sinfield, the title of whose important cultural-materialist book *Faultlines: Cultural Materialism and the Politics of Dissident Reading* (1992) is itself indicative of this view, agrees with Holderness in tracing this crucial difference back to the work of Raymond Williams:

> Much of the importance of Raymond Williams derives from the fact that at a time when Althusser and Foucault were being read in some quarters as establishing ideology and/or power in a necessarily unbreakable continuum, Williams argued the co-occurrence of subordinate, residual, emergent, alternative, and oppositional cultural forces alongside the dominant, in varying relations of incorporation, negotiation, and resistance.
>
> (1992, 9)

SECTION 3

A good example of such a cultural materialist approach, then, would be Holderness's chapter on E.M.W. Tillyard's *Shakespeare's History Plays* (1944) in his *Shakespeare Recycled*. Holderness suggests that this and other works all 'derive from a common problematic: the ideological crisis of British nationalism precipitated by the events of the 1930s and 1940s: the Depression, the crisis of Empire and particularly of course the Second World War' (1992, 22). He implies, too, that the continued life of such criticism can be understood only in the context of continued ideological crisis and struggle. One could say that for the cultural materialist the focus of study is not the text, but the birth and life of the text in culture and history.

The following scholars have been associated with New Historicism: Stephen Greenblatt, Louis Montrose, Jonathan Goldberg, Leonard Tennenhouse, Stephen Mullaney, and Hayden White. The best-known cultural materialists are Jonathan Dollimore, Alan Sinfield, Lisa Jardine, Graham Holderness, Catherine Belsey, and Francis Barker.

Postcolonialism

This is a label that can be used in a relatively neutral descriptive sense to refer to literature emanating from or dealing with the peoples and cultures of lands which have emerged from colonial rule (normally, but not always, relatively recently), but it can also be used to imply a body of theory or an attitude towards that which is studied. Exactly how precise a descriptive term *postcolonialism* is is a matter of some debate; Georg M. Gugelberger claims of 'Postcolonial Studies' that

> it is not a discipline but a distinctive problematic that can be described as an abstract combination of all the problems inherent in such newly emergent fields as minority discourse, Latin American studies, African studies, Caribbean studies, Third World studies (as the comparative umbrella term), *Gastarbeiterliteratur*, Chicano studies, and so on, all of which participated in the significant and overdue recognition that 'minority' cultures are actually 'majority' cultures and that hegemonized Western (Euro-American) studies have been unduly privileged for political reasons.
>
> (1994, 582)

As many different commentators have noted, both parts of the term are problematic. Does the 'post' imply temporal supersession or IDEOLOGICAL rejection? (If the latter, then clearly one can have postcolonial literature in lands which are still experiencing colonial rule.) So far as 'colonialism' is concerned, should one extend this to lands such as Australia, Canada, and the United States – which after all did emerge as independent nations after periods of colonial rule? Should 'colonialism' include 'neo-colonialism' – in other words that pursuance of the political objectives of colonial rule by means which (at least not overtly) do not involve the exercise of direct political sovereignty backed up by military might?

Many commentators have admitted that the term has caught on in part because it raises fewer hackles than do terms which contain words such as 'imperialism' or 'Third World', because it is more potentially all-embracing than are terms such as 'Commonwealth literature', and because it carries with it no fixed ideological baggage as does ORIENTALISIM. It is hard, after all, to be opposed to postcolonialism, in large part precisely because of the term's ambiguities and vagueness. Nevertheless, the term has created institutional space for the study of a wide variety of non-CANONICAL literatures, and has given academics (and, let us admit it, publishers) a focus for the development of new areas of study. Moreover, while the term carries no specific ideological baggage with it, a body of theoretical work is associated with the field and a range of terms associated with it can now be listed.

Feminism

Toril Moi makes a useful distinction between three cognate terms which provides a good starting point: *feminism* is a political position, *femaleness* a matter of biology, and *femininity* a set of CULTURALLY defined characteristics (1986b, 204). It should be recognized, of course, that Moi's suggested definitions here have a political edge: she is as much arguing for how these terms *should* be used as describing an actual, existing usage. Phrases such as 'the eternal feminine' make it clear that non-feminist usages can define femininity in universal, bio-logical rather than cultural terms – nor is it that uncommon to find 'female' used to refer to culturally acquired characteristics. (The *OED* definitions of feminin-ity make interesting reading in this context.)

However good a starting point this is it is not unproblematic – not least because ELAINE SHOWALTER, in her *A Literature of Their Own*, suggests a differ-ent way of using these three terms in the narrower field of women's writing. For Showalter, the feminine stage of women's writing involves a prolonged phase of imitating the prevailing modes of the dominant tradition and internalizing its standards of art; the feminist stage involves the advocacy of minority rights and values; and the female stage is the phase of self-discovery and search for identity (1982, 13).

Of the three terms, feminism is probably the most complex. The (original) *OED* described the word as 'rare', and defined it as 'the qualities of females', giv-ing an example from 1851. But from the end of the nineteenth century the word comes increasingly to be applied to those committed to and struggling for equal rights for women – including men: in Joseph Conrad's *Under Western Eyes* (first book publication 1911), for example, the CHARACTER Peter Ivanovitch is repeat-edly referred to (ironically) as a feminist. Moreover, not all those women fighting for women's rights accepted the term. In VIRGINIA WOOLF's *Three Guineas*, first published in 1938, Woolf writes

> What more fitting than to destroy an old word, a vicious and corrupt word that has done much harm in its day and is now obsolete? The word 'femi-nist' is the word indicated. That word, according to the dictionary, means 'one who champions the rights of women'. Since the only right, the right to earn a living, has been won, the word no longer has a meaning.
>
> (1977, 117)

Woolf goes on to describe a symbolic burning of the 'dead' and 'corrupt' word, and declares that once this has been done the air is cleared, and that we can see men and women working together for the same cause. Woolf argues, too, that the word *feminist* was one which was applied to those fighting 'the tyranny of the patriarchal state', 'to their great resentment' (1977, 118) – in other words, that the word was imposed on rather than chosen by women fighting for the rights of women. LUCE IRIGARAY's objection to the word in a 1982 interview was that *feminism* 'is the word by which the social system designates the struggle of women. . . . I prefer to say the struggles of women, which reveals a plural and polymorphous character' (Todd: 1982, 233).

Such arguments have not been successful in burying the word in question, however, and to a very large extent women (and men) fighting for women's rights have been happy to call themselves, and be called, feminists. But doubts about the term have remained. In an interview published in the *Guardian*, 18 May 1987, Margaret Atwood responds as follows when her interviewer suggests that in her book *Bluebeard's Egg* she seems mellower about men than in her other books.

> 'It depends how you count. (I was in market research,' she adds, very dead-pan.) 'If we all vote if women have souls, I vote on that side, if it's kill all the men, I'm not for it. I don't know what feminism means.'
>
> (Nadelson: 1987, 10)

Such doubts are probably more testimony to the health of the women's movement than the opposite, however. As the movement expands and develops, discussion about such a key descriptive term inevitably takes on a political character, and different interest groupings engage in struggle to impose their own MEANINGS on any term which has become a very important rallying point. To have feminism defined in such a way as to reflect one's own political objectives clearly does one's own political position and/or grouping no harm. It is perhaps worth recalling that Karl Marx was reported (by Engels) to have declared, 'all I know is that I am not a Marxist' when exasperated by some of his younger 'followers' (see the discussion in Draper: 1978, 5–11). What is indisputable is that feminism is a broad church, one within which many different emphases and persuasions (by no means necessarily opposed to one another) can be found. In the index entries for 'feminism' and 'feminist literary criticism' in the second edition of Mary Eagleton's *Feminist Theory: A Reader* (1996) one can find a representative list of sub-entries, including: academic/activist; Anglo-American; bourgeois; Black; competitive; cultural; cyberfeminism; French; international; Marxist; materialist; negative; object-relations; radical; separatist; socialist. Such diversity is surely a sign of health and energy.

In general usage the term 'feminist' is usually treated as an umbrella term to describe those (normally women but sometimes also men) who disagree with Virginia Woolf that there are no more rights to be achieved for women, and who think that it is necessary to struggle against the oppression of women on a number of different planes: social, economic, and IDEOLOGICAL. Such struggle takes varied forms and has differing objectives: if one can make the comparison with Marx and MARXISM again, one finds in both cases more unity over what is to be fought against than what is to be fought for.

Feminism as socio-political movement experienced a resurgence in the late 1960s and early 1970s, especially in Western Europe and the United States, a resurgence which continues and which has established a number of seemingly permanent changes in the developed countries – and which has not been without an effect in the developing world. Since that time feminism has become more and more of an international movement, with increasing contacts between activists and sympathizers in different parts of the world. From the start of this movement, the role of literature was considerable. This is partly because literary writing was less closed to women than most of the other arts, and other forms of writing, but also because the literature of the past written (especially) by women offered itself as a record and analysis of the past oppression of women. It should also be remembered that the modern resurgence of feminism had one of its most important sources in the universities and colleges of the developed world, amongst a group of widely read women.

Radical feminism is a term still current but perhaps more in use in the 1960s and 1970s. It is in its insistence upon the fundamental and all-embracing significance of GENDER differentiation that radical feminism's radicalness is normally taken to consist – along with (often but not always) a rejection of most or all forms of collaboration with men or with organizations containing men. Radical feminism is often (but again, not always) associated with a commitment to Lesbianism (as a moral-political commitment as much as a sexual orientation), and if it is possible for a man to be a feminist it seems impossible (or at the very least extremely difficult) for one to be a radical feminist. Radical feminism tends to be universalizing rather than to focus upon the socially, culturally, and historically specific characteristics of PATRIARCHY, although to this it needs to be added that radical feminists have led important campaigns against specific forms of oppression. Eve Kosofsky Sedgwick has commented, in criticism of radical feminism, that it

> tends to deny that the meaning of gender or sexuality has ever significantly changed; and more damagingly, it can make future change appear impossible, or necessarily apocalyptic, even though desirable. Alternatively, it can radically oversimplify the prerequisites for significant change. In addition, history even in the residual, synchronic form of class of racial difference and conflict becomes invisible or excessively coarsened and dichotomized in the universalizing structuralist view.
>
> (1993, 13)

Against such a view, in their own discussion of radical feminism Andermahr, Lovell and Wolkowitz stress the fact of some 'commitment to the goals of socialism' in the early stages of the radical feminist movement, a belief that 'the whole gender order in which people, things and behaviour are classified in terms of the distinction between masculine and feminine is socially constructed and has no basis in natural differences between the sexes', and a desire to annihilate sex-roles as important aspects of radical feminism (1997, 222–3). This suggests that the universalizing side of radical feminism is only part of the story, and indeed in their introductory essay 'Sexual Skirmishes and Feminist Factions: Twenty-five Years of Debate on Women and Sexuality', which is the first piece in their

Feminism and Sexuality: A Reader, Stevi Jackson and Sue Scott claim that radical feminists 'are often misrepresented as essentialist, as believing in an essential female nature and female sexuality'.

Of perhaps most specific interest to students of literature has been the radical feminist analysis of patriarchal and SEXIST elements in language. Representative radical feminists are Adrienne Rich, Mary Daly and Shulamith Firestone.

Queer theory

The recuperation of the term *queer* – originally a term of abuse aimed at homosexuals, but reclaimed by them to announce their pride in their identity as gays and lesbians – can be dated from the formation of the American group Queer Nation. As Ian Lucas reports, Queer Nation goes back to March 1990, when, after divisions amongst the ACT UP movement in New York, activists began to develop a new grouping.

> Queer Nation built activism based on sexual identity – not just lesbian, gay or bisexual, but *queer*. Queer was used as an in-your-face catch-all designer label. Its shocking tone caught some of the violence shown against lesbian and gay communities in America, and threw it right back. It was also a call to queer nationalism – a community that confronted homophobia and had collective responsibility for dismantling the power of 'the closet'.
>
> (Lucas: 1998, 14)

Following the widespread publicity achieved by Queer Nation, the term *queer* entered more and more into the vocabulary of gay and lesbian activism. According to an anonymous leaflet entitled 'Queer Power Now', distributed in London a year after the formation of Queer Nation, in 1991, and cited by Stevi Jackson and Sue Scott in their essay 'Sexual Skirmishes and Feminist Factions: Twenty-five Years of Debate on Women and Sexuality', 'Queer means to fuck with gender'. Jackson and Scott themselves go on to provide a rather less succinct definition.

> Among Left academics in particular, disillusionment with traditional Marxism rendered poststructuralist and postmodernist perspectives attractive. Once appropriated by feminists and gay theorists, and applied to sexuality, this tendency ultimately led to the development of Queer theory. Rather than setting up categories such as 'lesbian' as the basis of political identities, Queer sought to destabilise the binary oppositions between men and women and straight and gay. Such identities were not to be seen as authentic properties of individual subjects, but as fluid and shifting, to be adopted and discarded, played with and subverted, strategically deployed in differing context. . . . Radical lesbian perspectives were regarded as essentialist in that they cast lesbianism as a fixed point outside

of, and in opposition to, patriarchal relations. Politically the aim of Queer theory is to demonstrate that gender and sexual categories are not given realities but are 'regulatory fictions', products of discourse. Here Queer theory converges with Queer politics, in the latter's playing out of parodic performances at street level, for example holding public 'kiss-ins' and mock weddings, and the notion of 'gender-fuck' – challenging gender categories through dress and transgressive sexual performance.

(Jackson and Scott: 1996, 15)

Jackson and Scott express some reservations about this development, noting that 'much of the blurring of gender categories within gay culture is occurring at the level of style rather than politics' and allowing themselves the tart observation that they 'doubt whether wearing a tutu with Doc Martens will bring patriarchy to its knees' (1996, 16).

Catherine Grant (1994/5) is more guarded, noting that although 'Queer' has come to mean different things to different people, it

generally denotes the application of poststructuralist and postmodern ideas to interdisciplinary studies of the historical formations of lesbianism and homosexuality, and of the relationship between these formations and those of heterosexuality. It implies a shift from the consideration of lesbianism and homosexuality as discrete identities to one of homosexualities as kinds of discursive construct. 'Queer' theorists also often advocate the disruption or destruction of traditional categories of sex and gender.

(In Jackson and Scott: 1996, 166)

As we can see, the term 'queer' can invoke both high theory as well as a relatively unintellectualized activism, but at its heart is an anti-discriminatory view of GENDER as unfixed and certainly more complex than our neat BINARY distinctions would suggest. In his essay 'True love in queer times: romance, suburbia and masculinity', David Oswell has suggested that the 'notion that identity is not fixed but can be played with and contested has been a central element within the recent formation of "queer politics"' (1998, 161). He adds, however, that the practices associated with queer politics are 'far from unified', and that 'there is clear disagreement about the meaning of the term "queer"' (1998, 162). In spite of this he finds the term useful:

Although the term 'queer' is used to articulate a range of political positions, it has clearly come to signify an assault both on 'straight' sexual discourses and practices and on an earlier moment in lesbian and gay sexual 'identity politics' which called upon individuals to express the truth of their self. . . . [T]he queer politics of the late 1980s and 1990s has been deployed against

> the binary divide between heterosexual and homosexual and in favour of an enunciation of the pluralisation of sexual identities.
>
> . . .
>
> Likewise it has also come to define a wider articulation of 'perverse' sexual identities, communities, and practices. Sex-workers, lesbian and gay identified men and women, practitioners of S&M, body piercers and so on are articulated within the category of 'queer'. In this sense the politics of queer is neither assimilationist nor separatist.
>
> (1998, 163; S&M = sadism and masochism)

Oswell's article provides useful evidence of the way in which the term and the concept can be useful within literary criticism: it is devoted to a study of Hanif Kureishi's *The Buddha of Suburbia* (1990). The article is recommended as an excellent introduction to Queer studies.

Various coinages involving plays on the similarity of *queer* and *query* are popular at present. Thus *queer(y)ing* suggests that a queer READING of a literary WORK can serve to raise questions about conventional reading, and about conventions in general.

Section 4

Glossary of literary and theoretical terms

Absence Recent theorists have drawn particular attention to the issue of the absences lurking behind the seeming completeness of literary works, and since the publication of Pierre Macherey's *Pour une théorie de la production littéraire* (1966; translated as *A Theory of Literary Production*, 1978) such absences have been accorded more overt theoretical attention. According to Macherey the book is not self-sufficient but is necessarily accompanied by a certain absence without which it would not exist, and he draws our attention to the fact that Sigmund Freud relegated the absence of certain words to the UNCONSCIOUS. From this perspective a work's absences are as significant as was the dog that did not bark to Sherlock Holmes.

An absence can, according to such theorists, be *determinate*. In other words, it can be so central that it structures the work around itself, determining the final FORM of the work.

Abstract That which deals in general concepts (love, death, faith) rather than the CONCRETE particularities of person, place or thing.

Absurd The 'theatre of the absurd' refers to the work of MODERNIST playwrights such as Samuel Beckett and Eugene Ionesco, among others, whose work suggests a view of life as being farcically empty and meaningless. A sense of 'the absurd' is often said to characterize the writing of existentialists such as Albert Camus.

Acatelectic A term used to describe a line of poetry which is METRICALLY complete – that is, not missing a syllable in the final foot. An acatelectic line of iambic pentameter will have ten syllables. Its opposite would be CATALECTIC (with a missing syllable in the last foot: in iambic pentameter, this would result in only nine syllables), or extrametric or hypermetric (with an additional, metrically redundant, syllable: in iambic pentameter, eleven syllables).

Acrostic In poetry, a device whereby the first letters of the lines spell a message, name or word. When both the initial and final letters are used, this is a double acrostic.

Aesthetics The theory of what is beautiful in a work of art, and also the name given to that discipline or tradition of study that seeks to isolate the principles behind the beautiful – both in art and in natural phenomena. In the Anglo-American tradition aesthetics has tended to find its home in departments of Philosophy, and much recent literary theory has been suspicious of alleged universalizing and ESSENTIALIST tendencies in aesthetics; as Frank Kermode puts it in his *An Appetite for Poetry*, 'Despite their common devotion to the complexities of language, the newer criticism differs from the old New Criticism in that it challenges "the specificity of the aesthetic"' (1989, 10).

Affective The fifth meaning provided by the *OED* for 'affective' is nearest to that commonly associated with literary-critical usage: 'Having the quality of affecting; tending to affect or influence; influential, operative.' This usage owes much to two sources: I.A. RICHARDS's *Principles of Literary Criticism* (1924) and the essay 'The Affective Fallacy' by W.K. Wimsatt and Monroe Beardsley (1949). Richards's highly psychologizing approach led him to talk about 'affects' when discussing the READER's experience of literary WORKS, while the NEW CRITICAL commitments of Wimsatt and Beardsley led them to warn against paying attention to the *results* of a poem instead of the poem itself (Wimsatt: 1970, 21). By *results* they had in mind, in their own words, 'vivid images, intense feelings, or heightened consciousness' (Wimsatt: 1970, 32).

STANLEY FISH's *affective stylistics* stresses the regularity of affects within a particular INTERPRET[AT]IVE COMMUNITY. According to him the term (which replaces his earlier term *new stylistics*), describes a STYLISTICS 'in which the focus of attention is shifted from the spatial context of a page and its observable regularities to the temporal context of a mind and its experiences' (1980, 91).

Aleatory technique Aleatory means 'depending upon the throw of a die', or on chance: any work of art produced by an aleatory technique has reached its final FORM at least in part because of chance, unplanned events. The term is more common in film criticism, where it is used to describe films that have incorporated unplanned elements 'caught' during filming. William Burroughs's 'cut-out' and 'fold-in' techniques involve an aleatory element, as does the *objet trouvé* of experimental art.

Alienation effect From the German *Verfremdungseffekt* as defined and used by the German dramatist BERTOLT BRECHT. Terms such as *dislocation* and *estrangement effect* probably offer better translations of the Brecht's German term, and attempts have been made to establish them as the standard English terms, but *alienation effect* is probably too well established now to be displaced.

Alienation effects were aimed at dispelling the audience's empathy with what they witnessed on stage and at preventing their sinking into the 'world of the play' as well as preventing, too, the illusion that what they were witnessing was 'real life' and thus unchangeable. The concept accompanies Brecht's development of a theory of *epic theatre* designed to replace that of *dramatic theatre*. MIKHAIL BAKHTIN's distinction between the EPIC and the NOVEL in his essay 'Epic and Novel' is relevant here; Bakhtin argues that whereas the reader can enter the world of the novel he or she cannot enter the world of the epic (Bakhtin: 1981, 32).

Allegory Generally, a NARRATIVE involving persons, objects or actions which has two meanings: one literal and obvious and the other implied and less apparent. The most famous example is John Bunyan's *Pilgrim's Progress* (1676), in which the protagonist's journey represents the journey of every Christian through life to Heaven.

Alliteration The repetition of consonants at the beginning of words. This duplication of similar sounds comes under the general area of RHYME and is sometime called *head rhyme*. It can be used to achieve various effects including that of emphasis. Alliteration is one of the earliest FORMAL elements of ENGLISH poetry: in Anglo-Saxon and Old English verse, the line was characterized by four heavy stresses, generally marked by alliteration.

Allusion A reference within a TEXT to an event, object or person outside it, and which the writer presumes will be familiar to her or his audience.

Alterity See OTHER

Ambiguity In current usage the term owes much to WILLIAM EMPSON's *Seven Types of Ambiguity* (first published 1930). Empson defined *ambiguity* loosely, and by the third edition he was content to call an ambiguity 'any verbal nuance, however slight, which gives room for alternative reactions to the same piece of language' (1961, 1). What has rendered Empson's usage less fashionable, perhaps, is its location of multiple meaning in the WORK itself rather than in the READER or reading, or in the rules which define LITERARINESS itself. Thus alternative terms such as *polysemy* and *plurisignification* have emerged because they locate the lack of semantic CLOSURE elsewhere: in the reader, in language itself, or in the constituting rules of literariness.

Anachrony Also, following Bal (1985), *chronological deviation*. Any disparity between the ORDER in which EVENTS are presented in the PLOT or *sjužet*, and that in which they are reported in the STORY or FABULA, is termed an anachrony. Both ANALEPSIS and PROLEPSIS are examples of anachrony. Bal isolates two sorts of anachrony: *punctual anachrony*, when only one instant from the past or future is evoked, and *durative anachrony*, when a longer span of time or a more general situation is evoked.

    See also DURATION

Anagnorisis Literally, 'recognition', or a moment of intense revelation at which a CHARACTER suddenly becomes aware of something; 'seeing into the heart' of a situation at what is usually a moment of special intensity. In plot terms, *anagnorisis* often brings with it PERIPETEIA (or reversal).

Analepsis Also, following Prince (1988), *flashback, retrospection, retroversion, cutback* or *switchback*. An analepsis involves 'any evocation after the fact of an event that took place earlier than the point in the story where we are at any given moment' (Genette: 1980, 40).

    An *internal analepsis* does not reach back prior to the chronological point at which the STORY started, while an *external analepsis* does. A *completing analepsis*, according to GÉRARD GENETTE, fills in a gap or ELLIPSIS left earlier on in the

NARRATIVE, while a *repeating analepsis* or *recall* repeats that which has already been narrated. Analepses can be measured according to their *extent* (how long a period of time they cover), and *reach* (how far back in time they go) (Genette: 1980, 48; Prince: 1988, 5).

See also DIEGESIS AND MIMESIS (heterodiegesis and homodiegesis)

Analogy A comparison by means of which something familiar is used to explain something less familiar.

Analysis Analysis is conventionally distinguished from INTERPRETATION on the ground that it involves a separation of that which is to be studied into its component parts. Thus just as the chemical analysis of a substance would require that it be divided into the different chemical elements of which, in combination, it consists, so literary analysis would involve the dividing of a literary WORK (or in some cases a literary response) into the separate elements by which it is constituted.

Anapestic See METRE

Anaphora A rhetorical feature whereby a word or phrase is repeated at the beginning of successive lines, sentences, clauses or other units – especially in poetry. Walt Whitman uses it extensively, for example in the sixth section of 'Song of Myself', in which he begins three STANZAS with the phrase 'Or I guess . . .', providing alternative answers to a child who has asked him what grass is. He then addresses the grass directly, repeating the phrase 'It may be' three times in three lines, as he speculates further on its significance.

Androcentric Centred on the male. The term has been much-used recently by FEMINIST theorists wishing to describe a habit of mind and set of attitudes which are based upon a male perspective and which ignore female experience and interests. The opposite of androcentric is *gynocentric*: centred on the female.

Androgyny Technically, the union of both sexes in one individual. The *OED* gives this as a biological term and equates it with hermaphrodism, but in recent FEMINIST writing the term is used to refer to CULTURALLY acquired characteristics rather than to biologically determined ones. The writer who probably contributed most to this shift of emphasis was VIRGINIA WOOLF. Towards the end of her long essay, *A Room of One's Own* (1929), she reports the train of thought inspired in her by looking out of her window on what she claimed was a particular day (26 October 1928) and seeing a taxi-cab stopping for a girl and a young man (her terms), picking them both up, and driving off.

> [T]he sight of the two people getting into the taxi and the satisfaction it gave me made me also ask whether there are two sexes in the mind corresponding to the two sexes in the body, and whether they also require to be united in order to get complete satisfaction and happiness? . . . The normal and comfortable state of being is that when the two live in harmony together, spiritually co-operating. If one is a man, still the woman part of the brain must

> have effect; and a woman also must have intercourse with the man in her.
> Coleridge perhaps meant this when he said that a great mind is androgynous.
>
> (Woolf: 1929, 147–8)

A number of recent FEMINISTS writers have recognized that extension of the term beyond the realm of the biological was historically important, but that its use today is IDEOLOGICALLY problematic. Radical feminists in particular have expressed misgivings about the term.

Compare TRANSGENDER

Antithesis Contrasting two ideas by joining them together or juxtaposing them, as in Alexander Pope's 'To err is human; to forgive, divine'.

Anxiety of influence/authorship See REVISIONISM

Aphorism A concise and often memorable statement of belief or principle.

Aporia From the Greek for an apparently irresolvable logical difficulty, this term was traditionally used to describe statements by CHARACTERS in just that state – normally in SOLILOQUY. (Hamlet's 'To be or not to be' speech, for instance.)

More recently JACQUES DERRIDA has adopted and developed the term, and Alan Bass, the English translator of *Writing and Difference*, glosses Derrida's usage of it as follows:

> once a system has been 'shaken' by following its totalizing logic to its final consequence, one finds an excess which cannot be construed within the rules of logic, for the excess can only be conceived as *neither* this *nor* that, or both at the same time – a departure from all rules of logic.
>
> (Derrida: 1978, xvi)

For Derrida, according to Bass, this excess is often posed as an aporia. In the wake of Derrida the term has become more popular as a way of referring to those insoluble doubts and hesitations which are thrown up by the READING of a TEXT.

Apostrophe A rhetorical feature in which someone or something (e.g., a natural force, a deity) is formally addressed in their absence.

Apparatus See IDEOLOGY, and the discussion of BERTOLT BRECHT in Section 5

Arbitrary In Linguistics a SIGN is arbitrary if the relationship between it and whatever it stands for or represents is fixed by CONVENTION rather than by any intrinsic or inherent resemblance beyond the scope of the particular sign system to which it belongs. The French word *chien*, the German *Hund*, and the English *dog* are all used in their respective languages to represent the same animal; none of these words in spoken or written FORM resembles a dog independently of the conventions governing the use of the three languages in question. In contrast, speaking onomatopoeic words such as *pop* and *hiss* may be said to produce a noise not dissimilar to the sounds the words are used to represent. As signs, therefore, it can be said that these words are not totally arbitrary. FERDINAND DE SAUSSURE's insistence upon the arbitrary relationship between SIGNIFIER and SIGNIFIED has been very influential in the twentieth century.

The linked terms *motivated* and *unmotivated*, or *natural* and *conventional* are sometimes used to convey a similar point: a motivated or natural sign is one which is linked to that which it represents by a resemblance or connection existing independently of the conventions of the sign system to which the sign belongs.

Archaism The use of an outdated word or expression, normally for rhetorical or IDEOLOGICAL reasons.

Aside A dramatic CONVENTION, where an actor speaks unheard by the other actors, but in their presence. Like the SOLILOQUY, the convention allows for the display of a CHARACTER's private thoughts or secret motives, but in common with the soliloquy it came to be seen as somewhat artificial from the nineteenth century onwards.

Assonance The recurrence of identical or similar vowel sounds in verse. For example, in 'Ode to a Nightingale', John Keats describes the EPONYMOUS bird who, 'In some melodious plot | Of beechen green, and shadows numberless, | Singest of summer in full-throated ease'. The echoes created by the repetition (of 'e' and 'o' sounds) constitute an example of assonance.

Aubade A LYRIC poem about the morning.

Aura The German MARXIST writer WALTER BENJAMIN used the term aura (adj. auratic) to describe the mystical sense that surrounds artistic or ritual objects like a halo, an aura that, according to him, is ultimately destroyed by techniques of mechanical reproduction such as photography. In his essay 'The Work of Art in the Age of Mechanical Reproduction' (first published 1936; included in *Illuminations*, 1973), he writes that

> that which withers in the age of mechanical reproduction is the aura of the work of art. This is a symptomatic process whose significance points beyond the realm of art. One might generalize by saying: the technique of reproduction detaches the reproduced object from the domain of tradition.
>
> (1973, 221)

See also MODERNISM AND POSTMODERNISM; ORGANICISM

Authenticity In POSTCOLONIALIST usage, that which has originated in a culture rather than having been imposed upon it or adopted by it. The call for 'authenticity' has been attacked as an ESSENTIALIZING desire to fix 'native' peoples and their CULTURES in a timeless and static ethnic quaintness or difference, a requirement that 'native' peoples should stay safely STEREOTYPED as the OTHER of the Western observer, not challenging paternalistic or semi-racist assumptions by revealing that there is no reason why they should not have as close a relationship to technological advance or cultural modernity as Europeans or North Americans.

Author Subsequent to the publication of two essays in particular – ROLAND BARTHES's 'The Death of the Author' (1977) and MICHEL FOUCAULT's 'What is an Author?' (1980) – the term *author* has become the site of much complex discussion. Clearly, on a simple level an author is a person who writes a WORK: Emily Brontë is the author of *Wuthering Heights*. But as Foucault reminds us, one cannot be an author by writing just anything: a private letter may be signed by the person who wrote it, but it does not have an author, nor do we normally speak of the author of a scientific theory: such writing is seen to have a relationship to the person who wrote it which is different from an author's relationship to a literary work.

In other words, the term *author* does more than attach a piece of writing to its individual human origin: it has to be a special sort of writing, and the relation thus posited is more than a certificate of origin.

Foucault argues that the concept of authorship comes in the train of 'penal appropriation': it is when writers become subject to punishment for what they have written that works acquire authors, and he dates the emergence of authorship at the point at which writers entered the 'system of property that characterizes our society' (1980, 149). Barthes makes a similar point, claiming that the author is a modern figure, 'a product of our society insofar as, emerging from the Middle Ages with English empiricism, French rationalism and the personal faith of the Reformation, it discovered the prestige of the individual, of, as it is more nobly put, the "human person"' (1977, 142–3).

Perhaps the most challenging of Foucault's arguments is that *author* and *living person who wrote the work* are not to be equated, as the author function can give rise to several selves, several SUBJECTS, 'positions that can be occupied by different classes of individuals' (1980, 153). When we talk of an author, in other words, we have in mind a range of characteristic actions and relationships which we do not attribute to every writing individual. What these are is, of course, a complex matter – especially as (according to both Barthes and Foucault), the author function (those conventions and attributes which attach to authorship) is not a historically stable one.

Barthes in particular is keen (as the title of his essay suggests) to *challenge* the power of the author, a power to which he attributes a range of specifically IDEOLOGICAL functions. For him, to seek to explain a work by reference to the person who wrote it is (by implication) to be in thrall to a pernicious sort of individualism, and to imprison the work in the imagined self of its individual producer.

'The death of the author' represents, then, an aspect of the POSTMODERNIST and post-structuralist attack on *origins*, on the belief that we can explain (or even help to understand) anything by referring it to where we think that it comes from or to any process of cause and effect. And (as both proponents and opponents of such recent critical positions have argued) to reject such a belief involves an acceptance of the impossibility of arriving at a final meaning or INTERPRETATION of a text. Barthes closes his essay by claiming that the birth of the READER must be at the expense of the death of the author: in other words, to allow the reader unlimited interpretative play, the text must be removed from the author's control. See also the entry for PAUL RICOEUR in Section 5 for more on this issue.

The term *implied author*, along with the matching term *implied reader*, comes from Wayne C. Booth's *Rhetoric of Fiction* (1961). The term has entered into current critical vocabulary and is used to refer to that picture of a creating author behind a literary work that the reader builds up on the basis of elements in (or reading experiences of) the work.

To all intents and purposes the matched terms 'textual author' and 'textual reader'/'mock reader' are synonyms for 'implied author' and 'implied reader'. The term *career author*, in contrast, is used by Seymour Chatman to denote 'the subset of features shared by all the implied authors (that is, all the individual intents) of the narrative texts bearing the name of the same real author' (1990, 88).

Autodiegetic See DIEGESIS AND MIMESIS

Ballad A FORM of NARRATIVE verse, which relates a STORY through action and the extensive use of dialogue. Ballads typically employ four-line STANZAS with alternating lines of iambic tetrameter and iambic trimeter (see METRE), usually with an *abcb* rhyme scheme (known as 'ballad metre'). Since the ballad was originally meant to be sung and passed on by word of mouth, its vocabulary is usually simple. Ballads typically have a refrain, and often include supernatural elements. A good example of the traditional ballad is the anonymous 'Sir Patrick Spens'. 'La Belle Dame Sans Merci' by John Keats also has characteristics common to the FORM. Keats's poem is an example of the *literary ballad*, because it is *written* in imitation of the traditional ballad.

Baroque Often used to describe a style of architecture prevalent in the late sixteenth to early eighteenth centuries, in literary discussion *baroque* implies a complex and often ornate STYLE of expression associated with (for example) the use of CONCEITS (in Renaissance and metaphysical poetry). The GOTHIC NOVEL can be seen as a baroque FORM, as a result of its elaborate, exaggerated and FANTASTIC elements.

Base and superstructure Also *basis and superstructure*. Central to the traditional MARXIST analysis of society and history is the analytical distinction between base and superstructure. The most famous statement of this distinction is to be found in KARL MARX's *A Contribution to the Critique of Political Economy*, in which he states that

In the social production of their existence, men inevitably enter into definite relations, which are independent of their will, namely relations of production appropriate to a given stage in the development of their material forces of production. The totality of these relations of production constitutes the economic structure of society, the real foundation, on which arises a legal and political superstructure and to which correspond definite forms of social consciousness. The mode of production of material life conditions the general process of social, political and intellectual life. It is not the consciousness of men that determines their existence, but their social existence that determines their consciousness.

(1971, 20–1)

Working from the position outlined here, traditional Marxists have distinguished between elements in society which, with regard to their emergence and their historical effect, are either primary or secondary. On the one hand the *economic structure of society, the real foundation* (seen as primary), and on the other the *superstructure* (seen as secondary). Along with law and politics (mentioned by Marx), the superstructure has generally been taken to include other CULTURAL and intellectual phenomena such as (in some accounts) literature. Such an analytical position leads inexorably to the view that to understand literature one must understand the primary phenomenon of which it is the secondary product, reflection or extension: the economic base of society.

See also STRUCTURE OF FEELING

Bathos An (often unintentional) effect whereby a writer seeking to inspire pathos or sublimity only succeeds in invoking a contrary sense of the ridiculous.

Bildungsroman Also known as a NOVEL of education, this narrates the journey of a young person from adolescence and inexperience to a state of greater self-knowledge. It is a journey of discovery which leads to a more fully formed or mature identity. James Joyce's *A Portrait of the Artist* is often cited as an example; Kate Chopin's *The Awakening* has a heroine rather than a hero.

Binary/binarism Binary oppositions form the basis of DIGITAL systems of communication which involve the transformation of *continuous variations* to sets of *discrete either/or distinctions*. Binary distinctions are fundamental to much of modern Linguistics, and Jonathan Culler quotes the linguist Charles Hockett's remark that 'If we find continuous-scale contrasts in the vicinity of what we are sure is language, we exclude them from language' (Culler: 1975, 14).

STRUCTURALISM has adopted this principle of modern Linguistics and has given it a – perhaps *the* – central position in structuralist theory. Structuralist ANALYSIS typically searches for hierarchical strings of binary oppositions in the material or TEXT under investigation: a classic example is indicated in the title of Claude Lévi-Strauss's *The Raw and the Cooked*.

One general point of contention relating to binary oppositions concerns their status: are they useful *analytical tools*, or are they *fundamental linguistic (or other) units*? Many CULTURAL phenomena are based upon binary oppositions: 'If you are not with us you are against us' involves the forced cultural imposition of a binary opposition upon what is often a range of less sharply distinguished variations. The suspicion felt by many FEMINISTS with regard to binary distinctions is summed up in the following comment by Mary Eagleton: 'According to binary thinking the male and the masculine constitutes the norm, the positive and the superior; the female and the feminine is the aberration, the negative, the inferior' (1996, 287).

See also ANDROGENY; LINGUISTIC PARADIGM; TRANSGENDER

Blank verse and free verse Two verse-forms which are sometimes confused. The simplest definition of *blank verse* is that it consists of unrhymed iambic pentameters (see METRE), that is, verse with lines containing five *feet* but with no pattern of end-rhymes. The FORM has been much used by dramatists because of its closeness to the rhythms of ordinary English speech, allowing for a combination of naturalness with the discipline associated with a fixed form. The first use of blank verse is generally credited to Henry Howard, Earl of Surrey, in his mid-sixteenth-century translation of the *Aeneid*.

Free verse also reflects the stress and delivery patterns of natural speech, but has no regular metre or even line length. The term is derived from the French *vers libre*. Free verse may incorporate the use of rhyme, but it need not.

Bricoleur In his *The Savage Mind* Claude Lévi-Strauss distinguishes between the SIGN systems of modern human beings and those of primitive CULTURES. Modern man (Lévi-Strauss's GENDERED term), like an engineer, makes use of specialized and custom-made tools and materials, whereas primitive man resembles an odd-job man or *bricoleur*, who makes use of those odds and ends of material which he has to hand to construct pieces of *bricolage*.

> The characteristic feature of mythical thought is that it expresses itself by means of a heterogeneous repertoire which, even if extensive, is nevertheless limited. It has to use this repertoire, however, whatever the task in hand because it has nothing else at its disposal. Mythical thought is therefore a kind of intellectual 'bricolage' . . .
>
> (1972, 17)

As a literary example of a *bricoleur* Lévi-Strauss points to the CHARACTER Wemmick, from Charles Dickens's *Great Expectations*, because Wemmick creates a sort of MYTH from the raw materials at hand: the parts of his suburban villa are mythically transformed into a castle (1972, 17 and 150n.).

Compare ALEATORY TECHNIQUE

Burlesque Writing which sets out to deride a GENRE, STYLE, or subject matter, usually by imitating it in a distorted or exaggerated way, or by reversing its emphasis (so that the trivial is made absurdly momentous or serious, for example).

Caesura A pause or break in a line of verse, normally associated with the pattern of ordinary speech, but also governed by METRICAL or other poetic CONVENTIONS. A caesura is conventionally indicated by the sign ‖ or //.

Canon The term originates in debate within the Christian Church about the authenticity of the Hebrew Bible and books of the New Testament. That which was termed canonical was accepted as having divine authority within the Church, while writing of no, or doubtful, authority was termed apocryphal. Thus the Protestant canon and apocrypha differ slightly from those of the Catholic Church.

By extension the term in literary-critical usage came to be applied (i) to WORKS which could indisputably be ascribed to a particular AUTHOR, and (ii) to a list of works set apart from other literature by virtue of their literary quality and importance. By the middle of the twentieth century such a decision was to a large extent decided institutionally: just as the church (or different churches) decided upon the Biblical canon, so the universities attempted to legislate about which literary works the literary canon consisted. (Not without disputes, as the career of F.R. LEAVIS bears witness to.) But when FEMINIST critics started to construct a rival canon or canons, not always as a *replacement* for the 'official' canon but also as an *alternative* to it, then this struck at the *claim to universality* that lay behind the idea of a single canon.

For MIKHAIL BAKHTIN, *canonization* is a process towards which all literary GENRES have a tendency, in which temporary NORMS and CONVENTIONS become hardened into universal ones so that evaluations too are considered to reflect universal rather than CULTURE- or time-bound values.

Debates about the canon have, inevitably, led to the coining of a range of sub-terms. Thus a 'canon war' is what happens when members of an academic department engage in battle for and against proposals to change the syllabus in line with what is perceived to be a need to change (or to recognize that a change has taken place in) the canon. A 'canon buster' is a person or a proposal dedicated to overturning the accepted canon.

Carnival In the writings of MIKHAIL BAKHTIN the significance of the carnival in the Renaissance and Middle Ages assumes a representative importance, indicative of a particular form of popular counter-CULTURE. During this period, according to Bakhtin, 'A boundless world of humorous forms and manifestations opposed the official and serious tone of medieval ecclesiastical and feudal culture' (1968, 4). No matter how variegated and diverse these forms and manifestations they none the less, claimed Bakhtin, belonged to a single CULTURE of folk carnival humour (1968, 4). Bakhtin sees this culture as existing on the borderline between art and life, 'life itself, but shaped according to a certain pattern of play' (1968, 5). There is no firm distinction between actors and spectators, and during the period of the carnival it embraces all the people and there is no life outside of it.

By extrapolation Bakhtin dubs as *carnivalesque* all manifestations of a comparable counter-culture which is popular and democratic, and in opposition to a formal and hierarchical official culture. Important here is the idea of unity-in-diversity, of the heterogeneous unison or POLYPHONY of the many voices that make up the carnival. In his study of Dostoevsky Bakhtin suggests that the influence of carnival is responsible for a set of 'genres of the serio-comical', and that these have three main defining features. First, that 'their starting point for understanding, evaluating, and shaping reality, is the living *present*'; second, that they do not rely on *legend* but, *consciously*, on *experience* and *free invention*; and third, that they are deliberately 'multi-styled and hetero-voiced' (1984, 108).

Caroline age See PERIODS OF LITERATURE

Carpe diem A Latin phrase meaning 'seize the day'. The term is sometimes used to describe literature that promotes a philosophy of enjoying the moment, in defiance of death. Examples would include Marvell's 'To his Coy Mistress,' where human transience becomes part of a strategy to persuade the woman to give in to the lover's demands. Since we are dead for a long time, the speaker typically argues, then we should enjoy ourselves while we are still able.

Catachresis See INCORPORATION

Catalectic A line of poetry missing a syllable in the final foot; see ACATALECTIC.

Cavalier See PERIODS OF LITERATURE

Celtic revival (also Celtic renaissance, Irish literary revival, Irish literary Renaissance) A CULTURAL movement of the late nineteenth- and early twentieth century, characterized by a renewal of interest in traditional Gaelic language, literature, mythology, subjects and society. Associated writers included A.E. (George Russell), Lady Gregory, George Moore, J.M. Synge and William Butler Yeats, all of whom wrote in English, but sought to distinguish themselves from mainstream ENGLISH culture. The movement resulted in a great deal of cultural activity, but also in the founding of important institutions such as the Abbey Theatre and the Irish National Literary Society.

Centre In the work of JACQUES DERRIDA the term *centre* is used to represent 'a point of presence, a fixed origin' (1978, 278) which imposes a limit on the play of the STRUCTURE in which it is found or placed. Following Derrida, then, much of the energy of DECONSTRUCTIVE criticism is directed towards freeing structures from the tyranny of whatever centre or centres to which they are seen to be subject. Derrida also uses a range of other terms, including *origin*, *end*, *archē*, and *telos* as roughly equivalent to centre.

Building on such usages, Vincent Crapanzano explains that his own use of the term posits

an image, an event, or even a theoretical construct functioning as a nucleus or point of concentration that holds together a particular verbal sequence.

> The center gives coherence, a semblance of order at least, to what would otherwise appear to be a random, meaningless sequence of expressions.
>
> (1992, 28)

Louis Althusser's essay 'Freud and Lacan', which is reprinted in his *Lenin and Philosophy* (1971) was influential in suggesting that the SUBJECT could (and should) be decentred. A representative example of the POSTMODERNIST claim that the subject *has* been decentred can be found in MICHEL FOUCAULT's Introduction to *The Archaeology of Knowledge*:

> Lastly, more recently, when the researches of psychoanalysis, linguistics, and ethnology have decentred the subject in relation to the laws of his desire, the forms of his language, the rules of his action, or the games of his mythical or fabulous discourse, when it became clear that man himself, questioned as to what he was, could not account for his sexuality and his unconscious, the systematic forms of his language, of the regularities of his fictions, the theme of a continuity of history has been reactivated once again . . . .
>
> (1972, 13)

An unrelated use of *centre* can be found in the work of narratologist Seymour Chatman.

> 'Point of view' ('vision,' 'perspective,' 'focalization') has named still a third narrative function: that is, the presentation of a story in such a way that a certain character is of paramount importance. But this is quite different from filtration, since we may or may not be given access to that central character's consciousness. This function, I think, should be called *center*.
>
> (1990, 147–8)

See also LOGOCENTRISM

Centrifugal/centripetal MIKHAIL BAKHTIN uses these terms which describe the impulse either outwards or inwards, from or towards the centre, to refer to social and IDEOLOGICAL rather than physical forces. For Bakhtin, certain literary GENRES have a centripetal force, driving READERS towards a centre of conformity and uniformity, whereas others have the opposite effect, urging people away from conformity and towards diversity and heterogeneity. He accords poetry an essentially centripetal tendency, while the novel is granted the opposite, a centrifugal force. Not surprisingly, he argues that the novel flourishes during times of diversity and the slackening of central control.

Character The NEW CRITICS and F.R. LEAVIS were united in their disapproval of A.C. Bradley's alleged treatment of Shakespearian (and other) characters as if they were real people, and Alan Sinfield has reminded us that G. Wilson Knight set aside 'the character' as a category of analysis because of his belief that each play was a visionary whole, and was 'close-knit in personification, atmospheric suggestion, and direct poetic-symbolism' (Sinfield: 1992, 56–7, quoting from Knight's *The Wheel of Fire*). The continuing attack on literary character can be seen as an aspect of the anti-individualistic bias of much recent theory. To quote a representative example: in his *The Postmodern Condition: A Report on Knowledge* Jean-François Lyotard comments that

> A *self* does not amount to much, but no self is an island; each exists in a fabric of relations that is now more complex and mobile than ever before. Young or old, man or woman, rich or poor, a person is always located at 'nodal points' of specific communication circuits, however tiny these may be. Or better: one is always located at a post through which various kinds of message pass.
>
> (1984, 15)

To a large extent theorists who have questioned the concept of character are following in the wake of those MODERNIST and POSTMODERNIST writers whose works abandoned traditional forms of characterization. But even within the study of NARRATIVE, no doubt as a result of the STRUCTURALIST foundations of NARRATOLOGY, the individual character – whether traditional or modernist – is rigorously DECONSTRUCTED. Gerald Prince's definitions of the term 'character' – 'An existent endowed with anthropomorphic traits and engaged in anthropomorphic actions; an actor with anthropomorphic attitudes' (1988, 12) – suggests that considering a literary character as in some way equivalent to a real human being is akin to talking to one's cat. But just as people have gone on talking to their cats so too many theory-innocent critics and READERS have gone on treating literary characters as in certain ways equivalent to human individuals.

See also CHARACTER ZONE; CHORUS (for chorus character)

Character zone Coined by MIKHAIL BAKHTIN. According to his account, character zones are formed

> from the characters' semi-discourses, from various forms of hidden transmission for the discourse of the other, by the words and expressions scattered in this discourse, and from the irruption of alien expressive elements into authorial discourse (ellipsis, questions, exclamation). Such a zone is the range of action of the character's voice, intermingling in one way or another with the author's voice.
>
> (Quoted in Todorov: 1984, 73)

In other words, the READER of a NOVEL builds up a picture of the CHARACTER's identity not just from direct descriptions of his or her actions or from 'transcriptions' of his or her speech, but from a wider zone of verbal implication.

Chiasmus Originally a rhetorical figure in which the pattern AB BA is set up in more or less complicated versions. The last sentence of James Joyce's short story 'The Dead', for example, starts: 'His soul swooned slowly as he heard the snow falling faintly through the universe, and faintly falling . . .', and the repetition-with-inversion of the words *falling* and *faintly* gives us an example of chiasmus.

Brook Thomas has argued that chiasmus is the 'favourite figure' of the NEW HISTORICISTS, and that 'the historicity of texts and the textuality of history' (he is quoting from Montrose: 1989, 20) is both one of the most famous (or infamous) of New Historical catch-phrases and also a perfect example of chiasmus.

Chivalric romance See ROMANCE

Chorus Originating in Greek TRAGEDY, the chorus appears at regular intervals to comment upon the action of the play. By extension, any element in a literary work which has the function of commenting upon its action can be seen as a form of chorus. A *chorus character* is one who plays a role comparable to that played by the chorus in drama, providing necessary information and comments on characters, situation, or action. Very often applied to minor characters in NOVELS or short stories who themselves play little part in the events of the NARRATIVE.

Chronotope Coined by MIKHAIL BAKHTIN to designate 'the distinctive features of time and space within each literary genre' (Todorov: 1984, 83). According to Bakhtin he took the term from mathematical biology, but introduced it into literary studies in a METAPHORICAL sense (Bakhtin: 1981, 234). In his essay on the BILDUNGSROMAN, for example, Bakhtin suggests that the 'local cults' associated with particular literary works and linked to specific geographical locations in the mid-eighteenth century 'attest above all to a completely *new sense of space and time* in the artistic work' (1986, 47).

In the course of a discussion of Toni Morrison's novel *Beloved*, Lynne Pearce has proposed an extension of Bakhtin's term: *polychronotopic*, to describe the coexistence of multiple chronotopes within the same text (Pearce: 1994, 71).

Class Discussion of social class entered into literary-critical discourse most obviously with the emergence of a MARXIST literary criticism in the 1930s. Marxists define class by relation to the economic STRUCTURE of society, in contrast to more recent sociological views of class which emphasize such matters as status, individual wealth, CULTURAL and IDEOLOGICAL commitments, and so on. Accordingly, as Alan Hunt has pointed out, two men who clean windows for a living, earn identical amounts of money, and share a common CULTURE and lifestyle must from a traditional Marxist perspective be assigned to different classes if one is self-employed and the other is the employee of a large window-cleaning concern (1977, 89).

It is perhaps obvious that it is difficult to keep a concern with social class out of discussion of the work of a writer such as D.H. Lawrence, but it is arguable that light can also be thrown on the work of very different writers by an examination of their class origins and associations, along with a similar examination of READERS and critics of their work. A complicating factor which has to be confronted is that both writers and critics can occupy rather indefinite class positions (like window cleaners, their relation to the economic structure of society is not fixed by the job).

FEMINIST critics have directed a certain amount of criticism towards the tendency of more traditional Marxist discussions of class to limit themselves to the (male) 'heads of family' and assign women to the class to which their husbands or fathers belong.

Classicism In literature as in the arts generally, *classicism* refers to the AESTHETIC principles and products influenced by the art of ancient Greece or Rome (or by perceptions of the assumptions behind such art). *Neoclassicism* is used to refer mainly to the art of a subsequent phase in history (1660–1798), but embodying attitudes and models with their base in antiquity. Classicism and Neoclassicism are thus associated with a wide and often varying set of values, including a fondness for ABSTRACTION, elegance of expression, an attraction to FORM, harmony and idealism, an emphasis on logic and reason, a fondness for proportion, an attitude of restraint, and a predilection for society over the individual.

See also PERIODS OF LITERATURE (Classical period)

Closed texts See OPEN AND CLOSED TEXTS

Closure According to Barbara Herrnstein Smith, closure 'may be regarded as a modification of structure that makes *stasis*, or the absence of further continuation, the most probable event'. She further adds that closure allows the READER to be satisfied by the failure of continuation or, to put it another way, it creates 'the expectation of nothing' in the reader (1968, 34).

Closure, in other words, is more than just the ending of a literary work: it requires that the ending or discontinuation have a certain AESTHETIC force. It need not imply that the reader is so satisfied at the end of the work that he or she stops thinking or that the work leaves no problems to be resolved, only that the reader recognizes that the ending of the work at this point and in this way is of aesthetic significance. An absence of closure is frequently associated with MODERNIST or experimental art, including literature. *Consonant* and *dissonant* closures occur when the ending of a literary work either confirms and underwrites, or challenges and destabilizes, what has gone before.

Code The influence of Linguistics and SEMIOTICS has led to an increased recourse to the term *code* on the part of literary critics and theorists during the past two decades. This may be at least in part because the term implies that writer and READER are linked by their common possession of a set of CONVENTIONS governing systematic transformations, an implication which appeals to many contemporary theorists interested in issues raised by the sociology of literature and by the concept of LITERARINESS. The term also, of course, suggests that the literary work contains that which is hidden to those not possessed of the right codebook. (In this context, see also INTERPRET[AT]IVE COMMUNITY.)

In one of the more influential examples of the development of a theory of literary codes, ROLAND BARTHES has suggested five codes of reading which allow readers to recognize and identify elements in the literary WORK and to relate them to specific functions. The five codes are as follows.

■ The *proairetic code* controls the manner in which the reader constructs the PLOT of a literary work.

■ The *hermeneutic code* involves problems of INTERPRETATION, particularly those questions and answers that are raised at the level of plot.

■ The *semic code* is related to those TEXTUAL elements that develop the reader's perception of literary CHARACTERS.

■ The *symbolic code* governs the reader's construction of symbolic meanings.

■ The *referential code* is made up by textual references to CULTURAL phenomena.

(Based on Barthes: 1990, 19–20)

Jonathan Culler has raised one powerful objection to literary-critical use of these terms. He notes that 'listeners interpret sentences rather than decode them' (1975, 19).

The term *delayed decoding* was coined by Ian Watt in his *Conrad in the Nineteenth Century* (1980) to describe a particular impressionist technique of Joseph Conrad's whereby the experiences of a character who understands what is happening to him or her only while these experiences are taking place (or afterwards), is recreated in the reader. Thus in Conrad's *Heart of Darkness* we share Marlow's belief that lots of little sticks are dropping on the ship, up to the point when Marlow realizes that the 'sticks' are in fact arrows, and that the ship is being attacked.

See also HERMENEUTICS; INTERPRETATION

Colonial period See PERIODS OF LITERATURE

Comedy Generally speaking, a mode (frequently a dramatic work) which is chiefly meant to amuse and entertain, and/or which has a happy ending. Whereas TRAGEDY typically focuses on the life of a person with high status, comedies frequently depict more ordinary CHARACTERS and SETTINGS, using plain or colloquial language. Tragic heroes are special; comic CHARACTERS are not: nonetheless, both expose human frailties. Although comedies are characterized by humour, they often have a serious purpose: in Ancient Greece, the category known as old comedies (such as those of Aristophanes) were vehicles for political and social SATIRE. The new comedies (associated with Menander) are a forerunner of the romantic comedies of Shakespeare's time: typically, a comedy of that type will depict two lovers who must overcome obstacles before being united.

Within the general category of comedy, the following sub-types or sub-genres are generally recognized.

Comedy of humours According to medieval thought, human disposition and personality were affected by the proportion of certain 'humours', or bodily fluids:

too much blood made a person cheerful and assured; phlegm resulted in a person being apathetic and listless; choler (or yellow bile) created anger or temperament; black bile brought about melancholy. A humorous drama taking such a belief as its starting-point was known as a comedy of humours.

Comedy of manners A play which focuses on codes of behaviour among a specific and readily identifiable social group, and often on relations between men and women. It typically features witty dialogue and repartee. Restoration comedy is mostly of this type, with complex plots that centre on sexual intrigues and innuendo (rather than love), and that show clever characters outwitting dull, conventional ones in pursuit of immoral ends. SENTIMENTAL comedy, in contrast, emphasizes morality, respectability, and the rewards of virtue.

Dark comedy Plays that concern themselves with serious issues, which are not obviously funny, but which nonetheless have a happy ending, are occasionally referred to as dark comedies. Examples include *Measure for Measure* and *The Winter's Tale*. Not to be confused with *black comedy* which, like black humour in general, extracts humour from attitudes and experiences that are horrific or macabre.

High comedy Comedy which appeals primarily to the intellect, and which relies on wit and a skilful portrayal of CHARACTER. Oscar Wilde's *The Importance of Being Earnest* is an example.

Low comedy Comedy which emphasizes bodily humour and the visual. There are few plays which are entirely low: more frequently, as in Shakespeare, the 'low comedy' will provide a sub-plot.

Romantic comedy A drama which is constructed around a love affair, and where there is an obstacle which complicates this relationship. The complication is, following the CONVENTION, usually overcome.

Commedia dell'arte A type of sixteenth-century improvised Italian comedy, often involving stock CHARACTERS, and acted in masks. The PLOTS typically involve young couples allying with servants to outwit a father or older male relative and achieving emotional and material happiness. Characters such as Harlequin and Scaramouche derive from this tradition, which influenced farce, pantomime and light opera.

Comic relief A humorous interlude in an otherwise serious NARRATIVE or tragic drama. The famous 'gravedigger scene' in *Hamlet* is a classic example. The comedy provides a relief from the tension; it also serves to highlight the tragedy by contrast – throwing it into relief, so to speak.

Commonwealth period See PERIODS OF LITERATURE

Competence and performance A distinction introduced into Linguistics by Noam Chomsky, by means of which those language rules internalized by a native speaker which enable him or her to generate and understand grammatically correct sentences (competence), can be distinguished from the actual generation of particular correct sentences by such a speaker (performance). Competence also enables a native speaker to recognize whether or not a particular sentence is or is not grammatically well formed.

The distinction has been extended to literary criticism by a number of theorists who have sought to draw an ANALOGY between the internalized rules of a language and the internalized rules or CONVENTIONS which enable competent READERS to read and understand literary WORKS. The analogy has the virtue of reminding us that there is a difference between literacy and the ability satisfactorily to read and respond to literary works, but it has some shortcomings too. First, that whereas Chomsky's competence is mainly concerned with the *generation* of correct sentences, the posited literary competence has often been concerned mainly or exclusively with the *reading or reception* of literary works. Second, that literary competence seems to be based upon capacities which are transmitted by means of CULTURE rather than nature (there is no literary equivalent to Chomsky's genetically transmitted 'Language Acquisition Device'). And third, literary (unlike linguistic) competence is not universally present in adult human beings.

Compare attempts to apply the distinction between LANGUE AND PAROLE to literature.

Conceit A comparison, often far-fetched or ingenious, which is elaborated or developed over the period of (normally) a poem. The *Petrarchan conceit*, named after the Italian renaissance poet (1303–74), is a feature of Elizabethan poetry. It involves portraying the mistress as lovely but cruelly distant, thus rendering the lover miserable. In addition, the lover (always male) suffers from fever (caused by the heat of his attraction) and from intense cold (caused by neglect or rejection). This practice is SATIRIZED to some extent by Shakespeare in his SONNET 'Shall I Compare Thee to a Summer's Day?', in which the process of making METAPHORS is FOREGROUNDED.

Concrete poetry Concrete poetry creates an original visual FORM using (normally printed) language – by either making words into a shape or structure, or by scattering words across the page, or by fracturing them into letters made up from different typefaces and sizes. It appeals to the eye as well as – or more than – the ear. Concrete poetry can be seen as the modern equivalent of the *emblem poem* or *pattern poem*, popular in the sixteenth and seventeenth centuries, in which the printed form of the poem produces a design that complements the poem's meaning – as in George Herbert's 'Easter Wings'.

Concretization *Concrete* was a word much favoured by the NEW CRITICS and F.R. LEAVIS, used honorifically to distinguish literature (mostly poetry) which called particulars to mind, often by means of the direct evocation of the recalled testimony of the senses. Take, for example, Leavis's discussion of four lines from John Keats's 'Ode to Melancholy':

> Then glut thy sorrow on a morning rose,
>   Or on the rainbow of the salt sand-wave,
>   Or on the wealth of globed peonies;
> Or if thy mistress some rich anger shows . . .

Leavis comments: 'That "glut", which we can hardly find Rossetti or Tennyson using in a poetical place, finds itself taken up in "globed", the sensuous concreteness of which it reinforces; the hand is round the peony, luxuriously cupping it' (1964, 214).

According to Roman Ingarden's *Das Literarische Kunstwerk* (published in German in 1931 and in English translation as *The Literary Work of Art* in 1973) there are two types of concretization if one speaks purely ontically (i.e. 'of or having real being or existence'). On the one hand,

> the purely intentional concretization, ontically heteronomous in form and relative to the subjective operation [and on the other hand,] the objectively existing concretization, characteristic, in form, of the respective ontic sphere and thus, in a state of affairs that exists in the real world, in the form of an ontically autonomous realization of the corresponding essences or ideas.
>
> (1973, 162)

The distinction allows Ingarden to talk about the way in which the literary WORK is concretized by being read.

The PRAGUE SCHOOL theorist Felix Vodička adopts and develops Ingarden's category in his essay 'The History of the Echo of Literary Works'. For Vodička the study of the concretization of past and present literary works involves 'the study of the work in the particular form in which we find it in the conception of the period (particularly its concretization in criticism)' (1964, 73).

Condensation and displacement According to Sigmund Freud, a comparison of the dream-content with the dream-thoughts reveals that 'a work of *condensation* on a large scale has been carried out. Dreams are brief, meagre and laconic in comparison with the range and wealth of the dream-thoughts' (1976, 383). In other words, a large amount of meaning is *condensed* into a relatively small size by making individual SIGNS or IMAGES signify more than one thing: the dream-thoughts are thus OVERDETERMINED. Freud's INTERPRETATIONS accordingly involve a work of unpacking; out of a single scene or figure in a dream a number of different meanings can be salvaged. As Freud also points out, the interpretation of a dream may occupy six or twelve times as much space when written out as does the written account of the dream itself (1976, 383). Many aspects of Freud's dream ANALYSES are remarkably similar to aspects of NEW CRITICAL analyses of LYRIC poems.

For Freud, condensation is typically associated with *displacement*, and he argues that '*Dream-displacement* and *dream-condensation* are the two governing

factors to whose activity we may in essence ascribe the form assumed by dreams'
(1976, 417). Freud sees displacement as a means whereby censorship is outman-
œuvred; for example, if a person cannot consciously admit his or her hatred of
another as a result of the operation of the censor, this hatred may be transferred
to something associated with the person in question, *displaced* from one object
protected by the censor to another one about which the censor is unconcerned.
This again has been of interest to literary critics who have used the concept (often
in association with that of condensation) to explore the way symbolism functions
in literary WORKS.

Linguisticians use the term DISPLACEMENT in a rather different way: see the
separate entry. See also the discussion of METAPHOR and METONYMY in the
entry for SYNTAGMATIC AND PARADIGMATIC: following JACQUES LACAN, a number of commentators have observed that the condensation/displacement distinction has much in common with ROMAN JAKOBSON's distinction between
metaphor and metonymy (see the discussion in Scholes: 1982, 75–6, and the
entry for SYNTAGMATIC AND PARADIGMATIC).

In NARRATOLOGY, *condensation* is sometimes used to indicate that a passage of
Indirect or FREE INDIRECT DISCOURSE condenses the (implied) utterances of
many different people, perhaps made at many different times, into one represented utterance. Compare *pseudo-iterative*, in the entry for FREQUENCY.

Confessional poetry Many LYRIC poems can in some sense be thought of as confessional, inasmuch as they relate SUBJECTIVE experience. The term 'confessional
poetry' generally refers to writers from the 1940s, 1950s and 1960s who include
intimate and often harrowing details which are apparently about their private
lives: John Berryman, Robert Lowell, Sylvia Plath and Anne Sexton are some
examples. The phrase is nonetheless controversial, and its usefulness and accuracy have been disputed.

Connotation and denotation The two terms distinguish between two types of
REFERENCE: the word 'military' as defined in the dictionary involves that which is
connected to armies or soldiers (denotation), but it carries with it a range of associations which spring to the minds of those who share a common CULTURE – uni-
forms, marching, discipline, force, masculinity, rigid collectivity – and these are
the *connotations* of the word. Denotations are almost invariably more fixed than
connotations, changing only over much longer periods of time than it takes for a
word's connotations to alter.

A number of recent theorists have suggested that there are similarities between
the connotation/denotation distinction and the metonymy/metaphor distinction
(see the entry for SYNTAGMATIC AND PARADIGMATIC). This is because both connotation and metonymy involve relations of CONTIGUITY, whereas denotation
and metaphor involve relations mediated by CONVENTION. GÉRARD GENETTE
suggests that literature is the 'domain *par excellence*' of connotation (1982, 31).

Constatives See Section 3, p. 174

Convention In traditional usage, those fixed or unspoken rules that govern the composition, reading and performance of literary works. Thus it is a theatrical convention that the actors normally face towards the audience, while other conventions place a certain pressure on both poet and reader with regard to a poem's FORMAL STRUCTURE.

Generally speaking, a SIGN that derives its force from a system of conventions is said to be *unmotivated* (see the entry for ARBITRARY), whereas one which has a force independent of any such agreed or accepted conventions is said to be *motivated*. 'Agreed or accepted' is important: conventions may be technically *artificial*, that is to say they may be drawn up, agreed upon, and abided by on the basis of conscious human planning and acceptance. Alternatively, they may be more *natural*, growing in a more unplanned manner, as particular tasks require a set of rules to enable and standardize communication.

See also REGISTER

Conversation poem A kind of informal, colloquial poem which is said to reproduce some of the casual feel of a conversation. The term was originally applied by S.T. Coleridge to his 'The Nightingale,' and another poem of his – 'Frost at Midnight' – has many of the same qualities of intimacy and immediacy.

Co-operative principle See SPEECH ACT THEORY in Section 3, pp. 174–6

Courtly love A CONVENTION of medieval poetry whose influence extended well into the Romantic period and beyond, courtly love refers to a heavily stylized set of behavioural codes and regulations by which amorous relations between a man and woman are conducted. The convention typically involves the hopeless love for a married or otherwise unattainable woman on the part of a lover who undergoes a succession of tests and hardships for the object of his infatuation.

Crisis In traditional usage, the point at which the fortunes of the hero change. More recently, Mieke Bal (1985) distinguishes between *crisis* and *development*: the former a short span of time into which many events are compressed, the latter a longer span of time in which, as the name suggests, a development takes place.

Crux In textual scholarship, a problematic passage or disputed reading about which there is substantial editorial disagreement. The crux gets its name because the disagreements touch on competing editorial methods and principles, and therefore raise larger questions about different theoretical approaches to the editing of TEXTS. In literary INTERPRETATION, *crux* has come to refer to a crucially difficult or indeterminate passage of writing, which is central to an understanding of the work.

Cultural materialism/cultural poetics See Section 3, p. 186

Cultural Studies See Section 3, p. 183

Culture According to RAYMOND WILLIAMS'S *Keywords*, *culture* is 'one of the two or three most complicated words in the English language' (1976, 76). Williams attributes this complexity partly to the word's intricate historical development in several European languages, but mainly to the fact that it is now used for import-ant concepts in several different intellectual disciplines. His discussion of the word should be consulted in its entirety, but his isolation of three interrelated modern usages is worth summarizing here. These are, first: 'a general process of intellec-tual, spiritual and aesthetic development'; second: 'a particular way of life', of either a people, a period or a group; third: 'the works and practices of intellectual and especially artistic activity' (1976, 80).

Williams is also responsible for an influential proposal concerning certain sub-categories into which 'culture' can be divided. In his essay 'Base and Superstructure in Marxist Cultural Theory' he distinguishes first of all between dominant, alternative and oppositional cultures – thus making it clear that for him 'culture' is not to be understood as a monolithic concept. 'Alternative' and 'oppositional' cultures include, for Williams, both *residual* and *emergent* FORMS (1980, 40).

The term *popular culture* refers to the culture of a subordinate group or CLASS which is distinct from the dominant culture of a particular society, dominant in the sense either of more widely disseminated or highly valued, or in the sense of belonging to and reflecting the interests of a dominant group or class. The term *popular* is itself problematic, invoking either that which is *for*, or that which is *of*, the people (for which the term *folk culture* has sometimes been reserved).

See also BASE AND SUPERSTRUCTURE; STRUCTURE OF FEELING.

Cybernetics/-punk/-space From the Greek word meaning steersman, the term *cyber-netics* was coined by Norbert Wiener, whose book *Cybernetics: Or Control and Communication in the Animal and the Machine* (1949) introduced the term. Wiener was primarily interested in what became known as feedback systems, and in more scholarly circles *cybernetics* is still used to refer to complex feedback systems in (as Wiener's title has it) animals and machines – nowadays normally electronic 'machines'.

In less scholarly and more general usage *cyberspace* is used broadly to refer to the whole universe of electronic communication and (simulated) experience: missing e-mails are referred to as 'lost in cyberspace', electronic chat-lines allow for meetings in cyberspace, and so on. The term was coined by the American sci-ence FICTION writer William Gibson in his 1984 NOVEL *Neuromancer*. Gibson is one of a number of Canadian and American writers whose work has become known collectively as *cyberpunk*. This work extends science fiction through the incorporation of detail from existing and predicted electronic technologies, pre-sented in a format that owes much to the 'action' film. According to FREDRIC JAMESON, cyberpunk needs to be understood in terms of the social and historical contexts in which it emerged; for him, cyberpunk 'is fully as much an expression of transnational corporate realities as it is of global paranoia itself' (1991, 38).

Cyborg According to Nigel Wheale,

> [t]he term 'cyborg' was coined in 1960 as a definition of a 'self-regulating man-machine system' (Tomas 1989: 127) but every period has imagined such 'human-Things', entities which test or define the contemporary sense of intrinsic human value over against its simulacrum: the incubus or succuba in Christian tradition, the Golem in Jewish folklore, Prospero's Ariel and Caliban (and perhaps even Miranda too?), E.T.A. Hoffmann's Sandman, and of course Mary Shelley's Frankenstein. ... The robot also has a long and influential life in film history, beginning with Fritz Lang's eerie adaptation of the Golem legend in *Metropolis* (1926).
>
> (Wheale: 1995c, 102)

Andermahr, Lovell and Wolkowitz comment that if 'feminism hesitates before the figure of the cyborg, it is less because of the fears imagined by Mary Wings of a plot to bypass and control women's bodies (1988) than of cyborg manifestations in the form of cosmetic surgery and other body modifications in the direction of an idealized FEMININITY' (1997, 52).

Dactyl See METRE

Dark comedy See COMEDY

Death of the author See AUTHOR

Decadence In literary studies, *decadence* commonly refers to a literary movement of the late nineteenth century which emphasized 'art for art's sake', and which promoted the enjoyment of beauty, ceremony, pleasure and purity of FORM. AESTHETIC experience was part of a CULTURE of taste removed from the everyday: being bored was one of a number of signs of distinction. Decadents were controversial inasmuch as they rejected conventional values, both in life and in literature. A.C. Swinburne and Oscar Wilde are usually thought of as decadents. More generally, decadence can mean the final, declining, phase of other literary periods and movements.

Deconstruction See Section 3, p. 170, and the entry for JACQUES DERRIDA, Section 5, p. 326

Decorum The CONVENTION, commonplace in the eighteenth century, that certain CHARACTERS, events or subjects required a specific GENRE and/or STYLE of treatment. Decorum was thus used to underpin generic (and, indirectly, CLASS) hierarchies.

Deep structure See STRUCTURE

Defamiliarization Also *singularization*. From the Russian meaning 'to make strange', the term originates with the RUSSIAN FORMALISTS and, in particular, the theories of VIKTOR SHKLOVSKY. In his essay 'Art as Technique', Shklovsky argues that perception becomes automatic once it has become habitual, and that the function of art is to challenge automization and habitualization, and return a direct grasp on things to the individual perception.

> Habitualization devours works, clothes, furniture, one's wife, and the fear of war. 'If the whole complex lives of many people go on unconsciously, then such lives are as if they had never been.' And art exists that one may recover the sensation of life; it exists to make one feel things, to make the stone *stony*.
> (1965, 12; the quotation is from Leo Tolstoy's *Diary*)

The PRAGUE SCHOOL theorist Bohuslav Havránek provides useful definitions of both *automization* and *foregrounding* in his essay 'The Functional Differentiation of the Standard Language'.

> By *automization* we . . . mean . . . a use of the devices of the language, in isolation or in combination with each other, as is usual for a certain expressive purpose, that is, such a use that the expression itself does not attract any attention . . .
> By *foregrounding* . . . we mean the use of the devices of the language in such a way that this use itself attracts attention and is perceived as uncommon, as deprived of automization, as deautomized, such as a live poetic metaphor (as opposed to a lexicalized one, which is automized).
> (1964, 9, 10)

Nowadays, *foregrounding* and *defamiliarization* are often used interchangeably. Both concepts are related to the view that 'poetic language' is to be sharply distinguished from other forms of language; according to Jan Mukařovský, the 'function of poetic language consists in the maximum of foregrounding of the utterance', while the 'foregrounding of any one of the components is necessarily accompanied by the automatization of one or more of the other components' (1964, 19–20). *Foregrounding* has led to the coining of a complementary term: *backgrounding* – meaning the process whereby certain elements in a literary work are presented in such a way as *not* to stand out or be noticed.

The verb *to naturalize*, which also gives us the process of *naturalization*, is often used as an alternative term in English for automization. According to Gérard Genette, for ROLAND BARTHES the 'major sin of petty-bourgeois ideology' is the naturalization of culture and history (1982, 36).

Delayed decoding See CODE

Demotion See METRE

Denotation See CONNOTATION AND DENOTATION

Dénouement From the French meaning 'unknotting', and applied to that moment following the climax of a drama or NARRATIVE which provides the resolution and explanation of what has happened before. In detective FICTION, for instance, this involves the now clichéd scene of the investigator gathering together all of the suspects in a library to explain who the murderer is, and how and why the murder was brought about.

Desire Both as noun and as verb *desire* indicates a central but diffuse and by no means unified concept or set of concepts in a cluster of different contemporary theories, very often in connection with attempts to DECONSTRUCT or theorize the SUBJECT or subjectivity. According to MICHEL FOUCAULT, the more recent researches of psychoanalysis, linguistics and ethnology have 'decentred the subject in relation to', among other things, 'the laws of his desire' (1972, 13), and the concept of desire has assumed an important but varied function within theories concerned to see the subject as more site than determining origin or PRESENCE. For JACQUES LACAN, because the subject is split between a conscious mind the contents of which are unproblematically retrievable, and an unconscious set of drives and forces (*Trieb*), and because the subject knows that what it knows is not all that it is, desire for the OTHER is a constituting part of the subject. Moreover, according to Lacan, desire is necessarily linked to PHALLOCENTRISM because the child desires the mother's desire and thus identifies himself (Lacan's GENDERED term) 'with the imaginary object of this desire in so far as the mother herself symbolizes it in the phallus' (1977, 198).

It should not surprise anyone who has read this far to discover that FEMINIST critics have displayed both interest in and suspicion towards the concept of desire, variously defined. Catharine A. MacKinnon, for example, distances herself forcefully from the use of the term 'desire' to be found both in Jean-Paul Sartre's *Existential Psychoanalysis* and in *Anti-Oedipus: Capitalism and Schizophrenia* by Gilles Deleuze and Félix Guattari. In these works, MacKinnon argues, the concept of desire entails sexual objectification, which for her is 'the primary process of the subjection of women' (1982, 27). To substantiate her case she quotes first Sartre: 'But if I desire a house, or a glass of water, or a woman's body, how could this glass, this piece of property reside in my desire and how can my desire be anything but the consciousness of these objects as desirable?' (Sartre: 1973, 20), and then Deleuze and Guattari's view of man as 'desiring-machine'. She insists: 'Women are not desiring-machines' (1982, 27).

Robert J. C. Young's 1995 study *Colonial Desire: Hybridity in Theory, Culture and Race* has argued that (specifically sexual) desire is central to racist attitudes and colonial DISCOURSE. Young quotes Ronald Hyam's comment that one thing is certain: 'Sex is at the very heart of racism' (Young: 1995, 97, quoting Hyam: 1990, 203). Young's consideration of literary works is generally restricted to brief comments on writers such as Joseph Conrad and Jean Rhys, but his extended discussion of Matthew Arnold should be of interest to students of ENGLISH.

See also SYNTAGMATIC AND PARADIGMATIC (METONYMY as desire)

Deus ex Machina Latin term meaning 'god from a machine'. From CLASSICAL Greek drama, in which a god was lowered onto stage by means of a 'machine'. By extension, any intervention in literature which resolves a conflict or problem in a way that in real life would be extremely unlikely. In B-movies, this might involve a CHARACTER being rescued at a moment of extreme danger and in the face of impossible odds by the hero. More generally, the term is used to suggest a resolution of some kind that seems artificial or unbelievable. In Woody Allen's *Mighty Aphrodite* (1995), a film with many self-conscious jokes about classical conventions, the Deus ex Machina arrives literally in a machine – a helicopter.

Deviation The more that stress is laid upon NORMS and CONVENTIONS in a given theory or approach, the more significance is likely to be accorded to deviation from these norms and conventions. (We can only confidently refer to 'deviates' in a CULTURE in which we have, or think we have, a firm sense of what constitutes normality.) Clearly deviation is involved in the RUSSIAN FORMALIST concept of DEFAMILIARIZATION, in which the LITERARINESS of language consists in the extent to which it deviates from extra-literary language, or to which it encourages deviation from everyday habits of perception.

Deviation is also closely related to various usages of the terms difference and DIFFÉRANCE, as a deviation is significant as much (if not more) in terms of what it is *not* as in terms of what it *is*. Deviation has also become an important term in the fields of STYLISTICS and NARRATOLOGY: a style may be constituted at least in part by deviations from a linguistic norm, and according to GÉRARD GENETTE, Marcel Proust's *À la Recherche du temps perdu* deviates from then-accepted laws of NARRATIVE by its manipulation of the *singulative* and the *iterative modes* – basing the narrative rhythm of this work not, as in the classical NOVEL, on alternation between the summary and the scene, but on alternation between the iterative and the singulative mode (1980, 143). (For an explanation of these terms see the entry for FREQUENCY.)

Device See the entry for VIKTOR SHKLOVSKY, in Section 5, p. 385

Diachronic and synchronic A diachronic study or ANALYSIS concerns itself with the evolution and change over time of that which is studied: thus diachronic Linguistics is also known as historical linguistics, and is concerned with the development of a language or languages over time. A synchronic study or analysis, in contrast, limits its concern to a particular moment of time. Thus synchronic Linguistics takes a language as a working system at a particular point in time without concern for how it has developed to its present state. One of the main reasons why FERDINAND DE SAUSSURE is credited by some with having revolutionized the study of language early in this century is that he drew attention to the possibility of studying language synchronically, and thus established the possibility of a STRUCTURAL linguistics.

There have been attempts to study literature synchronically (diachronic literary study has, of course, a long pedigree). ROMAN JAKOBSON, for example, has argued that the synchronic description of literature concerns itself not just with present-day literary production, but also with that part of the literary tradition which has either remained vital or has been revived (1960, 352). GÉRARD GENETTE, taking up this suggestion from Jakobson, suggests that the structural history of literature 'is simply the placing in diachronic perspective of these successive synchronic tables' (1982, 21).

Dialogic Along with *dialogue, dialogical,* and *dialogism,* dialogic owes its current technical use to the influence that the writings of MIKHAIL BAKHTIN have had in the West following their translation into English during the 1970s and 1980s.

Dialogue in its everyday usage means verbal interchange between individuals, especially as represented in literary writing. Vološinov (1986) builds upon this familiar usage in a number of ways. First, he suggests that verbal *interaction* is the fundamental reality of language: both in the history of the individual and also in the history of the human species, language is born not within the isolated human being, but in the interaction between two or more human beings. The recent development of PRAGMATICS – both in Linguistics and Literary Studies – may make this obvious to the present-day reader, but highly influential theories of language have obscured this truth. Second, however, Bakhtin was increasingly to argue that even in DISCOURSE or UTTERANCE which was not overtly interactive, dialogue was to be found. Because all utterances involve the, as it were, 'importing' and naturalization of the speech of others, all utterances include inner tensions, collaborations, negotiations which are comparable to the process of dialogue (in its everyday sense). For Bakhtin, words were not neutral; apart from neologisms (of which he was, not surprisingly, rather fond) they were all second-hand and had belonged to other people, and in incorporating them into his or her own usage the individual had to engage in dialogue with that other person, struggle to wrest possession of them from their previous owner(s). Discussing language, Bakhtin habitually makes use of terms such as 'saturated','contaminated', 'impregnated'; a word for Bakhtin is like a garment passed from individual to individual which cannot have the smell of previous owners washed out of it. Spoken or written utterances are like PALIMPSESTS: scratch them a little and hidden meanings come to light, meanings which are very often at odds with those apparent on the surface.

The Bakhtinian view of the dialogic connects with the topics of INTERTEXTUALITY and transtextuality, and with HAROLD BLOOM's concept of the anxiety of influence (see the entry for REVISIONISM). For in using a word or an expression, an author will engage in some sort of dialogue with the text in which he or she first encountered this word, or the text in which the word has had a particular meaning embossed upon it.

The opposite of dialogue for Bakhtin is, logically, *monologue.* According to him,

Ultimately, *monologism* denies that there exists outside of it another consciousness, with the same rights, and capable of responding on an equal footing, another and equal *I (thou).* . . . The monologue is accomplished

> and deaf to the other's response; it does not await it and does not grant it
> any *decisive* force.
>
> (Quoted in Todorov: 1984, 107)

Polyglossia is Bakhtin's term for the simultaneous existence of two national
languages within a single CULTURAL system; in contrast, *monoglossia* indicates
that a culture contains but one national language.

Interest in Bakhtin has sent a number of commentators back to the work of
the German Hans-Georg Gadamer, in whose major work *Truth and Method* the
concept of dialogue also looms large. Gadamer distinguishes between AUTHEN-
TIC and inauthentic conversation and suggests that a reader's encounter with a
text is like authentic conversation – open, two-sided, unegocentric (1989, 385).

See also INTERIOR DIALOGUE

Diegesis and mimesis Both of these terms are to be found in the third book of
Plato's *Republic*, in which Socrates uses them to distinguish between two ways of
presenting speech. For Socrates, diegesis stands for those cases where the poet
himself is the speaker and does not wish to suggest otherwise, and mimesis stands
for those cases in which the poet attempts to create the illusion that it is not he
who is speaking. Thus a speech spoken by a CHARACTER in the play would represent mimesis, whereas if the writer spoke 'as him or herself' about characters, we
would have a case of diegesis.

Aristotle extended use of the term mimesis in his *Poetics* to include not just
speech but also imitative actions, and as these could of course be rendered in
indirect speech this extension had the effect of blunting Plato's rather sharper distinction. In his Appendix to Aristotle's *Poetics*, D.W. Lucas (1968) notes that it
is clear that not just poetry, painting, sculpture and music are forms of mimesis
for both Plato and Aristotle, but so too is dancing. Lucas further adds that the
word 'mimesis' has an extraordinary breadth of meaning which makes it difficult
to discover just what the Greeks had in mind when they used it to describe what
poet and artist do, and he suggests that to translate it we may at different times
need to use words such as 'imitate', 'indicate', 'suggest' and 'express', although
all of these words are related to human action ('praxis').

Since Aristotle, the term 'mimesis' has been pressed into service to describe the
more general capacity of literature to imitate reality, and has on occasions accumulated a somewhat polemical edge as a result of its use by those wishing to
establish imitation as central or essential to art – by MARXIST critics intent on
stressing that literature and art 'reflect' extra-literary reality, for example.

In modern NARRATIVE theory a number of theorists have equated diegesis and
mimesis with telling and showing, a distinction which can be traced back to
Henry James, and which was both adopted and simplified by Percy Lubbock.
This actually makes rather a large difference in the meaning of diegesis. For in
the case of almost any classic NOVEL, what the READER learns he or she acquires

through a *telling*, a *narration*, rather than as a result of a performance as in a play. One could thus defend referring to the work *in toto* as an example of diegesis, because even the direct speech of characters is *told* to the reader through a narrating. But any reader of the novel will recognize that such passages in the novel, in which dialogue and character interaction give a dramatic effect, cause the reader to forget about the NARRATOR and to feel as if one is witnessing the characters in dramatic interaction. (Note that we have now moved from a concern with the AUTHOR to a concern with the narrator.) From a Jamesian perspective such passages would be categorized as examples of showing rather than telling, so that if diegesis and mimesis are to be treated as equivalent to telling and showing, then clearly *Pride and Prejudice* is not an example of pure diegesis, but includes both diegetic and mimetic elements.

Modern narrative theory has introduced another use of these terms, one which is related to those discussed already, but which actually represents a significant change and extension of their meaning. Instead of relating them to telling and showing, it has equated them with PLOT and STORY, such that the diegetic level is the level of the 'story reality' of the events narrated, while the mimetic level is the level of the 'narrator's life and consciousness'. Both GÉRARD GENETTE and Shlomith Rimmon-Kenan, for example, use *diegesis* as 'roughly equivalent to my "story"' (Rimmon-Kenan: 1983, 47). This extension can lead us into some terminological contradictions. For if diegesis is equivalent to story, then *extradiegetic* must mean 'outside the story', and therefore could refer us to the actual *telling* of the story, the comments from a narrator who is not a member of the world of the story. But this is exactly the opposite of what we started with: for Socrates, we may remember, diegesis referred to those cases where the poet himself is the speaker, roughly what we have just termed *extradiegetic*! In narrative theorists such as Rimmon-Kenan and Genette, then, an extradiegetic narrator is a narrator who, like the narrator of *Pride and Prejudice*, exists on a different narrative level from the level of the events narrated or the story, whilst an intradiegetic narrator is one who is presented as existing on the same level of reality as the characters in the story he or she tells: Esther Summerson in Charles Dickens's *Bleak House*, for example.

To add to the confusion (as he himself admits), in his *Narrative Discourse* Gérard Genette uses the term *metadiegetic* to describe 'the universe of the second narrative', and the term *metanarrative* to refer to 'a narrative within the narrative' (1980, 228n). This is confusing because a METALANGUAGE is a language about a language – in other words, a 'framing' language and not a 'FRAMED' one. Indeed, Genette himself is not consistent, and in essays collected in his *Figures of Literary Discourse* he uses a different terminology: he defines a *metalanguage* here as a 'discourse upon a discourse' (he defines criticism as a metalanguage) and a metaliterature as 'a literature of which literature itself is the imposed object' (1982, 3–4). Rimmon-Kenan's alternative term for the level of the embedded narrative – *hypodiegetic* – avoids these confusions (1983, 92).

The terms *homodiegetic* and *heterodiegetic*, coined by Genette, introduce additional complications. Genette uses these terms to distinguish different types of ANALEPSIS or flashback: whereas a homodiegetic analepsis provides information about the same character, or sequence of events or milieu that has been the concern of the text up to this point, a heterodiegetic analepsis refers back to some character, sequence of events, or milieu *different from* that/those that have been the concern of the preceding text.

See also INTERTEXTUALITY; DISCOURSE; PALIMPSEST TEXT

Différance A portmanteau term coined by JACQUES DERRIDA, bringing together (in its French original) the senses of difference and deferment. For Derrida différance is the opposite of and alternative to LOGOCENTRISM; while logocentrism posits the existence of fixed meanings guaranteed by an extra-systemic PRESENCE or origin, différance sees meaning as permanently deferred, always subject to and produced by its difference from other meanings and thus volatile and unstable. Meaning is always relational, never self-present or self-constituted. Derrida uses and discusses the term throughout his writing, but perhaps the most accessible of his discussions is in *Positions* (1981), in which he identifies three main meanings for the term:

> *First, différance* refers to the (active *and* passive) movement that consists in deferring by means of delay, delegation, reprieve, referral, detour, postponement, reserving. ... *Second*, the movement of *différance*, as that which produces different things, that which differentiates, is the common root of all oppositional concepts that mark our language, such as, to take only a few examples, sensible/intelligent, intuition/signification, nature/culture, etc. ... *Third, différance* is also the production, if it can still be put this way, of these differences, of the diacriticity that the linguistics generated by Saussure, and all the structural sciences modeled upon it, have recalled is the condition for any signification and any structure. ... From this point of view, the concept of *différance* is neither simply structuralist, nor simply geneticist, such an alternative itself being an 'effect' of *différance*.
>
> (1981, 8–9)

Derrida has suggested a number of alternative terms for différance, including (in *Positions*) *gram*.

Differend See the entry for JEAN-FRANÇOIS LYOTARD, in Section 5, p. 369

Diglossia See HETEROGLOSSIA

Discourse Martin Jay describes discourse as

> one of the most loosely used terms of our time', adding that the term 'has been employed in a host of different contexts, from the communicative rationalism of a Jürgen Habermas to the archaeology of a Foucault; from

the computerized Althusserianism of a Michel Pêchaux to the sociolinguistics of a Malcolm Coulthard; from the textual analysis of a Zelig Harris to the ethnomethodology of a Harvey Sacks.

(1993, 15)

In Linguistics a renewed reliance upon the term is related to the growth in importance of PRAGMATICS; discourse is language in use, not language as an ABSTRACT system. (According to the *OED*, discourse as noun can mean [sense 4] 'Communication of thought by speech', and Samuel Johnson's definition is quoted: 'Mutual intercourse of language.' Interestingly, the use of the noun to mean 'talk' or 'conversation' is described as ARCHAIC.) But even within Linguistics there are varieties of meaning. Michael Stubbs comments on the use of the terms TEXT and discourse, and states that this is often ambiguous and confusing. He suggests that the latter term often implies greater length than does the former, and that discourse may or may not imply interaction (1983, 9). *Critical discourse analysis* is a term used within Linguistics to denote a non-FORMALIST analysis of written or spoken texts which pays attention to issues of social and CULTURAL context.

Gerald Prince isolates two main meanings for the term within NARRATIVE theory: first, the expression plane of a narrative rather than its content plane, the narrating rather than the narrated. Second, following Benveniste, *discourse* is distinguished from *story* (*discours* and *histoire* in the original French) because the former evokes a link between 'a state or event and the situation in which that state or event is linguistically evoked' (Prince: 1988, 21). Contrast 'John's wife was dead' (story) with 'He told her that John's wife was dead' (discourse). (Compare the distinction between *énonciation* and *énoncé* in the entry for ENUNCIATION.)

For MICHEL FOUCAULT, discourses are 'large groups of statements' – rule-governed language terrains defined by what Foucault refers to as 'strategic possibilities' (1972, 37), comparable to a limited extent to one possible usage of the term REGISTER in Linguistics. Thus for Foucault, at a given moment in the history of, say, France, there will be a particular discourse of medicine: a set of rules and CONVENTIONS and systems of mediation and transposition which govern the way illness and treatment are talked about – when, where, and by whom. All societies, following Foucault, have procedures whereby the production of discourses is controlled, selected, organized and redistributed, and the purpose of these processes of discourse control is to ward off 'powers and dangers' (1981, 52). These procedures govern, variously, what Foucault terms *discursive practices*, *discursive objects*, and *discursive strategies*, such that in all discourses *discursive regularities* can be observed.

The work of MIKHAIL BAKHTIN gives us yet further examples of the pressing of the word *discourse* into new services. According to the glossary provided in Bakhtin: 1981, *discourse* is used to translate the Russian word *slovo*, which can mean either an individual word, or a method of using words that presumes a type of authority (1981, 427). This is quite close to the usage argued for by Foucault, and this similarity can also be seen in some cognate terms used by Bakhtin. Thus *authoritative discourse* is the privileged language that 'approaches us from without; it is distanced, taboo, and permits no play with its framing context' (1981, 424). In contrast, *internally persuasive discourse* is discourse which uses one's own words, which does not present itself as 'other', as the representative of an alien power. *Ennobled discourse* is discourse which has been made more 'literary' and elevated, less accessible. TZVETAN TODOROV gives a number of brief quotations from Bakhtin which show, however, that even his use of the term (or its Russian near-equivalent) has its variations: 'Discourse, that is language in its concrete and living totality'; '*discourse*, that is language as a concrete total phenomenon'; '*discourse*, that is utterance (*vyskazyvanie*)' (Todorov: 1984, 25). In his *Problems of Dostoevsky's Poetics*, Bakhtin refers to '*discourse*, that is, language in its concrete living totality, and not language as the specific object of linguistics, something arrived at through a completely legitimate and necessary abstraction from various aspects of the concrete life of the word' (Bakhtin: 1984, 181). In the same work, Bakhtin also refers to 'double-voiced discourse', which he claims always arises under conditions of dialogic interaction (1984, 185).

Not surprisingly, the varied meanings which have accrued to 'discourse' are also active in the term 'discourse analysis'. Robert de Beaugrande (1994) has attempted to gather together some of the varied elements in discourse analysis, suggesting three areas of initial concentration: 'the cross-cultural study of stories and narratives' of the type carried out by Claude Lévi-Strauss, 'the discourse of schooling and education' (such as in the work of Michael Stubbs and others), 'and, with a sociological turn, the organization of conversation' (1994, 207). But as de Beaugrande points out, from the 1970s onwards the picture becomes much more complicated, as

> discourse analysis became a convergence point for a number of trends; 'text linguistics' on the European continent; 'functional' or 'systemic linguistics' in Czechoslovakia, Britain and Australia; 'cognitive linguistics,' 'critical linguistics,' 'ethnography of communication,' ethnomethodology, and the structuralism, post-structuralism, deconstruction, and feminism emanating from France; along with semiotics and cognitive science, both convergence points in their own right.
>
> (1994, 207–8)

For *monovalent discourse* and *polyvalent discourse* (Todorov), see the entry for REGISTER.

POSTCOLONIALIST theorists have applied the concepts of *master discourse* and *hegemonic discourse* to those ideologically charged ways of looking at and speaking about the world which presuppose and incorporate EUROCENTRIC and racist assumptions. Thus a master discourse is not just the chief among discourses, it is also the discourse of the masters.

See also ENUNCIATION; FREE INDIRECT DISCOURSE; GENRE; NEW HISTORICISM AND CULTURAL MATERIALISM (Section 3)

Displacement Within Linguistics, displacement refers to the human ability to refer to things removed from the utterer's immediate situation, either in time or in space. This ability seems to distinguish human beings from other living creatures, and it is language-dependent. Thus a question such as 'Do you remember the nice time we had on holiday in Bulgaria last year?' may appear trivial, but it exemplifies a resource not available in any significant way to other species.

In one sense literature is one of the most sophisticated exemplifications of this ability: members of other species can sham and mislead, but FICTION seems a specifically human resource (although it is arguably related to play, in both humans and animals).

Sigmund Freud's use of this term is rather different: see CONDENSATION AND DISPLACEMENT.

Dissociation of sensibility See the entry for T.S. ELIOT, Section 5, p. 331

Distance A term used with a range of related meanings in literary criticism, mostly within the theory of NARRATIVE. The most general meaning refers to READER involvement in a literary WORK. Thus whereas readers of Dickens's NOVELS typically became (and become) very involved in the fate of CHARACTERS in the course of reading (gathering on the quay in the United States to meet the latest instalment of *The Old Curiosity Shop* to learn of the fate of Little Nell, for example), much of Joseph Conrad's FICTION encourages the reader to observe characters and events more dispassionately, at more of an emotional distance.

This is not unrelated to more specific usages of the term within narrative theory. The reader of Conrad's 'An Outpost of Progress' feels relatively distanced from the fates of the characters of the work, but this is in part because the NARRATOR also seems detached and, if pitying, at a distance from the characters. Distance can, therefore, refer to the gap between STORY and NARRATION, and this gap can be temporal, geographical, or emotional – or traceable to a clash between the value-systems associated with characters and with the narrative. It can also be attributed to more technical matters: the more anonymous and covert the narration, the less distance there is between story and narration; the more the narrative draws attention to itself as narrative (through, for example, a PERSONIFIED narrator), then the greater the story–narrative distance. It should be remembered, however, that it is possible for the technical distance between narrative and story to be very small without necessarily producing very much reader or NARRATEE involvement in the work on an emotional level. Distance, in other words, can be technical, intellectual, moral, or emotional according to various usages.

See also ANALEPSIS

Dramatic irony Dramatic irony needs to be distinguished from IRONY, for which see the separate entry. Dramatic irony involves a discrepancy or distance between a CHARACTER's limited understanding and the fuller knowledge of the audience or reader. In Robert Browning's 'My Last Duchess' there is a contrast between the image of himself that the Duke thinks he is promoting (CULTURED, firm, a man of status and substance) and our sense of his personality (egocentric, vain, materialistic, superficial, brutal). In Mark Twain's NOVEL, Huckleberry Finn often finds himself caught up in situations that he does not properly understand: this gives us a sense both of his innocence and of society's corruption. Dramatic irony can be comic or tragic: for example, in Molière's *Tartuffe*, the villain Tartuffe voices his contempt for his PATRON, unaware that the latter is hiding beneath the table. But in TRAGEDY, dramatic irony often reveals how painfully limited human understanding can be; in Sophocles's *Oedipus the King*, Oedipus promises to revenge his father's murder, not knowing that he himself is the killer. Dramatic irony can also be anticipational, as when (for example) the character in a play with the greatest fondness for guns comes to be shot. *Situational irony* involves a comic duplication or parallelism: an inept detective searches the hotel room of a suspect while the suspect searches the hotel room of the detective, for instance.

Dramatic monologue A poem in which a single speaker who is not the poet addresses a (generally silent) listener. Conventionally, the delivery of the address often takes place not in a relaxed or contemplative situation, but at a moment involving at least some tension or drama. In the process of the delivery, something is revealed about the CHARACTER of the speaker and often about the time in which the poem is set. T.S. Eliot's 'The Journey of the Magi' and Robert Browning's 'My Last Duchess' are both dramatic monologues.

Dream vision A NARRATIVE in which a CHARACTER falls asleep, experiences a vision, and then relates its contents. Often, the dream features ALLEGORICAL elements. Most dream visions are medieval (the thirteenth-century *Roman de la Rose*, for example, or Dante's fourteenth-century *The Divine Comedy*). John Keats produces a more recent version of a dream vision, also strongly allegorical, in 'La Belle Dame Sans Merci'.

Duration In NARRATIVE theory, duration can refer either to the time covered by the STORY or part of it (an EVENT), or to the 'time' allotted to either by the TEXT (story-time and text-time). As Rimmon-Kenan points out, the latter concept is a highly problematic one as 'there is no way of measuring text-duration' (1983, 51). On a very rough basis it is possible to note that three years of story-time may be covered by three pages of text, while further on in the same text one hour of story-time may occupy 50 pages. But 'pages' do not give a particularly reliable measure: not only do some READERS read more quickly than others, the same reader will read more or less quickly depending upon such factors as textual complexity, reader involvement and tension, and so on. Gerald Prince points out that as a result many writers on narrative find *speed* or *tempo* more fruitful concepts in the analysis of narrative texts (1988, 24).

In some usages 'represented time' and 'representational time' are terms used to describe 'time-in-the-story' and 'time-it-takes-to-tell-the-story'.

According to GÉRARD GENETTE, the four basic FORMS of narrative movement are ELLIPSIS, pause, scene and summary. These constitute four different ways of varying duration (1980, 94).

See also ISOCHRONY

Eclogue Named after the *Eclogues* of the Roman poet Virgil, an eclogue normally involves a DIALOGUE between two CHARACTERS. It is typically applied to PASTORAL poems in which two shepherds speak to each other, but there are non-pastoral eclogues (Jonathan Swift's 'Town Eclogue' is one such).

Écriture French-English dictionaries give 'writing' as the equivalent of écriture, and in an article on DECONSTRUCTIVE criticism M.H. Abrams has glossed écriture as 'the written or printed text' (1977, 428), but the fact that many critics writing in English continue to use the French term suggests that this equivalence is very incomplete. Contemporary critical use of this term dates from ROLAND BARTHES's extension of the meaning of the French term in his *Le Degré zéro de l'écriture*, which was published in 1953. The English translation (Barthes: 1967b) has what, given the following comments, is arguably the misleading title *Writing Degree Zero*. In an article on écriture, Ann Banfield has named other 'landmark texts' which have contributed to the establishment of this term: Maurice Blanchot's 'The Narrative Voice' (1981); Michel Butor, 'L'Usage des pronoms personnels dans le roman' (1964), and MICHEL FOUCAULT, 'What is an Author?' (1980) (Banfield: 1985, 2). Barthes's translators point out in a note that although in everyday French *écriture* normally means only 'handwriting', or 'the art of writing', '[i]t is used here in a strictly technical sense to denote a new concept' (Barthes: 1967b, 7). This 'new concept' has to be explained by reference to Barthes's setting of écriture in opposition to *littérature*, a distinction related to that which he makes between *lisible* and *scriptible* or, as rendered in English translation, READERLY AND WRITERLY TEXTS. As Banfield points out, the distinction between écriture and *littérature* is the more striking in French because prose FICTION in French has appropriated to itself certain *grammatical* characteristics which distinguish it from other types of writing, notably the *passé simple* and the third-person NARRATIVE (Banfield: 1985, 4). If *littérature* is characterized by these overt grammatical markers, and by less overt and related IDEOLOGICAL ones, écriture seeks to escape from 'LITERARINESS' by a 'zero style' first, and most strikingly, seen in the French NOVEL in Albert Camus's *L'Étranger*, a novel told in the first and not the third person, and using not the *passé simple* but the *parfait composé*, a grammatical choice which has (or had) a shock effect in French which is lost in English translation. For Barthes, 'writing degree zero' is a 'colourless writing, freed from all bondage to a pre-ordained state of language' (1967b, 82), it represents an attempt 'to go beyond Literature by entrusting one's fate to a sort of basic speech, equally far from living languages and from literary language proper' (1967b, 83).

Banfield argues that although the grammatical markers of écriture are not so apparent in English, nonetheless the term points to a writing characterized by ABSENCE, a lack of the marks of literature, of human agency, which is not limited to French language or CULTURE. Écriture as substantive, says Banfield, 'is a product now divorced from the person and activity of its producer', it is 'the name for the coming to language of a knowledge which is not personal' (1985, 13), and she links it with the use of *style indirecte libre*, or FREE INDIRECT DISCOURSE in the novel.

Écriture féminine According to ELAINE SHOWALTER, 'the inscription of the feminine body and female difference in language and text' (1986, 249). The term was coined by French FEMINISTS, and represents more a description of an ideal, future achievement than of a particular type of writing of which there already exist many examples.

The name most frequently associated with the term is that of HÉLÈNE CIXOUS, although those described as practitioners of écriture féminine have, themselves, rarely used the term. Nor can one expect a tidy definition or theorization of the term from Cixous; as she writes in one of her best-known pieces, 'The Laugh of the Medusa':

> [i]t is impossible to *define* a feminine practice of writing, and this is an impossibility that will remain, for this practice can never be theorized, enclosed, coded – which doesn't mean that it doesn't exist. But it will always surpass the discourse that regulates the phallocentric system; it does and will take place in areas other than those subordinated to philosophico-theoretical domination. It will be conceived of only by subjects who are breakers of automatisms, by peripheral figures that no authority can ever subjugate.
>
> (1981, 253)

The concept has interesting forebears. Take the following comment from VIRGINIA WOOLF's essay 'Women and Fiction', which was first published in 1929.

> But it is still true that before a woman can write exactly as she wishes to write, she has many difficulties to face. To begin with, there is the technical difficulty – so simple, apparently; in reality, so baffling – that the very form of the sentence does not fit her. It is a sentence made by men; it is too loose, too heavy, too pompous for a woman's use.
>
> (1966, 145)

More recent feminist accounts of écriture féminine suggest that a woman's sense of her own body may become the source from which the new writing must stem. Madeleine Gagnon, for example, after noting that she has to take over a language which, although it is hers, is foreign to her, argues that there is an alternative: '[a]ll we have to do is let the body flow, from the inside; all we have to do is erase, as we did on the slate, whatever may hinder or harm the new forms of writing; we retain whatever fits, whatever suits us' (1980, 180).

SECTION 4

Not all have agreed with this proposal, and a forceful objection to proposals that 'place the body at the center of a search for female identity' is voiced by the Editorial Collective of *Questions Féministes* in an article entitled 'Variations on Common Themes'.

> To advocate a 'woman's language' and a means of expression that would be specifically feminine seems to us equally illusory. First, the so-called explored language extolled by some women seems to be linked, if not in its content at least in its style, to a trend propagated by literary schools governed by male masters. This language is therefore as academic and as 'masculine' as other languages. Secondly, it is at times said that women's language is closer to the body, to sexual pleasure, to direct sensations, and so on, which means that the body could express itself directly without social mediation and that, moreover, this closeness to the body and to nature would be subversive. In our opinion, there is no such thing as a direct relation to the body. To advocate a direct relation to the body is therefore not subversive because it is equivalent to denying the reality and the strength of social mediations, the very same ones that oppress us in our bodies. At most, one would advocate a different socialization of the body, but without searching for a true and eternal nature, for this search takes us away from the most effective struggle against the socio-historical contexts in which human beings are and will always be trapped.
>
> (Quoted in Mary Eagleton: 1996, 338)

Elegy A WORK of mourning or lamentation for the dead. There is no set FORM by which the elegy can be identified, but elegies generally impart a sense of loss and regret, and thus the TONE of the work is frequently the crucial element. The elegy typically attempts to find some measure of consolation, and often this is achieved by means of references to the seasonal regeneration of nature, implying the possibility of an afterlife.

Elizabethan See PERIODS OF LITERATURE

Ellipsis Alternatively *gap*. The omitting of one or more items in a NARRATIVE series: any gap of information in a temporal or other sequence. We never learn anything concrete, for example, of Heathcliff's history prior to his discovery in Liverpool by Mr Earnshaw, nor of what he does to become rich between the time of his disappearance and re-appearance in *Wuthering Heights*. In this case the ellipsis is relatively *unmarked* (or implicit), as it covers information not known to the PERSONIFIED NARRATORS. But when in Charles Dickens's *Bleak House* Esther Summerson seeks to explain why she finds Mrs Woodcourt irksome, and breaks off with the words, 'I don't know what it was. Or at least if I do, now, I thought I did not then. Or at least – but it don't matter', then we have a clearly *marked* (or explicit) ellipsis: the READER's attention is drawn to the fact that something that is known to the narrator is withheld from him or her.

GÉRARD GENETTE characterizes certain ellipses as *hypothetical*; these are those ellipses which are impossible to localize or – on occasions – to place in any spot at all, but which are revealed after the event by an ANALEPSIS (1980, 109).

Ellipses can be permanent or temporary: in most detective NOVELS certain marked gaps are sustained until the end of the WORK only to be filled in during the final pages.

See also ABSENCE; DURATION (narrative movements); PARALIPSIS

Emblem A term with a number of interconnected meanings, ranging from an illustration carrying SYMBOLIC force (often with the addition of an explanatory motto), to a standardized literary symbol. Emblems influenced the use of verbal IMAGERY in metaphysical poetry. *Emblem books* date from the early sixteenth century and generally involve illustrations accompanied by an explanatory moral or motto. For *emblem poems*, see CONCRETE POETRY.

Emplotment A term much used within NEW HISTORICIST theory to refer to the textualizing of historical 'facts' or 'events' to create a PLOT or NARRATIVE. Just as a novelist may create any number of NOVELS from a given set of CHARACTERS and events, so too (certain radical historians have argued) a given set of historical data can be emplotted in innumerable manners, all of which will present that material in different ways.

Those who use the term often draw on the distinction between STORY AND PLOT to be found in narrative theory, and suggest that just as we can get at a story only through a plot, so too it is an illusion to believe that the raw facts of history can be directly apprehended, as they too can be apprehended only in one emplotted FORM or another.

In their most extreme form such arguments espouse highly idealistic positions which deny the existence of historical facts or events as such, and argue that all the historian has is a set of different emplotments which cannot be judged against a reality that each claims to represent or reproduce, but which is actually produced and re-produced by these emplotments. Here JACQUES DERRIDA's notorious claim that there is nothing outside the TEXT (1976, 158) is taken to a logical extreme.

English This has long been considered to be an ideologically loaded or, at least, coloured word by those who have argued that the tendency within and outside Britain to substitute it for the often more accurate *British* compromises its use as a neutral descriptive term in other contexts (the 'English language', for example).

This suspicion of the word seems to have been at least partly responsible for the emergence of a new usage, current in British rather than American contexts, which can be summed up as 'that complex of attitudes and exclusions which accompanies the role played by English language and literature in the educational system, and which functions as a part of the dominant ideology'. Thus in an article from 1989 entitled 'Towards Cultural History – in Theory and Practice', Catherine Belsey writes that 'I start from the assumption that English as it has traditionally been understood, as the study of great literary works by great authors, has no useful part to play in a pedagogy committed to a politics of change' (Ryan: 1996, 82).

Enlightenment, the A term generally associated with the eighteenth-century intellectual movement that emphasized the centrality and potential of human reason. Central to Enlightenment thought was the notion of human progress, and the belief in the universe as regulated by observable laws and governed by a principle of systematic unity. Enlightenment thinkers promoted a rational approach to social and political issues, and saw the state as the supreme expression and upholder of order. After many centuries during which the term enjoyed unambiguously positive associations, POST-STRUCTURALIST theorists started to attack what they saw as a misguided belief in Enlightenment values, and in such circles the term may now be used pejoratively. See also the entry for JEAN-FRANÇOIS LYOTARD in Section 5, p. 369.

Enunciation Along with cognate words such as *enunciatee, enunciator* and *enunciated*, enunciation has now begun to replace the French loan-word *énonciation* and its cognates. However such translations often fail to carry the more specific meanings of the French originals. (The translator of ROLAND BARTHES's article 'To Write: an Intransitive Verb?', for example, regularly includes the French original terms alongside the English translation, and *énonciation* is translated on one occasion as *utterance* and on another as *statement*. UMBERTO ECO, in contrast, renders *énoncé* and *énonciation* as *sentence* and *utterance* [1981, 16].)

What is central to use of the various French terms is a distinction between the particular, time-bound *act* of making a statement, and the *verbal result* of that act, a result which escapes from the moment of time and from the possession of the person responsible for the act. We can note that the important distinction between *utterance* and *statement* is that the former term links that which is uttered to its human originator, whereas the latter term concentrates attention on to the purely verbal result. When *énonciation* is used in French it more usually has the meaning we attribute to *utterance*, that is to say, it calls to mind the *act* of producing a form of words which involves a human SUBJECT. In contrast, when *énoncé* is used the intention is normally to consider a form of words independently from their context-bound association with a human SUBJECT.

In addition, the French terms generally include the idea of a human target or audience (whereas a statement or UTTERANCE can be made in the absence of these). Thus some writers in English prefer to translate the term *énonciateur* as *addresser*, a usage which inevitably perhaps also brings with it *addressee* – the person at whom an utterance is aimed.

Envoi The short final STANZA of a poem, sometimes appended as a postscript, summarizing its contents or praising one or more of its CHARACTERS.

Epic An extended NARRATIVE (often equivalent to several books) which tells the story of a journey undertaken by a HERO or group of heroes, and their adventures. It is usually written in an elevated STYLE, and has many CONVENTIONS: invocations to the Muses, for example, catalogues (or lists of CHARACTERS, warriors, battles, achievements, episodes), and highly FORMAL addresses and speeches. Though not directly historical, the actions recounted are often disguised versions of actual events or processes (such as the battle at Troy, or the founding of Rome). Examples include Homer's *Iliad* and *Odyssey*, Virgil's *Aeneid* and Milton's *Paradise Lost*.

For MOCK EPIC, see the separate entry, and for BERTOLT BRECHT's 'epic theatre', see ALIENATION EFFECT.

Epigram A brief poem or part of a poem, often no more than a couplet (two lines) or quatrain (four lines). The term derives from the Greek word for 'inscription' ('epigramma'). Because of its extreme brevity, it encourages succinct, often witty, expression.

Epiphany According to Christian belief and practice, the feast of the Epiphany (January 6) celebrates the showing of the infant Jesus to the three Magi, 12 days after the Nativity. For James Joyce, the key elements of the epiphany were the moment of revelation and insight in combination with ordinary circumstances (Christ was born in a stable). In his writing, an epiphany was therefore a moment of extreme clarity, during which a CHARACTER understands something about her or himself, about other characters, or about a present or past situation. Such a moment occurs in his short story 'The Dead,' when the character Gabriel realizes that he is shallow and fallible – a realization which nevertheless may have its positive side. The epiphany can be linked to the concept of ANAGNORISIS in drama, where the tragic HERO achieves a measure of self-recognition.

Epistolary novel A NOVEL which is presented as a series of letters written by one or more of the CHARACTERS. This allows for a sense of intimacy (as if we were accessing the mind of the NARRATOR) and immediacy, as well as an illusion of linguistic transparency or sincerity. It also allows for interaction and tension between multiple points of view (see PERSPECTIVE AND VOICE). All of Samuel Richardson's novels are epistolary in FORM, as is Frances Burney's *Evelina; or, The History of a Young Lady's Entrance Into the World* (1778), and more recently, Alice Walker's *The Color Purple* (1982).

Epithalamion A poem or song composed in honour of a bride and groom, and in order to celebrate the joys of married love. Edmund Spenser's 'Epithalamion' is a famous early example.

Eponymous The eponymous CHARACTER of a literary TEXT is one whose name constitutes all or part of the title of the WORK, such as Anne Brontë's *Agnes Grey* or Charles Dickens's *David Copperfield*.

Essentialism The belief that qualities are inherent in objects of study rather than context-dependent. Essentialism is thus to be distinguished from dialectical, contextual or relational theories and approaches. All of these see reality not in terms of 'essential' units with a fixed identity, but in terms of shifting and interpenetrating elements the nature of which changes according to combination or context. The term 'essentialism' often carries with it the implication that the qualities of objects of study are self-evident and do not themselves need to be sought for or explained (see Cameron: 1985, 187).

HUMANISM is often accused of essentialism by its critics (see the entry for this term), and Alan Sinfield argues that '[t]he essentialist-humanist approach to literature and sexual politics depends upon the belief that the individual is the probable, indeed necessary, source of truth and meaning' (1992, 37). The opposite of essentialism is RELATIVISM, but it is possible (indeed, it is probably normal) for both of these terms to be used pejoratively. This seems to be because many believe that there are certain absolutes (which is denied by strict relativism), but that this does not commit one to being an essentialist. The term 'relationism' is sometimes used as a non-pejorative alternative to relativism.

A term associated with GAYATRI CHAKRAVORTY SPIVAK is *strategic essentialism*; the term carries the belief that the use of essentialist categories may be strategically necessary in the fighting of certain battles. See Spivak: 1984–5.

Eurocentric Perceived from the PERSPECTIVE of Europe. The term almost always refers to a set of beliefs or attitudes rather than simply a perspective in the geographical sense; it thus has a predominantly IDEOLOGICAL force. Very often the implication is that the perspective has been NATURALIZED, and is thus believed to represent a neutral or value-free outlook or point of view. At the same time, the assumption is that Europe represents a standard that the non-European can aspire to but cannot exceed or replace.

Compare GRAND AND LITTLE NARRATIVES (master narrative)

Exegesis Stemming from a tradition of Biblical study, exegesis traditionally involved a range of activities from the elucidation of textual cruces (see CRUX) and difficulties through commentary on the implications and applications of textual meanings. The Roman *exegetes* had as their official function the INTERPRETATION of such things as dreams, laws, omens and the pronouncements of the Oracle, so that in some usages exegesis is more or less interchangeable with INTERPRETATION. In current usage, however, the term is normally reserved for more careful commentary or *close reading* which stays near to the words on the page.

Exemplum A short NARRATIVE, true or FICTIONAL, used to illustrate an argument.

Expressionism A term borrowed from painting and used to describe art that abandons any attempt at a disengaged depiction of an external reality and chooses instead to express the inner self of the artist. Expressionists are thus anti-REALIST in tendency, focusing rather on SUBJECTIVE experience, and especially extreme states of consciousness (fear, horror). There is often an emphasis on stimulation rather than simulation: techniques such as distortion and exaggeration are often deployed to convey the uniqueness of the artist's vision of the world. Although the term dates from the very end of the nineteenth century, when it was applied to dramatists such as August Strindberg, it isolates an element in – for example – much Romantic literature.

Extradiegetic See DIEGESIS AND MIMESIS

Fable A didactic NARRATIVE exemplifying moral and social values, and often featuring animals. Aesop's *Fables* are the most celebrated example; George Orwell's *Animal Farm* is a more explicitly political, and recent, instance.

Fabula See STORY AND PLOT

Faction A portmanteau word (fact + FICTION) coined by the American author Truman Capote to describe works such as his *In Cold Blood* (1966) in which novelistic techniques are used to bring actual historical events and personages to life. A work of faction lies on the borderline between fact and FICTION: the people and events described are non-fictional, but the corroboratory detail is often imagined so as to bring the READER closer to them.

Fantastic The RUSSIAN FORMALISTS were the first extensively to theorize the fantastic. In his essay 'Thematics', for example, Boris Tomashevsky quotes an interesting passage from Vladimir Solovyev's Introduction to Alexey Tolstoy's NOVEL *The Vampire*, which Tomashevsky describes as 'an unusually clear example of fantasy'. According to Solovyev, the distinguishing characteristic of the genuinely fantastic is that it is never,

> so to speak, in full view. Its presence must never compel belief in a mystic interpretation of a vital event; it must rather point, or *hint*, at it. In the really fantastic, the external, formal possibility of a simple explanation of ordinary and commonplace connections among the phenomena always remains. This external explanation, however, finally loses its internal probability.
>
> (Tomashevsky: 1965, 83–4)

Christine Brooke-Rose has made a useful summary of the three conditions which TZVETAN TODOROV believes to be more or less standard components of the 'pure' fantastic. The READER must hesitate between natural and supernatural explanations of what happens in the WORK up to its conclusion; this hesitation may be represented – that is, it may be shared by a leading CHARACTER in the work; and the reader must reject both a poetic and an ALLEGORICAL reading of the work, as both of these destroy the hesitation which is fundamental to the pure fantastic (Brooke-Rose: 1981, 63). If there is no hesitation, then either we are in the realm of some variant of the *uncanny* (the events are seen by the reader to have a natural explanation), or of the *marvellous* (the events are seen by the reader to have a supernatural explanation).

Farce A SUB-GENRE of COMEDY, usually drama, involving highly improbable and ridiculous situations, stock CHARACTERS, mistaken identities, sexual innuendo and puns, and physical humour (the loss of clothing, the misplaced hairpiece, etc.) Farces are extremely popular forms of *low comedy* (see COMEDY). The British 'Carry On' films are mostly farces.

Feminism See Section 3, p. 191

Feuilleton Applied to a literary work, usually a NOVEL, published in serial FORM in a newspaper or magazine.

Fiction Literary critics have traditionally used the term *fiction* to denote imaginative WORKS (normally written NARRATIVES) which occupy a category distinct both from writing which purports to be true and also from forms of deceit and lying. This much is easy – but it is also clearly inadequate. The fictional MODE is a fundamental part of being human – being able to imagine 'what if', or to discuss 'as if' invented characters and events were actually true. Fantasy, play, role-playing and joking all seem to have *something* in common with literary fiction, although of course literary fiction in its different GENRES is regulated by sets of CONVENTIONS.

Fiction is much wider than 'prose fiction': jokes, imitations and parodies, songs, and narrative poems can all be described as fictions – and wider, non-literary usages include such things as legal fictions and (perhaps) folk tales and urban myths.

Although this is a complicated issue, it seems possible to argue that literary fiction is more a matter of the not-true (rather than the non-existent – novels *may* contain references to real people, places and events) treated imaginatively as if it were true. But a full definition of 'fiction' must encompass not just the 'work in itself' but also the way it is read. Thus it is arguable that although we can now read, say, Daniel Defoe's novel *Robinson Crusoe* as fiction, for Defoe's early readers who read it as a factual account it was not fiction.

First-person (narrator) See NARRATIVE SITUATION; STORY AND PLOT

Flâneur A (normally male) idler who wanders along crowded city streets and observes without involvement. The term is associated with the French poet Charles Baudelaire who popularized the figure, but later writers – most notably WALTER BENJAMIN – seized upon it as expressing something essential about modern life and the modern artist which was captured in MODERNIST art: the sense of semi-lonely detachment in the midst of the crowded urban scene.

Flashback See ANALEPSIS

Flashforward See PROLEPSIS

Focalization/focalizer See PERSPECTIVE AND VOICE; REFLECTOR (CHARACTER)

Foot (in poetry) See METRE

Foregrounding See DEFAMILIARIZATION

Form Most commentators agree that the form-content distinction involves oversimplification, but few are able entirely to dispense with it. If content refers to *what* is said, form means *how* it is said, the shape or STRUCTURE of the saying. 'Form' as a term overlaps with GENRE, and on occasions the two terms are used interchangeably.

Formalism See Section 3, p. 143

Formulaic literature A concern with the formulaic element in art and literature during the twentieth century is closely connected with investigations into popular and folk art, but has spread beyond the boundaries of such investigations. A key figure here is that of the Russian VLADIMIR PROPP, whose *Morphology of the Folktale* was first published in Russian in 1928. Propp based his work on the study of a corpus of nearly two hundred Russian folk tales, and attempted to abstract common elements from these, elements which he named functions. *Oral* performance typically involves a heavy reliance upon the formulaic, and the advent of writing leads to a lessening of the verbal artist's reliance upon formulaic elements.
See also ORALITY

Frame This is a term with a very wide variety of meanings in different discipline contexts. Andrew Gibson attributes a useful way of categorizing different sorts of usage within NARRATIVE theory to Ian Reid's 1992 book *Narrative Exchanges*:

> Reid distinguishes four kinds of narrative framing. The first is circumtextual, and a question of the physical adjuncts to the narrative, like title, footnotes, epigraph and so forth. The second is extratextual: the framing information, expectations and preoccupations that a reader brings to a text. The third is intratextual, taking place directly on the page itself. The fourth and last kind is intertextual, and a matter of the relationship between a narrative and other texts.
>
> (Gibson: 1996, 218)

Other relevant usages include the following.

1. According to Mieke Bal, 'the space in which the CHARACTER is situated, or is precisely not situated, is regarded as the *frame*' (1985, 94).

2. In her book *Reading Frames in Modern Fiction* (1985) Mary Ann Caws applies the term *frame* to the experience that many READERS have of finding that certain passages in works of prose FICTION 'stand out' from their surroundings. Caws suggests that such framing assumes an especial FORM in MODERNIST fiction as the idea of framing is called attention to or, we might say, FOREGROUNDED in modernist fiction (1985, xi).

3. Following Erving Goffman's *Frame Analysis* (1974) the term is also used to denote various ways in which works of art (among other things) are AESTHETICALLY bounded and, thus, require or invite a range of different

possible relationships with the art consumer, with other works of art, or generally with extra-artistic reality. Manfred Jahn's definition is similar: 'a frame will be understood as in Perry (1979) to denote the cognitive model that is selected and used (and sometimes discarded), in the process of reading a narrative text' (1997, 441–2).

4. A framed (or nested) narrative is either a 'narrative within a narrative', as in Henry James's *The Turn of the Screw*, or any narrative containing different narrative levels. In such a work the term *frame narrator* refers to the NARRATOR of the outer narrative (alternatively, the term *outer narrator* is often used). Inner, or framed narratives are also known as *embedded narratives* or *Chinese Box narratives*, and where multiple embedding occurs it is sometimes known as *staircasing*.

5. UMBERTO ECO adopts definitions from Eugene Charniak and Michael Riffaterre in order to suggest a distinction between common frames – which are the rules for practical life possessed by ordinary individuals – and INTERTEXTUAL frames, which are existing literary *topoi* or narrative schemes (1981, 21). (For *topoi* see TOPOS.)

6. In his introductory comments to an essay by Barbara Johnson, Robert Young discusses briefly JACQUES DERRIDA's use of the terms *parergon* (a term Derrida finds in Kant) and *ergon* as substitutes for *frame* and *work*: 'In the visual arts, the parergon will be the frame, or drapery, or enclosing column. The parergon could also be a (critical) text, which "encloses" another text' (Young: 1981, 226).

See also CLOSURE

Frankfurt School See Section 3, p. 186

Free Indirect Discourse Also *Free Indirect Speech* or *Style*; *Narrated Monologue*; *Erlebte Rede*; *Style Indirecte Libre*; *Quasi-Direct Discourse* or *Substitutionary Narration*. In some usages these all represent the same general NARRATIVE technique, subdivisions within which are indicated by distinguishing between *Narrated Speech* and *Narrated Thought*, or between *Free Indirect Speech* and *Free Indirect Thought* (thus making the former phrase slightly ambiguous as it can either represent the umbrella term or a subdivision within it).

Usages do vary, however, and some commentators use *narrated monologue* to refer to a variety of Free Indirect Discourse in which there is indirect quotation of the words used in a CHARACTER's speech or thought. This would mean that non-verbalized thought processes could not be represented by means of narrated monologue, and thus another term is called for: *psycho-narration*. According to Steven Cohan and Linda M. Shires, psycho-narration can be either *consonant* (following a character's own self-apprehension), or *dissonant* (moving back from a character's own perspective) (1988, 100).

The traditional way of defining what we can refer to as FID makes use of grammatical or linguistic evidence. This involves seeing FID as a midway point between Direct, and Indirect (or Reported) Discourse (DD and ID), or as a combination of the two which blends their grammatical characteristics in a distinctive mix. Thus Shlomith Rimmon-Kenan provides the following example, in which one can note that the third example retains the third person 'he' and past tense from ID, but in its truncation resembles the words in inverted commas in the DD example.

> DD: He said, 'I love her'
> ID: He said that he loved her
> FID: He loved her
>
> (1983, 111)

FID often resembles ID minus the normal accompanying tag phrases (e.g. 'he suggested', 'she thought'). The standard grammatical/linguistic signs of FID are taken to be such things as deictics referring to the character's own time or place (e.g. 'Tomorrow was Christmas'), the use of colloquialisms, etc. unlikely to have been used by the NARRATOR, abridgement such as is found in spoken but not, normally, written language, and the back-shift of tenses to be found in ID. When many of these characteristics are found together then a passage can be unambiguously FID, but FID may appear without any linguistic markers, such that only the semantic content of the passage in question can be adduced as evidence that one is dealing with FID.

More recent studies have exhibited increasing scepticism about approaches to FID that rely upon grammatical definitions. Richard Aczel, for example, argues that 'FID *can* be grammatically marked, but is not in any final sense grammatically *identifiable*' (1998, 477–8). Monika Fludernik has reported that with the exception of certain ambiguous Middle English examples, to her knowledge Aphra Behn is the first writer in English to employ free indirect discourse for the representation of consciousness (1996, 155).

A matter of some contention has been that of the 'dual voice' hypothesis, with Pascal (1977) and Banfield (1982) taking up positions for and against the suggestion that FID involves the combination of two voices, those of the narrator and the character. A related term noted by Wales (1989, 77), who attributes it to Graham Hough, is *coloured narrative*. In this case, as Wales points out, the narrative is seen to be 'coloured' by the speech of a character, whereas in FID it is, in a sense, the speech which is coloured by the narrative voice. Very similar to colouring is *mind style*, in which a passage which is not directly attributed to a character gives us, nevertheless, his or her style of thinking or speaking, or understanding.

Frequency Following GÉRARD GENETTE, the numerical relationship between events in a PLOT (or *sjužet*) and events in a STORY (or FABULA). This relationship can vary as follows:

1. a singular event which is narrated once (*singulative narration*);
2. an event which occurs x times and is narrated x times (*multiple narration*);
3. an event which occurs once but is narrated more than once (*repetitive narration*);
4. a repeated event which is narrated only once (*iterative narration*).

Gérard Genette uses the term *pseudo-iterative* to describe passages of narrative which claim to be iterative but which provide extended detail or include elements which by their very nature must be unique.

Function See entry for VLADIMIR PROPP, Section 5, p. 378

Gender In current FEMINIST usage, *gender* is used to refer to those characteristics of socio-cultural origin which are conventionally associated with the different biological sexes. Within Linguistics this usage is sometimes varied in order to avoid confusion with linguistic gender, but generally speaking feminist influence has succeeded in establishing that *gender* involves society and or CULTURE and *sex* involves biology. There are thus two sexes, but many different genders.

A *genderlect* is a term used to describe linguistic characteristics which in a given society or culture are specific to members of one gender. (Compare IDIOLECT.)

See also TRANSGENDER

Geneva School See Section 3, p. 157

Genre The traditional sense of genre as a literary type or class survives in the present day, with the term FORM sometimes confusingly used interchangeably with that of genre. Generic debates have become less heated during a time in which it is more generally accepted that genres have a CONVENTIONAL rather than an intrinsic justification, but the role of genres in forming audience and READER expectations and responses has been considered by a number of recent theorists and critics.

Georgic Named after the Roman poet Virgil's *Georgics*, this is a GENRE of PASTORAL poetry which contains practical (rather than moral or abstract) instruction.

Grand narratives and little narratives From the French terms *grand récit* and *petit récit*. *Grand récit* is sometimes rendered as *master narrative*. The terms have been given widespread currency by JEAN-FRANÇOIS LYOTARD's book *The Postmodern Condition: A Report on Knowledge* (1984; first published in French, 1979). Lyotard distinguishes the modern by its association with what he calls grand narratives:

> I will use the term *modern* to designate any science that legitimates itself with reference to a metadiscourse of this kind making an explicit appeal to

> some grand narrative, such as the dialectics of Spirit, the hermeneutics of
> meaning, the emancipation of the rational or working subject, or the cre-
> ation of wealth.
>
> (1984, xxiii)

A grand narrative, then, is a means for EMPLOTTING a life or a CULTURE; to give
one's actions or one's life meaning one pictures oneself as a CHARACTER within
an already-written narrative, one whose final conclusion is assured in advance. A
little narrative abandons such lofty goals and restricts itself to more local
explanatory models.

Grotesque The term shares a common root with 'grotto'; decorated Italian grottoes
often contained figures with exaggerated or monstrous appearances. The term
was applied to decorative figures from architecture, such as gargoyles and griffins,
which combined animal, human, and monstrous or supernatural features.
'Grotesque' has come to refer to literary CHARACTERS who seem abnormal or
unusual in some way, or to NARRATIVES that mix elements of the bizarre with the
commonplace.

Gynocriticism According to ELAINE SHOWALTER the term gynocriticism is an invention of hers to describe that FEMINIST criticism which studies women *as writers*,
'and its subjects are the history, styles, themes, genres, and structures of writing
by women; the psychodynamics of female creativity; the trajectory of the individual or collective female career; and the evolution and laws of a female literary
tradition' (1986, 248).
    See also ÉCRITURE; ÉCRITURE FÉMININE; FEMINISM

Haiku A Japanese GENRE of poetry, which has three unrhymed lines of five, seven
and five syllables. Haikus traditionally take nature – and especially the seasons –
as their subject, describing scenes or moments that are intense and charged with
implied meaning.

Hamartia A fatal flaw or weakness in a CHARACTER, or an error of judgement, which
leads to her or his downfall. In *Othello*, it is the EPONYMOUS character's jealousy
which has catastrophic consequences for himself and his wife, Desdemona.

Hegemony A term used by MARXISTS to describe the maintenance of power without
the use, or direct threat, of physical force; normally by a minority CLASS whose
interests are contrary to those over whom power is exercised. Its modern use
stems from the work of the Italian communist Antonio Gramsci, whose most
influential work was written while he was incarcerated by Mussolini's fascists,
and published in various collections after the Second World War.
    For *hegemonic discourse*, see the entry for DISCOURSE

Hemistich Half a METRICAL line of poetry, most often applied to Anglo-Saxon

SECTION 4

poetry, in which the hemistich was CONVENTIONAL. The division may be exact or approximate, and is signalled by the use of a CAESURA.

Hermeneutics See Section 3, p. 152

Hero and anti-hero See PROTAGONIST

Heroic couplet See STANZA

Heterodiegesis See DIEGESIS AND MIMESIS

Heteroglossia In the writing of MIKHAIL BAKHTIN, that multiplicity of social voices linked and interrelated DIALOGICALLY which enters the NOVEL through the interplay between authorial speech, NARRATOR speech, 'inserted genres', and CHARACTER speech (1981, 263).

In Bakhtin's usage, according to the same source, *polyglossia* refers more specifically to the co-existence of different national languages within a single CULTURE. *Diglossia*, in contrast, is a term used within Linguistics to denote the co-existence of two languages within one culture – normally where one of these languages enjoys greater status and authority.

See the longer entries for DIALOGIC and POLYPHONIC.

High comedy See COMEDY

Historical novel A NOVEL set in the past, often one in which fictional CHARACTERS are portrayed as taking part in actual historical events and interacting with historically specific individuals. Walter Scott began the trend, with novels such as *Waverley*, and both James Fenimore Cooper and Catherine Maria Sedgwick did the same in America, with (respectively) *The Last of the Mohicans* and *Hope Leslie*.

History play A drama that makes use of historical persons and SETTINGS, often concentrating on the life of an individual, as in Shakespeare's history plays.

Holograph An AUTHOR's manuscript TEXT – generally, a handwritten original.

Homodiegetic See DIEGESIS AND MIMESIS

Horizon of expectations See Section 3, p. 158–9

Hubris A term taken from the Greek and denoting excessive ambition and pride, which result in the overreaching and downfall of a tragic PROTAGONIST.

Humanism In the Renaissance, a more secular and human-centred outlook associated with an optimism in the power of human beings to understand and better their situation. Originally an honorific term, it has recently been used pejoratively by theorists – a change that can probably be dated from the publication of Louis Althusser's *For Marx* (1969; first published in French, 1966). Althusser declares at the beginning of this work that his aim is to oppose 'Marxist humanism' and the '"humanist" interpretation of Marx's work' (1969, 10). In his essay 'Marxism and Humanism' (1963; included in *For Marx*), Althusser makes clear that a key opposition for him is that between the insistence on the end of CLASS exploitation (the MARXIST goal), and the attainment of human freedom (which, he implies, is the goal of humanism) (1969, 221).

Hyperbole A heightened or exaggerated use of language which is in disproportion to the content. The effect is often comic.

Hypertext Fundamental to the idea of the hypertext is the replacement of linear and unidirectional progression between two fixed points ('beginning' and 'end') with a very large number of potential journeys through a TEXT-mass which is continually being added to, amended, and re-signposted and re-mapped. Hypertext is a child of the electronic media, and there are few below the age of 30 in the developed world who are unfamiliar with the experience of surfing the net by following a succession of links.

The electronic hypertext can be seen to realize some of the formal aspirations of certain experimental writers, who wished to break out of or away from the strict linearity and unidirectionality of the printed text. Thus B.S. Johnson's novel *The Unfortunates* (1969) was published in a box of 27 stapled gatherings, which could be read in any order.

Iambic See METRE

Icon Traditionally an image, especially painted and adhering to fixed CONVENTIONS, representing a holy figure or subject and itself considered to be holy. W.K. Wimsatt's book *The Verbal Icon* (first published 1954) introduced and popularized a NEW CRITICAL comparison of the literary work to an icon, and in his introductory note Wimsatt commented that the

> term *icon* is used today by semeiotic writers to refer to a verbal sign which *somehow* shares the properties of, or resembles, the objects which it denotes. ... The verbal image which most fully realizes its verbal capacities is that which is not merely a bright picture (in the usual modern meaning of the term *image*) but also an interpretation of reality in its metaphoric and symbolic dimensions.
>
> (1970, x)

Ideology No definition of this term can hope to provide a single and unambiguous meaning; instead a cluster of related but not always compatible meanings have to be indicated. What nearly all commentators agree upon is that the present-day use of the term refers to a *system of ideas*: according to some usages an ideology may include contradictory elements, but if so these elements are somehow brought into a functioning relationship which obscures these contradictions for the person or people by whom the ideology is lived. An ideology is thus a way of looking at and INTERPRETING – of 'living' – the world. A further point of agreement is that ideologies are *collectively held*.

In his book *Ideology: An Introduction*, TERRY EAGLETON suggests six broad definitions of the term: (i) 'the general material process of production of ideas, beliefs and values in social life'; (ii) 'ideas and beliefs (whether true or false) which symbolize the conditions and life-experiences of a specific, socially significant group or class'; (iii) 'the *promotion* and *legitimation* of the interests of such social groups in the face of opposing interests'; (iv) such promotion and legitimation when carried out by a 'dominant social power'; (v) 'ideas and beliefs which help to legitimate the interests of a ruling group or class specifically by distortion and dissimulation'; (vi) similar false and deceptive beliefs which arise 'not from the interests of a dominant class but from the material structure of society as a whole' (1991, 28–30).

For Louis Althusser, the ideas of the ruling class are imposed both by means of force and also by ideological means. In his view, class societies are maintained as much by a consensus produced ideologically, through what he calls Ideological State Apparatuses (ISAs), as by repression through Repressive State Apparatuses (RSAs). The ISAs include the educational ISA, the family ISA, the legal ISA, the political ISA, the trade-union ISA, the communications ISA and the cultural ISA. Althusser's short definition of ideology is that it is 'a "representation" of the imaginary relationship of individuals to their real conditions of existence' (1971, 152).

For ROLAND BARTHES's attempt to link connotation to ideology via rhetoric, see the entry for CONNOTATION AND DENOTATION; see also FORMATION; INCORPORATION.

Idiolect A term used by linguisticians to describe the features of a particular person's language which mark out him or her *individually* from others. An idiolect is thus distinguished from a *dialect*, which refers to the language characteristics marking out a *community* (geographical, social, educational) from others. Linguisticians normally restrict the primary reference of both terms to speech, but they are also applied by extension to written language as well.

Compare *genderlect* in the entry for GENDER.

Illocutionary act See Section 3, p. 174

Image This is a term which has become much less fashionable since the heyday of the NEW CRITICS, in whose criticism it frequently played a central and crucial role. One reason for this decline may be that doubts were raised concerning the extent to which it referred to something clear and unambiguous; P.N. Furbank's book *Reflections on the Word 'Image'* presented these doubts in a clear and polemical manner at an opportune time. Its central argument was that the 'trouble with "imagery" is that it appears to refer to some technical feature in literature – like "rhythm" or "STANZA" or "metaphor" – yet it is hard to discover *what*' (1970, 60). Furbank established that the term was used with very varied and even contradictory meanings, ranging from 'mental picture' to METAPHOR, SIMILE, or SYMBOL.

In spite of this loss of fashionability critics still make considerable use of *image* and *imagery* today. The terms retain the breadth of meaning pointed out by Furbank, being used to refer to figurative language in general or to those elements of literary works to which the word CONCRETE rather than ABSTRACT seems suited, and which appear to have a certain *sensuousness* – that is, that cause one sensuously to experience the taste, feel, smell, sound or appearance of something strongly and in a particularized way.

Imagism A literary movement dating from the early twentieth century, associated with the poetry of H.D. (Hilda Doolittle) and Ezra Pound. Influenced by Japanese art and writing, Imagists practised an extreme economy of expression, rejecting RHYME and conventional METRICAL structure, using as few words as possible, and often conveying ideas and emotions indirectly but suggestively through IMAGES, rather than by direct statement or via elaborate, ornate language.

Implied author See AUTHOR

Implied reader See READER-RESPONSE CRITICISM (Section 3), p. 159

Impressionism A nineteenth-century movement in art and literature, which abandoned the attempt to represent an 'objective' reality through accurate description, and sought instead to recreate a sense of experience by means of the impressions experienced by the writer. The term comes from the fine arts, and dates from the negative reactions to Claude Monet's painting *Impression: soleil levant*, first exhibited in 1874. Many critics are agreed that the label can be applied to the work of, among others, Joseph Conrad, although Conrad made a number of negative remarks about the movement. Nevertheless, his work does often focus upon a CHARACTER's subjective experiences: see the discussion of his 'delayed decoding' in the entry for CODE.

Incorporation In Freudian theory, that process of internalizing a lost or dead person as a way of coping with separation or (especially) bereavement. To the extent that that which has been internalized starts to exert power, incorporation may turn into possession. Elements of both incorporation and possession may be traced in the depicted relationship between Norman Bates and his mother in Alfred Hitchcock's film *Psycho*.

Within MARXIST political discussion the term is used to refer to the manner whereby opposition is neutralized by being incorporated into the dominant structures of power. Alan Sinfield's preferred terms are 'entrapment and containment'. Sinfield credits NEW HISTORICISTS with having developed the 'entrapment model' of IDEOLOGY and power, 'whereby even, or especially, maneuvers that seemed designed to challenge the system help to maintain it' (1992, 39), although he notes that entrapment is a concept found also in functionalism, STRUCTURALISM and Althusserian Marxism. Yet another related term is *recuperation*, used to describe a strategy whereby controlling authorities concede certain ideological positions to oppositional forces, but only so as to be able to incorporate these in a larger system of beliefs which reflects the interests of the controlling authorities.

The term *appropriation* has a similar force to incorporation, but the implied 'take-over' is more complete. Some writers have proposed that the term *abrogation* be used as an antonym for *appropriation*, especially in the context of a refusal of the categories of an imperial(ist) CULTURE. See Ashcroft *et al.* (1989, 38–9). Certain POSTCOLONIALIST writers have taken a cue from GAYATRI CHAKRAVORTY SPIVAK (1991) and have adopted the term *catachresis* (originally denoting a perverted or improper use of words) to refer to the way in which a subordinate group can adopt and redefine a term taken from the language of the oppressor (compare the entry for MIMICRY).

Index Edmund Leach distinguishes between an index and a signal as follows. Both are forms of SIGN, but whereas with an index the relationship involved is 'A indicates B', that with a signal is 'A triggers B'. Thus shivering is a signal produced by fever, whereas the word 'fever' is an index of the physical condition (1976, 12–13). For Leach a *natural index* is one in which the association is a natural (or MOTIVATED) one, but has been chosen by human beings to perform a signifying function (for example, smoke as an index of fire).

Along with ICON and symbol (see SIGN), *index* represents one of Charles Sanders Peirce's three essential forms of the sign, and Peirce's definition of an index is somewhat different from Leach's, and is, confusingly, very similar to Leach's definition of a signal. Robert Scholes glosses Peirce's view as follows: for Peirce, 'a sign is indexical to the extent that there is a phenomenal or existential connection between the sign and what it signifies' (1982, 144). Thus Robinson Crusoe takes Friday's footprint in the sand as an index of the fact that another man has been on his island, or, as Scholes puts it, 'Involuntary facial and bodily gestures are taken to be indices of emotional states and therefore truer than mere verbal reports on them (symbols)' (1982, 144).

In medias res Latin phrase meaning 'in the midst of things'. It is typically used to refer to those openings in which we join the action in the middle of events, without a formal scene-setting introduction.

Inscribed reader See READERS AND READING

Intention Intention has been an especially problematic and contentious issue in literary criticism and, especially, with regard to literary INTERPRETATION, since the publication in 1946 of the article 'The Intentional Fallacy' by W.K. Wimsatt and Monroe Beardsley. Wimsatt and Beardsley define intention as 'design or plan in the author's mind', and argue that although 'the designing intellect' might be the *cause* of a poem it should not be taken as the *standard* 'by which the critic is to judge the worth of the poem's performance'. Moreover, they add, if 'the poet succeeded in doing [what he tried to do], then the poem itself shows what he was trying to do. And if the poet did not succeed, then the poem is not adequate evidence, and the critic must go outside the poem – for evidence of an intention that did not become effective in the poem' (Wimsatt: 1970, 4). Others have refined such attempts at definition: Quentin Skinner has distinguished, usefully, between 'motives for writing' and 'intention in writing'.

The American critic E.D. HIRSCH has remained committed to the position that '[a] determinate verbal meaning requires a determining will' (1967, 46), and to the belief that to abandon the concept of intention is to plunge Literary Studies and, especially, literary interpretation, into an anarchic free-for-all in which there is no criterion to distinguish correct from incorrect interpretations.

Interior dialogue Alternatively (in Mikhail Bakhtin's usage) *internal dialogue* or *microdialogue*. A DIALOGUE between two well-defined voices within the single consciousness of a literary CHARACTER (or, in a wider usage, of a real human being), and the NARRATIVE representation of this process.

To count as genuine interior dialogue the questions and answers must stem from two voices which represent different and as it were PERSONIFIED attitudes, beliefs, or characteristics. A good example occurs towards the beginning of the tenth chapter of Charlotte Brontë's *Jane Eyre*, in which we have represented a long dialogue between different and personified aspects of Jane Eyre's personality or identity. MIKHAIL BAKHTIN gives another example from Book 11 of Part 4 of Feodor Dostoevsky's *The Brothers Karamazov* (Bakhtin: 1984, 255). Vincent Crapanzano provides a comparable concept with his term *shadow dialogue* (1992, 214).

Interior (internal) monologue See STREAM OF CONSCIOUSNESS

Interpellation According to the French MARXIST philosopher Louis Althusser, all IDEOLOGY '*hails or interpellates concrete individuals as concrete subjects*, by the functioning of the category of the subject' (1971, 162). Althusser (possibly as a result of the influence of JACQUES LACAN) is making use of a technical term used to describe what happens when the order of the day in a governmental chamber is interrupted so as to allow a Minister to be questioned. The implication is that, like the Minister, individuals are interrupted and called to account – but in this case, by different ideologies. As ideology calls them – so the argument goes – so they think that they recognize who they are. ('Think that', because actually they are being *told* who they are.)

On the theoretical level, the discussion by Etienne Balibar and Pierre Macherey in 'Literature as an Ideological Form' (1978) should be consulted. Some literary critics have applied Althusser's concept of interpellation to the way in which a reader adopts the 'subject' of a literary NARRATOR or CHARACTER as the consciousness through which the literary WORK or events in it are experienced and assessed. Thus Roger Webster refers to the reader's experience of Leo Tolstoy's *Anna Karenina*: 'The reader is drawn towards Levin and becomes through him the experiencing centre of the NOVEL's organic vision: unless we resist such positioning by reading against the grain, it is hard to avoid the process' (1990, 82–3).

Not to be confused with INTERPOLATION.

Interpolation To interpolate is to make insertions in something, and the term has been used in different ways by recent literary critics and theorists. The term *interpolated narration* (sometimes referred to as *intercalated narration*) is used to describe passages of NARRATIVE which come between two moments of action. Prince (1988, 44) points out that the EPISTOLARY NOVEL provides many examples: letters are normally written in between dramatic events rather than during them, although *Shamela*, Henry Fielding's PARODY of Samuel Richardson's *Pamela*, suggested that Richardson's CHARACTERS wrote letters at times and in situations when they would not have been written in real life.

In an essay on Virginia Woolf entitled 'Virginia's Web', Geoffrey Hartman (1970) argues that Woolf's subject is the activity of the mind, and he defines that activity as a work of interpolation: the mind is perpetually filling in gaps and adding explanatory information.

Not to be confused with INTERPELLATION.

Interpretation Literary critics have always argued about specific interpretations, but in the 1980s the focus of dispute shifted to the nature of interpretation itself. A revealing comment is to be found in an influential article by Steven Knapp and Walter Benn Michaels, 'Against Theory': 'By "theory" we mean a special project in literary criticism; the attempt to govern interpretations of particular texts by appealing to an account of interpretation in general' (1985, 11). The comment is revealing because of its assumption that literary theory is involved *only* with interpretation(s), and because of its implication that literary criticism itself is centrally concerned with the act (and principles) of interpretation. Jonathan Culler has seen the 'fundamental assumption' that 'the production of new interpretations is the task of literary study, the *raison d'être* of all writing about literature', as a legacy of the NEW CRITICS, and has himself argued for the more 'tendentious position' that to 'engage in the study of literature is not to produce yet another interpretation of *King Lear* but to advance one's understanding of the conventions and operations of an institution, a mode of discourse' (1981, 5).

John Wain's Introduction to the collection of essays which he edited under the title *Interpretations* in 1955 spends no time discussing what interpretation *is*; it is equated with the ANALYSIS of (in this case) poems, and treated as, theoretically, relatively unproblematic. Again symptomatic is the fact that the volume ends with an essay by G.S. Fraser 'On the Interpretation of the Difficult Poem', in which it is the poem (and perhaps its interpretation) rather than the concept of interpretation itself which is considered difficult (Wain: 1961, 211–37). T.S. ELIOT refers to *Interpretations* in his essay 'The Frontiers of Criticism' (first published in 1956), and this essay was influential in changing attitudes to what interpretation involved or entailed. Eliot suggested that one danger which the book might bring with it was that of assuming that there must be just one interpretation of the poem as a whole, that must be right, and went on to suggest 'the meaning [of the poem] is what the poem means to different sensitive readers' (1961, 126).

Some of these issues are traceable back to the term *interpretation* itself. When we talk of an actor's interpretation of the role of Hamlet we are using the word in a rather different sense from that which survives in the cognate term *interpreter* (at the United Nations, for example). Recent debates have oscillated between these two extremes: the literary interpreter as the translator, conveying the author's meaning as accurately as possible, and the interpreter as performer of a SCRIPT written by the author.

Interpret[at]ive communities The notion of the interpretive community stems from the American critic STANLEY FISH; British critics have sometimes adopted the term and modified it to *interpretative* communities so as to conform with more usual British English usage. Fish's view of the interpretive community is bound up with a related concept: that of the *interpretive strategy*:

> it is interpretive communities, rather than either the text or the reader, that produce meanings and are responsible for the emergence of formal features. Interpretive communities are made up of those who share interpretive strategies not for reading but for writing texts, for constituting their properties. In other words these strategies exist prior to the act of reading and therefore determine the shape of what is read rather than, as is usually assumed, the other way round.
>
> (1980, 14)

Fish thus claims that when READERS interpret a text in either the same or in varying ways this is because 'members of the same community will necessarily agree because they will see (and by seeing, make) everything in relation to that community's assumed purposes and goals; and conversely, members of different communities will disagree because from each of their respective positions the other "simply" cannot see what is obviously and inescapably there' (1980, 15).

Dealing with Fish's theory of the interpretive community in his book *Textual Power*, Robert Scholes indicates a key problem with the concept: only those who belong to the same community can discuss interpretive disagreements – but as they belong to the same community they shouldn't have any such disagreements to discuss (Scholes: 1985, 154–6).

Interregnum See PERIODS OF LITERATURE

Intertextuality A relation between two or more TEXTS which has an effect upon the way in which the *intertext* (that is, the text within which other texts reside or echo their PRESENCE) is READ. In some usages the term *transtextuality* is reserved for more overt relations between specific texts, or between two particular texts, while *intertextuality* is reserved to indicate a more diffuse penetration of the individual text by memories, echoes, transformations, of other texts. GÉRARD GENETTE has also coined the terms *hypertext* and *hypotext* to refer to the intertext and the text with which the intertext has some significant relation. Thus the relationship between James Joyce's *Ulysses* and Homer's *Odyssey* is that of hypertext to hypotext.

MIKHAIL BAKHTIN's insistence upon the DIALOGIC element in all UTTERANCES, and the range of different dialogues to be traced in literary works, undoubtedly sparked a more overt interest in the issue of intertextuality. A good example here is his extended discussion of 'the problem of quotation' in his essay 'From the Prehistory of Novelistic Discourse' (in Bakhtin: 1981). He pays particular but not exclusive attention to such forms as PARODY and travesty, and develops a theory of the linguistic hybrid to cover them, pointing out in passing parallels with the use of parody and travesty in the modern NOVEL (1981, 77).

Bakhtin seems himself to be an intertextual presence in ROLAND BARTHES's and JULIA KRISTEVA's development of theories of intertextuality. In her *Desire in Language* Kristeva defines the text as 'a permutation of texts, an intertextuality: in the space of a given text, several utterances, taken from other texts, intersect and neutralize one another' (1980, 36). Roland Barthes seems partly in agreement with this position, at least so far as the distinction between intertextuality and influence is concerned. But his usage seems significantly more diffuse and all-embracing than Kristeva's. According to him, all texts are intertexts: 'Any text is a new tissue of past citations' (1981b, 39). Of course, if 'any text whatsoever' is an intertext, then the term becomes tautologous.

See also PALIMPSEST TEXT, and discussion of the term *double-voiced* in the entry for DISCOURSE

Intrusive narrator A NARRATOR who breaks into the NARRATIVE to comment upon a CHARACTER, EVENT or situation – or even to introduce opinions not directly related to what has been narrated. The term is often reserved for situations in which the intrusion is felt to break into an established narrative TONE or illusion, although it is also used in a purely technical sense to describe 'own voice' comments from a narrator which may hardly be remarked by the READER because of their homogeneity with the rest of the narrative.

Invocation A formal address or appeal to an (often absent) person, entity (such as a god or a muse) or an ABSTRACT force. Invocations are associated with CLASSICAL EPICS. For a more recent example, see the opening of Percy Bysshe Shelley's 'Ode to the West Wind'.

Irony Verbal irony consists of saying one thing but implying a very different, even opposite, meaning, as when a woman standing in pouring rain says 'Beautiful weather' to the person next to her. The NEW CRITICS considered irony to be one of the most important techniques available to the poet, allowing him or her to inject a unifying tension into a poem. For NARRATIVE theorists, too, the use of irony on the part of a NARRATOR is often able to persuade a READER to view depicted events from a more distanced PERSPECTIVE.

See also DRAMATIC IRONY

Isochrony Borrowed by recent NARRATIVE theorists from a term used to describe poetic rhythm, isochrony denotes an *unvarying* or an *equal* relationship between

NARRATING-time and STORY-time. The two are not the same: if a story covers three hours and each or these hours is narrated by means of five thousand words, then the relationship between narrating-time and story-time is unvarying. But if a story covers three hours and each hour of the story takes approximately an hour to read, then the relationship between narrating-time and story-time can be said to be equal. It should be clear that whereas the former relationship can be measured with some degree of precision, the latter cannot.

The opposite of isochrony is *anisochrony*: either a varying or an unequal relationship between narrating-time and story-time – normally the former.

See also DURATION

Iterative See FREQUENCY

Jacobean See PERIODS OF LITERATURE

Jeremiad A lamentation, complaint, or even a stream of abuse. The term derives from the Old Testament prophet Jeremiah, who blamed the misfortunes of Israel on the lax morals of its people, and demanded reform. The jeremiad was especially prevalent in Puritan America, often following in the wake of an historical catastrophe, which was interpreted as God's punishment for backsliding and wrongdoing. At the same time, this direct intervention was a sign of God's continued commitment: change would restore His favour, and peace and prosperity might follow.

Jouissance This word can be found in the *OED*, although classified as obsolete and with examples cited from, among others, Carew and Spenser. Of the two main meanings given, that which is nearer to the current usage found amongst critical theorists is the second: pleasure, delight; merriment, mirth, festivity. This sounds very innocent, and is clearly different from the current usage – loaned from the French – that involves, among other things, *sexual* pleasure. The first meaning concerns the possession and use of something affording advantage, as in the *enjoyment* of a right, and jouissance is etymologically related to the word enjoyment.

Leon S. Roudiez dates the renewed critical interest in this term from the publication of JACQUES LACAN's discussion of it in his 1972–3 seminar, which in its French publication sported a cover picture of the *Ecstasy of St Theresa*, suggesting the prominent part played by sexual orgasm in jouissance. For Lacan, Roudiez claims, jouissance 'is sexual, spiritual, physical, conceptual at one and the same time' (Kristeva: 1980, 16).

Langue and parole Perhaps the most important – and influential – distinction introduced by FERDINAND DE SAUSSURE in his *Course in General Linguistics*. It is now common to use the French words to represent these paired concepts in English, but one can find attempts to render them in English, with langue represented by *language* (sometimes *a* or *the* language, as in the English translation of ROLAND BARTHES's *Elements of Semiology*, or as *language-system*), and parole as *speaking, speech, language-behaviour*, or, on occasions, phrases such as *the sum of all actual (possible) utterances*.

For the sake of clarity, where other terms are used in the following quotations, they will be replaced with either 'langue' or 'parole' in square brackets so that the substitution is MARKED.

According to Saussure,

> [i]f we could embrace the sum of word-images stored in the minds of all individuals, we could identify the social bond that constitutes [langue]. It is a storehouse filled by members of a given community through their active use of [parole], a grammatical system that has a potential existence in each brain, or, more specifically, in the brains of a group of individuals. For [langue] is not complete in any speaker; it exists perfectly only within a collectivity.
>
> (1974, 13–14)

A number of points need to be stressed here. First, that as the reference to 'a given community' makes clear, Saussure's mention of the minds of 'all individuals' should be taken to refer to all individuals within a particular language community. Second, that langue is supra-individual: were Martians to kidnap a single English speaker they could not extract the langue of English from him or her alone. Third, that langue is a *system*, and one that has generative power ('potential existence'). Thus, if those same Martians were able to gather every example of English speech and feed them into a super computer they still could not end up with our langue, for langue is that set of rules, that system, that is able not just to generate all those acts of English speech, but also all the *potential but as yet unuttered acts of speech* that *could* be generated by it. Fourth, it is also the system that allows native speakers to *understand* all the acts of speech correctly generated (in other individuals) by itself.

Saussure stresses that langue is not a function of the individual speaker: it is passively assimilated by the individual and does not require premeditation (contrast speaking in a *foreign* language). Parole, on the other hand, he insists is 'an individual act' which is wilful and intellectual (1974, 14).

The over-arching distinction between rule and rule-generated ACT has proved extremely fertile in a range of different contexts, although in our post-PRAGMATICS age there are rather fewer who are prepared unreservedly to accept Saussure's contention that the 'science of language is possible only if the other elements [of parole] are excluded' (1974, 15). Jonathan Culler assumes the possibility of a relatively unproblematic relating of langue and parole to Noam

Chomsky's COMPETENCE AND PERFORMANCE (1975, 9), and he seems to use these terms (here and elsewhere) relatively interchangeably.

There are some problems in applying the distinction to literature rather than language. Onega and Landa, for example, note that structuralists

> often hesitate, however, when it comes to deciding the level at which the analogy [between language and literature] should work: is it literature as a whole that works as a language, or is it the individual work that does so? Each work may be argued to constitute a *langue* of its own, may be seen as a self-regulating structure, since it creates, up to a point, the conditions for its own meaning and helps define the language in which it is interpreted.
>
> (1996, 5)

Leitmotif See THEME AND THEMATICS

Lexia See the entry for ROLAND BARTHES (Section 5)

Linguistic paradigm FERDINAND DE SAUSSURE established a number of extremely influential analytical distinctions in his work which, while originally applied by him to the study of language, have subsequently been extended METAPHORICALLY to other areas. Concepts such as SYNTAGMATIC AND PARADIGMATIC relations, LANGUE AND PAROLE, and SIGNIFIER AND SIGNIFIED have all been pressed into service by theorists concerned with a range of non-linguistic phenomena. All of these extensions of linguistic distinctions involve treating other SIGN-systems as if they were fundamentally similar to language: language, in other words, is taken as a *paradigm* for the study and analysis of other sign-systems.

Jonathan Culler gives an extended account of two such uses of the linguistic paradigm in his *Structuralist Poetics*: Claude Lévi-Strauss's structural analysis of MYTHOLOGY and ROLAND BARTHES's of fashion (Culler: 1975, 32–54). But once one has grasped the essential idea, the method has a potentially unending set of applications. Thus for example one can treat a meal with several courses like a sentence composed of several words: in a given CULTURE there are all sorts of different dishes that can be chosen as the first course, but once one is chosen it constrains what is chosen as the second course – and so on. Within the field of literary criticism one can refer to the way in which terminology and distinctions taken from the grammar of verbs have been applied to the study of NARRATIVE by GÉRARD GENETTE. JACQUES LACAN's claim that the UNCONSCIOUS is structured like a language represents a more global use of language as explanatory paradigm.

See also *BRICOLEUR*; PARADIGM SHIFT; SEMIOTICS and the entry for TZVETAN TODOROV in Section 5

Literariness This concept is introduced and discussed in the entries for RUSSIAN FORMALISM and the PRAGUE SCHOOL in Section 3, and its importance for ROMAN JAKOBSON and RENÉ WELLEK is detailed in the entries for these theorists in Section 5. Briefer references can be found in the present Section (4) in the entries for AMBIGUITY, CODE, DEVIATION, ECRITURE, LANGUE AND PAROLE, and STRUCTURE.

Litotes A specific kind of understatement, whereby one negates the opposite of the sentiment or opinion one wants to offer. Saying to a tourist edging too near a precipice that a further step might not be advisable would be an example of litotes, as would describing a poet as 'not uninspiring'.

Logocentrism JACQUES DERRIDA's coinage (sometimes used interchangeably with *phonocentrism*). Logocentrism refers to systems of thought or habits of mind which are reliant upon what Derrida, following Martin Heidegger, terms the metaphysics of PRESENCE – that is, a belief in an extra-systemic validating presence or CENTRE which underwrites and fixes linguistic meaning but is itself beyond scrutiny or challenge. For Derrida, such a position is fundamentally idealist, and he argues that the dismantling of logocentrism is simultaneously the DECONSTRUCTION of idealism or spiritualism 'in all their variants' (1981, 51).

In his 'Writing Before the Letter' (with which *Of Grammatology* opens), Derrida claims that the *history of metaphysics* has 'always assigned the origin of truth in general to the logos: the history of truth, of the truth of truth, has always been ... the debasement of writing, and its repression outside "full" speech' (1976, 3). Logocentrism, then, is associated by Derrida with the making of écriture subject to speech (the English translation of écriture as 'writing' may be misleading: see the entry for ÉCRITURE).

Derrida's much-quoted assertion that '*there is nothing outside of the text*' (1976, 158), which can also be rendered in English as 'there is no outside-text', has to be read in the light of his attack on logocentrism: the TEXT cannot be assigned a meaning that is underwritten by an origin, a presence, which resides in self-validating isolation beyond the confines of the text.

See also DIFFÉRANCE

Ludism From a Latin root meaning to play, *ludism* and *ludic* are used interchangeably in English with *play* and *playful* in DECONSTRUCTIONIST writing or by writers influenced by deconstructionist ideas.

The central idea behind the current use of these terms is that once the illusion of PRESENCE has been dispensed with, READING and INTERPRETATION no longer involve a decoding that is subject to the firm discipline of some CENTRE of authority that has access to the CODE book; instead the READER can observe and participate in the free play of SIGNIFIERS endlessly generating a succession of meanings none of which can claim superiority or authority. The main senses of 'play' involved here are: play as in 'to play a game', and play as in 'to play a fish' or 'to play a hose'. Vicki Mistacco expresses it as follows:

'Ludism' may be simply defined as the open play of signification, as the free and productive interaction of forms, of signifiers and signifieds, without regard for an original or an ultimate meaning. In literature, ludism signifies

> textual play; the text is viewed as a game affording both author and reader the possibility of producing endless meanings and relationships.
>
> (1980, 375)

This view is closely related to a belief in the (metaphorical) DEATH OF THE AUTHOR, the stern parent who would restrict the child's play.

Lyric The ancient Greeks distinguished between poetry that was meant to be sung by a single person to the accompaniment of a *lyre*, from poetry that was meant to be chanted (often by the CHORUS of a play, as with the ODE). From this distinction stems the category of the lyric, which came to be associated with personal expression and emotion. In recent times, lyric poetry is conventionally short and subjective, concerned with thought, emotion or feeling more than STORY (as with NARRATIVE poetry) or a situation and human interaction (as with dramatic poetry).

Magic realism In his book *Magic Realism Rediscovered, 1918–1981* (1983), Seymour Menton notes that although this term has been used with increasing frequency since 1955 to describe post-Second World War Latin American FICTION (1983, 9), it was in 1925 that Franz Roh first formulated the term and described its characteristics (1983, 13). Menton associates the term's juxtaposition of 'magic' and 'realism' with the psychological-philosophical ideas of Carl Jung, and suggests that the OXYMORON 'captures the artists' and the authors' efforts to portray the strange, the uncanny, the eerie, and the dreamlike – but not the fantastic – aspects of everyday reality' (1983, 13). The term is, as Menton notes, particularly associated with certain Central and South American novelists such as Gabriel García Márquez and Isabella Allende but it is being applied more and more liberally to a range of writers and WORKS from many different periods and CULTURES, including, especially, a number of recent female and FEMINIST European novelists.

In its current usage, magic realism seems typically to involve the sudden incursion of fantastic or 'magical' elements into an otherwise realistic PLOT and SETTING. A recent leading exponent of the GENRE is the British novelist Angela Carter. According to Paulina Palmer, in her earlier work Carter 'exploited this mode to evoke the individual's experience of anxiety, estrangement and isolation (the kind of emotions discussed by Sigmund Freud in his essay on "The Uncanny")'; in her more recent work 'she uses it as a vehicle for the expression of emotions which have a liberating effect', such as pleasure and wonder (Palmer: 1987, 182).

Marxist theory and criticism See Section 3, p. 184

Masque A FORM of (frequently light) court entertainment involving music and dance, such as Milton's *Comus*. CHARACTERS are usually ALLEGORICAL, and the dialogue is mostly in verse.

Masquerade Alternatively *parade*. Recent FEMINIST theorists of GENDER have gone back to Joan Riviere's 1929 theorizing about the behaviour of successful intellectual women who adopted a 'masquerade' of exaggerated feminine flirtatiousness when interacting with men. Women thus successful in traditionally male roles used womanliness as a mask or masquerade to hide the possession of 'masculinity' and to deflect the negative reactions that would stem from it.

Meaning and significance The pairing of *meaning* with *significance* is very much associated with one particular theorist: the American critic E.D. HIRSCH. In his book *Validity in Interpretation* Hirsch defines these two terms in ways that are matched and complementary:

> *Meaning* is that which is represented by a text; it is what the author meant by his use of a particular sign sequence; it is what the signs represent. *Significance*, on the other hand, names a relationship between that meaning and a person, or a conception, or a situation, or indeed anything imaginable.
>
> (1967, 8)

The definition has to be seen in the light of increasing debate about the respective roles and authority of AUTHOR and READER in the INTERPRETATION of literary WORKS, for it proposes a clear separation of powers: the author is responsible for meaning while significance comes from the interaction of this meaning with that which lies outside the work.

Medieval See PERIODS OF LITERATURE

Melodrama Coined in the late sixteenth century to refer to any drama that was accompanied by music and sometimes used interchangeably with 'opera', more recently the term has come to mean any NARRATIVE in which STEREOTYPED CHARACTERS and situations are used to evoke a strong emotional effect on an undemanding audience. Melodrama has an intimate relationship with the popular, and is typically looked down upon by the educated. However, although the term is often used derogatively, many respected writers were interested in and made use of melodrama, Henry James and Charles Dickens among them.

Metalanguage/metafiction A metalanguage is any language used to describe or refer to another language: 'a language about a language'. One of the characteristics of human word language is that it can function as its own metalanguage; we can discuss our language in that same language. This is a characteristic not shared by animal communication systems: dogs cannot bark about barking.

A *metanarrative* can be either a narrative which talks about other, embedded narratives, or a narrative which refers to itself and to its own narrative procedures.

Metafiction is, literally, fiction about fiction. To a certain extent the term overlaps with *metanarrative* because any work of fiction which contains a metanarrative will contain a metafictional element. It is generally used to indicate fiction which includes any *self-referential element* (not necessarily resulting from a metanarrative: thematic patternings can also contribute to the formation of a metafictional effect in a work). In their Introduction to an extract from Linda Hutcheon's *Narcissistic Narrative: the Metafictional Paradox* (1980), Onega and Landa suggest that

> Hutcheon's narcissistic narrative is more or less equivalent to such terms as Robert Scholes's 'fabulation', William H. Gass's 'metafiction', Raymond Federman's 'surfiction' and Ronald Binn's 'anti-novel', all of which were coined to account for the widespread tendency to introversion and self-referentiality of much postmodernist fiction.
>
> (Onega and Landa: 1996, 203)

Metaphor A figurative statement of similarity or identification between two elements, conventionally named 'tenor' and 'vehicle'. Thus 'my love is a rose', for instance, posits an imaginative equivalence between the woman (tenor) and the flower (vehicle). Contrast SIMILE.

For the metaphor/metonymy distinction, see the entry for SYNTAGMATIC AND PARADIGMATIC.

Metaphysical See PERIODS OF LITERATURE

Metaphysics of presence See LOGOCENTRISM; PRESENCE; and the entry for JACQUES DERRIDA (Section 5)

Metonymy and synecdoche These terms are often used interchangeably, but formally speaking metonymy is the use of an *attribute* to refer to a thing while synecdoche involves the use of a *part* to refer to the whole. With synecdoche, the part must always belong to the whole (as heads are connected to bodies), whereas in the case of metonymy, the part can simply be associated with the whole (as crowns are with kings). Clearly distinguishing the two is not always easy (take 'Address your remarks to the Bench': is Bench a part or an attribute of the Court?). For the metonymy/metaphor distinction, see the entry for SYNTAGMATIC AND PARADIGMATIC.

Metre (US meter) The metre of a poem in English consists of the pattern of stressed and unstressed syllables that it contains. Metre is one conventional way of distinguishing poetry from prose, and its study has produced various formal systems based upon patterns of syllables arranged according to either quantity, or stress, or a mixture of both.

Because there are different systems of metre, one problem is that much of the terminology we use is based on Greek and Latin verse, the metre of which was based on a *quantitative* measure – i.e. counting the *number* of syllables in a line. Although the metre of much English verse often involves a quantitative element, it is based primarily on the pattern of stressed and unstressed syllables in a line of poetry. In English, in words with two or more syllables, at least one of these will be emphasized (stressed) more than the others. Poets who compose in metre arrange words in such a way that they form a recurrent, rhythmic pattern of heavy and light stresses (or accents, or beats). For example: in a line with 10 syllables, more often than not you will find that five of these receive stress, and five do not. Moreover, the line will frequently be arranged in such a way that an unstressed syllable will follow a stressed one. Each metrical unit in this system (which may not coincide precisely with a single word) is called a *foot*. The concept of the foot is widely used in discussion of English poetry, although again its origin in systems of quantitative verse such as Greek or Latin means that its application to poetry written in English is often problematic. Many reference books on the analysis of poetry give long lists of the various types of foot, but learning up to 30 or so of these seems to us to be generally unhelpful, although it is worth remembering that a foot can contain more than two stressed or unstressed elements (to take an abstruse example, a 'ditroche' consists of a stressed, an unstressed, a stressed and an unstressed syllable [conventionally written ´ ˘ ´ ˘]).

It is useful to be able to identify the most characteristic or common feet used in English poetry, which are as follows:

- iambic (˘´) one unstressed followed by one stressed
- trochaic (´˘) one stressed followed by one unstressed
- dactylic (´˘˘) one stressed followed by two unstressed
- anapestic (˘˘´) two unstressed followed by one stressed
- spondaic (´´) two successive stressed syllables

The terms given above are the adjectival forms; the singular noun forms are iamb, trochee, dactyl, anapest and spondee.

If you want a neat way to remember the difference between the two most common feet in English poetry, Jon Stallworthy's useful account of versification printed at the start of the *Norton Anthology of Poetry* suggests New *York* as a model iamb and *Lon*don as a model trochee. Just remember the sentence 'I am in New York' (iamb in New York).

The most common terms for lines of different length are: *monometer* (one foot); *dimeter* (two feet); *trimeter* (three), *tetrameter* (four), *pentameter* (five) and *hexameter* (six).

In many cases there is no single 'correct' pattern of stress in a line of poetry, as the line can be read in different ways each of which is metrically acceptable. Thus one person's iambic pentameter is another one's *free verse* (see BLANK VERSE AND FREE VERSE). In other words, patterns of pronunciation vary according to age, CLASS, education, ethnicity and geographical location; INTERPRETATION may also make a difference (since you may choose to emphasize a particular word because of its centrality to the meaning of a line). In addition, not all stressed syllables receive the same amount of emphasis, and poets are fond of combining different kinds of feet (anapestic and iambic, for example). The theorist Derek Attridge (1996) has suggested that certain syllables which might normally be stressed are defined as unstressed when they appear between stronger syllables: this process he defines as *demotion*. The opposite can also work: a syllable which is normally unstressed may be counted as a stressed syllable in order to preserve the metrical scheme: this is called *promotion*. There is also substitution, especially at the beginning of a poem or a line, where the poet will use a trochaic foot in an otherwise predominantly iambic pattern, and one or two syllables may be omitted at the end of a line (causing it to be CATALECTIC: see also ACATELECTIC and HYPERMETRIC). Metre, then, is a much looser descriptive system than it sometimes appears. The natural rhythm of the poem is always primary, a formal metrical analysis or categorization is secondary.

See also the advice on analyzing poetry in Section 1, pp. 49–63

Mimesis See DIEGIS AND MIMESIS

Mirror stage In his essay 'The Mirror Stage as Formative of the Function of the I as Revealed in Psychoanalytic Experience', first delivered as an address in 1949 and reprinted in his *Écrits*, JACQUES LACAN argues for this *conception* (his term) as necessary to a full understanding of 'the formation of the *I*' (1977, 1). Lacan compares the behaviour of children and chimpanzees when confronted with their own image in a mirror; even at the age at which the child is outdone by the chimpanzee in instrumental intelligence, it can recognize its own image in a mirror. But whereas this act of recognition 'exhausts itself' for the chimpanzee, the child gives forth a series of gestures in which the relation between the real and the mirrored movements is played. This, Lacan suggests, leads to the creation of an 'Ideal-I' (from Freud's *Ideal-Ich*) which 'situates the agency of the ego, before its social determination' (1977, 2).

Lacan's further discussion of the conception is complex, but what it seems to stress is that the I is thus fixed in a fictive format: our conception of ourselves is necessarily a FICTION which we are then put to defend against the onset of the real. The ego should not then be regarded as centred on what Lacan calls the *perception-consciousness system*, or as organized by the 'reality principle', but on the function of *méconnaissance* (1977, 6).

Mise-en-abyme From the French meaning, literally, thrown into the abyss. The term is adapted from heraldry, and in its adapted FORM generally involves the recurring internal duplication of images of an artistic whole, such that an infinite series of images disappearing into invisibility is produced – similar to what one witnesses if one looks at one's reflection between two facing mirrors. Mieke Bal recommends the term *mirror-text* for literary examples of *mise-en-abyme*, as in verbal examples it is not the whole of the WORK which is mirrored but only a part. For Bal, when the primary FABULA and the embedded fabula can be paraphrased in such a manner that both paraphrases have one or more elements in common, 'the subtext is a *sign* of the primary text' (1985, 146; see the entry for SUB-TEXT). The possibilities for reflexivity and self-reference opened up by such repetitions are not limited to MODERNIST art and literature, but have been utilized by artists and writers over many centuries.

Mock epic A type of SATIRE that uses elevated and grandiose language, and many of the conventions of the GENRE of the EPIC, to describe commonplace CHARACTERS or events. Alexander Pope's *The Rape of the Lock* takes as its subject a feud between two families, sparked off when a young baron cuts a lock of hair from a society belle. Pope treats the resulting quarrel derisively by presenting it as if it were a major historical event. The poem opens with the kind of INVOCATION associated with the epics of Greece and Rome, and a trivial card-game is depicted as a major military engagement. *Mock heroic* is a less specific term: whereas the mock epic deliberately echoes and distorts the epic GENRE, 'mock heroic' refers to any literature that ridicules its subject by means of inappropriately exaggerated treatment.

Mock heroic See MOCK EPIC

Mode Apart from serving as a general synonym for 'type', *mode* enters into recent critical vocabulary mainly in connection with NARRATIVE theory. A usage associated with the linguistician M.A.K. Halliday equates mode with what can be termed the 'medium' of a TEXT or 'channel of communication'. Thus a telephoned message is in a different mode from a written one.

Alternatively, modifications of narrative DISTANCE can be said to produce different modes; thus a sudden shift into IRONY on the part of a NARRATOR involves a change of mode. Certain GENERIC categories such as TRAGEDY and COMEDY are also sometimes referred to as modes.

In Gerald Prince's definition, MOOD (see also the entry for PERSPECTIVE AND VOICE) consists of two sub-categories: *perspective* (or point of view) and *distance* (or mode) (1988, 54). In other words: one determines the mood of a narrative by finding out (i) what perspective on CHARACTERS and events the narrative has and (ii) how close to or distanced from these characters and events the narrative is.

Modernism and postmodernism Both of these terms reach beyond national-cultural and generic boundaries; they describe artistic and cultural artifacts and attitudes of (mainly) the twentieth century which are possessed of certain family resemblances. The term *postmodernism* can, further, be used to refer not just to art and CULTURE but also more comprehensively to a wide range of aspects of modern society.

David Harvey has suggested that there is more continuity than difference in the movement from modernism to postmodernism, and that the latter represents a crisis within the former in which fragmentation and ephemerality are confirmed while the possibility of the eternal and the immutable is treated with far greater scepticism (1989, 116).

A related term is *avant-garde*. The term comes from military terminology, and refers to the (normally small) advance guard which prepares the way for a larger, following army – what later became known as shock-troops. In the context of cultural politics the term was used in the early part of the twentieth century to refer to movements which had the aim of assaulting CONVENTIONAL standards and attitudes – particularly but not exclusively in the field of culture and the arts. Thus Cubism, Futurism, Dadaism, Surrealism and Constructivism are all conventionally described as avant-gardist in essence.

In general usage *modernism* describes that art (not just literature) which sought to break with what had become the dominant and dominating conventions of nineteenth-century art and culture. The most important of these conventions is probably that of REALISM: the modernist artist no longer saw the highest test of his or her art as that of VERISIMILITUDE. Instead, the modernist art-work is possessed, typically, of a *self-reflexive* element: we may lose ourselves in the FICTIONAL 'world' of, say, *Pride and Prejudice* when reading Jane Austen's NOVEL, but when reading James Joyce's *Ulysses* or VIRGINIA WOOLF's *The Waves* we are made conscious that we are reading a novel.

The work of modernists such as T.S. ELIOT, Ezra Pound, D.H. Lawrence, Franz Kafka, and Knut Hamsun is characterized by a pessimistic view of the modern world, a world seen as fragmented and decayed, in which communication between human beings is difficult or impossible, and in which commercial and cheapening forces present an insuperable barrier to human or cultural betterment. The modernist suspicion of science and technology is in many cases directly attributable to revulsion at the use of technology to slaughter millions in the First World War. It is one of the clearest ways of distinguishing modernism from much postmodernism.

The development of modernism seems to be associated with a certain 'masculinization' of art: in contrast to the dominant position of women novelists in the nineteenth century, women take a long time to regain this supremacy subsequent to the modernist revolution. Part of the explanation may relate to the association of modernism with social and geographical mobility, and the adoption of a bohemian lifestyle – much more difficult for women than for men, as Virginia Woolf pointed out (in the course of a different argument) in her *A Room of One's Own*. On the other hand, part of this masculinization may well lie in the eye of the (male) beholder, and interesting work is being done at present to rediscover neglected women modernists.

David Harvey has argued that modernism took on multiple PERSPECTIVISM and RELATIVISM as its epistemology for revealing 'what it still took to be the true nature of a unified, though complex, underlying reality (1989, 30). (Postmodernism, in contrast, tends to retain the relativism while abandoning the belief in the unified underlying reality, and David Harvey quotes JEAN-FRANÇOIS LYOTARD's definition of the postmodern as 'incredulity towards metanarratives' (1989, 45) – a definition which is itself, paradoxically, something of a METANARRATIVE; the resemblance between postmodernism and DECONSTRUCTION is strongly apparent at this point.) For the modernist, therefore, human beings are doomed to exist in an alienated state of social – and even existential – fragmentation, while yearning (unlike the postmodernist) to escape from this situation. Furthermore, this alienation also leads to – or is associated with – a problematizing of human individuality and identity. 'Who am I?' asks Virginia Woolf's Bernard, in her experimental novel *The Waves*, and his question is emblematic of a recurrent problem for modernist artists.

The term *postmodernism* only enters Anglo-American critical DISCOURSE in the 1950s, and only in a significant way in the 1960s. At first it seems to indicate a new periodization: postmodern art or culture is that art or culture which, in the years after the Second World War, extends or even breaks with modernist techniques and conventions without reverting to realist or pre-modernist positions. But before long critics start to use the term to refer to particular cultural, artistic – or even social – characteristics irrespective of when they manifested themselves. The use of the word 'social' is significant: *postmodernism* is typically used in a rather wider sense than is *modernism*, referring to a general human condition, or society at large, as much as to art or culture (a usage which was encouraged by Jean-François Lyotard's book *The Postmodern Condition: A Report on Knowledge* [English translation, 1984]). *Postmodernism*, then, can be used today in a number of different ways: (i) to refer to the non-realist and non-traditional literature and art of the post-Second World War period; (ii) to refer to literature and art which takes certain modernist characteristics to an extreme stage; and (iii) to refer to aspects of a more general human condition in the 'late capitalist' world of the post-1950s which have an all-embracing effect on life, culture, IDEOLOGY and art, as well as (in some usages) to a generally more welcoming attitude towards these aspects.

David Lodge has singled out five techniques typical of postmodernist fiction: *permutation*: postmodernist writers typically incorporate 'alternative narrative lines in the same text' (1977, 230); *discontinuity*: Beckett, according to Lodge, 'disrupts the continuity of his discourse by unpredictable swerves of TONE, metafictional asides to the reader, blank spaces in the text, contradiction and permutation' (1977, 231); *randomness* or a discontinuity produced by composing 'according to a logic of the absurd' (1977, 235); and finally *excess*: taking 'metaphoric or metonymic devices to excess [and testing them] to destruction' (1977, 235).

It is fair to say that there is far more debate around the term *postmodernism* than there is around the term *modernism*. One of the most powerful critiques of the term and the concept can be found in John Frow's essay 'What Was Postmodernism?' (1997). Frow argues that the concept is 'incoherent' for two reasons: first that no one can agree who actually was a postmodernist, and second that no one can agree about *when* postmodernism occurred or is occurring. It is probably fair to say that *modernism* as concept and term is relatively firmly established in present-day intellectual debate, but that the (generally left-wing) criticisms of theorists such as Frow have made *postmodernism* a rather more controversial term. Even so, it is probably relatively common to call the following writers and their works postmodernist: John Barth, John Ashberry, Thomas Pynchon, Donald Barthelme, William Burroughs, Walter Abish, Alain Robbe-Grillet, Peter Handke, Carlos Fuentes, and Jorge Luis Borges.

Two related terms describing postmodernist fiction are *fabulation* and *surfiction*. Both terms imply an aggressive and playful luxuriation in the non-representational, in which the writer takes delight in the artifice of writing rather than in using writing to describe or make contact with a perceived extra-fictional reality.

See also *BRICOLEUR*

Mood According to GÉRARD GENETTE, 'one can tell *more* or tell *less* what one tells, and can tell it *according to one point of view or another*; and this capacity, and the modalities of its use, are precisely what our category of *narrative mood* aims at' (1980, 161–2). The term is borrowed from grammatical mood, and its adoption by Genette is a good example of the reliance by NARRATOLOGISTS upon the LINGUISTIC PARADIGM. The word is also used in its everyday sense to describe the mood or emotional state evoked in a READER by a WORK.

See also MODE; PERSPECTIVE AND VOICE

Morality play A medieval play which makes use of ALLEGORY to impart moral lessons.

Motivated See ARBITRARY

Mystery play A popular FORM of medieval religious drama, which takes as its subject a scene from the Old or New Testament. *Passion plays* are mystery plays specifically concerned with Christ's trial, crucifixion and resurrection.

Myth Two of the most influential of contemporary thinkers – Claude Lévi-Strauss and ROLAND BARTHES – have helped to revivify the concept of myth in recent times. Lévi-Strauss's discussion of myth in *The Savage Mind* helped to establish the idea of myth as *a kind of thought*, one, as he puts it, based on elements that are 'half-way between percepts and concepts' (1972, 18). This is very different from the traditional view of myth, conveniently defined by Robert Scholes and Robert Kellogg as 'a traditional plot which can be transmitted' (1966, 12).

This shift of emphasis from myth as a sort of PLOT to myth as a way of thinking with close resemblances to (along with some differences from) IDEOLOGY, can also be found in Roland Barthes's highly original *Mythologies*. Barthes's great achievement was to bring myths home to contemporary life, to make present-day European READERS aware that myths were not just something that other people (remote African tribes, Russian peasants, the ancient Greeks) believed in and created – but were part of the stuff and fabric of everyday modern life in the West. *Mythologies* includes brief studies of such diverse topics as wrestling, soap powders, the face of Greta Garbo, steak and chips, and striptease. Barthes explained that for him the notion of myth explained a particular process whereby historically determined circumstances were presented as somehow 'natural', and that it allowed for the uncovering of 'the ideological abuse' hidden 'in the display of *what goes without saying*' (1973, 11).

See also the entry for ARCHETYPAL CRITICISM in Section 3, p. 180
See also *BRICOLEUR*

Narratee The 'target' at whom a NARRATIVE is directed. A narratee is not just the individual by whom a narrative is received; there has to be some evidence that the narrative is actually intended for a particular goal for it to count as the (or a) narratee. This leads Prince (1988) to argue that the narratee must be inscribed in the TEXT. He argues that there is a difference between a narratee and both the READER and the IMPLIED READER. In the final section of James Joyce's *Ulysses* therefore, if we follow Prince on this matter, the narratee is Molly Bloom herself (she aims her comments at herself), but the implied reader is rather a person who can, for example, pick up the CLASSICAL analogies contained within the text of *Ulysses* as a whole, with the real reader being anyone who actually reads the NOVEL.

Some NARRATOLOGISTS distinguish between *intra-fictional (or intra-diegetic) narratees* (such as Molly Bloom, or Lockwood in *Wuthering Heights*), who are FICTIONAL PERSONAE within the works concerned as well as having a narrative addressed to them, and *extra-fictional (or extra-diegetic) narratees*, who are not ('Dear Reader').

Narration This is a rather slippery term in contemporary NARRATIVE theory, and is given different weight by different theorists. By some it is used as a synonym for narrative, by others as the act or process whereby a narrative is produced. The second of these is the definition chosen by Shlomith Rimmon-Kenan, for whom narration is both (i) the *communication* process in which the narrative as message is transmitted and (ii) the *verbal* nature of the medium used to transmit the message (1983, 2).

Compare the distinctions listed in the entry for ENUNCIATION and its cognates.

Narrative A term which is much used but about which there is limited consensus when it comes to defining its meaning.

Gerald Prince defines this term as 'the recounting of one or more real or fictitious events' but as 'product and process, object and act, structure and structuration' (1988, 58). For Onega and Landa, narrative can be defined in a wider, Aristotelian sense as '"a work with a plot" (e.g. epic poetry, tragedy, comedy)' or in a narrower sense as '"a work with a narrator" (epic poetry, but not, in principle, drama or film)' (1996, 1). They compare the difference between their wider and narrower senses to the difference between TELLING AND SHOWING (1996, 2), and further define the term in a way that impinges on certain definitions of 'plot' (see STORY AND PLOT):

> A narrative is the semiotic representation of a series of events meaningfully connected in a temporal and causal way. Films, plays, comic strips, novels, newsreels, diaries, chronicles and treatises of geological history are all narratives in this wider sense.
>
> (1996, 3)

GÉRARD GENETTE points out that the word *narrative* (in French, *récit*) can refer to three separate things: either the oral or written narrative statement that undertakes to tell of an EVENT or events; or the succession of real or fictitious events that are the subject of the DISCOURSE, with their varied relations; or, finally, the act of narrating (1980, 25–6). In his own usage he reserves the word narrative for the first of these three, while the second he refers to as STORY or DIEGESIS and the third as *narrating*.

On two points there is, however, general agreement. First that a narrative must involve the recounting of an event or events, otherwise it is not a narrative but a description. And second that these events can be either real or fictitious.

See also REGISTER

Narrative situation Used by Mieke Bal in a technical sense, and fixed according to the answers evinced by a set of typical questions. Is the NARRATOR a CHARACTER or not? Does the narrator exist within the world of the STORY? Is the NARRATIVE FOCALIZED through the narrator? (1985, 126). In other words, narrative situation is defined according to the narrator's relationship to the narrative and the story.

Compare the discussion of *narrative levels* in the entry for STORY AND PLOT.

Narratology See Section 3, p. 168

Narrator Whereas Gerald Prince describes the narrator as 'the one who narrates' (1988, 65), and Katie Wales describes the narrator as 'a person who narrates' (1989, 316), Mieke Bal stresses that for her the narrator is the narrative agent, 'the linguistic subject, a function and not a person, which expresses itself in the language that constitutes the text' (1985, 119). The tension between these two approaches pinpoints a problem: whereas the term evokes a sense of a human individual for most people, many NARRATIVES do not stem from recognizably human or PERSONIFIED sources, but from a SUBJECT position within the text, although Claude Bremond (1966) has claimed that 'where there is no implied human interest (narrated events neither being produced by agents nor experienced by anthropomorphic beings), there can be no narrative, for it is only in relation to a plan conceived by man that events gain meaning and can be organized into a structured temporal sequence' (Onega and Landa: 1996, 63–4). On this account the 'Time Passes' section of VIRGINIA WOOLF's *To the Lighthouse* might not qualify as narrative. An alternative way round these problems is to reserve the term *covert narrator* for those instances in which a telling is delivered from a non-personified and non-intrusive source which does not address a NARRATEE.

Naturalism Often confused with REALISM because of its mode of presenting experience objectively, naturalism is governed by the dual premise that nature is all (there is no God), and that human lives are shaped by forces of nature, both external and internal (biology, environment, physical need or weakness, mental capacity), and socioeconomic influences, that are beyond the control of the individual. Such literature is often highly deterministic. The French novelist Émile Zola and the American Stephen Crane have both been described as naturalists, in spite of the many differences between their writings.

Neoclassicism See PERIODS OF LITERATURE

New Criticism See Section 3, p. 148

New Historicism and cultural materialism See Section 3, p. 186

Novel, novella, short story Definitions of the *novel* have been offered by many recent theorists and historians of the GENRE, and no single definition other than the broadest – such as the *OED*'s 'a fictitious prose narrative or tale of considerable length (now usually one long enough to fill one or more volumes) in which characters and actions representative of the real life of past or present times are portrayed in a plot of more or less complexity' – has been universally accepted. Even the *OED*'s definition raises questions concerning the force of a term such as 'real life'. Much recent fiction – MODERNIST and POSTMODERNIST in particular – is wary of or opposed to the requirements of a traditional PLOT, and these same movements have also attempted to downgrade and deconstruct the concept of CHARACTER. Not surprisingly, different definitions have implications for the age of the genre, and while a consensus existed for many years that the novel 'rose' in the late seventeenth and early eighteen centuries, other recent theorists have argued for the existence of novels way back to CLASSICAL antiquity.

Defining the *novella* is a more straightforward matter. The rise of the novella is normally associated with a specifically German tradition, and it is only comparatively recently that the term has been used to describe WORKS in ENGLISH fiction such as Henry James's *The Turn of the Screw*. A novella is normally short enough to be read in one sitting, but long enough to enable some development and complexity of plot and or character – let us say between fifteen and thirty thousand words, to set an arbitrary limit.

Most students of literature will also be faced with some study of the *short story*, and although this term is very widely accepted on present-day university syllabuses, it was long associated with more popular and superficial 'magazine' pieces, such that serious writers did not welcome their works being so described. Today it has a more open and non-evaluative force, and is conventionally used to describe pieces of prose fiction of up to about fifteen thousand words, although the borderline between the short story and the novella is impossible to draw with any precision.

See also BILDUNGSROMAN, EPIC, EPISTOLARY NOVEL, FACTION, FICTION, FEUILLETON, GOTHIC NOVEL, HISTORICAL NOVEL, MAGIC REALISM, METAFICTION (for *anti-novel*), MODERNISM AND POSTMODERNISM, NATURALISM, PICARESQUE NOVEL, POLYPHONIC (for *polyphonic novel*), ROMAN À CLEF, ROMANCE, SENTIMENTAL (for *sentimental novel*)

Objective correlative See the entry for T.S. ELIOT, Section 5, p. pp. 331–2

Occasional verse Poetry written in celebration of, or in connection with, a specific occasion such as a birthday, wedding or funeral, or a military victory.

Ode A LYRIC poem that is distinguished by a greater degree of formality and dignity from other lyrics. The ode is longer than more private lyrics, and although it shares the common lyric emphasis on the PERSONA's feelings and emotions it seems more conscious of its public. John Keats's major odes are representative of the FORM.

Onomatopoeia Words whose sound matches or mirrors their sense. For instance, words such as buzz, hiss, and smack are all said to be onomatopoeic, in that they imitate the sound they describe.

Open and closed texts The theorist who has done most to popularise the idea that TEXTS can be either open or closed is UMBERTO ECO. His formulation is, however, quite complex, and he defines 'open' and 'closed' in rather unexpected ways. As a result, the terms are often used in a sense that is the reverse of what he recommends.

The problem is very clear in the following discussion by Eco of texts such as Superman comic strips and NOVELS by Ian Fleming (the creator of 'James Bond'). For Eco, such texts are closed precisely because they are open to any sort of READING. In contrast, where the AUTHOR of the text has envisaged the role of the READER at the moment of generation, according to Eco the text is, paradoxically, open to successive INTERPRETATIONS. These interpretations and reinterpretations, according to Eco, echo one another, and operate within certain textually imposed constraints (unlike responses to what he calls closed texts): 'You cannot use the [open] text as you want, but only as the text wants you to use it. An open text, however "open" it be, cannot afford whatever interpretation' (1981, 19).

See also FORMULAIC LITERATURE; READERLY AND WRITERLY TEXTS

Orality A term used to denote an extended complex of elements associated with oral CULTURES – that is, cultures either unaffected by literacy and the written word or only marginally affected by them. One of the most influential (and accessible) theoretical contributions to the study of orality is Walter J. Ong's *Orality and Literacy* (1982), in which Ong argues that in a predominantly oral culture thought differs from the thought typical of a culture characterized by universal or near-universal literacy. The thought and expression of an oral culture, according to Ong, are *additive rather than subordinative, aggregative rather than analytic, redundant or 'copious', conservative or traditionalist, close to the human lifeworld, agonistically toned* (that is, polemical and emotive), *empathetic and participatory rather than objectively distanced, homeostatic,* and *situational rather than abstract* (1982, 37–57). Following Ong, a distinction is sometimes made between primary orality (orality in pre-literate societies) and secondary orality (orality in literate societies in which new technologies reintroduce forms of orality).

Organicism In literary criticism, particularly during the heyday of the NEW CRITICS, it came to be an item of faith that the work of literature (or art) had to be treated as an *organic* STRUCTURE – that is, having the qualities of a living unit with its parts organically rather than mechanically related.

During the same time F.R. LEAVIS extended the ANALOGY from the individual literary WORK to literature as a whole; in his essay 'Literature and Society' he argues that a literature 'must be thought of as essentially something more than a separation of separate works: it has an organic form, or constitutes an organic order, in relation to which the individual writer has his significance and his being' (1962, 184). Leavis also made much of the concept of 'the organic community', most notably in *Culture and Environment* which was written with Denys Thompson and first published in 1933, although directly comparable ideas can be found in the essay 'Literature and Society' (and in many other places in Leavis's writing) as well. The conservative-nostalgic concept of the organic community in Leavis's work owes much to T.S. ELIOT. It represents a lost unity in sharp contrast to the alleged disintegration and divisions of modern urban society, a unity both among human beings and between human beings and their environment, in which a CULTURE shared by all the community's members and interwoven with the realities of their daily lives could be found.

Nowadays a pejorative use of the term is current, one use to indicate a view of literature, or art, or culture, or social life as organic unities superior to material or economic determinants and untroubled by inner fissures, dissent, or tension.

Orientalism A term given new meaning by EDWARD SAID in his highly influential study of the same name (1979; first published 1978). Traditionally, an Orientalist was a scholar devoted to the study of 'the Orient' or the East. In this traditional usage the term had positive connotations – devotion to scholarship, a commitment to unearthing the secrets of another CULTURE, and so on.

Said's development of the term attempts to draw out its concealed political allegiances – the fact that Orientalists were complicit with imperialism and that they effectively provided Europe with 'one of its deepest and most recurring images of the Other' (1979, 1; see the entry for OTHER). According to Said,

> Orientalism can be discussed and analyzed as the corporate institution for dealing with the Orient – dealing with it by making statements about it, authorizing views of it, describing it, by teaching it, settling it, ruling over it: in short, Orientalism as a Western style for dominating, restructuring, and having authority over the Orient.
>
> . . .
>
> My contention is that without examining Orientalism as a discourse one cannot possibly understand the enormously systematic discipline by which European culture was able to manage – and even produce – the Orient polit-

ically, sociologically, militarily, ideologically, scientifically, and imaginatively during the post-Enlightenment period.

(1979, 3)

Other To characterize a person, group, or institution as 'other' is to place them outside the system of normality or CONVENTION to which one belongs oneself. Such an activity is referred to by some theorists by means of a verb form: *othering*. Processes of exclusion by categorization are central to certain IDEOLOGICAL mechanisms. If woman is other, then that which is particular to the experience of being a woman is irrelevant to 'how things are', to the defining conventions by which one lives. If members of a given racial group are collectively seen as other, then how they are treated is irrelevant to what humanity demands – because they are other and not human.

When granted a capital letter the term invokes JACQUES LACAN's theory of the way in which the SUBJECT seeks confirmation of itself in the response of the Other. In 'On a Question Preliminary to any Possible Treatment of Psychosis', Lacan comments that the Other is, 'the locus from which the question of [the subject's] existence may be presented to him' (1977, 194). Without its capital letter, 'other' in Lacan's usage designates the other, imaginary self, which is first formed during the MIRROR STAGE when the infant confronts his or her own reflected image. (See also Section 5, p. 362)

A recent coinage is that of the M/Other, often in the term 'the phallic M/Other'. As the formulation suggests, we are here dealing with a situation in which a child's or individual's mother represents the threatening Other, often by virtue of her allegedly having assumed patriarchal power or authority and having thus become a PHALLIC figure.

Alterity is frequently used as a synonym for otherness.

See also STEREOTYPE

Ottava rima Taken from the Italian, the term refers to a stanza FORM made popular by Byron's long poem *Don Juan*, which uses eight lines of iambic pentameter, rhyming ABABABCC.

Oxymoron A PARADOXICAL device which links two opposite concepts or words in the same phrase, such as John Milton's 'darkness visible' in *Paradise Lost*.

Palimpsest text A TEXT in which hidden or repressed meanings can be found between the lines or under the surface. (A palimpsest was originally a document with layers of writing on it, dating from times when paper or parchment was expensive and had to be regularly re-used: 'palimpsest text' transfers this layering from the literal to the METAPHORICAL level.)

See also INTERTEXTUALITY

Panegyric A highly formal and ornate poem of praise for a distinguished person or event.

Parable Any short NARRATIVE meant to illustrate a moral lesson, frequently religious (as with Christ's Biblical parables) but often taking a secular form in recent literature. The parable typically works on two levels, that of the familiar and simple events that will be immediately comprehensible, and that of a higher and often more ABSTRACT or complex meaning.

See also the entry for J. HILLIS MILLER in Section 5.

Paradigm shift A term introduced by Thomas S. Kuhn in his *The Structure of Scientific Revolutions* (1970; first published 1962). Kuhn suggested that particular learned communities or specialities rested upon acceptance of 'a set of recurrent and quasi-standard illustrations of various theories in their conceptual, observational, and instrumental applications'. These, he proposed, are the community's *paradigms*, which can be found revealed in its 'textbooks, lectures, and laboratory exercises' (1970, 43). Kuhn (as his title suggests) was particularly interested in how changes take place in scientific thinking, and his concept of the paradigm plays a central role in his explanation.

Readers of Kuhn's book from the Humanities were much struck by his account of cases of scientific evidence which was not recognized as such because it did not fit into known and accepted paradigms. MICHEL FOUCAULT's account of the reception of Mendel's work is presented in the context of Foucault's own concept of the DISCOURSE, but it could equally well exemplify the alleged inability of those located on different sides of a paradigm shift to communicate.

> People have often wondered how on earth nineteenth-century botanists and biologists managed not to see the truth of Mendel's statements. But it was precisely because Mendel spoke of objects, employed methods and placed himself within a theoretical perspective totally alien to the biology of his time.
>
> . . .
>
> Mendel spoke the truth, but he was not *dans le vrai* (within the true) of contemporary biological discourse: it was simply not along such lines that objects and biological concepts were formed.
>
> (Foucault nd, 224)

Compare LINGUISTIC PARADIGM

Paradox An apparent contradiction or incongruity. John Donne's SONNET 'Batter My Heart' is full of paradoxes; it explores the apparent inconsistency of a God who must punish to be merciful and suggests that it is only through suffering and pain in this life that salvation can be achieved in the next. Paradox is more extended than OXYMORON, which often involves no more than two words, and is meant to assert a truth in a strange or surprising manner.

Parallelism A rhetorical device by which two ideas are brought together through the use of identical or similar rhythmical, syntactic or verbal constructions. Grammatical or METRICAL equivalence in a few lines allows for an intense focus on the elements that are compared or contrasted, as well as creating memorable passages of writing. The opening of Charles Dickens's *A Tale of Two Cities* affords many examples, as with 'It was the best of times, it was the worst of times'.
 Compare ANTITHESIS

Parody Imitation with a comic or SATIRICAL intention, intended to mock its original, sometimes affectionately, but frequently with malice. Parody typically attempts to copy aspects of its target very closely, and the good parody may even be so close to its target that it is not recognized by all as a parody.

Pastiche From the Italian for 'paste' (as in 'cut and paste'), a WORK or part of a work of literature comprised of patches of other works or of passages which greatly resemble other works. As with PARODY, the effect can be mockery of the imitated or copied work. It is often seen as a characteristic of POSTMODERN literature – indeed, postmodern theories which question the notion of originality suggest that all representation must involve an element of pastiche. It is also used as a verb, and one who pastiches can be called a 'pasticheur'.

Pastoral A literary MODE originating in ancient Rome that ostensibly celebrates the simple and pure life of shepherds and shepherdesses. 'Ostensibly' because, as WILLIAM EMPSON argues in his extension of the term, pastorals typically projected the concerns and problems of the upper and privileged classes on to the imagined shepherds and shepherdesses of the mode. The mode has enjoyed periods of fashionability at different times and in different cultures, with one flowering in English literature around the late sixteenth and early seventeenth century in works by (among others) Sir Philip Sidney and Edmund Spenser. In his book *Some Versions of Pastoral*, which was first published in 1936, Empson extended the term to include works which projected the preoccupations of any relatively privileged group on to another deemed to be less powerful and more innocent – Lewis Carroll's *Alice* works, for example, in which (Empson argued), adult concerns were pursued in a story about a child. The sub-title of Empson's chapter on Alice – 'The Child as Swain' – is representative: 'swain' is a semi-archaic word much used in traditional pastoral to denote a young male rustic lover.

Pathetic fallacy A common literary device whereby human feelings or emotions are ascribed to non-human, natural objects. Typically a transferral of emotions is suggested, such that the charged object reflects the state of a human agent. John Ruskin invented the phrase as a derogatory term believing that such attributions wrongfully created false appearances, but the term is now used neutrally.

Pathos The quality of provoking feelings of compassion, pity or sorrow in the audience or READER. The technique is often looked down upon, and associated with popular modes such as MELODRAMA.

SECTION 4

Patronage The system by which writers are given political protection and/or financial support by an individual or institution. In return, the patron gains a certain amount of CULTURAL capital, either through association with a particular talent, or more specifically by having a WORK dedicated to him or her, or by being otherwise acknowledged. The decline of patronage coincided with eighteenth-century improvements in the technologies of distribution and publication, which enabled more writers to become economically independent. However, the system of patronage offered some freedoms not available in the new market-based system based on fees and royalties; a writer with a generous patron did not have to worry about pleasing the public to gain sales, for example.

Performatives See Section 3, p. 174

Periods of literature The concept of literary periods is often a confusing and controversial one. To begin with, the categories used are not systematic: some periods are associated with the reign of a particular monarch or dynasty, others with a philosophical movement. Already, we encounter inconsistencies and problems: why should a king bask in the reflected glory of writings produced in an age that coincided with his reign, but which were otherwise unrelated to his accomplishments? And why employ different modes of classification? There are in fact perfectly plausible (though not necessarily acceptable) answers to these questions: literature can sometimes have intimate connections with institutions of economic, political and social power, for instance, and the use of a monarch's name may not therefore be entirely inappropriate. In the case of more oppositional or minority movements, however, the opposite may be the case, which is why (for example) the Romantic age is linked to a wider intellectual movement with its origins in continental Europe, rather than to a British royal family.

These comments merely touch on the surface of broader and more complex issues of literary taxonomy: we offer them only to make you aware that organization according to period is not as straightforward as it might appear. Sometimes, the problem is one of accuracy: the Renaissance is seen as a time of great HUMANIST advancements, for example, but those who benefited from these advances were limited, numerically and in terms of CLASS, and they condoned activities (torture, public execution) that most people today would consider barbarous. Similarly, the eighteenth century is sometimes referred to as the Neoclassical or Augustan period, or the ENLIGHTENMENT, although there are countless aspects of cultural and social practice during this time that were neither CLASSICAL nor enlightened. But many critics and teachers make use of these temporal schemes, and you should be familiar with their meaning.

Generally speaking, these are the most important periods:

Classical literature, or the literature of antiquity, traditionally refers to compositions dating from the CULTURES of ancient Greece and Rome. Writers include the Greek EPIC poet Homer (author of the *Iliad* and the *Odyssey*) and the Roman poet Virgil (author of the *Aeneid*, and also the PASTORAL *Eclogues*); the dramatists Aeschylus, Aristophanes, Seneca, Sophocles, Euripides, and the philosophers Plato and Aristotle. Horace, Juvenal, Ovid and Pindar are others. Keep in mind that such a term covers a wide historical period, and many genres: EPIC, LYRIC, NARRATIVE (in poetry); TRAGEDY and COMEDY (in drama), as well as philosophy and rhetoric. It ends with the collapse of the Roman empire, in the 5th century AD.

The *medieval period* (also known as the Middle Ages, a direct translation of the matching Latin name) is a similarly broad term, encompassing different periods, languages and genres. It is traditionally divided into two eras: the Old English or Anglo-Saxon period begins around the first half of the fifth century, and refers to literature composed in the Anglo-Saxon language. The EPIC *Beowulf* is its most celebrated work. The Middle English or Anglo-Norman period stretches from around (AD) 1100 to 1500. It was during this time that Geoffrey Chaucer's *The Canterbury Tales* was produced (*c.* 1387).

The term *Renaissance* (French for 'rebirth') follows the medieval period, and in England covers (in approximate chronological order) literature also classified as Tudor, Elizabethan, Jacobean, Metaphysical, Caroline (and Cavalier) and Commonwealth (or Interregnum). Its beginning coincides with the commencement of the Tudor era (in 1485), and ends around 1660 (with the Restoration of the monarchy). See also RENAISSANCE HUMANISM.

The *Elizabethan period* designates writings from the reign of Elizabeth I (1558–1603): its authors conventionally include Ben Jonson, Christopher Marlowe, Sir Walter Raleigh, Sir Philip Sidney, William Shakespeare and Edmund Spenser. Jacobean is a term for English literature dating from the rule of James I (1603–25); Caroline (from the Latin for Charles, *carolus*) signifies literature authored during the reign of Charles I (1625–49). The Metaphysical poets (such as John Donne and George Herbert) are associated with the Elizabethan and Jacobean periods; the Cavalier or Royalist poets (Thomas Carew, Richard Lovelace, and Sir John Suckling among them) with the Caroline age.

In American literature, the *Colonial period* spans the years from the first English settlements (at the beginning of the seventeenth century) to 1776, when the Revolutionary period begins.

1649 is the date of Charles I's execution and the beginning of the *Commonwealth period* or Interregnum. Milton wrote before this, but is primarily linked with this time because of his sympathies for the Cromwellian cause. The end-point for the period denoted by the term is the restoration of Charles II in 1660, at which time the *Restoration period* begins. This period extends to the beginning of the eighteenth century though some scholars date it to 1688 (when James II was dethroned).

Eighteenth-century literature is (as the name suggests) writing that emerges during the eighteenth century: it is sometimes referred to as the *Augustan period*, the Enlightenment, or the Neoclassical period. The term Augustan more specifically designates literature written during the reign of Queen Anne (1702–14); nonetheless, it implies an adherence to values similar to those of neoclassicism (DECORUM, elegance, order, proportion, reason, restraint, and simplicity). Writers associated with this period include Frances (Fanny) Burney, Daniel Defoe, Henry Fielding, Eliza Haywood, Samuel Johnson, Alexander Pope, Laurence Sterne and Jonathan Swift.

The nineteenth century includes two periods: the Romantic and the Victorian. English *Romanticism* is conventionally taken to begin in 1789 (with the French Revolution), though some scholars date it to the publication of Wordsworth and Coleridge's *Lyrical Ballads* in 1798. Its major writers include William Blake, Lord Byron, Samuel Taylor Coleridge, John Keats, Mary and Percy Bysshe Shelley, Sir Walter Scott and William Wordsworth. Jane Austen's NOVELS derive from this period, but are not classified as Romantic. American Romanticism, associated with Ralph Waldo Emerson, Henry David Thoreau and Walt Whitman (the first two of these also known as Transcendentalists), begins slightly later, around the 1820s: the American Renaissance is an overlapping term that covers the middle years of the nineteenth century and encompasses writings as diverse as those of Emily Dickinson, Nathaniel Hawthorne, and Herman Melville (in addition to the Romantics).

The *Victorian period* in English history runs from 1837 to 1901, the year of Queen Victoria's death. The major British authors of the Victorian era include the novelists Anne, Charlotte and Emily Brontë, Charles Dickens, George Eliot, Elizabeth Gaskell, Thomas Hardy, Anthony Trollope, and William Thackeray, as well as poets Elizabeth and Robert Browning, Gerard Manley Hopkins, Christina Rossetti, and Alfred Lord Tennyson. Major movements of the period include NATURALISM, REALISM and SYMBOLISM.

The term MODERNISM usually designates literature and art from the early part of the twentieth century: though dated sometimes to the beginning of the First World War in 1914, modernist experiments such as IMAGISM (associated with H.D. [Hilda Doolittle] and Ezra Pound) began slightly earlier. Modernism is seen as continuing through the 1930s and up to the end of Second World War (in 1945). Among its CANONICAL writers are T.S. ELIOT, James Joyce, VIRGINIA WOOLF and Gertrude Stein. Surrealism is also a phenomenon of this era. *Postmodernism* is more difficult to date and define: readers are referred to the composite entry for MODERNISM AND POSTMODERNISM.

Peripeteia The sudden reversal of a CHARACTER's fortunes, as in the fall of a TRAGIC HERO.

Periphrasis A manner of speaking or writing in which an indirect and generalizing (and often ornate) phrase or IMAGE is substituted for something more straightforward. James Boswell reports (and mocks) the poet James Grainger's periphrastic use of 'whisker'd vermin tribes' to refer to rats, for instance. Its usage shades into euphemism, in which a dignified expression is used to mask something more unpleasant ('economic with the truth' instead of 'lying'). Periphrasis often results from a desire to deal with categories and ABSTRACTS rather than particulars, and thus to show the education and intelligence associated with CLASS privilege.

Perlocutionary act see Section 3, p. 175

Persona From the Latin meaning 'mask', an adopted identity which allows a writer to make utterances which are those of the 'speaker' rather than his or her own. Usually associated with poetry, as discussion of prose fiction more often makes use of the term NARRATOR.

Compare CHORUS

Personification The attribution of human qualities to inanimate objects, ABSTRACT things, or non-human life forms.

Perspective and voice The distinction made by GÉRARD GENETTE between MOOD and VOICE is perhaps the best way into a topic which was once conceptualized in relatively unproblematic terms under the rubric of *point of view*, but which with the advances in NARRATIVE theory of recent years has become a much more complex topic known by a range of terms, the most accepted of which is probably *perspective*.

Genette has drawn attention to the importance of a long-neglected distinction between *who sees?* and *who speaks?* Thus, for example, although the narrative voice in Joseph Conrad's *Under Western Eyes* is that of the PERSONIFIED narrator, the English 'Teacher of Languages', what is observed (in both senses of the word) frequently goes beyond his actual consciousness, and the reader is told things which he (the NARRATOR) could not possibly know if he were a living human being rather than a FICTIONAL character/narrator. (See the entry for PARALEPSIS.)

In Genette's terminology the distinction between *who sees?* and *who speaks?* is expressed in terms of the opposition between *mood* and *voice* (1980, 30). According to him, the category of mood gathers together the problems of DISTANCE which American critics have traditionally discussed in terms of the opposition between *telling and showing*, and he suggests that these terms represent a resurgence of the Platonic terms DIEGESIS AND MIMESIS. *Voice*, in contrast, he reserves to describe the way the NARRATIVE SITUATION, along with the narrator and his or her audience, is implicated in the narrative (1980, 29–31). To summarize: *mood* operates at the level of connections between STORY and narrative, while *voice* designates connections both between narrating and narrative, and narrating and story (1980, 32). Others following Genette have preferred to replace *mood* by *perspective*, as the pair 'perspective and voice' matches up more neatly with 'who sees/who speaks'.

Both Genette and Bal use the term *focalization*, and this term is now widely accepted. Accordingly, a narrative which has zero focalization is one in which it is impossible to fix the perspective in terms of which the narrated CHARACTERS, events and situations are being observed and presented. Many works of fiction which were traditionally described as characterized by an *omniscient* point of view are described by modern narratologists as having a zero focalization, although the two are not identical. An omniscient narrator is all-knowing: nothing is hidden from him or her. An omniscient narrator may or may not be personified (that is, may be presented as a person rather than just as a source of information), although omniscient narrators are normally not personified. But many narratives with zero focalization lay no claim to omniscience. The older term 'third-person narrator' is often used to denote a narrator standing outside the created world of the story. The term comes from the fact that such a narrator refers to characters as 'he' and 'she' rather than as 'I', as with a first-person narrator.

The term *focalized narrative* can also be rendered as *internal perspective*: the story is told from the perspective of a point (normally a consciousness) which is internal to the story, or *intra-diegetic* (see DIEGESIS AND MIMESIS). (Sometimes the term *intra-fictional* is preferred to intra-diegetic.) Thus a *focalizer* is a character or consciousness *in* a work who or which offers the reader 'positions' from which that which is narrated can be experienced.

Focalized narratives can be *fixed*, as in Jean Rhys's *Good Morning, Midnight* where everything we learn comes from the heroine/narrator Sasha Jansen, *variable*, as in Emily Brontë's *Wuthering Heights* in which some events are presented from the perspective of Mr Lockwood, some from that of Mrs Dean, and some from that of Isabella (in the long letter she writes), or *multiple* as in Tobias Smollett's *Humphry Clinker* in which the EPISTOLARY technique allows the same events to be presented more than once from different and contrasting perspectives. The term *double focalization* is normally used to indicate the simultaneous or co-terminous (rather than just consecutive or alternating) presentation of two narrative 'points of view'.

External focalization denotes a focalization that is limited to what, were the story true, the observer could actually have observed 'from the outside'; in other words, it involves no accounts of characters' thoughts, feelings, and emotions unless these are revealed in external behaviour or admitted to by the characters. According to Genette, external focalization involves a perspective which is intra-diegetic but outside that of the characters.

Because of variations in usage care needs to be exercised in the use of these terms. See also CENTRE; ENUNCIATION; FRAME; NARRATIVE SITUATION

Petrarchan conceit See CONCEIT
See also COURTLY LOVE, and SONNET

Phallocentrism A term associated with recent FEMINIST theory and used to refer to interlocking social and IDEOLOGICAL systems which accept and advance a patriarchal power symbolically represented by the phallus. 'Phallus' has to be understood as a *cultural* construction attributing symbolic power to the *biological* penis. Thus Carole-Anne Tyler has argued that some women do 'have' the phallus in our CULTURE because it is not just the penis but all the other signs of power and privilege, which stand in a METAPHORIC and METONYMIC relation not only to 'penis' but also to 'white' and 'bourgeois' – the signs of a 'proper' racial and class identity (1991, 58). (For the metaphor/metonymy distinction, see also the entry for SYNTAGMATIC AND PARADIGMATIC.)

Phallogocentrism A portmanteau term combining PHALLOCENTRISM and LOGOCEN-TRISM, coined by JACQUES DERRIDA in his critique of JACQUES LACAN in 'The Purveyor of Truth' (1975). For Derrida, Lacan's reading of Edgar Allan Poe's *The Purloined Letter* is guilty of phallogocentrism because Lacan sees the letter unproblematically as phallus, rather than recognizing that meaning cannot exist in such unproblematic one-to-one relationships.

Although the term was intended to imply criticism it has appealed to FEMI-NISTS and others eager to imply a connection between male, patriarchal author-ity, and systems of thought which LEGITIMIZE themselves by reference to some PRESENCE or point of authority prior to and outside of themselves. The hidden, legitimizing presence, in other words, is always, at root, that of the Father, whose authority is a starting point or unconsidered assumption rather than something that can be justified or admitted. The term implies that both phallocentrism and logocentrism have in common that they are both monolithic systems built round a single, ultimate determining CENTRE (the phallus, the word), a centre which ends indeterminacy and play and imposes meaning by the imposition of its unchallengeable authority.

Phenomenology See Section 3, p. 156

Picaresque novel The first picaresque NOVEL was *Lazarillo de Tormes* (1554), and fol-lowed the adventures of a *picaro*, Spanish for 'rogue'. Typically, then, such nov-els are episodic (based on one incident after another) and have a PROTAGONIST from a low social CLASS who encounters many different CHARACTERS from all walks of life in the course of a journey. Daniel Defoe's *Moll Flanders* gives us an English example with a heroine rather than a hero. *The Adventures of Huckleberry Finn* is also essentially picaresque in its structure, and in its central character, a young boy who is poor, naive, and (technically speaking) a criminal – since he aids a runaway slave. Such novels are often used to reveal hypocrisy and corruption in society – especially among the upper classes, and they can be associated with a venerable popular tradition in which a (normally male) protag-onist of low social class is shown to be more sharp-witted ('street-wise' in mod-ern jargon) than those of higher economic or social status.

Plot See STORY AND PLOT

Poetics The study of the theoretical principles governing literature generally, or of a particular branch of literature. The term is taken from Aristotle's *Poetics*, and does not necessarily denote a study of poetry – witness MIKHAIL BAKHTIN's book *Problems of Dostoevsky's Poetics* (1984).

Point of view See PERSPECTIVE AND VOICE

Polyphonic Literally, many-voiced. In his study of Dostoevsky, MIKHAIL BAKHTIN argues that Dostoevsky was the creator of the polyphonic NOVEL:

> *A plurality of independent and unmerged voices and consciousnesses, a genuine polyphony of fully valid voices is in fact the chief characteristic of Dostoevsky's novels.* What unfolds in his works is not a multitude of characters and fates in a single objective world, illuminated by a single authorial consciousness; rather a *plurality of consciousnesses, with equal rights and each with its own world,* combine but are not merged in the unity of the event.
>
> (1984, 6)

Bakhtin uses the word *voice* in a special way, to include not just matters linguistic but also issues relating to IDEOLOGY and power in society. Bakhtin's view that the polyphonic novel was born with Dostoevsky has been challenged, and he himself seems sometimes to have accepted that polyphonic elements can be found in many novels in many CULTURES and times. But his work on Dostoevsky has drawn attention to a representative lack of a single CENTRE of authority in the modern (or MODERNIST) literary WORK.

Brian McHale points out that a rather different use of the concept can be found in the work of the Polish PHENOMENOLOGIST Roman Ingarden. According to Ingarden, 'the literary artwork is not ontologically uniform or monolithic, but *polyphonic*, stratified. Each of its layers has a somewhat different ontological status, and functions somewhat differently in the ontological make-up of the whole' (McHale: 1987, 30). For Ingarden there are four such strata: that of word-sounds, that of meaning-units, that of 'presented objects' (which are distinguished from 'real-world objects'), and that of 'schematized aspects'. (Based on McHale: 1987, 33.)

See also DIALOGIC; HETEROGLOSSIA; and compare PERSPECTIVE AND VOICE.

Polysemy See AMBIGUITY

Postcolonialism See Section 3, p. 191

Postmodernism See MODERNISM AND POSTMODERNISM

Post-structuralism See Section 3, p. 169

Pragmatics See Section 3, p. 173

Prague School/Prague Linguistic Circle See Section 3, p. 146

Presence According to JACQUES DERRIDA in the early and influential article 'Structure, Sign and Play in the Discourse of the Human Sciences', 'all the names related to fundamentals, to principles, or to the center have always designated an invariable presence – *eidos, archē, telos, energeia, ousia* (essence, existence, substance, subject) *alētheia*, transcendentality, consciousness, God, man, and so forth' (1978, 279–80). All of these represent extra-systemic entities, points of reference or CENTRES of authority which escape from that play of difference which, following FERDINAND DE SAUSSURE, Derrida believes to be the sole source of meaning. The *metaphysics of presence*, then, is for Derrida a LOGOCENTRIC belief in and reliance upon some such extra-systemic point of authority.

Projection characters CHARACTERS into whom an AUTHOR projects (often contradictory) aspects of him- or herself. The term *projection* is taken from the work of Sigmund Freud, who used it to describe a process in which impulses or beliefs unacceptable to the ego are attributed to someone else.

Prolepsis Also, following Prince (1988), *anticipation, flashforward* or *prospection*. Any narrating of a narrative EVENT before the time in the STORY at which it will take place has been reached in the NARRATIVE. In some usages terms such as *prefiguring* and *foreshadowing* are reserved for the evocation of future events, while *prolepsis* implies a more overt narrative reference to such events. A *completing prolepsis* is one which is needed to achieve a full chronological coverage because of a later omission in the narrative; a *repeating prolepsis* or *advance notice* supplies information that will be provided afresh later on in the narrative.

GÉRARD GENETTE distinguishes between *internal prolepses*, which are sited within the time-span of the story, and *external prolepses*, which are sited outside of the story's temporal limits (1980, 68–71).

Promotion See METRE

Protagonist The central or leading CHARACTER of a literary WORK. In Greek drama, as in Shakespeare's time, the protagonist was conventionally a person of high rank. The person opposing the protagonist is the *antagonist*: their conflict is often what sets off the PLOT. The term 'hero' is often used synonymously with 'protagonist', though heroes traditionally are the main characters in EPICS, in which they achieve their status by performing feats of great courage. In modern literature, the anti-hero has come to mean something more than the rival of the hero: he or she is someone whose qualities and values are opposed to ideals or principles of heroism generally, and is thus often to be admired.

Psychological and psychoanalytic theories See Section 3, p. 176

Quantitative verse Poetry structured according to a regulated pattern of short and long syllables, rather than a succession of accented and unaccented syllables. Ancient Greek and Latin writers used this system, English poetry never fully succeeded in doing so.

Queer Theory See Section 3, p. 195

Quest narrative In Anne Cranny-Francis's definition, a linear NARRATIVE in which temporal sequence is taken to signify material causation. She sees this as the dominant STRUCTURE in nineteenth- and twentieth-century Western writing, a

structure which carries a particular IDEOLOGICAL and political charge, for it PRIV-
ILEGES linear sequence rather than, say, seasonal cycles, and thus underwrites
DOMINANT DISCOURSES in our CULTURE (1990, 10, 11).

Radical feminism See FEMINISM

Readerly and writerly texts Translated from ROLAND BARTHES's coinages *lisible* and
scriptible in his *S/Z* (1990, 4–5). Barthes uses the terms to distinguish between
traditional literary WORKS such as the classical NOVEL, with their reliance upon
CONVENTIONS shared by writer and READER and their resultant (partial) fixity or
CLOSURE of meaning, and those works produced especially in the twentieth century which violate such conventions and thus force the reader to work to produce
a meaning or meanings which are inevitably other than final or 'correct'. Thus,

> [t]he writerly text is a perpetual present, upon which no *consequent* language
> (which would inevitably make it past) can be superimposed; the writerly text
> is *ourselves writing*, before the infinite play of the world (the world as func-
> tion) is traversed, intersected, stopped, plasticized by some singular system
> (Ideology, Genus, Criticism) which reduces the plurality of entrances, the
> opening of networks, the infinity of languages.
>
> (1990, 5)

Readerly texts, in contrast, are products rather than productions, and they make
up the enormous mass of our literature (1990, 5). The distinction ties in with
Barthes's comments on the death of the author – see the entry for AUTHOR.

A comparable distinction is that provided by UMBERTO ECO in his *The Role of
the Reader* (1981) between OPEN AND CLOSED TEXTS.

Readers and reading See READER-RESPONSE CRITICISM, Section 3, p. 159

Realism Realist literary works are typically so-called because they are believed to
be in some way 'like life', or to be 'true to life', but the apparent simplicity of
this definition is belied by the history of bitter debates that have accompanied
this term. These debates go back a long way, and recent arguments need to be
seen as the latest attempts to grapple with certain perennial problems. (There is
an excellent historical account of the development of this term – not limiting
itself to literary or artistic usages – in RAYMOND WILLIAMS's *Keywords* [1976].)
David Lodge has pointed out that, as with the term 'literature', '[realism] is used
sometimes in a neutrally descriptive sense and sometimes as an evaluative
term', and he reminds us that 'the particular instances to which it is applied will
vary from one period to another . . . and it is not exclusively aesthetic in application' (1977, 22).

One of the more interesting recent debates about realism is that between
BERTOLT BRECHT and GEORG LUKÁCS. Their disagreement dates from the 1930s,

but Brecht's contributions were not made known to Lukács at that time nor were they published until much later. In his published writings Lukács had, by the mid-1930s, arrived at a definition of realism which placed a high premium upon the artist's (i) portraying the *totality* of reality in some form or other, and (ii) *penetrating beneath* the surface appearance of reality so as to be able to grasp the underlying laws of historical *change*. For Lukács, then, the artist's task is similar to that set for himself by Marx: to understand world history as a complex and dynamic totality through the uncovering of certain underlying laws. In practice this led Lukács to place a supreme value upon certain works of classical realism in the NOVEL – the names of Tolstoy, Balzac and Thomas Mann are frequently on his lips or at the tip of his pen – and to wage an unceasing campaign against different aspects of what he classified as MODERNISM. At the end of his *The Historical Novel* (written 1936–37) Lukács refers to the 'misunderstanding' of his position that 'we intended a formal revival, an artistic imitation of the classical historical novel' (1969, 422), but even so many commentators have seen his opposition to modernism to be so all-embracing that this is actually what would have been needed to satisfy his requirement that a literary WORK be 'realistic'.

So that when Brecht, writing about the concept of realism, states that we 'must not derive realism as such from particular existing works' (Bloch *et al.*: 1977, 81), the unstated target is clearly Lukács (especially as he goes on to refer to Balzac and Tolstoy). Brecht's argument is, in a nutshell, an anti-ESSENTIALIST one. In other words, realism for him is not INTRINSIC to a literary work, coded into it for all time like the genetic code in a living being, but a function of the role the work plays or can play in a given society at a particular historical moment. To simplify, we can say that whereas for Lukács a work is realistic or not depending upon whether it portrays a socio-historical totality in terms of its underlying laws of transformation, for Brecht a work is realistic not once and for all, but by reference to its ability at a particular time and place to allow individuals to understand and to change the conditions of their existence. As he says, reality changes and in order to represent reality modes of representation must also change (Bloch *et al.*: 1977, 82). Brecht's realism focuses not on questions of FORM or content, but of social function.

See also DEFORMATION; SYNTAGMATIC AND PARADIGMATIC

Reception theory See Section 3, p. 158

Reductionism A pejorative description of any explanation which allegedly ignores higher-level qualities in whatever is being studied and reduces the object of study to certain or all of its lower-level qualities. Thus 'literature is just words' is reductionist (the word 'just' is often a giveaway), for literature is more than words (or language, or marks on paper, and so on). Literature involves also the *arrangement* and *presentation* of words in particular ways which draw their force from CONVENTIONS established within different CULTURES, communities and traditions.

Reference To refer is to point or ALLUDE to, and thus to assert the existence or nature of something. In literary criticism from a very early time the term has been associated with controversies about whether literary WORKS make reference to extra-literary or extra-textual reality, and, if so, how. Many influential recent theories (and especially those associated with STRUCTURALISM and POST-STRUCTURALISM) have argued that literature is non-referential, that statements in literary works cannot be either true or false because they claim no reference to anything that really exists – a position that can be traced back to Sir Philip Sidney's *An Apology for Poetry* (1595) and beyond.

See also INTERTEXTUALITY; SENSE AND REFERENCE

Reflector (character) Alternatively *focalizer*. Following Henry James, the central consciousness or intelligence in a work of FICTION. More generally, a CHARACTER whose perception of events plays an important unifying or AESTHETIC role in a NARRATIVE. According to Jahn *et al.*, there is a simple test to find out who the focalizer is in a given passage: 'Since s/he is the grammatical subject that belongs to the verbs that express thought, feeling, and perception, one only has to ask: Who thinks?, feels, sees, hears, remembers, etc. whatever is being narrated in a given passage?' (1993, 16).

See also PERSPECTIVE AND VOICE for more discussion of focalization.

Refrain A phrase, line or lines which is (or are) repeated following some regular pattern during a poem or song. When the refrain recurs with slight variations, this is known as *incremental repetition*.

Register The concept of register comes originally from the study of music, where it refers to the compass of a musical instrument or of a human voice. From here a succession of metaphorical adaptations takes it to Phonetics where it is used to refer to the pitch of speech UTTERANCES, and to Linguistics in general in which it is used (with variations) to refer to context-dependent linguistic characteristics – either spoken or written, and encompassing any set of choices which are made according to a conscious or unconscious notion of appropriateness-to-context (vocabulary, syntax, grammar, sound, pitch, and so on).

From Linguistics the concept has, by a further metaphorical leap, been adopted within literary criticism and NARRATOLOGY. TZVETAN TODOROV, for example, in his *Introduction to Poetics*, lists a number of categories by which different *registers of DISCOURSE* may be recognized. These include the discourse's *concrete or ABSTRACT* nature, the ABSENCE or presence of *rhetorical figures*, the presence or absence of *reference to an anterior discourse* (giving, respectively, *polyvalent* and *monovalent* discourse), and, finally, the extent to which the language involved is characterized by 'subjectivity' or 'objectivity' (1981, 20–7).

It seems clear that the work done by the concept of register in Literary Studies to some extent duplicates that done by the concept of GENRE, and MIKHAIL BAKHTIN's essay 'The Problem of Speech Genres' (in Bakhtin: 1986) does in fact define what Bakhtin calls 'speech genres' in a way that brings together both 'register' and 'genre' as they are used today.

Renaissance humanism The Renaissance (see LITERARY PERIODS) forms a bridge between the medieval period and the modern age, and is associated culturally with a renewal of interest in the works of CLASSICAL antiquity – the art, languages, philosophies and writings of ancient Greece and Rome. A time of relative political stability, economic growth and urban expansion introduced a new era of civilized accomplishment, which in turn prompted a realignment of thought, whereby humanity's achievements and potential became legitimate and serious objects of study. This was a period during which there was a great emphasis on architecture and sculpture, on CULTURE, education, logic and science – on secular studies, rather than theology only. Human life was seen as meaningful in itself, and not simply as a form of preparation for the afterlife. And human beings were no longer seen as fallen: they were capable of greatness, if not of perfection. For an interesting critique of Renaissance humanism, see Robert Browning's poem 'My Last Duchess'.

Restoration See COMEDY (Restoration comedy); PERIODS OF LITERATURE

Revisionism In the work of the American critic HAROLD BLOOM, *revisionism* is used in a non-pejorative sense to indicate a general theory or set of theories concerning the manner in which the poet (Bloom uses this word in a wide sense) revises the work of his (Bloom's use of the female GENDER is very sparing) precursors. Thus, for Bloom, poetic influence 'is part of the larger phenomenon of intellectual revisionism' (1973, 28). Bloom sees this 'larger phenomenon' in terms of concepts much influenced by Freud; thus the poet's relation to these precursors is highly Oedipal in character: the struggle against them is the struggle of the son against the father (or, to stress patriarchal authority, the Father). Just as Oedipus has to kill his father, the aspirant poet has somehow to destroy the power of his precursors, and, normally, of one especially potent patriarchal precursor, while simultaneously absorbing and transforming his strength and authority. The *strong* poet is the poet who succeeds in this task, and in his *The Anxiety of Influence* Bloom restricts himself to the strong poets, those who have the persistence to wrestle with their major precursors, 'even to the death' (1973, 5). Bloom's insistence upon the *anxiety* associated with influence is consistent with this view: the poet's attitude to his precursors is characterized by the same anxious mixture of love and rivalry to which the Freudian term *Oedipus complex* has been assigned. For Bloom, the poet suffers always from a sense of *belatedness*, a sense that he or she has come after important things have been said, and after they have been said in ways which constrain the poet and against which he or she has to struggle.

Bloom argues challengingly that most 'so-called "accurate"' INTERPRETATIONS of poetry are worse than mistakes, and suggests that 'perhaps there are only more or less creative or interesting mis-readings', because every reading is necessarily a *clinamen*: Bloom's term for a poetic misreading – what he terms a misprision 'proper' (1973, 43).

Clinamen is the first of six 'revisionary ratios' outlined in *The Anxiety of Influence*. The others are as follows.

Tessera, or completion and ANTITHESIS. 'A poet antithetically "completes" his precursor, by so reading the parent-poem as to retain its terms but to mean them in another sense, as though the precursor had failed to go far enough.'

Kenosis, or a breaking device and movement towards discontinuity with the precursor, in which the poet's humbling of himself actually also empties out his precursor.

Daemonization, in which

> [t]he later poet opens himself to what he believes to be a power in the parent-poem that does not belong to the parent proper, but to a range of being just beyond that precursor. He does this, in his poem, by so stationing its relation to the parent-poem as to generalize away the uniqueness of the earlier work.

Askesis, or a movement of self-purgation in which the poet yields up part of his own self-endowment so as to separate himself from others, including the precursor (but see below for an additional usage).

Apophrades, or the return of the dead, in which the poet holds his work so open to that of the precursor that the impression is given that the work of the precursor was actually written by the poet.

(1973, 14–16)

Bloom's theories have been given a specifically FEMINIST emphasis by SANDRA M. GILBERT and SUSAN GUBAR, who use Bloom's theories concerning the male author's anxiety about his forebears to highlight the very different situation of the female writer. Asking how such a female writer fits in to Bloom's 'essentially male literary history', Gilbert and Gubar reply, 'we find we have to answer that a woman writer does *not* "fit in"'; the female writer

> must confront precursors who are almost exclusively male, and therefore significantly different from her. Not only do these precursors incarnate patriarchal authority . . . they attempt to enclose her in definitions of her person and her potential which, by reducing her to extreme stereotypes (angel, monster) drastically conflict with her own sense of her self – that is, of her subjectivity, her autonomy, her creativity.

(1979, 48)

Accordingly, for the woman writer, '"the anxiety of influence" that a male poet experiences . . . is felt as an even more primary "anxiety of authorship" – a radical fear that she cannot create, that because she can never become a "precursor" the act of writing will isolate or destroy her' (1979, 48–9).

Rhyme In poetry or music, a structural and/or semantic pattern formed by the repetition of syllables with identical or similar sounds. There are two main categories. *End rhyme* occurs at the close of a line. Traditionally, such rhyme is 'full' or 'perfect': it involves identical sounds (can/man, bright/night/sight). *Half rhyme* or *slant rhyme* involves a correspondence in the sounds that is not exact or identical (lad/led/lid, mat/gate). *Masculine rhyme* occurs when the rhyming elements comprise single, or final stressed, syllables (can/man). *Feminine rhyme* takes place when the rhyme comprises either a single, or a final, unstressed syllable (dreary/weary). *Eye rhyme* (alternatively *sight rhyme*) joins similarly spelled words that are pronounced differently (year and bear). *Internal rhyme* involves repeated elements that are placed within the line rather than at its close. ALLITERATION, ASSONANCE and consonance (the repetition of similar consonant sounds in words as with titter and tatter) are traditionally classified in this way.

Rhyme royal (Alternatively: rime royal.) STANZA form of seven iambic pentameters rhyming ABABBCC, first used by Geoffrey Chaucer (and sometimes called the Chaucerian stanza). King James I of Scotland also composed in it, which is probably why it was dubbed 'royal'.

Roman à clef Literally, a NOVEL with a key. A WORK in which historically identifiable personalities and events are portrayed in a disguised FORM, as FICTION. The early nineteenth-century novelist Thomas Love Peacock wrote many such works containing thinly disguised portraits of leading Romantics such as Percy Bysshe Shelley.

Romance Traditionally, a long and highly conventionalized medieval NARRATIVE (in poetry, or a combination of prose and poetry) involving the (often supernatural) experiences of a chivalrous knight. Often, the romance promoted the social values and manners of the royal court.

The *prose romance* grows out of the romance, and is generally seen as one of the traditions that contributed to the birth of the modern NOVEL, and continues to form a part of it. Thus Emily Brontë's *Wuthering Heights*, although not a romance, contains romance elements. In the nineteenth century, 'romance' often refers to any work which combines elements of REALISM with more imaginative and even marvellous features – such as Nathaniel Hawthorne's stories and longer prose works. The modern *popular romance* is a highly formulaic sub-GENRE involving STEREOTYPED figures and predictable PLOTS, with an emphasis on sexual courtship.

Romantic comedy See COMEDY

Romanticism and Romantic period See PERIODS OF LITERATURE

Russian Formalism See Section 3, p. 144

Satire A MODE that combines criticism with comic ridicule. Often light and witty, it is nonetheless undertaken with a serious purpose – to publicize and to rebuke hypocrisy, immorality and wrong-doing in order to improve conduct. Satire may use PARODY and IRONY as tools, and it typically gives the READER pleasure by inviting him or her to share a sense of superiority to the person or institution satirized. It is a type of protest, but also a form of correction which presupposes the existence of a shared set of values by which an individual or institution can be judged. Such accounts of misbehaviour can also be used to support the reader or listener's sense of the necessity of proper behaviour.

Horatian satire is named after the Roman poet Horace, and characteristically exposes human folly while also understanding its inevitability. Rather than naming specific individuals, Horatian satire tends to focus on recognizable types: the glutton or lecher, for example. It is therefore milder and more tolerant than *Juvenalian satire*, named after the Roman writer Juvenal. Such satire is more indignant, and criticizes historical individuals, either naming them directly or presenting them as fictional CHARACTERS with recognizable physical or verbal attributes. Jonathan Swift's 'Satirical Elegy on the Death of a Late, Famous General' is a classic, short piece of invective that can be described as Juvenalian. *Mennipean satire* (sometimes referred to as *Varonian satire*) is the least common of the three types: named after the Greek Cynic philosopher of the third century BC, it often involves a humorous overview of contemporary intellectual and philosophical topics. It frequently includes conventional SETTINGS, such as a banquet, and ABSURD arguments and conflicts.

Semiology/semiotics See Section 3, p. 165

Sense and reference The usual way in which a distinction made by the German philosopher Gottlob Frege between *Sinn* and *Bedeutung* is rendered in English, although sometimes *meaning and reference* has been preferred.

In the course of a complex discussion of the issue of what it is that language can be said to refer to, Frege noted that phrases such as 'The Morning Star' and 'The Evening Star' can be said to share the same REFERENCE (that is, the planet Venus) but to be possessed of a different sense (or meaning). It is not just that the one phrase refers to the planet as seen in the morning, and the other to the planet as seen in the evening, but that each phrase has accrued a complex set of CULTURAL and literary associations of its own.

The distinction has appealed to AESTHETICIANS and literary theorists concerned to avoid two polarized responses to the question as to whether WORKS of literature or art can be said to refer to the real world (however defined). Such theorists reject the views that (i) the literary work makes no reference to the real world, but rather creates its own reality, and (ii) the literary work has no meaning independent of its reference to the real world. Instead, they argue that the literary work does have a reference to the real world, but that it also has a sense which is not wholly dependent upon or restricted to its reference.

Sensibility As a modern critical term, 'sensibility' refers to an AUTHOR's intuitive sensitivity and manner of responding to stimuli, or to a critic's intuitive manner of responding to AESTHETIC creations. Such a use of 'sensibility' has lost considerable currency as notions of 'natural' or 'intuitive' SUBJECT positions have been widely questioned and destabilized. 'Sensibility' remains current in discussions of the eighteenth century, when it was used to refer to an individual's moral and emotional capacity – particularly the capacity to feel sympathy for the suffering of others and to respond to suffering through benevolent action (as such it is related to SENTIMENT). Because of the widespread valorization of this quality, and its expression in numerous literary works (the 'literature of sensibility'), the latter half of the eighteenth century is sometimes called the 'Age of Sensibility'. Sensibility is SATIRIZED by Jane Austen in her *Sense and Sensibility*, which clearly ranks the former ahead of the latter.

Sentimental The term is now generally applied pejoratively to mean 'excessively emotional' or 'mawkish', but when it became common in English in the eighteenth century, it had more positive CONNOTATIONS. A 'sentiment' was a 'mental feeling', a thought or reflection which was produced from or informed by emotion; often this feeling concerned moral conduct and it revealed a capacity to feel sympathy for others – as in Adam Smith's *Theory of Moral Sentiments* (1759). The adjectival derivative suggested 'capable of generating sentiments', as in 'the sentimental NOVEL': a sub-GENRE, popular in the second half of the eighteenth century, which typically describes highly-charged emotions and aims to produce emotional responses in READERS. Alternatively called 'novels of SENSIBILITY', examples include Samuel Richardson's *Pamela* (1740), Sarah Fielding's *David Simple* (1744 and 1753), and Henry Mackenzie's *The Man of Feeling* (1771).

Setting Used generally to indicate the historical period and the social and CULTURAL context in which the action of a literary WORK takes place. Setting can refer both to a created FICTIONAL context and to an actual historical or CULTURAL time and place. Recent critics have been suspicious of the idea that 'setting' can be neatly abstracted from other elements of a work, thus the 'London' of Daniel Defoe is different from the 'London' of Charles Dickens or VIRGINIA WOOLF, and not just because these novelists are writing at different times. Some literary GENRES carry with them certain requirements concerning setting: thus the traditional PASTORAL could not take place in the middle of a city.

The term can also be used to describe the use of scenery, props and lighting in a dramatic production.

Sibilance The use of 'hissing' sounds (sibilants) for poetic effect.

Sign Much modern literary and critical theory has been dominated by or founded on a version of SEMIOTICS – that is, upon a general theory (or 'science') of the nature of the sign and of its life in CULTURE and history. A useful starting point is to distinguish between *sign* and *symptom*. The key difference would appear to be that of the *conventional* nature of the sign: a symptom is fixed by and interpreted in the light of nature, a sign by and in the light of CONVENTION. Some theorists would be prepared to see a symptom as a sub-set of sign, while others distinguish sharply between the two. Clearly the issue of INTENTION, or MOTIVATION can be brought in here.

Probably the theory of the sign which has been most influential so far as literature is concerned is that of the Swiss linguistician FERDINAND DE SAUSSURE. It is worth remembering that Saussure's definition is not of the sign as such, but of the *linguistic* sign, although many of his followers have generalized his definition to include non-linguistic signs as well. Saussure denied the common-sense view that the linguistic sign was a name that could be attached to an object, and argued instead that the linguistic sign was a 'two-sided psychological entity' that could be represented by the diagram reproduced below (1974, 66; some translations have 'sound pattern' rather than 'sound image'). Saussure admits that this goes against then current usage (according to him the term *sign* was normally taken to designate only a sound-image), but argues that to avoid AMBIGUITY three related terms were needed: 'I propose to retain the word *sign* [*signe*] to designate the whole and to replace *concept* and *sound-image* respectively by *signified* [*signifié*] and *signifier* [*signifiant*]' (1974, 67). The English translations of *signifié* and *signifiant* given here have been questioned, and in one suggestion *significance* and *signal* have been proposed as alternatives.

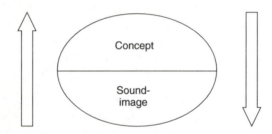

A *symbol* is anything which stands for something apart from itself. The cross, for example, stands for Christ's sacrifice and – in a larger sense – for Christianity. Symbols can be conventional and public, or private and personal. In literature, a writer can make use of a well-known symbol (a white wedding dress suggesting purity and virginity) or can build up a set of new symbolic associations, as E.M. Forster does when the Marabar caves increasingly come to symbolize a European experience of India in *A Passage to India*.

For *symbolic order*, see the entries for HÉLÈNE CIXOUS and JACQUES LACAN in Section 5.

Signification/*signifié*/signified/signifier See SIGN

Signifying practice In his Introduction to JULIA KRISTEVA's *Desire in Language* Leon S. Roudiez quotes Kristeva's definition of this term from her *La Traversée des signes*:

> I shall call signifying practice the establishment and the countervailing of a sign system. Establishing a sign system calls for the identity of a speaking

subject within a social framework, which he recognizes as a basis for that identity. Countervailing the sign system is done by having the subject undergo an unsettling, questionable process; this indirectly challenges the social framework with which he had previously identified, and it thus coincides with times of abrupt changes, renewal, or revolution in society.

(Kristeva: 1980, 18)

See also DISCOURSE (discursive practice); IDEOLOGY; UTTERANCE

Simile A statement of comparison or equivalence which uses a grammatical conjunction such as 'like', 'as', or 'as if'. One example is 'my love is like a red, red rose' where certain qualities of the flower are associated with the lady. Contrast METAPHOR.

Simulacrum (pl. simulacra) An image, representation, or copy. Associated with English translations of the work of Jean Baudrillard, who argues that we now live in a world in which such representations precede, and indeed create, that which they ostensibly represent.

Sjužet See STORY AND PLOT

Skaz A mode or technique of narration that mirrors oral NARRATIVE. A useful alternative definition of the term is given by Ann Banfield, who points out that apart from the EPISTOLARY form, *skaz* 'is the only type of literary first person narrative which clearly has a second person' (1982, 172). The term comes from the Russian, as RUSSIAN FORMALIST theorists were the first to tackle the issues raised by *skaz*, but there are many non-Russian examples. For example, from a technical point of view much of Joseph Conrad's *Heart of Darkness* can be described as *skaz*, as much of what we read represents the CHARACTER Marlow's ORAL address to listeners.

Soliloquy A speech made by a single CHARACTER in a drama, and assumed to be heard only by the audience. The soliloquy represents an early attempt to represent a character's most intensely private emotions and ideas. Examples can be found in *Hamlet*, in which the PROTAGONIST debates whether to seek revenge for his father's murder, or kill himself. At this point his grief threatens his sanity, and the soliloquy affords us an insight into the extremes of his mental suffering. Compare ASIDE.

Sonnet A fourteen-line LYRIC poem, traditionally written in iambic pentameter and associated with love, and capable of a variety of fixed rhyme schemes. The word derives from the Italian 'sonnetto,' or little song. The *Petrarchan* or *Italian Sonnet* is divided into two main sections, the *octave* (first eight lines) and the *sestet* (last six lines). The octave allows the writer to develop an idea or a mood, and then (after the *volta* or turn in the eighth line) to change direction in some way. John Milton often uses this FORM in his sonnets: in 'How Soon Hath Time', the speaker agonizes over a choice to be made between serving God and writing poetry: by the seventh line, he has found that writing poetry is the way to serve God. Petrarchan sonnets can be identified by their rhyme schemes, the most common of which is ABBA ABBA CDE CDE (though the rhyme in the sestet can vary).

The *English* or *Shakespearean Sonnet* (perfected but not invented by Shakespeare), contains three *quartets* (sometimes inaccurately referred to as *quat-rains*, see STANZA), and a *couplet*, and is more technically challenging in the sense that it involves a greater number of rhyming words. The most common rhyme scheme is ABAB CDCD EFEF GG. Though it varies, the form of the poem encourages the deliberate and thorough consideration of an argument or idea, which is then wittily illustrated or summed up in some way by the final couplet – which tends to be EPIGRAMMATIC. The *Spenserian sonnet* uses an interlaced rhyme scheme, or ABAB BCBC CDCD EE, so that each quartet links with, and develops from, the next. A sonnet sequence or cycle is a group of sonnets written by one poet, and often linked by a common theme or source of inspiration. There are many poems which without being full sonnets seem to resemble the form. (Examples include Shelley's 'Ode to the West Wind' and Keats's 'Ode to a Nightingale'.) Not all sonnets are about love in the conventional, romantic, sense, either: Wordsworth expresses his patriotism and sense of empire in his sonnet 'Composed Upon Westminister Bridge'.

Speech act theory See Section 3, p. 174

Spondee See METRE

Stanza A more formally correct term for what is often referred to as a 'verse'. A stanza is formed by a group of lines in a poem which constitute a separate unit. Moreover, a stanza has a construction that exhibits formal features repeated in comparable units. 'Verse' originally denoted a single line of poetry, which is why the term 'stanza' is to be preferred. A simple rule-of-thumb test is whether groups of lines exhibiting formal similarities are separated by spaces from preceding and succeeding lines. Not all poems are composed of separate stanzas. A long poem may lack subdivisions, and extended 'books' or sections in a long poem that exhibit no regular formal patterning are not normally referred to as stanzas.

The following are the most common examples of stanza: tercet (three lines); quatrain (four lines); quintain (five lines); sextain (six lines); septet (seven lines).

Sometimes these terms are used to refer to units of lines within a poem which do not constitute separate stanzas, but more correct terms for such units (especially when referring to the parts of a SONNET) are: couplet (two lines); triplet (three lines); quartet (four lines); quintet (five lines); sestet (six lines).

A *heroic couplet* is a rhyming pair of ten-syllable lines, usually in iambic pentameter form.

The terms *octave* and *octet* both refer either to an eight-line stanza or a group of eight lines within a poem.

Stereotype Originally taken from a process in printing, the term has become a Standard English phrase for a concept, term, or description that is fixed and unchanging – normally with a pejorative ring, suggesting that oversimplification and prejudice are involved in its formation and use. It has played an important part in recent FEMINIST theory in connection with the description of fixed and, normally, patriarchal or SEXIST views of GENDER roles and characteristics.

Thus the central third chapter in Mary Ellmann's very influential book *Thinking About Women* (first published 1968) is devoted to 'Feminine Stereotypes', and lists formlessness, passivity, instability, confinement, piety, materiality, spirituality, irrationality and compliancy – along with 'two incorrigible figures': the shrew and the witch.

Stereotyping is not directed only at women, of course: we can isolate stereotypes based on race or CULTURE, on age, on profession, and so on.

Story and plot With this item we are concerned with an essentially very simple distinction which is of fundamental importance in NARRATOLOGY but which is surrounded by minefields of confusing vocabulary. The distinction is between, on the one hand, a *series of real or fictitious events, connected by a certain logic or chronology, and involving certain ACTORS*, and on the other hand, the *NARRATION of this series of events*. Thus were one to be asked to give the story of *Wuthering Heights*, a suitable response would be to start with the first arrival of the child Heathcliff at Wuthering Heights and then proceed to recount the events of the NOVEL in chronological order until the death of Heathcliff and the (possible) reuniting of him with Cathy. But the plot of *Wuthering Heights* is these events *in the order that they are actually presented in Emily Brontë's novel*. Thus the same story can give rise to many different plots, as FORMULAIC literature reveals very clearly.

The 'minefields' mentioned earlier arise from the fact that the same distinction is also referred to by means of the Russian words *fabula* (story) and *sjužet* (plot), and in some translations these are rendered in ways that conflict with the usage associated with story and plot. Mieke Bal, for example, renders our story and plot as *fabula* and *story* (1985, 5), a usage which is also adopted by Onega and Landa (1996), which gives *story* the opposite meaning from that with which we started.

Meanwhile other translators of RUSSIAN FORMALIST texts have suggested that *fabula* be rendered as *plot* – thus giving *plot* exactly the opposite meaning from that suggested in our 'story and plot'. (Other translators have suggested FABLE and *subject* for *fabula* and *sjužet*, which introduces yet further possibilities of confusion.)

Stream of consciousness As the term suggests, this refers to a NARRATIVE technique whereby a single CHARACTER's consciousness is represented – often as a loose sequence of associated emotions and thoughts, in language which is not structured or constrained by the conventions of grammar or logic. *Interior monologue* (or internal monologue) overlaps with stream of consciousness, and is sometimes used as a synonym for it, but should be distinguished from it. The key difference is that internal monologue gives us the words actually used by a character in thought, whereas stream of consciousness uses words to convey mental processes which may not themselves be wholly or even partly verbal. The final section of James Joyce's *Ulysses* is thus both stream of consciousness and interior monologue (we are given the words Molly Bloom actually uses in her thoughts), but much of Virginia Woolf's fiction is stream of consciousness but not internal monologue.

Stress See METRE

Structuralism See Section 3, p. 163

Structure It is usual to make a distinction between a literary work's structure and its plot (see STORY AND PLOT): whereas a work's plot can be seen as the NARRATIVE arrangement of its story, *structure* refers to its total (or total AESTHETIC) organization.

A more technical definition developed both from STRUCTURALISM and Systems Theory is given by Anthony Wilden: 'Structure is the ensemble of laws which govern the behavior of the system' (1972, 242). Moreover, these laws control elements or components which are interchangeable – thus an economic system stays the same even though the economic acts which it enables and controls are all unique. This takes us to the structuralist commitment to a set of enabling rules ('LITERARINESS') which remain the same even though the literary WORKS or acts of READING enabled or controlled by the rules change.

The paired terms *deep structure* and *surface structure*, originated by the linguistician Noam Chomsky, denote elements in his Standard Theory. According to this theory, the following sentences would be seen to have the same deep structure, but different surface structures:

The ploughman homeward plods his weary way.
Weary, the ploughman plods his way homeward.
The ploughman plods his weary way homeward.

Surface structure is derived from deep structure by means of transformations: hence transformational grammar. Chomsky's theory is controversial amongst linguisticians, and amongst non-linguisticians (literary critics, for example) it seems fair to say that the terms *deep structure* and *surface structure* are used only METAPHORICALLY.

See also PRAGUE SCHOOL, p. 146

Structure of feeling The term is the coinage of the Welsh CULTURAL theorist and novelist RAYMOND WILLIAMS. In his *Raymond Williams: Literature, Marxism and Cultural Materialism* (1999), John Higgins traces this term in Williams's work from its first appearance in *Drama in Performance* (1954) through to later works and interviews. Higgins argues that in its inception the term was 'used as a deliberate challenge and alternative to the existing explanatory framework of Marxist literary and cultural analysis', although by 'the time of the interviews with the New Left Review team . . . structure of feeling had become known as one of Williams's most characteristic concepts, a keyword of Williams's own vocabulary, and just as shifting and unstable in its conceptual identity as any item in *Keywords* itself' (1999, 37; for the interviews mentioned, see Williams: 1979).

Williams's most extended definitional and explanatory treatment of the term comes in a single chapter of his book *Marxism and Literature*. According to Williams, the term is deliberately chosen to emphasize a distinction from more formal concepts such as *world-view* or IDEOLOGY; the reason for this, he states, is that we are 'concerned with meanings and values as they are actively lived and felt', and with 'characteristic elements of impulse, restraint, and TONE; specifically affective elements of consciousness and relationships: not feeling as against thought, but thought as felt and feeling as thought: practical consciousness of a present kind, in a living and interrelating continuity' (1977, 132).

So far as its relation to literature is concerned, Williams gives a relevant example. He argues that whereas early Victorian ideology specified the exposure caused by poverty, debt or illegitimacy as social failure or deviation, the structure of feeling represented in the works of Dickens, Emily Brontë and others specified exposure and isolation as a general condition, and poverty, debt, or illegitimacy as its connecting instances – a view represented at the ideological level only later (1977, 134). In this view structures of feeling are pre-ideological formations developed almost unconsciously, antagonistic to existing ideological formations, and expressed through (among other things) art and literature.

Style and stylistics The noun *style* has a long history and wide set of meanings: the *OED* devotes over six page-columns to its various definitions. It derives from a Latin term meaning stake, or pointed instrument for writing (it shares a broad etymology with *stylus*), and modern meanings involve metaphorical and metonymic extensions of this meaning (see the entry for SYNTAGMATIC AND PARADIGMATIC). It is the thirteenth of the *OED*'s definitions that is most relevant to our present concerns: 'The manner of expression characteristic of a particular writer (hence of an orator) or of a literary group or period; a writer's mode of expression considered in regard to clearness, effectiveness, beauty, and the like.'

In the second half of the twentieth century Stylistics grew up as a recognized academic discipline, situated on the borderline between the study of language and of literature (although stylistic ANALYSIS can be and is applied to non-literary TEXTS), and concerned to engage in technical study and analysis of what the *OED* calls 'manners of expression'. It is important for students of literature because – as a result of its close relation to and impingement on Literary Studies – it has brought a number of more specifically linguistic terms and methods of analysis into literary criticism and theory.

Styles can be categorized according to a number of principles: deliverer's intention (a humorous style); receiver's evaluation (an imprecise style); context (an inappropriate style or REGISTER); AESTHETIC (an ornate style); level of formality (a colloquial style); social CLASS (an urbane style) – and so on. For a linguistician these are relatively imprecise categories, of course, and the academic study of style typically involves an attempt to analyze what are perceived impressionistically as distinctive styles in more formal and objective ways, often through the use of statistical analysis directed at syntax, vocabulary, grammar, and so on.

At this level Stylistics involves an attempt to back up the hunches of Common Readers ('Hemingway has a distinctive, plain style') with statistical evidence. At another level, Stylistics can involve an attempt to go beyond the hunches of the Common Reader, detailing significant stylistic differences which may be functional but which are not necessarily noticed by the reader or listener.

For *Affective Stylistics*, see the entry for AFFECTIVE.

Subaltern See the entry for GAYATRI CHAKRAVORTY SPIVAK in Section 5

Subject and subjectivity The traditional sense of *subject* as an abbreviation of *the conscious or thinking subject*, meaning the self or ego (*OED*), or individual *cogito*, has been pressed into service in a largely pejorative sense in recent theoretical writing. The main targets for attack in this process have been (i) the view that the human subject is somehow a point of origin for larger historical, social or even personal movements and events, and (ii) the belief that the individual human being is possessed of valid self-knowledge and is self-actuating – in a phrase, in charge and control of him/herself.

A more detailed account of one particular example of this use of *subject* can be found in the entry for INTERPELLATION, in which the position of the French MARXIST philosopher Louis Althusser is outlined. According to Althusser, all IDEOLOGY '*hails or interpellates concrete individuals as concrete subjects*, by the functioning of the category of the subject' (1971, 162). Thus *subject* represents the individual's self-consciousness and consciousness of self after having been 'body-snatched' by ideology. Althusser's position here forms the theoretical basis for a discussion by Etienne Balibar and Pierre Macherey of the specific role played by literature in this process. According to them, through the endless functioning of its TEXTS,

> literature unceasingly 'produces' *subjects*, on display for everyone. So paradoxically using the same schema we can say: literature endlessly transforms (concrete) individuals into subjects and endows them with a quasi-real hallucinatory individuality.
>
> (1978, 10)

These subjects are not just the Readers of literature, but also the Author and his Characters (Balibar and Macherey's capitals).

According to such views the subject is site rather than CENTRE or PRESENCE, is where things happen, or that to which things happen, rather than that which makes things happen: extra-individual forces use the subject to exert their sway, the subject does not use them (although it thinks that it does, and this is part of the cunning of the system). This is the stance generally adopted by POST-STRUCTURALISM, for which a major target is the view of the subject as primary, unified, self-present, self-determining, autonomous, and homogeneous. For post-structuralism the subject is, rather, secondary, constructed (by language, or ideology, for instance), volatile, standing in its own shadow, and self-divided.

If we turn to recent FEMINIST theory we find a rather more nuanced attitude to the subject and to subjectivity. During the earlier years of the rebirth of the Women's Movement in the 1960s and 1970s one finds evidence of a far less antagonistic view of the subject – a belief that the subjective might actually provide a rallying point *against* SEXIST ideas, and against the ideology of patriarchy.

For discussion of decentring the subject, see the entry for CENTRE, and compare the entry for INTERSUBJECTIVITY.

Sub-text That which is implied but not directly or overtly stated. The term originates in theatrical usage, and is associated with the so-called *Theatre of Silence* – the normal English translation of the *Théâtre de l'Inexprimé* founded by Jean-Jacques Bernard in the 1920s. The modern dramatist most associated with the term is Harold Pinter, whose plays typically have, critics agree, sub-texts of a violent or sexual nature which is unstated on the surface. The term typically also implies a certain consistency in implied meaning: thus the sub-text of a given work is unlikely to consist of a sequence of meanings which have nothing in common with one another.

Superstructure See BASE AND SUPERSTRUCTURE

Symbol See SIGN

Symbolists Applied mainly to certain French writers of the late nineteenth century, who reacted against prevailing techniques of NATURALISM and REALISM in literature. The GENRE associated with Symbolism is poetry: writers concentrated on SUBJECTIVE experience, and conveyed intense emotional experience through association and suggestion, the manipulation of sound patterns, and the deployment of private SYMBOLS.

Synaesthesia The employment of words associated with one sense in order to describe another. For example, in the fifth STANZA of John Keats's 'Ode to a Nightingale', the speaker refers to the perfume of flowers hanging upon the boughs of the trees. He responds so intensely to the scent that he imagines it suspended from the branches like any other visible object. But smells cannot be seen: the poet uses synaestheia to suggest how tangible the aroma is to him. The language of sight is transferred to the language of smell.

Synecdoche See METONYMY AND SYNECDOCHE

Syntagmatic and paradigmatic According to FERDINAND DE SAUSSURE's account of language in the *Course in General Linguistics*, '[c]ombinations supported by linearity are *syntagms*', while those 'co-ordinations formed outside discourse' that are 'not supported by linearity' but are 'a part of the inner storehouse that makes up the language of each speaker', 'are *associative relations*' (1974, 123). Present-day usage tends to favour the term *paradigms* over *associative relations*. Thus to construct a grammatical sentence we have to select words according to one set of rules, and combine them according to another set. The first are *paradigmatic* (or *associative*) rules and the second are *syntagmatic* rules. Take the following sentence.

The cat sat on the mat.

Here the first word could be replaced by 'A' or 'No'; the second word could be replaced by 'dog' or 'boy'. The relations between the words within these groups of alternatives (alternative according to the rules of grammar and syntax, but not, of course, *semantically* interchangeable) are *paradigmatic*; that is to say, they involve rules which govern the *selection* (not the combination) of words used in a sentence. But once one has chosen 'The' as the first word, one's selection of the second word is constrained: it cannot, for example, be 'a'. This is because there are rules governing the *combination* of words in a sentence: *syntagmatic* rules.

Another way of expressing the distinction is as Jonathan Culler puts it: syntagmatic relations bear on the possibility of combination; paradigmatic relations determine the possibility of substitution (1975, 13).

In 1956 ROMAN JAKOBSON published an article entitled 'Two Aspects of Language and Two Types of Aphasic Disturbances' which relied heavily upon a distinction between what Jakobson referred to as the metaphoric and the metonymic modes. In traditional usage METONYMY is a figure of speech in which the name of one item is given to another item, either an attribute of it or one associated by *contiguity* to it. Thus 'The pen is mightier than the sword' works by means of metonymy: *pen* and *sword* stand for those activities with which they are closely associated. Under the heading of 'metonymy' Jakobson includes SYNEC-DOCHE – that is, the use of a part to represent a whole: 'bloodshed' for war, for example. METAPHOR, in contrast, relies upon *similarity* rather than contiguity.

Through reference to the varying forms of aphasia experienced by patients with cerebral impairments, Jakobson was able to argue that the metaphoric and metonymic processes were governed by localized brain functions. These different processes (or modes) Jakobson related, in turn, to what he described, following Saussure, as the selection and combination axes of language. Metaphor and metonymy were thus, according to Jakobson, governed by specific brain functions which also governed these two fundamental axes of language. According to Jakobson, all examples of aphasic disturbance consisted of some impairment of either the faculty for selection or of that for combination and contexture.

Jakobson did not stop here, but attempted to generalize his discoveries and to claim that although both processes were operative in normal verbal behaviour, the influence of CULTURAL pattern, personality or verbal STYLE could lead to preference being given to one of the two processes over the other. From here, Jakobson then moves to consider literature. He claims that whereas the metaphoric process is primary in Romanticism and Symbolism, metonymy is predominant in REALISM (Jakobson and Halle: 1971, 91–2).

Jakobson's article has itself been very influential; JACQUES LACAN refers to it in his essay 'The Agency of the Letter in the Unconscious or Reason Since Freud' (in Lacan: 1977, 146B78), and David Lodge structures his book *The Modes of Modern Writing* (1977) around an attempt to apply and extend what Jakobson says about metaphor and metonymy to the ANALYSIS and INTERPRETATION of literary TEXTS.

Jakobson's work has not been without its critics, however, and in 1998 in an article entitled 'The Naming Disease: How Jakobson's Essay on Aphasia Initiated Postmodern Deceits', James Drake launched an uncompromising frontal attack on Jakobson. Drake claimed that Jakobson distorted the nineteenth-century aphasiologist Hughlings Jackson's work by selective quotation, and he used formulations such as 'Jakobson's frauds'.

According to Robert Scholes, 'neo-Freudians' such as 'Jacques Lacan and his circle' have reminded us that Jakobson's metaphor and metonymy are very close in meaning to Freud's CONDENSATION AND DISPLACEMENT (1982, 75–6).

Telling and showing A distinction that can be found in Percy Lubbock's *The Craft of Fiction* (1921), but which Lubbock probably got from Henry James. The distinction is between the use of *direct statement* in a NARRATIVE (telling), and other more indirect techniques such as suggestion, implication, enactment – all of which display certain qualities, characteristics or events to a reader who has to use his or her powers of deduction to work them out.

Text and work In his essay 'Theory of the Text' ROLAND BARTHES suggests that whereas the work is 'a finished object, something computable, which can occupy a physical space', 'the text is a methodological field', and that '[t]he work is held in the hand, the text in language'. Barthes continues, suggesting that one can put the matter in another way:

> [I]f the work can be defined in terms that are heterogeneous to language (everything from the format of the book to the socio-historical determinations which produced that book), the text, for its part, remains homogeneous to language through and through: it is nothing other than language and can exist only through a language other than itself. In other words, 'the text can be felt only in a work, a production': that of 'signifiance'.
>
> (1981b, 39–40)

(Barthes's quotation is from his own *Image-Music-Text*;
for *signifiance*, see the entry for SIGN)

Barthes's distinction suggests a different definition of *work*, at any rate, from that current in most contemporary literary-critical usage. JEROME J. McGANN provides us with this more current usage:

> ['Works'] refer to cultural products conceived of as the issue of a large network of persons and institutions which operate over time, in numbers of different places and periods. 'Texts' are those cultural products when they are viewed more restrictively, as language structures constituted in specific ways over time by a similar network of persons and institutions. Barthes' critique of the concept of the poetical 'work' was a salutary move against the naive idea of poems as stable and defined objects. His related effort to install the concept of 'text' in literary discourse has much less to recommend it, since

> this concept – while it has promoted certain forms of dialectical thinking in criticism – has also broadened the gap between the empirical and the reflective dimensions of literary studies.
>
> (1985, 20 n. 27)

In another usage, *text* is a synonym of *edition*, so that when in Section 1 we advise students to buy the recommended texts of prescribed works, we are in effect talking about the recommended editions of these works.

Theme and thematics In traditional literary-critical usage the term *theme* suffers from a certain AMBIGUITY. Whereas for some critics it implies a certain claim, doctrine or argument raised either overtly or implicitly throughout a literary WORK (or by the work as a whole), for others the term *thesis* is used with this meaning, and theme is reserved for what one can better call an issue. Prince suggests the useful distinction that whereas a thesis involves both a question and a proposed answer or answers, a theme 'does not promote an answer but helps to raise questions' (1988, 97).

A theme is generally also distinguished from a *motif* (or *leitmotif*) by its greater ABSTRACTION: motifs are generally linked to specific, concrete forms of manifestation whereas, for example, one can trace 'the theme of working-class socialization' in Alan Sillitoe's *Saturday Night and Sunday Morning* through a range of very different concrete examples. In contrast, Cedric Watts provides the reader of Joseph Conrad's *Lord Jim* in the Penguin edition with a list of *leitmotifs*, and these are all much more concrete or linked to specific and recurrent forms of words than this: 'butterflies and beetles'; 'dream, dreams'; 'glimpse (of Jim's CHARACTER) through mist or fog'; ' "in the ranks" '; 'jump, leap'; ' "nothing can touch me" '; ' "one of us" '; 'romance, romantic'; ' "under a cloud" '; 'veiled opportunity' (Conrad: 1986, 377). It will be noted that one can *attach* issues to some of these motifs, but they do not raise them overtly, and thus they cannot according to current CONVENTIONS be called either themes or theses.

To show how shifting is the use of these different terms, one can note that M.H. Abrams suggests that motif and theme are sometimes used interchangeably, but that theme is more usefully applied to a general claim or doctrine (1988, 111) – which of course is what Prince (see above) would dub a thesis.

GÉRARD GENETTE has borrowed 'from certain linguists' the distinction between *theme* (what one talks about) and *rheme* (what one says about it) (1997, 78), thus enabling him to distinguish between thematic and rhematic titles.

Thesis See THEME AND THEMATICS

Third-person narrator See STORY AND PLOT

Tone The sense of an AUTHOR's or NARRATOR's attitude to his or her CHARACTER, situation, or subject, as conveyed by the words he or she chooses. Sometimes used in a wider sense to describe the MOOD engendered in a READER by a particular WORK.

Top-down and bottom-up theories See Section 3, p. 139

Topos (pl. topoi) A traditional term, from the Greek meaning a 'commonplace', often referring to certain CONVENTIONALIZED places or SETTINGS consisting of a fixed combination of characteristic and stylized objects – a meadow, a tree, a running stream, for example (Bal: 1985, 96–7). The term is often used in a broader sense to include conventional collocations of MOTIFS, or THEMES, and in some present-day usages is very close to certain usages of STEREOTYPE.

Tragedy A GENRE or MODE in which suffering and calamity are used to explore aspects of the human condition.

According to Aristotle's *Poetics* (4th century BC), the purpose of tragedy was to arouse pity (*eleos*) and fear (*phobos*) to induce a feeling of emotional purging (or *katharsis*) in the audience. CLASSICAL and Elizabethan tragedy typically focused on the life of a PROTAGONIST of high birth (usually a king or queen, prince or princess) who, because of a fatal moral flaw or an error of judgement (HAMARTIA), experienced a disastrous reversal of fortune (*katastrophe* or *peripeteia*), and proceeded from happiness into suffering and even death. The success of the drama depends a great deal on the protagonist's mixture of pride, status and vulnerability: the audience must feel that he or she is not too perfect (and therefore distant from their own experience) or too evil (in which case, his or her fall would be entirely justified). Traditional tragedy suggests a view of the universe as indifferent to human fate, and essentially unjust: although protagonists have some weakness or fault which is the catalyst for their fall, they are caught up in circumstances over which they have no control, and their fate seems frequently out of proportion to the actual mistake that they made or weakness that they had. What they learn, however, is not so much acceptance as a greater insight into the human condition, and their appeal to their audience depends on the combination of dignity and self-knowledge they acquire.

Medieval theories of tragedy centred more specifically on the rise and fall of people with political and social power – rulers, in short. At a time when even the privileged often died young so that royal succession was rapid, the idea of the 'wheel of fortune' had a strong appeal: those on top one day would be at the bottom the next. Also important are the contributions of the Roman playwright Seneca (first century AD): he introduced the five-act play, used ghost-CHARACTERS and messengers to supply important details of plot, and showed a world where evil often overcame good. His plays were often very violent, and this bloody dimension can be seen in the Elizabethan 'revenge tragedies', among them Thomas Kyd's *The Spanish Tragedy*, as well as Shakespeare's *Hamlet*.

Speculation concerning the alleged or desired 'death of tragedy' has returned regularly in modern times, often in association with the idea of the death of God. But so far tragedy has proved capable of adaptation to the vicissitudes of modern life.

Transgender A term used in a number of ways, but generally suggesting a lifestyle or an identity that mixes or transgresses CONVENTIONAL sex-gender associations. The term can imply that a person is born with the characteristics of both sexes or has had surgery to change his or her physical sexual characteristics. But it may also be used to describe the adoption of dress or behaviour that is conventionally associated with those of a different biological sex.

Much interesting study of CANONICAL literature concerned to show how it explores such challenges to the public GENDER system has resulted from recent work by those within such areas as QUEER THEORY and masculinity studies. In Henry James's short story 'The Death of the Lion', for example, the NARRATOR discovers that a newspaper journalist named Guy Walsingham is actually a woman, while one named Dora Forbes is referred to as 'he'. John Carlos Rowe suggests that this and other of James's tales have 'been rediscovered as tours de force of a gay aesthetic' (1998, 104). Such examples of James's whimsical humour are now being reinterpreted as partly concealed challenges to the dominant gender system, to the idea that the whole of humanity can be divided in BINARY terms between the male and the female.

Trochee See METRE

Trope From the Greek word for 'a turn', a trope was originally part of the vocabulary of rhetoric, and refers to a word or phrase that is used in a consciously different or figurative sense – and thus turned away from its literal meaning. METAPHOR, METONYMY and SIMILE are all classified as tropes.

Type Traditionally used to signify a fictional CHARACTER who represents a certain quality in people, or a specific kind of person. The term overlaps with STEREOTYPE but lacks its pejorative edge, and can be compared with E.M. Forster's concept of the 'flat character'. In earlier periods of literature, a set of conventional types was well known to both writers and readers or audiences.

Uncanny See FANTASTIC

Unconscious Sigmund Freud's development of a theory of the Unconscious is part of a general movement of thought that places a great emphasis upon the individual or collective mind's dark or hidden areas. The theory can be seen emerging in *Studies on Hysteria* – both in the parts of this work written by Freud and in those written by Joseph Breuer. Both writers were able to draw on a number of important traditions in Psychology in forming a coherent theory, but their actual case-histories also played an important role in this. Much could be written about the Freudian Unconscious, but for our present purposes it is probably most important to indicate the connection between the concept and the idea of *repression*. This has proved very convenient again to literary critics interested in explaining why a given literary work may have a tendency seemingly much at odds with the AUTHOR's expressed or consciously held beliefs and opinions.

Since Freud, various theorists have developed or challenged his theory of the Unconscious. Most influential in literary-critical circles is probably JACQUES LACAN, who makes his position clear when he talks of Freud's *discovery* of the Unconscious. Lacan defines the unconscious (he does not grant the term a capital letter) as 'that part of the concrete discourse, in so far as it is transindividual, that is not at the disposal of the subject in re-establishing the continuity of his conscious discourse' (1977, 49), and as 'that chapter of my history that is marked by a blank or occupied by a falsehood: it is the censored chapter' (1977, 50), and it shows us 'the gap through which neurosis recreates a harmony with a real – a real that may well not be determined' (1979, 22). Even so, it can be rediscovered – in monuments, in archival documents such as childhood memories, in semantic evolution, in traditions, and in surviving (conscious) traces (1977, 50).

Lacan provides a rather more accessible account of the unconscious in his lecture 'Of Structure as an Inmixing of an Otherness Prerequisite to Any Subject Whatsoever', in which he insists that the unconscious has nothing to do with instinct or primitive knowledge or preparation of thoughts in some underground. 'It is a thinking with words, with thoughts that escape your vigilance, your state of watchfulness.'

FREDRIC JAMESON's *The Political Unconscious* attempts to rehistoricize Freud's concept of the Unconscious and to reassign the CENTRE of the Freudian INTERPRETATIVE system (which Jameson sees as wish-fulfilment) to history and society rather than to the individual SUBJECT and individual psychobiology. Thus a number of associated Freudian concepts – repression, censorship, and so on – are resituated in a socio-historical context by Jameson, and thence applied to the reading of literary works.

See also CONDENSATION AND DISPLACEMENT

Unities According to Ludovico Castelvetro's 1570 Italian translation of Aristotle's *Poetics*, a TRAGEDY must be seen to observe three unities: of time, place and action. Ideally, the play should portray the events of a single day; there should be a single SETTING or location in which the action took place; and the play should have a single, coherent, plot. Although a commentary on, rather than a straight translation of, Aristotle's theories, Castelvetro's ideas proved influential because of their association with the Greek philosopher. Samuel Johnson's *Preface to Shakespeare* (first published in 1765) subjects the CONVENTION to scorn.

Utterance An utterance is generally regarded as a natural unit of linguistic *communication*. In her editorial Preface to her translation of M.M. BAKHTIN's *Problems of Dostoevsky's Poetics*, Caryl Emerson claims that the distinction between *utterance* and *sentence*

> is [Bakhtin's] own: a sentence is a unit of language, while an utterance is a unit of communication. Sentences are relatively complete thoughts existing within a single speaker's speech, and the pauses between them are

'grammatical,' matters of punctuation. Utterances, on the other hand, are impulses, and cannot be so normatively transcribed; their boundaries are marked only by a change of speech subject.

(Bakhtin: 1984, xxxiv)

In like manner, Jan Mukařovský attributes 'uniqueness and nonrepeatability' to the utterance in his essay 'The Esthetics of Language' (1964, 63).

See also DISCOURSE; ÉCRITURE; ENUNCIATION; LANGUE AND PAROLE; SPEECH

Verisimilitude Appearing real and resembling actual experience. In literature, the term refers to a sense of accuracy and credibility evoked by the inclusion of convincing details in the description of people and places. It is a CONVENTIONAL feature of REALISTIC or NATURALISTIC fiction.

Victorian See PERIODS OF LITERATURE

Voice This is a term used in a bewildering variety of ways, from the straightforwardly literal to the purely metaphorical. These usages can be mapped in the following entries: CARNIVAL; CHARACTER ZONE; CHRONOTOPE; DISCOURSE; FREE INDIRECT DISCOURSE; HETEROGLOSSIA; INTERIOR DIALOGUE; LINGUISTIC PARADIGM; PROJECTION CHARACTERS; PERSPECTIVE AND VOICE; POLYPHONIC; REGISTER; *SKAZ*; STORY AND PLOT.

Vraisemblance A French loan-word meaning 'appearance as real', close to the English VERISIMILITUDE, and used in discussions of REALISM. The term is not new (its use in discussion of art dates from the seventeenth century), but what is new is that it is used in an increasingly pejorative or dismissive sense the more the status of realism has been brought into question.

Weak ending The final syllable of a line of poetry which is assigned a stress by the METRICAL pattern, but which in normal pronunciation would be unstressed.

Well-made play A term that has come to have slightly negative CONNOTATIONS when applied to modern drama, but which is used to describe any play with a well-crafted PLOT. The key to such a plot is that there must always be something happening to drive it forward and to keep the audience entertained and interested. There are generally few CHARACTERS, but the relations between them are complex and changing. Oscar Wilde's *The Importance of Being Earnest* manages to be both a well-made play and a PARODY of its CONVENTIONS.

Work See TEXT AND WORK

Writerly See READERLY AND WRITERLY TEXTS

Section 5

Guide to Theorists

In this section you will find brief accounts of some of the most important recent figures in literary theory and criticism whose work you are likely to encounter in an undergraduate course. These entries are not included so as to allow you to avoid any first-hand acquaintance with the work of the individuals in question. On the contrary, our aim has been to allow you to situate these figures in an over-all map of the range of critical theories and approaches that covers the period during which modern literary studies developed, so that you can then plan for a direct engagement with the work of those individuals whose ideas are relevant to your own course of study.

Throughout this section you will see that frequent cross-references are made to entries in Sections 3 and 4. We advise you to get into the habit of following up such cross-references so as to build up a sense of the relationship between influential figures, critical and theoretical movements, and important terms and concepts.

For ease of reference, entries in this section are arranged alphabetically on the basis of the surnames of the individuals in question.

BAKHTIN, Mikhail Mikhailovich (1895–1975)

Main works

Rabelais and his World (1968; in Russian 1965)
The Dialogic Imagination: Four Essays (1981; in Russian 1975)
Problems of Dostoevsky's Poetics (1984; in Russian 1963, with an earlier version 1929)

Key terms

CARNIVAL ■ CENTRIFUGAL/CENTRIPETAL ■ CHARACTER ZONE ■ CHRONOTOPE ■ DIALOGIC ■ DISCOURSE ■ HETEROGLOSSIA ■ POLYGLOSSIA ■ POLYPHONIC ■ UTTERANCE

Bakhtin was born in Orel in Russia 1895. His father (though of the nobility) was a propertyless bank official. Bakhtin's childhood was spent in Orel, Vilnius and Odessa, and after a brief spell at university in Odessa he moved to study Greek and Latin at St Petersburg University, at just the time when major debates around what became known as RUSSIAN FORMALISM were taking place. He moved to Nevel in 1918 and Vitebsk in 1920. By this time what was later to be dubbed the 'Bakhtin circle' had been formed, consisting of individuals from disciplines and professions ranging from music to archaeology and philosophy. The group also included two writers who, Bakhtin was later to claim, lent their names to books that he had written: V.N. Vološinov (*Freudianism: A Marxist Critique*; *Marxism and the Philosophy of Language*), and P.N. Medvedev (*The Formal Method in Literary Scholarship*). The debate about the authorship of these works has not been fully resolved, and for the purpose of this entry they will not be considered as part of Bakhtin's *œuvre*. Medvedev's book is discussed briefly in Section 3, p. 145, while Vološinov's book on language is also discussed briefly in the same section, p. 167. For further brief discussion of Vološinov's book on formalism, see the entry for DIALOGIC in Section 4. One of Bakhtin's foremost English-speaking commentators, Caryl Emerson, has argued that the work of Vološinov and Medvedev is, unlike that of Bakhtin, situated within MARXISM, and a careful reading of the work of all three writers suggests that this view has much to recommend it.

For the next two and a half decades Bakhtin led a precarious and unsettled existence, working as a teacher between periods of political exile and imprisonment and unemployment. He wrote constantly, and at the end of the Second World War he became Professor of Russian and World Literature at the University of Saransk. He remained a somewhat suspect figure politically as his work was (correctly) adjudged to be at odds with the official line of socialist realism, and his dissertation on Rabelais (the basis of his later book) was awarded the degree of Candidate rather than Doctor in 1947 after very heated public debate about its merits. As Stalinism thawed or at least defrosted, his earlier writings were published: much that appeared in print for the first time in his later years had been begun very much earlier.

Bakhtin suffered from ill-health all his life; a bone disease (possibly helped by his lifelong chain-smoking) cost him a leg in 1938.

As the list of terms given above indicates, Bakhtin's influence on theoretical and critical thought in the English-speaking world has been massive ever since his work started to appear in English translation from the late 1960s onwards. In order to avoid duplication we refer readers to the discussion of these terms in Section 4, while limiting ourselves here to some general comments on the possible reasons for this great interest in Bakhtin's work.

First, the appearance of Bakhtin's work in English coincided with a renewed and reinvigorated attempt to theorise seriously about the NOVEL. Much of his best-known work focuses on the novel, its history and its GENERIC distinctiveness.

Second, Bakhtin's work became accessible in English at about the time that the influence of the NEW CRITICISM was definitely on the decline, and critics were keen to replace its insistence on the autonomy of the TEXT with approaches which respected the particularity of the text while exploring its dependency on – and contribution to – specific historical and intellectual contexts.

Third, and related to this, Bakhtin's intellectual position was consistently anti-individualist, stressing instead forms of social collaboration or conflict ranging from DIALOGUE to dethroning. His stressing of the importance of the UTTERANCE of living, interactive speech over the formal autonomy of the sentence chimed in with movements that would lead to developments in PRAGMATICS (see Section 3, p. 173) that opposed the formalism of not just the New Criticism but also of STRUCTURALISM.

Fourth, Bakhtin's work was infused with a consistently democratic and anti-authoritarian spirit, perhaps best exemplified in his concept of CARNIVAL.

Further reading

Michael Holquist, *Dialogism: Bakhtin and his World* (London: Routledge, 1990); Lynne Pearce, *Reading Dialogics* (London: Arnold, 1994); Tzvetan Todorov, *Mikhail Bakhtin: The Dialogical Principle* (Minneapolis: University of Minnesota Press, 1984).

BARTHES, Roland (1915–80)

Main works

On Racine (1964; in French, 1963)
Writing Degree Zero (1967; in French, 1953)
Elements of Semiology (1967; in French, 1964)
Mythologies (1972; in French, 1957)
S/Z (1974; in French, 1973)
The Pleasure of the Text (1975; in French, 1975)
Image–Music–Text (1977; contains essays published separately in French)
A Lover's Discourse: Fragments (1978; in French, 1977)

Key terms

codes of reading (see CODE) ■ death of the author (see AUTHOR) ■ ÉCRITURE ■ JOUISSANCE ■ MYTHOLOGY ■ READERLY AND WRITERLY TEXTS

Born in Cherbourg, France, Barthes was a student at the University of Paris, where he took a degree in Classics in 1939 and in Grammar and Philology in 1943. After positions at the *Centre National de la Recherche Scientifique* and the *École Pratique des Hautes Études*, he was the first to occupy the Professorship of Literary Semiotics at the *Collège de France*.

There are no neat ways to categorize or summarize Barthes's work as a whole. This is partly because his intellectual positions and associations with different artistic and other movements were constantly changing and developing, and partly because his writings deal with so many aspects of CULTURE, politics and art – although language and literature loom large in his *œuvre*. Barthes is the lexicographer's friend: a great coiner of terms and neologisms.

Barthes's *Elements of Semiology* introduced not just SEMIOTICS but also the basic ideas of STRUCTURALISM to English-speaking readers, while the extremely influential *Mythologies* was a key text in the development of CULTURAL STUDIES, demonstrating that familiar elements of everyday life in developed countries could be treated as cultural TEXTS and analyzed in such a way as to reveal their IDEOLOGICAL content and semiotic function.

Barthes approaches MYTHS as 'ideological abuse' hidden in the '*what-goes-without-saying*'. What he means by this, is that those assumptions and attitudes that are so generally accepted in a culture that they are invisible, contain and act out the motives of particular interest groups. Barthes's analysis of myths demonstrates how textual analysis can be politically challenging. A closing theoretical section in *Mythologies* dealing with 'Myth Today' argues, among other things, that myth is 'depoliticized speech' that deprives the object of which it speaks of all history.

For students of literature, three texts have been directly influential. *On Racine* precipitated an enormous row in French literary circles about the French new criticism or *nouvelle critique*, and called forth a book by Raymond Picard in 1965 entitled *Nouvelle critique ou nouvelle imposture?* ('New Criticism or New Imposture?'). Picard attacked Barthes for failing to enter into Racine's INTENTIONS, for relying upon illegitimate psychoanalyses, and for repeatedly and inappropriately dragging sexuality into his argument.

S/Z is structured around a detailed analysis of Honoré de Balzac's *Sarrasine*, which Barthes cuts up into 'units of reading' which he terms *lexias*, and analyzes in terms of five CODES OF READING. Perhaps of more importance than such technical issues is Barthes's engagement with the complexities of GENDER in Balzac's text. Certainly *S/Z* has played an important part in the development of FEMINIST literary theory and of such later developments as QUEER THEORY, although Barthes's own homosexuality was publicly revealed only after his death (which was caused by a traffic accident). Later works such as *The Pleasure of the Text* and *A Lover's Discourse: Fragments* have also been influential in the development of gender-oriented literary studies (introducing the term JOUISSANCE to English-speaking readers) and, particularly, in the development of a socio-historical interest in the body.

Perhaps Barthes's most influential text so far as literary studies is concerned is his essay 'The Death of the Author', which is reprinted in *Image–Music–Text*. Along with Michel Foucault's 'What is an Author?' this essay reinvigorated the attack on biographical forms of criticism just at the time when the decline of the NEW CRITICISM seemed to be weakening such attacks. Unlike the New Critics, however, Barthes's murderous intentions *vis-à-vis* the AUTHOR were aimed at strengthening the rights and influence not so much of the WORK but more of the READER, who '(re)writes' the text with every reading. The article contains what is perhaps Barthes's most quoted line: 'the birth of the reader must be at the cost of the death of the Author' (the selective use of capitalization is deliberate). See also the discussion in the entry for AUTHOR in Section 4.

Further reading

Louis-Jean Calvet, *Roland Barthes: A Biography* (Cambridge: Polity Press, 1994); Jonathan Culler, *Barthes* (London: Collins, 1990).

BEAUVOIR, Simone de (1908–86)

Main works

The Second Sex (1953; in French, 1949)

Key terms

FEMINISM ■ sexual politics ■ self and OTHER ■ STEREOTYPE ■ MYTH ■ existentialism

Simone de Beauvoir was an immensely prolific philosopher, novelist and political activist, who is now best known for her pioneering FEMINIST treatise, *The Second Sex*, first published in 1949 as *Le Deuxième Sexe*. It is this work that has proved influential within literary studies, where Beauvoir's analysis of the subordination of women within patriarchal societies has stimulated many of the concerns of modern feminist theory.

Beauvoir was born in Paris in 1908 into a traditional, bourgeois, Catholic family, the conservatism of which she reacted against as an adolescent and in her later career as an intellectual. An outstanding student from an early age, Beauvoir studied literature, classics and mathematics, before studying philosophy at the Sorbonne. In 1929 she excelled in the Sorbonne's notoriously difficult final examination, the *agrégation de philosophie*, which was taken the same year by Jean-Paul Sartre, the existentialist philosopher with whom Beauvoir had a life-long intellectual and personal relationship. She taught philosophy in various French schools until the mid-1940s, after which she devoted herself to writing.

Her literary output includes memoirs, letters, essays, travelogues and NOVELS, all of which are marked by a strong autobiographical content. Her novels, including the Prix Goncourt-winning *Les Mandarins* (1954), are largely fictional explorations of existentialist philosophy, with which, along with Sartre, she is associated. As a political activist she opposed French imperialism in Algeria and campaigned for many causes including improved safety for factory workers, women's abortion rights and social status, and, in later life, the rights of the elderly.

The Second Sex is a cornerstone of twentieth-century feminism. It had a powerful and controversial impact when it first appeared, and it has remained a CANONICAL work of feminist thought. The book adopts a number of perspectives – historical, biological, sociological, psychoanalytical, literary critical – to explore the question 'what is a woman?' Beauvoir argues that femininity is neither ESSENTIAL nor natural to females, but rather is a construction that is imposed upon and imprisons women. In a famous statement from the book, she asserts that 'one is not born, but rather becomes, a woman' – in other words, women's identities are created through social and cultural processes. In this way, her concerns have informed POST-STRUCTURALIST notions of subjectivity. Beauvoir argues that, historically and in contemporary Western societies, women have been defined by men and have been defined not as autonomous beings in their own right but as 'OTHERS', standing in a negative relation to men. Thus patriarchal IDEOLOGIES not only designate what 'woman' is, but they subordinate women in the process. These ideas have been further explored by theorists such as KATE MILLETT. Like VIRGINIA WOOLF, Beauvoir also reflects upon the constrictions imposed by women's secondary status upon women writers.

The Second Sex examines several literary works and shows how literature has functioned so as to propagate and uphold misogynist MYTHS of womanhood. Beauvoir's own critical practice, therefore, focuses upon literary representations and STEREOTYPES, but her influence upon subsequent feminist theorists and critics goes beyond the advancement of this critical methodology, and must include her generation and popularization of feminist politics in a more general sense. Her impact is most profound within Anglo-American feminism; more recent French feminist theorists – HÉLÈNE CIXOUS, LUCE IRIGARAY, JULIA KRISTEVA – have reacted against Beauvoir's anti-essentialism, which is not reconcilable with their emphasis upon women's difference as an agent of liberation (see ÉCRITURE FÉMININE).

Further reading

Margaret Crosland, *Simone de Beauvoir: The Woman and her Work* (London: Heinemann, 1992); Toril Moi, *Feminist Theory and Simone de Beauvoir* (Oxford: Blackwell, 1990); Toril Moi, *Simone de Beauvoir: The Making of an Intellectual Woman* (Oxford: Blackwell, 1994).

BENJAMIN, Walter (1892–1940)

Main works

Illuminations (1968; a translation of part of *Schriften* [1955])
Understanding Brecht (1973; in German, 1966)

Key terms

against the grain ■ AURA ■ FLÂNEUR ■ mechanical reproduction

Walter Benjamin was born into a German-Jewish middle-class family and educated in Switzerland during the First World War. His MARXISM dates from the early 1920s, partly as a result of friendships with influential Marxists and partly from his reading, which included GEORG LUKÁCS's *History and Class Consciousness*. Benjamin's Marxism was never (by the standards of the 1920s and, especially, the 1930s) orthodox, however, as is witnessed by his association with the FRANKFURT SCHOOL (he accepted commissions from the Institute of Social Research) and his defence of the work of both BERTOLT BRECHT and Franz Kafka against the attacks on them from theorists such as Lukács. *Understanding Brecht* contains some of the earliest and most valuable attempts to grapple with the playwright's profound originality, and 'Conversations with Brecht' (included in this collection and in Bloch *et al.*: 1977) reports fascinating snippets of conversation from Brecht from the years 1934–38.

In 1940, after trying to flee Nazi-occupied France (where he had been living), Benjamin committed suicide on the Spanish border when it became apparent that he would probably be returned to France.

Within the discipline of literary studies, Benjamin is best known for his activity as a defender, promoter and theorist of MODERNISM, especially in conjunction with his staunch support of the work and the theories of his friend Brecht. However, his importance is not limited to these activities. Although Benjamin's work and ideas were known to key figures in the Left of the inter-war period – Lukács, Adorno, Brecht – his work became widely known in English-speaking circles only in the 1970s. His most influential work up to now is certainly the essay 'The Work of Art in the Age of Mechanical Reproduction', which dates from 1936 and is included in *Illuminations*. In this essay Benjamin argues that mechanical reproduction represents something new, and that when applied to art (Benjamin suggests a date of around 1900 by which time the technical standards of reproduction had reached a significantly higher level) this caused 'the most profound change in their [transmitted works of art] impact upon the public'. Involved in this profound change, according to Benjamin, are a number of elements: a loss of authenticity or AURA, detachment from the realm of tradition, and the far greater accessibility of art to people at large. In losing its uniqueness, then, the work of art assumes a historically quite new identity. Benjamin has much of interest to say about film in the essay, at a time when serious investigation into the medium or APPARATUS of film was relatively rare. Among other things, Benjamin suggests that film actually enriches the field of human perception.

Also included in *Illuminations*, the essay 'The Storyteller' brings the same sharp sense of historical change to the issue of NARRATIVE, and includes illuminating comment on the relationship between the decline of ORAL storytelling and the rise of the NOVEL.

Further reading

Momme Brodersen, *Walter Benjamin: A Biography* (London: Verso, 1996); Terry Eagleton, *Walter Benjamin: Or, Towards a Revolutionary Criticism* (London: Verso, 1991); David S. Ferris (ed.), *Walter Benjamin: Theoretical Questions* (Stanford, CA: Stanford University Press, 1996).

SECTION 5

BHABHA, Homi K. (1949–)

Main works

Nation and Narration (ed.) (1990)
The Location of Culture (1994)

Key terms

POSTCOLONIAL ■ identity ■ 'in-between' ■ interstices ■ hybridity ■ 'third space'

Since the publication in 1994 of *The Location of Culture*, Homi Bhabha has had a major impact upon POSTCOLONIAL theory and has stimulated a radical rethinking of how colonial encounters are articulated. His primary preoccupation has been to re-conceive EUROCENTRIC representations of the 'location of CULTURE' which have tended to uphold BINARY oppositions between the poles of East and West, master and slave, self and OTHER, and so on. Bhabha insists that a 'third space' should be recognized and celebrated – an 'in-between' space in which different identities interact, not in relations of pure dominance and subjection but in creative hybrid relations.

Bhabha's own cultural identity is notably 'in-between'. He grew up and took his first degree in Bombay. He comes from the Parsis, an Indian minority group that Bhabha describes as necessarily hybridized both within India, where the ethnic and religious Parsi identity must negotiate with Hindu customs, and in interaction with other cultures throughout the globe. Moving from India, Bhabha took Masters and Doctoral degrees at Oxford – undertaking research on colonial experience – and from 1978 he taught English at Sussex University. Following work at the universities of Princeton and Pennsylvania, Bhabha has been Professor of English, Art History and Southern Asian Studies at the University of Chicago.

The Location of Culture is a collection of previously-published essays treating a variety of writers and THEMES with a singularity of purpose outlined in the introduction and conclusion. Taking leads from EDWARD SAID's explorations of the cultural ramifications of imperialism, Bhabha asserts the centrality of the postcolonial condition to modern experience and explores how issues of nationhood are mediated by AUTHORS including Joseph Conrad, Toni Morrison, Salman Rushdie and Derek Walcott, and in other TEXTS such as documents from the Indian mutiny. Bhabha homes in on texts which articulate or embody encounters between different races and classes, and he explores the limitations of the simple view that the colonizer's power reshapes the colonized SUBJECT, arguing instead that colonial encounter transforms identities on both sides of the power relation. He is drawn to instances where cultures overlap: 'It is in the emergence of the interstices – the overlap and displacement of domains of difference – that the intersubjective and collective experiences of *nationness*, community interest, or cultural value are negotiated.' There are POST-STRUCTURALIST leanings in his breaking down of ESSENTIALIZED notions of self and OTHER, first world and third world, and in his insistence that it is no longer possible to conceive of national identities in any 'pure', unitary sense. Identities, for Bhabha, are 'performative' (see SPEECH-ACT THEORY, Section 3) – they are formed and renegotiated through acts of ENUNCIATION within changing contexts. He draws on PSYCHOANALYTIC conceptions of how identities develop: intercultural encounters function as mirrors, providing visions of difference which contribute to NARRATIVES of self-image (see JACQUES LACAN).

It can be said that Bhabha's work is both an analysis of interculturally-marked texts and a manifesto promoting a view of cultural 'in-betweenness' as a matrix of potentially positive, creative interactions. A 'willingness to descend into that alien territory', he writes, 'may reveal that the theoretical recognition of the split-space of enunciation may open the way to conceptualizing an *inter*national culture, based not on the exoticism of multiculturalism or the *diversity* of cultures, but on the inscription and articulation of culture's *hybridity*'. Within literary studies, Bhabha's work has significantly re-inflected postcolonial approaches to criticism, and it has massively popularized the analysis (and even writing) of texts which articulate colonial encounter.

Further reading

Bill Ashcroft, Gareth Griffiths and Helen Tiffin, *The Empire Writes Back: Theory and Practice in Postcolonial Literatures* (London: Routledge, 1989); Robert Young, *Colonial Desire: Hybridity in Theory, Culture and Race* (London: Routledge, 1995).

BLOOM, Harold (1930–)

Main works

The Anxiety of Influence (1973)
A Map of Misreading (1975)
The Western Canon (1994)

Key terms

ANXIETY OF INFLUENCE ▪ Balkanization ▪ CANON ▪ precursors ▪ misreading ▪ misprision ▪ REVISIONISM

Born in the East Bronx area of New York City in 1930, Harold Bloom was the youngest child of Orthodox Jewish immigrants from Russia. He obtained his BA from Cornell University in 1951, and his doctorate from Yale in 1955. Staying at Yale, he joined the English faculty as a junior lecturer. In 1977, he was appointed DeVane Professor of Humanities; since 1988, he has also been Berg Professor of English at the New York University. He is a prolific and sometimes controversial writer, with more than 20 books of literary and religious criticism to his credit.

Bloom's intellectual range and output are so prodigious that any short description must necessarily reduce and simplify the scale of his achievement. Certain key aspects of his career are of particular importance to students of literature, however. During the 1970s, he authored two major works: *The Anxiety of Influence* (1973) and *A Map of Misreading* (1975). In the first of these, he proposed a dynamic model of repression in the relation between new and old poets, since at least the Renaissance. He argued that in the young poet's desire to emulate and at the same time escape the influence of 'precursors' (the great writers of the past), considerable creative and motivational energies were released. Although these energies emerged from a kind of fear and were in one sense oppositional, they allowed the successful writer to fulfil greater aspects of his imaginative potential.

Bloom's model was loosely based on Freud's theory of the Oedipus complex, whereby the son competes with and revolts against the father, in order to outdo him and realize himself. In *A Map of Misreading*, he extends this insight into a fundamental theory: poetry results from poets repressing the works that influence them through conscious and unconscious acts of correction and improvement, or misreading. This process Bloom also called 'misprision'. Interestingly, Bloom proposed a similar understanding of critical practice: in order to free themselves and to create original readings, critics had to 'misread' the literature of the past. (See also the entry for REVISIONISM.)

Because Bloom happened to teach at Yale during the 1970s, he was briefly associated with the DECONSTRUCTION practised by several of his prominent colleagues, including PAUL DE MAN and J. HILLIS MILLER. But the logic of Bloom's thinking, his emphasis on imaginative originality and the importance of the Western literary heritage, is opposed to the basic tenets of deconstruction. This is especially clear in *The Western Canon: The Books and School of the Ages*, a study of 26 canonical writers. In *The Western Canon*, Bloom takes issue with what he sees as the 'Balkanization' of literature as an academic discipline, by which he means its division into enclaves of CLASS, ethnicity, GENDER or religion. He attacks critics who promote political and sociological approaches to reading and evaluating literary documents. Among those schools he berates are FEMINISM, MARXISM, and NEW HISTORICISM, and as a result Bloom has often (and wrongly) been described as spokesperson for the political right. In fact, although strongly committed to a CANON of great books and writers, he emphatically denounces those who would judge works according to their moral content. Nevertheless, his model of literature is not a democratic one: there are only a few minds capable of creating, appreciating and understanding it.

Among the criticisms levelled at Bloom, perhaps the most serious are that his list of great writers includes very few women, that his list is based upon arbitrary selections, and that the Oedipal model of inter-generational rivalry and imaginative originality is notoriously chauvinist. There are alleged inconsistencies in his work: since criticism (in his view) is essentially an act of misreading, it could be argued that feminists, Marxists or LACANIANS can hardly be blamed for applying the wrong criteria to literary works.

Further reading

Graham Allen, *Harold Bloom: A Poetics of Conflict* (New York: Harvester Wheatsheaf, 1994); Peter De Bolla, *Harold Bloom: Towards Historical Rhetorics* (London: Routledge, 1988); Lars Ole Sauerberg, *Versions of the Past, Visions of the Future* (Houndsmill: Macmillan Press, 1997).

BRECHT, Bertolt (1898–1956)

Main works

Brecht on Theatre: The Development of an Aesthetic (1964)
The Messingkauf Dialogues (1965; in German, 1963)
Collected Plays (1970–)
Poems 1913–1928 (3 vols, 1976)
'Against Georg Lukács' (1977; in German, 1967 but written 1938)

Key terms

ALIENATION EFFECT ■ apparatus

Bertolt Brecht's activity as poet and (especially) dramatist, as political activist, and as theorist cannot and should not be seen in isolation from one another. Brecht is the opposite of an ABSTRACT theorist: his theoretical work is committed rather than disinterested. It arose out of particular cultural, artistic and political situations, chief amongst which have to be the political struggles of the left in Germany prior and subsequent to the Nazi takeover in 1933, and the attempt to harness cultural activity involving the working class to these struggles. Brecht was consistently interested in an art that did what W.H. Auden (in his poem 'In Memory of W.B. Yeats') was later to claim that poetry could not do: make things happen.

Brecht's intellectual tendencies are very clearly expressed in his polemic 'Against Georg Lukács', written in 1938 but not published in German until 1967. In his argument with LUKÁCS about the concept of REALISM, for example, Brecht effectively argues that there is no satisfactory intrinsic or ESSENTIALIST definition of the term: a work of art's 'realism' will vary according to the circumstances of its reception, circumstances that include specifically artistic CONVENTIONS and traditions but that extend also to matters of audience and to social and political realities outside the theatre or the study. Brecht used the term *apparatus* to describe those often invisible or disregarded conventions, traditions, and material elements – from theatres, actors and audiences to censors and subsidies – which together constitute the conditions for producing a play. Brecht is thus a genuinely dialectical thinker, one who seeks always for connections and contexts rather than essences and absolutes, and whose ideas are fundamentally and self-consciously rooted in specific historical and political realities. His unrelenting dedication to the left and opposition to fascism (which forced him into a succession of exiles) did not blend well with the essentialist certainties of Stalinism, and his loyalty to

SECTION 5

the positions of Communist Parties in power and in opposition was always a qualified one (he was never a party member).

For students of literature two aspects of his work are of particular importance. First, his resistance to the condemnation of MODERNISM advanced by Lukács and others, and second, his advocacy of a distanced, intellectual response to art rather than an empathic, emotional one. The latter aspect of Brecht's work has retained a topicality and a challenge that the former has lost with the passing of 'socialist realist' opposition to modernism. See the entry for ALIENATION EFFECT.

Further reading

Walter Benjamin, *Understanding Brecht* (London: New Left Books, 1973).

CIXOUS, Hélène (1937–)

Main works

'The Laugh of the Medusa' (1976; in French, 1975)
The Newly Born Woman (1986; in French, 1975)
Coming to Writing (1991; in French, 1977)
Stigmata (1998)

Key terms

ÉCRITURE FÉMININE ■ writing the body ■ white ink

Hélène Cixous's concern with imperialism, with forms of political oppression and resistance, and the role of language in mediating these, can be partly attributed to her being born and raised in Oran, Algeria, which was then a French colony, and to the fact that German was her first language. She also taught at the University of Bordeaux and at the Sorbonne during the 1960s, at a time when many French students and academics were politically active. She is multi-lingual, and was appointed to a professorship of English literature at the University of Paris VIII-Vincennes, which she helped to establish, in 1968. In 1974, she was instrumental in the founding of the Centre for Research on Women's Studies, which she later directed. Apart from editing a literary review and being a critic and theorist, Cixous is a novelist and playwright.

Cixous's writing combines FEMINISM, PSYCHOANALYTIC theory and DECON-STRUCTION. She develops JACQUES LACAN's idea that children enter a SYMBOLIC order, a structure of language, and that they then inherit different SUBJECT positions according to their sex. For Cixous, this system of differences is patriarchal – or PHALLOGOCENTRIC. For Cixous, women become part of a system characterized by BINARY oppositions: male/female, speech/writing, presence/absence, light/dark, good/evil, where one value is opposed by, and inferior to, the other.

In addition, Cixous argues that when the child enters the realm of the Symbolic, she leaves behind the mother. As a result, learning a language is associated with the absence of the female body, and female sexuality is therefore impossible to represent within a phallogocentric order. According to the masculine tradition of psychoanalysis begun by Freud, women are further defined by lack: they have no penis, and therefore no active sexuality. In any system whereby subjectivity and pleasure are defined in relation to the phallus, its absence suggests non-existence, invisibility, passivity. Moreover, since language itself is a system anchored by the idea of a masculine CENTRE and perspective, women who use language inevitably inherit and inhabit male views of themselves. In using a language which excludes them, women inevitably reproduce the masculine order.

Cixous's solution is to argue that the norms of language have to be deconstructed and complicated by a writing of the female body (see ÉCRITURE FÉMININE). As she sees it, women are uniquely placed to put in practice POST-STRUCTURALIST theories of language, since they are already at a further remove from the centre than men. Occupying a marginal position enables them to see things differently, and to use a discourse marked by subjective flexibility, fluidity and plurality, rather than the simplistic dualisms of phallocentric speech and writing.

Cixous's language is characterized by puns, by a kind of playfulness: when she says that a 'woman must write herself', she means both that women should tell their own stories, and that 'women' ought to correct, to right, the stories of themselves that they have inherited from, and that are embodied in, men's language.

Cixous also relates her idea of women's writing closely to women's bodies, aligning creative writing in particular with clitoral self-stimulation, something that society denounces but which can involve intense and prolonged JOUISSANCE. She sees poetry as representing the best possibility of such a language, since its meanings are less fixed and stable than in prose – and particularly the prose of the classic NOVEL. Poetry, in Cixous's view, is closer to what has been repressed – the realm of the imaginary, the unconscious, that she associates with the mother and the female. She uses the METAPHOR of 'white ink', writing in breast milk, to suggest a link between her idea of a feminine writing and a return to the maternal body, to a site which precedes the prejudices and divisions of Western thought.

Critics of Cixous argue that her identification of men with reason, order, logic and women with the body simply reinforces male STEREOTYPES of women – though Cixous has always argued that the feminine is not a literal or physical entity, but an imaginary one that suspends and deconstructs such conventional oppositions. By extension, critics have taken issue with the idea of the feminine language, which does not proceed in a linear fashion (like prose): again, this it could be argued could be used to confirm prejudices about women's speech being nonsense, illogical, or trivial in some form. Such objections seem to miss the point of Cixous's arguments, however, which promote a kind of linguistic bisexuality, a performative rejection of divisions between male and female, self and other (see TRANSGENDER).

Further reading

Verena Conley, *Hélène Cixous: Writing the Feminine* (Lincoln: University of Nebraska Press, 1984); Morag Shiach, *Hélène Cixous: A Politics of Writing* (London: Routledge, 1991); Helen Wilcox *et al.*, (eds), *The Body and the Text: Hélène Cixous, Reading and Teaching* (Hemel Hempstead: Harvester Wheatsheaf, 1990).

DERRIDA, Jacques (1930–)

Main works

Of Grammatology (1976; in French, 1967)
Writing and Difference (1978; in French, 1967)
Dissemination (1981; in French, 1972)
A Derrida Reader: Between the Blinds (1990; ed. Peggy Kamuf)

Key terms

ABSENCE ■ LOGOCENTRISM ■ DIFFÉRANCE ■ DECONSTRUCTION ■ OTHER

Born in Algeria, Derrida began his education there before moving to France in 1949, where he studied at the prestigious *École Normale Supérieure* in Paris. From 1960 to 1964 he taught philosophy at the Sorbonne, then returned to the *École Normale Supérieure*, where he worked from 1965 to 1984, teaching and researching in the history and theory of philosophy. 1967 saw him publish two massively important collections of essays, *L'Écriture et la différance* (*Writing and Difference*) and *De la grammatologie* (*Of Grammatology*).

Derrida's concept of DIFFÉRANCE shows the influence of FERDINAND DE SAUSSURE, and his theory of the arbitrary relationship between signifier and signified (see SIGN). Words, according to Saussure, were not the things they represented: there was no divine, natural, or rational connection between the word 'cat' and a four-legged feline. Instead, the word 'cat' (signifier) represented the concept of the animal (signified) by virtue of its difference from other words such as 'bat' and 'fat'. Derrida extends this position by arguing that all language is governed by the principle he called 'différance', which in French is a pun combining the senses of deferral and differentiation. Words do not allow PRESENCE (i.e. direct contact with a denoted object), they defer it; at the same time, their meaning is a function of their difference from other words.

In *Of Grammatology*, Derrida focuses on the opposition between speech and writing in the Western tradition, and argues that speech is preferred to writing because it is associated with presence, and therefore with truth, authority and legitimacy. The presence of a speaker guarantees the value of what he or she is saying; more importantly, it guarantees that there is a real self doing the speaking. Derrida refers to the importance of an original being behind speech as part of a 'metaphysics of presence' (see LOGOCENTRISM and PRESENCE) which is central to the Western tradition. Writing, on the other hand, is seen as more problematic and unreliable, since the person who does the writing is not always physically present at the time of reading. As a result, difficulties and indeterminacies arise, as well as doubts and uncertainties. Moreover, writing is seen as secondary to speech, and even parasitic upon it, and therefore at a greater remove from accurate and pure expression.

The privileging of speech and presence is what Derrida refers to as LOGO-CENTRISM. Speech and writing, presence and absence, are typical elements of a society and culture that operate according to a system of BINARY oppositions: light and dark, good and evil, man and woman. Derrida points out that one is always privileged over an inferior or undesirable 'other', but that both depend on each other for their meaning: presence can only be defined and understood in terms of its opposite.

'Deconstruction' is a term that Derrida developed from Heidegger, and though represented and explained in various ways, it typically combines the meanings of 'destruct' and 'construct': one attacks the structure of a literary or philosophical argument in order to construct new understandings and insights. As a theoretical method, it was first demonstrated in 1966, when Derrida delivered a paper entitled 'Structure, sign and play in the discourse of the human sciences' (this would later appear in *Writing and Difference*). In the paper, Derrida looked at the concept of STRUCTURALISM as it was embodied in the work of the anthropologist Claude Lévi-Strauss. In particular, he scrutinized the anthropologist's language, which aspired to be objective, rational and scientific, but in fact often relied on assumptions that had their only basis either in CONVENTION or in METAPHOR. It was this ability to reveal that scientific arguments were often founded on untested beliefs (in God, in truth, in a CENTRE, in an origin) or the existence of a 'transcendental signifier' (a concept that had no proven reality outside language), which had the greatest consequences for literary theory and criticism during the next decade. Readers could seize upon an image or term in a given work, and show that it had no objectifiable existence: language, then, always betrayed its own figurative nature, its inability to deliver a reality or experience outside itself. For Derrida, there is always the existence of a law of the 'supplement' that subverts any claim to absolute truth, some apparently incidental or repressed element that contradicts the central logic, but which the logic depends on at the same time. Footnotes, metaphors, rhetorical devices, or unintended linguistic ambiguities are employed in order to reveal contradictions and complacencies.

Derrida's critics argue that deconstructionist techniques constitute a programme for dismantling, and not explaining, texts. A more disturbing development has been the misuse of his arguments by others to suggest that the Holocaust, for example, did not take place, and that it exists only as an historical fabrication, a trick of language. Such misrepresentations unfairly abuse and grotesquely PARODY Derrida's techniques, however, which are rigorously deployed in the service of confounding received certainties.

Further reading

Jonathan Culler, *On Deconstruction* (Ithaca: Cornell University Press, 1982); Christopher Norris, *Deconstruction: Theory and Practice* (London: Methuen, 1982).

EAGLETON, Terry (1943–)

Main works

Shakespeare and Society (1967)
Exiles and Émigrés (1970)
Myths of Power (1975)
Criticism and Ideology (1976)
Marxism and Literary Criticism (1976)
Walter Benjamin, or Towards a Revolutionary Criticism (1981)
The Rape of Clarissa: Writing, Sexuality and the Class Struggle in Samuel Richardson (1982)
Literary Theory: An Introduction (1983)
The Ideology of the Aesthetic (1990)
Ideology: An Introduction (1991)
Heathcliff and the Great Famine (1995)

Key terms

IDEOLOGY ■ POSTMODERNISM

Born in Salford, Lancashire, Terry Eagleton graduated from Trinity College, Cambridge in 1964. He was then a Fellow of Jesus College Cambridge until 1969, when he became a Fellow of Wadham College, Oxford. He now holds the Wharton Professorship of English at Oxford. He is an extremely prolific writer who in addition to the literary-critical and theoretical books listed above (the list is far from exhaustive), has written fiction, drama, a screenplay – and a very substantial amount of (typically combative) journalism and reviewing. He became known in the mid-1960s as one of a number of academic 'Catholic Marxists', and he addressed the relationship between Christianity and socialism in his contributions to the 1966 '*Slant*' *Manifesto: Catholics and the Left*: a long essay entitled 'Christians against Capitalism', co-written with Adrian Cunningham, and an essay on 'The Roots of the Christian Crisis'. From this point onwards, however, he soon became Britain's best-known MARXIST literary critic, theorist, and intellectual, a position which by general assent he still fills. His *Marxism and Literature* and, especially, *Literary Theory: An Introduction* have found their way on to very large numbers of Eng. Lit. 'set texts' lists, and their influence is hard to overestimate. He writes clearly and accessibly even when dealing with complex issues, and his textbooks never patronize their readers. A selection of his work is available in *The Eagleton Reader*, edited by Stephen Regan (Oxford: Blackwell, 1998).

In spite of the consistency of Eagleton's commitment to Marxism there have been shifts and developments in his intellectual and political allegiances and enthusiasms. He has played an important part in introducing important bodies of theory to English-speaking students, among them the Marxism of Louis Althusser, STRUCTURALISM, the work of WALTER BENJAMIN, and aspects of POST-STRUCTURALISM (of which he is now critical). His semi-oedipal relationship with RAYMOND WILLIAMS can be traced through a number of positions, ending up with the tribute of *Raymond Williams: Critical Perspectives* (1989), which he edited. Eagleton has probably done more than any other single figure to make students of literature aware of the importance of IDEOLOGY to their studies, and he was also a central figure in those debates about POSTMODERNISM which took place in the 1990s.

Eagleton is one of those writers who is arguably best in opposition. When playing the role of champion (of Althusser, for example), his intellectual edge seems somewhat blunted in contrast to those times when he is on the attack. (The Althusserian *Criticism and Ideology* is perhaps the book of his that has worn least well, falling at times into just the sort of mechanical reductionism typical of the Stalinism to which he has always been implacably opposed.) When on the attack he often writes to provoke, and rarely fails to do so when he tries. The more conventional literary criticism of his earlier years – on Shakespeare, the Brontës, Richardson, and 'exiles and émigrés' such as Conrad – is very well worth reading, as is his more contentious later study of Emily Brontë's Heathcliff. In recent years he has explored his Irish roots, spending much time in Ireland and writing on Irish themes and issues.

Further reading

Stephen Regan (ed.), *The Year's Work in Critical and Cultural Theory*, Part II, 'Barbarian at the Gate: Essays in Honour of Terry Eagleton' (Oxford: Blackwell, 1991).

ECO, Umberto (1932–)

Main works

A Theory of Semiotics (1976) (a revised version of *La struttura assente* (1968))
The Role of the Reader: Explorations in the Semiotics of Texts (1979)
The Name of the Rose (1983; in Italian, 1980)
Semiotics and the Philosophy of Language (1984)
Travels in Hyperreality (1986)
The Open Work (1989) (an expanded trans. of *Opera aperta* (1962))
Foucault's Pendulum (1989; in Italian, 1988)
The Limits of Interpretation (1990)
Apocalypse Postponed (1994; partials trans. and expansion of *Apocalittici e integrati* (1964))
The Island of the Day Before (1995; in Italian, 1994)
Kant and the Platypus (1999; in Italian, 1997)

Key terms

SEMIOTICS ▨ SIGN ▨ CODE ▨ OPEN AND CLOSED TEXTS ▨ 'model reader' ▨ READER RESPONSE

Umberto Eco is a semiotician, literary critic, novelist, and journalist whose intellectual interests embrace a range of topics of a breadth that defies simple categorization. His field of analysis stretches from the medieval to the modern period, and includes a vast array of CULTURAL productions – both 'high' and 'low', both literary and visual – from (chiefly but not exclusively) Europe and North America. Most known for *The Name of the Rose*, his best-selling murder mystery set in a medieval monastery and filled with a complex interplay of philosophy, Latinate allusion and sexual intrigue, Eco is as at home discussing James Joyce as analyzing James Bond NOVELS or Superman.

He was born in 1932 in Alessandria, a small city in Piedmont, Italy. He studied at the University of Turin, where he initially read law – the profession his father wished him to pursue – but he soon turned to the study of medieval literature and philosophy. He received his doctorate in 1954 for a thesis on Thomas Aquinas and aesthetics, which became the basis for his first book. He subsequently worked as a newspaper journalist, writing on diverse aspects of modern CULTURE, and for the Italian state television network (RAI) – through these positions he became associated with several *avant-garde* artists and critics with whom, in 1963, he formed 'Gruppa 63'. In 1956 he began lecturing in Turin, and with no reduction of his journalistic work his career has since straddled academia and the popular media. Following lecturing positions in Milan, Eco was appointed Professor of Semiotics at the University of Bologna in 1971. He remains at Bologna, but has also been a visiting professor at many other universities, mostly in North America.

Eco pursues and theorizes a culturally-engaged version of SEMIOTICS. His analytical approach, developing from the semiotic theories of Charles Sanders Peirce, aims to explain the CODES and SIGN systems at work in cultural productions, but, in contrast to more purely synchronic STRUCTURALIST approaches (see DIACHRONIC AND SYNCHRONIC), he views these codes and signs as meaningful only in relation to specific INTERPRETATIVE contexts. There are resemblances between aspects of Eco's work and the ROLAND BARTHES of *Mythologies* (1957) – particularly due to their shared interest in 'popular', mass culture – but Eco's work has a greater concern with audience and reception.

Eco has developed his theories of sign production and reception through several books, notably *Opera aperta* (which made him popular in Italy), *La Struttura assente*, *The Role of the Reader* and *The Limits of Interpretation*. His comments on the multivocal meanings of TEXTS and on the role of the READER in determining an interpretation may now sound familiar given the prominence of reader-oriented approaches to literature – in fact, Eco's work has been instrumental in the emergence of reader-response theory (and what Barthes calls the 'birth of the reader'). Arguing that interpretation of a text must depend in part upon the COMPETENCE of the reader, Eco stresses in *The Open Work* that 'every reception of a work of art is both an *interpretation* and a *performance* of it, because in every reception the work takes on a fresh perspective for itself'. But Eco is insistent that while textual meanings may be multiple, they are not infinite: a text may allow the production of different meanings, but only within a range of possibilities determined by the text. While Eco's theories of reception have become widely accepted, his sometimes paradoxical applications of 'open' and 'closed' have not gained widespread currency (see OPEN AND CLOSED TEXTS).

Eco suggests, furthermore, that the reader plays a role in shaping the text at the point of its writing. A writer will typically imagine a 'model reader', an ideal addressee whose assumed competence will determine features of the text: its form of address, range of ALLUSIONS, and so on (see Section 3, p. 160).

Eco's embrace and celebration of popular culture have led him, in *Apocalittici e integrati* and elsewhere, to distinguish between different ways in which the intellectual can confront mass culture. The 'apocalyptic' intellectual feels disgust at mass communication's supposed debasement of cultural values and thus withdraws to seek the refined sands of high art in which to hide the head. The alternative 'integrated' position is that which Eco has himself clearly espoused throughout his career. The integrated intellectual takes it as read that mass culture is an inescapable fact, and rather than retreat from it will engage with it, analyze it, decode its signs, and explain the competing IDEOLOGIES that are expressed through it. In Eco's own case, the intellectual will also contribute to mass culture and will aim to sustain cultural values through the creation of challenging works.

Further reading

Peter Bondanella, *Umberto Eco and the Open Text: Semiotics, Fiction, Popular Culture* (Cambridge: Cambridge University Press, 1997); Michael Caesar, *Umberto Eco: Philosophy, Semiotics and the Work of Fiction* (Malden, MA: Polity Press, 1999).

ELIOT, T[homas] S[tearns] (1888–1965)

Main works

The Sacred Wood (1920)
The Use of Poetry and the Use of Criticism (1933)
Notes Towards a Definition of Culture (1948)
The Three Voices of Poetry (1954)

Key terms

tradition ■ dissociation of SENSIBILITY ■ objective correlative

Thomas Stearns Eliot was born in St Louis, Missouri, to a distinguished family with roots in New England. His father, Henry Ware Eliot, was a successful businessman; his mother, Charlotte (Stearns) Eliot, a prominent woman of society. Eliot was educated mostly at St Louis, completing his studies at Smith Academy (of Washington University) and spending a year at Milton Academy. He was at Harvard University from 1906 to 1910 and completed his BA and Masters there. From 1910 to 1911 he studied at the Sorbonne and returned to Harvard as a graduate student, finishing his PhD in 1914. He studied briefly in Germany on a travel scholarship and later attended Oxford University for a year. In 1915, he married Vivienne Haigh-Wood and settled in London, teaching at Highgate School and then working as a clerk in the foreign department at Lloyds Bank from 1917 to 1925.

Although Eliot's reputation is founded on his poetry, during the 1920s he established and solidified a position as one of the leading critical voices of his generation. A series of articles for the *Times Literary Supplement* on Elizabethan and Jacobean dramatists (including Shakespeare, Marlowe, and Jonson) formed the core of his first major book of essays, *The Sacred Wood*. The most influential essay in the collection, 'Tradition and the Individual Talent', emphasizes the importance of situating creative and critical writing within a larger literary heritage, in order to arrive at a fuller sense of its significance. He argues not only that new writers have to be seen in relation to the old, but that our comprehension of previous writers is modified by the achievements of contemporary authors.

In the introduction to the collection, Eliot discussed the ideas of Matthew Arnold and identified himself as a serious critic whose writing would extend and to some extent improve on Arnold's work. Like Arnold, and to some extent HAROLD BLOOM, Eliot subscribed to the idea of a great tradition of writing in English: unlike Bloom, Eliot's thinking reflected a need for the individual to find his place within a hierarchy and acknowledge authority. Like Arnold, again, Eliot believed that great literature conveyed essentially timeless values and was central to any civilization. His considerable influence and power as a literary critic can be explained in part by his strategic association with the world of publishing: in 1922 he founded *The Criterion* and in 1925 joined Faber & Faber as an editor.

Central to Eliot's views on art were the need for impersonality and an emphasis on objectivity. In a celebrated formula, he claimed that poetry was 'not a turning loose of emotion, but an escape from emotion'. Related to these ideas was his theory of the 'objective correlative', where subjective experience is expressed through something external – an object, place, event or situation which corresponds to it. In his essay 'The Metaphysical Poets', Eliot lamented a 'dissociation of sensibility' that (in his view) took place around the seventeenth century: whereas writers had previously managed to describe reality in ways that combined emotion and intellect, thought had now become divorced from feeling. It is was for this reason that Eliot attacked Milton (as being emotionally remote) and the Romantics (for over-emphasizing feeling). But his opposition to these writers can also be related to his conservative, royalist, politics: Milton was anti-royalist, and many of the Romantics (Byron and Shelley in particular) were social dissidents.

Further reading

Gregory Jay, *T.S. Eliot and the Poetics of Literary History* (Baton Rouge: Louisiana State University Press, 1983); David Newton-de Molina (ed.), *The Literary Criticism of T.S. Eliot: New Essays* (London: Athlone Press, 1977); Tom Paulin, Introduction to *The Faber Book of Political Verse* (London: Faber & Faber, 1986).

EMPSON, Sir William (1906–84)

Key terms

AMBIGUITY ■ PASTORAL

Sir William Empson (he was knighted in 1979) was born in the family house, Yokefleet Hall, at Howden in Yorkshire. In 1925 he went up to Magdalen College, Cambridge, to read mathematics. Only in the autumn of 1928 did he switch to English, starting work on *Seven Types of Ambiguity* at the same time. In 1929 he gained a first class degree with 'special distinction' in Part I of the English Tripos, was elected to a 'Bye-Fellowship', but was almost immediately deprived of it when a college servant found contraceptives in his room. From this point to 1940 he alternated between spells as a freelance writer in London, and lecturing appointments in Japan (1931–4) and China (1937–9). Arriving in China at the time of the Japanese invasion he travelled with the exiled Peking universities, an experience on which his poem 'Autumn on Nan-Yueh' is based. After war-work with the BBC, more teaching in China followed, then a permanent appointment as Professor of English at the University of Sheffield in 1953.

Empson is still best known for his first volume of criticism, *Seven Types of Ambiguity*, in spite of the fact that he published much subsequent to it. In addition to the titles listed above there is a body of poems recently published in a complete edition (from which the biographical details given above are taken), based mainly on two volumes of poetry published in the 1930s, and a number of posthumous collections of previously unpublished or uncollected work. *Seven Types of Ambiguity* was not the first example of exhaustive interpretative ANALYSIS of literary TEXTS but it occupied a central position in what T.S. ELIOT dubbed the 'lemon-squeezer school of criticism', and was cited by Cleanth Brooks as a key TEXT in the development of what became known as the NEW CRITICISM. Empson's originality lay in his challenge to the idea that AMBIGUITY meant imprecision, vagueness, or sloppiness on the part of the writer. He saw ambiguity in quite the opposite way, as the packing of several meanings together in a text in a manner that explored their tensions and connections.

For the university English undergraduate *Seven Types of Ambiguity* is still an ideal way to explore the power of poetry to produce complex patterns of highly concentrated meaning. Empson's analyses are never aridly FORMALIST: although praised by the New Critics, the much later *Using Biography* confirms that he never accepted the embargo on reference to the AUTHOR or his or her INTENTION, and his analyses typically trace the force of a range of 'extrinsic' influences or elements. Very often he writes to provoke: a typical ploy is to adopt a chatty and seemingly anachronistic way of describing authors or characters that appears unhistorical – but that often turns out to be informed by a more detailed and sensitive understanding of historical specificities than more soberly presented criticism. (See also Section 3, p. 150.)

Some Versions of Pastoral expands the concept mentioned in its title so as to render it applicable to any literary WORK in which issues and problems associated with one (normally privileged) group are explored through a concern with another (see the entry for PASTORAL).

The Structure of Complex Words took Empson's techniques of unpacking interwoven complexities down to the level of the individual word, so that by tracing the meanings of a word such as 'honest' in Shakespeare's *Othello* he is able to show how the accumulated experience of a CULTURE can be released by a writer's tracing of the semantics of one word.

Empson was a HUMANIST, both in the sense that he was anti-Christian and also in the sense that his writing assumes that historical change does not prevent human beings living at different times and in different cultures from sharing common characteristics and problems.

It is arguable that Empson's work became progressively less good-tempered, and it has been criticized for becoming more IDEOLOGICAL and less open to the variety of the works with which he was concerned. But he is always worth reading. The reader who disagrees with him finds that he or she must go back to the literary work to express and consolidate such disagreement – and this insistence upon the primacy of the work arguably remains his greatest legacy.

Further reading

The Introduction and notes to John Haffenden (ed.), *The Complete Poems of William Empson* (London: Allen Lane, the Penguin Press, 2000) contain much useful discussion and information; Christopher Norris and Nigel Mapp, *William Empson: The Critical Achievement* (Cambridge: Cambridge University Press, 1993).

FISH, Stanley (1938–)

Main works

Surprised by Sin: The Reader in Paradise Lost (1967)
Self-Consuming Artifacts: The Experience of Seventeenth-Century Literature (1972)
Is There a Text in this Class? The Authority of Interpretive Communities (1980)
Why Not Say What Happened?: Change, Rhetoric, and the Practice of Theory in Literary and Legal Studies (1988)
There's No Such Thing As Free Speech, and It's a Good Thing, Too (1994)
The Trouble with Principle (1999)

READER-RESPONSE ■ INTERPRETIVE COMMUNITY ■ AFFECTIVE SYLISTICS

Fish's principal contribution to literary studies lies in his emphasis upon the active role of the READER in literary INTERPRETATION. His criticism has stressed that TEXTS themselves are not the only determiners of meaning during an act of reading; rather, readers inevitably play a creative role in assigning meaning to a literary work. Fish, then, has been a key figure within the emergence and growth of READER-RESPONSE criticism and his work has generated several useful and widely applied terms within that field.

He was born into a working-class Rhode Island family, and was the first of his family to go to college. Far from subsuming his working-class identity within what was a mostly middle- and upper-class American academy, Fish has consistently brandished his origins and has adopted a combative approach to academic debate and to the practice of literary criticism. Such is shown in his early *John Skelton's Poetry* (1965), in which he launches an attack on reductively historical approaches to literature so as to advance a view of the text as an artifact marked by history but available for abstraction from its original context as an expression of AUTHORIAL psychology.

Fish would move away from an early sympathy with the NEW CRITICISM as he developed his reader-oriented approach to literature through further writing on Renaissance poetry. In *Surprised by Sin*, he stressed the central position of the reader in Milton's EPIC poem *Paradise Lost*, arguing that it was crucial to Milton's poetic performance to 'harass' the reader as part of a morally-didactic process. The reader, Fish asserted, was the *subject* of the poem, which coercively encourages a bracing re-creation of Adam's Fall to take place within the reader's mind. In such an account of the reading process, readers' experiences are *formed* by the text – their participation in the reading contract does not involve what they might *bring* to the text.

However, Fish developed the idea of the reader as an *active* creator of meaning in *Self-Consuming Artifacts*, in which he introduces the term 'affective stylistics'. (In this regard, his work elaborates ideas put forward in E.D. HIRSCH's *Validity in Interpretation* (1967).) Fish disputes the notion of the 'Affective Fallacy' (see AFFECTIVE), as advanced in a famous essay of 1949 by W.K. Wimsatt and Monroe Beardsley. These New Critics insist that criticism should pay attention to what the text *is* and *means* independent of who reads it, rather than to the *results* or the *affective* power that a text may achieve when it is read. Fish, on the other hand, argues that literary meaning is an *event* that takes place 'in the reader' and is inseparable from the process of textual consumption. 'Affective stylistics', then, describes the impact of a text upon a reader, and Fish stresses that this impact must be seen as linear and temporal, since the consumption of literature is always an activity that occurs and develops over time. Here, again, his work rejects New Criticism, with its emphasis upon literary works as finely-balanced wholes which can claim an almost spatial existence as their various parts play off against one another in the untemporality of 'final meaning'. Fish stresses the temporal aspect of reading, demonstrating how interpretation is the result of a progressive word-by-word, stanza-by-stanza process of interaction between text and reader.

In his work from the 1970s, Fish comes close to advancing a relativist argument that interpretation is purely subjective, but he maintains that texts have the power to manipulate readers. In *Is There a Text in this Class?* (perhaps his most interesting and influential book), Fish further restrains the relativist implications of the reader's apotheosis, by arguing that readers tend to exist within and be inseparable from INTERPRETIVE COMMUNITIES. He introduces this term to describe the context of shared values and practices within which readers typically function. Readers are not solitary beings, Fish argues, but are caught up within particular networks of authority and interpretive expectation which will always mediate textual consumption and partially govern interpretation. Thus it is typical that readers within particular cultural circumstances will discover a significant degree of communal consensus with regard to a text's meaning.

Fish's later work has been less literary in its application and more relativist and anti-foundationalist (i.e. rejecting fundamental truths or belief systems) in its character. His relativism (alongside a habit of audacious self-promotion) has made him a highly controversial figure within (particularly American) academia, and he is regularly and virulently attacked in the press. This controversiality should not obscure the usefulness to literary criticism and history of the terms and concepts advanced in his earlier work.

Further reading

Robert C. Holub, *Reception Theory: A Critical Introduction* (London: Methuen, 1984); H. Aram Veeser (ed.), *The Stanley Fish Reader* (Oxford: Blackwell, 1999).

FOUCAULT, Michel (1926–84)

Main works

Madness and Civilisation: A History of Insanity in the Age of Reason (1965; in French, 1961)
The Order of Things: An Archaeology of the Human Science (1970; in French, 1966)
The Archaeology of Knowledge (1972; in French, 1969)
Discipline and Punish: The Birth of the Prison (1977; in French, 1975)
'What is an Author?' (first published in English in Bouchard, Donald F. (ed.), *Language, Counter-memory, Practice: Selected Essays and Interviews* (New York: Cornell University Press, 1977)
The History of Sexuality, 3 vols (1990, 1990, 1988; in French, 1976, 1984, 1984)

Key terms

DISCOURSE ■ AUTHOR ■ power ■ POST-STRUCTURALISM ■ NEW HISTORICISM ■ panopticon

Paul-Michel Foucault was born in Poitiers, France in 1926, the son of a surgeon and professor of medicine. He was schooled in Poitiers and Paris, and from 1946 studied at the *École Normale Supérieure* in Paris, where he took degrees in philosophy and psychology. He was briefly associated with the Parti Communiste Français, but ultimately rejected MARXISM, and was more drawn to the influence of the German philosophers Frederick Nietzsche and Martin Heidegger. Nietzsche's emphasis upon 'power' as fundamental to human relations (in contrast to the economic emphasis of Marxism), and Heidegger's critique of existing understandings of 'being' had important effects upon the development of Foucault's thought. Foucault taught at the ENS and at the University of Lille, also observing in hospitals and writing about the treatment of mental illness, before leaving France in 1955 to teach in Sweden, Poland – where he wrote *Madness and Civilisation* – and in Germany. He returned to France in 1961 to work at the University of Clermont-Ferrand and the University of Paris at Vincennes, before being appointed, in 1970, to the prestigious position of chair in the History of Systems of Thought at the *Collège de France*, which he held until his death.

There is no simple category into which the work of Foucault fits. He did not confine his work within traditional disciplinary boundaries – indeed such divisions of knowledge are among the topics he explored – and his writings straddle history, philosophy, psychology, sociology, and literary and CULTURAL theory. Developing a methodology he dubbed 'archaeology', he addressed a range of social THEMES through the analysis of which he aimed to uncover structuring principles of Western societies and of how human identities are formed in relation to institutional, political and cultural structures and practices. Principal themes he explored include: the treatment of the mentally ill (and relatedly the construction of the category of 'madness'); the manner in which categories of knowledge are organized and authorized; institutions of punishment; and the definition and regulation of human sexuality. Foucault's 'archaeological' method presents a revisionary history of thought, whereby the formations and transformations of DISCOURSES are analyzed, not in terms of the truths those discourses may or may not contain, but in terms of the rules which allow collections of statements to attain coherence and authority as patterns of thought.

Foucault's work thus contributes to late twentieth-century anti-HUMANISM and can be seen as POST-STRUCTURALIST in the sense that it dismisses liberal notions of the autonomous individual, and instead sees identity as the product of cultural construction. Humans, Foucault argues, are inevitably SUBJECT to systems of power (or 'power/knowledge'), which will structure patterns of thought and behaviour, and which, at the same time, may veil the fact of that construction by means of naturalizing rhetoric.

Foucault's attention to disadvantaged groups – the mentally ill, the incarcerated, and those with non-mainstream sexual orientations – was not merely descriptive, but was partly aimed towards bettering the conditions for such groups in modern society, and Foucault actively campaigned for their causes. The political engagement of Foucault's work – its insistence that empowered discourses typically function at the expense of subjected groups – has informed political approaches to literature. FEMINIST critics, for example, have depicted patriarchal discourse in Foucauldian terms (and have also criticized Foucault for neglecting in his analyses the GENDERING of power and knowledge); POSTCOLONIALIST critics, such as EDWARD SAID, have applied Foucault's thinking to the study of national and international discursive formations; and Foucault's critique of fixed categories of gender has been influential within QUEER THEORY. Foucault's development of the notion of discourse has probably had its greatest impact in the emergence of NEW HISTORICISM – as practised and popularised by such critics as STEPHEN GREENBLATT – and in the spread of new-historical methods to other approaches. Indeed, Foucault's depiction of literary TEXTS as components of wider discourses – involving other texts (literary and non-literary), institutions and social practices – has overturned and largely supplanted the traditional notion that a text might be studied alongside a consideration of its 'background'. For Foucault and for new-historically inclined followers, a literary work and a 'background' are unreifiable, but must rather be recognized as elements inseparably conjoined within a shared discourse.

More specifically within literary studies, Foucault's essay 'What is an Author?' – alongside ROLAND BARTHES's 'The Death of the Author' (1977) – has stimulated considerable debate over the once mostly unproblematized notion of 'the author' (see the entry for AUTHOR in Section 4 for further discussion).

Foucault's extended discussion of the significance of Jeremy Bentham's 'Panopticon' in *Discipline and Punish* has also had its effect on literary studies. Bentham's Panopticon was a circular building containing cells in the centre of which was an observation tower. Foucault argues that the experience of knowing that he or she could be observed at any time, but could never be sure whether he or she was actually being observed, caused prisoners to *internalize* the discipline attached to surveillance. In short: prisoners began to act as their own surveillance agents. Foucault sees this as an aspect of that more general move away from the use of external constraints such as execution and torture towards that internalized self-discipline that he finds characteristic of MODERNITY.

Theorists of IDEOLOGY were able to relate such processes of internalization to concepts such as INTERPOLATION, and literary critics have explored these ideas in a number of directions, including that of the 'surveillance' that the omniscient NARRATOR of the classic nineteenth-century NOVEL conducts on his or her characters. (A novel such as Charles Dickens's *Oliver Twist* is full of acts of spying, both by characters on one another but also by the author-NARRATOR on his characters.) Foucault's other general point, that knowledge obtained by looking constitutes power ('power/knowledge') has also been seen to have implications for the forms of knowledge granted to – or withheld from – narrators and READERS.

Foucault is not without his critics. Historians, particularly, frequently take him to task for making massive generalizations on the basis of insufficient empirical evidence, and for producing historical narratives so as to confirm *a priori* positions rather than discovering a position on the basis of empirical research. Foucault's choice of topics has consequently been criticized as idiosyncratic; furthermore, his style is sometimes seen as overly poetic for intellectual writing. Foucault remains, nevertheless, one of the most influential intellectuals of the twentieth century, and – perhaps because of a 'poetic' style – one of the most readable.

See also the entries for: CENTRE; DESIRE; ÉCRITURE; PARADIGM SHIFT.

Further reading

Gary Gutting (ed.), *The Cambridge Companion to Foucault* (Cambridge: Cambridge University Press, 1994); David Macey, *The Lives of Michel Foucault* (New York: Pantheon Books, 1993); Lois McNay, *Foucault: A Critical Introduction* (Cambridge: Polity Press, 1994); Paul Rabinow (ed.), *The Foucault Reader* (New York: Pantheon Books, 1984).

FRYE, Northrop (1912–91)

Main works

Anatomy of Criticism (1957)
The Critical Path (1971)

Key terms

ARCHETYPE ▪ MYTH

Born in the Canadian province of Quebec in 1912, and educated mostly in New Brunswick, Frye studied English and philosophy at Victoria College, Biblical studies and theology at Emmanuel College (both at the University of Toronto), and English at Merton College, Oxford. For most of his life, from 1939 onwards, he taught at Victoria College, eventually becoming its Chancellor. In 1967, he became the first University Professor of the University of Toronto.

Frye's work can be seen as a reaction against the NEW CRITICAL and FORMAL-IST schools of criticism that dominated literary studies during the 1940s and 1950s. Frye was interested in recurrent and ABSTRACT patterns in literature, rather than techniques of close reading applied to single WORKS or writers. In his view, criticism was a science and literature the object of its study: rather than relating literature to historical or biographical contexts, or to subjective evaluation, one could identify a work according to certain definite criteria, and use a specialized vocabulary to do this, because literature was a closed system which behaved according to identifiable laws and orderly processes.

As its name suggests, the *Anatomy of Criticism* attempts to describe the physical structure of literature as a whole, or the total aggregate of its elements – MODES, SYMBOLS, MYTHS and GENRES. Each work can be identified according to a set of taxonomic maps: there are seven categories of IMAGERY, five primary literary modes, five principles of NARRATIVE structure, five literary epochs (or periods) and four ARCHETYPAL narratives. The five primary modes he identified were mythical, romantic, high mimetic (TRAGEDY and EPIC), low mimetic (COME-

DY and REALISM) and ironic, and these could be further related to about twenty categories of FORM and THEME.

The most influential of his theories is the one on MYTHS, or archetypes (see the entry for ARCHETYPAL CRITICISM in Section 3). According to this, literature can be categorized in four ways, which correspond to the seasons: comedy is the myth of spring, ROMANCE the myth of summer, tragedy the myth of autumn, and IRONY the myth of winter. These four genres are also linked to the role of the HERO, states of mind, and to different stages in the historical development of society. In comedy, for example, the hero appears in a controlling, restrictive society and succeeds in liberating it: falsehood is replaced with truth, illusion with reality. IRONY and SATIRE (winter) are linked to a world from which the hero has been vanquished, and where meaning is lost. All of these phases are cyclical: one dominates literature for a while, before giving way to the next. The postmodern period, for example, emphasizes PARODY and irony: eventually, it will be replaced by a new phase with its associated modes, forms and genres.

The importance of Frye's thinking lies less in his tendency to systematize, than in his belief that education enables people to see beyond and behind the surface to an underlying structure. His commitment to education as a form of enlightenment, and the universities as leading engines in the democratic process, links him to Matthew Arnold, while his use of mythological traditions has clearly influenced HAROLD BLOOM. Especially evident in Frye's *The Critical Path* is an Arnold-like view of teaching literature as a replacement for religion in society, and as a purveyor of humanist, middle-class values, with literature striking a balance between the conservative tendency towards order and authority (the 'myth of concern') and the need for liberalism (the 'myth of freedom').

Further reading

John D. Denham, *Northrop Frye and Critical Method* (University Park: Pennsylvania State University Press, 1978); A.C. Hamilton, *Northrop Frye: An Anatomy of his Criticism* (Toronto: The University of Toronto Press, 1990).

GATES, HENRY Louis, Jr (1950–)

Main works

Figures in Black (1987)
The Signifying Monkey (1988)
Loose Canons (1992)

Key terms

signifyin(g) ■ talking book

Henry Louis Gates, Jr was born in Keyser, West Virginia. He travelled widely through Africa on a fellowship in 1970 and 1971, and returned to study for his

BA at Yale in 1973. He subsequently travelled on a Mellon scholarship to Clare College, Cambridge, where he met and befriended the Nigerian novelist Wole Soyinka during the writing of his Master's thesis (1974). His PhD thesis, which he completed at Cambridge in 1979, was on the reception of Black literature during the Enlightenment period. Afterwards he returned to teach at Yale, before being appointed to the W.E.B. DuBois chair in literature at Cornell in 1985. Since 1990, he has worked at Harvard.

His friendship with Soyinka led Gates to study the Yoruba and Fon CULTURES of West Africa, and the 'trickster' figures of Èsù-Elégbara and Legba in particular. Gates combined this research with POST-STRUCTURALIST and DECONSTRUC-TIONIST theories to develop his idea of 'signifyin(g)', whereby he argued that African and African-American culture existed in an often PARODIC relationship to what had preceded it, both revising and reinterpreting what had gone before. Traditional African and Caribbean folk tales told of figures who listened to tales and then repeated them in modified or ironized forms, exposing their contradictions: Gates uses this tradition to describe a process of 'mediation' that takes place when Black novelists write in English. By paying serious attention to aspects of African culture, Gates hoped to counter the limitations of theoretical DISCOURSES in the European heritage, within which Blacks were often marginal or absent. The 'talking book', meanwhile, was his term for slave NARRATIVES, which uniquely synthesized aspects of Black vernacular, writing, folk tradition and SUBJECTIVITY, in ways that DECONSTRUCTED normal boundaries.

In *Loose Canons* (1992), Gates argued courageously for a continuing spirit of multiculturalism in the humanities, during an historical period when conservatives were defending the literary CANON. For Gates, the greater inclusion of African-American literature is not simply a political gesture; it is vital for the continued health of the Western tradition generally. The new perspectives imparted by marginal voices and traditions help to sustain and renew mainstream literature and criticism. But his contribution to the study of African-American literature has been to FOREGROUND its literary as against its extra-literary qualities. Whereas critics had often adopted a political or historical approach to Black literature, overlooking its formal and linguistic qualities and focusing on its content, Gates argued for a knowledge of both. He has been criticized for preferring the more difficult and experimental work of Ralph Ellison to that of Richard Wright, thereby privileging a form of writing that fits more successfully into high cultural traditions. But his writing has revealed culturally-specific aspects of African-American literature and therefore broadened the scope of literary criticism and theory generally.

Further reading

Ralph Cohen (ed.), *The Future of Literary Criticism* (London: Routledge, 1989).

GENETTE, Gérard (1930–)

Key terms

See the terms listed at the end of the second paragraph, below.

Genette's higher education was at the *École Normale Supérieure* in Paris. After some school teaching he then taught at the Sorbonne (1963–7), and at the *École des Hautes Études en Sciences Sociales*. Probably the single most important figure in the creation of an independent discipline or study of narrative – NARRATOLOGY – Genette has undoubtedly been foremost in the fruitful application of STRUCTURALIST concepts and terminology to the study of NARRATIVE. Our present-day use of a range of terms from ANACHRONY to VOICE owes a major debt to Genette, especially subsequent to the publication in English of his *Narrative Discourse*. This is a book that has revolutionized the study of fiction in many CULTURES and languages, and terminology and concepts popularized by it can be found in most analyses of FICTION written today.

Genette writes directly about his debt to structuralism in the essay entitled 'Structuralism and Literature' (included in *Figures of Literary Discourse*). In this essay he explains how the temporary warrant to ignore 'content' granted by FORMALISM and structuralism has a cathartic value which enables the theorist to study literature's system of conventions. The CONVENTIONS uncovered by Genette are, following structuralist principle, isolated and described with the aid of the LINGUISTIC PARADIGM. Thus Genette attempts to isolate a LANGUE behind the literary system that is equivalent to the *langue* that underlies the use of language by native speakers. Formal grammars are raided for a vocabulary, and terms applied by linguisticians to the analysis of a sentence are applied to the analysis of narrative method. Many of the terms to be found in the glossary pages of this book owe their existence as specifically narratological terms to Genette, and the reader interested in an overview of Genette's contribution to narratology might begin by looking at the entries for ANALEPSIS, CONNOTATION AND DENOTATION, DEVIATION, DIEGESIS AND MIMESIS, ELLIPSIS, FREQUENCY, INTERTEXTUALITY, LANGUE AND PAROLE, MOOD, NARRATIVE, PERSPECTIVE AND VOICE, and PROLEPSIS.

Genette's theorizing rests upon a solid base of specific literary analyses. His favoured writer is undoubtedly Marcel Proust, but *Narrative Discourse* also takes examples and underpins arguments by means of references to a range of other writers, from Laurence Sterne to Alain Robbe-Grillet.

Further reading

Gerald Prince, *Narratology: The Form and Function of Narrative* (The Hague: Mouton, 1982); Shlomith Rimmon-Kenan, *Narrative Fiction: Contemporary Poetics* (London: Methuen, 1983).

GILBERT, Sandra (1936–) and GUBAR, Susan (1944–)

Main works

The Madwoman in the Attic (1979)
No Man's Land (1987, 1989, 1994)

Key terms

FEMINISM ■ anxiety of authorship (see REVISIONISM)

Sandra M. Gilbert was born in New York in 1936. She graduated with a BA degree in English literature from Cornell University in 1957, subsequently earning an MA from New York University in 1961. She obtained her doctorate from Columbia in 1968. She has worked as an assistant professor at California State University at Hayward, at Indiana University, as well as at Princeton and Stanford. She joined the faculty of the University of California at Davis as an Associate Professor in 1975 and is now a full professor of English there. Susan Gubar was born in Brooklyn, New York, in 1944. She graduated with a BA in English literature from City University of New York in 1965, and did graduate work at the University of Michigan (MA, 1968) and the University of Iowa (PhD, 1972). Gubar taught for a year at the University of Illinois at Chicago before beginning a long association with Indiana University in 1973. She is currently a Distinguished Professor of English and Women's Studies at Indiana.

Although they have also published separately, it is with their joint *The Madwoman in the Attic* (1979) that Gilbert and Gubar have had the greatest impact on literary criticism. The book's title refers to Rochester's mad first wife in Charlotte Brontë's *Jane Eyre* (1847), who is kept locked in the attic of his mansion, but who then sets fire to it, killing herself in the process but also burning the house down, wounding and blinding her husband. Gilbert and Gubar look at the ways in which British and American women writers in the nineteenth century respond to different degrees of confinement within patriarchal CULTURE and society. The study has proved extremely useful to generations of students, offering many close readings of particular TEXTS. Gilbert and Gubar focus on FORMAL and NARRATIVE structures and THEMATIC concerns and patterns of IMAGERY, tracing their reappearance and revision across different texts by the same and by different writers. In particular, they point out how women's anger at their literary disenfranchisement manifests itself in different ways – sometimes in the same text (as when Rochester is maimed by his first wife but then marries Jane, who gains a measure of authority over him). At times, such rage and rebelliousness are dramatized by a CHARACTER, a story, an IMAGE or SYMBOL: at other times, it manifests itself in the use of a fragmented or experimental language.

Gilbert and Gubar can in many ways be seen as arguing for the existence of a separate tradition of great writing by women – something that is partly supported by their edition of *The Norton Anthology of Literature by Women: The Tradition in English* (1985). Indeed, they first met at Indiana University, where they taught a course in 1974 on a female literary tradition that their first book goes a long way towards defining. Their work can therefore be usefully compared with that of ELAINE SHOWALTER, and their emphasis on the imagination within a larger tradition can be related to the work of T.S. ELIOT and HAROLD BLOOM. For example, their key concept of the 'anxiety of authorship,' where nineteenth-century women writers have to confront patriarchal notions of femininity, is clearly a rewriting of Bloom's largely male-oriented theory of the 'anxiety of influence' (see the entry for REVISIONISM). Gilbert and Gubar have now completed a critical trilogy, under the collective title of *No Man's Land*, that comprises *The War of the Words* (1987), *Sexchanges* (1989), and *Letters From the Front* (1994), and which looks at twentieth-century texts by both men and women. In response to earlier charges that their work suggested a kind of ESSENTIALISM, or the idea that women had shared experiences because of their sex which were independent of their ethnicity or CLASS, the writers also looked at Zora Neale Hurston, Toni Morrison and others in order to map out the complicated nexus of sexual oppression and cultural resistance to it in the twentieth century.

Gilbert and Gubar's combination of the literary technique of close reading inherited from NEW CRITICISM with cultural and historical analysis situates them in an Anglo-American or PRAGMATIC tradition of feminism that is often distinguished from a tradition of POST-STRUCTURALIST feminism associated with French writers.

Further reading

William E. Cain (ed.), *Making Feminist History: The Literary Scholarship of Sandra M. Gilbert and Susan Gubar* (New York: Garland, 1994).

GOLDMANN, Lucien (1914–70)

Main works

The Hidden God: A Study of Tragic Vision in the Pensées of Pascal and the Tragedies of Racine (1964; in French, 1959)
The Human Sciences and Philosophy (1969; in French, 1966)
Immanuel Kant (1971; in French, 1945, revised 1967)
Towards a Sociology of the Novel (1975; in French, 1965)
Essays on Method in the Sociology of Literature (1980)

Key terms

genetic structuralism ■ homology

Born Sergiu-Lucian Goldmann in Bucharest, Goldmann's father, who died when Goldmann was seven years old, worked in the legal profession. Goldmann's family belonged to the cultured, political and persecuted Jewish community in Romania, and some published reports claim that his father was a rabbi, but this appears to be incorrect. Mitchell Cohen (see below) reports that his family was 'relatively secularized'. As a student at the University of Bucharest, Goldmann's early Zionist-socialism hardened into active work for the Communist underground, and here he made initial acquaintance with the writings of GEORG LUKÁCS, which were to constitute an important influence on him, especially during his time in Switzerland during the Second World War.

Goldmann moved to Paris in 1935 where he earned degrees in public law and political economy, and heard lectures by (among others) WALTER BENJAMIN and Nikolai Bukharin. After a number of academic jobs in France, Goldmann fled to Switzerland in October 1942, and remained there for the rest of the war, writing a doctoral thesis which formed the basis of his later book on Kant. While in Switzerland Goldmann came into contact with child psychologist Jean Piaget, whose ideas played an important part in developing the STRUCTURALIST side of Goldmann's 'genetic structuralism'.

Back in Paris after the war his second doctorate (from the Sorbonne in 1956) was in turn the basis of his most influential work, *The Hidden God*. His final academic post was as director of his own research institute (in the sociology of literature) in Brussels from 1961.

The book on Kant manifests the strong influence of Hegelian MARXIST ideas, stressing that Hegelian totality is founded upon (i) the concrete, (ii) change and (iii) development as a result of contradiction. These ideas inform much of Goldmann's subsequent work, in which actual (concrete) socio-economic contradictions are projected into (among other things) literature as part of a process of change.

Goldmann's work exhibits a consistently non-dogmatic and anti-Stalinist Marxism, and the influence of *The Hidden God* can be explained in terms of its provision of a more mediated and less mechanical theory of the determination of (or influence on) literature by socio-economic factors. Writing of Pascal and Racine, Goldmann sees their work as the product not of a direct expression of their CLASS background – that of the *noblesse de la robe* – but of an intermediate formation, that of Jansenism, which Goldmann argued was an IDEOLOGICAL formation that expressed the tensions within this class background. Contradictions at the level of the social class or class fraction suffer two stages of mediation or transformation – from social class to ideology, and from ideology to literary or philosophical expression. The tragic vision in Racine or the wager in Pascal can thus be traced back to stresses in a particular socio-economic group, but not directly or mechanically. The writer does not express a merely private vision, but as a result of 'trans-individual mental structures' is able to depict in concealed or displaced form underlying contradictions in a social grouping. It is the structure of relationships in Racine's tragedies rather than their overt content that expresses the plight of the *noblesse de la robe*, just as Jansenism expresses the same plight through its theology of human beings trapped between a sinful world and a 'hidden God'. Thus structural patterns in the plays and in the religious belief are *homologous* with the problems of a social group caught in an impossible position between an embattled monarchy and aristocracy on the one hand and a rising bourgeoisie on the other.

In the year of Goldmann's death, that seminal collection of essays that hovered on the borderline between structuralism and POST-STRUCTURALISM – Richard Macksey's and Eugenio Donato's *The Languages of Criticism and the Sciences of Man: The Structuralist Controversy* (1970) – included an essay by Goldmann entitled 'Structure: Human Reality and Methodological Concept'. In this essay Goldmann states bluntly that 'all reality is made up of overlapping structures, every structure fulfils a function within a larger structure and that structure is defined as rational only by its ability to solve a practical problem', concluding that to forget this is to run the risk of denying history. Here in a nutshell we have the attempt to combine the SYNCHRONIC and the DIACHRONIC and to produce a (paradoxically) historical structuralism.

Although he subsequently distanced himself from aspects of it, Goldmann's work exerted an important influence on RAYMOND WILLIAMS, who published an essay on it after Goldmann's death. The 1970s generally saw a diminution in his influence: he tended to be too Marxist for structuralists and post-structuralists, and too HUMANIST for Althusserian Marxists (in an interview with Brigitte Devismes published in French in 1970 he averred that the work of Louis Althusser represented a return to mechanical materialism, a damning characterization for such a dialectical, non-mechanical thinker as was Goldmann).

Further reading

Mitchell Cohen, *The Wager of Lucien Goldmann: Tragedy, Dialectics, and a Hidden God* (Princeton: Princeton University Press, 1994).

GREENBLATT, Stephen Jay (1943–)

Main works

Sir Walter Raleigh: The Renaissance Man and His Roles (1973)
Renaissance Self-Fashioning: From More to Shakespeare (1980)
Shakespearean Negotiations: The Circulation of Social Energy in Renaissance England (1988)
Learning to Curse: Essays in Early Modern Culture (1990)
Marvelous Possessions: The Wonder of the New World (1991)
New World Encounters (ed.) (1993)
Practicing New Historicism (co-authored with Catherine Gallagher) (2000)

Key terms

NEW HISTORICISM ■ cultural poetics ■ DISCOURSE

Stephen Greenblatt was born in Cambridge, Massachusetts, the grandson of Lithuanian Jews who moved to America in the 1890s. Greenblatt has described himself as loosely associated with this religious and cultural heritage, but he recognizes its erosion through the generations of the family living in America. He grew up and was schooled in Newton, Massachusetts, before studying English at Yale, where he took a BA (1964) and a PhD (1969). With a Fulbright scholarship, he also studied at Cambridge, England, taking an AB (1966) and an MA (1968). At Cambridge he performed with several of the team who would go on to form Monty Python's Flying Circus (he is mentioned in one of their sketches), but he would pursue his own career within academia. From 1969 he taught English Literature at the University of California, Berkeley, becoming a full professor in 1980. Since 1997 he has been a professor of literature at Harvard University, where in 2000 he was appointed John Cogan University Professor of the Humanities.

Greenblatt is a leading scholar of Renaissance literature and CULTURE whose work as a writer and editor has been instrumental in the emergence of 'NEW HISTORICISM' – indeed it was Greenblatt who coined the phrase in 1982 (although he himself prefers the alternative 'cultural poetics' – see the entry for NEW HISTORICISM AND CULTURAL MATERIALISM in Section 3, p. 186). He has expressed surprise at the widespread adoption of 'new historicism' as a term, and he often asserts a deep mistrust of all-embracing *theories* of literature or culture – he is not, in other words, comfortable with being identified as a 'theorist', which role has in some ways been thrust upon him. He has written (almost by popular demand, it seems) on the meanings and implications of 'new historicism', but when he takes a step back to discuss his practice in isolation from a particular object of investigation he is at pains to point out that, if 'new historicism' is to be recognized at all, it should be seen as a group of malleable interpretative practices rather than as any type of fixed doctrine. This is seen in the careful wording of the title *Practicing New Historicism*, and in the recurrent insistence in that work that 'new historicism is not a repeatable methodology or a literary critical program'. In some respects, then, Greenblatt's influence on critical practice has worked through example rather than prescription – through his illuminating examinations of *particular* cultural productions rather than through the *abstraction* of modes of thought or critical approaches from those particular cases.

Greenblatt may downplay his role as a generator of critical tools, but his work has nevertheless significantly shifted the sands of literary studies in England and America since the early 1980s. His analyses of Renaissance TEXTS – particularly the drama of William Shakespeare and Christopher Marlowe, but also travel NARRATIVES and poetry – have radically influenced the manner in which historical criticism is conducted. Greenblatt's development of what would become New Historicism can be seen as a reaction against the ahistorical approaches of NEW CRITICISM and DECONSTRUCTION which dominated literary studies in America in the 1960s and 1970s. Where these approaches tended to divorce literary works from the environments in which they were produced, Greenblatt has always emphasized the embeddedness of literary works within their cultural, political, religious and other contexts. For Greenblatt, literary works and other representations are never historically-transcendent vessels of universal truth: literature may very well still 'speak to us' (and Greenblatt is fascinated by the fact that literature from the past can do this), but that does not alter the fact that the identity of a literary work is intricately marked by the CULTURAL circumstances of its writing. And furthermore, Greenblatt argues, literature is typically more than a mere product of its circumstances but can feed back into and change the conditions in which it was created – in other words, literature, for Greenblatt, is frequently the politically-charged site of IDEOLOGICAL struggle. Shakespeare's plays, he argues in *Shakespearean Negotiations*, 'negotiate' the struggles for power and authority of Early Modern England, and as publicly performed WORKS they actively *participate* in these struggles. Renaissance travel accounts, he argues in *Marvelous Possessions*, often functioned as sites where identities were negotiated through plotting encounters with the OTHERS of newly-discovered lands.

Unlike many examples of what we might call 'old historicism', Greenblatt's historicism does not view literature within a privileged category of 'Art' which stands somehow distinct from a historical 'background'. Literary works, for Greenblatt, are not autonomous creations but are inevitably enmeshed within wider DISCOURSES embodied in other works and in social, cultural and political practices: he writes, with Catherine Gallagher, of their 'fascination with the possibility of treating all of the written and visual traces of a particular culture as a mutually intelligible network of signs'. In this sense Greenblatt's approach is clearly indebted, as he acknowledges, to the DISCOURSE analysis of MICHEL FOUCAULT. Indeed, Greenblatt's new historicism owes much to several other key POST-STRUCTURALIST concerns, particularly the mistrust of language as a transparent medium through which to see 'the world' and the idea that SUBJECTS are constructed by discourse. In Greenblatt's hands, the former of these concerns becomes a rigorous attention to the *textuality* of history (there are resemblance between his work and that of Hayden White), and such a problematization of what actually constitutes 'history' can be seen as a central distinction between 'old' and 'new' historicisms. As Greenblatt writes: 'methodological self-consciousness is one of the distinguishing marks of the new historicism in cultural studies as opposed to a historicism based upon faith in the transparency of signs and interpretative procedures'.

Greenblatt is also influential as an editor, both of literary texts and of criticism. He edits *Representations*, a Berkeley-based journal which developed from a reading group he was involved in and which publishes articles of a broadly new-historical stamp. He was the general editor of *The Norton Shakespeare* (1997) and was an associate general editor of *The Norton Anthology of English Literature* (2000). As an editor of Shakespeare, Greenblatt advances his efforts to read the plays back into their historical situations: the introductions and annotations in *The Norton Shakespeare* assert the political engagement of the plays and provide expansive documentation of the cultural circumstances of their writing. Reviewing the edition in the *Times Literary Supplement*, Peter Holland suggests that the drive to historicize the plays is to the neglect of their subtleties in terms of stagecraft and performance, and that by prioritizing the Early Modern context the edition 'offers no means to negotiate between a view of the works as cultural tokens and their subsequent accommodation to other cultures, other histories and geographies'.

Even those inclined to grant that this criticism has some force must recognize that Greenblatt's influence on both Renaissance studies and on literary criticism and theory more generally has been both substantial and valuable. His work can be credited with changing critical practice more than any other single figure during the past two decades.

Further reading

Richard Dutton and Richard Wilson (eds), *New Historicism and Renaissance Drama* (London and New York: Longman, 1992); H. Aram Veeser (ed.), *The New Historicism* (London and New York: Routledge, 1989).

HIRSCH, E[ric] D[onald], Jr (1928–)

Main works

Wordsworth and Schelling: A Typological Study of Romanticism (1960)
Innocence and Experience: An Introduction to Blake (1964)
Validity in Interpretation (1967)
The Aims of Interpretation (1976)
Cultural Literacy: What Every American Needs to Know (co-authored with Joseph Kett and James Trefil) (1987)
The Dictionary of Cultural Literacy (co-authored with Joseph Kett and James Trefil) (1988)

Key terms

cultural literacy ■ INTENTION ■ MEANING AND SIGNIFICANCE ■ objectivism

Born in Memphis, Tennessee, E.D. Hirsch obtained his doctorate from Yale University in 1957. He taught at the same university until 1966, when he was appointed professor at the University of Virginia. Hirsch's academic career can conveniently be divided into three main stages. First, that of the respected scholar-critic of the Romantic period; second, that of the literary theorist concerned to argue for an 'objectivist' view of literary meaning based upon authorial INTENTION, and finally, that of the CULTURAL and educational polemicist fighting for traditional educational methods and against 'progressive' attempts to replace an accepted cultural CANON.

Hirsch's books *Validity in Interpretation* and *The Aims of Interpretation* raised significant controversy for arguing against what in 1967 was a fashionable INTER-

PRETATIVE pluralism. The former book effectively raised its standard against the view that the meaning of a literary work could be divorced from what its AUTHOR intended it to mean. This was a view which had been advanced most forcefully by W.K. Wimsatt and Monroe Beardsley in their influential essay 'The Intentional Fallacy', and which had subsequently been endorsed by, among others, T.S. ELIOT, who had publicly conceded that his own poetry could legitimately be interpreted in ways that had never occurred to him. In addition to Wimsatt and Beardsley, Hirsch attributed such views to a minority within the German HERMENEUTIC tradition represented by Martin Heidegger and Hans-Georg Gadamer, whose 'relativism' he contrasted to the 'objectivism' of an alternative tradition of general hermeneutics.

Those opposed to Hirsch asked why it was that literary works went on being interpreted from generation to generation: if it is the case that the meaning of a literary work is what its author intended it to mean, then one might expect that once this authorial intention had been uncovered there would be nothing left for the interpretative critic to do but to repeat this uncovered truth. Hirsch, however, has used his distinction between MEANING AND SIGNIFICANCE to explain why literary works can always elicit something new from those reading them without sacrificing a unitary authorial meaning. Furthermore, he in his turn was able to ask how relativist critics could with a good conscience mark student essays and examinations if they felt that there was no way of adjudicating between the validity of different interpretations once the 'standard' of authorial intention was removed. Subsequent commentators have suggested that it was perhaps a limitation of the debate that it focused too much upon *meaning*, as we do not read literary works to discover a meaning but rather in order to experience both emotional and intellectual *responses*.

For more on Hirsch's contribution to debates with the hermeneutic tradition, see the entry for HERMENEUTICS in Section 3.

The third and most controversial stage of Hirsch's career (to date) has involved his linked defence of the traditional canon of learning and his attack on 'progressive' educational methods that (according to him) replace the authority of a cultural tradition and the hard work of learning with the vagaries and sloppiness of pupil/student choice. Hirsch claims that the replacement of the traditional canon of learning with IDEOLOGICALLY motivated alternatives (created by ethnic minorities, FEMINISTS, MARXISTS and others) is producing an America ignorant of the (note the definite article) Western cultural heritage. His opponents accuse him of wanting to return to authoritarian schools and universities based upon the rote learning of facts about dead white males. Hirsch's co-authored books on cultural literacy have been best sellers, and their success has encouraged Hirsch to set up the Cultural Literacy Foundation in Charlottesville, Virginia (Hirsch holds a professorship in the English Department at the University of Virginia).

Hirsch has denied that he is politically a conservative, and indeed in an article entitled 'Why Traditional Education is Progressive' he has described himself as a liberal and has cited the communist intellectual Antonio Gramsci's 1932 attack on a 'democratic education' that stressed naturalistic approaches over hard work. However Hirsch's alleged lack of respect for cultural traditions other than the dominant Graeco-Roman and Anglo-Saxon ones has raised the ire of ethnic and other minorities.

Further reading

Paul B. Armstrong, *Conflicting Readings: Variety and Validity in Interpretation* (Chapel Hill and London: University of North Carolina Press, 1990); Frank Lentricchia, *After the New Criticism* (Chicago: University of Chicago Press, 1980).

hooks, bell (1952–)

Main works

Ain't I a Woman: Black Women and Feminism (1981)
Outlaw Culture: Resisting Representations (1994)

Key terms

white supremacist capitalist patriarchy ■ politics of domination

Born in 1952 in Hopkinsville, Kentucky, bell hooks is the pseudonym of the American scholar Gloria Jean Watkins. Watkins grew up in the segregated South. She obtained her BA in English literature from Stanford University in1973, then completed an MA on Toni Morrison's fiction and its relation to Black CULTURE at the University of Wisconsin in 1976 and her doctorate at the University of California, Santa Cruz in 1983. Upon graduation, she taught African and Afro-American studies at Yale University, and women's studies at Oberlin College until 1994. Since 1994 she has been Distinguished Professor of English at the City College of New York.

Her first full-length book, *Ain't I a Woman: Black Women and Feminism* (1981), reviewed FEMINIST criticism and found that it was often written from and for the perspective of White, middle-class women; in it she also looked at the marginalization of Black women involved in the struggle for equal rights. Her work was an attempt at challenging and simultaneously expanding feminist agendas to include a greater awareness of economic, ethnic and historical contexts. In the 1980s, hooks founded a support group for Black women called the Sisters of the Yam, which she later used as the title of a 1993 book celebrating the sense of community among African-American women.

The theoretical flexibility that is in many ways her trademark is partly demonstrated by her use of a pseudonym, which is actually the name of her maternal great-grandmother. By using it, Watkins immediately suggests herself as a spokesperson for a larger cultural tradition: at the same time, she problematizes the idea of the author as the sole origin of what he or she produces (a technique

SECTION 5

that is accentuated by her refusal to use upper-case letters for the name, suggesting a sense of identity that is almost POST-STRUCTURALIST in its view of identity as a position within, rather than outside, language and history).

Typical of hooks and her idea of cultural theory is her critique of the style of pop music known as 'gangsta rap', which she sees as misogynist and sexist, but which she further relates to White STEREOTYPES of Black male behaviour. For hooks, 'gangsta rap' allows white listeners and spectators to take part in a culture of aggression towards women, without being held directly responsible for it: at the same time, rappers who express themselves in this way confirm a sense of Black male behaviour as violent and brutal, especially towards women, and therefore uncivilized. In addition, 'gangsta rap' is funded and exploited by the system hooks repeatedly refers to as 'white supremacist capitalist patriarchy' (which in itself suggests her unique blend of ethnic, FEMINIST and MARXIST thinking): the moguls of the music industry make money from such singers and at the same time make the latter agents in their own humiliation.

hooks is attentive to the politics of domination in its entirety, and does not restrict herself to the oppression of Black women. For her, the oppression of Black men by Whites, or White women by men, prevents either from further oppressing or silencing other groups. She therefore introduces a sense of complexity into the issue of identity, one which is very much influenced by political experience and by POSTMODERN theories of subjectivity. But her commitment to public debate and to the importance of education combine to make her in some ways like a latter-day, radical version of Matthew Arnold.

Further reading

Patricia Hill Collins, *Black Feminist Thought: Knowledge, Consciousness and the Politics of Empowerment* (London: Routledge, 1991); Stanlie M. James and Abena Busia (eds), *Theorizing Black Feminisms: The Visionary Pragmatism of Black Women* (London: Routledge, 1993).

IRIGARAY, Luce (1932–)

Main works

Speculum of the Other Woman (1985; in French, 1974)
This Sex Which is Not One (1985; in French, 1977)
An Ethics of Sexual Difference (1993; in French, 1984)

Key terms

double I / two lips ■ speculum ■ woman-as-subject

Born in 1932 in Belgium, Luce Irigaray worked as a schoolteacher in Brussels for three years after receiving an MA from the University of Louvain (in Belgium) in 1955. In 1961 she received her second Master's, this time in psychology, from the University of Paris. From 1962–64 she worked for the *Fondation Nationale de la Recherche Scientifique* in Belgium. In 1968 she received a Doctorate in

Linguistics. From 1969–74 she taught at the University of Paris VIII-Vincennes, where she became a member of the Freudian School of Paris, directed by JACQUES LACAN. Irigaray's second Doctoral thesis, later published as *Speculum of the Other Woman* (1974) led to her being dismissed from Vincennes for politicizing PSYCHOANALYSIS. Later, she went to work as a research assistant at the *Centre National de la Recherche Scientifique* in Paris: she is currently Director of Research at the Commission of Philosophy there.

Irigaray has been classified as (among other things) a psychoanalyst, a philosopher, a POST-STRUCTURALIST and a theorist of FEMINISM, and all of these classifications have some justice to them. Her work is iconoclastic and strikingly original, but it has also been accused of pretentiousness and of word-spinning.

Irigaray's work on the speculum, a curved mirror used by women to examine their sexual organs, is both engagement with and direct challenge to JACQUES LACAN's theory of the MIRROR STAGE, during which the child sees his reflection in the flat mirror and becomes aware of himself as a SUBJECT, with an identity that is visible and separate from that of the mother. Irigaray argues that this ideal is exclusively masculine: identity is based on the male child's rejection of the mother. At the same time, the woman is seen as the mirror image of man: she is described and understood in male terms, and is a product of his CULTURAL, historical, social and theoretical imagination. This is rejected in the image produced by the speculum. In addition, Irigaray uses the speculum to critique the notion of language or art as something mimetic (faithfully reproducing reality, like a flat mirror): the curved mirror produces an image that folds back into itself, and which has no obvious beginning or end.

Like the work of HÉLÈNE CIXOUS, then, Irigaray's writings can be seen as a feminist engagement with the work of Lacan. Combining psychoanalysis, feminism and post-structuralist linguistics in her work, Irigaray attacks male views of female SUBJECTIVITY, which are predicated on the Freudian idea that women do not have a phallus and are therefore defined by lack and by a need for what they do not have. For Irigaray, humanity is trapped by the male notion of identity based on a single, unified, fixed position predicated on the penis: women have a much more fluid sense of self which can be related to the vaginal labia, which are double. In *This Sex Which is Not One*, Irigaray proposes a theory of identity based on the 'double I', or the two lips, by which she means not the literal female body but a symbolic identity formed by the idea of the female. The two lips suggest an intersection of selves, a DIALOGUE of languages (social and personal), that correspond to a plurality of subjective experience opposed to the single 'I' advanced by Sigmund Freud and others. The title of her book suggests that women are not a sex within the male system (they are an absence, the OTHER, that which is not male) and at the same time that they are more than one.

Irigaray's theories are useful when looking, for example, at Emily Dickinson's writing, which is characterized by its multiplicity of perspective and voice. According to Irigaray, such writing is typical of both the woman's search for subjectivity within a male culture that denies her identity or defines it in negative terms, and of a woman's subjectivity, which is shifting, ambiguous, excessive, disruptive, always 'other'. There are two ideas expressed by her phrase 'woman-as-subject', then: that of women's oppression, and that of women's search for SUBJECTIVITY.

Further reading

Carolyn Burke, Naomi Schor, and Margaret Whitford (eds), *Engaging with Irigaray* (New York: Columbia University Press, 1994); Margaret Whitford, *Luce Irigaray: Philosophy in the Feminine* (London: Routledge, 1991).

ISER, Wolfgang (1926–)

Main works

The Implied Reader: Patterns of Communication in Prose Fiction from Bunyan to Beckett (1974)
The Act of Reading: A Theory of Aesthetic Response (1978)
Prospecting: From Reader Response to Literary Anthropology (1989)
The Fictive and the Imaginary: Charting Literary Anthropology (1993)
The Range of Interpretation (2000)

Key terms

gap ■ implied reader (see AUTHOR) ■ imaginary ■ indeterminacy ■ READER-REPONSE THEORY

The German critic and theorist Wolfgang Iser has remained a consistently influential figure within Anglo-American literary studies for almost three decades, during a period within which a succession of different movements, critics and theorists have risen to prominence only to fade out of view after a few years. Iser was a pupil of the German philosopher and AESTHETICIAN Hans-Georg Gadamer, and his ideas owe much to Gadamer's HERMENEUTICS with its stress upon the DIALOGIC nature of the encounter between READER and TEXT. Indeed, if one wanted to isolate the most important founding principle of Iser's thought then one might well highlight its anti-ESSENTIALISM and stress upon the DIALOGIC or dialectical nature of the literary process. Iser is critical of any form of reification, whether of TEXT or of INTERPRETATION. Together with his colleague at the University of Konstanz in Germany Hans Robert Jauss, Iser is a leading member of what has become known as the Konstanz School, a theoretical grouping that built on the work of Gadamer and of other leading representatives of a Germanic tradition of aesthetic theorizing such as Ingarden and Husserl. In spite of their shared interests and positions, however, Iser's concern with aesthetic response (which generally homes in on the individual READER or viewer) should be distinguished from Jauss's reception theory, which has a much wider scope, focusing on broad patterns of readership or audience 'reception'. In Anglo-American circles both writers are often referred to as reader-response critics, and the list above will reveal how often the word 'reader' appears in the title of Iser's books. For Iser's relationship with phenomenology and reader-response criticism, see Section 3, pp. 157–8.

In addition to holding a position at Konstanz, Iser has worked at the University of California at Irvine, and his association with the journal *New Literary History* has done much to make his work known outside the German-speaking world. Iser's first article for this journal, 'The Reading Process: A Phenomenological Approach', published in 1972 then reprinted both in a popular anthology of articles from the journal *New Directions in Literary History* (1974) and in Iser's book of the same year *The Implied Reader*, has remained one of his most widely read and influential pieces. Building on dialogic and interactive elements in the German PHENOMENOLOGICAL tradition, Iser argued in this article for a shift of focus from the text itself to the text plus the actions involved in responding to the text, and he then moved to distinguish the literary text from the literary WORK by characterizing the work as the text when realized or CONCRETIZED through a reading. Such a view was clearly anti-FORMALIST, and struck a chord in the minds of those interested in looking at literature not in terms of object-like works, or (as in vulgar MARXISM) as mechanical reflections of a socio-economic reality, but as a component in an interactive and creative process. Or, rather, as component in many interactive and creative processes, as the same work might be realized in different ways through different readings. Thus if the text already contains an implied reader, the reader also contains the results of reading previous texts.

Iser's subsequent work has retained this emphasis upon the dynamic nature of literary response, arguing that reading is a creative activity which fills in 'gaps' in the text and illuminates it from different angles in a kaleidoscopic manner. His later writing has attempted to extend ideas developed in literary theorizing to life in general, on the assumption that if a literary text *does* something to readers it can also *tell us* something about them and about the human need for the fictive and the 'imaginary' – a concept that, Iser admits, resists definition but that we experience in such a way as to place it beyond doubt. This larger project of Iser's has been dubbed 'literary anthropology'.

Critics of Iser, including TERRY EAGLETON in his very widely read book *Literary Theory*, have accused Iser of advocating an apolitical, neutral and non-ideological reader's stance, in the belief that any IDEOLOGICAL commitment closes off possible responses by the reader to a text. There may be some truth in this criticism, and Iser's youthful desire to distance himself from the cultural legacy of the German Nazi period may, some commentators have argued, explain Iser's suspicion of the overtly ideological. But Eagleton's characterization of Iser as a liberal humanist is probably too restricted in scope to capture the subtlety of Iser's response to socio-political elements in particular texts.

Among the authors about whom Iser has written, Beckett occupies a special place, and Iser deserves respect for the seriousness of his initially unfashionable grappling both with Beckett and also with literary MODERNISM more generally.

Further reading

The special issue of *New Literary History* (31(1), 2000), *On the Writings of Wolfgang Iser*, contains a range of accessible articles on Iser's career and publications.

JAKOBSON, Roman Osipovich (1896–1982)

Main works

'Two Aspects of Language and Two Types of Aphasic Disturbance' (1956; revised 1971)
'Closing Statement: Linguistics and Poetics' (1960)
Selected Writings (8 vols; 1962–88)
'Charles Baudelaire's "Les Chats"' (co-written with Claude Lévi-Strauss) (1970; in French, 1962)
'The Dominant' (1971; in Czech, 1935)

Key terms

dominant ■ LITERARINESS ■ SYNTAGMATIC AND PARADIGMATIC

Born in Russia, the son of an industrialist, Roman Jakobson took his first degree at Moscow University then moved to Czechoslovakia in 1920, receiving his doctorate from the University of Prague. He remained teaching in Czechoslovakia until the German invasion in 1939, when he fled first to Scandinavia (working in the universities of Copenhagen, Oslo and Uppsala) and subsequently (in 1941) to the USA. A founding member of both the Moscow Linguistic Circle and also the PRAGUE SCHOOL, Jakobson is a hard figure to classify. His work ranges from relatively 'straight' linguistics (studies in phonology, language acquisition and child language, and the use of aphasic disorders to investigate language processes) to the study of the folk tale, general poetics, and the linguistic study of literary WORKS. His *Selected Writings* bears testimony to a massive production, but within literary studies his influence has rested on a relatively small number of seminal articles, and he has played a leading part in a variety of influential movements – RUSSIAN FORMALISM, STRUCTURALISM in its early and later manifestations (the work of FERDINAND DE SAUSSURE exerted a significant influence on him), SEMIOTICS, general poetics, STYLISTICS, and even (mainly through his association with Claude Lévi-Strauss) anthropology.

Matejka and Pomorska's 1971 collection of Russian Formalist and Structuralist TEXTS *Readings in Russian Poetics* contains no fewer than four essays by Jakobson, including his influential essay 'The Dominant' in which he argues that the work of art contains a 'focusing element' that orders all other components. Another essay in the collection, 'On Realism in Art' (written in Czech in 1921) argues for a relational rather than an ESSENTIALIST understanding of the concept of REALISM in a manner that predates similar arguments by BERTOLT BRECHT.

One of the most influential concepts developed by the Russian Formalists is that of 'LITERARINESS', and in his essay 'The Theory of the "Formal Method"'

Boris Eichenbaum quotes tellingly from Jakobson's 'Recent Russian Poetry, Sketch 1', first published in Prague in 1921. In the extract quoted, Jakobson makes the polemical claim that the object of study in literary science is not literature but literariness – that is, that which makes a given work a work of literature. The argument is directed *outwards* against using the methods of history, anthropology, psychology, politics or philosophy to analyze the literary work, and *inwards* towards the text itself, upon whose features the scholar of literature is enjoined to concentrate.

Jakobson's 'Closing Statement: Linguistics and Poetics' had considerable impact within literary studies when published in 1960. In his statement Jakobson outlined diagrammatically what he described as the constitutive facts in any act of verbal communication, ranging from an addresser through context, message, contact and code to an addressee. (The model almost certainly owes much to what is known as the Shannon and Weaver model of communication, although this source is not acknowledged by Jakobson.) Each of Jakobson's 'facts' is granted an attached basic function of human communication: emotive, referential, poetic, phatic, metalingual and conative. Jakobson then proceeds with a gnomic but much-quoted claim: '*The poetic function projects the principle of equivalence from the axis of selection into the axis of combination.*' In common with much of Jakobson's most influential pieces of writing, the article had its detractors as well as its champions. It seemed to define the poetic in terms of self-referential language (a focusing upon the message for its own sake), it included no clear indication as to how bad poetry was to be distinguished from good, and it seemed to include no clear role for prose in its POETICS.

Jakobson's use of research into aphasia to illuminate language processes has also been both influential and controversial: the reader is here referred to the entry for SYNTAGMATIC AND PARADIGMATIC in Section 4. Also controversial has been Jakobson's application of linguistic analysis to literary works. The article on Baudelaire's 'Les Chats' which Jakobson co-authored with Claude Lévi-Strauss was very widely read as a result of being included (along with Jakobson's 'On Russian Fairy Tales') in English translation in Michael Lane's best-selling *Structuralism: A Reader* in 1970, at the start of structuralism's period of great influence in literary studies. The article attempts to trace structural patterns in Baudelaire's poem at an almost exclusively ABSTRACT level: comparisons and contrasts are drawn between masculine and feminine rhymes, subordinate and main clauses, animate and inanimate substantives, and singular and plural verb-forms. Comment on the 'phonic texture' of the poem contains statements such as 'in the second quatrain, the role of dominant phonic passes from the vowel-sounds to the consonant phonemes, in particular to the liquid consonants', and the article contains box diagrams indicating shifts between extrinsic and intrinsic, empirical and mythological, and real, unreal and surreal. The essay was negatively reviewed by, among others, Jonathan Culler in his *Structuralist Poetics* (1975). Culler remarked (after having criticized Jakobson's 'careless' treatment of grammar), that

Jakobson's way of proceeding with the poem indicated the tenuousness or even irrelevance of the kind of numerical symmetry argued for in the article.

Further reading

Jonathan Culler, *Structuralist Poetics: Structuralism, Linguistics and the Study of Literature* (London: Routledge, 1975); David Lodge, *The Modes of Modern Writing: Metaphor, Metonymy and the Typology of Modern Literature* (London: Edward Arnold, 1977).

JAMESON, Fredric R. (1934–)

Main works

Marxism and Form: Twentieth-Century Dialectical Theories of Literature (1971)
The Prison-House of Language: A Critical Account of Structuralism and Russian Formalism (1972)
The Political Unconscious: Narrative as a Socially Symbolic Act (1981)
The Ideologies of Theory: Essays 1971–1986 (2 vols; 1986)
Signatures of the Visible (1990)
Postmodernism, or, The Cultural Logic of Late Capitalism (1991)

Key terms

hyperspace ▓ mediation ▓ political unconscious ▓ POSTMODERNISM

Fredric Jameson is one of the most intellectual of contemporary literary and CUL-TURAL critics, and perhaps also one of the most European of American intellectuals. His doctorate was awarded by Yale University for a thesis on Jean-Paul Sartre which became his first published book, and an immersion in certain key European intellectual and academic traditions is a hallmark of his work. His political commitment to MARXISM may also seem more European than American (early on in *Marxism and Form* he suggests that little in contemporary American art or culture is worth salvaging), although this commitment seems to carry fewer implications for political activism than it does for, for example, TERRY EAGLETON.

But if Jameson's theoretical forebears are largely European, his analytical concerns are more truly global than most of his contemporaries (in 1998 he co-edited a volume entitled *The Cultures of Globalization*). In *Marxism and Form* Jameson engages with what has come to be known as Western Marxism: the work of Adorno, BENJAMIN, Marcuse, Bloch, LUKÁCS and Sartre is subjected to a critique which ends with a call for a dialectical criticism. Even at this stage in his career Jameson recognized that a key problem facing Marxist literary or cultural analysis was that of mediation, and in his preface to this book he suggests that the essential value of Sartre's *Critique of Dialectical Reason* is that it poses this problem. If the mechanical-Marxist view that literature and other cultural products 'reflect' a society's economic base directly was unacceptable, then the problem became that of demonstrating how large socio-economic forces, formations and interests none the less had a formative and determining effect upon such products through complex sequences of transforming mediations, mediations which Jameson accepts must also constantly expand the observer's relationship to historical fact. Ten years later, in his *The Political Unconscious*, Jameson is still teasing away at this issue, suggesting that mediation is the classical dialectical term for the establishment of relationships between the FORMAL analysis of a WORK of art and its social ground. The very concept of a 'political unconscious' can be seen as an attempt to appropriate a concept from Freud for Marxist use.

In between these two books, Jameson had published his critique of FORMAL-ISM and STRUCTURALISM, *The Prison-House of Language*. As the title suggests, Jameson's main criticism of both traditions is that their reliance upon the linguistic paradigm locks human beings into a totalizing prison from which there is no escape, and Jameson extends this criticism to later structuralist Marxists such as Louis Althusser who, according to Jameson, believes that 'we never really get outside our own minds'.

It is with his contribution to debates about the POSTMODERN that Jameson achieves perhaps his widest readership. Once again, a chosen title sums up his position: *Postmodernism, or, the Cultural Logic of Late Capitalism* – postmodernism is not just a cultural fashion or a social trend, it represents a *logic*, one produced by the particular socio-economic formation to which Jameson (indulging in either optimism or wish-fulfilment) dubs late capitalism. 'Cultural' is not a euphemism for literature: Jameson has always been able to appeal to arts such as music, film and architecture in his writings, and the scope of his book is impressive. It is packed with genuinely challenging insights and suggestions – for example, that film gothic is ultimately a class fantasy or nightmare in which the dialectic of privilege and shelter is exercised: privileges seal you off from others, but by the same token they constitute a protective wall behind which all kinds of envious forces may be plotting against you. Alluding to Hitchcock's *Psycho*, Jameson refers to this as 'the shower-curtain syndrome'!

The example serves as a useful token of Jameson's method: a detail is picked up from one TEXT, generalized across a group of texts, and then related to an element in a larger socio-economic unit. The required set of mediations is there, and such examples are often genuinely thought-provoking and enlightening. But sometimes the jumps involve seven-league boots and do less than adequate justice to the texts considered. In an essay published in 1985 (see below), Jacques Berthoud offered a detailed critique of *The Political Unconscious* and, in particular, of Jameson's treatment of Joseph Conrad's *Lord Jim*. For Berthoud, Jameson's reading was just too capricious and reductive, manufacturing spurious rifts and discontinuities in the text. Jameson's fondness for drawing lines of connection between the telling textual detail and the large sociopolitical context can, it may be conceded, involve paying less attention to the significance of the AESTHETIC totality of the individual text than could be hoped for. (A 1990 essay of Jameson's, 'Modernism and Imperialism' is representative in its leaps between large generalizations about imperialism and three relatively short quotations from E.M. Forster's *Howards End*, with some additional comments on VIRGINIA WOOLF.)

Further reading

Jacques Berthoud, 'Narrative and Ideology: A Critique of Fredric Jameson's *The Political Unconscious*', in Jeremy Hawthorn (ed.), *Narrative: From Malory to Motion Pictures* (London: Edward Arnold, 1985); Clint Burnham, *The Jamesonian Unconscious: The Aesthetics of Marxist theory* (Durham, NC: Duke University Press, 1995); Sean Homer, *Fredric Jameson* (Cambridge: Polity Press, 1997).

KRISTEVA, Julia (1941–)

Main works

Desire in Language: A Semiotic Approach to Literature and Art (1980; in French, 1969, 1971 and 1977)
Strangers to Ourselves (1991; in French, 1988)

Key terms

SEMIOTICS ■ INTERTEXTUALITY

Born in Bulgaria in 1941, Kristeva emigrated to France in 1966 after receiving a degree in linguistics from the University of Sofia. As a doctoral fellow, she was research assistant to the STRUCTURALIST and MARXIST critic LUCIEN GOLDMANN; she also studied with ROLAND BARTHES at the same time. She soon became a member of the group of intellectuals (including Barthes and MICHEL FOUCAULT) associated with the journal *Tel Quel*, an avant-garde literary review published from 1960 to 1982: she joined its editorial board in 1970. Her doctoral dissertation at the University of Paris VII, *La Révolution du langage poétique* (1974; *Revolution in Poetic Language* [1984]), combined PSYCHOANALYTIC theory with linguistics and literature. She was awarded a Chair at the university on the strength of it, and has worked there as Professor of Linguistics since that time, in addition to being a Visiting Professor at Columbia University, sharing the Chair of Literary Semiology with UMBERTO ECO and TZVETAN TODOROV. She is also Executive Secretary of the International Association of Semiology, and in 1997 was the recipient of one of France's highest honours, the 'Chevalière de la légion d'honneur'.

In *Revolution in Poetic Language*, Kristeva introduced her concept of INTERTEXUALITY, which involves 'the passage from one sign system to another'. For Kristeva, intertextuality is especially evident in the NOVEL, which often involves several SIGN systems competing and interacting. Kristeva's knowledge of Russian meant that she was acquainted first-hand with the work of MIKHAIL BAKHTIN, and her theory of intertextuality can be linked both to the concept of the DIALOGIC and his idea of the CARNIVALESQUE. 'Intertextuality', however, is not confined to literature: in Kristeva's view it can equally well be traced in political history and even psychoanalysis.

Central to Kristeva's work is her distinction between the 'semiotic' and the 'symbolic'. The second of these terms relates to JACQUES LACAN's theory of child development, whereby the move into language involves entrance into the realm of the 'symbolic', dominated by the 'Law of the Father'. Language is structured by grammar, by divisions, by rules and regulations that divide the world into an 'I' and a set of objects outside the self. For Kristeva, however, there are still residues of a pre-linguistic state that involves perceptions, emotions, forces and 'pulsions' that are associated with the site of the maternal, and which involve all kinds of sensations – including apparently contradictory ones. These 'pulsions' can be accessed or felt through music, or rhythms of any kind: they also manifest themselves in silence, absence, contradictions, noise and linguistic playfulness. She argues that although this element is feminine, and opposed to the patriarchal, it is not biologically female: since all human beings are carried in the womb, and nursed after birth, then all have experienced or felt the same movements and rhythms and are capable of responding to and recreating them to some extent. Unlike HÉLÈNE CIXOUS and LUCE IRIGARAY, whose 'writing of the feminine' is much more closely identified with the female body (see ÉCRITURE FÉMININE), Kristeva's SEMIOTIC state is equivalent to a phase of existence during which the social distinctions of GENDER are not recognized. (See also Section 3, p. 168.)

Kristeva differs then from Sigmund Freud and Jacques Lacan in emphasizing the continuing importance of the maternal in the development of subjectivity and language. For Freud and Lacan, entrance into the social and linguistic realms involves a move away from the mother which stems from the child's fear of castration. Kristeva also defines identity in terms of a 'subject-in-process': we are never finished, complete, unified, singular, but always in a process of becoming, negotiating between different states.

Although Kristeva's work is most often described as FEMINIST, she has in fact been critical of its two main branches. She criticizes liberal, Anglo-American, feminism on the grounds that it regards experience as being universal and non-problematic, and because it seeks power within the same terms as the bourgeois system (that is, feminists want equal power rather than a different kind of power system). She also criticizes feminists – like SIMONE DE BEAUVOIR (who though French, is regarded as the founding theorist of American feminism) – whose attitude to motherhood is allegedly hostile. On the other hand, Kristeva has not joined forces with those writers whose work is often identified with her own – Cixous and Irigaray, for example – who argue for a feminine language outside and against patriarchal culture, and who oppose Lacan. Rather than reject what she calls the sphere of the symbolic, Kristeva claims that it is important to combine it with a sense of the semiotic: indeed, for her, the two can be interdependent, as in poetry, which is both a means of signification, a sequence of references, and a form of language which foregrounds its own materiality in the shape of rhythms, noises and imagistic skill. In short, Kristeva prizes poetry for combining both the CONSTATIVE and PERFORMATIVE aspects of DISCOURSE, which correspond to the SYMBOLIC and semiotic dimensions of the human mind.

SECTION 5

Further reading

John Lechte, *Julia Kristeva* (London: Routledge, 1990); Michael Payne, *Reading Theory: An Introduction to Lacan, Derrida and Kristeva* (Oxford: Blackwell, 1993).

LACAN, Jacques (1901–81)

Main works

Écrits (1977; in French, 1966)
The Four Fundamental Concepts of Psychoanalysis (1977; in French, 1973)

Key terms

MIRROR STAGE ■ PHALLOCENTRIC ■ the symbolic ■ the real ■ the imaginary

Born in Paris in 1901 into a bourgeois Catholic family, Jacques-Marie Emile Lacan studied medicine at the Sorbonne, earning his full medical degree by 1932 before proceeding to study psychiatry under Henri Claude and Gatian de Clerambaut, working at a special clinic attached to the Prefecture of Police. Lacan became a full member of the *Société Psychoanalytique de Paris* in 1938, but after a number of disputes he formed a breakaway faction that eventually became the *École Freudienne de Paris* in 1964. Lacan's prominence grew after he began giving regular weekly seminars at the *École Normale Supérieure* in 1953: many of these were eventually published as essays in *Écrits* in 1966, which gave him celebrity status. The seminars for 1964 were published in French in 1973 and in English as *The Four Fundamental Concepts of Psychoanalysis* (1977). The organization called the Freudian School of Paris was disbanded by Lacan himself in 1980, because of what he claimed was its failure to adhere with sufficient strictness to Freudian principles.

Lacan's work is essentially a development of Sigmund Freud's theory that there is a radical split between consciousness and the unconscious (the ego and the id). Whereas most of us work from the assumption that we are largely in control of our own actions, Freud claimed that we are in fact often motivated by impulses and forces of which we are not even aware. For Lacan, there are three main phases in the development of the child, which he identifies as corresponding to the concepts of need, demand, and desire, or the Real, the Imaginary, and the Symbolic. (These develop from Freud's theory of the Oedipus complex, where the infant passes through the seduction, primal, and castration phases.)

In the first phase, the infant is incapable of distinguishing between itself and the mother, or between the baby and anything that is not the baby: it is driven by the need for food and comfort, which it gets mostly from the breast. At this stage, there is no distinction between the breast which satisfies, and the need to be satisfied: they are part of a continuum, a state which Lacan identifies with nature, and with a kind of fullness and completeness which he identifies as the real. The phase ends when the child begins to become aware of itself as separate, when it changes from pure need to 'demand' – which involves someone else to satisfy the demand.

The next phase, the move into the imaginary, coincides with the MIRROR STAGE. The child sees its reflection in the mirror, then looks back at another person (most often, the mother) and then again at the mirror image. The child anticipates that it will one day become whole, complete, unified again, like the image in the mirror, which becomes an ideal. The encounter with the mirror acts as a catalyst, initiating a sense of self-awareness, enabling the child to think of itself as a subject-in-the-making, soon to be an 'I', and therefore creating the ego. According to Lacan, the idea of this self is always a vision, a fantasy of wholeness, which is why he refers to this stage as the 'imaginary'.

The Symbolic realm overlaps with the 'imaginary', and is necessary for the process of adulthood to come about. Lacan associates the 'symbolic' with the acquisition of language: speaking confers an identity upon us, an 'I' position, and language further enables us to structure the world. Language also encodes the rules and conventions of a given CULTURE, the dimension of law, which according to Lacan operates under the assumption of some CENTRE of authority, what he calls the 'Name of the Father' or patriarchal order (sometimes referred to as the phallus: language is 'PHALLOCENTRIC', or based on the idea of a controlling centre identified with the system of the phallus). Entering into this structure is a necessary stage in the acquisition of a social identity. Language exists outside the self, like the mirror, in order to provide the self with an image of itself, like the mirror.

Also central to Lacan's ideas are his theories of the 'OTHER'. When the child is made conscious that it is separate from the world, the idea of the 'other' is created. This is accompanied by a sense of anxiety and loss. The child desires a return to the original sense of fullness and non-separation that it had in the Real. By extension, the Other (with a capital O) is made a structural position in the Symbolic order: it is a state that everyone is trying to access, to merge with, in order to get rid of the separation between 'self' and 'other'. At the same time, fulfilling this need is by definition impossible, because the sense of self comes about through an apprehension of separateness. So, the existence of the Other creates and sustains a ceaseless state of lack, which Lacan calls 'DESIRE'. By extension, language works the same way: it does not allow us to access reality directly, but mediates between the speaker and the object he wishes to represent. Such a view of discourse echoes the work of SAUSSURE and DERRIDA, for whom language involves both desire for the object and the deferral of desire: words are substitutes, not things.

At the same time, many of Lacan's ideas are related to a patriarchal system, where separation from the mother is compensated for by the acquisition of language and culture, and where the masculine is primary or central. Lacan does not necessarily support this, but his emphasis on the male has been criticized by several writers, including HÉLÈNE CIXOUS and LUCE IRIGARAY, among others.

SECTION 5

The relevance of Lacan to the study of literature would seem at first sight to be very limited, yet many literary theorists and critics have found his ideas to be of great value to their work. Feminist writers in particular have used concepts such as that of the symbolic order to explore the female writer's PARADOX: the need to work within the dominant order while challenging and disrupting it. Others have suggested that Lacan's work on gender formation, although not without its patriarchal assumptions, can be commandeered by feminists interested in the contribution made by literary works to gender division and formation. The concept of ÉCRITURE FÉMININE clearly owes much to Lacan, and has been important in charting alternative strategies for women writers. More generally, by some of those unexpected shifts of influence to which EDWARD SAID has given the name 'travelling theory', the apparently anti-individualist element in Lacan's theories led to their adoption by various MARXIST writers, including Louis Althusser.

Further reading

Barbara Freedman, *Staging the Gaze: Postmodernism, Psychoanalysis and Shakespearean Comedy* (Ithaca: Cornell University Press, 1991); John P. Muller and William J. Richardson (eds), *The Purloined Poe* (Baltimore: Johns Hopkins University Press, 1988).

LEAVIS, F[rank] R[aymond] (1895–1978)

Main works

Mass Civilisation and Minority Culture (1930)
New Bearings in English Poetry (1932)
Culture and Environment: The Training of Critical Awareness (with Denys Thompson) (1933)
Revaluation: Tradition and Development in English Poetry (1936)
The Great Tradition (1948)
The Common Pursuit (1952)
D.H. Lawrence: Novelist (1955)
Two Cultures? The Significance of C.P. Snow (1962)
'Anna Karenina' and Other Essays (1967)
Dickens the Novelist (with Q.D. Leavis) (1970)

Key terms

CANON ■ concrete (see CONCRETIZATION) ■ enactment ■ ORGANICISM

F.R. Leavis had a life-long connection with the town and the University of Cambridge. He was born in the town (in which his father owned a shop that sold musical instruments), was educated at the Perse School and at the University, and was successively associated with the University as Fellow of Downing College (1937–62), University Reader in English (1959–62) and Honorary Fellow (1962–64). In 1965 he was Chichele Lecturer at Oxford, and then held a number of visiting professorships at the universities of York, Wales and Bristol, and he also lectured in the USA. He was founder and editor of the very influential journal *Scrutiny* between 1932 and 1953. During the First World War he served as stretcher-bearer, suffered in a gas attack (hence his perpetual open-necked shirt) and, as he himself reported, read Milton in the trenches. It is necessary to stress that his wife Queenie Dorothy Leavis (formerly Roth, whom he married in 1929) was a major critic in her own right, and the lifelong collaboration between the two has to be recognized as crucial to the work of each. Q.D. Leavis's own research into journalism and what is now known as POPULAR CULTURE, as well as her literary critical writings, constituted a continuing influence on Leavis.

Moreover, limiting any commentary to Leavis's published work provides at best an incomplete account. Much in Leavis's published books started life as lecture material, and his followers had typically had him as tutor or had heard him lecture. His work as teacher and as journal editor was extremely influential, and helped to create a sense of mission – complete with disciples and demons, items of faith, sanctifications and excommunications.

For Leavis, as he put it in 'Sociology and Literature' (in *The Common Pursuit*),

> to insist that literary criticism is, or should be, a specific discipline of intelligence is not to suggest that a serious interest in literature can confine itself to the kind of intensive local analysis associated with 'practical criticism' – to the scrutiny of the 'words on the page' in their minute relations, their effects of imagery, and so on: a real literary interest is an interest in man, society and civilization, and its boundaries cannot be drawn.

If this indicates Leavis's distance from conventional FORMALIST or NEW CRITICAL positions, it should be added that he was equally far from any conventionally MARXIST or sociologizing conception of the relationship between literature and 'man, society and civilization'. His writing is consistently driven by an evaluative and moral (or moralizing) imperative that adds a set of forceful associations to the favoured word 'life'. Thus recent readers of Leavis are typically surprised to find that in spite of his passionate advocacy of University English, words such as 'academic' and 'scholarship' are given negative connotations, while words such as 'CONCRETE', 'ORGANIC' and 'enact' have only positive associations.

Leavis's work was responsible for the emergence of a revised and more exclusive (if contested) CANON in the first half of the twentieth century, and again a religious METAPHOR – this time of the saved and the damned – seems appropriate to the operation of a set of (another favoured word) discriminations. The much quoted (and often parodied) opening words of *The Great Tradition* are (again a favoured word) representative: 'The great English novelists are Jane Austen, George Eliot, Henry James, and Joseph Conrad'. Even within an accepted author's production, sharp discriminations are made: Swift's *Gulliver's Travels* – but especially the fourth book; Dickens (subsequently promoted after a somewhat grudging inclusion in *The Great Tradition*) but especially *Hard Times*. A significant number of Leavis's positive assessments have, however, stood the test of time, and there is no doubt that he played a pivotal role in establishing the pre-eminent importance of a number of key MODERNIST writers such as T.S. ELIOT, D.H. Lawrence, and Joseph Conrad, and in closing the door of history on a snobbish and self-satisfied tradition of *belle-lettrist* appreciation of the 'beauties' of literature.

The moral judgements have a CULTURAL and not a narrowly 'literary' force. Leavis was consistently opposed to commercialism, middlebrow culture, and what he dubbed Technologico-Benthamism, which he saw culturally manifested in and through a range of institutions and individuals, ranging from the British Sunday newspapers, the Arts Council, the Common Market, C.P. Snow (attacked in the widely disseminated Rede Lecture 'The Two Cultures?'), Kingsley Amis and Margaret Drabble.

Leavis's importance probably lies most of all in his insistence on the seriousness of literary studies, distinguishing ENGLISH as discipline from self-enclosed and technical FORMALIST analysis, on the one hand, and from vulgar Marxist views of literature as 'reflection' of socio-economic realities, on the other. In his book *Hitchcock's Films Revisited* (1989), film critic Robin Wood pays tribute to Leavis, a literary critic who, Wood acknowledges, showed not the slightest knowledge of or interest in the cinema. In spite of his own commitment to Marxist and FEMINIST principles, Wood usefully sums up Leavis's importance in an extended Introduction. For Wood, Leavis was uncompromisingly hostile to the critical and cultural establishment, he assumed that a seriousness about art is inseparable from a seriousness about life, he opposed consumer capitalism, and his critical practice was complex, flexible and subtle.

On the negative side, it is hard to deny that under a claimed openness lurked an intolerance to opposition or dissent which hardened with age, and which became associated with positions that were increasingly conservative and reactionary. Leavis's position was always embattled, and while Wood is right to blame a lot of this on opposition from the Establishment in Cambridge and elsewhere, the experience hardened into a style that became progressively more and more self-generated. Leavis's role in encouraging (or at least in not actively discouraging) too slavish forms of discipleship, can be criticized, and these disciples were typically less open-minded and creative in their use of Leavis's legacy than is Wood. Modern readers often find, too, that Leavis's belief that key passages of great literature speak for themselves is unsatisfactory, and this may be why his literary criticism is less read today than is that of his contemporary WILLIAM EMPSON.

Further reading

Gary Day, *Re-reading Leavis: Culture, and Literary Criticism* (London: Macmillan, 1996); Andrew Gibson, *Postmodernity, Ethics and the Novel: From Leavis to Lévinas* (London: Routledge, 1999).

LUKÁCS, Georg (György) (1885–1971)

Main works

The Historical Novel (1962; in Russian, 1937)
The Meaning of Contemporary Realism (1963; in German, 1957)
Essays on Thomas Mann (1964)
Writer and Critic (1970; essays first published in 1930s and 1940s)
History and Class Consciousness (1971; in German, 1919–23)
The Theory of the Novel (1971; in German, 1916)
Essays on Realism (ed. Rodney Livingstone; 1980)

Key terms

REALISM ■ reification ■ typicality

Lukács was born into a Jewish family in Budapest, then part of the Austro-Hungarian empire. His father was a banker who had been ennobled by the Hapsburgs, and Lukács only dropped the honorific 'von' after 1918. He was both precocious and prolific; his first published work was in 1902, in 1906 he obtained his doctorate from Budapest University, and in 1908 he received a prize for his *Development of the Modern Drama*. Also in 1908 his influential *The Soul and the Forms* was published. After a winter in Florence he settled in Heidelberg in 1912, and continued to form contacts with many of the leading intellectuals of his day (he knew Georg Simmel, Max Weber and Ernst Bloch).

Lukács responded with shock and outrage to the carnage of the First World War. In a later (1962) preface to his *The Theory of the Novel* he writes of his 'vehement, global and . . . scarcely articulate rejection of the war', and in a preface to a 1969 edition of his essays in Hungarian he described the war as 'the crisis of the whole of European culture'. He was especially bitter about the *volte-face* of those many Social Democratic parties that supported the war. The war and a movement from the influence of Immanuel Kant to that of G.W.F. Hegel can in retrospect be seen as important components in Lukács's journey towards MARXISM. In 1918 he joined the newly formed Hungarian Communist Party. Heavily involved in the uprising that led to the short-lived 1919 Hungarian Soviet Republic in which he was Minister of Education, Lukács was forced to go underground and to flee after its suppression. In Viennese exile, only a petition signed by Paul Ernst, and Thomas and Heinrich Mann allowed him to escape deportation back to a certain death in Hungary. His later advocacy of Thomas Mann's work is probably not devoid of an element of personal gratitude.

The rest of Lukács's life and work involved complex acts of juggling the often contradictory demands of exile (first in Germany and then the Soviet Union), practical politics, intellectual belief and CULTURAL sympathy. He maintained a commitment to Marxism and Communism to the end of his life, and it was a commitment that involved responsibilities as much practical-political as they were intellectual and moral. Although he is often dismissed as a Stalinist, or seen as a tragic victim of his attempt to appease Stalinism, he was never a mere party hack, and he came up against political orthodoxy on a number of occasions: criticized by Lenin in 1920, forced to recant his views concerning a democratic transition to socialism in Hungary in 1929, and serving briefly as Minister of Culture in the government of Imre Nagy in 1956. After the Soviet invasion yet another period of exile (in Romania) ensued. Those who accuse Lukács of being a mere puppet of successive bureaucrats need to remember how often in his life he narrowly escaped being sentenced to death.

Lukács's writing on literature is concerned most of all with the 'classical' European NOVEL: in another Hungarian preface, written in 1969, he talks of his youthful rejection of bourgeois Budapest life, and of his discovery of modern European literature as a 'serious counter-force' to it. From today's perspective the PARADOX of Lukács's mature writings on literature and AESTHETICS is that while he was steadfastly and implacably anti-MODERNIST, upholding the REALISM of novelists such as Balzac, Tolstoy and Thomas Mann as superior to the DECADENCE of modernists such as Beckett, BRECHT, Kafka and Joyce, he also claimed with fair justification to have been a consistent anti-Stalinist. There seems little doubt that his anti-modernism made him more acceptable to Stalinist authority, but his lack of enthusiasm about mediocre socialist realism kept him out of favour until the demands of Popular Front politics made his commitments politically expedient.

At the heart of Lukács's commitment to classical realism (what he termed 'critical realism') was his belief that a realist novel involved a 'correct reflection' of the totality of a society – totality both in terms of its structure and, importantly, its movements and inner forces. Modernism, in contrast, Lukács saw as a matter of presenting fragments and appearances so as to *reify* them, seeing them in themselves rather than as tokens of a larger dynamic totality. In *The Meaning of Contemporary Realism* Lukács sees a disintegration of personality that is matched by a disintegration of the outside world to be characteristic of modernism. The greatest realist writers, in contrast, Lukács insists again and again throughout his career, are able to present a social totality by means of concrete details that capture the whole through their *typicality*. In his Introduction to *Essays on Realism* Rodney Livingstone has drawn attention to Lukács's liking for 'contrasting concepts' (what we might now term BINARY oppositions): the 'partisan' as opposed to the 'tendentious' writer, realist 'portrayal' as against modernist 'reportage', and (as the middle section of *The Meaning of Contemporary Realism* is entitled), 'Franz Kafka or Thomas Mann?' The concept of the class struggle doubtless had its formal appeal for Lukács.

BERTOLT BRECHT lumped Lukács together with others who, he claimed, wanted 'to play the *apparatchik*', telling WALTER BENJAMIN: 'Every one of their criticisms contains a threat'; and he dubbed Lukács's theory of realism 'formalistic', PARODYING Lukács in the much-quoted injunction, 'Be like Tolstoy – but without his weaknesses! Be like Balzac – only up-to-date!'

That today it is generally accepted that Lukács failed to appreciate that the triumph of many modernist TEXTS lay in their ability to capture the *experience* of fragmentation and loss of unity that modern life provided, does not necessarily render aspects of his critique of modernism – or of his defence of the classical realist novel – without merit. It should moreover be noted that it is in large part thanks to Lukács that there is now general agreement that certain writers are understood to have in common features that allow us to refer to them all as modernists.

Further reading

Arpad Kadarkay, *Georg Lukács: Life, Thought, and Politics* (Oxford: Basil Blackwell, 1991); Galin Tihanov, *The Master and the Slave: Lukács, Bakhtin and the Ideas of Their Time* (Oxford: Clarendon Press, 2000).

LYOTARD, Jean-François (1924–98)

Main works

The Postmodern Condition: A Report on Knowledge (1984; in French, 1979)
The Differend: Phrases in Dispute (1988; in French, 1983)
Peregrinations: Law, Form, Event (1988)
The Lyotard Reader (ed. Andrew Benjamin; 1989)
Heidegger and 'the jews' (1990; in French, 1988)
Phenomenology (1991; in French, 1954)

Key terms

différend ■ GRAND/LITTLE NARRATIVES ■ POSTMODERNISM

Born in Versailles, Lyotard studied in Paris and then moved to a teaching post in Algeria in 1950. He remained in Algeria until 1959, when he took up the first of a number of university posts in philosophy in Paris. He held many visiting professorships outside France – in universities in the United States and in Brazil.

Lyotard's shifts of position were as much intellectual and political as geographical. While in Algeria he was head of the radical MARXIST group *Socialisme ou barbarie*, and during the 'events' of May 1968 when France was paralysed by student demonstrations, he was actively involved in demonstrations against the French government at the University of Nanterre. But subsequent to 1968 he turned against Marxism. His essay 'A Memorial for Marxism' (in *Peregrinations*) reveals, perhaps, how this personal journey of political change became a model for the larger scepticisms which crystallized most clearly (and influentially) in *The Postmodern Condition*. In the essay Lyotard speaks of Marxism having been a 'universal language' for him, and of his present belief that the history of his Marxist radicalism needed 'to be thought and written in its own language'.

This movement from the universal or totalizing DISCOURSE to the self-enclosedness of certain systems of thought forms the structural core of Lyotard's most influential work, *The Postmodern Condition*, in which it is traced as the movement from GRAND NARRATIVES to LITTLE NARRATIVES. In his Introduction to the study,

Lyotard states that he uses 'the term *modern* to designate any science that legitimates itself with reference to a metadiscourse … making an explicit appeal to some grand narrative', while '[s]implifying to the extreme, I define *postmodern* as incredulity toward metanarratives'. The 'Postmodern Condition' is thus one involving separate 'language games' (Lyotard adopts this term from Wittgenstein); little NARRATIVES 'play their own game' and cannot legitimate one another.

Following on in the same logic, Lyotard's concept of the *differend* involves 'a conflict between at least two parties that cannot be equitably resolved for lack of a rule of judgment applicable to both arguments', as he puts it in the Preface to *The Differend*. Lyotard is thus one of a number of recent thinkers associated with POSTMODERNISM and/or POST-STRUCTURALISM (MICHEL FOUCAULT, STANLEY FISH and Jean Baudrillard are arguably others) who see the contemporary or postmodern world as one of a set of self-contained systems of thought lacking any grand narrative on the explanatory (or moral) plane. There is a strong case for calling Lyotard not a theorist but an anti-theorist.

Such arguments have come under considerable fire in recent times for the problem they leave us with regard to the making of moral judgements concerning crimes against humanity such as that of the Holocaust. If Lyotard associates grand narratives with terror and terrorism, the loss of grand narratives might seem to imply throwing up one's hands at the impossibility of talking about or condemning the terror of the Holocaust. Lyotard has not shied away from confronting such problems – for example in his *Heidegger and 'the jews'* ('the jews' in lower case so as to distinguish the anti-Semitic idea of Jewishness from actual Jews). In this work Lyotard associates 'the Heidegger affair' (i.e. the accommodation and perhaps worse that the philosopher Martin Heidegger made with the Nazis) with the universalism of the Enlightenment. This defends by means of attack: the Enlightenment project of reason is not what allows us to condemn terror, but what underpinned the terror in the first place. It seems fair to say that such arguments have won at best a sceptical response in recent years.

For Lyotard, literature has a role in revealing and representing in words what representations miss, what is 'unnamable'. Thus if there are no longer any grand narratives for Lyotard, there are forms of writing which may come near to representing (for example) evil.

Lyotard shares many stylistic features with other French theorists; his writing is extremely discursive, regularly going off at tangents, interrogating itself and its terminology, presenting spots of insight rather than a logical chain of reasoned conclusions. For students of literature his importance is probably mainly as initiator of major debates about the nature (and even the existence) of postmodernism.

Further reading

Andrew Benjamin (ed.), *Judging Lyotard* (London: Routledge, 1992); Geoffrey Bennington, *Lyotard: Writing the Event* (Manchester: Manchester University Press, 1988); Gary Browning, *Lyotard and the End of Grand Narratives* (Cardiff: University of Wales Press, 2000).

McGANN, Jerome J. (1937–)

Main works

The Romantic Ideology: A Critical Investigation (1983)
A Critique of Modern Textual Criticism (1983)
The Beauty of Inflections: Literary Investigations in Historical Method and Theory (1985)
Social Values and Poetic Acts (1987)
The Textual Condition (1991)
Black Riders: The Visible Language of Modernism (1993)
Poetics of Sensibility (1996)

Key terms

NEW HISTORICISM ■ visible language ■ CONCRETE

Of mixed Canadian and American parentage, Jerome McGann was born in 1937. He was educated at LeMoyne College before taking his MA at Syracuse University in 1962 and completing his doctorate at Yale University in 1966. He worked as an Assistant Professor at the University of Chicago (1966–69) and as an Associate Professor and Professor at Johns Hopkins University from 1969 till 1975. He has also taught at the California Institute of Technology, where he was Dreyfuss Professor of Humanities (1980–86), at the University of Southern California (1983–86) and at the University of Virginia, where he was Commonwealth Professor between 1986 and 1993. In 1999, he became the Thomas Holloway Professor of Victorian Studies at the University of London.

McGann's concept of 'visible language' has been most recently explored in *Black Riders* (1993), where he argued that certain works of literature experiment with the graphic and physical properties of language – the shape of its letters, different typefaces, the relation of print to blank space, the appearance and texture of the page, and the kind of binding – and therefore increase its expressive and distinctively human potential. Such an approach is not original in itself, but is pursued with a scholarly rigour and an attention to detail that sets it apart from its intellectual predecessors. It continues McGann's previous concern with bibliography (the history and description of a book and its editions), and indeed part of McGann's project involves showing that textual variants and critical responses are not simply matters of FORM or technique, but may be intimately related to wider social factors. His work is also inflected by MARXISM, and by an interest in the possibility of producing an 'unalienated' literature: certain writing (that of William Blake and Emily Dickinson, among others) gestures in the direction of a craft that is not standardized by mechanical technology and commodified by the market, and thus removed from its unique human origins.

More recently, McGann has involved himself extensively in the implications of new electronic technologies of reproduction and distribution for the reading and writing of literature. Like others, McGann has recognized that the Internet offers the possibility of making all kinds of resources that were previously difficult to access (on the grounds that the materials were fragile, or were held in libraries and institutions that were geographically remote to many), more freely available for all. But again he has explored the implications of this insight more rigorously than others have done. He sees use of the Internet as 'the beginning of a great scholarly revolution' – not least because it allows an expansion and redefinition of the literary canon: previously undiscovered or little-known writers, as well as those regarded as minor, who might have been thought uneconomic for publication, can be made widely available. Hypermedia Archives allow almost unlimited space, so that all kinds of materials (notes, manuscript poems, images) can be displayed, thus contributing to a greater knowledge of the processes by which literature is brought about. Computer technologies can present more aspects of a writer's work, including potentially significant aspects which editors might traditionally have regarded as unimportant and to be excluded from a printed text.

McGann's approach to literary study is broadly NEW HISTORICAL, and his work on the Romantic poets (especially Byron and Rossetti) is a direct challenge to the Yale critics (such as PAUL DE MAN, Geoffrey Hartman and HAROLD BLOOM), who wrote on the Romantics but emphasized mostly FORMAL aspects of their work. He attempts to recover as much of the social-historical field of original publication as possible, looking (for instance) at where a poem was first published and what kinds of IDEOLOGICAL alliances this might suggest. Presented with a poem included in a magazine, McGann asks how much it cost, what kind of readership it attracted, and whether the poem's IMAGERY challenged or supported or simply avoided the magazine's political views. In the case of a book he will examine its cover, price and circulation to see what kinds of signals this might suggest as to the writer's own ideology. The Romantics in particular, he argues, developed a kind of writing that disguised its own collusion with particular social and political forces.

Though McGann's work would appear to oppose DECONSTRUCTION, it should be registered that his preoccupation with ABSENCES, DISPLACEMENTS and erasures in literary texts (what they try to avoid or silence, rather than what they say explicitly) combines more traditional historical approaches with traces of deconstruction. He is one of the most readable and exciting of contemporary literary theorists.

For McGann's term *radial reading*, see Section 3, p. 161.

Further reading

Jeremy Hawthorn, *Cunning Passages: New Historicism, Cultural Materialism and Marxism in the Contemporary Literary Debate* (London: Arnold, 1996).

MAN, Paul de (1919–83)

Blindness and Insight (1971)
Allegories of Reading (1979)
The Resistance to Theory (1986)
Aesthetic Ideology (1996)

ALLEGORY ■ APORIA ■ IRONY ■ undecidability

Born in Antwerp, Belgium, de Man studied science and philosophy at the University of Brussels, graduating in 1942. For five years he worked as a writer and translator, before emigrating to America in 1947. He lived and taught in New York from 1949 to 1951, before enrolling at Harvard University, where he was awarded an MA in 1958 and a PhD in comparative literature in 1960. He subsequently taught at the universities of Harvard, Cornell, Johns Hopkins, and finally (in 1970) Yale. He remained at Yale for the rest of his life, becoming the Sterling Professor of Humanities, and the Chairman of the Department of Comparative Literature. Other members of the faculty at Yale were Geoffrey Hartman, J. HILLIS MILLER, and JACQUES DERRIDA, with whom de Man helped to develop the theoretical approach known as DECONSTRUCTION. After his death from cancer in 1983, it was revealed that from 1940 to 1942 he had written 170 literary and cultural articles, including one overtly anti-Semitic piece, for *Le Soir*, a Belgian pro-Nazi newspaper. What is less well known is that de Man attempted unsuccessfully to escape from Belgium after the German invasion, and that upon leaving *Le Soir*, he went to work for the publisher Agence Dechenne, from which post he was fired in 1943 for aiding in the publication of the journal *Messages*, which published various writers associated with the Resistance. (For more on de Man's wartime record, see the entry for J. HILLIS MILLER.)

During the 1970s and early 1980s, de Man became one of the most prominent and influential literary theorists in the United States. Like other deconstructionist critics, he combined a theoretical interest in philosophy, language and literature with a practical attention to close reading which, though different in its conclusions, links him with NEW CRITICISM and FORMALISM. De Man typically practised a mode of reading which involved looking at the view of the world implicit in a TEXT, and then focusing on a METAPHOR, series of metaphors, or rhetorical technique which problematized or completely undermined the 'claims' of the text. The text as a descriptive or conceptual system was thus shown to be opposed by its own language, and indeed the capacity of any DISCOURSE to refer to a world outside itself was thereby brought into question.

For de Man, the main difference between literature and, say, the law is that the former is aware that it is not literally true while the latter is blind to this. There is a neat reversal of the conventional hierarchies here: language that aspires to knowledge and authority is blind, whereas language that is aware of its blindness (its figurative or rhetorical status) has at least the insight of its own limitations. Metaphors, traditionally seen as figures of speech by means of which one object is compared to another, are regarded by de Man as central to his theory that language does not refer to a world outside itself, but simply replaces one SIGN with another sign (or set of signs). Literature is moreover linked to a specialized sense of IRONY, in that it purports to refer to the world while also denying the possibility of ever being able to do so.

De Man's attraction to ALLEGORY as against SYMBOL, in his discussion of Romantic writers, can be understood as being consistent with his criticism of any view of language as a transparent bearer of meaning, a communicative medium. According to him a symbol attempts to fuse subject and object, signifier and signified (see SIGN), in one unit: whereas in an allegory, what is represented, and the terms of the representation, are kept apart. 'Whereas the symbol postulates the possibility of an identity or identification, allegory designates primarily a distance in relation to its own origin, and renouncing the nostalgia and the desire to coincide, it establishes its language in the void of this temporal difference.'

According to de Man, reading typically involves moments of APORIA, or irreconcilable uncertainty, which to all intents and purposes is akin to his concept of undecidability. Whereas WILLIAM EMPSON wrote about AMBIGUITY as a condition where the critic was presented with several, objective, meanings simultaneously, in de Man's view the critic is unable to decide what is and is not an objective meaning. We cannot distinguish between ambiguity in ourselves and ambiguity as a condition of the text, and an aporia is a kind of blind spot when this recognition takes place.

Two of de Man's works were left incomplete at this death, but were edited and then published posthumously. In the first, *The Resistance to Theory*, he investigated the theoretical climate of his day and explored why rhetorical reading was strongly resisted in the academies. In the second, *Aesthetic Ideology*, he continued a lifelong interest in nineteenth-century German philosophy, looking again at AESTHETIC traditions and their deconstruction by language.

Further reading

Rodolphe Gasché, *The Wild Card of Reading: On Paul de Man* (Cambridge, MA: Harvard University Press, 1998); Ortwin de Graef, *Serenity in Crisis: A Preface to Paul de Man, 1939–1960* (Lincoln: University of Nebraska Press, 1993).

MILLER, J. Hillis (1928–)

Charles Dickens: The World of his Novels (1958)
Fiction and Repetition: Seven English Novels (1982)
Tropes, Parables, Performatives: Essays on Twentieth-Century Literature (1990)
Theory Then and Now (1991)
Hawthorne and History: Defacing It (1991)
Black Holes (1999)

black hole ■ PARABLE ■ repetition

After gaining his doctorate at Harvard University in 1952, Hillis Miller taught at Johns Hopkins University from 1953 to 1972, and then for 14 years at Yale University. Reference to the 'Yale critics' generally has to do with Miller, HAROLD BLOOM, Geoffrey Hartman and PAUL DE MAN – all at Yale and all associated with DECONSTRUCTION to a greater or lesser extent. In 1986 Miller became Professor of English and Comparative Literature at the University of California at Irvine – an appointment that led to a small flurry of media interest and prompted the sub-head: 'UCI Will Try Deconstructing with Yale Critic' in the *Los Angeles Times*. In the same year (1986) he was President of the Modern Language Association of America, and put the weight of his office behind attempts to interest America in deconstruction.

Miller is a prolific critic (*Hawthorne and History* contains a useful bibliography of his work between 1955 and 1990). He has, however, returned regularly to certain authors: in his Preface to *Tropes, Parables, Performatives* he mentions especially 'Kafka, [Wallace] Stevens, [William Carlos] Williams . . . Conrad, [and especially] Hardy'. This line of continuity is matched by another element of consistency in his criticism: what in the same Preface he describes as his 'irresistible penchant for "close-reading" of individual texts'. This penchant, Miller claims, is not an inheritance from the NEW CRITICISM but is the result of 'an initial and persistent fascination with local strangenesses in literary language'. Manuel Asensi supports Miller's self-assessment: in his *J. Hillis Miller, or, Boustrophedonic Reading* (1999) he argues that although Miller has been accused of 'translating' the ideas of (among others) W. K. Wimsatt, Georges Poulet, JACQUES DERRIDA, PAUL DE MAN and JACQUES LACAN, in fact these writers and their movements have actually themselves translated Miller's own essential concerns.

Whatever the case, Miller's criticism has regularly succeeded in bringing together the challenge of recent theoretical arguments with detailed close READINGS of individual TEXTS.

The 'recent theoretical arguments' have as Miller himself admits, gone in waves, or what in the Preface to *Theory Then and Now* he describes as three dis-

tinct 'episodes': the GENEVA SCHOOL and PHENOMENOLOGY; the 'reception, assim-
ilation, and transformation in America of so-called "deconstruction"'; and 'the
negotiation between deconstructionisms and the almost universal turn in the
1980s to forms of literary study oriented toward society, toward history, toward
ethical questions and questions of institutional organization, towards questions
of race, class, and gender, towards the reformation of the canon'. If this suggests
the modishness of a critical Vicar of Bray it should be stressed that Miller's
involvement with theoretical movements has always been principled, inquiring,
and conditional.

During the furore over the revelations concerning Paul de Man's wartime
journalism, Miller played an extremely principled role, going over the evidence
for de Man's alleged anti-Semitism extremely conscientiously, and exposing much
careless journalistic attribution of guilt without in any way attempting to white-
wash his by-then deceased friend from Yale.

Miller has played an invaluable role in introducing Anglo-American READERS
to continental theories of varying sorts, while having remained faithful to the aim
to be true to his reading experience of individual TEXTS. For many years he represented 'deconstruction with a human face', and the student who comes across
an essay of his on a CANONICAL work (it is hard not to do so) will invariably find
much to challenge and illuminate.

He has also made important contributions to academic politics, and his recent
book *Black Holes* (1999) moves from a tough and perceptive account of the new
situation facing the humanities in universities in the United States, to suggestions
for building a new role for (in particular) the university study of ENGLISH in the
days of the HYPERTEXT, the rise of cultural studies (see Section 3, p. 183), and the
loss of public funding for universities. The 'black holes' of his title are (among
other things) those cores of incomprehensibility that an encounter with a literary
work reveals and engenders, black holes which, he reports, have the power to dis-
possess his self of its 'seemingly secure self-possession'.

Further reading

Manuel Asensi, *J. Hillis Miller; or, Boustrophedonic Reading* (Stanford, CA: Stanford University
Press, 1999); Imre Salusinszky, *Criticism in Society* (London: Methuen, 1987) [interview with Hillis
Miller]; Daniel R. Schwarz, *Critical Theories of the Novel from James to Hillis Miller* (London:
Macmillan, 1986).

MILLETT, Kate (1934–)

Main works

Sexual Politics (1970)
Going to Iran (1982)
The Loony Bin Trip (1990)
The Politics of Cruelty (1994)

patriarchy ■ FEMINISIM

Born in St Paul, Minnesota, in 1934, Katherine Murray Millett gained a BA from the University of Minnesota in 1956, and an MA (with first-class honours) from St Hilda's College at the University of Oxford two years later. She briefly taught English at the University of North Carolina at Greensboro, and then moved to New York in order to pursue a career as a performance artist, working at a kindergarten in Harlem in order to support herself. She moved to Tokyo in 1961, teaching at Waseda University and studying sculpture. After the break-up of her marriage to the Japanese sculptor Fumio Yoshimura, Millett returned to New York in 1965, teaching English and philosophy at Barnard College. At the same time, she studied for a doctorate at Columbia University, and was awarded a PhD (with distinction) in 1970. Her thesis, which linked anthropology, literature, sociology and feminist politics, was published the same year as *Sexual Politics*.

In her book, Millett – like SIMONE DE BEAUVOIR before her – argues that differences between the sexes are constituted by CULTURE, and not biology, and that the social domination of the male is reinforced by the family unit, which is the chief institution of patriarchy. Although Millett argues that women are oppressed as a group, she acknowledges that CLASS plays a factor in establishing rivalries and antagonisms between them. None the less, Millett sees GENDER politics as being fundamentally more significant than issues of class: patriarchy uses class to reinforce the economic superiority of the male, allowing women little access to professional avenues of self-realization, and paying them less than their male counterparts. Education is a means of furthering the male–female hierarchy: women are encouraged to study the humanities, while men are channelled into areas such as economics, law, mathematics, politics, science and theology, which have strong links with the institutions of power in society. Millett also looks at how patriarchy uses violence to suppress women, both legally and illegally: women are punished for adultery and prostitution, and are denied the right to control their own fertility (through abortion and contraception); they are also the victims of domestic and sexual abuse (both physically, in the shape of rape, and culturally, in the form of pornography). Millett argues that psychoanalysis, and in particular the theories of Sigmund Freud, are a powerful form of propaganda against women.

The last section of *Sexual Politics* examines those male writers who for Millett embody and reproduce patriarchal ideologies, and it focuses on how these writers often presuppose the presence of a male reader or a male point-of-view: women readers are therefore asked either to collaborate with male views of their identity, or relegated to the margins of the TEXT, forced into the role of passive spectator rather than agent and participant.

There is no doubt that Millett's work had a very marked effect on both the study and the production of literary WORKS. Creative writers were given the confidence to write for other than a male readership, while feminist critics were encouraged to treat the work of CANONICAL authors with less awe and more scepticism.

Further reading

Cora Kaplan, *Sea Changes: Essays on Culture and Feminism* (London: Verso, 1986); Toril Moi, *Sexual/Textual Politics* (London: Methuen, 1985); Rosemarie Tong, *Feminist Thought: A Comprehensive Introduction* (London: Unwin Hyman, 1989).

PROPP, Vladimir (1895–1970)

Main works

Morphology of the Folktale (1968; first published in Russian, 1928)

Key terms

function ■ morphology

Vladimir Propp was born in St Petersburg (Leningrad for most of the Soviet period) and remained there with few absences. He studied languages as a student, and subsequently lectured in folklore at Leningrad University.

Propp's main importance for students of literature is in the way in which his STRUCTURALIST method of analysis served as model for later theories of NARRATIVE. Fundamental to Propp's approach was his concept of the *function*, which can be seen as a sort of ABSTRACT unit of narrative. In his *Morphology of the Folktale* Propp defines a narrative function as an act of a CHARACTER, defined from the point of view of its significance for the course of the action. Propp argued that although folk tales contain an extremely large number of different characters, they contain a relatively small number of functions, functions which constitute the fundamental components of the folk tale.

Propp's approach is structuralist to the extent that it assumes a 'grammar' of the folk tale. From this perspective, functions play a role in an individual folk tale analogous to that played by parts of speech in a well-formed sentence. Thus just as the same word can perform different grammatical functions in different sentences (compare 'I set the table' with 'You win the first set'), so too can the same act perform a different narrative function in different folk tales (the appearance of a dragon could represent struggle in one tale, pursuit in another). As a result, while the number of different CHARACTERS in a corpus of folk tales will be large, the number of functions they perform is small. Although not all functions will be used in any given tale, the *order* in which they are used will be determined by the 'grammar' of the GENRE – just as not all parts of speech will be used in any given sentence, but *how* those that are used, are used, will be determined grammatically.

Propp's use of the terms such as 'function' and 'morphology' betrays a representatively structuralist reliance upon the LINGUISTIC PARADIGM (morphology studies the structures of words; in Propp's usage a tale is thus treated like a word, and broken down into its component parts).

Propp's work has been subject to certain criticisms, some detailed (how many functions are there, and how rigid are the grammatical rules governing their use?), and some more general (do the rules apply only to Russian folk tales, can contextual issues be excluded as Propp suggests?). In spite of such criticisms, Propp was a truly influential figure in developing an abstract model for the analysis of highly formulaic narratives. He demonstrated how details of content can be ignored by the isolation of content elements which are to be found at a deeper level than that of surface meaning. Later analyses of formulaic GENRES such as the ROMANCE or the film western owe much to his example.

Further reading

Claude Lévi-Strauss, 'Structure and Form: Reflections on a Work by Vladimir Propp', in *Structural Anthropology 2* (Harmondsworth: Penguin, 1973).

RICHARDS, I[vor] A[rmstrong] (1893–1979)

Main works

The Meaning of Meaning (co-written with C.K. Ogden; 1923)
Principles of Literary Criticism (1924)
Practical Criticism (1929)
Coleridge on Imagination (1934)

Key terms

basic English ■ practical criticism

I.A. Richards was educated at Cambridge, and held a lecturing post there between 1922 and 1929. He came to literary studies from psychology and after having written about semantic theory in *The Meaning of Meaning*. There is a sense in which Richards's next two books provided two of the three pillars upon which modern English Studies has been constructed, for if the subject developed as an amalgam of historical scholarship, verbal analysis, and criticism and critical theory, then Richards provided the modern starting-point for the second and third of these.

Given the authority and pervasiveness of literary theory today it is perhaps hard to understand the extent to which Richards's attempt to systematize the value of literature and thus the function and responsibility of the critic in *Principles of Literary Criticism* was seen as a frontal attack on what was deemed to be appropriate critical procedure. Instead of the exercise of taste and the unsubstantiated display of one's reading pleasures, Richards argued that criticism was, or should be, the endeavour to discriminate between experiences and to evaluate them. This required 'some understanding of the nature of experience [and] theories of valuation and communication'. More hackles were raised by Richards's casting doubt on the existence of a separate or unique AESTHETIC mode or attitude, consistent with his pouring of scorn on 'Ultimates' or 'ABSTRACT entities'. This was a significant tactical move on his part, as 'the aesthetic' was often considered to be *sui generis* and unanalyzable: to dispense with the concept was thus to remove an objection to the possibility of investigating 'aesthetic experiences'. For Richards, the arts were not a closed room or an ivory tower, but our 'storehouse of recorded values' springing from and perpetuating hours in the lives of exceptional people, when 'their control and command of experience [were] at its highest'. And the storehouse door could be opened by painstaking analysis and appropriate critical training.

Given Richards's background it is not surprising that a key component in *Principles of Literary Criticism* was the attempt to argue for a psychological theory of value. While modern readers may find Richards's sense of the CULTURAL relativity of value and his attack on nationalism appealing, his vocabulary of 'appetencies' and 'AFFECTS' will probably seem mechanistic and outmoded. The chapter entitled 'The Analysis of a Poem' shares some of these shortcomings, but it also can be seen as a precursor of Richard's next book, *Practical Criticism*, which is structured around students' written responses to 'unseen' poems ranging from the CANONICAL (Donne and Lawrence) to the popular (a First World War padre who wrote under the name of 'Woodbine Willie'). Richards was shocked by his students' inability to discriminate between good and bad poetry, and the reason for this, he argued, was their inability to *read* poetry properly. The book suggested ways to rectify this situation, and Richards's book was the foundation of what became a key element in the teaching of literature: close reading or practical criticism. In a 1978 conference paper, Ian Watt described *Practical Criticism* as 'certainly the most influential text as far as the Cambridge English School was concerned'; many universities introduced examinations in which students had to write about unseen texts, and this way of forcing close attention to verbal detail is undeniably a key element in the development of the NEW CRITICISM.

Practical Criticism was again vigorously attacked. An early piece by WILLIAM EMPSON, who was a student and disciple of Richards, is a response to an attack on the book by John Sparrow, who had been at Winchester with Empson. (The response is entitled 'O Misselle Passer!' – O poor little Sparrow! – and is reprinted in Empson's *Argufying* [1987].) For Empson the key point of debate is whether the meaning of a poem and its mode of action should be analyzed; clearly what Richards's book did was to legitimize the sort of analysis that formed the substance of Empson's own highly influential *Seven Types of Ambiguity* (1930).

In the 1930s Richards devoted most of his energies to developing 'Basic English', a form of English with a minimal (850 word) vocabulary that could be taught to non-native English speakers so as to promote international communication (he was in China with Empson in the 1930s), and in 1942 he published a translation of Plato's *Republic* in Basic English. Empson reports in a 1973 review of a *festschrift* for his old tutor that Richards had been a very popular lecturer at Cambridge, so much so that he was forced to lecture in the street because the hall would not hold all those who turned up to hear him. This commitment to teaching underpins and informs his books on criticism.

Further reading

William Empson, *Argufying: Essays on Literature and Culture* (London: Chatto & Windus, 1987 [section on Richards and Basic English]); Jerome P. Schiller, *I.A. Richards' Theory of Literature* (New Haven, CT: Yale University Press, 1969).

RICOEUR, Paul (1913–)

Main works

The Conflict of Interpretations (1974; in French, 1969)
The Rule of Metaphor (1978)
Hermeneutics and the Human Sciences (1981)
Time and Narrative (1984, 1985, 1988)

Key terms

HERMENEUTICS ■ act of reading ■ act of writing

Born in Valence in Western France, Paul Ricoeur was orphaned at an early age and was a prisoner-of-war in Nazi Germany. He had graduated from the University of Rennes in 1932, going on to study philosophy at the Sorbonne and earning his Master's in 1935. After the war, he completed his Doctorate there in 1950. He also taught at a number of institutions, before being appointed as a professor at the University of Strasbourg, where he worked from 1948 to 1956. He then moved to the University of Paris-Nanterre in 1956. He has been a visiting professor at numerous universities, in particular at the University of Chicago, and is the recipient of over 30 honorary degrees. Much of his work has been in the field of HERMENEUTICS, or theories of meaning and understanding, which traditionally has concerned itself with studies of the Bible, and with moral philosophy and theology.

One of Ricoeur's most important contributions to the specific study and theory of literary practice is his distinction between DISCOURSE (writing) and DIALOGUE (hearing and speaking). Discourse differs from dialogue in that it is removed from the original circumstances of its production (compare the distinctions outlined in the entry for ENUNCIATION). The intentions of the author are not always clear or recoverable, and the 'act of writing' assumes an address to a general audience rather than to an individual. In the case of historical work (where the author is dead), not all the references can be fully contextualized. (Indeed, Ricoeur has stated that 'to read a book is to consider its author as already dead and the book as posthumous'.) Thus, INTERPRETATION, or the 'act of reading' is necessarily detached from the author's subjective experience and INTENTIONS, allowing a greatly increased number of possible and acceptable readings. Thus meaning is not just the transmission of the author's wishes on to a passive

SECTION 5

READER, but is constructed by the reader and influenced by her or his world view. Clearly, Ricoeur's distinction can be related to READER-RESPONSE CRITICISM, and is also a challenge to theories that are grounded in the mind of the author, or in intentionalism: just as clearly, they contradict NEW HISTORICAL approaches that attempt to situate meaning as much as possible in social and historical contexts.

Ricoeur's theory is not quite the same as the notion of the 'death of the author' proposed by ROLAND BARTHES and others (see AUTHOR). Meaning is still an activity that presupposes human subjectivity. According to Ricoeur, the reader forms a number of possible hypotheses about the text that he or she is reading, and has these guesses validated by certain objective information. Ricoeur is (like E.D. HIRSCH) arguing that meaning is not a fully arbitrary process, but a kind of negotiation, where the guesses are informed ones and where the text can supply not absolute proof but a degree of confirmation. Certain criteria (of coherence, for example, or interconnections within the writing) can be applied to judge how plausible or likely a reading will be, especially in comparison with other readings. In addition, as more and more of the text is read, the interpreter comes closer to the world view of the author, and is increasingly likely to understand the text with something approaching accuracy. The text demonstrates patterns of meaning that give rise to the possibility of objectivity without suspending or erasing the subjectivity of the author or the reader.

Further reading

David E. Klemm, *The Hermeneutical Theory of Paul Ricoeur* (Lewisburg: Bucknell University Press, 1983); Mario J. Valdés, *A Ricoeur Reader: Reflection and Imagination* (Toronto: University of Toronto Press, 1991).

SAID, Edward (1935–)

Main works

Beginnings: Intention and Method (1975)
Orientalism: Western Conceptions of the Orient (1978)
The World, The Text, and The Critic (1983)
Musical Elaborations (1991)
Culture and Imperialism (1993)

Key terms

POSTCOLONIALISM ■ ORIENTALISM ■ contrapuntal reading

Since the publication in 1978 of his celebrated and influential *Orientalism: Western Conceptions of the Orient*, Edward Said has made an immensely significant impact upon literary studies and he can be said to be one of the principal founders of POSTCOLONIAL literary theory and criticism. Said has argued forcefully that literary TEXTS written within the era of imperialism are typically and significantly marked by their contexts of imperialist DISCOURSE. As such, texts are in part the product of existing power relations, and these relations are typically replicated and re-enforced by a 'colonial' text's pattern of representation. Specifically, Said has argued that Western cultural discourse, in which imaginative literature plays a crucial role, has consistently constructed an IMAGE of the 'Orient' (as in the Middle East) not with a view towards truthful representation but so as to serve Western imperial interests and to bolster a particular Western self-image.

Said has focused attention upon the struggles for identity faced by SUBJECTS embroiled in empire, an acute sense of which he has clearly acquired through his own experience as an imperial subject and as an exile. He was born in Palestine (which since the early 1920s had largely been controlled by a British administration) and with his Arabic background his position was threatened by the internationally-supported plans to annex Palestine for the foundation of modern Israel. In 1948, following the United Nations' approval of Palestine's partitioning, he fled with his family to Egypt where he attended American and British schools. In 1951 he moved to America, where he studied literature at Princeton and Harvard and where he has since worked as a literature professor, principally at New York's Columbia University. His own identity, and his literary criticism, have thus been informed by his dual position as an active participant within Western culture and as an exile from the 'Orient' who is denied a sense of stable statehood by international power.

Said's analysis and impassioned critique of ORIENTALISM build on and develop MICHEL FOUCAULT's theories concerning the relationship between power and discourse (an engagement with which forms part of Said's early *Beginnings: Intention and Method*). Orientalism, for Said, is not, as the term was traditionally applied, the worthy scholarly study of Eastern cultures; rather, it is a representational enterprise which emerges from and is complicit with imperial power. In *Orientalism*, Said considers a wide range of literary WORKS relating to the Middle East – FICTION, travel accounts, political works – written mostly by French and British AUTHORS from the late eighteenth to the middle of the twentieth century. He argues that, consciously or unconsciously, authors of such works produced and sustained demeaning MYTHS and STEREOTYPES which constructed conceptions of the Orient and the Oriental as, for example, exotic, sensual, devious and fanatical. Collectively, such representational practices constitute an institution through which the Orient is defined, controlled and dominated; and by constructing the Orient as a cultural OTHER, orientalism has the further function of supporting notions that rationality and civilization underpin Western identity.

Said has been criticized for being overly polemical and for painting too monolithic a picture of Western discourse (one which downplays its internal contradictions and variations), and he has been accused of producing a type of 'Occidentalism' in his critique of the West. But his work has also been hugely influential and has been a major impetus behind the now common postcolonial reading practice which seeks to uncover relations between texts (by both 'colonized' and 'colonizing' authors) and the metanarratives of empire. Elaborating a means to describe this mode of reading, he has developed (particularly in *Culture and Imperialism*) the useful concept of 'contrapuntal reading': an interpretative strategy which aspires to discover a *simultaneous* awareness of a text's 'official' discourse and the concealed history (or the counter-narrative of the oppressed) which is typically suppressed by imperial discourse.

Said has also written widely for the cause of Palestinian self-determinism (he has been a member of the Palestinian parliament in exile, although his relations with Palestinian leaders including Yasser Arafat have frequently been marked by dissent), and, with a strong sense that the intellectual should be politically engaged in society, he regularly functions within the American media as a spokesman for the Palestinian cause.

Further reading

Bill Ashcroft and Pal Ahluwalia, *Edward Said: The Paradox of Identity* (London: Routledge, 1999); Leela Gandhi, *Postcolonial Theory: A Critical Introduction* (St Leonards, New South Wales: Allen & Unwin, 1998).

SAUSSURE, Ferdinand de (1857–1913)

Main work

Course in General Linguistics (1959; new translation 1983; in French, 1915)

Key terms

ARBITRARY ■ LANGUE AND PAROLE ■ SIGN (signifier and signified) ■ SYNTAGMATIC AND PARADIGMATIC

Saussure was born in Switzerland, studied chemistry and physics at the University of Geneva (1875–76) and then linguistics in Germany (Berlin from 1878 to 1879, and Leipzig in 1880). Interesting in view of his association with the SYNCHRONIC study of language is the fact that he taught historical linguistics both in Paris (at the *École des Hautes Études* between 1881 and 1891) and at the University of Geneva, where he was Professor of Indo-European linguistics and Sanskrit (1901–13) and of general linguistics (1907–13).

Often credited with laying the foundation of modern linguistics, Saussure's most influential work (in Anglo-American literary studies effectively his *only* influential work) is the *Course in General Linguistics*, which was actually constructed (or reconstructed) from notes taken by a number of his students at the University of Geneva during three courses of lectures (1907; 1908–9; 1910–11). The only work he published during his lifetime (while he was still a student) was concerned with the vowel system of ancient Indo-European languages.

From the point of view of the student of literature, Saussure's importance lies first of all in his having drawn attention to the possibility of two dominant approaches to the study of language: the *historical* or DIACHRONIC, and the *structural*, or SYNCHRONIC. This distinction is crucial to the development of STRUCTURALISM, and once established it was capable of being applied not just to language but also to myth (Lévi-Strauss and later BARTHES), to literature (GOLDMANN and many others), and to a whole range of other CULTURAL and artistic institutions and products (see the entry for LINGUISTIC PARADIGM). Contrary to what is often asserted, Saussure certainly did not want to outlaw historical linguistics, and a careful reading of the *Course* demonstrates that he believed that synchronic and diachronic approaches to the study of language were both necessary and complementary (see the entry for DIACHRONIC AND SYNCHRONIC).

Saussure's characterization of language as a system of differences (i.e. a system based upon defining *relationships* between items recognized as *different*, rather than a system of items adjudged to be *absolutes* in themselves), is a key element in first structuralism and later POST-STRUCTURALISM. (English speakers do not all pronounce the word 'big' in exactly the same way, but all can distinguish and recognize the difference between 'big', 'bag', 'bug', 'beg', and 'bog' – and between 'big', 'dig', and 'bit'.) Such a view of language underlies, for example, the system of 'functions' found by VLADIMIR PROPP in the Russian folk tale, and subsequently applied by others to additional examples of formulaic literature and art. Saussure is an important founding influence on both RUSSIAN FORMALISM and the PRAGUE SCHOOL (see Section 3).

More detailed commentary on Saussure's importance for students of literature can be found in the individual entries in the glossary (see the list of 'key terms' above). There is little doubt that for such students, the most fruitful and successful application of Saussure's theories is to be found (i) in the study of the formulaic, and (ii) in the field of NARRATOLOGY.

For more critical comments on attempts to apply the distinction between LANGUE AND PAROLE to literature, the entry for this topic should be consulted.

Further reading

Jonathan Culler, *Saussure* (London: Collins, 1976); Raymond Tallis, *Not Saussure: A Critique of Post-Saussurean Literary Theory* (London: Macmillan, 1988).

SHKLOVSKY, Viktor Borisovich (1893–1984)

Main works

'Art as Technique' (1965; in Russian, 1917)
'The Mystery Novel: Dickens's *Little Dorrit*' (1971; in Russian, 1925)
'On the Connection Between Devices of *Syuzhet* Construction and General Stylistic Devices' (1972; in Russian, 1919)
Theory of Prose (1991; in Russian, 1925)

DEFAMILIARIZATION ■ device ■ FRAME ■ *sjužet* (see STORY AND PLOT)

Shklovsky (his name is sometimes transliterated as Shklovskii or Šklovskij) was born in St Petersburg and studied literary history at university there, subsequently teaching at the Institute of Art History. Shklovsky's shifting political positions in the months prior to and succeeding the October revolution included certain anti-Bolshevik stances, and he experienced exile to the Ukraine in 1918 and, after a return to Russia in 1919, to Berlin (1922–23). Along with Osip Brik and Lev Iakubinsky he was a founder member of OPOIAZ (alternatively OPOYEZ), an acronym standing for the Society for the Study of Poetic Language. The Society was concerned to encourage the FORMAL and technical rather than the contextual or historical study of literature, and it became the chief begetter and popularizer of RUSSIAN FORMALISM. Shklovsky was also associated with the 'Serapion Brothers', a group that began meeting in St Petersburg (by now Petrograd) in 1921, and with the short-lived LEF (Left Front of Art). Shklovsky's ideas were criticized from a non-Stalinist MARXIST perspective in 1928 in P.N. Medvedev's *The Formal Method in Literary Scholarship* (see below), which some have attributed in whole or in part to MIKHAIL BAKHTIN.

By 1930 the growing pressure of socialist realist orthodoxy forced a public recantation from Shklovsky ('Monument to a Scientific Mistake'), and there were further brushes with the authorities later on during the same decade. Shklovsky also wrote a number of NOVELS, and from very early on involved himself in discussion of the cinema.

Shklovsky's importance lies in his demonstration that matters of literary content could be at least temporarily ignored while more ABSTRACT issues of technical and formal organization and construction were explored. Such a procedure is fundamental to formalism in its Russian (but not its Anglo-American NEW CRITICAL) manifestation, and it is also at the heart of STRUCTURALIST approaches to (among other things) literature. It is of course arguable that the study of poetry had long recognized that formal devices such as RHYME and METRE could be considered independently of 'content', but Shklovsky and other formalists were able to demonstrate that the same was true of the study of fictional prose. Shklovsky very often used as his structural unit the 'device', a concept comparable to VLADIMIR PROPP's 'function'. The modern field or discipline of NARRATOLOGY undoubtedly owes certain debts to Russian Formalism in general and to Shklovsky in particular, especially with regard to the distinction between fabula and *sjužet* (see STORY AND PLOT.)

Shklovsky is, however, best known for his concept of DEFAMILIARIZATION ('ostranenie', sometimes translated as *estrangement*), one which has stood the test of time and which is regularly appealed to by critics of both literature and film. The examples he gives have become well known (the Lilliputian examination of Gulliver's watch, for example), and the force of the concept has reached into theorizing about the social function of art and literature – ironically, in view of Shklovsky's formalist suspicion of sociological approaches to the arts. Also important is Shklovsky's understanding of the way in which FRAMING devices work in a READER's experience of a TEXT; in the essay on *Little Dorrit*, for example (see above), he argues that the plot of the novel is framed by two basic mysteries ('the watch' and 'the dreams') to which readers are introduced at the start of the novel.

Further reading

M.M. Bakhtin / P.N. Medvedev, *The Formal Method in Literary Scholarship: A Critical Introduction to Sociological Poetics* (Baltimore and London: Johns Hopkins University Press, 1978); Richard Sherwood, 'Viktor Shklovsky and the Development of Early Formalist Theory on Prose Literature' (*20th Century Studies*, December 1972, special issue on Russian Formalism), 26–40.

SHOWALTER, Elaine (1941–)

Main works

A Literature of Their Own: British Women Novelists From Brontë to Lessing (1977)
The Female Malady: Women, Madness and English Culture 1830–1980 (1985)
Sexual Anarchy: Gender and Culture at the Fin de Siècle (1990)
Sister's Choice: Tradition and Change in American Women's Writing (1991)
Hystories: Historical Epidemics and Modern Culture (1997)

Key terms

GYNOCRITICISM ■ hystoria

Born Elaine Cottler in Cambridge, Massachusetts, Showalter studied for a BA in English at Bryn Mawr College (1962), an MA from Brandeis University (1964), and received her PhD from the University of California at Davis (1970). She joined the faculty of Douglass College, the women's division of Rutgers University, in 1969, where she was among the first to teach courses dedicated specifically to women writers and CULTURE. In 1985 she moved to Princeton, where she was Professor of Humanities. She has recently served as President of the Modern Language Association in America.

Showalter's doctoral thesis became her first major publication, *A Literature of their Own* (1977). Looking at established as well as comparatively minor and unknown writers, Showalter argued that there was a separate tradition of women's writing in English, which demonstrated certain THEMATIC, GENERIC and even stylistic continuities. In her view, women's writing had progressed through a series of phases, from a pre-1880 period she characterized as 'feminine', and very much linked to the dominant male tradition, to a 'FEMINIST' phase between 1880 and 1920, marked by a rebellion against this tradition and by the attempt to find alternatives to it. The final, 'female' stage, since 1920, allowed for women to express themselves fully and freely, without recourse to the kinds of disguise and role-playing that characterized many nineteenth-century writers. (See also the entry for FEMINISM.)

Showalter was subsequently criticized, mainly by feminist writers aligning themselves with the French tradition of HÉLÈNE CIXOUS, LUCE IRIGARAY and JULIA KRISTEVA, for a kind of 'presentism' (believing that the best literature was contemporary) and for judging literature on the basis of the authenticity of experience and the directness of its presentation: all art thus becoming an extension of autobiography, an unproblematic reproduction of self and world, rather than a system with intricate laws and CONVENTIONS of its own. In other words, Showalter was accused of being so naive as to operate with a view of language as transparent, and of ignoring an emerging theoretical consensus that denied that language referred unproblematically to a reality outside itself.

In response, Showalter meshed her views with theories of 'ÉCRITURE FÉMININE' to develop her theory of 'GYNOCRITICISM', focusing on forms of writing by women that are uniquely female in their style and logic, as well as in their silences.

In her subsequent work Showalter has widened the scope of her writing beyond the purely literary to encompass changing ways in which the medical professions have colluded in the oppression of women. *The Female Malady* (1985) looks at the historical mistreatment of women by the health professions in Great Britain, and how they diagnosed unconventional women as patients suffering from hysteria. For Showalter this was to interpret creative and intellectual originality as a pathological disorder requiring medical intervention and supervision. Showalter shows how women were regarded as being more prone to depression and other mental illnesses during the Victorian era, eventually outnumbering men in asylums and clinics.

Showalter's preoccupation with hysteria continued in her latest, and most controversial, book *Hystories* (1997), which looks at chronic fatigue syndrome, Gulf War syndrome, recovered memory, multiple-personality syndrome, satanic-ritual abuse, and alien abduction, and arguing that these are essentially epidemics or plagues which reflect psychological problems. Her critics have claimed that Showalter seems to have come full circle here, agreeing with those she formerly criticized for interpreting physical ailments as expressions of mental unease.

Further reading

Toril Moi, *Sexual/Textual Politics* (London: Methuen, 1985); Janet Todd, *Feminist Literary Theory* (New York: Routledge, 1988).

SPIVAK, Gayatri Chakravorty (1942–)

Main works

Translation of and introduction to Jacques Derrida, *Of Grammatology* (1976)
'Three Women's Texts and a Critique of Imperialism' (1985)
In Other Worlds: Essays in Cultural Politics (1987)
'Can the Subaltern Speak?' (1988)
The Postcolonial Critic: Interviews, Strategies, Dialogues (1990)

Outside in the Teaching Machine (1993)

A Critique of Postcolonial Reason: Toward a History of the Vanishing Present (1999)

Key terms

ABSENCE ■ DECONSTRUCTION ■ FEMINISM ■ OTHER ■ POSTCOLONIALISM ■ subaltern

Introducing Gayatri Chakravorty Spivak requires a bombardment of labels: she is a DECONSTRUCTIVIST FEMINIST MARXIST POSTCOLONIALIST theorist and critic of literature and of other cultural TEXTS. The ordering of these terms is not random – 'deconstructivist' comes first for it is by applying the tools of deconstruction that Spivak has interrogated DISCOURSES of GENDER and imperialism as well as influentially intervening in debates about feminism, Marxism and postcolonialism. And the choice of these terms, it should be added, is contestable: Spivak herself has endeavoured, in her most recent work, to distance her position from the 'postcolonial' camp, but it nevertheless remains that she is generally seen as one of the pillars of what has come to be known as 'postcolonial' theory. Her work is committed to the cause of the 'subaltern' (literally, someone 'of inferior rank'), and it is given an active application through her engagement in world politics, particularly the politics of Third World/First World relations and of the exploitation of Third World labour.

Spivak was born into a middle-class family in Calcutta, West Bengal, five years before the end of British colonial rule in India – she has described this period, with its immense political tensions, as deeply important to her development as an intellectual. She studied English at Presidency College in Calcutta, graduating in 1959, and attended graduate school in Calcutta, before moving in 1962 to Cornell University where she took an MA in comparative literature. Her PhD, supervised by PAUL DE MAN, was also based at Cornell but while working on it she moved to a teaching position at the University of Iowa. Her dissertation addressed the life and poetry of W.B. Yeats, and a version of it was published in 1974. She has taught at several North American Universities and has lectured and held fellowships at numerous others around the world. Since 1991 she has been the Avalon Foundation Professor of the Humanities at Columbia University in New York.

She became prominent as an intellectual with her 1976 translation of JACQUES DERRIDA's *De la grammatologie* (1967). Her preface to the translation is, in many ways, typical of her writing and of deconstructivist writing more generally: it uses the occasion to reflect at length on the actual business of writing prefaces, and such self-conscious attention to the conditions of her own written UTTERANCES and an attention to the conditions of the literary (and other) utterances she examines can be said to be hallmarks of her work. Her preferred form of writing is the essay – her books are primarily collections of previously published essays – but she also exploits the interview as an intellectual outlet. (In general, the interviews provide the clearest paths to her arguments.) She has also translated (into English) FICTION by the Bengali writer Mahasweta Devi.

Her approach to theory is typically confrontational, and her confrontations emerge from multiple intellectual vantage points, such that her *œuvre* cannot be aligned with any single political/theoretical position. As she herself says, in a much-quoted remark from *The Postcolonial Critic*, 'I am viewed by the Marxists as too codic, by feminists as too male-identified, by indigenous theorists as too committed to Western theory.' And typically for a deconstructivist keen to resist CENTRED positions, she adds, 'I am uneasily pleased about this.' The shifting intellectual stance is described well by Robert Young (see Further reading):

> Instead of staking out a single recognizable position . . . she has produced a series of essays that move restlessly across the spectrum of contemporary theoretical and political concerns . . . To read her work is not so much to confront a system as to encounter a series of events.

This volatility in Spivak's work renders it resistant to generalized description, but a key thread that runs through the *œuvre* is an endeavour to create CULTURAL space in which oppressed voices – of women, of colonial subjects, of the poor – might be articulated. Spivak's inflection of deconstruction is the tool by which she challenges the authority of those empowered discourses which suppress other voices. 'Deconstruction', she says in an interview (in *The Spivak Reader* – see Further reading), 'does not say there is no subject, there is no truth, there is no history. It simply questions the privileging of identity so that someone is believed to have the truth . . . . It is constantly and persistently looking into how truths are produced.' Like EDWARD SAID and HOMI BHABHA, she aims to overturn the epistemological authority of imperial discourse, and importantly this deconstructive project resists *replacing* one discourse with another (with the potential to oppress), but rather demands, as she suggests, constant and persistent interrogation of truth claims.

Her essay 'Can the Subaltern Speak?' has proved to be one of the most influential contributions to this project, not least for popularizing the use of 'subaltern' as a term. In the essay Spivak builds on ANTONIO GRAMSCI's anti-HEGEMONIC application of 'subaltern', which he used to describe those groups within a society who are subject to the power of the ruling classes. Spivak writes that the 'development of the subaltern is complicated by the imperialist project', and notes that this issue has been 'confronted by a collection of intellectuals who may be called the "Subaltern Studies" group'. The group's project, according to Spivak, 'is to rethink Indian colonial historiography from the perspective of the discontinuous chain of peasant insurgencies during the colonial occupation' – what EDWARD SAID has termed 'the permission to narrate'. From this point she moves into a complex discussion of the consciousness of the oppressed, marginal, and subordinate groups, building on Pierre Macherey's formula that '[w]hat is important in a work is what it does not say', a focus which, Macherey suggests, may lead to the task of *measuring silences* (see ABSENCE). As Spivak puts it, when addressing the 'question of the consciousness of the subaltern, the notion of what the work *cannot* say becomes important'.

For Spivak, there is an element of double oppression for women in the colonial situation: '[if], in the context of colonial production, the subaltern has no history and cannot speak, the subaltern as female is even more deeply in shadow'. (Indeed, Spivak observes that 'if you are poor, black, and female you get it in three ways'.) The subaltern's mute and shadowy existence stems from the fact that history is written by the rulers, and the ruled are assigned walk-on (or work-on) parts in a historical play that is not their own. The moral imperative of Subaltern Studies is thus to retrieve the suppressed and erased voices of the subaltern – even if it means measuring silences.

Spivak's essay 'Three women's texts and a critique of imperialism' provides a good example of how these endeavours are advanced through literary criticism. Here Spivak reads Charlotte Brontë's *Jane Eyre* (among other texts) to expose its complicity with nineteenth-century British imperialism. She argues that the character of Bertha Rochester, the Creole first wife of Mr Rochester, is constructed by the text as a monstrous OTHER in order to legitimate the ultimate authority of the English heroine Jane Eyre. The novel is typically read by feminists as a triumph of female individualism, but by focusing on the character of Bertha, Spivak demonstrates how this triumph is achieved at the expense of the silenced colonial subject. Typically for Spivak, her critique is two-pronged: she exposes what she sees as political failings in the novel, while at the same time confronting the limitations of a feminism which is blind to NARRATIVES extrinsic to white, imperialist experience.

Spivak is always alert to the implications of voicing a SUBJECT's silences. She pays considerable attention to the 'situatedness' of the Western intellectual and explores the paradox that measuring silences can involve speaking *for* the subaltern from the privileged position within an academic institution, and thus continuing his or her voicelessness. This paradox underlies her reservations about postcolonialism, and particularly about the transformation of postcolonialism into something of a commodity in modern academia and in cultural exchange more broadly. At the beginning of *A Critique of Postcolonial Reason*, she describes how she had set out to 'track the figure of the Native Informant', but after 1989 'began to sense that a certain postcolonial subject had, in turn, been recoding the colonial subject and appropriating the Native Informant's position'. Spivak, then, continues to critique dominating DISCOURSES – including those which must be regarded as, at least in part, of her own making.

Further reading

Bill Ashcroft, Gareth Griffiths and Helen Tiffin, *The Empire Writes Back: Theory and Practice in Postcolonial Literatures* (London: Routledge, 1989); Leela Gandhi, *Postcolonial Theory: A Critical Introduction* (St Leonards, New South Wales: Allen & Unwin, 1998); Donna Landry and Gerald MacLean (eds), *The Spivak Reader* (London and New York: Routledge, 1996); Robert Young, *White Mythologies: Writing History and the West* (London and New York: Routledge, 1990).

TODOROV, Tzvetan (1939–)

Main works

The Fantastic: A Structural Approach to a Literary Genre (1973; in French, 1970)
The Poetics of Prose (1977; in French, 1971)
An Introduction to Poetics (1981; in French, 1973)
The Conquest of America: The Question of the Other (1982)
Genres in Discourse (1990)

Key terms

FANTASTIC ■ NARRATOLOGY ■ POETICS ■ STRUCTURALISM

Tzvetan Todorov was born in Sofia, Bulgaria, and studied Slavic philology for his first degree (in 1961), before moving to France, where he studied language and literature at the University of Paris. His doctoral thesis (finished in 1966) was supervised by ROLAND BARTHES, and he was awarded the title of Doctor of Letters in 1970. From 1968 to the present he has held a position at the *Centre National de la Recherche Scientifique* (CNRS) in Paris, and is currently a Director there. He has taught at several universities in the United States, including Yale and Columbia.

Todorov is identified with STRUCTURALISM, and his work has links to the ideas of GÉRARD GENETTE, ROMAN JAKOBSON and VLADIMIR PROPP, as well as to those of FERDINAND DE SAUSSURE. Developing Saussure's distinction between LANGUE AND PAROLE, Todorov has striven to apply this distinction to NARRATIVE and to literature in general. Rather than being preoccupied solely with meaning, then, Todorov looks at the ways in which meaning is brought about. For him, all narratives can be identified according to a kind of grammar, and it was he who first used the term 'NARRATOLOGY' in *Grammaire du Décaméron* (1969; 'The Grammar of the Decameron') to describe a science of narrative in which structural elements inherent in a narrative are studied so as to arrive at an understanding of the rules that govern them and their relation to a universal logic.

Todorov focused on three aspects of literary DISCOURSE that he identified as being part of a system, a pattern of CODES: the semantic, the syntactic and the verbal. The semantic deals with meaning or content in the traditional sense, as an accumulation of thematic concerns. The verbal looks at the relations between the grammatical units, the sentences, of the TEXT. The syntactic, which is the area that he is most interested in, examines the connections between the various structural elements of the text. Essentially, he takes rules associated with language – agency, noun, adjective and verb, tense, etc. – and applies them to narrative (see the entry for LINGUISTIC PARADIGM). Thus, characters are related to nouns, what they do to verbs, and their attributes to adjectives. Each text is organized according to three basic levels: there is the proposition (where an agent, or character, wants to be or do something); there is the sequence (where a group of propositions are linked in fairly predictable ways), and there is the text (the total organization of propositions). The sequences can be divided into five main categories, which can be ordered and mixed differently, as follows: Equilibrium (first type); Force (first type); Disequilibrium; Force (second type); Equilibrium (second type). These different phases can be linked to more traditional critical terms such as exposition, complication and resolution: they suggest that most narratives have elements that are fairly similar, and that point to patterns of human understanding that are universal and that can be objectively ascertained.

Todorov is also known for his work on the FANTASTIC, which he describes as a literary GENRE positioned between the 'uncanny' and the 'marvellous'. The uncanny explains the strange in terms of the rational; the marvellous accepts the strange or supernatural without attempting to explain it away. The fantastic is poised between these genres, and the reader is unable to decide which he or she is reading.

Further reading

Mieke Bal, *Narratology: Introduction to the Theory of Narrative* (2nd edn) (Toronto: University of Toronto Press, 1980); Christine Brooke-Rose, *A Rhetoric of the Unreal: Studies in Narratives and Structure, Especially of the Fantastic* (Cambridge: Cambridge University Press, 1981); Wallace Martin, *Recent Theories of Narrative* (Ithaca and London: Cornell University Press, 1986).

WELLEK, René (1903–)

Main works

Theory of Literature (with Austin Warren, 1949)
Concepts of Criticism (1963)
The Attack on Literature (1982)
A History of Modern Criticism (8 vols; 1965–92)

Key terms

LITERARINESS ■ extrinsic ■ intrinsic ■ perspectivism

Born in Austria in 1903, Wellek studied English and German Philology at Charles University in Prague, and then went to England from 1924 to 1925. He was awarded his doctorate in 1926, and then went to the United States, where he worked at Princeton University from 1927 to 1930. He was an active member of the PRAGUE SCHOOL (the Prague Linguistic Circle), and from 1935 to 1939 lectured on Czech literature and language at the School of Slavonic Studies in London, before emigrating to the United States at the outbreak of the Second World War. He worked at the University of Iowa, and in 1946 was appointed the Director of Comparative Literature at Yale University, where he remained until his retirement in 1972.

From 1947 to 1975, Cleanth Brooks, one of the critics most closely associated with NEW CRITICISM, also worked at Yale, and Wellek's main importance was in promoting and adapting the ideas of the Prague School in America. Essentially, he believed that literature was a system of SIGNS with its own norms, and his interest was in defining the 'literariness' of an object of study, explaining in what ways it demonstrated the principles of this larger system. The writing of literature was an autonomous creative activity that was to be judged primarily on AESTHETIC grounds, and not only on its relation to history – though Wellek did believe in 'perspectivism', by which he meant a combination of criticism, history and theory that allowed a greater knowledge of the meanings in a TEXT. This commitment to historical norms is often ignored or overlooked in attacks on his writing.

Wellek made a number of distinctions that were central to New Critical practice. An intrinsic approach focused on the aesthetic qualities of the literary text as a whole; an extrinsic approach looked at the text from the perspective of another discipline (such as psychoanalysis or sociology). He also categorized writers as either Makers, who are very deliberate, methodological and elegant writers, like the neo-Classicists, or Possessed, who are more spontaneous and obsessive, like the Romantics. Wellek's *Theory of Literature* (1949), co-authored with Austin Warren, was enormously popular and influential.

Further reading

Martin Bucco, *René Wellek* (Boston: Twayne, 1981); Joseph Strelka (ed.), *Literary Theory and Criticism: Festschrift in Honor of René Wellek* (Zurich: Peter Lang, 1984).

WILLIAMS, Raymond (1921–88)

Main works

Reading and Criticism (1950)
Drama from Ibsen to Eliot (1952; 2nd edn 1954; revised and retitled *Drama from Ibsen to Brecht*, 1968)
Drama in Performance (1954; revised edn 1991)
Culture and Society 1780–1950 (1958)
The Long Revolution (1961)
Modern Tragedy (1966)
The English Novel from Dickens to Lawrence (1970; new edn 1984)
Television, Technology and Cultural Form (1974)
Keywords: A Vocabulary of Culture and Society (1976; revised edn 1983)
Marxism and Literature (1977)
Politics and Letters: Interviews with New Left Review (1979)
Problems in Materialism and Culture: Selected Essays (1980)
Culture (1981)
The Politics of Modernism: Against the New Conformists (1989)

Key terms

CULTURAL MATERIALISM ■ STRUCTURES OF FEELING

Two aspects of the work of Raymond Williams are of especial importance for students of literature. The first of these is his view of literature as a component part of a wider, more all-embracing CULTURE (and thus of literary studies as an integral part of the larger project of CULTURAL STUDIES). The second is his development of a type of social and historical criticism different from that (or those) proposed by MARXISTS. Both of these elements of his work place him firmly in the camp of the anti-FORMALISTS: for Williams, works of art and literature are the products of, and need to be related to, the experiences of living individuals. Given such emphases, Williams's writing on literature has perhaps had more of a CANONICAL slant than one might have expected; although sceptical about the notion of 'great literature' his literary criticism has extended to relatively few marginal or oppositional writers.

Born into a Welsh working-class family (his father was a railway signalman in Pandy, South Wales), Williams's perception of the crucial importance of his own background to who and what he was formed the basis of a general belief in the need to trace back the products of the mind to the particular social, historical, *material* circumstances in and by which they were formed. He won a scholarship to Cambridge in 1939 but his university studies were interrupted by service as a tank commander in the Second World War, taking part, as John Higgins (see below) reports, in some of the bloodiest battles of the war. Finishing his studies with, revealingly, a thesis on the socially committed Henrik Ibsen, he then spent 14 years working in adult education. In 1961 he returned to Cambridge as an academic, and spent the rest of his working life there, first as lecturer and then from 1974 as Professor of Drama.

Williams maintained a lifelong commitment to left-wing and socialist politics, as activist and not just as 'supporter', and a militant and polemical strain runs through all of his writing. Apart from a brief period in the Communist Party at Cambridge prior to his war service, Williams was associated with the left both within and outside the Labour Party.

The structure of Williams's *Culture and Society* (1958) – his first book to achieve wide general sales and to give him a readership beyond the academic – is representative in its bringing together social history, linguistic development, and literary writing so as to explore the development of the 'idea of culture'. In his Introduction Williams considers certain 'key words' such as 'industry', 'democracy', 'class', 'art' and 'culture', all of which either assumed a changed meaning at the end of the eighteenth and beginning of the nineteenth century, or first came into common use at this time. Arguing that there is a general pattern of change in these words and that they can be treated as a 'special kind of map' to examine wider changes in life and thought, Williams engages in a characteristic move, that of linking very large patterns of social and historical change to new ways of thinking through the mediation of significant shifts of local linguistic usage. New words and new usages thus both reflect or refer to such changes but they also in part enable them.

If *Culture and Society* brings with it a mention of 'key words' – later the title of a book by Williams – it also includes use of another term very much associated with his work. Talking about Elizabeth Gaskell's NOVEL *Mary Barton*, Williams suggests that this novel 'begins' from a 'STRUCTURE OF FEELING' that is a combination of sympathetic observation and an attempt at imaginative identification. As John Higgins has pointed out, the term 'structure of feeling' first appears in Williams's work in the early *Drama in Performance* (1954), and is regularly refined in succeeding works through to Williams's death. In *Drama in Performance* Williams talks of a structure of feeling which 'is adequate to communicate, not merely the acknowledged and apparent, but the whole and unified life of man'. As Higgins has also pointed out, there is little doubt that for Williams the concept of the structure of feeling was always advanced in opposition to what Williams saw as the ABSTRACTIONS of Marxist cultural theory, and in particular its reliance on concepts such as BASE AND SUPERSTRUCTURE, which Williams attacks directly in his essay 'Base and Superstructure in Marxist Cultural Theory', in *Problems in Materialism and Culture* (1980).

But if Williams attempted to develop a cultural theory and criticism which avoided what he saw as the rigid and mechanistic abstractions of Marxist theory, he had no time for the AESTHETICISM and formalism that he saw in 'Cambridge English' (by which he meant, in particular, the work of F.R. LEAVIS and his followers), or the NEW CRITICISM. His social and cultural analyses consistently move out to the actual lived experiences of those ordinary people who either produced, or supported those who produced, the TEXTS, artifacts and ideas that more conservative, élitist writers took to be the whole of culture. For Williams culture is always a 'whole way of life', and he consistently resists its reduction either to a few highly valued cultural products (what he saw as the conservative-élitist view) or to large socio-economic abstractions (what he saw as the Marxist view).

By late 1970s, Williams was prepared to give his general position a name: CULTURAL MATERIALISM. The position is implicit in his *Marxism and Literature* (1977), and is stated overtly in his essay 'Notes on Marxism in Britain Since 1945'. At this time Williams starts to associate himself with an oppositional, anti-Stalinist tradition within Marxism, one including such diverse figures as LUCIEN GOLDMANN, Antonio Gramsci, and V.N. Vološinov (see the entry for MIKHAIL BAKHTIN). For him, then, Cultural Materialism is 'cultural' because of its insistence upon the centrality of language and communication as formative social forces and not (as in 'vulgar Marxism') mere secondary elements in the superstructure 'reflecting' the primary reality of the economic base, and it is materialist because it involves a theory of culture as a social and material productive process, rooted in the actualities of the life and consciousness of ordinary people.

Throughout his writing life Williams took up a position in opposition to various forms of what he deemed to be crude determinism. His *Television, Technology and Cultural Form* (1974), for example, performed a valuable role in exposing and critiquing simplistic notions of technological determinism. At the same time, however, Williams by no means dismissed the importance of technological innovation, but (as always) he insisted that human beings were not just automatons who were reacted on by forces beyond their understanding or control, but people who individually and collectively made conscious decisions about their lives. This anti-deterministic, humanistic element in Williams led him to see a continuity from vulgar Marxism through Althusserianism and to various forms of anti-HUMANIST POST-STRUCTURALISM – all of which he opposed.

If we imagine, very crudely, a continuum from the minutiae of linguistic detail, through cultural products, to large social and economic movements and processes, then Williams's strengths can be located at the ends rather than in the middle of this continuum. Books such as *Keywords* have drawn important attention to the congealed history of experience, struggle and change contained in familiar words, while others such as *Culture and Society* have spread awareness about the need to situate cultural and literary works in large and complex processes of social and historical change, much of which is not immediately visible in them. Williams's studies of individual literary works are less memorable.

Williams spent a life in polemic and argument, and accordingly has been much criticized. Marxists have found a concept such as 'structures of feeling' too vague, shifting and imprecise to be of use in concrete analysis, while historians have reacted against a social history based too exclusively upon a few selected cultural texts. Formalists and Leavisites have disliked Williams for reasons less clearly articulated, but having much to do with his insistence upon moving out of texts and into the hidden social and IDEOLOGICAL realities of the societies from which they emerged. But no British writer in the twentieth century did more to change the way in which literary and cultural texts were discussed. Williams's contribution to the development of an academic discipline of Cultural Studies (see Section 3, p. 183) is enormous and unique, and deserves admiration and respect.

Further reading

John Higgins, *Raymond Williams: Literature, Marxism and Cultural Materialism* (London: Routledge, 1999).

WOOLF, Virginia (1882–1941)

Main works

'Modern Fiction' (1925, revised from 'Modern Novels', 1919)
'Mr Bennett and Mrs Brown' (1923)
The Common Reader (1925; a collection of earlier published essays)
'The Art of Fiction' (1927)
'Women and Fiction' (1929)
The Common Reader: Second Series (1932; a collection of earlier published essays)
A Room of One's Own (1929)

SECTION 5

ANDROGYNY ■ ÉCRITURE FÉMININE ■ FEMINISM ■ MODERNISM ■ STREAM OF CONSCIOUS-
NESS

Best known as a writer of MODERNIST NOVELS, Virginia Woolf was also a prolific reviewer and essayist, whose numerous WORKS on literary topics have had a
deep and continuing impact upon literary studies, particularly upon FEMINIST
theory and criticism. Woolf was born into an upper-middle class London family,
and like most women growing up in England in the nineteenth century she
received no formal education. She nevertheless gained a vast knowledge of literature through avid reading in the library of her father, the Victorian biographer
and editor Sir Leslie Stephen. Woolf was acutely aware of the inequalities
between the sexes, and her exclusion from university – coupled with her close
association with her Cambridge-educated brothers and their male friends –
intensified her reaction against patriarchy. Such aversion became a driving force
in her work, and much of her writing explores and condemns the conditions
which support the inferior status of women. In 1904 Woolf published her first
essay, and thereafter she published frequently on a wide range of topics in such
titles as the *Times Literary Supplement* and *The New Statesman*. In 1912 she
married Leonard Woolf with whom, in 1917, she set up the Hogarth Press. This
small-scale press published the work of a number of experimental modernist
writers, including T.S. ELIOT and Katherine Mansfield, as well as several of
Woolf's own works; it also published some of the first English translations of
Sigmund Freud's studies in psychoanalysis. Woolf's first novel appeared in 1915
and it was followed by eight more – including the modernist classics *Mrs
Dalloway* (1925), *To the Lighthouse* (1927) and *The Waves* (1931) – through
which Woolf became increasingly popular and famous. Throughout her life
Woolf suffered periods of depression, the last of which contributed to her sui-
cide in 1941.

In terms of GENRE, no neat distinction can be made between Woolf's FICTION
and her literary criticism and theory. Woolf often used the novel to advance points
of a critical or theoretical nature, while her more explicitly critical works exploit
devices associated with fiction. The works listed above provide some of the clearest expressions of her most influential thinking about literature, but these same
arguments are present, explicitly or implicitly, in many of her other works.

'Modern Fiction' and 'Mr Bennett and Mrs Brown' are important as mani-
festos for literary modernism – the essays promote the value of the type of fiction that Woolf strove to write herself and they advertise the radical break from
old CONVENTIONS that such fiction represents. In 'Modern Fiction' she argues
that the Edwardian novelists H.G. Wells, Arnold Bennett and John Galsworthy
are severely limited by their attention to *external* detail. She dubs these writers
'materialists', and argues that their approach to fiction fails to achieve what she
sees as the goal of the novelist: the representation of 'life'. For Woolf, 'life' is not

found in external matter, but in that chain of experience that occurs *within* an individual's consciousness, and it is the novelist's duty, she argues, to delve into these inner realms of the psyche. 'Let us record', she writes, 'the atoms [of experience] as they fall upon the mind in the order in which they fall, let us trace the pattern, however disconnected and incoherent in appearance, which each sight or incident scores upon the consciousness'. The essay, then, is an early assessment and promotion of the STREAM OF CONSCIOUSNESS technique (although it does not employ the term). Such a technique was, of course, used by Woolf and by other modernists including James Joyce who is praised in the essay (albeit with reservations about his indecency). 'Mr Bennett and Mrs Brown' develops the argument with a close focus on characterization.

Woolf, then, was an important 'eye-witness' theorist of modernism and of Modernist literary FORM, but it is as a feminist that her impact has been most lasting, particularly through *A Room of One's Own*, a long essay exploring the past and present conditions for women writers. (See, however, the entry for FEMINISM in Section 4 for Woolf's reservations about this term.) Based on lectures delivered in 1928 to one of the few British colleges for women, the essay blends anecdotes, fantasy and scholarship in its discussion of women's multiple exclusions (from education, economic independence, history, literary history) and of the disabling consequences of these exclusions for the production of literature. Woolf's basic premise is simple: if a woman is to write she needs a stable income and a private room. In approaching this conclusion from several angles, the essay has stimulated a number of distinct strands in feminist studies.

Woolf argues that while the ordinary lives of women are barely represented in history (with its focus upon 'masculine' subjects like war), false projections of women have regularly been created so as to reflect and uphold the male ego and patriarchal IDEOLOGY. The essay campaigns for the writing of women's social history, a discipline which has certainly grown since Woolf wrote, and the argument has likewise been a stimulus for feminist criticism focusing upon representations of women. Woolf furthermore argues that the exclusion of women from *literary* history, is a major problem for women writers. '[W]e think back through our mothers if we are women', she states, but women writers suffer the absence of literary mothers, in the sense that there is no CANON or known tradition of women's writing. Again Woolf calls for new historical approaches, and her discussion of early writers, such as Margaret Cavendish and Aphra Behn, gestures towards the feminist literary history which, since the 1960s, has 'rediscovered' numerous women writers. Women write differently from men, Woolf insists, and she contrasts a man's sentence with a woman's sentence in an analysis which, in many ways, foreshadows French feminist discussions of ÉCRITURE FÉMININE. There are, then, ESSENTIALIZING tendencies in *A Room of One's Own*, but Woolf also develops an idea of GENDER as floating free from the BINARY divisions of sex when she advances an influential and controversial discussion of androgyny as the ideal psychological state for creativity (see the entry on ANDROGYNY for fuller discussion).

Woolf has also been recognized as proto-DECONSTRUCTIVIST in her approach to language. Her writing strategies often fracture monologic, CENTRED perspectives – ' "I" is only a convenient term for somebody who has no real being', she writes in *A Room of One's Own* – and this tendency has been read as a critique of PHALLOGOCENTRISM. Woolf's writing, then, has been read in support of many different critical methodologies, and because of this breadth of appeal Woolf must be recognized as one of the most influential pioneers of modern feminist studies.

Further reading

Rachel Bowlby, *Virginia Woolf: Feminist Destinations* (Oxford: Blackwell, 1988); Mark Goldman, *The Reader's Art: Virginia Woolf as Literary Critic* (The Hague: Mouton, 1976); Toril Moi, 'Who's afraid of Virginia Woolf?' in *Sexual/Textual Politics: Feminist Literary Theory* (London: Methuen, 1985).

Bibliography

This bibliography lists all works from which extracts are quoted in Sections 3 and 4.

Abrams, M.H. (1977). The limits of pluralism: the deconstructive angel. *Critical Inquiry*, **3**, 425–38.

Abrams, M.H. (1988). *A Glossary of Literary Terms* (5th edn). London: Holt, Rinehart & Winston.

Aczel, Richard (1998). Hearing voices in narrative texts. *New Literary History*, **29**, 467–500.

Althusser, Louis (1969). *For Marx* (first published in French, 1966). Brewster, Ben (trans.). London: Allen Lane.

Althusser, Louis (1971). *Lenin and Philosophy and Other Essays*. Brewster, Ben (trans.). London: New Left Books.

Althusser, Louis and Balibar, Etienne (1977). *Reading 'Capital'*. London: New Left Books.

Andermahr, Sonya, Lovell, Terry and Wolkowitz, Carol (1997). *A Glossary of Feminist Theory*. London: Arnold.

Ashcroft, Bill, Griffiths, Gareth and Tiffin, Helen (1989). *The Empire Writes Back: Theory and Practice in Post-Colonial Literatures*. London: Routledge.

Ashcroft, Bill, Griffiths, Gareth and Tiffin, Helen (eds) (1995). *The Post-Colonial Studies Reader*. London: Routledge.

Attridge, Derek (1996). *Poetic Rhythm: An Introduction*. Cambridge: Cambridge University Press.

Atwood, Margaret (1983). *Murder in the Dark: Short Fictions, and Prose Poems*. Toronto: Coach House Press.

Austin, John (1962). *How to Do Things with Words*. Oxford: Clarendon Press.

Bakhtin, M.M. (1968). *Rabelais and his World*. Iswolsky, Helene (trans.). Cambridge, MA: MIT Press.

Bakhtin, M.M. (1981). *The Dialogic Imagination: Four Essays*. Holquist, Michael (ed.), Emerson, Caryl and Holquist, Michael (trans.). Austin: University of Texas Press.

Bakhtin, M.M. (1984). *Problems of Dostoevsky's Poetics*. Emerson, Caryl (ed. and trans.). Manchester: Manchester University Press.

Bakhtin, M.M. (1986). *Speech Genres and other Late Essays*. McGee, Vern W. (trans.). Austin: University of Texas Press.

Bal, Mieke (1985). *Narratology: Introduction to the Theory of Narrative*. Van Boheemen, Christine (trans.). Toronto and London: University of Toronto Press.

Balibar, Etienne and Macherey, Pierre (1978). Literature as an ideological form. McLeod, Ian, Whitehead, John and Wordsworth, Ann (trans.). *Oxford Literary Review*, **3**(1), 4–12.

Banfield, Ann (1982). *Unspeakable Sentences: Narration and Representation in the Language of Fiction*. London: Routledge.

Banfield, Ann (1985). Écriture, narration and the grammar of French. In Hawthorn, Jeremy (ed.), *Narrative: from Malory to Motion Pictures*. London: Arnold, 1–22.

Barrett, Michèle (1991). *The Politics of Truth: From Marx to Foucault*. Cambridge: Polity Press.

Barthes, Roland (1967a). *Elements of Semiology*. Lavers, Annette and Smith, Colin (trans.) (first published in French, 1964). London: Cape.

Barthes, Roland (1967b). *Writing Degree Zero*. Lavers, Annette and Smith, Colin (trans.) (first published in French, 1953). London: Cape.

Barthes, Roland (1973). *Mythologies*. Lavers, Annette (ed. and trans.) (first published in French, 1957). Frogmore: Granada.

Barthes, Roland (1976). *The Pleasure of the Text*. Miller, Richard (trans.) (first published in French, 1975). London: Cape.

Barthes, Roland (1977). The death of the author. In Heath, Stephen (ed. and trans.), *Image–Music–Text*. London: Collins, 142–8.

Barthes, Roland (1981a). Textual analysis of Poe's 'Valdemar'. Bennington, Geoff (trans.). In Young, Robert: 1981, 133–61.

Barthes, Roland (1981b). Theory of the text. McLeod, Ian (trans.). In Young, Robert: 1981, 31–47.

Barthes, Roland (1990). *S/Z*. Miller, Richard (trans.) (first published in French, 1973). Oxford: Blackwell.

Barthes, Roland (1991). *The Responsibility of Forms: Critical Essays on Music, Art and Representation*. Howard, Richard (trans.). Berkeley and Los Angeles: University of California Press.

Benjamin, Walter (1973). *Illuminations*. Arendt, Hannah (ed.), Zohn, Harry (trans.) (first published in German, 1955; English trans. first published 1968). London: Collins.

Blanchot, Maurice (1981). The narrative voice (the 'he', the neuter). In Davis, Lydia (trans.), *The Gaze of Orpheus and Other Literary Essays*. New York: Station Hill Press.

Bloch, Ernst, Lukács, Georg, Brecht, Bertolt, Benjamin, Walter and Adorno, Theodor (1977). *Aesthetics and Politics*. London: New Left Books.

Bloom, Harold (1973). *The Anxiety of Influence: A Theory of Poetry*. Oxford and New York: Oxford University Press.

Bodkin, Maud (1934). *Archetypal Patterns in Poetry*. London: Oxford University Press.

Booth, Wayne C. (1961). *Rhetoric of Fiction*. Chicago and London: University of Chicago Press.

Bowlt, John (1972). Introduction to special issue on Russian Formalism. *20th Century Studies*, **7/8**, December.

Bremond, Claude (1966). La logique des possibles narratifs. *Communications*, **8**, 60–76. Published as 'The logic of narrative possibilities' (Cancalon, Elaine D., trans.) in *New Literary History*, **11** (1980), 387–411, and repr. in abridged form in Onega and Landa: 1996, 61–75.

Brooke-Rose, Christine (1981). *A Rhetoric of the Unreal: Studies in Narrative and Structure, Especially of the Fantastic*. Cambridge: Cambridge University Press.

Brooks, Cleanth (1946). Empson's criticism. In Quinn, Kerker and Shattuck, Charles (eds), *Accent Anthology* (first published 1944). New York: Harcourt Brace.

Brooks, Cleanth (1983). In search of the New Criticism. *The American Scholar*, **53**(1), Winter 1983/4, 41–53.

Brooks, Cleanth and Warren, Robert Penn (1958). *Understanding Poetry* (rev. edn; first published 1938). New York: Henry Holt.

Brooks, Peter (1994). *Psychoanalysis and Storytelling*. Oxford: Blackwell.

Bryson, Norman, Holly, Michael Ann, and Moxey, Keith (1994). *Visual Culture: Images and Interpretations*. Hanover and London: Wesleyan University Press. (Published by University Press of New England).

Butor, Michel (1964). L'usage des pronoms personnels dans le roman. In *Répertoire II*. Paris: Les Editions de Minuit.

Callinicos, Alex (1989). *Against Postmodernism*. Cambridge: Polity Press.

Cameron, Deborah (1985). *Feminism and Linguistic Theory*. London: Macmillan.

Caws, Mary Ann (1985). *Reading Frames in Modern Fiction*. Princeton: Princeton University Press.

Chatman, Seymour (1990). *Coming to Terms: The Rhetoric of Narrative in Fiction and Film*. Ithaca and London: Cornell University Press.

Cixous, Hélène (1981). The laugh of the Medusa. In Marks, Elaine and de Courtivron, Isabelle (eds), Cohen, Keith and Cohen, Paula (trans.), *New French Feminisms: An Anthology* (first published in French, 1975; translation is of the revised French version of 1976). New York: Schocken Books, 245–64.

Cohan, Steven and Shires, Linda M. (1988). *Telling Stories: A Theoretical Analysis of Narrative Fiction*. London: Routledge.

Cohn, Dorrit (1978). *Transparent Minds: Narrating Modes for Presenting Consciousness in Fiction*. Princeton: Princeton University Press.

Conrad, Joseph (1986). *Lord Jim*. Hampson, Robert (ed.), Watts, Cedric (Introduction and Notes). Harmondsworth: Penguin.

Cranny-Francis, Anne (1990). *Feminist Fiction: Feminist Uses of Generic Fiction*. Cambridge: Polity Press.

Crapanzano, Vincent (1992). *Hermes' Dilemma and Hamlet's Desire: On the Epistemology of Interpretation*. Cambridge, MA: Harvard University Press.

Culler, Jonathan (1975). *Structuralist Poetics: Structuralism, Linguistics and the Study of Literature*. London: Routledge.

Culler, Jonathan (1980). Prolegomena to a theory of reading. In Suleiman, Susan R. and Crosman, Inge (eds), *The Reader in the Text*. Princeton: Princeton University Press, 46–66.

Culler, Jonathan (1981). *The Pursuit of Signs: Semiotics, Literature, Deconstruction*. London: Routledge.

Culler, Jonathan (1988). *Framing the Sign: Criticism and its Institutions*. Oxford: Blackwell.

de Beaugrande, Robert (1994). Discourse analysis. In Groden, Michael and Kreiswirth, Martin (eds), *The Johns Hopkins Guide to Literary Theory and Criticism*. Baltimore: Johns Hopkins University Press, 207–10.

Deleuze, Gilles and Guattari, Félix (1983). *Anti-Oedipus: Capitalism and Schizophrenia* (first published in French, 1972 and in English, 1977). Minneapolis: University of Minnesota Press.

Derrida, Jacques (1975). The purveyor of truth. *Yale French Studies*, **52**, 31–113.

Derrida, Jacques (1976). *Of Grammatology*. Spivak, Gayatri Chakravorty (trans.) (first published in French, 1967). Baltimore: Johns Hopkins University Press.

Derrida, Jacques (1978). *Writing and Difference*. Bass, Alan (trans.). London: Routledge.

Derrida, Jacques (1981). *Positions*. Bass, Alan (trans.). London: Athlone Press.

Drake, James (1998). The naming disease: how Jakobson's essay on aphasia initiated post-modern deceits. *The Times Literary Supplement*, issue **4979**, 4 September, 14–15.

Draper, Hal (1978). *Karl Marx's Theory of Revolution: The Politics of Social Class*. New York: Monthly Review Press.

Eagleton, Mary (ed.) (1996). *Feminist Theory: A Reader* (2nd edn). Oxford: Blackwell.

Eagleton, Terry (1983). *Literary Theory: An Introduction*. Oxford: Blackwell.

Eagleton, Terry (1991). *Ideology: An Introduction*. London: Verso.

Eco, Umberto (1972). Towards a semiotic inquiry into the television message. Splendore, Paola (trans.) (first read as a paper in Italian, 1965). *Working Papers in Cultural Studies*, **3**, 1972, 103–21. (Repr. in Corner, John and Hawthorn, Jeremy [eds], *Communication Studies: An Introductory Reader*. London: Arnold, 1980, 131–49.)

Eco, Umberto (1981). *The Role of the Reader: Explorations in the Semiotics of Texts*. London: Hutchinson.

Eichenbaum, Boris (1965). The theory of the 'formal method' (first published in Ukrainian, 1926; this translation from the Russian version, 1927). In Lemon, Lee T. and Reis, Marion J. (eds and trans.), *Russian Formalist Criticism: Four Essays*. Lincoln, NE: University of Nebraska Press.

Èjxenbaum, Boris M. (1971). The theory of the formal method (first published in Russian, 1927). In Matejka, Ladislav and Pomorska, Krystyna (eds), Titunik, I.R. (trans.), *Readings in Russian Poetics: Formalist and Structuralist Views*. Cambridge, MA and London: MIT Press, 3–37. See also Eichenbaum: 1965.

Eliot, T.S. (1920). *The Sacred Wood*. London: Methuen.

Eliot, T.S. (1922). *The Waste Land*. London: Hogarth Press.

Eliot, T.S. (1961). *On Poetry and Poets*. New York: Noonday Press.

Ellmann, Mary (1979). *Thinking about Women* (first published 1968). London: Virago.

Empson, William (1961). *Seven Types of Ambiguity* (3rd edn; first edn published 1930). Harmondsworth: Peregrine.

Empson, William (1966). *Some Versions of Pastoral: A Study of the Pastoral Form in Literature*. (First published in 1935.) Harmondsworth: Peregrine.

Ermarth, Elizabeth Deeds (1992). *Postmodernism and the Crisis of Representational Time*. Princeton: Princeton University Press.

Fiedler, Leslie (1966). *Love and Death in the American Novel* (rev. edn; first published 1960). New York: Stein & Day.

Fish, Stanley (1980). *Is There a Text in this Class? The Authority of Interpretive Communities*. Cambridge, MA and London: Harvard University Press.

Fludernik, Monika (1996). *Towards a 'Natural' Narratology*. London: Routledge.

Foucault, Michel (1972). *The Archaeology of Knowledge*. Sheridan Smith, A.M. (trans.). London: Tavistock.

Foucault, Michel (1980). What is an author? (first published in English, 1977, in Bouchard, Donald F. (ed.), *Language, Counter-memory, Practice: Selected Essays and Interviews*. New York: Cornell University Press. In Harari, J.V.: 1980, 141–60.

Foucault, Michel (1981). The order of discourse. Originally Foucault's inaugural lecture, delivered at the Collège de France, 2 December 1970. McLeod, Ian (trans.). In Young, Robert: 1981, 48–78.

Foucault, Michel (nd). The discourse of language. (First delivered as a lecture in French, 1970, and published in French and English, 1971.) In *The Archaeology of Knowledge*. Sheridan Smith, A.M. (trans.). New York: Pantheon Books, 215–37.

Freud, Sigmund (1976). *The Interpretation of Dreams*. Strachey, James (ed., assisted by Alan Tyson), Strachey, James (trans.). The Pelican Freud Library, **4**. Harmondsworth: Penguin.

Frow, John (1997). *Time and Commodity Culture: Essays in Cultural Theory and Postmodernity*. Oxford: Clarendon Press.

Furbank, P.N. (1970). *Reflections on the Word 'Image'*. London: Secker & Warburg.

Fuss, Diana (1991). *Inside/Out: Lesbian Theories, Gay Theories*. New York and London: Routledge.

Gadamer, Hans-Georg (1989). *Truth and Method* (2nd, rev. edn). Trans. rev. by Weinsheimer, Joel and Marshall, Donald G. London: Sheed & Ward.

Gagnon, Madeleine (1980). Body I. An excerpt from 'Corps I' (first published in French,

1977). In Marks, Elaine and Courtivron, Isabelle de (eds), Courtivron, Isabelle de (trans.), *New French Feminisms: An Anthology*. Amherst: University of Massachusetts Press.

Garvin, Paul (ed. and trans.) (1964). *A Prague School Reader on Esthetics, Literary Structure, and Style*. Washington, DC: Georgetown University Press.

Genette, Gérard (1980). *Narrative Discourse*. Lewin, Jane E. (trans.). Oxford: Blackwell.

Genette, Gérard (1982). *Figures of Literary Discourse*. Sheridan, Alan (trans.). Oxford: Blackwell.

Genette, Gérard (1997). *Paratexts: Thresholds of Interpretation* (*Literature, Culture, Theory*, 20; first published in French, 1987). Lewin, Jane E. (trans.). Cambridge: Cambridge University Press.

Gibson, Andrew (1996). *Towards a Postmodern Theory of Narrative*. Edinburgh: Edinburgh University Press.

Gilbert, Sandra M. and Gubar, Susan (1979). *The Madwoman in the Attic: The Woman Writer and the Nineteenth-Century Literary Imagination*. New Haven: Yale University Press.

Goffman, Erving (1974). *Frame Analysis: An Essay on the Organization of Experience*. Cambridge, MA: Harvard University Press.

Gramsci, Antonio (1971). *Selections from the Prison Notebooks of Antonio Gramsci*. Hoare, Quintin and Nowell Smith, Geoffrey (eds and trans.). London: Lawrence & Wishart.

Grant, Catherine (1994/5). Queer theorrhea (and what it might mean for feminists). *Trouble and Strife*, 29/30 (repr. in Jackson and Scott: 1996, 166–71).

Greenblatt, Stephen J. (1990). *Learning to Curse: Essays in Early Modern Culture*. London: Routledge.

Gugelberger, Georg M. (1994). Postcolonial cultural studies. In Groden, Michael and Kreiswirth, Martin (eds), *The Johns Hopkins Guide to Literary Theory and Criticism*. Baltimore: Johns Hopkins University Press, 581–5.

Hall, Stuart and Whannel, Paddy (1964). *The Popular Arts*. London: Hutchinson.

Hampton, Christopher (1990). *The Ideology of the Text*. Milton Keynes: Open University Press.

Harari, Josué V. (ed.) (1980). *Textual Strategies: Perspectives in Post-structuralist Criticism*. London: Methuen.

Harland, Richard (1987). *Superstructuralism: The Philosophy of Structuralism and Post-structuralism*. London: Methuen.

Hartman, Geoffrey (1970). *Beyond Formalism*. New Haven: Yale University Press.

Harvey, David (1989). *The Condition of Postmodernity*. Oxford: Blackwell.

Havránek, Bohuslav (1964). The functional differentiation of the standard language (first published in Czech, 1932). In Garvin: 1964, 3–16.

Higgins, John (1999). *Raymond Williams: Literature, Marxism and Cultural Materialism*. London: Routledge.

Hirsch, E.D. (1967). *Validity in Interpretation*. New Haven and London: Yale University Press.

Hirsch, E.D. (1976). *The Aims of Interpretation*. Chicago: University of Chicago Press.

Hoggart, Richard (1970). Contemporary cultural studies: an approach to the study of literature and society. In Bradbury, Malcolm and Palmer, David (eds), *Contemporary Criticism*, Stratford-upon Avon Studies, 12. London: Arnold, 154–70.

Holderness, Graham (1982). *D.H. Lawrence: History, Ideology and Fiction*. Dublin and London: Gill and Macmillan.

Holderness, Graham (1991). Production, reproduction, performance: Marxism, history, theatre. In Barker, Francis, Hulme, Peter, and Iversen, Margaret (eds), *Uses of History:*

Marxism, Postmodernism and the Renaissance. Manchester: Manchester University Press, 153–78.

Holderness, Graham (1992). *Shakespeare Recycled: The Making of Historical Drama*. Hemel Hempstead: Harvester Wheatsheaf.

Holland, Norman N. (1975). *5 Readers Reading*. New Haven: Yale University Press.

Hunt, Alan (1977). Theory and politics in the identification of the working class. In Hunt, Alan (ed.), *Class and Class Structure*. London: Lawrence & Wishart, 81–111.

Hutcheon, Linda (1980). *Narcissistic Narrative: The Metafictional Paradox*. Waterloo, Ontario: Wilfred Laurier University Press (repr. 1984 by Methuen).

Ingarden, Roman (1973). *The Literary Work of Art: An Investigation on the Borders of Ontology, Logic, and Theory of Literature* (first published in German, 1931). Grabowicz, George G. (trans.). Evanston: Northwestern University Press.

Iser, Wolfgang (1974). *The Implied Reader: Patterns of Communication in Prose Fiction from Bunyan to Beckett*. Baltimore and London: Johns Hopkins University Press.

Jackson, Stevi and Scott, Sue (eds) (1996). *Feminism and Sexuality: A Reader*. Edinburgh: Edinburgh University Press.

Jahn, Manfred (1997). Frames, preferences, and the reading of third-person narratives: towards a cognitive narratology. *Poetics Today*, **18**, 441–68.

Jahn, Manfred, Molitor, Inge and Nünning, Ansgar (1993). *COGNAC: A Concise Glossary of Narratology from Cologne*. Cologne: Englisches Seminar.

Jakobson, Roman (1960). Closing statement: linguistics and poetics. In Sebeok, Thomas A. (ed.), *Style in Language*. Cambridge, MA: The Technology Press/MIT; New York: John Wiley.

Jakobson, Roman and Halle, Morris (1971). *Fundamentals of Language* (2nd rev. edn). The Hague: Mouton.

James, Henry (1948). *The Lesson of the Master and Other Stories by Henry James*. (Place of publication not given): John Lehmann.

Jameson, Fredric (1981). *The Political Unconscious: Narrative as a Socially Symbolic Act*. London: Methuen.

Jameson, Fredric (1991). *Postmodernism, or, The Cultural Logic of Late Capitalism*. Durham, NC: Duke University Press.

Jauss, Hans Robert (1974). Literary history as a challenge to literary theory. In Cohen, Ralph (ed.), *New Directions in Literary History*. London: Routledge, 11–41.

Jay, Martin (1973). *The Dialectical Imagination: A History of the Frankfurt School and the Institute of Social Research 1923–50*. Boston: Little, Brown.

Jay, Martin (1993). *Downcast Eyes: The Denigration of Vision in Twentieth-Century French Thought*. Berkeley: University of California Press.

Johnson, Pauline (1984). *Marxist Aesthetics: The Foundations Within Everyday Life for an Enlightened Consciousness*. London: Routledge.

Kaplan, E. Ann (1990). *Psychoanalysis and Cinema*. New York and London: Routledge.

Kermode, Frank (1989). *An Appetite for Poetry: Essays in Literary Interpretation*. London: Collins.

Knapp, Steven and Michaels, Walter Benn (1985). Against theory. In Mitchell, W.J.T. (ed.), *Against Theory: Literary Studies and the New Pragmatism*. Chicago and London: University of Chicago Press.

Knights, L.C. (1937). *Drama and Society in the Age of Jonson*. London: Chatto & Windus.

Kristeva, Julia (1980). *Desire in Language: A Semiotic Approach to Literature and Art*. Roudiez, Leon S. (ed.), Gora, Thomas, Jardine, Alice and Roudiez, Leon S. (trans). Oxford: Blackwell.

Kristeva, Julia (1984). *Revolution in Poetic Language* (first published in French, 1974). Waller, M. (trans.). New York: Columbia University Press.

Kuhn, Thomas S. (1970). *The Structure of Scientific Revolutions* (2nd edn). Chicago and London: University of Chicago Press.

Lacan, Jacques (1977). *Écrits: A Selection*. Sheridan, Alan (trans.). London: Tavistock.

Lacan, Jacques (1979). *The Four Fundamental Concepts of Psychoanalysis*. Miller, Jacques-Alain (ed.), Sheridan, Alan (trans.) (first published in French, 1973, and in English translation, 1977). Harmondsworth: Penguin.

Lanser, Susan Sniader (1981). *The Narrative Act: Point of View in Prose Fiction*. Princeton: Princeton University Press.

Lawrence, D.H. (1961). *Selected Literary Criticism*. Beal, Anthony (ed.). London: Mercury Books.

Leach, Edmund (1976). *Culture and Communication: The Logic by which Symbols are Connected*. Cambridge: Cambridge University Press.

Leavis, F.R. (1962). *The Common Pursuit* (first published 1952). Harmondsworth: Peregrine.

Leavis, F.R. (1964). *Revaluation: Tradition and Development in English Poetry* (first published 1936). Harmondsworth: Peregrine.

Leavis, Q.D. (1932). *Fiction and the Reading Public*. London: Chatto & Windus.

Leech, Geoffrey N. and Short, Michael H. (1981). *Style in Fiction: A Linguistic Introduction to English Fictional Prose*. Harlow: Longman.

Lessing, Doris (1973). *The Golden Notebook* (new edition; first published 1962). Frogmore: Panther.

Levinson, Stephen C. (1983). *Pragmatics*. Cambridge: Cambridge University Press.

Lévi-Strauss, Claude (1972). *The Savage Mind*. London: Weidenfeld & Nicolson.

Lodge, David (1977). *The Modes of Modern Writing: Metaphor, Metonymy and the Typology of Modern Literature*. London: Arnold.

Lotman, Yuri (1976). *Analysis of the Poetic Text*. Johnson, D. Barton (ed. and trans.). Ann Arbor: Ardis.

Lubbock, Percy (1921). *The Craft of Fiction*. London: Jonathan Cape.

Lucas, D.W. (1968). Appendix to Aristotle, *Poetics*. Oxford: Clarendon Press.

Lucas, Ian (1998). *Outrage! An Oral History*. London: Cassell.

Lukács, Georg (1969). *The Historical Novel* (first published in German, 1937). Mitchell, Hannah and Mitchell, Stanley (trans.). (Trans. first published 1962.) Harmondsworth: Peregrine.

Lyotard, Jean-François (1984). *The Postmodern Condition: A Report on Knowledge* (first published in French, 1979). Bennington, Geoff and Massumi, Brian (trans.). Minneapolis: University of Minnesota Press.

McGann, Jerome J. (ed.) (1985). *Historical Studies and Literary Criticism*. Madison: University of Wisconsin Press.

McGann, Jerome J. (1991). *The Textual Condition*. Princeton: Princeton University Press.

McHale, Brian (1987). *Postmodernist Fiction*. London: Methuen.

Macherey, Pierre (1978). *A Theory of Literary Production* (first published in French, 1966). Wall, Geoffrey (trans.). London: Routledge.

Machin, Richard and Norris, Christopher (eds) (1987). *Post-structuralist Readings of English Poetry*. Cambridge: Cambridge University Press.

MacKinnon, Catharine A. (1982). Feminism, Marxism, method, and the state: an agenda for theory. In Keohane, Nannerl O., Rosaldo, Michelle Z., and Gelpi, Barbara C. (eds), *Feminist Theory: A Critique of Ideology*. Brighton: Harvester, 1–30.

Macksey, Richard (1997). Foreword to Genette, Gérard, *Paratexts: Thresholds of Interpretation*. In Genette: 1997, xi–xxii.

Maclean, Ian (1986). Reading and interpretation. In Jefferson, Ann and Robey, David (eds), *Modern Literary Theory: A Comparative Introduction* (2nd edn). London: Batsford, 122–44.

Makaryk, Irena R. (ed.) (1993). *Encyclopedia of Contemporary Literary Theory*. Toronto: University of Toronto Press.

Marx, Karl (1971). *A Contribution to the Critique of Political Economy*. Ryazanskaya, S.W. (trans.). London: Lawrence & Wishart.

Marx, Karl and Engels, Frederick (1962). *Selected Works* (2 vols). London: Lawrence & Wishart.

Marx, Karl and Engels, Frederick (1970). *The German Ideology*. Part 1, with selections from Parts 2 and 3. Arthur, C.J. (ed.). London: Lawrence & Wishart.

Medvedev, P.N./Bakhtin M.M. (1978). *The Formal Method in Literary Scholarship* (first published in Russian, 1928). Wehrle, Albert J. (trans.). Baltimore and London: Johns Hopkins University Press.

Menton, Seymour (1983). *Magic Realism Discovered, 1918–1981*. Philadelphia: The Art Alliance Press.

Miller, J. Hillis (1991). *Theory Then and Now*. Hemel Hempstead: Harvester Wheatsheaf.

Mistacco, Vicki (1980). The theory and practice of reading *nouveaux romans*: Robbe-Grillet's *Topologie d'une cité fantôme*. In Suleiman, Susan R. and Crosman, Inge (eds), *The Reader in the Text*. Princeton: Princeton University Press, 371–400.

Mohanty, Satya P. (1997). *Literary Theory and the Claims of History: Postmodernism, Objectivity, Multicultural Politics*. Ithaca and London: Cornell University Press.

Moi, Toril (ed.) (1986a). *The Kristeva Reader*. Oxford: Blackwell.

Moi, Toril (1986b). Feminist literary criticism. In Jefferson, Ann and Robey, David (eds), *Modern Literary Theory: A Comparative Introduction* (2nd edn). London: Batsford, 204–21.

Montrose, Louis (1989). Professing the Renaissance. The poetics and politics of culture. In Veeser: 1989, 15–36.

Mukařovský, Jan (1964). Standard language and poetic language, *and* The esthetics of language (both articles first published in Czech, 1932). In Garvin: 1964, 17–30 and 31–69.

Mulhern, Francis (ed.) (1992). *Contemporary Marxist Literary Criticism*. Harlow: Longman.

Mulvey, Laura (1989). *Visual and Other Pleasures*. London, Macmillan.

Mulvey, Laura (1996). *Fetishism and Curiosity*. London: BFI Publishing.

Nadelson, Regina (1987). Eating out with Atwood. Interview with Margaret Atwood. *Guardian*, 18 May.

Newman, Judie (1995). *The Ballistic Bard: Postcolonial Fictions*. London: Arnold.

Norrman, Ralf (1982). *The Insecure World of Henry James's Fiction: Intensity and Ambiguity*. London: Macmillan.

Norrman, Ralf (1985). *Samuel Butler and the Meaning of Chiasmus*. London: Macmillan.

Nostbakken, Faith (1993). Cultural materialism. In Makaryk: 1993, 21–4.

Onega, Susana and Landa, José Ángel García (eds) (1996). *Narratology*. Harlow: Longman.

Ong, Walter J. (1982). *Orality and Literacy: The Technologizing of the Word*. London: Methuen.

Oswell, David (1998). True love in queer times: romance, suburbia and masculinity. In Pearce and Wisker: 1998, 157–73.

Palmer, Paulina (1987). From 'coded mannequin' to bird woman: Angela Carter's magic flight. In Roe, Sue (ed.), *Women Reading Women's Writing*. Brighton: Harvester, 179–205.

Palmer, Richard E. (1969). *Hermeneutics: Interpretation Theory in Schleiermacher, Dilthey, Heidegger, and Gadamer*. Evanston: Northwestern University Press.

Pascal, Roy (1977). *The Dual Voice: Free Indirect Speech and its Functioning in the Nineteenth-century European Novel*. Manchester: Manchester University Press.

Pearce, Lynne (1994). *Reading Dialogics*. London: Arnold.

Pearce, Lynne (1997). *Feminism and the Politics of Reading*. London: Arnold.

Pearce, Lynne and Wisker, Gina (1998). *Fatal Attractions: Rescripting Romance in Contemporary Literature and Film*. London: Pluto Press.

Perry, Menakhem (1979). Literary dynamics: how the order of a text creates its meanings. *Poetics Today*, **1–2**, 35–64; 311–61. Towne, Frank (trans.). Seattle: Washington State University Press.

Plekhanov, G.V. (1974). *Art and Social Life* (repr. of 1957 edn; first published in Russian, 1912). Fineberg, A. (trans.). Moscow: Progress Publishers.

Plimpton, George (ed.) (1989). *Women Writers at Work: The 'Paris Review' Interviews*. Harmondsworth: Penguin.

Pratt, Annis (1982). *Archetypal Patterns in Women's Fiction*. Brighton: Harvester.

Pratt, Mary Louise (1977). *Toward a Speech Act Theory of Literary Discourse*. Bloomington: Indiana University Press.

Prince, Gerald (1988). *A Dictionary of Narratology*. Aldershot: Scolar Press.

Richards, I.A. (1924). *Principles of Literary Criticism*. London: Routledge & Kegan Paul.

Richards, I.A. (1964). *Practical Criticism: A Study of Literary Judgment* (first published 1929). London: Routledge.

Riffaterre, Michael (1978). *Semiotics of Poetry*. London: Methuen.

Rimmon-Kenan, Shlomith (1983). *Narrative Fiction: Contemporary Poetics*. London: Methuen.

Rodway, Allan (1970). Generic criticism: the approach through type, mode and kind. In Bradbury, Malcolm and Palmer, David (eds), *Contemporary Criticism*, Stratford-upon-Avon Studies, **12**. London: Arnold, 82–105.

Rowe, John Carlos (1998). *The Other Henry James*. Durham, NC: Duke University Press.

Ryan, Kiernan (ed.) (1996). *New Historicism and Cultural Materialism: A Reader*. London: Arnold.

Said, Edward (1979). *Orientalism* (first published 1978). New York: Vintage Books.

Said, Edward (1984). *The World, the Text, and the Critic*. London: Faber.

Salusinszky, Imre (1987). *Criticism in Society*. London: Methuen.

Sartre, Jean-Paul (1973). *Existential Psychoanalysis*. Barnes, Hazel E. (trans.). Chicago: Henry Regnery.

Saussure, Ferdinand de (1974). *Course in General Linguistics*. Bally, Charles and Sechehaye, Albert (eds), Buskin, Wade (trans.) (rev. edn). London: Peter Owen.

Scholes, Robert (1982). *Semiotics and Interpretation*. New Haven: Yale University Press.

Scholes, Robert (1985). *Textual Power: Theory and the Teaching of English*. New Haven: Yale University Press.

Scholes, Robert and Kellogg, Robert (1966). *The Nature of Narrative*. London: Oxford University Press.

Scott, William T. (1990). *The Possibility of Communication*. Berlin: Mouton de Gruyter.

Searle, John R. (1969). *Speech Acts: An Essay in the Philosophy of Language*. Cambridge: Cambridge University Press.

Searle, John R. (1976). A classification of illocutionary acts. *Language in Society*, **5**, 1–23 (first presented as a lecture, 1971).

Sedgwick, Eve Kosofsky (1993). *Between Men: English Literature and Male Homosocial Desire* (repr. with a new preface by the author; first published 1985). New York: Columbia University Press.

Sell, Roger (ed.) (1991). *Literary Pragmatics*. London: Routledge (contains Sell's own essay, 'The politeness of literary texts', 208–24).

Seung, T.K. (1982). *Semiotics and Thematics in Hermeneutics*. New York: Columbia University Press.

Shea, Victor (1993). New historicism. In Makaryk: 1993, 124–30.

Shklovsky, Victor (1965). Art as technique (first published in Russian, 1917). In Lemon, Lee T. and Reis, Marion J. (eds and trans.), *Russian Formalist Criticism: Four Essays*. Lincoln: University of Nebraska Press.

Showalter, Elaine (1982). *A Literature of Their Own*. London: Virago.

Showalter, Elaine (1986). Feminist criticism in the wilderness (first published 1981 in *Critical Inquiry*, **8**, 179–205). In Showalter, Elaine (ed.), *The New Feminist Criticism: Essays on Women, Literature and Theory*. London: Virago, 243–70.

Sinfield, Alan (1992). *Faultlines: Cultural Materialism and the Politics of Dissident Reading*. Oxford: Clarendon Press.

Smith, Barbara Herrnstein (1968). *Poetic Closure: A Study of How Poems End*. Chicago: University of Chicago Press.

Spivak, Gayatri Chakravorty (1984–5). Criticism, feminism and the institution. Interview with Elizabeth Gross. *Thesis Eleven*, **10–11**, 175–87.

Spivak, Gayatri Chakravorty (1991). Identity and alterity: an interview. *Arena*, **97**, 65–76.

Stierle, Karlheinz (1980). The reading of fictional texts. In Suleiman, Susan R. and Crosman, Inge (eds), Crosman, Inge and Zachrau, Thekla (trans.), *The Reader in the Text*. Princeton: Princeton University Press, 83–105.

Stubbs, Michael (1983). *Discourse Analysis: The Sociolinguistic Analysis of Natural Language*. Oxford: Blackwell.

Thomas, Brook (1991). *The New Historicism and Other Old-Fashioned Topics*. Princeton: Princeton University Press.

Tillyard, E.M.W. (1944). *Shakespeare's History Plays*. London: Chatto & Windus.

Todd, Janet (ed.) (1982). *Women Writers Talking*. New York: Holmes & Meier.

Todorov, Tzvetan (1975). *The Fantastic: A Structural Approach to a Literary Genre*. Ithaca, NY: Cornell University Press.

Todorov, Tzvetan (1981). *Introduction to Poetics*. Howard, Richard (trans.). Brighton: Harvester.

Todorov, Tzvetan (1984). *Mikhail Bakhtin: The Dialogical Principle*. Minneapolis: University of Minnesota Press.

Tomas, David (1989). The technophilic body. On technicity in William Gibson's cyborg culture. *New Formations*, **8**, 113–29.

Tomashevsky, Boris (1965). Thematics (first published in Russian, 1925). In Lemon, Lee T. and Reis, Marion J. (eds and trans.), *Russian Formalist Criticism: Four Essays*. Lincoln, NE: University of Nebraska Press.

Trilling, Lionel (1966). *Beyond Culture*. London: Secker & Warburg.

Tyler, Carole-Anne (1991). Boys will be girls: the politics of gay drag. In Fuss: 1991, 32–70.

Veeser, H. Aram (ed.) (1989). *The New Historicism*. New York and London: Routledge.

Vodička, Felix (1964). The history of the echo of literary works (first published in Czech, 1942). In Garvin: 1964, 71–81.

Vološinov, V.N. (1986). *Marxism and the Philosophy of Language*. Matejka, Ladislav and Titunik, I.R. (trans.) (first published in English, 1973). Cambridge, MA: Harvard University Press.

Vygotsky, L.S. (1986). *Thought and Language*. Kozulin, Alex (rev. and ed. version of the previous trans. by Hanfmann, Eugenia and Vakar, Gertrude, 1962). (First published in Russian, 1934.) Cambridge, MA: MIT Press.

Wain, John (ed.) (1961). *Interpretations: Essays on Twelve English Poems* (first published 1955). London: Routledge.

Wales, Katie (1989). *A Dictionary of Stylistics*. Harlow: Longman.

Watt, Ian (1980). *Conrad in the Nineteenth Century*. London: Chatto & Windus.

Webster, Roger (1990). *Studying Literary Theory*. London: Arnold.

Weisgerber, Jean (1988). *Le Réalisme magique: roman, peinture, cinéma*. Lausanne: Editions l'Age d'homme.

Weston, Jessie L. (1993). *From Ritual to Romance* (first published 1920). Princeton: Princeton University Press.

Wheale, Nigel (ed.) (1995a). *The Postmodern Arts: An Introductory Reader*. London and New York: Routledge.

Wheale, Nigel (1995b). Postmodernism: from elite to mass culture? In Wheale: 1995a, 33–56.

Wheale, Nigel (1995c). Recognizing a 'human-Thing': cyborgs, robots and replicants in Philip K. Dick's *Do Androids Dream of Electric Sheep?* and Ridley Scott's *Blade Runner*. In Wheale: 1995a, 101–14.

Wiener, Norbert (1949). *Cybernetics: Or Control and Communication in the Animal and the Machine*. Cambridge, MA: The Technology Press.

Wilden, Anthony (1972). *System and Structure: Essays in Communication and Exchange*. London: Tavistock.

Willett, John (ed. and trans.) (1964). *Brecht on Theatre: The Development of an Aesthetic*. London: Eyre Methuen.

Williams, Raymond (1954). *Drama in Performance*. London: Frederick Muller.

Williams, Raymond (1958). *Culture and Society 1780–1950*. London: Chatto & Windus.

Williams, Raymond (1976). *Keywords*. Glasgow: Collins.

Williams, Raymond (1977). *Marxism and Literature*. Oxford: Oxford University Press.

Williams, Raymond (1979). *Politics and Letters: Interviews with New Left Review*. London: New Left Books.

Williams, Raymond (1980). *Problems in Materialism and Culture: Selected Essays*. London: Verso.

Williams, Raymond (1989). *What I Came to Say*. London: Hutchinson Radius.

Wimsatt, W.K. (1970). *The Verbal Icon: Studies in the Meaning of Poetry* (first published 1954). London: Methuen.

Wimsatt, W.K. and Beardsley, Monroe (1946). The intentional fallacy. In Wimsatt: 1970, 3–18.

Wimsatt, W.K. and Beardsley, Monroe (1949). The affective fallacy. In Wimsatt: 1970, 21–39.

Wings, Mary (1988). *She Came in a Flash*. London: The Women's Press.

Woolf, Virginia (1929). *A Room of One's Own*. London: Hogarth Press.

Woolf, Virginia (1966). Women and fiction. *Collected Essays*, **2**. London: Hogarth Press, 141–8.

Woolf, Virginia (1977). *Three Guineas* (first published 1938). Harmondsworth: Penguin.

Wright, Iain (1984). History, hermeneutics, deconstruction. In Hawthorn, Jeremy (ed.), *Criticism and Critical Theory*. London: Arnold, 83–96.

Young, Robert (ed.) (1981). *Untying the Text: A Post-structuralist Reader*. London: Routledge.

Young, Robert J.C. (1995). *Colonial Desire: Hybridity in Theory, Culture and Race*. London: Routledge.